Court of Protection H

A user's guide

Available as an ebook at www.lag.org.uk/ebooks

The purpose of the Legal Action Group is to promote equal access to justice for all members of society who are socially, economically or otherwise disadvantaged. To this end, it seeks to improve law and practice, the administration of justice and legal services.

Court of Protection Handbook

A user's guide

Alex Ruck Keene, Kate Edwards,
Professor Anselm Eldergill
and Sophy Miles

Legal Action Group
2014

This edition published in Great Britain 2014
by LAG Education and Service Trust Limited
3rd floor, Universal House, 88–94 Wentworth Street, London E1 7SA
www.lag.org.uk

British Library Cataloguing in Publication Data
a CIP catalogue record for this book is available from the British Library.

Crown copyright material is produced with the permission of the Controller of HMSO and the Queen's Printer for Scotland.

This book has been produced using Forest Stewardship Council (FSC) certified paper. The wood used to produce FSC certified products with a 'Mixed Sources' label comes from FSC certified well-managed forests, controlled sources and/or recycled material.

Print ISBN   978 1 908407 39 9
ebook ISBN   978 1 908407 40 5

Typeset by Regent Typesetting, London
Printed in Great Britain by Hobbs the Printers, Totton, Hampshire

Foreword

by Sir James Munby, President of the Court of Protection

Once again we are all indebted to the Legal Action Group. Its latest Handbook, *Court of Protection Handbook: a user's guide*, handsomely lives up to the well-deserved reputation of its various predecessors.

The Handbook is, as it says, a user's guide. It is a very practical guide, written by those whose expert knowledge of the law and procedure of the Court of Protection is more than matched by their deep understanding, based on experience, of the realities of how the Court of Protection works. Aimed not just at the lawyers who practise in the Court of Protection but also at the increasing number who, whether by choice or otherwise, appear before the Court as litigants in person, the Handbook will, I am sure, be of great benefit to all who use it.

The organisation of the Handbook, explained in the Introduction, is clear, sensible and user-friendly. Particularly useful, not least as an important way of explaining what might otherwise appear complex, are the various tables, flow-charts and other diagrams which are such a valuable feature of the Handbook.

The authors are to be congratulated for giving us such a useful and practical work. It should be in the hand of every practitioner and, more particularly, of every lay user of the Court of Protection.

James Munby
30 June 2014

Preface

The Mental Capacity Act (MCA) 2005 is an extraordinarily wide-reaching piece of legislation: any of us at any time could find ourselves incapable of taking decisions about our health, our welfare, or our finances. The Court of Protection, the specialist court established by the MCA 2005 as the ultimate decision-maker in relation to those lacking capacity to take those decisions, is in consequence a court with a very wide reach.

There are many books which deal with the MCA 2005, and there are also a number of books which deal with the Court of Protection. However, this is the first book to set out to address in detail the practice and processes of the court – across the whole range of its work – in terms that are aimed not solely at lawyers who are advising those bringing or responding to applications but also to the increasing numbers of people who either by choice or otherwise are involved in proceedings before the Court of Protection without the help of lawyers or specialist advisers.

The book is accompanied by a website: www.courtofprotection handbook.com, upon which will be found links to relevant statutory materials and other guidance that space precluded us from including in the appendices, together with updates on practice and procedure before the Court of Protection cross-referenced to the relevant paragraphs in the book.

We are very grateful to all those who have contributed their thoughts and expertise at various stages of this book's life, and in particular Alastair Pitblado (the Official Solicitor to the Senior Courts), Neil Allen, Romana Canneti, Gordon Ashton OBE, Victoria Butler-Cole, Helen Clift, Janet Ilett, Nicola Mackintosh QC (Hon), Michelle Pratley, Lucy Series, Beverley Taylor, Aswini Weereratne and Susan Thompson. We are grateful to Floyd Porter and the other partners at Miles and Partners LLP for allowing us to reproduce some of their precedents.

Special thanks are due to Stephen Knafler QC for his invaluable input at the planning stages and his work in pulling together resources and to Mark Neary for taking the time to describe a Court of Protection case from the perspective of those most affected by the outcome – his son Steven and himself. We are also very fortunate that Dr Ian Hall was kind enough to contribute a concise account of how to get the best from an expert witness.

We would also like to thank those who have kept the authors going through the darker nights of the soul. Alex thanks, above all, his wife Pieta, for her unswerving support and (very well-feigned) toleration of his disappearing into the ether of the internet at odd hours of the day and night in pursuit of a thought; he would also like to thank Zoë and Benjamin for making it so clear when Daddy has done enough for the day. Kate would like to thank her husband, Stephen Elliott, for his support and encouragement throughout the many hours spent shut away writing. Anselm would like to thank his wife Helen, and his cat Captain Haddock for keeping him company. Sophy would like to thank Guy, Frank and Rebecca for everything including remarkable forbearance.

We state the law as at 28 April 2014, although we have sought to incorporate where possible developments to 13 June 2014.

We welcome feedback, which should be sent to the editors at courtofprotectionhandbook@gmail.com.

Alex Ruck Keene
Kate Edwards
Anselm Eldergill
Sophy Miles

June 2014

Authors

Alex Ruck Keene is a barrister at Thirty Nine Essex Street. Alex has been recommended as a leading expert in the field of mental capacity law for several years, appearing in cases involving the Mental Capacity Act 2005 at all levels up to and including the Supreme Court. He also writes extensively about mental capacity law and policy – works to which he has contributed including *The International Protection of Adults* (forthcoming, 2014, Oxford University Press), Jordan's annual *Court of Protection Practice* and the third edition of *Assessment of Mental Capacity* (Law Society/BMA 2009). He is an Honorary Research Lecturer at the University of Manchester, has sat on both the ad hoc committees convened to review the Court of Protection Rules 2007, is a member of the Law Society's Mental Health and Disability Committee, and the creator of the website www.mentalcapacitylawandpolicy. org.uk. In addition to editing this book, Alex wrote chapters 12 (to which Sophy also contributed), 15, 16, 18, 19 and 23–27.

Kate Edwards is an Associate Solicitor and professional property and affairs deputy with the Court of Protection team at Slater & Gordon Lawyers. She is a member of STEP (Society of Trusts & Estates Practitioners) and the founder and chair of the Court of Protection Practitioners Association (CoPPA). Kate wrote chapters 7 and 21 and co-wrote, with Sophy, chapters 10 and 17.

Professor Anselm Eldergill is a district judge in the Court of Protection and a visiting professor at University College, London. Before becoming a judge he was a practising legal aid solicitor specialising in mental health law for over 25 years, and then led the mental health team at Eversheds. He was President of the Mental Health Lawyers Association and of the Institute of Mental Health Act Practitioners, and ranked 1 in the Chambers Directory. He is an Alexander Maxwell Scholar and the author of *Mental Health Review Tribunals: Law and Procedure* (Sweet & Maxwell 1997) and articles for journals such as the Princeton University Law Journal, Journal of Forensic Psychiatry and The Guardian. He was chairman of the Mental Health Act Commission's Law and Ethics Committee. Anselm wrote chapters 3–5.

Sophy Miles qualified as a solicitor in 1989. She was a founding partner at Miles and Partners LLP where she led the mental health and capacity team for 16 years, and where she is now a consultant. She has been involved in significant cases under the inherent jurisdiction and in the Court of Protection, including *JE v DE and others* and *Hillingdon v Neary*. Sophy holds rights of audience in the higher civil courts and regularly appears in the Court of Protection. She is a fee-paid judge of the First-tier Tribunal (Mental Health). Sophy writes and trains on mental health and mental capacity issues and writes the regular Court of Protection updates in *Legal Action*. She chairs the Law Society's Mental Health and Disability Committee and is an active member of the Mental Health Lawyers Association committee. She is an accredited mediator (Regent's University London). Sophy wrote chapters 6, 8, 9, 14, 20 and 22, co-wrote (with Kate) chapters 10 and 7, and contributed to chapter 12.

Contents

Table of cases

Table of statutes

Table of statutory instruments

Table of European and International Conventions and Treaties

Table of guidance

Abbreviations

ABE	Achieving best evidence
ACO	Authorised court officer
ADR	Alternative dispute resolution
AJA 1960	Administration of Justice Act 1960
AMHP	Approved mental health professional
CAFCASS	Children and Family Court Advisory and Support Service
CCG	Clinical commissioning group
CEA 1972	Civil Evidence Act 1972
CEA 1995	Civil Evidence Act 1995
CES	Customer Enquiry Service
CFO	Court Funds Office
CHC	NHS continuing healthcare
CICA	Criminal Injuries Compensation Authority
CMC	Civil Mediation Council
COPR	Court of Protection Rules 2007 SI No 1744
CQC	Care Quality Commission
CRPD	UN Convention on the Rights of Persons with Disabilities
CSSIW	Care and Social Services Inspectorate Wales
CTO	Community treatment order
DOLS	Deprivation of Liberty Safeguards
DPA 1998	Data Protection Act 1998
ECHR	European Convention on Human Rights
ECtHR	European Court of Human Rights
EPA	Enduring power of attorney
EqA 2010	Equality Act 2010
FNC	NHS-funded nursing care
FPR	Family Procedure Rules 2010 SI No 2955
GMC	General Medical Council
HCPC	Health and Care Professions Council
HMCTS	Her Majesty's Courts and Tribunals Service
HMRC	Her Majesty's Revenue and Customs
IMCA	Independent mental capacity advocate
IMHA	Independent mental health advocate
LAA	Legal Aid Agency
LASPO Act 2012	Legal Aid, Sentencing and Punishment of Offenders Act 2012
LPA	Lasting power of attorney
LSC	Legal Services Commission
MCA 2005	Mental Capacity Act 2005

MHA 1983	Mental Health Act 1983
MHA 2007	Mental Health Act 2007
MoJ	Ministry of Justice
NAA 1948	National Assistance Act 1948
NMC	Nursing and Midwifery Council
OPG	Office of the Public Guardian
P	The relevant person
PACE 1984	Police and Criminal Evidence Act 1984
PALS	Patient advice and liaison service
PCT	Primary care trust
PD	Practice direction
PGO	Public Guardianship Office
PHA 1997	Protection from Harassment Act 1997
PSU	Personal Support Unit
RPR	Relevant person's representative
RTM	Round table meeting
SRA	Solicitors Regulation Authority
VHCC	Very high costs case

CHAPTER 1

Introduction

The scheme of the book

1.1   The book is divided into four parts.

1.2   In the first section, we set out an overview of the Mental Capacity Act (MCA) 2005 and of the Court of Protection. In order to ensure that the book's focus is where it should be – on the people whose lives are affected by its decisions – this section starts with a chapter written by Mark Neary, the father and carer of Steven Neary, whose story[1] illustrates both the potential for misuse of the MCA 2005 by statutory authorities and the powers of the Court of Protection.

1.3   In the second section, the book proceeds in chronological order through the life of an application (or, to be precise, from the point before an application is even prepared – by asking, first, the often overlooked question of whether it is actually appropriate to bring an application to the Court of Protection). We then trace the process through from the drafting of the application, issue, response and then on to any directions hearings necessary before the final determination of the application, before dealing with the questions of costs, enforcement and appeals.

1.4   In a series of – mostly – shorter chapters in the third section, we address a number of specific issues that arise in connection with the Court of Protection's jurisdiction, such as applications in relation to authorisations granted under the deprivation of liberty safeguards (DOLS) regime and the interaction between the Court of Protection and Administrative Court.

1.5   The fourth section, the appendices, contain the key statutory materials and guidance, together with precedent orders, samples of important documents such as letters of instruction, as well as useful contact addresses and resources.

---

1 Encapsulated in the judgment in *Hillingdon LBC v Neary* [2011] EWHC 1377, [2011] COPLR Con Vol 623.

Approach

1.6   We need to make four important – linked – points at the outset of the book as to the approach that we have taken.

1.7   First, while it has deep historical roots, the Court of Protection in its new incarnation with jurisdiction to take decisions not solely in regard to the property and affairs of those without capacity but also in regard to their health and welfare has been in existence only since October 2007, and it is still therefore a comparative newcomer. Its practices and processes are in significant measure still being worked out. This book is, in part, a contribution to the development of those practices and processes, although we have sought to make clear whenever we move beyond description into prescription.

1.8   Second, this book covers the span of the Court of Protection's work. However, only a very small number of applications relating to property and affairs received by the court are contentious; the vast majority are decided 'upon the papers' by either a judge or (in a relatively recent development) an authorised court officer. Those sections of the book which relate to the determination of contested applications, and, in particular, to hearings, are very much focused upon health and welfare applications. It is a legitimate question as to whether the priorities of the Court have been distorted by the fact that health and welfare cases, which make up such a small percentage of its overall work, have generated so much of its jurisprudence since 2007. That discussion is beyond the scope of this book but will hopefully be held in the forum of a Rules Committee in short order.

1.9   Third, insofar as the book deals with the determination of health and welfare applications in particular, it does so from a starting point that there is a wealth of valuable guidance to be found from proceedings relating to children (and especially care proceedings). It is vital to emphasise, however, that we are *not* saying that incapacitated adults[2] are to be equated with 'big children'. Very far from it – the law that Court of Protection judges have to apply and the factors to take into account when considering what substantive decision to take upon an application relating to an incapacitated adult are – and should be – very different from the law and factors that apply in relation to a child. However, the forensic processes in both types of proceedings are – we suggest – very similar, and for very good reason: they are

---

2   The Court of Protection can, of course, take decisions in relation to children of 16 and 17. This jurisdiction is not often invoked. This edition of the book touches on the position of the children where relevant; it may be that their position merits consideration in a separate chapter in a future edition.

above all designed to ensure that, as best as possible, a judge is put in a position to take the decision that it right for a person who is not a protagonist in the proceedings but their subject.[3]

1.10 Fourth and finally, hanging over the entirety of the book as it stands is a very large question as to whether the MCA 2005 is compatible with the United Nations Convention on the Rights of Persons with Disabilities. There is a strong argument that the MCA 2005 is not, in particular because it allows for substituted decision-making (by both informal decision-makers and the Court of Protection) on the basis of an objective analysis of where the best interests of 'P' lie. We summarise the key points in relation to this issue in chapter 28, but note that it is one that is likely to rise further up the agenda as the Committee on the Rights of Persons with Disabilities turns its attention to the position of the UK in 2015.

1.11 It should be noted that the law relating to capacity issues is significantly different in both Northern Ireland and Scotland; this book should not be used as a guide to the principles and practices adopted in those jurisdictions.[4]

In this book we use 'P' to refer to the person whom it is said lacks capacity to take the material decisions.

---

3 See, in this regard, The Honourable Mr Justice Baker, 'Reforming the Court of Protection: lessons to be learned from the Family Justice Reforms' [2014] 4 *Elder Law Journal* 1, 45–50.
4 Readers are directed, in particular, to Part X of Ashton et al, *Court of Protection Practice 2014*, Jordans; and also, for a fuller discussion, to Frimston et al, *The international protection of adults*, Oxford University Press, forthcoming, 2014.

PART 1

Overview of the Mental Capacity Act 2005 and the Court of Protection

CHAPTER 2

Steven Neary's story

This chapter is written by Steven Neary's father, Mark Neary

2.1   My experience of the Court of Protection comes through being caught up in the deprivation of liberty safeguards (DOLS). I am the father of Steven Neary, who for nearly the whole of 2010 was held in a positive behaviour unit under four successive DOLS authorisations. When the case eventually came before the Court of Protection in December 2010, Steven was immediately released and allowed to return to his home. The standard authorisation was terminated. At a subsequent hearing in May 2011,[1] the judge found that the local authority had breached Steven's rights under articles 5 (right to liberty and security) and 8 (right to respect for private and family life) of the European Convention on Human Rights (ECHR) for the whole year, and all four DOLS authorisations had been unlawful.

2.2   In the light of that successful outcome after a truly horrendous year when my family was needlessly torn apart, you'd expect my view of the Court of Protection to be a positive one. And it is, I have nothing negative to report about the experience, although I have concerns about accessing the court in the first place.

2.3   Mr Justice Peter Jackson quoted the Magna Carta in his introduction to his judgment in our case. His reference induced a powerful emotional reaction in me and from commentaries on our case, I know that it resonated with a lot of people. I can see why. Issues that the Court of Protection regularly address usually involve matters of liberty, best interests and the role of the state in the lives of incapacitated people. Steven's case rested heavily on all those things and as

---

1   *Hillingdon LBC v Neary* [2011] EWHC 1377 (COP), [2011] COPLR Con Vol 623. See also *Hillingdon LBC v Neary* [2011] EWHC 3522 (COP) on the question of costs.

I've become more acquainted with the Mental Capacity Act (MCA) 2005, I can see that what was articulated in the Magna Carta is relevant to our lives today. Thank goodness. In Steven's case, the local authority behaved appallingly and a running thread of the judgment is their lack of frankness towards Steven and me. The judge concluded one part of his judgment with the sentence that, had Hillingdon had their way: 'Steven would have faced a life in public care that he did not want and does not need'.[2] Since our case moved into the public domain, I have been approached by many families where what nearly happened to Steven, has actually happened to them. Sadly, more and more people are encountering what Steven and I had to face – challenging state decisions about incapacitated people is seldom successful through internal processes. This is for a number of reasons. First, the family is always outnumbered by large multidisciplinary teams of professionals. Second, often, the real agendas are withheld from families, making challenge impotent. In our case, the local authority led Steven and me to believe that we were in a 'transition home plan' for six months. Although we were unhappy about the timescale, there did seem to be light at the end of the tunnel. But as Mr Justice Peter Jackson held:

> Between April and July 2010 Hillingdon pursued two inconsistent agendas. The professionals were opposed to Steven returning home, whether or not a final decision had been taken. The agenda so far as Steven and Mr Neary were concerned was a return home under the transition plan. It was only when the transition plan was about to lead to an actual return home that the pursuit of two agendas became unfeasible and the true view of the professionals was disclosed. The records show that the professionals were at times uneasy about this lack of frankness, but it happened nonetheless.[3]

2.4   In August 2010, after (as Mr Justice Peter Jackson put it) 'the cat of Hillingdon's thinking was out of the bag',[4] the local authority promised to refer the disagreement over the DOLS to the court. It should have been a straightforward challenge to a DOLS submission. But it took them two-and-a-half months to make a submission, and when they did, they applied for welfare deputyship. Mr Justice Peter Jackson remarked on the 'extraordinarily wide ranging'[5] orders the court was asked to make, but the DOLS authorisations were not mentioned

---

2 [2011] EWHC 3522 (COP) para 28.
3 Para 155(3).
4 Para 155(5).
5 Para 122.

at all in the local authority's submission. I can't know for sure, but it looks to me like they were hoping to be granted welfare deputyship and then they would have had full control and their DOLS authorisations wouldn't have come under the spotlight. Faced with this sort of conduct, the odds seem very stacked against P or their family.

2.5 Once Hillingdon's real agenda was exposed on 8 July 2010, I knew that the only possible way of challenging their plan to move Steven to a hospital in Wales was through the Court of Protection. In his judgment, Mr Justice Peter Jackson declared that the onus was on the local authority to bring the matter before the court, but throughout the year, I was repeatedly told by Hillingdon that if I disagreed with their plans, it was down to me to instigate proceedings. I know differently now, but at the time I believed them. It is very common, and a deeply unsettling fact for many families, that when their children are 'transitioned' into adult social care services, the parents are effectively side-lined. My twenty years of experience of Steven counted for nothing in the year that Steven was in the unit – in one document, I wasn't even recognised as his next of kin, that role went to his 'care champion' within the unit. So it's not surprising that many families, like me at the time, don't realise they can challenge state decisions, far less know how to go about it. When the DOLS were authorised, I was told that I was Steven's 'relevant person's representative' (RPR) but did not have a clue what that meant in practice. All I knew was that, by this time, I had been attending meetings for four months and had absolutely no say in any of the care planning for Steven's future. My role as Steven's RPR was never fully explained to me. If it had, I would probably have triggered the court process myself much sooner.

2.6 Once the penny dropped in July 2010 that the matter could only be resolved through the Court of Protection, the next big hurdle was accessing the court. I used the Internet to put out a call for help, and someone sent me a list of solicitors who might be prepared to take our case on. It was a dispiriting exercise. Most of the firms I contacted confessed to insufficient knowledge of the Mental Capacity Act to take the case on. The vast majority didn't return my calls. I had a hopeful few days with one firm until they told me that I didn't qualify for legal aid. I didn't know it at the time, but under the DOLS legislation I was automatically entitled to legal aid as Steven's RPR. And that was just me – I had not been told, or considered, that *Steven*, as the person being deprived of his liberty, was entitled to legal aid. That was partly because (as the judge found) they had failed to press for Steven to be allocated an independent mental capacity advocate

(IMCA). This is someone who could have led professional backing for Steven's case and opened up legal doors that had remained firmly closed to me. Even when an independent psychologist reported on the lack of advocacy for Steven or me on 16 August 2010, his report was deliberately suppressed (a fact that the judge described as deplorable[6]) and it took until 29 October for Hillingdon to appoint an IMCA for Steven (coincidentally, the day after they submitted their own court application). When the IMCA came on board, the effect was transformative. Three weeks later we had a solicitor and three weeks after that, we were in court.

2.7   I have told the story of how we eventually got a solicitor many times, and people often think I've exercised some dramatic license in the narrative. A member of the Facebook group I set up is an expert in the DOLS and offered to contact a law firm in Cornwall (bear in mind, we live in west London) who she felt had the necessary experience to take our case on. On the day she contacted him, he happened to be at, of all things, a DOLS conference in London. It was a turgid event and he was prepared to bunk off for the afternoon and travel across London to meet me. Three weeks after this unexpected meeting, we were in court and Steven was released.

2.8   I know that Steven and I were blocked every step of the process by Hillingdon, but there must be a better, quicker way of accessing the Court of Protection. It took from 15 April 2010 (the date the first DOL was authorised) until 26 October 2010 (two weeks before the fourth DOL was authorised) before Steven got an IMCA. It took until 22 November 2010 before we found a solicitor. When it comes to the issue of the liberty of an incapacitated person, I would suggest that this is hardly enabling the detained person 'to have the lawfulness of his detention reviewed speedily by the court' as required by ECHR article 5(4). I accept that the main reason for the delay was the approach adopted by Hillingdon, which was severely criticised by the judge, but actually getting through the doors of the Court of Protection for a family member can be extremely difficult without legal representation.

2.9   My apologies if I have laboured the point, but when things get as serious as our case had become, the MCA 2005 only has a value if the people who fall within the scope of it are able to access justice. To have that access either effectively blocked for eleven months or for it to be downright inaccessible, has major implications for the court that was set up to help the most vulnerable people in our society.

6 [2011] EWHC 3522 (COP) para 114.

2.10   Even if it would not help directly with getting to court, it would definitely help if the detained person or their representative was allowed to approach the IMCA service directly, rather than having to rely on the supervisory body who authorised the DOL to refer you for one. To put it bluntly, if the local authority do not want you to have external advocacy from an IMCA, you are not going to get one. As I write this chapter, the House of Lords have just published their recommendations following their review into the MCA 2005.[7] One of their proposals is that P or his representative be given direct access to IMCA services. That can only be good news if the recommendation is taken up.

2.11   On a happier note, at the first hearing in the Court of Protection on 21 December 2010, Steven was represented by the Official Solicitor and I had my own counsel. Mr Justice Mostyn terminated the current DOLS authorisation and allowed Steven home. On Christmas Eve 2010 Steven returned home – 359 days after he walked out of the front door, setting off for three days' respite.

2.12   Of course, the scrutiny didn't end with Steven's return home. Between then and the hearing in February 2011, we had the visits from the two court-appointed experts (one a psychologist; the other a social work expert), plus a further visit from the Official Solicitor. Although things at home had been going very well since Steven's return, I found these visits very anxiety-provoking. Once again, I felt like I was having to prove and to put a case for the most important, fundamental aspects of Steven's life, and if I was unable to present his life properly, the consequences could have been dire. The local authority had not revised its 'care plan', so a move to a hospital in Wales was still a possibility. I felt that if one little thing was misinterpreted, or if the experts did not share the view of Mr Justice Mostyn, then the whole nightmare might start up again. I know that for the Court of Protection to make a thorough, robust decision it needs as much information as possible, but it seems to me that life under the microscope applies more to the learning disabled than any other member of our society, and it's terrifying. I'd had a year of Hillingdon interpreting every aspect of Steven's life negatively. Steven loves engaging in endless conversations about his favourite things – Mr Bean, Take That, flavours of crisps – but at the unit, these conversations were viewed through a negative, judgmental prism. His love of

---

7   *Mental Capacity Act 2005: post-legislative scrutiny*, Select Committee on the Mental Capacity Act 2005, Report of Session 2013–14, HL Paper 139, published March 2014; available at: www.publications.parliament.uk/pa/ld201314/ ldselect/ldmentalcap/139/139.pdf.

Mr Bean was seen as obsessive and obstructive to him engaging in more 'acceptable, mature interactions'. The thought that the court-appointed psychologist might share that view scared the hell out of me. Thankfully, he didn't, and when we returned to court in February 2011, the order for Steven to live in his own home was made permanent. The Official Solicitor then pushed for the lawfulness of Hillingdon's actions throughout 2010 to be judged and the judge agreed with him. All of a sudden, the spotlight was off Steven and me. We no longer had to put a good case – that task now fell on Hillingdon.

2.13   Two weeks before the hearing before Mr Justice Peter Jackson at which the lawfulness of Hillingdon's actions were to be examined, we encountered another setback. Because Mr Justice Mostyn had terminated the DOLS authorisation, I was no longer entitled to legal aid. Steven would still be represented by the Official Solicitor, but I lost the team that had been so successful in December 2010 and February 2011. This meant that I had to appear as a litigant in person. Thankfully, the Official Solicitor put together a fabulous case, because it would have been impossible for me on my own to cover all the legal arguments that the case before Mr Justice Peter Jackson was built on.

2.14   Obviously, the most important aspect of the entire case was to get the DOLS authorisations withdrawn and allow Steven to return home, but as events have demonstrated since the case, the importance of having the DOLS legislation and process examined and the actions of the supervisory body looked into has had a major impact across the country in terms of practice. Since 2011, I have regularly been invited to speak at events involving social care, legal and best interests professionals and have seen how our judgment has shaped the way many of these professionals work. I'm not sure the case would have had that impact if it had ended in February 2011 with the termination of the authorisation and the decision to allow Steven to live at home permanently.

2.15   Finally, I am regularly asked about the publicity our case attracted (and still does) and whether it has been in Steven's best interests. In the first instance in 2010, I turned to social media and the wider national media out of desperation. The motivation was to find some guidance and support which must surely have been in Steven's best interests. I was always confident that I was acting in Steven's best interests but approaching the press was quite a dramatic manoeuvre. I was also fairly confident that I could shield Steven from any external situation that he'd find difficult to cope with, as I had done all his life. I knew that I would never put him in a public situation that would cause him anxiety or distress. I can honestly say, as I did in court, that I don't think Steven has been affected at all by the publicity. He continues to live his life in his own idiosyncratic, Steven Neary way. He is interested whenever we appear in the press or on the television, but then gets back to watching Fawlty Towers or whatever he is doing at the time. For me, the most important thing about the court's decision to allow the case to be reported openly is that it has enabled people to engage with a very human story. It's a son and father story. And because son and father were identified as Steven and Mark, the judgment clearly comes alive as a story of two human beings caught in a horrendous situation. When I speak publicly and tell the story, people laugh, cry and rage because they connect with the three-dimensional characters at the heart of the story. I met a judge a few weeks back and he said it was a very 'filmatic' story. I'm not sure that could happen if we were '*SN and MN vs A local authority*'. The learning disabled are a pretty invisible, unacknowledged section of our society and I believe it is important for our stories to be told. I continue to write about our lives because if attitudes are going to change in the future, we have to move away from the mindset that sees people like Steven as not quite human. Steven Neary is a fully rounded human being – SN (or P) is not an object or a case study. And that for me is ample reason to have our case in the public arena and for the push for the Court of Protection to be more open in its reporting of its cases. Mr Justice Peter Jackson's judgment is often referred to as 'landmark judgment'. I am delighted that it is used as a key reference point in social work, legal and best interest assessor training. But more importantly, I am glad that it is in the public domain to help other Stevens and other Marks who suddenly find themselves in the same awful situation we got trapped in, back in 2010. On a weekly basis, I am contacted by people with relatives trapped in care homes or hospitals where either the person or their family want them to live at home. Worryingly, in many cases, there is no DOLS authorisation, so there is no way of challenging the detention. I always suggest people push for a DOLS authorisation as at least that will give them the opportunity to take the matter to court. *Hillingdon v Neary* has given hope to lots of families and I am proud of that. If our experience helps just one person, that can only be a good thing.

An overview of the Mental Capacity Act 2005

continued

Introduction

3.1   The Mental Capacity Act (MCA) 2005 received the royal assent on 7 April 2005. Most of its provisions came into effect on 1 October 2007. Prior to the MCA 2005:

- The Court of Protection only had jurisdiction over an incapacitated person's property and financial affairs. The relevant legal provisions were set out in Part VII of the Mental Health Act (MHA) 1983 and in rules made under that Act.
- Most treatment and care decisions were governed by the common law, in other words by laws and principles set down by judges rather than in legislation.
- The test which the judges formulated was beautifully simple: If the individual had capacity to make their own decision, treatment or care required their consent. If they lacked capacity, the clinician was under a duty to give any treatment or care necessary to preserve their life, health or well-being which was in their best interests.

3.2   The beauty of the scheme was its simplicity and the fact that it was non-prescriptive; it left much to the discretion of those providing the treatment or care. The weakness of the scheme was its simplicity and the fact that it was non-prescriptive; it left much to the discretion of those providing the treatment or care.

3.3   Because of the decision-making discretion given to professionals and family carers, few cases came to court. Only cases which involved especially significant or difficult decisions – such as life-sustaining treatment and sterilisation – tended to be referred.

3.4   As the years went by, many people became concerned by the lack of any structured process for deciding more commonplace personal welfare matters – issues such as where and with whom an incapacitated person should live, how much contact they should have with family members and friends, how to help them to develop their activities and skills, what medication they should receive, and so on.

3.5   Depending on the values, resources and time of family members and professionals, great to little or no care might be taken to establish which decisions the person could make for themselves. Similarly, if incapacitated, the individual might have considerable involvement in decisions about their welfare and future or none at all.

The Law Commission's work

3.6   Much useful work was done by the Law Commission to address these difficult issues. The Commission's fourth programme published in September 1989 noted the view that existing legal mechanisms were 'complicated, inflexible and piecemeal' and stated that the recent House of Lords decision in *Re F*[1] could not provide a comprehensive solution.[2]

3.7   Lady Hale (then Brenda Hoggett) was an important driver of the reform programme, and the Law Commission's Report of 1995[3] which had a draft Bill appended to it was preceded by a number of consultation and discussion papers.

3.8   The Law Commission's proposals were debated and in some respects modified over the following years, eventually emerging as the MCA 2005.

3.9   Subsequently, a number of important insertions to the Act were made by the MHA 2007. In particular, a new scheme for authorising deprivation of liberty under the MCA 2005 was introduced.

Statutory principles (section 1)

3.10   The MCA 2005 starts with a number of fundamental statutory principles which apply, and must be applied, whenever a person does something under the Act.

THE STATUTORY PRINCIPLES
Section 1(1) provides that the following principles apply for the purposes of the Act:

1	A person must be assumed to have capacity unless it is established that he lacks capacity (MCA 2005 s1(2)).
2	A person is not to be treated as unable to make a decision unless all practicable steps to help him to do so have been taken without success (MCA 2005 s1(3)).

1   Reported as *Re F (mental patient: sterilisation)* [1990] 2 AC 1.
2   Fourth Programme of Law Reform (1989) Law Com NO 185, Item 9; Cm 800.
3   *Mental incapacity (report)* [1995] EWLC 231, 15 January 1995. The report can be downloaded from the BAILII website: www.bailii.org/ew/other/ EWLC/1995/231_s.html.

3	A person is not to be treated as unable to make a decision merely because he makes an unwise decision (MCA 2005 s1(4)).
4	An act done, or decision made, under the Act for or on behalf of a person who lacks capacity must be done, or made, in his best interests (MCA 2005 s1(5)).
5	Before the act is done, or the decision is made, regard must be had to whether the purpose for which it is needed can be as effectively achieved in a way that is less restrictive of the person's rights and freedom of action (MCA 2005 s1(6)).

3.11   It is important to emphasise the importance of these principles at the outset, and useful to illustrate one or two of the situations in which they can be significant.

The presumption of capacity

3.12   The first principle is that the relevant person 'must be assumed to have capacity unless it is established that he lacks capacity'.

3.13   The starting point, therefore, is *always* that this person has capacity to make this particular decision for themselves. That remains the legal position until it is established that it is more likely than not that they lack this capacity.[4]

3.14   A fair number of cases brought to the Court of Protection are brought because the evidence is quite finely balanced and there is a dispute about the person's capacity. In such cases, the presumption of capacity may be decisive. In medical practice, for example in an A&E setting, it is not uncommon for a doctor when asked about a person's capacity to say that it is 'fifty-fifty'; evidently, the presumption of capacity has not been displaced. And, when it comes to depriving someone of their liberty under the Act, it follows that the presumption that they can make their own decision about whether to not to be in the particular hospital or care home must first be displaced.

---

4 MCA 2005 s2(4). In proceedings under the MCA 2005 'or any other enactment, any question whether a person lacks capacity within the meaning of this Act must be decided on the balance of probabilities'. The reference to proceedings under 'any other enactment' is likely to be relevant to certain proceedings taken under the MHA 1983.

Duty to help the person make their own decision where possible

3.15   The second principle is that a person is not to be treated as unable to make the particular decision for themselves unless all practicable steps to help them to do so have been taken without success.

3.16   What is practicable – that is, capable of being put into practice – depends on the circumstances at the time.

3.17   If a person in need of urgent medical treatment is unconscious after a serious motorway accident it will not be practicable before intervening to take any steps to help them make their own decision about the particular medical intervention.

3.18   At the other end of the scale is the situation where it is practicable to assist a person with a learning disability to make their own will. If there is no urgency, the fact that the person lacks capacity to make their own will today is not decisive if with assistance over weeks or months they can develop the necessary understanding. It may be possible to break the relevant information down into a more understandable form, to repeat key points over a number of weeks, to devise helpful visual aids and so on.

3.19   Likewise, an unwell person in hospital who is asked about a return home or a move into residential care may appear to lack capacity to make the decision at this moment. However, with more time to reflect, clearer explanations, and the benefit of discussing the options with family members, trusted friends or an advocate, they may well have capacity to make their own decision.

Unwise decision-making

3.20   The third principle is that 'A person is not to be treated as unable to make a decision merely because he makes an unwise decision'.

3.21   One can rephrase this by saying that a person is not to be treated as being unable to make their own decision merely because the decision they make *or propose making* is considered by some person or persons to be unwise.

3.22   Although a person cannot be found to lack capacity *merely* because their proposed decision is unwise, fairly obviously an unwise or irrational decision may raise significant doubts and so trigger an assessment of their capacity.

3.23   In practice this principle is often in play, particularly when it comes to decisions about whether to remove older people into residential care. There are many older people who prefer to 'take their chances' at home rather than live in a care home, notwithstanding the risk of falls and some physical suffering. Some of them, in common with all generations, will have a stubborn streak, 'unreasonably' refuse good or well-meant advice, or demonstrate a lifelong antipathy to being told what to do. The fact that others think they are being unwise is insufficient. They only lack capacity if their ability to understand, retain and weigh the information relevant to the decision, including the foreseeable benefits and risks of deciding one way or the other, is undermined in some significant way by an impairment or disturbance of their mind or brain. Otherwise, their decision is essentially no different to that of a person who goes mountaineering, hang-gliding or motor racing – risky and the doctor might not do it, arguably unwise, could end unhappily, but they are within their rights.

Duty to act in the person's best interests

3.24   The fourth principle is that, 'An act done, or decision made, under the Act for or on behalf of a person who lacks capacity must be done, or made, in his best interests'.

3.25   This was also part of the old common law test which, it may be recalled, required a clinician, social worker or other professional carer to give the incapacitated person any treatment or care necessary to preserve their life, health or well-being 'which was in their best interests'.

3.26   The final phrase drew attention to the fact that providing treatment or care is not always in a person's best interests. Obvious examples are where further prolonging a terminally ill patient's life would cause them considerable suffering for little benefit, and where a patient's fierce resistance to treatment means that it is not in their best interests to attempt to give it by restraint.

3.27   If a person lacks capacity to make a decision, so that someone else must make it for them, applying the best interests requirement does not mean that other people's interests are always irrelevant and must be given no weight. As an example, almost all parents want their children to be happy and free from worry. The Court of Protection may therefore authorise making a gift from the incapacitated person's funds to a child in need. If the incapacitated person still had capacity to make the gift they would wish to help in this way; and it is in their best interests to do on their behalf that which they themselves would obviously do if they could. Similarly, most people with capacity consider and take into account the wishes, feelings and needs of their spouse or partner when making decisions which affect them. It is in the incapacitated person's best interests to have regard to these historic genuine feelings and values if they can no longer hold or express them.

3.28 The critical error to avoid is an analysis of the person's best interests which disregards or downplays their wishes, feelings, values and beliefs in the perverted belief that critical objectivity is undermined by subjective considerations.

3.29 The law requires objective analysis of a subject not an object. The incapacitated person is the subject. Therefore, it is *their* welfare in the context of *their* wishes, feelings, beliefs and values that is important. This is the principle of beneficence which asserts an obligation to help others further *their* important and legitimate interests, not one's own.[5]

3.30 Why would anyone wish a person to receive care otherwise than in accordance with their wishes if they can be cared for adequately in accordance with their wishes?

Duty to consider less restrictive options

3.31 The fifth principle is that: 'Before the act is done, or the decision is made, regard must be had to whether the purpose for which it is needed can be as effectively achieved in a way that is less restrictive of the person's rights and freedom of action'.

3.32 This principle is sometimes paraphrased as 'one must choose the least restrictive option', which risks being misleading. The 'least restrictive option' of those available may be to do nothing and to neglect the person. That is not what the principle requires. The decision-maker must have regard to whether the necessary purpose or aim (eg treating a severe illness which is causing considerable suffering) can be as effectively achieved in a less restrictive way (eg in a way which is acceptable to the person or more acceptable to them). Why an act or decision is now needed, and the effectiveness of less restrictive approaches, must be considered.

---

5 From *Westminster City Council v Sykes* [2014] EWHC B9 (COP), (2014) 17 CCLR 139 at section 10.

Who lacks capacity (sections 2 and 3)

3.33   The purpose of the MCA 2005 is to provide a structure and appropriate mechanisms for making a decision on behalf of a fellow citizen who lacks capacity to make their own decision.

3.34   The first consideration therefore is, 'does this person lack capacity?' Does this person lack or now lack the capacity necessary to exercise a citizen's usual constitutional right to make their own decision? Does a decision now need to be made for them, in their best interests?

3.35   This is a matter of constitutional importance for a second reason. Those capable of acting are responsible for their actions and omissions and, being responsible for them, accountable to others. The counterpart of freedom and autonomy is accountability for acts freely and autonomously done.

3.36   The law takes what some people call an 'issue specific' or 'functional' approach to capacity. It assesses a person's ability to make a particular decision at a particular time, not their ability to make decisions generally.

3.37   As has been seen, everyone is assumed to have capacity to make the decision(s) in question unless and until it is established that they lack this capacity, which must be established on the balance of probabilities. Furthermore, a person is not to be treated as lacking capacity to make the decision in question unless all practicable steps to help them to do so have been taken without success.

3.38   A person does not lack capacity simply because they have a mental disorder or disability (sometimes described as a 'status approach' to capacity). Nor are they to be treated as lacking capacity to make the decision(s) in question merely because they propose making a decision which others consider to be unwise (sometimes called an 'outcome approach').

3.39   Furthermore, a lack of capacity cannot be established merely by reference to their age or appearance, a condition of theirs such as mental illness or a learning disability, or an aspect of their behaviour, which might lead others to make unjustified assumptions about their capacity.[6] One needs to be especially careful in the case of those who may merely be stubborn or eccentric. The correct test of capacity must be applied and lack of capacity be established.[7]

---

6   MCA 2005 s2(3).
7   See *Court of Protection Practice 2014*, Ashton et al, Jordans, at p991 et seq.

The incapacity test

3.40 For the purposes of the Act, a person lacks capacity in relation to a matter 'if at the material time he is unable to make a decision for himself in relation to the matter because of an impairment of, or a disturbance in the functioning of, the mind or brain'.[8]

3.41 Accordingly, capacity is both:

- *time-specific*, focusing on the particular time when a decision has to be made – so the loss of capacity can be temporary, partial or fluctuating, and
- *decision- or issue-specific*, concentrating on the particular matter to which the decision relates, rather than the ability to make decisions generally – so, someone may lack capacity in relation to one particular matter but not another.

3.42 The fact that a temporary impairment or disturbance of the mind or brain suffices brings within the Act those who are unable to make a decision because of the effects of alcohol or drugs. This is particularly relevant for A&E staff.

What is meant by 'unable to make a decision'

3.43 This is the 'section 3 test'. For these purposes, a person is unable to make a decision for themselves if they are unable:

- to understand the information relevant to the decision;
- to retain that information;
- to use or weigh that information as part of the process of making the decision; or
- to communicate their decision (whether by talking, using sign language or any other means).

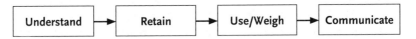

3.44 It can be seen that being 'unable to decide' does not literally mean that. Demonstrating incapacity involves establishing that the person's capacity to make the decision in question is in some way fundamentally compromised by the fact that the functioning of their mind or brain is impaired or disturbed. In other words, because of an impairment or disturbance of their mind or brain they are unable

---

8 It does not matter whether the impairment or disturbance is permanent or temporary.

to understand, retain or weigh the information relevant to the decision, or are unable to communicate their decision. A link must be demonstrated.

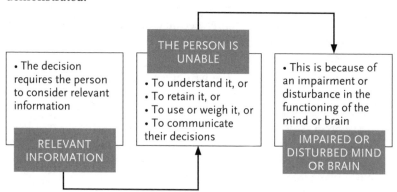

3.45   The test is not purely about cognition or capacity to reason. A person may understand the relevant information, be able to retain it, and intellectually able to acknowledge its significance, but be unable to give it weight because of an overwhelming phobia, obsessive thoughts, compulsive behaviour, abnormally impulsive behaviour or some other impairment or disturbance. It is therefore going too far to say that the quality of the decision is irrelevant as long as the person 'understands' what he or she is deciding.[9]

How much information is relevant information

3.46   How much information is relevant – the level and amount of information which the person must be capable of understanding, retaining and weighing in order to have capacity to make the decision – turns on the significance and complexity of the decision in question.

3.47   The MCA 2005 states that: 'The information relevant to a decision includes information about the reasonably foreseeable consequences of (a) deciding one way or another, or (b) failing to make the decision' (section 3(4)). This therefore is relevant information that needs to be

9   As Ashton notes, 'in *Mitchell v Alasia* [2005] EWHC 11 (QB), Cox J relied on qualities such as impulsiveness and volatility when deciding that the claimant was incapable of managing and administering his own affairs'. Similarly, in *NHS Trust v Ms T* [2004] EWHC 1279 (Fam), (2005) 8 CCLR 38, although there was no problem in respect of Ms T's intellectual capacity, and she was able to acknowledge intellectually that her belief was delusional, her wishes were driven by a delusional belief that any transfusion would only add to the evil circulating within her system: *Court of Protection Practice 2014*, Jordans, at p995.

understood, retained, used and weighed in order to have capacity to make the decision.

3.48 Some decisions are relatively insignificant and involve understanding and weighing very little information; other decisions are more complicated or have foreseeable consequences that are more significant.

3.49 Regardless of whether a person has capacity, the aim of all explanations is to simplify matters as far as possible but no further. Once the information relevant to a decision has been communicated in as understandable a way as possible – by breaking it down and using plain language and aids, but without resorting to omitting information which is relevant if more difficult to understand and weigh – one is still left with a spectrum of decisions ranging from those which are simple and require understanding relatively little to those that require understanding and weighing more.

3.50 In the case of a simple and trivial gift, such as giving a small present to a friend, there is not much to it and very little to grasp in order to make a valid gift. By definition, more significant transactions – those where the reasonably foreseeable consequences are more significant for the person concerned – require the capacity to understand and weigh the more significant consequences. Thus, in the old case of *Re Beaney*,[10] where the person was giving her house and only main asset to one of three children at the end of her life instead of by will, and the significance was to disinherit the other two children, the degree of understanding required was as high as that required for a will: the donor had to understand the claims of all potential donees and the extent of the property being disposed of. Unless she understood that, she would be entirely failing to grasp the significance, the essence, of the transaction.

3.51 It follows from the fact that capacity is issue-specific, and partly depends on the nature or complexity of the decisions to be made, that a person may have capacity to make some decisions for themselves (eg capacity to marry) but lack capacity to do other things (eg to make a will). A person may have capacity to bring or defend a small, relatively trivial claim in court, where the nature of the dispute and the issues are simple to understand and weigh, but lack capacity to litigate a case where the nature of the dispute or the issues are more significant or complex. Likewise, they may have capacity to consent to a simple medical procedure but not something much more significant.

---

10 *Re Beaney* [1978] 1 WLR 770, [1978] 2 All ER 595.

Capacity to understand the relevant information

3.52   The first of the four parts of the section 3 test concerns the person's capacity 'to understand' the relevant information.

3.53   The Act says that a person is not to be regarded as being unable to understand the information relevant to a decision if they are able to understand an explanation of it given to them in a way that is appropriate to their circumstances (using simple language, visual aids or any other means).[11] A relatively common example of a person being unable to understand the information relevant to a medical treatment decision would be an inability to understand the meaning of even common words, as a result of a very profound brain injury, learning disability or dementia.

Capacity to retain the relevant information

3.54   The fact that a person is able to retain the information relevant to a decision for a short period only does not prevent them from being regarded as able to make the decision.[12] However, by definition, before one can weigh relevant information one must be able to retain it long enough to do so. As an example, even a clear and simple explanation of the information relevant to a treatment decision involves communicating what is wrong (the diagnosis), what is proposed (the treatment), the likely outcome with and without treatment (the prognosis) and any significant treatment risks (adverse effects). If a person understands the diagnosis but has forgotten it by the time the proposed treatment is being explained, they are unable to retain all of the relevant information for long enough to enable them to weigh it and make a decision.

Capacity to weigh the relevant information

3.55   This is the ground which has proved to be the most difficult and controversial in practice.

3.56   Even though a person can understand and retain all of the information relevant to a decision, and can communicate their preferred decision, they will still be held to be unable to make the decision if they cannot 'use or weigh' the information as part of the process of making the decision.

---

11   MCA 2005 s3(2).
12   MCA 2005 s3(3).

3.57   A simple example is that of a person who because of mental ill-ness believes that their consultant psychiatrist is an imposter. The individual can understand and retain the relevant information given to them by the psychiatrist about their diagnosis, the proposed treat-ment, and so forth. They can also communicate the decision they intend to make. However, because they do not believe the doctor is a doctor, and give no weight at all to what the person says, they can-not 'use or weigh' the information as part of the process of making the decision. Therefore, they will be held to lack capacity to make the decision, on the weighing ground.

3.58   In the old case of *Re MB (Caesarean section)*,[13] MB consented to a Caesarean operation but then refused to be given anaesthesia by injection because she had a phobia of needles. When MB went into labour, the hospital obtained a declaration that it would be lawful to perform any necessary Caesarean upon her because she was incap-able of consenting to or refusing treatment.

3.59   In that kind of case, the individual can understand and retain the relevant information about the proposed treatment and the foresee-able consequences of deciding one way or the other, repeat it back word for word and communicate their decision to refuse. That is not the issue. However, as in MB, it may be held that she is unable to use or weigh this information as part of the process of making the deci-sion because her mind is disturbed by a terror of needles. She is petri-fied. This is so overwhelming as to prevent her from being able to use or weigh the relevant information about the foreseeable consequences of declining the intervention.

3.60   All cases are, of course, fact-specific. The important point is that the weight a person gives to relevant information, and their ability to use it when making the decision, are legally important considerations.

3.61   Some say that as soon as you refuse or discontinue treatment against medical advice you risk being found to lack capacity because it will be said that you have not understood or used the medical informa-tion properly, or have given it insufficient weight. That may happen in practice to a degree but it is not a correct statement of the law. It has to be demonstrated that the person is *unable* to use or weigh the informa-tion given to them and that this inability is *because of* an impairment or disturbance of the mind or brain. A link must be established.

3.62   What is true when it comes to serious medical treatment deci-sions is that the more autonomy the law sanctions the more deaths there will be. Freedom to make 'unwise' decisions comes at a price

13 [1997] EWCA Civ 3093, [1997] 2 FLR 426.

in terms of safety, and safety bears a price in terms of freedom. It is not possible to have it both ways.

3.63   It is important to be aware of any temptation to overcome this uncomfortable truth by a misuse of the intellect or evidence. One must not give in to 'the self-interested lie' and construct a contrived incapacity argument in order to release *oneself* from an almost unbearable burden.

Capacity to communicate one's decision

3.64   This applies to people who are unconscious or in a coma and those with the rare condition sometimes known as 'locked-in syndrome', who are conscious but cannot speak or move at all. If a person cannot communicate their decision in any way, the MCA 2005 says they should be treated as if they are unable to make that decision. However, before deciding that this is so, it is necessary to take all practicable steps to help them communicate; for example, one might involve speech and language therapists, specialists in non-verbal communication and other appropriate professionals. Communication by simple muscle movements can show that somebody may have capacity to make a decision.[14]

Best interests (section 4)

3.65   If it is the case that the relevant person is unable to make their own decision, then by definition unless the decision can be postponed someone else must make it for them.

3.66   The decision made for them must be made in their 'best interests'. The MCA 2005 provides that one must not determine what is in a person's best interests merely on the basis of their age or appearance, or a condition of theirs, or an aspect of their behaviour, which might lead others to make unjustified assumptions about what might be in their best interests.[15]

Matters to consider

3.67   The person making the determination must consider all of the relevant circumstances. Rather unhelpfully, the Act says that 'relevant

14   See Code of Practice paras 4.23–4.25: www.justice.gov.uk/downloads/protecting-the-vulnerable/mca/mca-code-practice-0509.pdf.
15   MCA 2005 s4(1).

circumstances' are those which the person determining best interests is aware of and which it would be reasonable to regard as relevant.[16] However, the person making the decision must in particular consider the matters set out in the following table.

BEST INTERESTS CONSIDERATIONS (MCA 2005 s4)	
The person determining what is in the person's best interests must in particular (MCA 2005 s4(2)):	
1	Consider whether it is likely that the person will at some time have capacity in relation to the matter in question and, if it appears likely that he will, when that is likely to be (MCA 2005 s4(3)).
2	So far as reasonably practicable, permit and encourage the person to participate, or to improve his ability to participate, as fully as possible in any act done for him and any decision affecting him (MCA 2005 s4(4)).
3	Consider, so far as is reasonably ascertainable, the person's past and present wishes and feelings (and, in particular, any relevant written statement made by him when he had capacity); the beliefs and values that would be likely to influence his decision if he had capacity; and the other factors that he would be likely to consider if he were able to do so (MCA 2005 s4(6)).
4	If it is practicable and appropriate to consult them, take into account the views of the following people: • anyone named by the person as someone to be consulted on the matter in question or on matters of that kind; • anyone engaged in caring for the person or interested in his welfare; • any donee of a lasting power of attorney granted by the person; and • any deputy appointed for the person by the court as to the matters mentioned in paragraph 3 and what would be in the person's best interests (MCA 2005 s4(7)).
5	Not be motivated by a desire to bring about his death where the determination relates to life-sustaining treatment and considering whether the treatment is in the best interests of the person concerned (MCA 2005 s4(5)). ('Life-sustaining treatment' means treatment which in the view of a person providing healthcare for the person concerned is necessary to sustain life: s4(10)).

16 MCA 2005 s4(11).

3.68   As to these five considerations:

1) The first of them differs from the second guiding principle, which stated that a person is not to be treated as unable to make a decision unless all practicable steps to help them to do so have been taken without success.

    Even if the person cannot *presently* make their own decision (even, for example, with the assistance of family members and simple, clear explanations) and so lacks capacity to decide the matter, one must consider if and when they are likely to have that capacity.

    It may be that with more time to reflect, further treatment, improved health, reduced medication levels, clearer explanations and the benefit of discussing the options with family members, trusted friends or an advocate, they are likely to develop or recover the capacity to decide.

    If so, this must be considered when deciding what is in their best interests. Depending on the urgency, it may be in their best interests to postpone the decision until they can make it for themselves.

2) The second makes a different point to that made by the second guiding principle. The point here is that, if the person cannot make their own decision because all practicable steps to help them to do so have failed, they must still be permitted and encouraged to participate in the decision-making process and any act done on their behalf. This is, of course, provided that this is reasonably practicable.

3) The third consideration draws attention to five matters:
    i) the person's present wishes and feelings;
    ii) the person's past wishes and feelings;
    iii) the beliefs and values that would be likely to influence their decision if they had capacity;
    iv) any relevant written statement made by the person when they had capacity (this could be a written statement about the treatment which the person wishes to receive rather than to reject);
    v) the other factors that they would be likely to consider if they were able to do so.

4) Provided that it is practicable and appropriate, the fourth consideration imposes a requirement to consult carers, nominated persons and persons appointed under the MCA 2005 about the person's wishes, feelings, beliefs and values, and the factors

which they would have been likely to take into account if they still had capacity to make their own decision.

Clearly, family members and non-professional carers will often know much more than the professionals about the person's wishes, feelings, beliefs, values, life goals and views concerning care and treatment. Proper consultation and sharing of information is critical to building up a true picture of the person's best interests.

5) The final listed matter provides that any person determining whether life-sustaining treatment is in the best interests of the person concerned must not be motivated by a desire to bring about their death. This legal requirement ties in with section 62 which states that nothing in the Act constitutes a defence to a charge of manslaughter or murder or is to be read or taken as legalising or authorising assisted suicide.

3.69 None of the listed considerations has automatic precedence.[17] This would be impossible given that the person determining best interests must also consider any other (unlisted) relevant considerations of which he or she is aware.

3.70 The weight to be attached to the various factors depends on the circumstances of the particular individual. A feature or factor which in one person's situation may carry great, possibly even preponderant, weight may in another, superficially similar, case carry much less, or even very little, weight. Sometimes one or more features or factors may be of 'magnetic importance' in influencing or even determining what is in the person's best interests.[18]

3.71 The person who determines best interests does not incur any legal liability for their determination simply because a court later comes to a different view. The Act provides that there is sufficient compliance with section 4 if, having complied with the requirements of the section, the person 'reasonably believes' that what they do or decide is in the best interests of the person concerned.[19] Unless one takes a peculiarly authoritarian view, in many situations more than one belief can reasonably be held. It is quite possible that family members and/ or members of the multi-disciplinary team may 'reasonably' believe something different.

17 See *ITW v Z* [2009] EWHC 2525 (Fam), (2009) 12 CCLR 635, per Munby J (as he then was) at para 32.

18 *ITW v Z* at para 32.

19 MCA 2005 s4(9).

Best interests and substituted judgment

3.72   To what extent must the aim of the person determining best interests be to identify and make the decision which they believe the person themselves would have made if they had, or still had, capacity to make it?

3.73   'Substituted judgment' is a principle which holds that surrogate decisions should be made by establishing as accurately as possible the decision which the incapacitated person would have made for themselves if they had capacity.

3.74   The Law Commission argued that 'best interests' on the one hand and 'substituted judgment' on the other were not in fact mutually exclusive. It favoured a 'best interests' criterion which contained a strong element of 'substituted judgment'.[20]

3.75   A main reason for rejecting a pure substituted judgment test was not that the views, beliefs and values of an incapacitated person were unimportant but that they are important:

> One of the failings of a pure 'substituted judgment' model is the unhelpful idea that a person who cannot make a decision should be treated as if his or her capacity were perfect and unimpaired, and as if present emotions need not also be considered.[21]

3.76   One must take into account and give weight to the person's present wishes and feelings, and what they now view as important, and not just the values and beliefs which they held when they had capacity, even if more objective.

3.77   Furthermore, as the Commission noted when rejecting a pure substituted judgment approach, if a person has never had capacity then 'substituted judgment' is impossible and there is no viable alternative to a best interests approach.

Safety, health, care, treatment and liberty

3.78   It must not be assumed that because the decision concerns care or medical treatment that therefore the person's care and medical treatment, and physical safety, are the most important considerations. There will usually be many other competing factors to consider, such as a person's attachment to their home, their privacy and sense of security at home, their attitude towards institutional life and the importance to them of their freedom.

---

20 Law Com No 231 para 3.25.
21 Law Com No 231 para 3.29.

3.79   The importance of individual liberty is of the same fundamental importance to incapacitated people who still have clear wishes and preferences about where and how they live as it is for those who remain able to make capacitous decisions. This desire to determine one's own interests is common to almost all human beings. Society is made up of individuals, and each individual wills certain ends for themselves and their loved ones, and not others, and has distinctive feelings, personal goals, traits, habits and experiences. Because this is so, most individuals wish to determine and develop their own interests and course in life, and their happiness often depends on this. The existence of a private sphere of action, free from public coercion or restraint, is indispensable to that independence which everyone needs to develop their individuality, even where their individuality is diminished, but not extinguished, by illness. It is for this reason that people place such weight on their liberty and right to choose.

Wishes, feelings and objectivity

3.80   The fact that the individual's past and present wishes, feelings, beliefs and values must be considered tells us that this is not a sterile objective test of best interests.

3.81   It is not a case of trying to determine what some hypothetical objective or rational person would decide in this situation when presented with these choices. Nor are we seeking to do anything more sophisticated than impose on the individual an objective and rational analysis based on professional expertise of what they ought sensibly to do in that situation.

3.82   The law requires objective analysis of a subject not an object. The incapacitated person is the subject. Therefore, it is *their* welfare in the context of *their* wishes, feelings, beliefs and values that is important. This is the principle of beneficence which asserts an obligation to help others further *their* important and legitimate interests, not one's own.

3.83   That this is so is emphasised by Lady Hale in the *Aintree* case:[22]

> Finally, insofar as Sir Alan Ward and Arden LJ were suggesting that the test of the patient's wishes and feelings was an objective one, what the reasonable patient would think, again I respectfully disagree. The purpose of the best interests test is to consider matters from the patient's point of view. That is not to say that his wishes must prevail, any more than those of a fully capable patient must prevail. We cannot always have what we want. Nor will it always be possible to ascertain

22 *Aintree University Hospitals NHS Foundation Trust v James* [2013] UKSC 67, (2013) 16 CCLR 554 at para 45.

what an incapable patient's wishes are. Even if it is possible to determine what his views were in the past, they might well have changed in the light of the stresses and strains of his current predicament. In this case, the highest it could be put was, as counsel had agreed, that 'It was likely that Mr James would want treatment up to the point where it became hopeless'. But insofar as it is possible to ascertain the patient's wishes and feelings, his beliefs and values or the things which were important to him, it is those which should be taken into account because they are a component in making the choice which is right for him as an individual human being.

3.84   It also emerges from various decisions of the President of the Court of Protection. Naturally, precisely how much weight to give to a person's present wishes and feelings will depend on the particular context and the individual's circumstances. The relevant circumstances will include the degree of their incapacity; the strength and consistency of their views; the possible impact on them of knowing that their wishes and feelings are not being given effect to; the extent to which their wishes and feelings are, or are not, rational, sensible, responsible and pragmatically capable of sensible implementation; and the extent to which their wishes and feelings, if given effect to, can properly be accommodated within the overall assessment of what is in her best interests. However, while the weight to be attached to the person's wishes and feelings will always be case-specific and fact-specific, their wishes and feelings will always be a significant factor to which the court must pay close regard.[23]

3.85   The drawing up of a 'balance sheet' in personal welfare cases, listing the actual and potential advantages and disadvantages of each alternative,[24] should not be a dry accountant's exercise which omits what is personal, but one that includes the 'personal' element of 'personal welfare'.

3.86   Whatever weight is given to the person's wishes and feelings, it is imperative not to reformulate them and claim to know better than they do what they truly wish, feel or will; in other words, not to be an 'aesthetic bully'.[25]

---

23 *ITW v Z* [2009] EWHC 2525 (Fam), (2009) 12 CCLR 635, per Munby J at para 35.

24 *Re S (adult's lack of capacity: carer and residence)* [2003] FLR 1235.

25 Care must be taken not to treat humanity as the raw material upon which the professional imposes her or his creative will, for the last century exposed the dangers of this way of thinking. It is, Berlin suggested, a form of thinking to which the scientist may be especially prone; for if, as Comte believed, scientific method will in due course reveal all truths, then what case is there for freedom of opinion or action, at least as an end in itself, and why should any conduct be

Summary – waypoint

3.87 There is a lot here for a reader new to the subject to grapple with, so it is worth summarising where we have got.

3.88 So far, in general terms, we have looked at three things:

1) the statutory principles to be applied to anything and everything done under the MCA 2005;
2) what we mean by lacking capacity to make a decision for oneself;
3) what we mean by best interests, and how to go about determining what is in a person's best interests.

We have also seen that the decisions which may be made for someone under the Act can relate to their personal welfare or to their property and financial affairs.

3.89 In diagrammatic form, this is where we have reached:

The circumstances require the person concerned to make a decision

↓

Someone is concerned about whether the person has capacity to make the decision

↓

The person's capacity to make the particular decision is assessed: is it the case that because of an impairment or disturbance of their mind or brain they are unable to understand, retain or weigh the information relevant to this decision, or are unable to communicate their decision?

If this cannot be established on the balance of probabilities, the law regards the person as having capacity to make their own decision. Who decides? They decide.	If this is established on the balance of probabilities then, by definition, if they cannot make the decision for themselves someone must decide for them.

↓

The way we do this is by applying the MCA 2005. That is why it exists: it is an Act which sets out the framework to be used when making a decision for someone who cannot make their own decision.

↓

When using and applying the Act, a person making a decision for someone must always act in their best interests, rather than eg in their own interests.

tolerated that is not authorised by appropriate experts? See Sir I Berlin, *Four essays on liberty*, OUP, 1969, pp150–151.

The statutory mechanisms

3.90   That helps but takes matters only so far.

3.91   What does the phrase, 'The way the person does that is by applying the MCA 2005', mean in practice? Are there forms or documents to complete, does an application need to be made to a court, does a decision-maker need to be formally appointed, and so on?

3.92   Put differently, we now know the principles, but what are the mechanisms – the mechanics of getting the job done?

Four main mechanisms

3.93   There are four main decision-making mechanisms, four ways of making decisions under the MCA 2005.

3.94   All of them are relevant to personal welfare decision-making. Only two of them – lasting powers of attorney (LPA) and the Court of Protection – are relevant to financial and property-related matters.

Arrangements made by the person themselves when they had capacity	
1. Advance decisions to refuse treatment	An adult with capacity to do so may make an advance decision to refuse a particular treatment at a later date if they lack capacity at that time to decide whether or not to receive it. Because the decision was made when the person still had capacity, subject to certain exceptions it is binding on clinicians.
2. Lasting powers of attorney (LPA)	An adult with capacity to do so may make an LPA appointing one or more trusted persons to make decisions for them at a later date which they lack capacity to make for themselves.
	There are two types of LPA. One is used to authorise the person's chosen attorney(s) to make personal welfare decisions; the other is used to authorise making financial and property-related decisions on the individual's behalf.
	(LPAs replaced the old-style enduring powers of attorney (EPAs), which were limited to authorising financial and property-related decisions and could not provide for personal welfare matters. Previously made EPAs continue to have effect but no new ones may be created.)

Arrangements which can be made for them after capacity has been lost	
3. Court orders	The Court of Protection can make the particular decision(s) on the person's behalf or appoint a person called 'a deputy' to make personal welfare and/or financial and property-related decisions for the person as and when they arise.
4. Section 5	MCA 2005 s5 relates only to personal welfare matters and is an exemption from legal liability provision. In general terms, it states that a carer (paid or unpaid) will not be liable for non-negligent care and treatment given to an incapacitated person provided they comply with the conditions set out in section 5.

3.95   It is helpful to say a little more about this overall decision-making structure.

Above and below the line

3.96   The first two mechanisms – the 'above the line' mechanisms in the table above – are things which adults with capacity can do for themselves to plan for the day when they lose capacity:

- As regards personal welfare matters, they can make a decision in advance to refuse a particular treatment or treatments they dislike and/or appoint a person or persons they trust to make future personal welfare decisions for them which they lack the capacity to make.

    From this it can be seen that if a person lacks capacity to make the decision in question the first thing to do is to check whether they made their own arrangements to cater for this situation when they had capacity. If so then, unless their arrangement is invalid or inapplicable for some proper legal reason, apply this mechanism. If not 'go below the line' and – unless there are appropriate ways of dealing with the situation outside the MCA 2005 – make an application to the Court of Protection or rely on the protection afforded by section 5.

- As regards financial and property-related matters, the only mechanism 'above the line' is an LPA for property and financial matters.

    If the person has made an LPA (or previously an old-style EPA) then unless it requires registration, or is invalid or inapplicable for some proper legal reason, this is the appropriate mechanism to use.

- Because only adults (people aged 18 or over) can make these 'above the line' arrangements, necessarily it follows that if the incapacitated person is a child there cannot exist a valid LPA, EPA or advance decision to refuse treatment. In their case it will always be necessary either to go 'below the line' or to seek an alternative to the MCA 2005, such as parental authority or a provision of the Children Act 1989 or MHA 1983.

Going below the line

3.97   If the incapacitated person did not make their own 'above the line' arrangements in anticipation that subsequently they might lack capacity to make this decision, it will be necessary to resort to the two remaining mechanisms, 'below the line':

- As regards financial and property-related matters, the only mechanism 'below the line' is a court application. The usual application is to apply to the court for it to appoint a 'deputy for property and affairs' on the incapacitated person's behalf. The person appointed, who is often a close relative or a solicitor, is authorised by the court to deputise for the incapacitated person and to make financial and property-related decisions for them, subject to any restrictions in the court order. Because routine financial decisions – for example, paying bills – are needed on a day-to-day or week-to-week basis, this is more practical than going to court each time a financial decision is required.
- As regards personal welfare matters – for example, decisions about providing care or treatment to the individual – there are two options: making an application to court or applying section 5.

3.98   For reasons that may not always be valid, the Court of Protection has sometimes discouraged the appointment of personal welfare deputies.

3.99   An application for a court order should be made if it is in the person's best interests – for example, because the care or treatment is particularly intrusive, there is a significant dispute about what is in the person's best interests or apponting a personal welfare deputy is in the person's best interests.

3.100   In practice, almost all routine care and treatment is provided under the protection of section 5 without a court order or deputy in place. Many routine treatment and care decisions are not opposed by the incapacitated person, their family or paid carers. For example, decisions about bathing and treating an unconscious person or a decision to dress and help feed someone with severe dementia. Other decisions, where there is some difference of opinion, can be resolved by holding a best interests meeting at which the options are discussed and a resolution reached. In all of these cases, what is happening in legal terms is that the care and treatment is being provided in reliance on the last mechanism, section 5, and there will be no application to the Court of Protection for it to authorise the step in question.

3.101   Section 5 does not as such authorise providing any care or treatment; rather, it exempts a person who does provide an incapacitated person with care or treatment from any legal liability, provided they reasonably believe it is in the individual's best interests and the other section 5 conditions are satisfied.

More about advance decisions

3.102   The purpose of this chapter is not to provide an exhaustive statement of the law but to introduce the reader to the basic MCA 2005 principles and structures applicable to Court of Protection work. There are a few points concerning advance decisions which it is useful to know at the outset.

An advance decision 'to refuse treatment'

3.103   MCA 2005 s24(1) provides that an 'advance decision' means a decision made by an adult 'when he has capacity to do so' that if:

(a) at a later time and in such circumstances as he may specify, a specified treatment is proposed to be carried out or continued by a person providing health care for him, and

(b) at that time he lacks capacity to consent to the carrying out or continuation of the treatment,

the specified treatment is not to be carried out or continued.

3.104   From this, it can be seen that:

• An advance decision can only relate to 'treatment' proposed by someone providing health care, not personal care. The term 'treatment' includes 'a diagnostic or other procedure'.[26] The intention presumably is that a person cannot refuse basic personal care which they may require upon becoming incapacitated such

26 See MCA 2005 s64(1).

as shelter, feeding, drinking, clothing and washing. There is no right to die in squalor.

- Second, a person with capacity may decide in advance what treatment to refuse but not what treatment to receive. A clinician cannot be required to give treatment which they consider is clinically inappropriate.[27]
- Third, on a literal reading, the right is to refuse a particular specified treatment, not to refuse treatment by a specified health care provider or treatment at a specified hospital or place.

Effect of advance decisions

3.105   The effect of a valid advance decision which it is accepted is applicable to the particular treatment is that the incapacitated person is treated as having made the decision with capacity on the future date when they would otherwise be given the treatment.[28] In other words, notwithstanding that the person now lacks capacity to consent or to refuse consent to the treatment, it operates as a valid and binding refusal of that treatment.

Formalities

3.106   In terms of the formalities, an advance decision can be expressed 'in layman's terms',[29] provided of course it is sufficiently clear what treatment is being ruled out and the circumstances in which it is not to be given.

3.107   An advance decision to refuse treatment need not be in writing unless it relates to life-sustaining treatment. In this instance, to be applicable it must be in writing and include a statement 'to the effect that it is to apply to that treatment even if life is at risk'. It must then be signed by the relevant person (or by someone in their presence and at their direction) in the presence of a witness who then signs as a witness.[30] These formalities exist because the individual may literally be signing their life away.

---

27 A person can of course set out in writing in advance what treatment they wish to receive if and when they lack capacity and this must be taken into account when deciding what treatment (if any) is in their best interests: see MCA 2005 s4(6)(a). However, such a statement is not binding in the way that an advance decision made under section 24 is. Since it is not binding, nothing has been decided in advance.

28 MCA 2005 s26(1).

29 MCA 2005 s24(2).

30 MCA 2005 s25(5).

3.108   The person concerned may withdraw or alter their advance decision at any time they have capacity to do so,[31] and a withdrawal (including a partial withdrawal) of an advance decision which relates to life-sustaining treatment need not be in writing.[32]

Validity and applicability of advance decisions

3.109   A person does not incur liability for the consequences of withholding or withdrawing a treatment if at the time the person reasonably believes that an advance decision refusing the treatment exists which is 'valid and applicable' to the treatment.[33]

3.110   Conversely, a person is liable in law to the incapacitated person if the person carries out or continues a particular treatment when at the time he or she is satisfied that an advance decision refusing the treatment exists which is 'valid and applicable' to it.[34]

3.111   The Court of Protection may make a declaration as to whether an advance decision exists, is valid or is applicable to a particular treatment.[35]

3.112   Nothing in an apparent advance decision stops a person providing life-sustaining treatment, or doing any act that the person reasonably believes to be necessary to prevent a serious deterioration in the person's condition, while a decision as respects any relevant issue is sought from the court.[36]

3.113   In any disputed case, it can be seen that the two key issues are validity and applicability.

Validity	• An advance decision is not binding if it is not valid. • An advance decision is not valid if the person lacked capacity to make it at the time. • An advance decision is not valid if the person withdrew it at any time when s/he had capacity to do so. • An advance decision is not valid if the person has done anything else clearly inconsistent with it remaining their fixed decision.

31   MCA 2005 s24(3).
32   MCA 2005 s24(4).
33   MCA 2005 s26(3).
34   MCA 2005 s26(2).
35   MCA 2005 s26(4).
36   MCA 2005 s26(5).

Applicability	• An advance decision is not binding if it is not applicable to the particular treatment. • An advance decision is not applicable if the person still has capacity to make this particular treatment decision (simply ask them for their decision). • An advance decision is not applicable if the treatment is not the treatment specified in the advance decision. • An advance decision is not applicable if any circumstances specified in the advance decision are absent. • An advance decision is not applicable if there are reasonable grounds for believing that circumstances exist which the person did not anticipate at the time of the advance decision which would have affected their decision. • An advance decision is not applicable to life-sustaining treatment unless it is verified by a statement to the effect that it is to apply to that treatment even if life is at risk, and the decision is in writing, signed and witnessed.

More about LPAs

3.114   Although not fully appreciated, the new personal welfare LPA was the 'game-changer' in the MCA 2005.

3.115   The previous common law position in relation to incapacitated persons was that the clinician, social worker or other professional carer was under a duty to give any treatment or care necessary to preserve their life, health or well-being which was in their best interests. In other words, the best interests care or treatment decision was taken by the relevant professional.

3.116   Where a registered LPA is in force, the position now is that there is always someone from whom the relevant professional requires a consent. For as long as the receiver of the proposed care or treatment has capacity, treatment and care requires their consent. If they lack capacity to consent or refuse consent, the professional must go to the person nominated by them to make the decision.

3.117   This represents a considerable shift in the balance of power. Any adult with capacity can now nominate a trusted family member, friend, colleague or professional to make personal welfare decisions for them which they are unable to make in the future, in preference to leaving the best interests determination to the relevant professional.

3.118   The necessary detail is dealt with in the relevant chapters. However, it is probably helpful to emphasise the following points about LPAs at the outset:

- The person who makes the LPA is called the 'donor'. Strictly speaking, a person appointed is a 'donee'. However, in practice most people prefer 'attorney' because it is more natural and was the term used for many years in relation to the old-style EPAs.
- More than one attorney can be appointed but, if more than one, the document creating the LPA must state whether they are only authorised to make decisions jointly or can act alone or jointly ('jointly and severally').
- An LPA is not valid unless and until it has been registered (that is, stamped and entered on a register) by the Public Guardian.
- Completing an LPA is not difficult but involves using the prescribed form, and there are separate forms for the creation of a personal welfare LPA and for the creation of a property and financial affairs LPA.
- An attorney must act in accordance with the statutory principles and best interests requirements in MCA 2005 s4.
- What constitutes a 'personal welfare' decision is not exhaustively defined. However, the range of best interests decisions which may be made by a personal welfare attorney on behalf of an incapacitated person is likely to be extensive. The main Code of Practice suggests that they include decisions about:
  - where the incapacitated person should live and whom they should live with;
  - their day-to-day care, including diet and dress;
  - whom they may have contact with;
  - consenting to or refusing consent to medical examination and treatment;
  - necessary arrangements for medical, dental or optical treatment;
  - community care assessments and the provision of community care services;
  - participation in social activities, leisure activities, education or training;
  - personal correspondence and papers;
  - rights of access to personal information about the donor;
  - complaints about their care or treatment.[37]

---

37 See Code of Practice para 7.21.

- This decision-making authority is subject to the restriction that a donee may only make personal welfare decisions which he or she reasonably believes the donor lacks capacity to make for themselves.[38] Furthermore, a personal welfare donee has no authority to give or to refuse consent to life-sustaining treatment unless the LPA document expressly permits this.[39]
- A donor may revoke the power at any time he or she still has capacity to do so.[40]
- The Court of Protection can revoke an LPA in certain circumstances, for example where a donee has contravened their authority or has behaved in a way which is not in the person's best interests.[41]

Interplay between advance decisions and LPAs

3.119 An advance decision to refuse a particular treatment is not valid if the person later makes an LPA authorising an attorney to decide whether or not to consent to the particular treatment in the event they lack capacity to make the decision.[42]

3.120 That restriction aside, the existence of an LPA does not in itself prevent an advance decision from being valid and applicable.[43] Indeed, a valid and applicable advance decision made by a person with capacity after making an LPA prevents their donee from consenting to that treatment. This is because, other than the statutory exception just referred to, a donee's authority is subject to the person's advance decision 'rights' in MCA 2005 ss24–26.[44] Furthermore, a donee may only make those personal welfare decisions which he or she reasonably believes the donor lacks capacity to make[45] and the advance decision has effect as if the refusal of treatment was made with capacity at the time the treatment is proposed.[46]

---

38 MCA 2005 s11(7)(a).
39 MCA 2005 s11(7)(c) and (8).
40 MCA 2005 s13(2).
41 MCA 2005 s22(3).
42 MCA 2005 s25(2)(b).
43 MCA 2005 s25(7).
44 MCA 2005 s11(7)(b).
45 MCA 2005 s11(7)(a).
46 MCA 2005 s26(1).

More about court orders and deputies

3.121 Court orders and deputies are dealt with in greater detail later. However, in brief, MCA 2005 s15 provides that the Court of Protection may make declarations as to:

- whether a person has or lacks capacity to make a decision specified in the declaration;
- whether a person has or lacks capacity to make decisions on such matters as are described in the declaration;
- the lawfulness or otherwise of any act done, or yet to be done, in relation to that person.

3.122 Section 16 applies if a person lacks capacity in relation to a matter or matters concerning their personal welfare or property and affairs.[47] It enables the court by order to make such decisions on their behalf or to appoint a deputy to make the decisions for the person.

3.123 Without prejudice to MCA 2005 s4, the court may make an order or appoint a deputy on such terms as it considers are in the incapacitated person's best interests – and may do so even though no application is before it 'on those terms'.

3.124 Naturally, if the judge can make the decision, it will generally be inappropriate for him or her to authorise someone else to make it.

3.125 Consequently, the Act provides that a decision by the court is to be preferred to the appointment of a deputy to make a decision; and that the powers conferred on the deputy should be as limited in scope and duration 'as is reasonably practicable in the circumstances': see MCA 2005 s16(4).

Personal welfare deputies

3.126 Personal welfare deputy orders are considerably less common than property and affairs deputyships for reasons which seem invalid or inconsistent to some incapacitated people and their families.

3.127 The circumstances in which it is appropriate to appoint a personal welfare deputy are explained in *Re P*,[48] *G v E, Manchester City Council and F*,[49] *SBC v PBA and others*[50] and *A Local Authority v TZ (No 2)*.[51]

---

47 MCA 2005 s16(1).
48 [2010] EWHC 1592 (Fam), (2010) 13 CCLR 610.
49 [2010] EWHC 2512 (COP).
50 [2011] EWHC 2580 (Fam), [2011] COPLR Con Vol 1095.
51 [2014] EWHC 973 (COP).

3.128   Roderic Wood J observed in *SBC v PBA and others* that the test to be applied when determining whether to appoint a deputy (whether to manage a person's property and affairs or take decisions regarding their health and welfare) is to be derived from the unvarnished words of the MCA 2005. What is in the person's best interests is the governing criterion, as with all other decisions made under the Act.

3.129   As His Lordship noted, nothing in the then two leading cases on the appointment of deputies compelled a different conclusion: *Re P (vulnerable adult: deputies)*[52] and *G v E (deputyship and litigation friend)*.[53]

3.130   Naturally, it will rarely be appropriate for a judge to effectively deputise someone to judge a dispute or make a decision brought before the court for a judicial decision.

3.131   However, sometimes it may well be in a person's best interests to authorise their spouse or life partner, or the parent of a severely learning disabled young adult, to deputise for them in day-to-day personal welfare matters as well as day-to-day property matters.

3.132   That individual will often be best placed to make good quality decisions on the incapacitated person's behalf which best promote their interests in connection with community care assessments and services; access to personal information about them; complaints about their care, or treatment; arrangements for dental and optical treatment; GP appointments, medical appointments and examinations; social activities; and day-to-day care, education and training.[54]

3.133   In each of these instances, if the incapacitated person still had capacity they would decide whether or not to consent to proposed treatment or care and it may well be in their best interests that their 'nearest and dearest' now deputises for them in this capacity. The marriage vows are a relevant statement made when the person had capacity. Cohabitation, devotion and mutual commitment over many years are a relevant circumstance.

3.134   One advantage of an approach that takes each case on its merits is that a symmetry emerges from the shadows which is consistent with the ethos of the legislation in enabling a judge to advance the best interests of people who have lost capacity. An individual who still had capacity when the Act came into force was or is able to appoint a trusted person such as a spouse or partner to make future decisions for them which they cannot make. What, though, of the person who

52 [2010] EWHC 1592 (Fam), (2010) 13 CCLR 610.
53 [2010] EWHC 2512 (COP).
54 See Code of Practice para 7.21.

lost capacity to appoint their spouse or partner before the Act was in force? As in the case of their property, surely the court has the option of appointing as their deputy the person they would have appointed as their attorney. That is, of course, provided on the evidence that the advantages are real and it is in their best interests.

3.135 On this construction, the argument that property and financial affairs deputyship is somehow always different in kind to personal welfare deputyship is artificial. For many incapacitated people, just as many personal welfare decisions as financial decisions are made for them each week.

3.136 The fact that a person who provides routine care is given legal protection by MCA 2005 s5 does not mean that it is not in their best interests to have a personal welfare deputy any more than the fact that a person who provides necessary goods and services is given legal protection by section 7 means that it is not in their best interests to have a financial deputy. Sections 5 and 7 both exist to ensure that people who are incapacitated do not go without what they need.

3.137 It may be significant that the same subsection (MCA 2005 s6(6)) provides that section 5 does not authorise a person to do an act which conflicts with a decision made by a donee or a deputy, which perhaps points away from a suggestion that the statutory norm is that donees but not deputies will commonly make personal welfare decisions in preference to reliance on section 5.

3.138 Ultimately, the decision in each case ought to turn on what is in that person's best interests. It would be strange if the statutory framework is that a judge ought not to appoint a personal welfare deputy even if he or she is satisfied that it is in the person's best interests. Where does this leave their wishes and feelings? What of their beliefs and values, and the views expressed by the persons consulted? MCA 2005 s4 says that the judge must have regard to these considerations. The position of a spouse or partner of 50 years' duration or the parent of a brain-damaged child who is having their 18th birthday is not the same as that of a paid carer.

Who may be a deputy

3.139 A deputy must be an adult (aged 18 or over) or, in the case of property and affairs deputyships, a trust corporation.[55]

---

55 MCA 2005 s19(1).

3.140   A person may not be appointed as a deputy without their consent.[56]

3.141   The court may appoint the holder of a specified office or position as the person's deputy,[57] for example the holder of a particular local authority finance office. This avoids the need for a new order when the current holder of the post moves on and is replaced.

Two or more deputies

3.142   The court may appoint two or more deputies to act jointly, jointly or alone ('severally'), or jointly in respect of some matters and jointly or alone in respect of others.[58]

A deputy's powers and duties

3.143   Subject to certain restrictions dealt with below, the court may confer on a deputy such powers and/or impose on them such duties as it thinks necessary or expedient for giving effect to, or otherwise in connection with, their appointment.[59]

3.144   A deputy:

- is appointed to make decisions on the incapacitated person's behalf, not on the court or judge's behalf (in other words, the deputy is deputising for the person concerned, not for the judge or court);
- is to be treated as that person's agent in relation to anything done or decided within the scope of their appointment and in accordance with the Act;[60]
- must act in accordance with the authority conferred by the court.

3.145   With regard to property and affairs deputyships, the court may confer on a deputy powers to:

- take possession or control of all or any specified part of the person's property;

---

56 MCA 2005 s19(3).
57 MCA 2005 s19(2).
58 MCA 2005 s19(4).
59 MCA 2005 s16(5).
60 As a general proposition, whatever P has power to do for themselves (eg request a community care assessment) may be done by their agent and, conversely, what a person cannot do for themselves (eg force a doctor to give a particular drug) cannot be done by their agent.

- exercise all or any specified powers in respect of it, including such powers of investment as the court may determine.[61]

Interplay between advance decisions and deputyship

3.146 A personal welfare deputy may not consent to treatment which is prohibited by an advance decision because the authority conferred on a deputy is subject to the provisions of the Act.[62] Furthermore, MCA 2005 s20(1) provides that a deputy does not have power to make a decision for the person if he or she knows or has reasonable grounds for believing that the person has capacity to decide the matter, and the advance decision has effect as if the refusal was made with capacity at the time the treatment is proposed.[63]

Restrictions on deputies

3.147 The Act provides that certain powers may not be conferred on or exercised by a deputy:

Powers which a deputy does not have	Powers which the court may not give a deputy
With regard to the person's personal welfare	
A deputy does not have power to make a decision in relation to a matter if he or she knows or has reasonable grounds for believing that the person concerned has capacity in relation to that matter (MCA 2005 s20(1)).	The court may not give a deputy power to prohibit a named person from having contact with the incapacitated person (MCA 2005 s20(2)(a)). Power to prohibit such contact is reserved to judges (and personal welfare attorneys).
A deputy may not refuse consent to the carrying out or continuation of life-sustaining treatment in relation to the relevant person (MCA 2005 s20(5)).	The court may not give a deputy power to direct a professional responsible for the relevant person's health care to allow a different professional to take over that responsibility (MCA 2005 s20(2)(b)).

---

61 MCA 2005 s19(8).
62 MCA 2005 s20(6).
63 MCA 2005 s26(1).

Powers which a deputy does not have	Powers which the court may not give a deputy
A deputy may not do an act that is intended to restrain the person unless the four conditions set out in MCA 2005 s20(7) are satisfied.	The court may not give a deputy power to make a decision on the relevant person's behalf which is inconsistent with a decision made, within the scope of their authority and in accordance with the Act, by a donee of a lasting power of attorney (MCA 2005 s20(4)).
A deputy is not authorised to deprive the person of their liberty.	
With regard to the person's property and affairs	
A deputy does not have power to make a decision in relation to a matter if he or she knows or has reasonable grounds for believing that the person concerned has capacity in relation to that matter (MCA 2005 s20(1)).	The court may not give a deputy power to make a decision on the relevant person's behalf which is inconsistent with a decision made, within the scope of their authority and in accordance with the Act, by a donee of an LPA (MCA 2005 s20(4)).
	A deputy may not be given powers with respect to the execution of a will for the person concerned (MCA 2005 s20(3)(b)).
	A deputy may not be given powers with respect to the settlement of any of the person's property, whether for P's benefit or for the benefit of others (MCA 2005 s20(3)(a)).
	A deputy may not be given powers with respect to the exercise of any power (including a power to consent) vested in the person whether beneficially or as trustee or otherwise (MCA 2005 s20(3)(c)).
General limitations imposed by the Act	
The authority conferred on a deputy is subject to the provisions of the Act and, in particular, to MCA 2005 s1 (the principles) and s4 (best interests): MCA 2005 s20(6).	

Powers of deputies compared with donees and the court

3.148   It can be seen that deputies have fewer powers than donees and judges:

	Court	LPA donee	Deputy
Power to refuse life-sustaining treatment	✓	✓	×
Power to give or refuse consent to other forms of treatment and care	✓	✓	✓
Power to restrain P to give care or treatment	✓	✓	✓
Power to prohibit contact with a named person	✓	✓	×
Power to allow another person to take charge of P's treatment	✓	✓(?)	×
Power to deprive P of their liberty	✓	×	×

A donee's powers are subject to any conditions and restrictions in the LPA and any authority to give or refuse life-sustaining treatment is conditional on it being expressly provided for in the LPA. Similarly, a deputy's authority is subject to any duties and conditions specified in the order appointing them. A donee, deputy or judge may not make a decision for a person if they know or reasonably believe that the person has capacity to make their own decision. There may be other qualifications in a particular case such as the existence of an advance decision and the table compares the maximum powers which each decision-maker may possess.

More about section 5 ('acts in connection with a person's care or treatment')

3.149   Everyone is liable to an incapacitated person for criminal acts such as ill-treatment or neglect and for negligent treatment or care. MCA 2005 s5 does not affect these liabilities.[64]

3.150   Instead, it provides that a professional or non-professional carer is regarded as having the person's consent for any treatment or care given to them if five conditions are satisfied.

3.151   Because of this presumed consent, the legal effect is that the carer need not worry that technically he or she may be committing

---

64 MCA 2005 s5(3).

an assault because the person concerned lacks capacity to consent to the operation, treatment or piece of care being provided.[65] Likewise, provided that the conditions are satisfied, the carer is protected even if later it is held that a person who objected to care or treatment did in fact have capacity at the time and a right to refuse it.

3.152   The essential thrust of the provision is that those who care for people without capacity should be protected from legal liability provided that the care is reasonably believed to be in the person's best interests and is performed without negligence.

3.153   Because section 5 is a 'freedom from legal liability' provision, it is of a different kind to those sections of the MHA 1983 which authorise treatment or care without consent but which require applications and medical recommendations to be completed before the power arises.

3.154   There are no statutory forms to complete under section 5, although in non-routine situations it is sensible to keep some kind of written record of the decision. Rather, the section is there to be invoked and relied on as a defence if the carer is later challenged and it is suggested that they are legally liable to the incapacitated person for their act.

---

65 MCA 2005 s5(2). The person who does the act (D) does not incur any liability in relation to the act that he would not have incurred if P had had capacity to consent in relation to the matter, and had consented to D's doing the act.

THE FIVE SECTION 5 CONDITIONS		
1	The act is one undertaken 'in connection with' another person's care or treatment.	• This embraces nursing, medical and dental treatment, speech and language therapy, psychological interventions, social work, community care and also personal care such as assistance with washing, dressing, personal hygiene and feeding. • The phrase 'in connection with' indicates that section 5 also covers diagnostic examinations and tests, assessment procedures, taking a person to see their doctor, arranging the provision of a care service, etc.
2	The person doing it takes reasonable steps to establish whether the recipient has capacity.	Unless the carer has given it to the lawyers 'on a plate', they will have taken reasonable steps to establish lack of capacity – which does not necessarily require a capacity assessment – and reasonably believe that the person lacks capacity to make this particular treatment or care decision for themselves.
3	The person reasonably believes that the recipient lacks capacity.	
4	The person reasonably believes that it will be in their best interests for the act to be done.	• This involves applying the best interests considerations in section 4. • More than one thing can reasonably be believed and the level of protection to a carer is generous to that extent.
5	If the person uses restraint, he or she reasonably believes *both* that it is necessary to do the act in order to prevent harm to the person and that the act is a proportionate response to the likelihood of their suffering harm and the seriousness of that harm.	• The Act states that for these purposes one person restrains another if he or she a) uses, or threatens to use, force to secure the doing of an act which he or she resists, or b) restricts their liberty of movement, whether or not they resist. • Restricting someone's liberty or using force is always undesirable. If used to give care or treatment, the requirement here is essentially that the care or treatment is necessary and does more good than the restraint does harm; it is the lesser of two evils.

3.155   When providing care or treatment, it may seem tempting to seek to rely on section 5 in all situations, and thereby to avoid the complexities of advance decisions, LPAs and court orders.

3.156   This would be a mistake. For example, the Act provides that:

- nothing in section 5 affects the operation of sections 24–26 (advance decisions to refuse treatment);[66] and that
- section 5 does not authorise a person to do an act which conflicts with a decision properly made within the scope of his authority by a donee of a lasting power of attorney or a deputy appointed by the court.[67]

3.157   It is not possible therefore simply to leap to section 5 as a way around having to learn the framework. The first step is to consider whether the person made an applicable advance decision or LPA. Only if they did not provide for this situation, or their advance decision or LPA is irrelevant or invalid, does one move on to considering the need for a court application or relying on section 5.

3.158   Furthermore, one cannot reasonably believe that it is in the person's best interests to delay going to court and to continue to provide the care or treatment under section 5 if there is a significant disagreement about whether it is in the person's best interests which cannot be resolved.

A general framework

3.159   It is now possible to set out a framework that is generally applicable to all personal welfare decisions made under the MCA 2005:

---

66   MCA 2005 s5(4).

67   MCA 2005 s6(6). This prohibition does not prevent a person providing life-sustaining treatment, or doing any act which he or she reasonably believes to be necessary to prevent a serious deterioration in P's condition, while a decision as respects any relevant issue is sought from the court: see MCA 2005 s6(7).

	Step	Example
1	The circumstances require a person to make a decision in connection with their own care or treatment	Mr Smith is being examined at hospital and it is apparent that he has a significant heart condition. Treatment is recommended.
2	Someone is concerned about whether this person has capacity to make the decision for themselves	Mr Smith also suffers from quite severe dementia. The doctor is concerned that he appears not to understand the relevant information being conveyed concerning the diagnosis, the treatment which is necessary medically and the prognosis with and without treatment.
3	The person's capacity to make this particular decision for themselves is assessed: Is it the case that because of an impairment or disturbance of their mind or brain they are unable to understand or retain or weigh the information relevant to this decision, or are unable to communicate their decision?	Mr Smith's capacity to make his own decision about whether or not to have the proposed assessment procedures and treatment is assessed.
4	If this cannot be established on the balance of probabilities, the law regards the person as having capacity to make their own decision. Who decides? They decide. If it is established on the balance of probabilities that the person cannot make the decision for themselves, then (unless it can be postponed) someone will have to make it for them.	On the evidence, the doctor is satisfied that the presumption of capacity has been rebutted. Because of an impairment of the brain (dementia) Mr Smith is unable to understand, retain and weigh the information relevant to the treatment decision.

	Step	Example
5	**The way the person does this is by applying the MCA 2005. It is an Act which sets out a framework to be used when making a decision for someone who lacks the capacity to make their own decision.**	The doctor applies the treatment and care framework set out in the MCA 2005. The Act contains four mechanisms in relation to providing a person with care and/or treatment. The person must take each in turn and work out which is applicable.
6	**When the relevant person still had capacity to do so, did he or she make a valid advance decision to refuse this particular treatment?**	There are caveats, but in general terms if Mr Smith did then this is the relevant mechanism to apply.
7	**When the relevant person still had capacity to do so, did he or she make a (registered) LPA which covers care or treatment decisions of this kind?**	There are caveats, but in general terms if Mr Smith did then this will be the relevant mechanism to apply. Ask the attorney (donee) whether or not he or she consents to this treatment on Mr Smith's behalf.
8	**If there does not appear to be a relevant advance decision or LPA, is this a situation where it is necessary or appropriate as being in the person's best interests to apply for a court order as to whether the care or treatment should be given?**	If it is such a situation, apply to the court. If not, then there are only four mechanisms and, since three of them are properly 'not in play', there is only one left. Therefore, the care or treatment can be given under the MCA 2005 if the section 5 conditions are satisfied but not otherwise.
9	**Apply MCA 2005 s5 – are the five section 5 conditions satisfied?**	(a) Is this something connected with the person's care or treatment? (b) Have reasonable steps been taken to establish whether the person has capacity to make their own decision about whether or not to receive this particular piece of care or treatment? (c) Does the person providing the care or treatment reasonably believe that the other person lacks capacity to decide this?

Step	Example
	(d) Does the person reasonably believe that it will be in their best interests to receive this piece of care or treatment (or for an act connected with it to be done)? (e) If restraint is used to provide the care or treatment, does the person reasonably believe that the care or treatment is necessary and does more good than the restraint does harm (see above for the precise criteria)?

3.160   This gives us a fairly clear framework for providing care and/or treatment to an incapacitated person who has a physical health problem such as a heart or liver disorder. Indeed, once one has learned this basic framework, it can be used in relation to all treatment and care decisions, from helping an incapacitated person to dress to a decision to switch off life-support:

Example 1

3.161   P was recently involved in a car accident and has sustained severe brain injury. P's life is being sustained artificially. There is no prospect of recovery. Medical professionals and family members agree that the situation is hopeless and must now consider whether to stop treatment.

3.162   Taking each of the listed steps in turn:
a) The circumstances require P to make a decision about his care or treatment, ie to consent or refuse consent to what is proposed.
b) Someone is concerned that P lacks capacity to make this decision for himself.
c) P's capacity to make this particular decision is assessed.
d) Because of an impairment or disturbance of P's mind or brain, P is unable to understand, retain or weigh the information relevant to the treatment decision or is unable to communicate his decision.
e) Because P cannot make the decision for himself, someone must decide for P. The way this is done is by applying the MCA 2005 which sets out the framework to be used when making a decision for someone who lacks the capacity to make their own decision.
f) The MCA 2005 contains four mechanisms to consider in turn.

g) If P made a valid advance decision refusing life-sustaining treatment in such circumstances when he had capacity, the general rule is that it must be respected.

h) If P has a registered LPA appointing a trusted person to make decisions for P about life-sustaining treatment in such circumstances, generally that person has the right to decide.

i) If there is no advance decision or LPA which resolves the matter, is this a case where an application to the Court of Protection is necessary or in P's best interests, for a judge to decide whether or not further treatment is hopeless? That would be unusual. Sadly, following serious road traffic accidents, it is not uncommon in intensive care settings for professionals and family members to agree that the situation is now hopeless. A judge would have to decide any application on the evidence and here all of the evidence is consistent and to the same effect. In reality, a court application would simply cause delay and avoidable distress to no benefit.

j) If the first three mechanisms are not applicable, the only one left is MCA 2005 s5.

k) Is this decision something connected with P's care and treatment? Yes.

l) Have reasonable steps been taken to assess P's capacity? Yes.

m) Is it reasonably believed that P lacks capacity to make this decision for himself? Yes.

n) Is it in P's best interests to stop treatment? This is the issue. Address it by considering the best interests requirements and considerations in MCA 2005 s4 ('The person making the determination must consider all the relevant circumstances and, in particular, must ...'):

o) The restraint condition adds little here if stopping treatment is in P's best interests. Insofar as this technically involves the use of a degree of restraint, it is reasonable to believe that this is a necessary and proportionate response.

Example 2

3.163   P has developed very advanced dementia and now lives in a care home. Sadly, he seems to have lost the ability to respond to his environment, to speak and to control movement. He cannot sit without support. He requires a wheelchair, is doubly incontinent and needs help with all personal care. He is being taken to a local park and, because it is raining, needs his footwear changing. A care assistant, Ms Q, puts some boots on before taking him out.

3.164   If this was ever challenged then, taking each of the listed steps in turn:

a) The circumstances require P to make a decision about his care or treatment, ie to consent or refuse consent to what is proposed.

b) Based on their long acquaintance, his care assistant's concern is that he no longer has capacity to make this decision for himself, or indeed even to understand that a change of footwear needs to be considered.

c) P's capacity to make this particular decision is assessed. In reality, the care assistant is not aware that she is assessing P's capacity but, if she was ever asked why she acted as she did, she might say that:

- she knows P and his needs very well;
- for some time P has been unable to make his own decisions about what to wear because his cognitive decline is now such that he cannot understand or use relevant verbal or visual information;
- medical and nursing assessments have confirmed this; and
- P did not demonstrate any awareness of or response to the suggestion or prompt that his footwear was changed.

In other words, because of an impairment or disturbance of P's mind or brain he is unable to understand, retain or weigh the information relevant to the care decision or is unable to communicate his decision.

d) Because P cannot make this care decision for himself, someone must decide for him. The way this is done is by applying the MCA 2005 which sets out the framework to be used when making a decision for someone who lacks the capacity to make their own decision.

e) The Act contains four mechanisms to consider in turn.

f) Any advance decision which P has made will relate only to treatment, not care, and will not be relevant.

g) If there is a registered LPA appointing a trusted person to make care decisions, then P's care must be consistent with any consents and refusals of consent made by his attorney on his behalf in relation to his care plan.

h) This is not a case where an application is going to be made to the Court of Protection for an order permitting the care assistant to change his footwear. If P already has a personal welfare deputy appointed for him by the court then, as with an LPA, his care must be consistent with any consents and refusals of consent made by his deputy in relation to his care plan.

i) If none of the first three mechanisms are applicable, apply MCA 2005 s5.

j) Is this decision something connected with P's care and treatment? Yes.

k) Have reasonable steps been taken to assess P's capacity? Yes. It is not necessary in the circumstances to do a fresh formal capacity assessment.

l) Is it reasonably believed that P lacks capacity to make this decision for himself? Yes.

m) Is it in P's best interests to have this piece of care? Yes. If the care assistant was ever asked to justify the decision, she might say:
  – that P's care plan is devised to promote his best interests;
  – that it includes visits to local places;
  – that P seems to enjoy the outings and there is a health benefit.

  In section 4 terms, it is in P's best interests to give him this piece of care having regard to his known wishes and feelings, the views concerning his best interests of family members and professional carers and other relevant considerations, such as the care plan which addresses his health and welfare needs.

n) The restraint condition adds little here. If changing P's footwear before going out is in his best interests then, insofar as this technically involves a degree of force, it is reasonable to believe that it is a necessary and proportionate response.

3.165   The second example may seem rather artificial, although relatives and care home staff are sometimes involved in disagreements about clothing and dressing. Its main function here is to emphasise that once one has learned the above model it can be used as a framework for any situation, from routine care to intensive care. It is therefore worth considering.

Deprivation of liberty

3.166   To recap, the MCA 2005 in its original form included a fairly clear framework in relation to providing care or treatment to an incapacitated person.

3.167   It did not adequately address the problem that an incapacitated person who did not wish to receive this care or treatment was often not permitted to leave the hospital, care home or other place where it was being given.

3.168   In certain circumstances, MCA 2005 s5 permitted a carer to restrict the person's liberty of movement and to use reasonable and proportionate force in order to give the care or treatment. Likewise, if the individual had a personal welfare donee or deputy appointed for them, that person could authorise such restraints in identical circumstances.[68]

3.169   What no one other than a judge of the Court of Protection could do was to authorise depriving the person of their liberty in order to give them the care or treatment. The authority conferred by section 5, deputyship and an LPA was limited to restrictions of liberty which did not amount to deprivation of liberty:

Restriction of liberty	Deprivation of liberty
Permitted	**Not permitted**
A person restrains another person if he (a) uses, or threatens to use, force to secure the doing of an act which s/he resists, or (b) restricts their liberty of movement, whether or not they resist.	The person doing the act ('D') does more than merely restrain the other person if s/he deprives that person of their liberty within the meaning of article 5(1) of the European Convention on Human Rights, whether or not D is a public authority

3.170   This was a problem for three reasons:

a) First, if the reality was that many care homes were depriving residents of their liberty, it was not practical for them to obtain a court order authorising this for every such resident. They would soon be bankrupt given the relatively modest fees paid by local authorities and the costs involved in applying for court orders.

b) Second, if the reality was that many incapacitated people were being deprived of their liberty in relatives' homes or in supported living accommodation, it was similarly unrealistic to expect families and housing providers to obtain court orders for each person affected.

68 MCA 2005 ss11 and 20.

c) Third, there was uncertainty as to the dividing-line between restricting someone's liberty of movement (permitted without a court order) and depriving them of their liberty (not permitted without a court order). It was not always clear to care providers where the line was, nor therefore whether it had been crossed and a court order was required.

3.171   Even allowing for some uncertainty, it was obvious that a considerable number of incapacitated hospital patients and care home residents were being deprived of their liberty without any proper legal order or authority permitting it, without the use of clear and explicit criteria, with no proper application process and no adequate form of judicial review.

3.172   In essence, this was what was commonly referred to as the 'Bournewood gap' as a result of a famous case in which the European Court of Human Rights found that this lacuna in English and Welsh law breached the European Convention on Human Rights (ECHR).

3.173   The eventual consequence was that a new scheme was inserted in the MCA 2005 (by the MHA 2007) which enables hospitals and care homes to obtain a legal authority to deprive people of their liberty under the MCA 2005 without having to obtain an order from a court.

3.174   This authority – called a standard authorisation – can be obtained from the relevant local authority (or initially in the case of hospitals, from the relevant primary care trust (PCT)), with the incapacitated person having a right to apply to court for a review of the authorisation.[69]

3.175   The new 'deprivation of liberty safeguards' scheme – known colloquially as the 'DOLS scheme' – commenced operation on 1 April 2009. The detail is set out as necessary in the relevant chapters. However, briefly, it applies only to hospitals and care homes. It seeks to ensure that the relevant person is assessed at least annually by two suitably qualified and independent professionals. They must certify that the care and treatment arrangements made for the incapacitated person are in their best interests, necessary to protect them from harm, proportionate and so forth.

---

69   The new authorisations are commonly referred to as 'DOLS orders'. Most of the relevant provisions are set out in two new schedules at the end of the MCA 2005: Schedules A1 and 1A. Even now it is not known publicly who devised the scheme and drafted the schedules, which were not put out to prior consultation.

The six requirements

3.176   The new Schedule A1 to the MCA 2005 provides that deprivation of liberty under the scheme requires that six requirements are satisfied: the age, mental health, mental capacity, best interests, no refusals and eligibility requirements.

3.177   The purpose of the requirements is the same as in the case of the 'sectioning criteria' in the MHA 1983, ie to prevent people who do not meet the statutory requirements from being deprived of their liberty.

The age requirement

3.178   The age requirement is simply that the person must be an adult. A child may not be deprived of their liberty under a standard authorisation.

The mental health requirement

3.179   The second requirement is simply that the person suffers from a mental disorder within the meaning of the MHA 1983 (but disregarding the requirement in the 1983 Act sometimes to demonstrate that a learning disability is associated with abnormally aggressive or seriously irresponsible conduct).

The mental capacity requirement

3.180   The requirement here is that the person lacks capacity to make their own decision about whether or not to be accommodated in the particular hospital or care home in order to receive the care or treatment in question.

The best interests requirement

3.181   This is really four requirements masquerading as one. It is satisfied only if all of the following conditions are satisfied:

1) the person is being detained in the hospital or care home for the purpose of being given care or treatment in circumstances which amount to a deprivation of their liberty;[70]
2) this is in their best interests;
3) this is necessary in order to prevent harm to them; and

---

70   More precisely, they are a 'detained resident'. By MCA 2005 Sch A1 para 6, a 'detained resident' is 'a person detained in a hospital or care home – for the purpose of being given care or treatment – in circumstances which amount to deprivation of the person's liberty'. If this is not the case, then no authorisation is required, because there is no deprivation that requires authorisation.

4) their detention in the care home or hospital for the purpose of being given care or treatment in circumstances which amount to a deprivation of their liberty is a proportionate response to the likelihood of them suffering harm, and the seriousness of that harm (if they were not so detained).

3.182   If one or more of the four conditions is not satisfied, the person does not meet the best interests requirement; and, because a standard authorisation may only be given if all six requirements are satisfied in their totality, that person may not be deprived of their liberty under the scheme.

The no refusals requirement

3.183   The essence of this oddly phrased requirement is to ensure that the relevant person does not have in place a valid LPA or advance decision which a standard authorisation would breach.

3.184   Specifically, a person may not be deprived of their liberty in a care home or hospital in order to give them treatment or care which by virtue of their advance decision may not be given to them under the MCA 2005.

3.185   Nor may they be deprived of their liberty in order to give them treatment or care which their personal welfare donee under an LPA has refused consent to on their behalf.

3.186   The underlying premise is that one cannot use the MCA 2005 to break the MCA 2005.

The eligibility requirement

3.187   This requirement is concerned with the inter-relationship between the MHA 1983 and the MCA 2005.

3.188   In certain situations where the MHA 1983 is 'in play', detention or compulsory treatment or care takes place under that Act, not the MCA 2005. This requirement is dealt with below, after some relevant provisions of the MHA 1983 have first been considered.

The DOLS scheme and the four mechanisms

3.189   The four care and treatment mechanisms set out in the original MCA 2005, which were explained above, remain unaffected and are still good law.

3.190   Where a person lacks capacity to consent to treatment or care, their treatment or care is subject to any relevant advance decision,

LPA or court order, or is given under the protection of MCA 2005 s5. All that has changed is that if it is necessary and in their best interests to deprive them of their liberty so that this care or treatment can be given, then a standard authorisation is required alongside (or a court order).

3.191   So, for example, a person may be deprived of their liberty at a care home under a standard authorisation in order to give them the care determined to be in their best interests, which in practice most often is provided under the protection of section 5.

Ten commandments

3.192   The legislative framework is intended to be a protective scheme. Anyone who is deprived of their liberty – that is, who is under another person's complete and effective control and is not free to leave – is vulnerable to abuse.

3.193   The subject is dealt with in detail in chapter 22. However, at this preliminary stage, the relevant domestic and convention law can be understood as imposing ten commandments:

1) Deprivation of liberty requires that the person has been confined in a particular restricted space 'for a not negligible length of time'. This is the 'objective condition'.

2) In addition, a 'subjective condition' must be met before a person is deprived of their liberty. This is that they have not validly consented to their confinement.

3) However, a person cannot consent to being confined if they lack capacity to consent to it.

4) The distinction between deprivation of liberty and restriction of liberty is one of degree or intensity, not one of nature or substance.

5) The starting-point is the specific situation of the individual concerned. Account must be taken of a whole range of factors arising in the particular case, such as the type, duration, effects and manner of implementation of the measure in question.

6) The critical issue is whether the professionals exercise 'complete and effective control' over the person's care and movements, so that the individual is 'under continuous supervision and control and is not free to leave'.

7) The state's obligations under the convention are engaged if a public authority is directly involved in the detention (it is 'imputable to the state'), but also where the state has breached its positive

obligation to protect the person against interferences by private persons.

8) This is because article 5(1) ECHR imposes a positive obligation on the state to protect the liberty of its citizens. The state is obliged to take measures providing effective protection of vulnerable persons, including reasonable steps to prevent a deprivation of liberty of which the authorities have or ought to have knowledge.

9) It is also essential that the person concerned should have access to a court and the opportunity to be heard in person or, where necessary, through some form of representation. Fundamental procedural safeguards are called for in order to protect the interests of detained persons who, on account of their mental disabilities, are not fully capable of acting for themselves.

10) With regard to persons in need of psychiatric treatment in particular, the state is also under an obligation to secure to its citizens 'their right to physical integrity' under article 8 ECHR. Private psychiatric institutions, in particular those where persons are held without a court order, need not only a licence, but also competent supervision by the state on a regular basis of whether confinement and medical treatment is justified.

Detention and deprivation of liberty

3.194   A critical thing to understand is that in law there is a distinction between 'detention' and 'deprivation of liberty'. This is counter-intuitive because most people use these words interchangeably in everyday conversation.

3.195   At first blush, the first commandment appears to be one of those vague legal statements which are of no use to anyone. However, that is not so.

3.196   In our field of interest, the particular restricted space in which the relevant person is confined will often be a hospital, a part of a hospital such as a ward or A&E department, a police station or a care home. A person who is prevented from leaving hospital for a brief period, say for one hour, until he can be assessed by a doctor is being 'detained' there but is not in fact being 'deprived of his liberty'. This is because his confinement is, in this sense, for a 'negligible length for time'.

3.197   Compare that with the case of an older person in a care home. Their situation for the next hour may be exactly the same: they are not allowed to leave. However, it may be the case that nor will they be allowed to leave tomorrow or next week or next month. Their confinement in a particular restricted space is 'for a not negligible length of time', in which case the objective condition for a deprivation of liberty is met.

3.198   The doctor's action is an emergency measure which does not carry with it any general claim to a right to control the person's liberty of movement; to prevent that person from being 'at liberty'. It is only in the second case that the 'confiner' claims a general power or right to control the person's liberty of movement to the extent that a right to confine is claimed. Unlike me or you, the concrete reality is that their liberty is no longer theirs and is in the hands of another: they do not decide whether and when to leave, where to go, when if at all to return, what they do when they leave, and so on.

Interplay with the MHA 1983

3.199   The final matter to deal with in any overview of the personal welfare provisions is the interplay between the MCA 2005 and the MHA 1983.

Treating physical disorders

3.200   We have seen that it is relatively easy to understand when the MCA 2005 mechanisms apply in the case of care or treatment for a physical disorder such as a heart or liver disorder:

Physical disorders

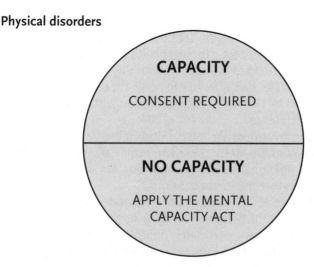

CAPACITY

CONSENT REQUIRED

NO CAPACITY

APPLY THE MENTAL CAPACITY ACT

3.201   Because the MHA 1983 is only concerned with the treatment of mental disorders, (subject to one small caveat) the legal position of 'sectioned' patients with regard to treating their physical health problems is exactly the same as for everyone else, and is that set out in the diagram above.

Treating mental disorders

3.202   What then is the legal position where the proposed treatment is treatment for a mental disorder? Does the MHA 1983 or the MCA 2005 apply?

3.203   It is easier to understand the position if one considers first the simpler scheme set out in the MCA 2005 as originally enacted, before considering the modifications introduced by subsequent amendments.

The scheme set out in the original MCA 2005

3.204   The simpler scheme set out in the MCA 2005 as originally enacted was as follows:

- The general rule is (and remains) that the MCA 2005 applies whenever you wish to give care or treatment to an incapacitated person outside the terms of the MHA 1983.
- In other words, if the patient's treatment is covered by the terms of the MHA 1983 then that Act applies.
- If their treatment falls outside the MHA 1983 then the MCA 2005 will apply.
- Treatment may fall outside the MHA 1983 because it is treatment for a physical health problem (see above); or it may fall outside because it is treatment for a mental health problem but the MHA 1983 does not authorise giving it without the person's consent.
- In the second case, one then has to see if there is legal authority outside the MHA 1983 to give the treatment without the person's consent, which takes us to the MCA 2005.
- When then is treatment for mental disorder without consent not authorised under the MHA 1983? The simple answer is: when the individual is not subject to a section of that Act which authorises psychiatric treatment without consent.
- As is well-known, if a person has been 'sectioned' under the MHA 1983 the fact that the person is 'under a section' may permit professionals to give them psychiatric treatment without consent. If this is the case then the treatment is authorised under the MHA

1983 and it is not necessary to establish whether it is authorised under the MCA 2005.

• However, relatively few sections of the MHA 1983 in fact authorise treating an individual without their consent:

TREATING MENTAL DISORDER WITHOUT CONSENT	
Authorised by the MHA 1983 (or MHA 1983 rules apply)	**Not authorised – Apply the MCA 2005**
Section 2 patients (those liable to be detained in hospital for assessment and any necessary treatment for up to 28 days)	Informal patients (those in hospital and in the community who are not presently subject to a section of the MHA 1983)
Section 3 patients (those liable to be detained in hospital for treatment for up to six or 12 months at a time)	Patients detained under the short-term sections of the MHA 1983 that have a maximum duration of 72 hours or less (ss4, 5(2), 5(4), 135, 136)
Patients subject to a Community Treatment Order	Patients subject to guardianship under the MHA 1983
	Conditionally discharged restricted patients
	Persons remanded to hospital by a criminal court for a report on their mental condition under MHA 1983 s35
	Persons in prison, eg prison medical units

3.205　Naturally, many people find this confusing. When studying the right-hand column, it seems odd to them that a person may be detained or subject to a MHA 1983 'order' – such as short-term detention or guardianship – but their treatment or care be governed by a different Act, the MCA 2005.

3.206　The reason for this relates to the framework of the MHA 1983 and its interplay with the old common law rules which the MCA 2005 replaced. As enacted, the framework constructed by the MHA 1983 was more liberal than much of today's legislation.

3.207　Subject to complying with various procedural safeguards set out in Part IV of the Act, such as obtaining a second-opinion, persons who were liable to be detained in hospital for up to 28 days (section 2) or for up to six months or more (section 3 and its criminal law equivalents) could be treated without their consent. In their case, their compulsory admission was founded on an application made, in most cases, by an independent approved social worker supported by two medical recommendations, one provided by a specialist.

3.208   People who were not considered to be so unwell as to require detention in hospital for those sorts of period were not liable to treatment without their consent under the Act, and therefore could only be so treated in the limited circumstances then permitted by the common law. These are all the people in the right-hand column now covered by the MCA 2005.

3.209   As can be seen from the right-hand column, the vast majority of people with mental health problems fell within this category, because on any given day relatively few people are subject to one of the more Draconian sections in the left-hand column.

3.210   Looking at who is in the right-hand column, the purpose of the holding sections with a maximum duration of 72 hours or less is to enable a person to be assessed, most often with a view to making an application under section 2 or 3. Because they have not yet been detained on the basis of an application supported by two medical recommendations, the MHA 1983 does not authorise their treatment without consent. Any treatment during this period had to be justifiable under common law.

3.211   The MCA 2005 replaced the common law in this area; hence the person is detained under one Act but potentially treatable under another.

3.212   Similarly, the MHA 1983 did not authorise giving treatment without consent to persons on community orders such as guardianship and those who had been conditionally discharged. Only patients who were liable to detention were liable to treatment without consent under the Act; and only then if the person was subject to the longer sections and certain legal formalities were observed. Similarly, therefore, any treatment without consent was given under the common law, which now has been replaced by the MCA 2005.

3.213   In diagrammatic form, therefore, the relationship with the MHA 1983 set out in the MCA 2005 in its original form was as follows:

Mental disorders

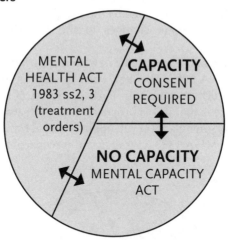

3.214   Looking at the diagram, where it was proposed to give a person treatment for mental disorder – antipsychotics, antidepressants, other medication, ECT, etc – that person's situation would come within one of three legal groups, each of which is represented by a segment of the circle:

- If the person was subject to section 2 or one of the treatment orders in the MHA 1983, such as section 3, the rules in (Part IV of) the MHA 1983 applied and, subject to complying with the procedural safeguards set out there, the patient was liable to treatment without their consent.

- If the citizen was not subject to one of those MHA 1983 sections, they retained a citizen's usual rights and were in the same legal position as everyone else. If they had capacity (or, strictly speaking, it could not be established that they lacked it) then treatment required their consent; in short, they could refuse it. If they lacked capacity to make a decision about the treatment then the MCA 2005 applied – unless the patient was 'sectioned' at that point and taken into section 2 of the Act or one of its treatment sections, such as section 3.

3.215   And that is the purpose of the connectors in the diagram. The individual's situation is fluid, not static – the membranes (lines) separating the three segments are permeable and the individual will move across the lines from one segment to another as their mental health and capacity fluctuates, they are sectioned under section 2 or 3 or released from liability to detention under section 2 or 3.

3.216   That was the situation when the MCA 2005 first came into force but it has now been complicated by the MHA 2007.

3.217   There were two main changes to the simpler structure just described.

3.218   First, the MHA 2007 inserted a new 'community treatment order' (CTO) in the MHA 1983. The legal rules governing the treatment of patients on a CTO are set out in Parts 4 and 4A of the MHA 1983. The general rule is that if it is proposed to give treatment for mental disorder to a person on a CTO you apply the legal framework in Parts 4 and 4A of the MHA 1983. Our diagram now becomes:

Mental disorders

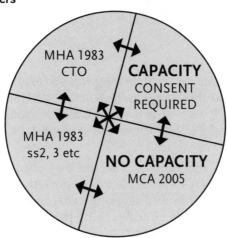

3.219   As can be seen, the individual may now be in one of four groups, and be moving between four groups.

3.220   As with most post-1983 mental health legislation, it is questionable whether the practical benefits justify the extra complexity and the legislation is poorly constructed.

3.221   The second significant change related to ECT. As far as antipsychotic and other medication for mental disorder is concerned, sectioning a person under section 2 or 3 still has the same effect as before: the MHA rules apply, not the MCA 2005. Because, as we have seen, the former permit treatment without consent, from a psychiatrist's point of view this may be a 'trump card' in terms of overcoming a patient's refusal to take prescribed medication. (Once the section comes to an end and the patient reverts to informal status, the same problem may of course represent itself.)

3.222   When it comes to ECT, however, taking a person into one of the treatment sections of the MHA (ss2, 3, etc) no longer necessarily has the effect of 'trumping' or circumventing the protections of the MCA 2005.

3.223   The new ECT rules inserted into the MHA 1983 by the MHA 2007 provide that a section 2 or treatment order patient with capacity cannot be given ECT to which they do not consent unless it can be justified as urgent treatment which is necessary to save their life or immediately necessary to prevent a serious deterioration of their condition.[71]

3.224   Likewise, unless it can be justified as urgent treatment on these terms, an incapacitated section 2 or treatment order patient cannot be given ECT if it would conflict with a relevant advance decision or with a decision made by the Court of Protection, a Court of Protection appointed deputy or a donee appointed under a personal welfare LPA.

3.225   What we see here for the first time is the autonomy provisions in the MCA 2005 starting to infiltrate and cut down the compulsory treatment provisions in the MHA 1983, at least as far as ECT is concerned, and the position is very similar with regard to CTOs.[72]

Deprivation of liberty and the MHA 1983

3.226   Turning to the interplay between the detention provisions in the MHA 1983 and the deprivation of liberty provisions in the MCA 2005, the MHA 1983 only permits detention in a hospital. The standard authorisation scheme in the MCA 2005 applies to hospitals and care homes; and the Court of Protection can also authorise deprivation of liberty in any other location.

3.227   Where a person requires detention in a hospital for psychiatric treatment, the MCA 2005 is not to be used (in preference to the MHA 1983) if the individual falls within any of the following groups:

- People who are currently detained in a hospital under one of the following sections of the MHA 1983: sections 2, 3, 4, 35–38, 44, 45A, 47, 48, 51.
- People who, though not currently detained, are subject to one of these sections or to a CTO, if the care or treatment in question consists wholly or partly of medical treatment for mental disorder in a hospital.

71   For the precise criteria, see MHA 1983 s62.
72   See eg MHA 1983 s64D.

- People who, though not currently detained, are subject to one of these sections, or to a CTO or guardianship, if accommodating them in the hospital or care home under the MCA 2005 would conflict with a requirement imposed on them under their MHA 1983 section.
- People who are subject to guardianship under the MHA 1983, if they object to being accommodated in the particular hospital for the purpose of being given some or all of the proposed medical treatment for their mental disorder (unless they have a donee or deputy who consents to each matter to which they objects).
- People who meet the criteria for being sectioned under section 2 or 3 of the MHA 1983, if they object to being accommodated in the particular hospital for the purpose of being given some or all of the proposed medical treatment for their mental disorder (unless they have a donee or deputy who consents to each matter to which they object).

Principles of mental health law

3.228   That then is the basic relationship between the MCA 2005 and the MHA 1983.

3.229   As a final point, when legislating in this area it is useful to bear the following principles in mind:[73]

1)   It is unsatisfactory to seek to determine principles by reason only, without regard for human experience of the world within which principles are formulated and applied. Our value judgments are judgments about experienced objects.

2)   There are many reasons to limit state intervention in people's lives: errors in law spread their negative effects throughout the nation as opposed to individual errors that are limited in scope; the damage of erroneous laws affect citizens more than legislators, who are thus less inclined to repeal them; it takes longer to repair the damage done by legislation than the damage done by individuals by their own private choices; because of the constant watch of critics, politicians are less inclined to publicly admit error and undo the damage done; politicians are more inclined

---

73   A Eldergill, 'Is anyone safe? civil compulsion under the draft Mental Health Bill', *Journal of Mental Health Law*, January 2003.

than citizens to make decisions based on political gain and prejudice, rather than principle.[74]

3) The British constitution separates powers, the aim being to keep executive powers in check and under proper scrutiny, and so to secure good government. This is necessary because the 'whole art of government consists in the art of being honest',[75] and 'it is not by the consolidation, or concentration of powers, but by their distribution, that good government is effected'.[76]

4) Promoting liberty, protecting individuals from harm caused by those at liberty, and those not at liberty from abuse by those who are, alleviating suffering, and restoring to health those whose health has declined, are all legitimate objectives, in that they reflect values embraced by virtually all members of our society.[77]

5) We are, however, 'faced with choices between ends equally ultimate, and claims equally absolute, the realisation of some of which must inevitably involve the sacrifice of others'.[78] Whether individuals 'should be allowed certain liberties at all depends on the priority given by society to different values, and the crucial point is the criterion by which it is decided that a particular liberty should or should not be allowed, or that its exercise is in need of restraint'.[79]

6) When enacting mental health legislation, parliament has generally sought to erect a balanced legal structure that harmonises three things: individual liberty; bringing treatment to bear where treatment is necessary and can be beneficial; and the protection of the public.[80] Those we describe as 'patients' are themselves members of the public, so that the law must seek to ensure that members of the public are not unnecessarily detained, and also that they are protected from those who must necessarily be detained.

---

74 Benjamin Constant, *Political writings* (Biancamaria Fontana (trans and ed)), Cambridge University Press, 1988.

75 Thomas Jefferson, *Rights of British America, 1774. The writings of Thomas Jefferson, memorial edition* (Lipscomb and Bergh (eds)), Washington DC, 1903-04.

76 *Thomas Jefferson: Autobiography, 1821. The writings of Thomas Jefferson, memorial edition* 1:122.

77 AC Eldergill, *Mental health review tribunals – law and practice*, Sweet & Maxwell, 1997, p45.

78 Berlin, Sir I, *Four essays on liberty*, OUP, 1969, p168.

79 RWM Dias, *Jurisprudence*, Butterworths, 5th edn, 1985, p109.

80 *Hansard*, HC Vol 605 col 276.

7) The use of compulsion has been permitted when significant harm is foreseeable if an individual remains at liberty. Its purpose is to protect the individual or others from those risks that arise when a person's capacity to judge risks, or to control the behaviour giving rise to them, is impaired by mental disorder.

8) Other risks are, constitutionally, matters for citizens to weigh in their own minds. The purpose of compulsion is not to eliminate that element of risk in human life that is simply part of being free to act and to make choices and decisions. A person who obeys our laws is entitled to place a high premium on their liberty, even to value it more highly than their health. Subject to the stated limits, people are entitled to make what others regard as errors of judgment, and to behave in a manner which a doctor regards as not in their best interests, in the sense that it does not best promote health.

9) This desire to determine one's own interests is common to human beings, and so not to be portrayed as an abuse of liberty. On the one hand stands liberty, a right which Parliament and the law should always favour and guard, on the other licence, a wilful use of liberty to contravene the law, which the law must of necessity always punish.

10) Any power given to one person over another is capable of being abused. No legislative body should be deluded by the integrity of their own purposes, and conclude that unlimited powers will never be abused because they themselves are not disposed to abuse them.[81] Mankind soon learns to make interested uses of every right and power which they possess or may assume.[82]

11) This risk of abuse is multiplied if the individual is not free to escape abuse, is incapacitated or otherwise vulnerable, or their word is not given the same weight as that of others. Children and adults with mental health problems are particularly at risk and the law has usually afforded them special protection.

12) This protection involves imposing legal duties on those with power, conferring legal rights on those in their power, and independent scrutiny of how these powers and duties are exercised. The effectiveness of such schemes depends on whether, and to what extent, they are observed.

13) This is a matter of constitutional importance, for the observance of legal rights and the rule of law are the cornerstones of all

---

81   *Thomas Jefferson: Notes on Virginia Q.XIII, 1782. Memorial edition,* 2:164.
82   *Thomas Jefferson: Notes on Virginia Q.XIII, 1782. Memorial edition,* 2:164.

liberal democracies. The rule of law 'implies the subordination of all authorities, legislative, executive [and] judicial ... to certain principles which would generally be accepted as characteristic of law, such as the ideas of the fundamental principles of justice, moral principles, fairness and due process. It implies respect for the supreme value and dignity of the individual.'[83]

14) In any legal system, 'it implies limitations on legislative power, safeguards against abuse of executive power, adequate and equal opportunities of access to legal advice and assistance, ... proper protection of the individual and group rights and liberties, and equality before the law ... It means more than that the government maintains and enforces law and order, but that the government is, itself, subject to rules of law and cannot itself disregard the law or remake it to suit itself'.[84]

15) In framing these principles and laws, Parliament has sought to be just, justice being 'a firm and continuous desire to render to everyone that which is his due'.[85]

16) When new laws are necessary, they should impose minimum powers, duties and rights; provide mechanisms for enforcing duties and remedies for abuse of powers; be unambiguous, just, in plain English, and as short as possible.

17) Because there is a long record of experimentation in human conduct, cumulative verifications give these principles a well-earned prestige. Lightly to disregard them is the height of foolishness.[86]

83 David M Walker, *The Oxford companion to law*, Clarendon Press, 1980, p1093.
84 David M Walker, *The Oxford companion to law*, p1093.
85 Justinian, Inst, 1, 1.
86 J Dewey, *Human nature and conduct*, Allen & Unwin, 1922.

The Court of Protection

continued

Introduction and background

4.1   Prior to the Mental Capacity Act (MCA) 2005 coming into force, the Court of Protection's jurisdiction was limited to dealing with an incapacitated person's property and financial affairs.

4.2   The court was an office of the Supreme Court with a full-time Master and nominated officers. The relevant legal provisions were set out in Part VII of the Mental Health Act (MHA) 1983, supplemented by Court of Protection Rules[1] which regulated its procedures. Appeals from the Master were to the Chancery Division of the High Court.

4.3   Hearings were in London and usually took the form of an inquiry around a conference table rather than a trial. The great advantages were sometimes said to be informality and flexibility, and the perceived disadvantages too much informality and flexibility, in terms of case management, pleadings, advance disclosure and witness statements.

4.4   The Public Guardianship Office (PGO) was responsible for administering the court and it also supervised the affairs of those under the court's jurisdiction.

Establishment and constitution

4.5   The new Court of Protection established by the MCA 2005 is a Superior Court of Record.[2]

4.6   It has 'in connection with its jurisdiction the same powers, rights, privileges and authority as the High Court',[3] for example in relation to witnesses, contempt of court and enforcement.

4.7   Its jurisdiction includes much of the personal welfare and healthcare jurisdiction previously exercised by judges of the Family Division of the High Court, in addition to the property and financial decision-making jurisdiction which it already had under the Mental Health Acts.

---

1 Court of Protection Rules 2001 SI No 824.
2 According to *Halsbury's Laws of England,* prima facie no matter is deemed to be beyond the jurisdiction of a superior court unless it is expressly shown to be so, while nothing is within the jurisdiction of an inferior court (such as a magistrates' court) unless it is expressly shown on the face of the proceedings that the particular matter is within the cognisance of the particular court: *R v Chancellor of St Edmundsbury and Ipswich Diocese ex p White* [1948] 1 KB 195 at 205–206, [1947] 2 All ER 170 at 172, CA, per Wrottesley LJ.
3 MCA 2005 s47(1).

4.8   The court is based at First Avenue House, 42–49 High Holborn, London WC1V 6NP. All applications are filed in London. However, where appropriate and convenient, the case can then be transferred to a nominated Court of Protection judge sitting outside London.

4.9   The court has a President and Vice-President and a resident Senior Judge:

President	Rt Hon Sir James Munby, President of the Family Division of the High Court and Court of Protection
Vice-President	Hon Sir William Charles, Vice-President of the Court of Protection
Senior Judge	Senior Judge Lush (formerly Master of the Court of Protection)

4.10   All High Court (Family and Chancery) judges are nominated to sit as Court of Protection judges and some applications must be heard by a judge of at least that seniority.

CASES WHICH MUST BE HEARD BY A HIGH COURT JUDGE,[3] etc	
Type of application	Must be heard by:
• Applications in relation to the lawfulness of withholding or withdrawing artificial nutrition and hydration from a person in a permanent vegetative state, or a minimally conscious state.	The President or by another judge nominated by the President: Court of Protection (COP) Rules SI No 1744 r86 and Practice Direction (PD) 12A
• Cases where a declaration of incompatibility is sought pursuant to section 4 of the Human Rights Act (HRA) 1998; • applications in relation to a case involving an ethical dilemma in an untested area; • other cases in relation to serious medical treatment (as to which, see the definitions in PD 9E paras 3 and 4), eg non-therapeutic sterilisation, certain terminations of pregnancy, experimental or innovative treatments, medical treatments or procedures that involve a degree of force or restraint, cases involving organ or marrow donation by an incapacitated person.	The President, [Vice-President], Chancellor of the High Court, High Court judge: COPR rr83, 86 and PD 11A, PD 12A

---

4   Technically, a 'puisne judge of the High Court': in other words a 'full' judge of the High Court, rather than a deputy: MCA 2005 s46(2)(c).

Circuit judges and district judges

4.11 The Senior Judge, who has circuit judge rank, is supported by 3.8 resident district judges at First Avenue House in London and by circuit judges and district judges across England and Wales who are nominated ('ticketed') to undertake Court of Protection work as required.

Independence of the judiciary

4.12 Because the office of Lord Chancellor is a political appointment and the holder need not have any legal or judicial qualification or experience, it is the Lord Chief Justice who is responsible for judges and their management, performance and discipline. In terms of their Court of Protection work, the judges are led by, and responsible to, the President.

4.13 In order to further ensure judicial independence and the rule of law, section 2(5) of the Courts Act 2003 provides that: 'The Lord Chancellor may not enter into contracts for the provision of officers and staff to discharge functions which involve making judicial decisions or exercising any judicial discretion'.

HMCTS and court administration

4.14 The Lord Chancellor is under a duty to ensure that there is an efficient and effective system to support the carrying on of the business of the Court of Protection and that appropriate services are provided for it.[5]

4.15 In practice, this duty is discharged day-to-day on the Lord Chancellor's behalf by an agency called Her Majesty's Courts & Tribunals Service (HMCTS).

COURT OF PROTECTION JUDGES	HMCTS
Managed and led by the Lord Chief Justice and the President	A responsibility of the Lord Chancellor
Support system provided by HMCTS	Responsible for ensuring that the judges have the system and support which they require

---

5 Courts Act 2003 s1(1)(aa).

4.16   The Lord Chancellor may appoint such officers and other staff as appear to him or her appropriate for the purpose of discharging this general duty.[6]

4.17   As at June 2014, the court has an agreed complement of 86 HMCTS staff, and there is an agreed plan to recruit seven more staff. In addition, the Office of the Public Guardian funds five staff members to scan court orders.

4.18   HMCTS court staff ('officers') are organised into a number of branches or sections, as described in the table below:

COURT OF PROTECTION – ADMINISTRATION AND CASE WORK	
Branch/Section	Responsibilities
G1 Branch (Receiving and Issuing Applications team)	• Making up case files • Issuing applications • Interim directions • Fast-tracking cases • Applications for permission
G2 Branch (Draft Orders team)	• Processing applications to appoint a deputy • Processing routine personal welfare applications • Processing applications from existing deputies • Receiving and processing certificates of service and acknowledgments of service (including objections to applications) • Applications within proceedings • Preparing standard drafts of court orders
G3 Branch (Issuing Orders team)	• Issuing and dispatching final orders • Dispatching security bond forms • Dealing with bond defaulters • Scanning orders to the Public Guardian

6   Courts Act 2003 s2(1).

Branch/Section	Responsibilities
Listing and Appeals Branch (including the regional and appeals team)	• Ushering hearings • Dealing with cases that require listing for an attended or telephone hearing • Case transfers to and from a regional court • Issuing most orders and directions made by a judge at a hearing • Dealing with applications to vacate or re-list a hearing • Appeals
Authorised court officers (ACOs)	• ACOs are civil servants who have been authorised to exercise designated court functions of a purely formal or administrative character which previously were exercised by the judges
Technical specialists	• Deprivation of liberty applications • Applications for personal welfare orders • Statutory will, gift and settlement applications • New trustee applications • Enduring power of attorney (EPA) and lasting power of attorney (LPA) objections and directions • Public Guardian applications • Requests for visitor reports under MCA 2005 s49 • Appointing panel deputies • Orders discharging deputies (recovery/retirement)
Customer Enquiry Service (CES)	• Court's telephone service • General email inquiries • Dispatching court forms to users

Authorised court officers

4.19   A few civil servants known as ACOs are now authorised under the rules to exercise designated functions 'of a purely formal or administrative character' in relation to court applications.

4.20   The functions that must be performed by a judge and those which may be performed by an authorised court officer are set out in PD 3A.

4.21   An authorised officer may not conduct a hearing and must refer to a judge any application or question arising in an application which is contentious or which, in the opinion of the officer, is complex, requires a hearing or for any other reason ought to be considered by a judge. The relevant person concerned ('P'), a party and any other person affected by an order can apply to have an authorised officer's order reconsidered by a judge.

APPLICATIONS THAT MAY BE DEALT WITH BY AUTHORISED COURT OFFICERS (COPR r7; PD 3A para 2.1)

2.1 Subject to paragraphs 2.2, 3 and 4.2 an authorised court officer may deal with any of the following applications:
   (a) applications to appoint a deputy for property and affairs;
   (b) applications to vary the powers of a deputy appointed for property and affairs under an existing order;
   (c) applications to discharge a deputy for property and affairs and appoint a replacement deputy;
   (d) applications to appoint and discharge a trustee;
   (e) applications to sell or purchase real property on behalf of P;
   (f) applications to vary the security in relation to a deputy for property and affairs;
   (g) applications to discharge the security when the appointment of a deputy for property and affairs comes to an end;
   (h) applications for the release of funds for the maintenance of P, or P's property, or to discharge any debts incurred by P;
   (i) applications to sell or otherwise deal with P's investments;
   (j) applications for authority to apply for a grant of probate or representation for the use and benefit of P;
   (k) applications to let and manage property belonging to P;
   (l) applications for a detailed assessment of costs;
   (m) applications to obtain a copy of P's will;
   (n) applications to inspect or obtain copy documents from the records of the court; and
   (o) applications which relate to one or more of the preceding paragraphs and which a judge has directed should be dealt with by an authorised court officer.

4.22   The case management powers of authorised officers are limited to those matters referred to in PD 3A para 3.

Workload and number of applications

4.23　On average there was an eight per cent year-on-year increase in the number of applications to the Court of Protection during the four-year period between 2008/09 and 2011/12.

Year	Number of applications
2008/09	19,528
2009/10	21,042
2010/11	23,093
2011/12	24,586

4.24　There was also a 42 per cent increase in hearings in 2012 compared with 2011. Internal court data indicates that there were 882 attended hearings in London during 2013 and 745 attended hearings in the regions.

The court's budget

4.25　Published Ministry of Justice (MoJ) data is quite old because of the time it takes to collect data and the need for auditing. Consequently, it is difficult to establish the court's current budget. However, the HMCTS management accounts for 2011/12 indicate an annual expenditure of £4.1 million.[7]

Where to find the law and guidance

4.26　The relevant law and guidance is found in several places:
- Primary legislation: the Mental Capacity Act 2005
- Secondary legislation: orders, rules and regulations made under the authority of the Act
- Practice Directions, Practice Guidance and Codes of Practice
- Case-law decisions of judges
- European Convention on Human Rights
- Textbooks and textbook opinion

7　In line with civil courts generally, the Court of Protection fees are expected to fully cover the cost of administering the court although some funding from central government is inevitable because provision is made for fee exemptions, remission and postponement.

4.27   The precise legal status of these different documents is not always easy to discern. However, the following brief points may help non-lawyers unfamiliar with the various documents and how to refer to them. By convention –

4.28   Acts of Parliament (*'primary legislation'*) are divided into sections (s), subsections (subs), paragraphs (para) and subparagraphs (sub-para). If a document refers to s22(3)(a)(i) of the MCA 2005, this is a reference to subparagraph (i) of paragraph (a) of subsection (3) of section 22 of the Act.

4.29   Primary legislation takes precedence over *'secondary legislation'*, that is over orders, rules and regulations made by the Lord Chancellor or by some other minister with Parliament's permission, ie under the authority of an Act of Parliament.

- The term 'rules' is used for secondary legislation which is concerned with court procedures, eg the COPR. A set of rules is divided into rules (r), paragraphs (paras) and sub-paragraphs (sub-para). Thus, r5(2)(b) of the COPR refers to sub-paragraph (b) of paragraph (2) of rule 5 of those rules.

- The term 'regulations' is used for secondary legislation that relates to non-court executive procedures, eg the procedures of the Public Guardian. A set of regulations is divided into regulations (reg), paragraphs (para) and sub-paragraphs (sub-para).

- The term 'order' has no single meaning. In relation to the MCA 2005, it is used for secondary legislation that deals with matters directly relating to the Act's implementation, such as transitional arrangements, consequential provisions and prescribed fees. An order is divided into articles (art), paragraphs (para) and sub-paragraphs (sub-para).

4.30   In recent times, primary and secondary legislation has been augmented by a proliferation of *codes of practice, practice directions and practice guidance*:

- *Practice directions*: section 52 of the MCA 2005 provides that the President of the Court of Protection may, with the concurrence of the Lord Chancellor, give directions 'as to the practice and procedure of the court'. Such directions may not be given by anyone else (for example, by the Vice-President or Senior Judge) without the approval of the President of the Court of Protection and the Lord Chancellor.

- *Practice guidance*: section 52(3) expressly states that providing for practice directions in this way does not prevent the President of the Court of Protection without the concurrence of the Lord

Chancellor giving directions which 'contain guidance as to law or making judicial decisions'.

- *Codes of Practice*: the two codes do not have statutory force, but professionals and some carers must have regard to their provisions, and the courts must take them into account where relevant.

4.31 *Case-law*: judges' decisions that settle or interpret significant points of law – for example, the precise meaning of a section of the Act – may be 'reported', that is published, in one of three historic series of law reports. These are the Official Law Reports; the Weekly Law Reports (WLR); and the All England Reports (All ER). The former should be referred to ('cited') in court if the case is reported in it.

4.32 Transcripts of 'unreported' judgments often appear on the website of the British and Irish Legal Information Institute (Bailii).[8] These transcripts have an uncertain status. They should not usually be cited unless they contain a relevant statement of legal principle not found in reported authority.[9] Many such decisions are simply illustrative of how the law was applied in a novel legal situation or one of obvious public interest. Most often, they are aids to understanding the law and its application rather than legal precedents.

4.33 Many new series of law reports have been established in recent years, the most important of which in this context are Jordan's Court of Protection Law Reports.[10] In practice, they are considered to be wholly reliable, and so are relied upon by the court.

4.34 *Legal textbook opinion* may be quoted if it is likely to assist the court as to the meaning of a disputed or difficult legal provision.

4.35 The *European Convention on Human Rights* (ECHR) is essentially a modern-day Magna Carta. So far as is possible, all primary and secondary legislation must be interpreted so as to be compatible with it.

Mental Capacity Act 2005

4.36 The MCA 2005 consists of 69 sections in three parts. These sections are followed by nine schedules which deal with legal technicalities and formalities that would clog up and make unreadable the main body of the Act if placed there.

---

8 See: www.bailii.org.
9 PD of 24 March 2012: *Citation of authorities* para 10.
10 See also *Community Care Law Reports* published by LAG covering a significant number of Court of Protection cases.

Mental Capacity Act 2005		
Part of Act	**Title**	**What it includes**
Part 1	Persons who lack capacity	• Statutory principles • Definitions of incapacity and best interests • Legal protection for professionals and other carers in respect of care and treatment given informally • Payment for necessary goods and services; LPAs • Court declarations and orders • Appointment of deputies by the court • Court's powers in relation to personal welfare matters, property and financial matters, deprivation of liberty, LPAs and advance decisions to refuse treatment • Research • IMCAs (independent mental capacity advocacy service)
Part 2	The Court of Protection and the Public Guardian	• Establishment, jurisdiction and powers of the Court of Protection and the Public Guardian • Court of Protection visitors
Part 3	Miscellaneous and general	• Scope of the Act • International protection of adults • Interpretation • Making of rules, regulations and orders
Schedule 1	Lasting powers of attorney: formalities	Technicalities and formalities relating to LPAs
Schedule 2	Property and affairs: supplementary provisions	Additional provisions relating to matters such as wills and the effect of the court disposing of part of an incapacitated person's property on the distribution of their estate on their death (either by will or under the intestacy rules)

Part of Act	Title	What it includes
Schedule 3	International protection of adults	The schedule gives effect in England and Wales to the Hague Convention (the Convention on the International Protection of Adults, 2000). See also MCA 2005 s63
Schedule 4	Provisions applying to existing enduring powers of attorney	The MCA 2005 repealed the Enduring Powers of Attorney Act 2005. Its provisions are, however, repeated here because, although no new EPAs may be made, EPAs made before the new Act continue to have effect, may be challenged in court on the old terms, etc. See also MCA 2005 s66
Schedule 5	Transitional provisions and savings	
Schedule 6	Minor and consequential amendments	
Schedule 7	Repeals	
Schedule A1	Hospital and care home residents: deprivation of liberty	These schedules set out the 'deprivation of liberty' scheme inserted into the MCA 2005 by the MHA 2007
Schedule 1A	Persons ineligible to be deprived of liberty by this Act	

Rules, practice directions, practice guidance, regulations and orders, and codes

4.37   The MCA 2005 provides for issuing rules, regulations and orders, and the publication of codes of practice. The following are some of the most important for court users.

Rules	
COPR 2007 SI No 1744	These rules govern the procedures of the court. They are cumbersome: 202 rules in 22 parts, supplemented by 62 practice directions, numerous prescribed forms and where necessary the Civil Procedure Rules 1998 and Family Procedure Rules 2010.
Practice directions[a]	
The practice directions are essentially of two kinds. Some do no more than repeat in plainer English what is said in a part of the rules; others, such as those on the right, are substantive.	• PD 9D – Applications by currently appointed deputies, attorneys and donees in relation to [the person's] property and affairs • PD 9E – Applications relating to serious medical treatment
Practice guidance	
Practice guidance	• *Committal for Contempt of Court,* Practice Guidance issued on 4 June 2013 by Sir James Munby, President of the Court of Protection (supplements guidance issued on 3 May 2013)[b] • *Transparency in the Court of Protection: publication of judgments,* Practice Guidance issued on 16 January 2014 by Sir James Munby, President of the Court of Protection[c]

a   See: www.judiciary.gov.uk/publications-and-reports/practice-directions/cop-practice-directions.

b   See: www.judiciary.gov.uk/publications-and-reports/guidance/2013/family-division-practice-direction-committal-contempt-of-court-june-2013.

c   See: www.judiciary.gov.uk/publications-and-reports/guidance/2014/index.

Regulations and orders	
Lasting Powers of Attorney, Enduring Powers of Attorney and Public Guardian Regulations 2007 SI No 1253	These regulations deal with matters such as the completion and registration of Lasting Powers of Attorney, the registration of enduring powers of attorney, the reports required of deputies and the registers maintained by the Public Guardian.
Codes of Practice	
There are separate codes on the MCA 2005 as originally passed and the deprivation of liberty provisions added in 2007.	• *Mental Capacity Act 2005: Code of Practice* (Department for Constitutional Affairs, 2007)[d] • *Deprivation of liberty safeguards: Code of Practice to supplement the main Mental Capacity Act 2005 Code of Practice* (Ministry of Justice, 2008)[e]

Textbooks

4.38   The main textbook on court practice and procedure is Jordans' *Court of Protection Practice*, a new edition of which appears annually in the spring. The other four standard publications used by practitioners are:

- *Court of Protection Law Reports* (Jordans), which contain decisions made by senior judges on important legal issues;
- *Heywood & Massey: Court of Protection Practice* (looseleaf) (Sweet & Maxwell);
- *Cretney & Lush on Lasting and Enduring Powers of Attorney* (Jordans, 2013);
- the monthly *Mental capacity law* newsletter produced by Thirty Nine Essex Street (A Ruck Keene, V Butler-Cole, N Allen and A Bicarregui (eds)) and published at www.39essex.com, and by (free) subscription by contacting marketing@39essex.com.

d See: www.justice.gov.uk/downloads/protecting-the-vulnerable/mca/mca-code-practice-0509.pdf.

e See: http://webarchive.nationalarchives.gov.uk/20130107105354/http://www.dh.gov.uk/prod_consum_dh/groups/dh_digitalassets/@dh/@en/documents/digitalasset/dh_087309.pdf.

European Convention on Human Rights

4.39   The HRA 1998 makes it unlawful for a public authority, such as the NHS or a local authority, to act in a way which is incompatible with a convention right unless legislation requires it to act in that way. So far as is possible, all primary and secondary legislation must be interpreted so as to be compatible with the ECHR. If this is impossible, one of the higher courts will make a declaration of incompatibility.

4.40   The articles of the ECHR which are most often 'in play' in Court of Protection proceedings are articles 5 (right to liberty and security) and 8 (right to respect for private and family life).

4.41   Article 5 is engaged when an incapacitated person is deprived of their liberty. The state is obliged to take effective measures to protect vulnerable persons, including reasonable steps to prevent a deprivation of liberty of which the authorities have or ought to have knowledge. A proper authorisation or court order is required. The person concerned should have access to a court and the opportunity to be heard in person or, where necessary, through some form of representation.

4.42   Article 8 provides a qualified right to respect for one's private and family life, home and correspondence. Any interference with an incapacitated person's family or private life must be authorised by law, proportionate ('necessary in a democratic society') and for a permitted purpose, eg for the protection of their health. The court should consider the nature and strength of the evidence of any alleged risk of harm and there must be a proper, factual basis for such concerns.

Jurisdiction of the Court of Protection

4.43   The court's jurisdiction derives from the MCA 2005 which sets out a number of different types of applications and orders that can be made.

Exempt matters to which the MCA 2005 does not apply

4.44   The MCA 2005 does not apply to some legal situations and cannot be used to authorise certain kinds of interference with a person's life. These exclusions are set out in sections 27–29.

People falling outside the Act

4.45   Depending on the type of decision to be made, the court's jurisdiction may be restricted to adults (eg statutory wills, lasting powers of attorney) or to persons aged 16 or over (eg personal welfare issues).[11]

Family matters falling outside the Act (section 27)

4.46   Nothing in the MCA 2005 permits a decision on any of the following matters to be made on behalf of a person:

- consenting to marriage or a civil partnership;
- consenting to have sexual relations;
- consenting to a decree of divorce being granted on the basis of two years' separation;
- consenting to a dissolution order being made in relation to a civil partnership on the basis of two years' separation;
- consenting to a child's being placed for adoption by an adoption agency;
- consenting to the making of an adoption order;
- discharging parental responsibilities in matters not relating to a child's property;
- giving a consent under the Human Fertilisation and Embryology Act 1990.[12]

Mental Health Act matters (section 28)

4.47   Section 28 excludes certain MHA matters from being dealt with under the MCA 2005. The precise inter-relationship between the two statutes was considered in chapter 3 above.

Voting rights (section 29)

4.48   Nothing in the MCA 2005 permits a decision on voting at an election for any public office, or at a referendum, to be made on behalf of an incapacitated person.[13]

---

11 MCA 2005 s2(5) and (6).
12 MCA 2005 s27(1).
13 MCA 2005 s29(1).

The range of applications and orders that may be made

4.49   The different types of application and orders that may be made are dealt with in greater detail in the appropriate chapters. However, it is useful at the outset to have an understanding of the range of orders that can be made:

- Declarations
- Court orders and decisions under section 16
- Appointing deputies under section 16
- Powers in relation to Lasting Powers of Attorney
- Powers in relation to Advance Decisions to Refuse Treatment
- Powers in relation to Enduring Powers of Attorney
- Other powers
- Interim Orders

Declarations

4.50   Section 15 of the MCA 2005 provides that the Court of Protection may make declarations as to:

- whether a person has or lacks capacity to make a decision specified in the declaration;
- whether a person has or lacks capacity to make decisions on such matters as are described in the declaration;
- the lawfulness or otherwise of any act done, or yet to be done, in relation to that person.

Section 15(2) provides that the term 'act' includes an omission and a course of conduct.

4.51   As its name suggests, a declaration involves the court declaring the law or a person's rights or interests in relation to a particular matter, historically without any reference to enforcement. It registers what exists and declares what it finds. However, it is not an academic process. There has to be a real issue to resolve between the parties and declaring that something is lawful or otherwise clarifies for the parties what may and may not be done under the Act.

Court orders and decisions under section 16

4.52   MCA 2005 s16 applies if a person lacks capacity in relation to a matter or matters concerning their personal welfare or property and affairs.[14] It enables the court by order to make the necessary decisions on their behalf or to appoint a deputy to make those decisions for the person. The powers of the court are subject to the provisions of the Act and, in particular, to sections 1 (the principles) and 4 (best interests).[15] Any order of the court may be varied or discharged by a subsequent order.[16]

Section 16 and personal welfare matters

4.53 The court's section 16 powers as respects an incapacitated person's personal welfare extend in particular to:[17]

- deciding where the person is to live;
- deciding what contact, if any, the person is to have with any specified persons;
- making an order prohibiting a named person from having contact with the person;
- giving or refusing consent to the carrying out or continuation of a treatment by a person providing health care for the person;
- giving a direction that a person responsible for the person's health care allow a different person to take over that responsibility.

Section 16 and property and financial matters

4.54 The court's section 16 powers as respects an incapacitated person's property and affairs extend in particular to:[18]

- the control and management of their property;
- the sale, exchange, charging, gift or other disposition of their property;
- the acquisition of property in their name or on their behalf;
- the carrying on, on their behalf, of any profession, trade or business;
- the taking of a decision which will have the effect of dissolving a partnership of which the person is a member;
- the carrying out of any contract entered into by the person;
- the discharge of the person's debts and any of their obligations, whether legally enforceable or not;

---

14 MCA 2005 s16(1).
15 MCA 2005 s16(3).
16 MCA 2005 s16(7).
17 MCA 2005 s17(1), (2).
18 MCA 2005 s18(1).

- the settlement of any of their property, whether for their benefit or for the benefit of others;
- the execution for them of a will (although no will may be made under this power at a time when the person has not reached 18 years of age[19]);
- the exercise of any power (including a power to consent) vested in the person whether beneficially or as trustee or otherwise;
- the conduct of legal proceedings in the person's name or on their behalf.

Appointing deputies under section 16[20]

4.55   MCA 2005 s16 provides that the court may:

- by making an order, make the decision or decisions on the person's behalf in relation to the matter or matters, or
- appoint a person (a 'deputy') to make decisions on the person's behalf in relation to the matter or matters.[21]

4.56   Naturally, if the judge can make the decision, it will generally be inappropriate for him or her to authorise someone else to make it.

4.57   Consequently, the Act provides that a decision by the court is to be preferred to the appointment of a deputy to make a decision; and that the powers conferred on the deputy should be as limited in scope and duration 'as is reasonably practicable in the circumstances': see section 16(4).

4.58   Without prejudice to section 4, the court may make an order or appoint a deputy on such terms as it considers are in the incapacitated person's best interests, and may do so even though no application is before it 'on those terms'.[22]

Who may be a deputy

4.59   A deputy must be an adult (aged 18 or over) or, in the case of property and affairs deputyships, a trust corporation.[23]

4.60   A person may not be appointed as a deputy without their consent.[24]

---

19   MCA 2005 s18(2).
20   See further chapter 7.
21   MCA 2005 s16(2).
22   MCA 2005 s16(6).
23   MCA 2005 s19(1).
24   MCA 2005 s19(3).

4.61   The court may appoint the holder of a specified office or position as the person's deputy,[25] for example the holder of a particular local authority finance office. This avoids the need for a new order when the current holder of the post moves on and is replaced.

Two or more deputies

4.62   The court may appoint two or more deputies to act jointly, jointly and separately ('severally'), or jointly in respect of some matters and jointly and separately in respect of others.[26]

Appointment of successors

4.63   When appointing a deputy or deputies, the court may at the same time appoint one or more other persons to succeed the deputy or deputies in such circumstances, or on the happening of such events, as may be specified, and for such period as may be so specified.[27]

Property and affairs deputyships

4.64   With regard to property and affairs deputyships, the court may confer on a deputy powers to:
- take possession or control of all or any specified part of the person's property;
- exercise all or any specified powers in respect of it, including such powers of investment as the court may determine.[28]

Restrictions on deputies

4.65   The MCA 2005 provides that certain powers may not be conferred on or exercised by a deputy. These restrictions are described in chapter 3 above.

Security, reports and the Public Guardian

4.66   The court may require a deputy:
- to give to the Public Guardian such security as the court thinks fit for the due discharge of his functions; and

---

25 MCA 2005 s19(2).
26 MCA 2005 s19(4).
27 MCA 2005 s19(5).
28 MCA 2005 s19(8).

- to submit to the Public Guardian such reports at such times or at such intervals as the court may direct.[29]

Reimbursement and remuneration

4.67   The deputy is entitled:

- to be reimbursed out of the incapacitated person's property for their reasonable expenses in discharging their functions; and
- if the court so directs when appointing them, to remuneration out of the incapacitated person's property for discharging them.[30]

Revoking a deputy's appointment

4.68   The court may revoke the appointment of a deputy or vary the powers conferred on them if it is satisfied that the deputy:

- has behaved, or is behaving, in a way that contravenes the authority conferred on them by the court or is not in P's best interests; or
- proposes to behave in a way that would contravene that authority or would not be in P's best interests.[31]

Powers in relation to LPAs[32]

4.69   MCA 2005 ss22 and 23 set out the court's powers where a person has:

- executed[33] or purported to execute a document ('an instrument') with a view to creating an LPA; or
- such a document has been registered as an LPA by the Public Guardian.[34]

Determining whether an LPA exists or still exists

4.70   The court may determine any question relating to:

---

29 MCA 2005 s19(9).
30 MCA 2005 s19(7).
31 MCA 2005 s16(8).
32 See further chapter 7.
33 'Executed' simply means to sign a document and to complete any other necessary formalities to give it legal effect, such as having it sealed (which does not apply here). The document or 'instrument' is simply the standard LPA form prescribed under the MCA 2005.
34 MCA 2005 s22(1).

- whether one or more of the requirements for the creation of an LPA have been met;[35]
- whether the power has been revoked or has otherwise come to an end.[36]

Impropriety or failure to act in P's best interests

4.71 MCA 2005 s20(4) applies if the court is satisfied:

- that fraud or undue pressure was used to induce the relevant person to execute an instrument for the purpose of creating a lasting power of attorney, or to create a lasting power of attorney; or
- that the donee (or, if more than one, any of them) of an LPA (i) has behaved, or is behaving, in a way that contravenes his authority or is not in the person's best interests, or (ii) proposes to behave in a way that would contravene his or her authority or would not be in the person's best interests.[37]

4.72 In such a case, the court may:

- direct that an instrument purporting to create the lasting power of attorney is not to be registered; or
- if the person lacks capacity to do so, revoke the instrument or the LPA.[38]

4.73 If there is more than one donee, the court may revoke the instrument or the LPA so far as it relates to any of them.[39]

Powers of court in relation to the operation of lasting powers of attorney

4.74 MCA 2005 s23(1) provides that the court may determine any question as to the meaning or effect of an LPA or an instrument purporting to create one. The court may:

- give directions with respect to decisions which the donee of an LPA has authority to make, and which the person lacks capacity to make;[40]

---

35 An LPA is not created unless section 10 is complied with, the prescribed document is registered, the person creating it is an adult who had capacity to execute it: MCA 2005 s9(2).
36 MCA 2005 s22(2).
37 MCA 2005 s22(3).
38 MCA 2005 s22(4).
39 MCA 2005 s22(5).
40 MCA 2005 s23(2)(a).

- give any consent or authorisation to act which the donee would have to obtain from the person if the person had capacity to give it.[41]

4.75   Where the relevant person lacks capacity to do so, the court may:
- give directions to the donee with respect to the rendering by them of reports or accounts and the production of records kept by them for that purpose;[42]
- require the donee to supply information or to produce documents or things in their possession as donee;[43]
- give directions with respect to the remuneration or expenses of the donee;[44]
- relieve the donee wholly or partly from any liability which they have or may have incurred on account of a breach of their duties as donee.[45]

Gifts

4.76   The court may authorise the making of gifts which are not permitted gifts (such as customary birthday presents and charitable donations) within the meaning of section 12(2).[46]

Powers in relation to advance decisions to refuse treatment

4.77   The court may make a declaration as to whether an advance decision exists; is valid; or is applicable to a treatment.[47]

4.78   Nothing in an apparent advance decision stops a person from providing life-sustaining treatment, or from doing any act they reasonably believe to be necessary to prevent a serious deterioration in the relevant person's condition, while a decision in respect of any relevant issue is sought from the court.[48]

---

41 MCA 2005 s23(2)(b).
42 MCA 2005 s23(3)(a).
43 MCA 2005 s23(3)(b).
44 MCA 2005 s23(3)(c).
45 MCA 2005 s23(3)(d).
46 MCA 2005 s23(4).
47 MCA 2005 s26(4).
48 MCA 2005 s26(5).

Powers in relation to EPAs

4.79 The court's powers in relation to EPAs are set out in Schedule 4 to the MCA 2005 and derive from the Enduring Powers of Attorney Act 1985. The case-law on that Act therefore continues to be relevant. It is undecided whether and to what extent the main body of the MCA 2005 applies to EPAs.

Objections to the registration of an EPA

4.80 If the Public Guardian receives a valid notice of objection to the registration of an EPA from a person entitled to notice then he or she must not register it unless the court directs that it is registered.

4.81 A notice of objection to registration is valid if made on one or more of the following grounds:

1) that the power purported to have been created by the instrument (ie EPA form) was not valid as an EPA;
2) that the power created by the instrument no longer subsists;
3) that the application is premature because the donor is not yet becoming mentally incapable;
4) that fraud or undue pressure was used to induce the donor to create the power;
5) that, having regard to all the circumstances and in particular the attorney's relationship to or connection with the donor, the attorney is unsuitable to be the donor's attorney.

4.82 If any of these grounds is established to the satisfaction of the court, it must direct the Public Guardian not to register the instrument. If the court is not satisfied that any of the grounds are established then it must direct registration.

4.83 If the court directs the Public Guardian not to register an instrument on the fraud, undue pressure or unsuitability ground then it must by order revoke the EPA. This is not necessary under the first two grounds because no EPA exists, and it would be premature under the third ground because it does not rest on a finding of fault and the EPA may require registration in the future.

4.84 In all cases other than the no-fault prematurity ground, the EPA document must be delivered up to the Public Guardian to be cancelled, unless the court otherwise directs. Again, this is logical. In all of the other cases, the EPA document either has no legal effect (in which case one usually one does not want it circulating in someone's possession) or at best the attorney has been found to be unsuitable (in which case one usually does not want them retaining possession of it).

Powers in connection with a registered EPA

4.85   Once an EPA has been registered, the court may be asked to revoke it or to give directions to the attorney as to the management of the donor's property.

Giving directions concerning the operation of the EPA

4.86   Where an instrument has been registered the court may:

a) determine any question as to the meaning or effect of the instrument;

b) give directions with respect to:
   i) the management or disposal by the attorney of the property and affairs of the donor;
   ii) the rendering of accounts by the attorney and the production of the records kept by them for the purpose;
   iii) the remuneration or expenses of the attorney whether or not in default of or in accordance with any provision made by the instrument, including directions for the repayment of excessive or the payment of additional remuneration;

c) require the attorney to supply information or produce documents or things in their possession as attorney;

d) give any consent or authorisation to act which the attorney would have to obtain from a mentally capable donor;

e) authorise the attorney to act so as to benefit themselves or others otherwise than in accordance with Schedule 4 para 3(2).

Revocation of a registered EPA

4.87   Once an EPA has been registered, because the donor is becoming mentally incapable, it can only be revoked by the donor if the court confirms the revocation. On such an application, the court must confirm the revocation of the power if it satisfied that the donor:

a) has done whatever is necessary in law to effect an express revocation of the power; and

b) was mentally capable of revoking a power of attorney when they did so (whether or not they are still capable of doing so by the time the court considers the application).

Objections to a registered EPA

4.88   The court must direct the Public Guardian to cancel the registration of a registered EPA in any of the following circumstances:

a) on confirming the revocation of the power by the donor (see immediately above);

b) on directing under MCA 2005 Sch 4 para 2(9)(b) that the power is to be revoked (this is where the court makes a deputy order and when doing so directs that a pre-existing EPA shall be revoked);

c) on being satisfied that the donor is and is likely to remain mentally capable;

d) on being satisfied that the power has expired or has been revoked by the mental incapacity of the attorney;

e) on being satisfied that the power was not a valid and subsisting enduring power when registration was effected;

f) on being satisfied that fraud or undue pressure was used to induce the donor to create the power;

g) on being satisfied that, having regard to all the circumstances and in particular the attorney's relationship to or connection with the donor, the attorney is unsuitable to be the donor's attorney.

4.89   If the court directs the Public Guardian to cancel the EPA's registration on one of the fault grounds (fraud, undue pressure or unsuitability) then it must also revoke the EPA itself, ie the EPA document is no longer valid and therefore there can be no future attempts to re-register it.

4.90   In all cases other than the no-fault 'donor is and is likely to remain mentally capable' ground, the EPA document must be delivered up to the Public Guardian to be cancelled, unless the court otherwise directs. Again, this is logical. In all of the other cases, the EPA document either has no legal effect or at best the attorney has been found to be unsuitable.

Other powers

4.91   The court's other main powers relate to COPR r202 and MCA 2005 Sch 3.

Applications under COPR r202

4.92   The court receives applications from persons subject to a deputyship order for the deputy order to be revoked on the ground that the person concerned no longer lacks capacity in relation to the matter or matters in question and therefore no longer falls within the court's jurisdiction.

Applications under MCA 2005 Sch 3

4.93   The court sometimes receives applications in relation to Schedule 3 to the Act which is concerned with the Hague Convention and the international protection of adults with incapacity. For example, a person may apply to the court for a declaration that a protective measure taken in a country other than England and Wales is enforceable in England and Wales. The Convention and Schedule 3 are dealt with in chapter 27.

Interim orders where there is reason to believe person lacks capacity

4.94   The Court of Protection's jurisdiction is directed towards making decisions on behalf of people who lack capacity to make their own decision. By the end of the case there is usually ample evidence on which the judge can determine whether or not the person concerned has that capacity.

4.95   What, though, is the position where it appears that a person lacks capacity to make a decision for themselves, and in consequence is at risk, but that person will not agree to a capacity assessment and the evidence which can be put before the court is incomplete?

4.96   The answer is that the court has power to make interim orders and directions under MCA 2005 s48 if there is reason to believe that the relevant person lacks capacity in relation to the matter and it is in their best interests for the court to do so.

4.97   The specific issue raised in the case of *Re F*[49] was whether the court has any jurisdiction to hear an application about a person unless and until the presumption of capacity is first rebutted. What if the medical evidence concerning capacity is equivocal?

4.98   It was observed by HHJ Hazel Marshall QC that there are two stages to the court's jurisdiction under section 48. The section enables the court to make 'Interim orders and directions' provided, firstly, that 'there is reason to believe that [the person] lacks capacity in relation to the matter'. This is plainly a lower threshold than 'proof on balance of probability that [the person] lacks capacity'. What is required is simply sufficient evidence to justify a reasonable belief that the person may lack capacity in the relevant regard. There are various phrases which might be used to describe what is required, such as 'good' or 'serious cause for concern' or 'a real possibility' that the person lacks capacity, but the concept behind each is the same and quite easily recognised.

4.99 It is the second stage which provides the real protection for the citizen against undue interference with their affairs and their right to make their own decisions. The first stage involves considering whether there is evidence giving good cause for concern that the person may lack capacity in some relevant regard. Once that is raised as a serious possibility, the second stage requires the court to consider whether 'it is in the person's best interests to make the order or give the directions, without delay'.

Court of Protection procedures

4.100 The court's procedures are dealt with in the relevant chapters. However, it is helpful to emphasise the following points by way of general introduction.

The overriding objective

4.101 COPR r3 sets out the overriding objective of the rules which is to enable the court to deal with a case justly 'having regard to the principles contained in the Act'.

4.102 The principles contained in the MCA 2005 are those set out in section 1. So, for example, a person should not be held to lack capacity to make litigation decisions merely because they make what others regard as an unwise decision or until all practicable steps to help them litigate their own case have been taken without success.

THE OVERRIDING OBJECTIVE
(COPR r3)

The overriding objective

3.–(1) These Rules have the overriding objective of enabling the court to deal with a case justly, having regard to the principles contained in the Act.

(2) The court will seek to give effect to the overriding objective when it–
    (a) exercises any power under these Rules; or
    (b) interprets any rule or practice direction.

(3) Dealing with a case justly includes, so far as is practicable–
    (a) ensuring that it is dealt with expeditiously and fairly;
    (b) ensuring that P's interests and position are properly considered;
    (c) dealing with the case in ways which are proportionate to the nature, importance and complexity of the issues;
    (d) ensuring that the parties are on an equal footing;
    (e) saving expense; and
    (f) allotting to it an appropriate share of the court's resources, while taking account of the need to allot resources to other cases.

Duty of the parties

4.103   COPR r4 then provides that 'the parties are required to help the court to further the overriding objective'. Thus, for example, so far as practicable they must help to save litigation expense and deal with the case in ways which are proportionate to the nature, importance and complexity of the issues. In an appropriate case, the penalty for not doing so would be not to allow the party all of their costs in a property and financial affairs case or to require them to contribute to another party's costs in a case involving, eg health and welfare.

Who are the parties to the proceedings

4.104   Unlike proceedings in other courts, the parties do not define themselves – although they will generally be the applicant(s), any objectors and, in significant personal welfare cases, the person said to be incapacitated. The district judge dealing with a case initially must identify the persons who should be parties and ensure that notice is given to other relevant people to enable them to be joined if they wish.

Involvement of the person concerned

4.105 The rules represent a compromise of different perspectives. COPR r3 requires the court to ensure that the relevant person's interests and position are properly considered, and rule 88(1) provides that the court may hear them on the question of whether or not an order should be made. However, rule 73(4) provides that the relevant person should not be named as a respondent, and thereby made a party to the proceedings, 'unless the court orders otherwise' and the court may proceed in the person's absence if it considers that is appropriate.[50]

4.106 The judge is given a wide discretion, subject to exercising it in a manner which is consistent with the rules of natural justice, the overriding objective and the individual's rights under ECHR articles 5 (right to liberty and security) and 6 (right to a fair trial). A flexible approach is best, which has regard to the person's wishes and feelings and seeks to facilitate their attendance and participation in decisions affecting them. Depending on the particular circumstances, this can be achieved by:

- the person's attendance at hearings;
- telephone hearings;
- inviting and considering their letters and written representations;
- the use of advocates;
- the judge visiting the person at their home, hospital or place where they are detained; or
- a combination of all of these approaches.

See further in this regard chapter 16.

Litigation friends

4.107 Because the COPR are based on the Rules of the Supreme Court, rather than the Mental Health Tribunal Rules, they require the relevant person to have a litigation friend if they are made a party to the proceedings (or intend to be a party) and lack capacity to conduct the proceedings.[51] This issue is dealt with in chaptes 6 and 12.

---

50 COPR r88(2).
51 COPR r141(1).

Case management[52]

4.108   By COPR r5, the court is required to further the overriding objective of dealing with cases justly by actively managing cases.

COURT'S DUTY TO MANAGE CASES
(COPR r5)

Court's duty to manage cases
5.–(1) The court will further the overriding objective by actively managing cases.
(2) Active case management includes–
    (a) encouraging the parties to co-operate with each other in the conduct of the proceedings;
    (b) identifying at an early stage–
        (i) the issues; and
        (ii) who should be a party to the proceedings;
    (c) deciding promptly–
        (i) which issues need a full investigation and hearing and which do not; and
        (ii) the procedure to be followed in the case;
    (d) deciding the order in which issues are to be resolved;
    (e) encouraging the parties to use an alternative dispute resolution procedure if the court considers that appropriate;
    (f) fixing timetables or otherwise controlling the progress of the case;
    (g) considering whether the likely benefits of taking a particular step justify the cost of taking it;
    (h) dealing with as many aspects of the case as the court can on the same occasion;
    (i) dealing with the case without the parties needing to attend at court;
    (j) making use of technology; and
    (k) giving directions to ensure that the case proceeds quickly and efficiently.

Hearings

4.109   Most hearings take place in court, but they can take place in a hospital, nursing home or other agreed venue where this is necessary in order to enable the relevant person to participate. As now retired District Judge Gordon Ashton OBE has observed on many occasions,

---

52   See further chapter 11.

the approach may be adversarial, inquisitorial or conciliatory according to the needs of the case.

4.110 The general rule is that hearings are held in private. This reflects the personal, private, nature of the information which the court is usually considering. However, the rules provide that the court may by order authorise any person or class of persons (such as members of the press) to attend a private hearing or part of it. See further chapters 14 and 16.

Legal aid

4.111 For property and affairs cases, public funding is not available. In most kinds of personal welfare cases it is severely restricted, and where available generally means-assessed. This issue is dealt with in chapter 6.

Personal Support Unit (PSU)

4.112 The PSU volunteers at First Avenue House do not give legal advice. However, subject to resources, they may be able to support litigants in person by:

- prompting them to order their thoughts;
- tidying paperwork into a rational order, and indexing it;
- helping them to find out which forms they need to fill in, to complete them if they know what they want to say, and to take the paperwork to the appropriate customer service desk or court office;
- helping people find their way around the court building;
- assisting in discussions with court staff;
- going into court with the person to offer support;
- signposting clients to free legal advice or representation, or to access relevant advice online.

McKenzie friends and lay representation

McKenzie friends

4.113 Litigants who cannot arrange legal representation have the right to have reasonable assistance from a suitable layperson, sometimes called a 'McKenzie friend'.

4.114 A McKenzie friend may:

- provide moral support;
- take notes;

- help with case papers;
- quietly give advice on any aspect of the conduct of the case.

4.115   A McKenzie friend may not act as advocate or to carry out the conduct of litigation. Specifically, they may not:

- act as the litigant's agent in relation to the proceedings;
- manage the litigant's case outside court, for example by signing court documents;
- address the court, make oral submissions or examine witnesses.

Lay representation

4.116   Lay representation is not generally allowed. The court should only be prepared to grant a right of audience or a right to conduct litigation to a layperson where there is good reason to do so, taking into account all the circumstances of the case, which are likely to vary greatly. Such grants should not be extended to laypersons automatically or without due consideration, and should not be granted for mere convenience.

4.117   Examples of the type of special circumstances which have been held to justify the grant of a right of audience to a layperson, including a McKenzie friend, are that:

- the person is a close relative of the litigant;
- health problems preclude the litigant from addressing the court, or conducting litigation, and the litigant cannot afford to pay for a qualified legal representative;
- the litigant is relatively inarticulate and prompting by that person may unnecessarily prolong the proceedings.[53]

Appeals

4.118   The appellate court will interfere with the original decision unless the judge erred in principle or reached a conclusion that was wrong. See further chapter 19.

---

53 In this respect, see the Practice Guidance: *McKenzie friends (Civil and Family Courts)* issued on 12 July 2010 by Lord Neuberger of Abbotsbury (the then Master of the Rolls) and Sir Nicholas Wall (the then President of the Family Division).

Enforcement of orders and declarations

4.119　The court has all the powers of the High Court within the scope of its jurisdiction, and the COPR incorporate many of the enforcement provisions contained in the Civil Procedure Rules 1998. See further chapter 18.

PART 2

Stages of an application

CHAPTER 5

Is an application appropriate?

Introduction

5.1   There are many reasons why people 'go to law'. Not all of them are well thought out, and many people have later regretted doing so in haste. It is sensible, therefore, to consider carefully whether an application to the Court of Protection is necessary as a matter of law, or appropriate as being in the person's best interests.

5.2   The matters to think through before applying include the following:

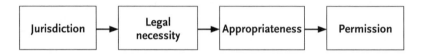

JURISDICTION	
Does the Court of Protection have jurisdiction to consider the proposed application?	• There is little point applying to the court unless it has power to grant the remedy sought. • The court's jurisdiction is defined by the Mental Capacity Act (MCA) 2005. Most obviously, it is a jurisdiction exercisable only over people who lack (or, on an interim basis, appear to lack) capacity. • Remember that a person must be assumed to have capacity unless it is established that they lack capacity. Furthermore, a person is not to be treated as being unable to make their own decision unless all practicable steps to help them to do so have been taken without success, or merely because they make or propose making an unwise decision. • Even if the person is incapacitated, certain family law matters (such as consenting to the making of an adoption order) and Mental Health Act (MHA) matters (treatment without consent under that Act) are excluded from its jurisdiction: see sections 27 and 28. • Depending on the type of decision to be made, the court's jurisdiction may be restricted to incapacitated adults (eg statutory wills, lasting powers of attorney (LPAs)), to persons aged 16 or over (eg treatment or care issues) or available to people of all ages (property and financial affairs matters where the child's incapacity is likely to last into adulthood). • Court of Protection Rules (COPR) 2007 SI No 1744 r87 and Practice Direction (PD) 12B contain provisions for disputing the court's jurisdiction.

	LEGAL NECESSITY
Is an application necessary?	In various situations, an application is a legal necessity. For example, in the personal welfare sphere, a case involving non-therapeutic sterilisation or organ donation; in the financial sphere, situations where there is a need for someone with capacity to manage an incapacitated person's property.
	APPROPRIATENESS
Is an application appropriate?	Even if an application is not necessary, it may still be appropriate to apply because an application is reasonably believed to be in the relevant person's best interests. This is case-specific and depends on many things. For example: • Whether what is required can be done lawfully and in the person's best interests without the court's involvement (ask what is in their best interests having regard to their legal rights and circumstances). • The person's wishes, feelings, beliefs and values and all of the other relevant circumstances. • The likely benefits for the person concerned (ask in what ways the application will benefit them). • The likely cost for the person concerned, not just financially but emotionally if personal or family discord is likely to result (ask in what ways the application may cause them harm). • The affordability of proceedings for the relevant person. Even relatively modest costs may be unaffordable. The Court of Protection has the same status as the High Court and the fees charged for applications, legal assistance and reports tend to reflect this. It is essential to avoid *Jarndyce v Jarndyce* situations where the costs of litigation approach or exceed the value of the estate. Everyone involved is under a duty to deal with the underlying issues in a proportionate and cost-effective manner. • Who is at risk of bearing the litigation costs. It should not be assumed that whatever the merits of the application each party will pay their own litigation costs or that the costs will be recoverable from the incapacitated person's estate. The rules enable the court to have regard to the conduct of the parties, which includes their conduct before as well as during the proceedings, whether it was reasonable for them to raise, pursue or contest a particular issue, etc. *continued*

	• The strength of the evidence and the chances of the application succeeding (is there sufficient evidence in support of it and is the court likely to be persuaded to exercise its powers?). • The suitability and appropriateness of the applicant (ought it to be obvious that another person such as a spouse or partner is better placed to apply and will reasonably object?). • Relevant guidance in the Codes of Practice. • The availability of more appropriate alternative procedures or remedies: – Can the matter wait until the person recovers capacity and is able to take the decision for themselves? – Is this the simplest and most appropriate legal way to address this person's needs? – Can the purpose which the applicant has in mind be as effectively achieved in another way which is less restrictive of the person's rights and freedom of action? – Where relevant, does the person still have capacity to complete an LPA or advance decision? – Can what is proposed lawfully and appropriately be done in the person's best interests under MCA 2005 s5? – Does anyone such as an attorney or deputy already have authority to make this decision for the person? – Is it more appropriate to proceed under a different statute, eg guardianship under the MHA 1983, the Children Act 1989 or public health legislation? – If the matter is contentious, are discussions and negotiations really at an end? Is there a possibility of mediation? Would the appointment of an independent mental capacity advocate (IMCA) or a person with a similar independent role help?
PERMISSION	
If permission to make the application is required, is it likely to be granted?	• In order to prevent applications which are frivolous, vexatious, an abuse of process or otherwise an illegitimate interference with the interests and rights of the relevant person, the court's permission is required to make some applications: see MCA 2005 s50 and COPR rr50–52. • When deciding whether to grant permission, MCA 2005 s50(3) requires the court to consider: (a) the applicant's connection with the person concerned; (b) the reasons for the asking the court to appoint a deputy to make personal welfare decisions for the person concerned;

> (c) in what ways the person concerned will benefit from having a deputy appointed to make personal welfare decisions for them;
> (d) whether those benefits can be achieved in any other way.
> • Even when permission is required, it is simply a filtering stage. Permission ought to be granted where, having regard to these and any other relevant considerations, on the material available to the court the application deserves fuller investigation by it and, realistically, the order sought may be in the best interests of the relevant person.

Maxims and principles

5.3   Opinion varies otherwise it would not be an opinion. Having acknowledged that, there is a good case for saying that the following common-sense maxims and principles have proved their utility when it comes to reflecting on whether to intervene in someone else's life:

1) First, do no harm – there are many we cannot help, but none we cannot avoid harming. This principle is as important to the practice of law as it is to the practice of medicine.[1]

2) Give due weight to the importance for the person concerned of their liberty and wish to determine their own course in life.

3) In order to avoid disappointment later, be realistic about the proper function of the law and its limits. One can legislate for marriage but not for a happy marriage. The law provides a useful framework for managing conflict, conferring authority, enforcing legal duties and restraining the unlawful exercise of power. It cannot solve family conflict and underlying resentment, that feeling of not being a loved or favoured child, a scarcity of resources, the disease process itself or the fact that the person concerned must soon die.

4) Accept that risk cannot be avoided. All personal welfare decisions involve balancing competing risks of which the risk to the person's physical safety is but one. Where appropriate, in order to avoid practising too defensively consider applying (or applying in

---

1   'The wicked are wicked, no doubt, and they go astray and they fall, and they come by their deserts; but who can tell the mischief which the very virtuous do?,' Thackeray, *The Newsomes*, Book 1 chapter 20. There is a great deal to be said for 'legal homeopathy': the application of minute, sub-clinical, doses of law. That is tongue-in-cheek, but the lightest touch is often the best.

the alternative) for a declaration that it *is* lawful and in the person's best interests to take the conventional safeguarding risk rather than to avoid it (by, for example, separating them from their life-partner and removing them to a care home). Let the judge take the strain; that is why they are there.

5) Consider the adequacy of your evidence.

Considering the evidence

5.4   Lawyers spend much time discussing new case-law and the nuances of particular sections. However, for every case lost on a point of law, a thousand are lost for want of evidence; and a few more for proced-ural reasons such as missing time-limits and non-compliance with directions.

5.5   The lawyers' old maxim 'only a fool bags himself as a brief' acknowledges that everyone finds it difficult to be objective about a case in which they have a strong personal interest.

5.6   Much litigation in the Court of Protection is the result of historic family tensions, in particular disagreements between siblings and step-relations. Strained relationships over many years now colour each child's personal assessment of the evidence as to which of them is best placed to take on day-to-day decision-making for an incapaci-tated parent.

5.7   Where there are longstanding family issues and an application is likely to be opposed, it is sensible to take legal advice on the evidence and merits of a possible application. Litigation is easy to start, often demanding to pursue and sometimes costly to withdraw or settle.

5.8   Given human nature, it is also often quite easy for a person to satisfy themselves that an application for a proposed gift or will in their favour is one in the incapacitated person's best interests. Again, it is prudent to take neutral advice on the weight of the evidence and what to expect before setting out. At this point the question to ask is not 'What do I make of it?' but 'What is a judge likely to make of it?'

5.9   In the case of local authority safeguarding applications, evidential problems often have a different cause. Local safeguarding investiga-tions rarely involve full disclosure, forensic questioning or independ-ent scrutiny. Consequently, in court the findings reached may not withstand that level of scrutiny.

5.10   To summarise, before embarking on litigation that is likely to be contested it is particularly important to assess objectively the strength of one's case and the adequacy of one's evidence.

Example

5.11   Mrs Smith is a 95-year-old widow who suffers from moderate to severe dementia. She lives with her son and daughter-in-law, Ms Jones. She is taken to a day centre three times a week by a paid carer. Staff at the day centre notice that she has a bruise and Mrs Smith says that her daughter-in-law caused it and that she is frightened of her. Wessex County Council are contacted and place Mrs Smith in a care home under a 'DOLS order' (Deprivation of Liberty Safeguards), ie a standard authorisation. Several months later, an adult safeguarding investigation concludes on the balance of probabilities that the bruising was non-accidental. The family start Court of Protection proceedings seeking a declaration that it is in Mrs Smith's best interests to return home.

What is the local authority's submission?	That it is in Mrs Smith's best interests not to return to the family home and that she should remain in the care home.
What is the local authority trying to prove?	Ill-treatment by her family.
How does it prove this?	By evidence.
What is the evidence?	The evidence consists of: i) the fact that bruising was observed by care home staff; and ii) Mrs Smith's statement as to its cause.
How reliable is the evidence?	Given that the family deny ill-treatment, the key evidential questions are: a) What is the evidence that the bruising is of a kind consistent with non-accidental injury? b) What is the evidence that Mrs Smith is or is not a reliable witness of events, eg that her dementia has not affected her reliability, that she was not led in her account and that she is not motivated by malice?

5.12   As to a), bruising may be related to factors such as age, gender, health status and medication. It is necessary to consider the location, age and pattern of the bruising and any other injuries, the physical indicators of abuse, the behavioural indicators of abuse and the pool of possible perpetrators. Ideally, an applicant requires expert contemporaneous mapping and recording of the injuries by a forensic medical examiner and expert interpretation of the evidence recorded by this examination.

5.13   Although one would never take a child care order application to court without obtaining this evidence, strangely, in the case of alleged elder abuse this is very rarely obtained; and by the time the case comes to court, it is too late to obtain it.

5.14   As to b), there are clear evidential problems given the severity of Mrs Smith's dementia, the passage of time, the fact that the allegations are strongly denied and the number of demonstrably inaccurate allegations made by her in respect of other people.

5.15   By the time of the trial, the situation facing the local authority is that there are a number of possible explanations and a pool of possible perpetrators of any non-accidental injury. The alleged perpetrator has no relevant history and Mrs Smith has been living with her family for some years with no previous concerns of this kind being raised. On the evidence, it is accepted that Mrs Smith has made other allegations which must be the result of confusion. The key evidential omission was not obtaining contemporaneous medical evidence and a forensic opinion on the significance (if any) of the bruising.

Analysing one's own case and evidence

5.16   The approach adopted in the following table is not a substitute for analysing the evidence and taking appropriate advice in each particular case. It is merely an example of how one can devise a simple structure to test the quality and internal consistency of one's own case.

	Example 1	Example 2	Example 3
Type of case	Place of residence dispute	Suitability of a deputy	Contact dispute
Jurisdiction: can the court do what you want? (the application)	The court may determine P's place of residence (MCA 2005 s17)	The court may revoke a deputy's appointment (MCA 2005 s16)	The court may decide contact issues (MCA 2005 s17)
The local authority's best interests submission (the submission)	It is in P's best interests to reside at care home X, not at her own home	It is in P's best interests to remove his current deputy	It is in P's best interests not to have unsupervised contact with Y
What the local authority is alleging/seeking to prove (the findings sought)	Ill-treatment at home by relatives	The existing deputy has stolen money from P	Sexually inappropriate behaviour by Y
The evidence for the allegation (the facts which prove the allegation)	• Bruising • P's oral account	• Bank statements • Failure to account • Failure to explain	• Staff observations • P's oral account
Possible alternative explanations which will need to be ruled out on the balance of probabilities (likely defences)	• Innocent alternative cause of the bruising • P is an unreliable witness	• P gifted the money • P has capacity • P owed the money • Money spent on P	• P has capacity/ consents • P enjoys sexual contact • Faulty observation • P is an unreliable witness
Evidence re any less restrictive options	• Exclude a particular relative or restrict contact with them? • Arrange alternative carers?	Retrospective validation of the transaction if no dishonesty, etc	The friendship is in P's best interests
P = the incapacitated person			

Admissibility and weight of the evidence

5.17   Nowadays there are few strict rules concerning the admissibility of evidence, particularly in the Court of Protection.

5.18   Part 14 of the COPR deals with evidence and the court's power to control it. Subject to complying with the rules, the court's discretion and the odd caveat, the general position is simply that to be admissible evidence must be relevant. 'Relevance' means relevant to the issues which the court must decide and evidence is relevant if it makes a matter which requires proof more or less probable.[2]

5.19   If evidence is relevant, one must next consider the weight which a court is likely to give it, that is how credible and persuasive it is. The case may consist of a mixture of agreed first-hand evidence (things actually said to or observed by a witness), disputed first-hand evidence, valid and invalid inferences from agreed or disputed first-hand evidence, hearsay (agreed or disputed 'facts' communicated to a witness), inferences from hearsay, assumptions and suspicions ('It must be, or is likely to be, the case that ...'), professional presumptions, professional opinions, 'independent expert opinions'.

5.20   If a matter is likely to be contested, some of the questions to consider at this stage are:

- Can all of our 'evidence' be used in court? (This often raises issues of confidentiality; the availability, willingness and compellability of witnesses; and the unrepeatability of some suspicions and corridor conversations.)
- What are the gaps in our evidence?
- Assuming the facts are as stated, are the inferences that have been drawn valid?
- What are the weaknesses in our case?
- How impressive are our witnesses and how expert is our expert evidence?
- What will the other side be saying or putting to our witnesses?
- Does the other side have any good points and is their evidence accurate and reliable?
- Even if our witnesses are right, do we have sufficient evidence that we can provide a better alternative for the incapacitated person to the situation which we are trying to remedy?

---

2   See *Director of Public Prosecutions v Kilbourne* [1973] AC 729, 756. As Lord Bingham once noted, contested trials last long enough as it is without spending time on evidence which is irrelevant and cannot affect the outcome.

The standard of proof

5.21 The standard of proof in Court of Protection proceedings is always 'the balance of probabilities'. However, to leave it there is an over-simplification. The more serious the allegation the less likely it is that the event occurred. Hence, the stronger should be the evidence before the court concludes that the allegation is established on the balance of probability:[3]

> The balance of probability standard means that a court is satisfied an event occurred if the court considers that, on the evidence, the occurrence of the event was more likely than not. When assessing the probabilities the court will have in mind as a factor, to whatever extent is appropriate in the particular case, that the more serious the allegation the less likely it is that the event occurred and, hence, the stronger should be the evidence before the court concludes that the allegation is established on the balance of probability. Fraud is usually less likely than negligence. Deliberate physical injury is usually less likely than accidental physical injury. A step-father is usually less likely to have repeatedly raped and had non-consensual oral sex with his under age stepdaughter than on some occasion to have lost his temper and slapped her. Built into the preponderance of probability standard is a generous degree of flexibility in respect of the seriousness of the allegation.

> Although the result is much the same, this does not mean that where a serious allegation is in issue the standard of proof required is higher. It means only that the inherent probability or improbability of an event is itself a matter to be taken into account when weighing the probabilities and deciding whether, on balance, the event occurred. The more improbable the event, the stronger must be the evidence that it did occur before, on the balance of probability, its occurrence will be established. Ungoed-Thomas J expressed this neatly in *In re Dellow's Will Trusts* [1964] 1 WLR 451, 455:

>> 'The more serious the allegation the more cogent is the evidence required to overcome the unlikelihood of what is alleged and thus to prove it.'

> This substantially accords with the approach adopted in authorities such as the well known judgment of Morris LJ in *Hornal v Neuberger Products Ltd.* [1957] 1 QB 247, 266. This approach also provides a means by which the balance of probability standard can accommodate one's instinctive feeling that even in civil proceedings a court should be more sure before finding serious allegations proved than when deciding less serious or trivial matters.

---

3 *Re H (minors) (sexual abuse: standard of proof)* [1995] UKHL 16 paras 73–75; [1996] AC 563, D–H.

5.22   It is also necessary to consider the setting within which the 'evidence' was given; as to this, see the observations of McFarlane J (as he then was) in *Re SA*:[4]

> 68. When looking at evidence from a witness who is engaged in providing therapy to an individual who then, during the course of the therapeutic relationship, makes statements which are then produced as evidence of the truth, the words of Butler-Sloss LJ in *Re D (Child Abuse: Interviews)* [1998] 2 FLR 10 must be borne in mind:
>
> > 'It is essential to distinguish between interviewing the child to ascertain the facts and interviewing to provide the child with help to unburden her worries. The therapeutic interview would seem to me to be generally unsuited to use as part of the court evidence, although there may be rare cases in which it is necessary to use it.'
>
> 69. Often the therapist will alert others to matters of concern arising from the therapeutic interview and the child or vulnerable person may then be subject to an interview aimed at the forensic process – as indeed happened here with the ABE interview. In the event the ABE interview did not provide any evidence to support the local authority case and thus reliance is made on the original statements made to AL. I do not regard AJ's reports as being inadmissible or to be automatically of no weight, but I do have regard to the observations of Butler-Sloss LJ and, the reasons behind them, in being cautious as to the amount of weight that can be attached to the material that originates from the drama therapy sessions.'

Evidence meeting

5.23   Time and resources permitting, there is a lot to be said for having an evidence meeting before issuing what is likely to be a contested application.

Possible alternative remedies

5.24   The practice of law is concerned with remedies – people go to a lawyer or a court for the same reason they see a doctor, in order to obtain a remedy.

5.25   Sometimes there will be a more appropriate alternative to making an application to the Court of Protection.

5.26   Most courts deal only with litigious matters. The Court of Protection is unusual in that much of its work, particularly on the property

4   [2010] EWHC 196 (Admin).

and financial side, is non-litigious. Here there is often a common goal, which is to put in place a protective legal framework for a person who is unable to protect and promote their own personal interests.

5.27 The remainder of this chapter considers or lists possible alternative remedies under the following headings:

- Non-contentious property and financial matters
- Contentious property and financial matters
- Non-contentious personal welfare matters
- Contentious personal welfare matters.

Non-contentious property and financial matters

Steps to take

5.28 Where a person appears to be incapable of managing their property and affairs or a particular transaction, the first step is to verify this. Capacity often fluctuates, no one is to be found incapable unless all practicable steps to help them make their own decision have been taken unsuccessfully, the correct legal test must be applied and the answer may depend on the significance and complexity of the matter in hand.

5.29 If the person does lack capacity, the second step is to establish if and when they may recover capacity, and whether the decision(s) can be postponed until they are able to act for themselves.

5.30 If a decision is required now, the third step is to check whether arrangements are already in place for managing the situation. For example, did the person execute an enduring power of attorney (EPA) or LPA when they had capacity, or has a deputy already been authorised to make decisions of this kind?

5.31 If not, the fourth step is the check whether the person's affairs are sufficiently complicated to require the appointment of a deputy or whether an alternative procedure will or may suffice.

5.32 The court process for appointing a deputy is not onerous in most cases. It consists of ensuring that there is adequate evidence of incapacity, information about the person's finances, identifying possible conflicts of interest and ensuring that close family members are notified and have an opportunity to object to the proposed arrangement.

5.33 However, the appointed deputy must then usually take out security, file annual reports with the Public Guardian, pay an annual supervision fee and so forth. It is therefore worth considering whether there are any other suitable ways of managing the person's finances in their best interests which avoid supervision of what hitherto has been the individual's private life and all the expense that goes with that.

5.34   Some of the main options are those given in the following table, which is based on one in Ashton's *Elderly people and the law:*[5]

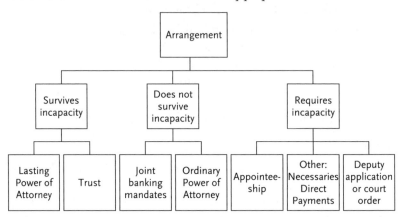

Lasting power of attorney

5.35   The best way of avoiding the need for a court-appointed deputy is for the relevant person to execute an LPA, provided of course that they still have capacity to do so.

5.36   The important point to bear in mind is that a person may lack capacity to manage their property and affairs in a general sense, so that the court could lawfully appoint a deputy to manage their estate, but still have sufficient capacity to execute an LPA.

5.37   In other words, the person concerned may retain sufficient capacity to be able to make their own arrangements for the future management of their estate. If so, they can appoint (say) their spouse or partner as their attorney, which avoids the need for the latter to apply to be appointed as their deputy.

5.38   The possibility arises because capacity is 'issue-specific' and depends on the transaction or decision in hand.

5.39   Because the relevant individual's capacity is borderline in such cases, it is imperative to ensure that the certificate of capacity is completed by an independent professional such as a general practitioner or solicitor and to establish that close family members and any other key individuals accept the capacity finding.

---

5   G Ashton, *Elderly people and the law*, Butterworths, London, 1995, p299.

5.40   Provided there is nothing untoward, the arrangement has clear advantages in terms of maintaining the historic privacy, simplicity and trust of a long-standing relationship. Although there is a fee to be paid for registering an LPA, this is less than the standard court fee payable when filing a deputy application.

Enduring power of attorney

5.41   Once the MCA 2005 came into force on 1 October 2007 it was no longer possible to execute an EPA. However, EPAs made before then were not revoked by the Act and continue to have legal effect, subject to the need for registration if the attorney has reason to believe that the donor is becoming mentally incapable of managing and administering their property and affairs.

Trusts

5.42   It is possible for a person who is concerned that they may be becoming mentally incapacitated to create a trust. This involves transferring money and assets to trustees on terms that require the trustees to manage the trust fund for the benefit of the individual who has created it (and perhaps for the benefit of others also). The relevant test is whether the person has capacity to make the trust at the same time and *Re Beaney*[6] provides some guidance as to this.

5.43   As Ashton noted in 1995, this approach lost some popularity once it became possible for an individual who was beginning to lose capacity to create an EPA. It was then easy for them to enter into a lasting arrangement with a trusted person for the latter to manage the former's property as their agent without the need to create a trust and give up legal ownership of the property to trustees.

There is usually a tension between the settlor's various objectives. He or she will often wish to retain ultimate control over the money and to be able to call for it to be spent on them. However, to obtain tax advantages or to avoid it being taken into account in the assessment of means-tested benefits, it is usually necessary to give up any form of control.

5.44   The tax consequences of placing money in trust need to be carefully considered, as do the extent to which the trustees will be legally obliged to maintain the person who created it. In addition, unless the trust was of a very specific nature, and entered into before there was any reason to believe that the settlor may need residential or nursing

---

6   [1978] 2 All ER 595.

care it is extremely unlikely that the trust would be effective at sheltering assets from local authority assessment. Professional advice is essential if a trust is being contemplated. For these reasons the trust is no longer popular as a vehicle for planning for future incapacity.

Banking arrangements

5.45   Joint accounts and other banking arrangements often seem an attractive proposition from a planning point of view compared with other more formal mechanisms. However, as with all mechanisms, they also have limitations and drawbacks.

Third-party mandates

5.46   An account holder who has mental capacity can authorise someone to access their account, for example because they have physical disabilities. This is called a 'third-party mandate'.[7] A common alternative is for an individual to appoint someone to act as their agent under an ordinary power of attorney. However, neither arrangement survives mental incapacity.

Joint bank accounts

5.47   It is, of course, common for people to operate a joint account with a spouse, partner, child or other trusted person. A joint account involves two different kinds of legal relationship:

Legal relationship between the joint account holders	This is a private matter for the individuals. The individuals agree who pays what amounts in, what may be withdrawn, how the money in the account is split, how any borrowing on the account will be repaid.
Their legal relationship with the bank	• This is controlled by a document called a mandate or authority which each joint-account holder must sign. Often this document forms part of the joint-account application form. Depending on the terms of the mandate, either or both account-holders can withdraw money separately or two signatures may be required.

---

7 *Guidance for people wanting to manage a bank account for someone else*, AE254, March 2013, British Bankers' Association, Pinners Hall, 105–108 Old Broad Street, London EC2N 1EX.

> • Either way, the general position is that both are individually as well as jointly responsible for all debts on the account, even if one of them puts all the money in and one of them takes all of it out. For this reason, on becoming aware that one of the joint account-holders lacks capacity, a bank will often cancel the joint authority to withdraw funds and effectively 'freeze' the account.
> • The legal justification is that authority to sign on a joint account entails a continuing consent which is broken by mental incapacity. From the bank's viewpoint, there is also a risk management issue if one of the account holders lacks capacity to monitor the account and understand how the funds are spent.
>
> Source: 'You and your joint account' (AE256), British Bankers' Association Enterprises, July 2013.

5.48 There is no single procedure which all banks and building societies adopt when a joint account-holder loses capacity. Different banks have different procedures. The degree of flexibility may sometimes depend on their knowledge of the account and their relationship with the account-holders. In some cases the bank may continue to pay pre-existing direct debits and standing orders for utilities, household bills, residential care fees and living expenses until a deputy has been appointed or a power of attorney has been registered.

Joint accounts and attorneys

5.49 If one joint account holder loses the capacity to operate their account and a registered EPA or LPA is in place, the bank will allow the attorney and account holder with capacity to operate the account independently unless the account holder with capacity objects. In such cases the bank will then usually only allow the account to continue to operate on a 'both-to-sign' basis.[8]

Limitations and disadvantages

5.50 The effect of the death of either account holder may be a particularly relevant consideration if one of them is frail. The general (but rebuttable) rule is that on death money in a joint account passes to the surviving account holder. This leaves room for disagreement in

---

8 *Guidance for people wanting to manage a bank account for someone else* (see fn 7 above).

some cases if a parent's will provides for dividing their estate equally among all of their children. In practice, in the event of a dispute about the ownership of funds in an account this will come down to evidence as to the sources of the funds in the account.[9]

5.51   A second disadvantage relates to local authority means assessments. There can be a risk that some of the non-incapacitated account holder's funds are means-assessed by the local authority when it comes to assessing the contribution payable towards the incapacitated person's care home costs.

5.52   A third disadvantage materialises where a person added to the account then withdraws funds from it for their own benefit. If both had authority to draw on the account, it can be very difficult to prove that the withdrawals were not authorised and difficult to recover the funds.

Ordinary power of attorney

5.53   An ordinary or general power of attorney can be effective for a specified period of time (for example, to cover a trip abroad) or run indefinitely until the donor brings it to an end by revoking it. The authority granted by the document is automatically revoked if the donor becomes mentally incapacitated.

5.54   Because the donor must be legally competent, an ordinary or general power of attorney does not need to be registered by the Public Guardian.

Appointeeships

5.55   A deputyship may be unnecessary where the person's income consists solely of a state pension or benefits and they have no savings or equity in a house that needs to be sold.

---

9 The mere fact that the legal title to an account is held in two names does not mean that the beneficial title is held in the same manner – an example of the money in a joint bank account belonging beneficially to one of its signatories can be found in *Day v Harris* [2013] COPLR 254. The beneficial ownership of joint bank accounts is often a difficult question. One difficulty is often proving what was intended, and is often complicated by the competing presumptions of result trust and advancement. *Re Figgis* [1969] 1 Ch 123 is a case where the presumption of advancement was held to apply when a husband in ailing health put an account in his, and his wife's, joint names. In *Re Bishop* [1965] Ch 540 a husband and wife who had contributed unequally to a joint account were each held to be entitled to draw on the proceeds for joint purposes or for their own purpose (the presumption of advancement is to be abolished from a date to be appointed: Equality Act 2010 s199).

5.56   In such cases, a spouse, partner or other suitable person can apply to the Department for Work and Pensions (DWP) for the pension or benefits to be paid to them as the person's 'appointee'. The appointee is authorised to receive the benefits and manage the benefit income. The appointee has various responsibilities and functions. The appointee:

- must report any change in the person's circumstances that may affect benefit entitlement;
- may sign on behalf of the person if they are a non-tax payer to enable bank and building society interest to be paid without deducting income tax;
- can only deal with the person's income from benefits, except for small amounts of savings which can be used to meet unforeseen emergencies.

5.57   Once the proposed appointee has completed the usual form, a representative from the DWP may visit the relevant person or ask for evidence confirming that they are no longer able to act on their own behalf.

5.58   Current departmental guidance is that the appointee should, wherever possible, be a close relative who lives with the person or visits them frequently. In certain circumstances, the appointee may be a friend, neighbour or professional carer.

5.59   An appointee who does not wish to continue in the role can resign and the DWP can revoke an appointeeship if it has evidence that the appointee is not acting in the person's best interests.

5.60   The regulations provide that a court-appointed deputy automatically becomes the relevant person's appointee in place of any existing appointee, but are silent as to the effect of registering an EPA or LPA.

Limitations and disadvantages

5.61   The limitations of an appointeeship arrangement are fairly obvious: an appointee does not have authority to deal with capital or with other income belonging to the incapacitated person. A court order and/or the appointment of a deputy will be necessary if authority is required to manage other assets which the relevant person lacks capacity to manage, such as real property, personal possessions, cars, shares and so on.

5.62   Unspent pension and benefits may constitute capital. The general view for some time now has been that a deputy application is unnecessary provided that the appointee only holds a 'reasonable sum' of accrued savings. However, some banks set limits on the amount of money that a person can have in an appointeeship account.

Other options

5.63   A number of other provisions are helpful on occasion.

Payment for necessary goods and services

5.64   MCA 2005 s7(1) provides that: 'If necessary goods or services are supplied to a person who lacks capacity to contract for the supply, he must pay a reasonable price for them.' By subsection (2), 'necessary' means suitable to a person's condition in life and to his actual requirements at the time when the goods or services are supplied.

5.65   This provision combined the old common law rule relating to services with the statutory rule in the Sale of Goods Act 1979 relating to goods. Thus, if the milkman carries on delivering milk to the house of someone who has a progressive dementia, they can expect to be paid. If, however, a roofer puts a completely unnecessary new roof on to that person's house, when all that was required was a minor repair, then the rule will not apply.

Expenditure on the person's behalf

5.66   MCA 2005 s8(1) provides that where someone does an act to which section 5 applies which involves expenditure in connection with another person's care or treatment then it is lawful for them to pledge payment from the person's estate and also to apply money in the person's possession to meet the expenditure.

5.67   Furthermore, if expenditure is borne on the person's behalf by the individual acting under section 5, it is lawful for the latter to reimburse themselves from any money in the person's possession or to be otherwise indemnified by them.

5.68   This restates the common law rules which provided that a person acting as an 'agent of necessity' for another person should not be out of pocket as a result. However, nothing in the clause allows a carer to gain access to the relevant person's funds where they are held by a third party such as a bank or building society.

Direct payments

5.69   Direct payments are local authority cash payments for people who have been assessed as being entitled to help from social services and who would like to arrange and pay for their own, independently contracted, care and support services.

5.70   Where a person with eligible needs lacks capacity to consent to the making of direct payments, a suitable person can be appointed to manage the payments on their behalf.[10] This could be an attorney, deputy, DWP appointee or other person such as a carer.

5.71   The suitable person is the only person who can access and manage the direct payment. The account should be in their name but identified as being held on behalf of the person the payments are for (for example, 'Joan Smith on behalf of Edward Smith').[11]

Personal health budgets

5.72   From April 2014, people receiving NHS Continuing Healthcare at home have the right to ask for a personal health budget. This can be paid to someone suitable on behalf of an incapacitated person.

5.73   The scheme is at an early stage but potentially, once the person's healthcare plan has been agreed, the money in their personal health budget can be managed in a number of different ways. An organisation or trust could hold the money and help them decide what they need; the local NHS team could buy the care and support which the person has chosen; or the person or their representative could buy and manage the services.

Court orders other than deputyship

5.74   Where the authority of the Court of Protection is required, it is not always necessary to appoint a deputy.

5.75   The court is frequently asked to make single orders dealing with matters such as authorising an individual to sign or surrender a tenancy agreement, to litigate on an incapacitated person's behalf, to access their health or social care records, to challenge NHS funding decisions, to ratify a gift and so on. In some cases it ought not to be necessary to obtain a court order, for example in relation to access to records, but the applicant has been frustrated in their attempts to persuade the relevant authority that they are suitable or that the step is in the incapacitated individual's best interests.

5.76   Apart from one judge who occasionally does so, the court no longer makes the kind of old-style 'short order' previously made under the pre-MCA legislation or any contemporary variant of it. However, the legislation does include the principle that a single order is to be

---

10 See Community Care, Services for Carers and Children's Services (Direct Payments) (England) Regulations 2009 SI No 1887.
11 *Guidance for people wanting to manage a bank account for someone else* (see fn 7 above).

preferred to the appointment of a deputy and some estates are small and simple enough that what is required can be achieved in a single order.

Contentious property and financial matters

5.77   Litigation or some formal action may be inevitable if a matter is contentious. The alternative ways forward then need to be explored. Consider the time limits for each possible court action[12] or complaint, the funding options for each and the remedies afforded by each. The aggrieved person needs to be clear about the outcome they wish to achieve – damages, the reversal of a funding decision, better services, disciplinary proceedings, the investigation and deregistration of a care home or service provider, an injunction, a prosecution, an apology, publicity – and who has power to provide that kind of remedy. Remember that the Court of Protection is not a regulatory, investigatory or complaints body, nor is it an inspectorate. Ombudsmen and regulators usually require that a complaint has been investigated locally and the service provider been given a fair opportunity to deal with the situation before considering a complaint.

5.78   Where possible, take professional legal advice or advice from Citizens Advice or a similar organisation. Be fair. Avoid multiple complaints to multiple bodies. This demoralises professionals, creates chaos and delay and damages the complainant's case. Be polite – apart from the fact that unpleasant emails and tweets are upsetting for those concerned, and may constitute a criminal offence, they are damaging when later produced in court and may have a bearing on who pays the litigation costs. Most important of all, if any step is being taken on behalf of an incapacitated person, remember that you must act in their best interests. Therefore apply the MCA 2005 s4 considerations and try to maintain a good relationship, or at least a working relationship, with their professional carers, family members, representatives and friends.

---

12 Where the claim is not for damages but what is known as equitable relief, for example an injunction, the equitable defence of laches (unreasonable delay in bringing the claim) may be raised.

PROPERTY AND FINANCIAL AFFAIRS – POSSIBLE ALTERNATIVE REMEDIES	
Remedy	Possible relevance
MCA 2005 matters	
Best interests meetings	If the contentious matter is connected with different opinions as to what is in an incapacitated person's best interests with regard to their property and finances, consider whether there is a professional such as a solicitor or a neutral family member who could convene a best interests meeting. Explore what kinds of formal mediation and alternative dispute resolution (ADR) are available locally.
Complaints about a deputy or donee	• The Public Guardian supervises court-appointed deputies and deals with representations (including complaints) about the way in which a deputy or donee of an LPA is exercising their powers. These functions may be discharged in co-operation with any other person who has relevant safeguarding functions such as a local authority or the police. • On application by the Public Guardian, the Court of Protection can order that any security bond in place is 'called in' to make good the loss.
Complaints about court funds	Contrary to inaccurate press reports, the Court of Protection does not hold or administer funds on behalf of incapacitated people. It is the Court Funds Office (CFO) which provides a banking and administration service for the civil courts throughout England and Wales. See the Court Funds Rules 2011 SI No 1734 or contact the Court Funds Office, Glasgow G58 1AB.
Complaints about an NHS or social services funding decision	
NHS	As to appeals against NHS decisions that a person does not qualify for NHS continuing healthcare, see the section below dealing with personal welfare matters.
Local authority	As to local authority community care means assessments and charges, see the section below dealing with personal welfare matters.

Remedy	Possible relevance
Ombudsmen and regulatory bodies	
Ombudsmen	Depending on the nature of the grievance, a number of ombudsmen and regulatory bodies may exercise a relevant function: • The Financial Ombudsman Service deals with complaints about banking, insurance, loans, credit and other financial services. • The Pensions Ombudsman deals with complaints and disputes about the way that occupational pension schemes and personal pensions are run. The complainant must usually have asked the Pensions Advisory Service for assistance first. • The Solicitors Regulation Authority (SRA) is a regulatory body which deals with failures to comply with professional obligations such as the duty to keep the person's affairs confidential or the duty to act honestly and with integrity. • The Bar Standards Board (BSB) is the equivalent regulatory body for barristers. • The Legal Ombudsman deals with complaints that a poor service has been provided by a barrister, solicitor or legal executive, eg a failure to keep the client properly informed. • The Housing Ombudsman Service deals with complaints from people who receive a direct service from registered social landlords in England and certain other landlords who are members of the scheme, including bodies which take over homes transferred from local authorities.
Raising the matter with an elected representative or publicising it	
MP	A request to the relevant person's MP concerning the provision of a public service often produces positive action. However, MPs cannot properly become involved in litigation issues being dealt with by a court.
Councillor	Similarly, a request to the person's local councillor about the provision of social services by (or through) the local authority can be effective.

Remedy	Possible relevance
Media/press	This may be an option but it is a legal minefield and one to be exercised with tremendous caution in relation to someone who lacks capacity to decide for themselves whether to waive their usual right to privacy and confidentiality. Consider their capacity to make the decision for themselves, whether *you* have any legal right to waive their right to privacy or confidentiality, whether therefore you may be liable to the incapacitated person, the best interests considerations in MCA 2005 s4, the law relating to defamation (libel, slander) and the legal rights and remedies of the other people involved.
Other kinds of legal proceedings (civil)	
Actions relating to vulnerable or incapacitated persons	• As to the enforceability of contracts entered into by an incapacitated person, a contract is not enforceable against them if a) the relevant person was incapable of understanding the nature of the contract they were entering into and b) the other contracting party knew of their incapacity at the time, or knew of such facts and circumstances that they must be taken to have known of the incapacity. A separate rule applies to the supply of necessary goods and services, which is now set out in MCA 2005 s7. • A gift made by an incapacitated person may be avoided in the circumstances set out in *Re Beaney* ([1978] 2 All ER 595 at 600). In the case of a simple and trivial gift, such as giving a small present to a friend, there is not much to it and very little to grasp in order to make a valid gift. More significant transactions – those where the reasonably foreseeable consequences are more significant for the person concerned – by definition require the capacity to understand and weigh the more significant consequences. • Unless the commission of a tort (civil wrong) requires specific intention, such as malice, avoiding legal liability may be limited to acts done while in a state of automatism, although there is a lack of recent authority. *continued*

Remedy	Possible relevance
	• The common law duties of an attorney include duties a) of utmost good faith, b) to keep accounts, c) to disclose all relevant facts in certain transactions, d) not to make secret profits, e) to discharge duties with reasonable care.
Standard actions	The relevant person has the usual range of available remedies in relation to breach of trust, breach of contract and torts (other civil wrongs which give rise to a right to a remedy, eg conversion, deceit, trespass to land, trespass to goods, nuisance, negligence).
Other kinds of legal proceedings (criminal)	
Offences relating to vulnerable or incapacitated persons	Fraud Act 2006 s4 (abuse of position) makes it a criminal offence where a person intentionally and dishonestly takes advantage of their position.
Standard offences	Incapacitated persons have the protection of the usual criminal laws relating to property, theft, fraud, false accounting, etc. Where justified, a concerned person may ask for an investigation to be undertaken by the police, the local authority adult safeguarding team, the DWP Fraud Investigation Unit or the fraud unit of a bank or other financial institution.

Non-contentious personal welfare matters

5.79   Non-contentious routine care and treatment is usually provided under the protection of MCA 2005 s5 without any application to a court.

5.80   If the relevant person still has capacity to appoint an attorney in relation to their future care and treatment, or some aspect of it, then this mechanism ensures that decisions are always made either with their own consent or that of a trusted person. They may also wish to consider making an advance decision to refuse treatment.

5.81   Direct payments and personal health budgets paid to a suitable person acting for, and hopefully with, the individual also enable care and treatment to be provided in a way which is consistent with the principles of the MCA 2005.

5.82   Guardianship under the MHA 1983 can provide a useful light-touch safety-net for citizens who are vulnerable to self-neglect or abuse but historically it is not favoured by local authorities, for reasons that appear to be almost entirely irrelevant.

5.83 The Children Act 1989 provides an alternative age-dependant framework in some cases.

Contentious personal welfare matters

5.84 Most personal welfare litigation in the Court of Protection involves either:

- a public authority (such as a local authority or NHS trust) in dispute with a person alleged to lack capacity and/or one or more family members; or
- a dispute between family members, in particular siblings, as to what personal welfare arrangements are in an incapacitated person's best interests.

5.85 Before commencing court proceedings, it is important to:

1) Remember the duty to act in the relevant person's best interests, not one's own.
2) Remember that the normal rule in personal welfare proceedings is that each party bears their own legal costs and that the cost of independent expert reports is usually apportioned between the parties. Unless legally aided, the expense can be significant.
3) Remember that the Court of Protection cannot review NHS and local authority funding decisions. Provided they do not act so irrationally that it constitutes acting unlawfully, etc, it is for local and other public authorities, not judges, to decide how to allocate their limited resources. Furthermore, the funds available to public authorities, and levels of taxation and public expenditure, are political decisions, that is matters for all of us, ie for voters not judges.
4) Consider the likely emotional cost of being involved in prolonged litigation.

PERSONAL WELFARE MATTERS – POSSIBLE ALTERNATIVE REMEDIES	
Remedy	Possible relevance
MCA 2005 matters	
Best interests meetings, ADR	• Consider, and where practicable explore, non-litigious ways of resolving the outstanding issues. The court expects those involved in an incapacitated person's care to co-operate where possible in seeking to ascertain and promote that person's best interests before asking a court to intervene and rule on the matter. • Where relevant, ask the local authority or NHS body to convene a 'best interests meeting' at which the outstanding issues can be discussed and hopefully a way forward agreed. • Alternatively, or in addition, ask the local authority or NHS body for a professional second opinion as to the matter in dispute and the person's best interests. • Explore what kinds of formal mediation and ADR are available locally. • Consider whether a neutral family member or professional such as a solicitor not involved in the dispute may be willing and able to mediate.
Alleged unlawful deprivation of liberty	If an incapacitated person is being deprived of their liberty in a care home or hospital without there existing any legal order or authority which authorises this, consider requesting the relevant local authority to review whether there is an unauthorised deprivation of liberty before applying to the Court of Protection. The non-court procedures relating to unauthorised deprivation of liberty are set out in MCA 2005 Sch A1 paras 67–73.
Deprivation of liberty: requesting a Part 8 review	An application may be made to the Court of Protection challenging a standard authorisation authorising a deprivation of liberty. An alternative procedure in appropriate cases which does not rule out applying to the court if the outcome is adverse is to ask the local authority to undertake a 'Part 8 review'. In general, it must do so if it receives a request from the person concerned or their representative. The procedure is set out in MCA 2005 Sch A1 Part 8.

Remedy	Possible relevance
Complaints about a deputy or donee	The Public Guardian supervises court-appointed deputies and deals with representations (including complaints) about the way in which a donee of an LPA or a court-appointed deputy is exercising their powers. These functions may be discharged in cooperation with any other body with relevant statutory functions such as a local authority or police.
Complaints about an NHS or social services decisions in relation to funding and services	
NHS	• 'NHS continuing healthcare' (CHC) refers to a package of ongoing care arranged and funded solely by the NHS where it has been assessed that the individual's primary need is a health need. It can be provided in any setting. In a person's own home, it means that the NHS funds all of the care required to meet the person's assessed health needs. In care homes, it means that the NHS makes a contract with the care home and pays the fees for the person's accommodation as well as all their care. • The *National framework for NHS continuing healthcare and NHS funded nursing care* sets out the principles and processes for determining eligibility. (Available at: https://www.gov.uk/government/publications/national-framework-for-nhs-continuing-healthcare-and-nhs-funded-nursing-care.) • The initial assessment consists of a screening checklist completed by a healthcare professional or social worker. Depending on the outcome, the relevant person will either be found to be ineligible for NHS continuing healthcare or be referred for a full multi-disciplinary assessment. A 'decision support tool' (ie detailed form) must then be completed which records the person's assessed needs – no needs, low, moderate, high, severe, priority – across a number of 'domains' (behaviour, cognition, psychological needs, communication and mobility, etc) in order 'to inform' the final decision as to whether the person does have a primary health need. *continued*

Remedy	Possible relevance
	• There is a three-stage appeals process: Stage one involves an appeal to the relevant clinical commissioning group (CCG). Stage 2 involves a request to NHS England for an independent review. Stage three involves requesting a review by the Parliamentary and Health Service Ombudsman (see below). • NHS continuing healthcare should not be confused with NHS-funded nursing care. A person who lives in a care home who requires care from a registered nurse may be entitled to NHS-funded nursing care (FNC). The standard rate is £110.89 per week, and the higher rate £152.61 per week.
Local authority	• If the relevant person does not qualify for NHS continuing healthcare, their local authority will be responsible for their care needs and for providing services for which they are eligible. Care services from the local authority are usually means-tested. In other words, if the person is eligible for local authority community care services, their finances are assessed and they may be required to pay some or all of the cost of the services. • Complaints about community care assessments and services are subject to the Local Authority Social Services and National Health Services Complaints (England) Regulations 2009 SI No 309. • The complaint is made initially to the local authority. A further complaint to the Local Government Ombudsman may then be possible if the complainant remains dissatisfied. • The Local Government Ombudsman cannot question the merits of community care funding decisions or professional judgements which have been reached properly. However, the Ombudsman can consider how those decisions were reached and whether they have been implemented properly (maladministration and service failure issues).

Remedy	Possible relevance
Judicial review	In some cases, it may be possible to apply to the Administrative Court (a specialist court within the Queen's Bench Division of the High Court) for judicial review of a funding decision on the basis that the decision was unlawful. This might be because the decision of the NHS body or local authority was irrational, procedurally unfair, outside its legal powers, in breach of the Human Rights Act (HRA) 1998 or in breach of European Union law.
Other complaints about the person's treatment or care	
NHS complaints	• The NHS Constitution explains people's rights when it comes to making a complaint. • In England, every NHS organisation must make arrangements for dealing with complaints in accordance with the Local Authority Social Services and National Health Services Complaints (England) Regulations 2009. Regulation 14 imposes a duty on NHS bodies to provide a written response to complaints. • The standard complaints procedure is a two-tier procedure. The complaint must initially be made to the service provider (eg the GP or hospital) or to the commissioner of the service. Since the abolition of primary care trusts (PCTs) in 2013, NHS England commissions most primary care services, such as GP and dental services, while CCGs oversee the commissioning of secondary care such as hospital care and some community services. • A patient advice and liaison service (PALS) is available in all hospitals. It offers confidential advice, support and information to patients, families and carers. • In addition, an NHS Complaints Advocacy Service was established on 1 April 2013. Local authorities now have a statutory duty to commission independent advocacy services to provide support for people making, or thinking of making, a complaint about their NHS care or treatment. <div align="right">*continued*</div>

Remedy	Possible relevance
	• Where a complaint is not resolved at the first-tier, the complainant may take it to the second stage, which is to refer the matter to the Ombudsman. • In England, the Parliamentary and Health Service Ombudsman is the final step for people who want to complain about being treated unfairly or receiving a poor service from the NHS, government departments (including the Ministry of Justice, the Department of Health and the DWP) and other public organisations (such as the Care Quality Commission (CQC)). • Much of the primary legislation governing the Ombudsman's remit is set out in the Parliamentary Commissioner Act 1967; Health Service Commissioners Act 1993; Parliamentary and Health Service Commissioners Act 1987; Health Service Commissioners Act 1993; Health Service Commissioner (Amendment) Act 1996. • In Wales, the bodies which the Public Services Ombudsman for Wales may investigate include the Welsh Assembly Government; a local health board; an NHS trust managing a hospital or other establishment or facility in Wales; an independent health provider; and a family health service provider. • See the Public Services Ombudsman (Wales) Act 2005.
Local authority and other care services	• The Local Authority Social Services and National Health Service Complaints (England) Regulations 2009 apply if a local authority provided or commissioned the care service. • The complainant must normally make the complaint initially to the local authority or to the person or body which provides the commissioned service. If the complaint cannot be resolved at this level, the second stage is to refer it to the Local Government Ombudsman.

Remedy	Possible relevance
	• Where the care is provided under a private contract with the provider, rather than commissioned by a local authority, the CQC requires all registered care providers to have an effective complaints process. The Local Government Ombudsman may now also investigate the complaint but expects the complaint to be made to the service provider in the first instance. • Provided that (in most cases) the local authority or care provider has had a reasonable opportunity to deal with the matter, the Ombudsman can investigate complaints about issues such as alleged poor-quality care, fees and charges, poor complaint handling, delay, assessments of need, safety and safeguarding. The Ombudsman's remit in some matters extends to personal care at home and supported living services for someone with learning disabilities. • A complaint may be made by a suitable representative if the person is incapable of nominating someone to make it for them. • Much of the relevant primary legislation is set out in the Local Government Act 1974 Parts III and IIIA; Health Act 2009; Regulatory Reform (Collaboration etc between Ombudsmen) Order 2007 SI No 1889. • In Wales, the bodies which the Public Services Ombudsman for Wales may investigate include local authorities (including county/county borough councils and community councils); independent social care providers and social landlords such as housing associations.
Access to health and social care records	
NHS and social services records	• The Data Protection Act (DPA) 1998 applies to the records of living persons. • It provides that an individual who makes a request in writing and pays the relevant fee is generally entitled to given a copy of information held about them in an intelligible and permanent form unless this would involve 'disproportionate effort'. *continued*

Remedy	Possible relevance
	• There is a discretion to disclose information to the carers of an incapacitated adult in order to allow them to exercise their rights as carers where the consent of the person being cared for cannot be obtained. • Special rules apply to health and social work records. Access to health records may be refused on medical advice by the information holder ('data controller') if disclosure would be 'likely to cause serious harm to the physical or mental health or condition of the data subject or another person'. The information holder can only do this after consulting the 'appropriate health professional' (meaning the person most recently responsible for the patient's clinical care in connection with the subject matter of the request). • There is a similar provision in relation to social work records. In this case, however, the decision rests with the social work authority alone, with no obligation to consult the relevant professional. • The Access to Health Records Act 1990 now applies only to records of deceased persons created since 1 November 1991. • The Access to Medical Reports Act 1988 concerns medical reports prepared for employers and insurance companies. • Complaints that information has been disclosed to a third-party without a court order requiring or authorising this usually turn on whether there has been an unlawful breach of confidentiality or privacy or a breach of the DPA 1998 principles in relation to processing personal data fairly and lawfully.
The Information Commissioner	The Information Commissioner enforces and oversees the DPA 1998 and the Freedom of Information Act 2000, for both England and Wales. A person denied access to records may complain using the NHS and local authority complaints procedures and then, if a local resolution is not achieved, to the Information Commissioner's Office.

Remedy	Possible relevance
Other Ombudsmen and Commissioners	
Older People's Commissioner for Wales	The Commissioner may review the way in which the interests of older people are safeguarded and promoted when public bodies discharge, propose to discharge or fail to discharge their functions. It can also investigate whether certain bodies' advocacy, whistle-blowing and complaints arrangements are effective in safeguarding and promoting the interests of relevant older people in Wales. The Commissioner may examine the case of an older person in relation to a matter which affects the interests of a wider group of older people and not just the individual concerned. See the Commissioner for Older People (Wales) Act 2006.
Regulatory bodies	
NHS hospitals, local authority care services, private and voluntary sector	• The CQC is the regulator of health and social care in England. In general terms, it registers and inspects all health and social care provision and seeks to ensure that they meet essential standards of quality and safety. • The Health and Social Care Act 2008 (Regulated Activities) Regulations 2010 SI No 781 set out the essential standards of quality and safety expected from service providers of regulated activities, such as care homes. These are set out in regs 9–24 and are supported by compliance guidance. • The CQC deals with complaints about the standards of care homes, hospitals and other registered services as a whole rather than with the kind of individual complaint of poor service dealt with by ombudsmen. • Monitor is responsible for authorising, monitoring and regulating NHS foundation trusts. Whereas the CQC is responsible for service standards and safety, Monitor is concerned with governance issues – the ability of an NHS foundation trust board to do their job and to provide the necessary service. *continued*

Remedy	Possible relevance
	• In Wales, the Care and Social Services Inspectorate Wales (CSSIW) is the body equivalent to the English CQC. It regulates and inspects domiciliary services and care homes for adults including those providing nursing care in order to ensure that they meet national minimum standards.
Individual practitioners	• The General Medical Council (GMC) regulates doctors. • The Nursing and Midwifery Council (NMC) regulates nurses and midwives. • The Health and Care Professions Council (HCPC) regulates psychologists, social workers in England (in Wales, this is done by the Care Council for Wales) and speech and language therapists.
	**Other 'avenues' for complaints and grievances**
MPs, local authority councillors, media/press	As to these options, see the section above dealing with property and financial affairs.
	**Other kinds of legal applications and proceedings (civil)**
	*The relevance of these options depends on whether a public authority or family member is seeking a safeguarding-type remedy or an incapacitated person (or someone on their behalf) is seeking to enforce their legal rights.*
	*Possible remedies for public authorities*
Application under the High Court's inherent jurisdiction	• The exercise of the High Court's inherent jurisdiction may be used to obtain appropriate orders where a person not incapacitated by mental disorder or mental illness is vulnerable and is reasonably believed to be (i) under constraint; or (ii) subject to coercion or undue influence; or (iii) for some other reason deprived of the capacity to make the relevant decision, or disabled from making a free choice, or incapacitated or disabled from giving or expressing a real and genuine consent. See *DL v A local authority* [2012] EWCA Civ 253, (2012) 15 CCLR 267.

Remedy	Possible relevance
	• The purpose of the jurisdiction is facilitative rather than dictatorial. Its purpose is to facilitate the process of unencumbered decision-making by those with capacity free from external pressure or physical restraint.
MHA 1983 powers	The MHA 1983 includes various provisions relating to compulsory admission to hospital, in particular sections 2, 3 and 4. The community provisions include reception into guardianship and sections 115 (entry to and inspection of private premises); 135 (warrants to search private premises and to remove to a place of safety persons suspected to suffer from mental disorder); and 136 (removal by police to a place of safety of persons in public places who appear to be suffering from mental disorder and to be in immediate need of care or control).
Removal under the National Assistance Act (NAA) 1948	• Section 47 of the NAA 1948 and section 1 of the National Assistance (Amendment) Act 1951 remain in force but will be repealed when the Care Bill is enacted. • An application may be made by a specified local authority officer to magistrates for the removal and detention in a hospital or other suitable place of people who a) are suffering from grave chronic disease or, being aged, infirm or physically incapacitated, are living in insanitary conditions; and b) are unable to devote to themselves, and are not receiving from other persons, proper care and attention. • The relevant medical officer of health must have certified after thorough inquiry that he or she is satisfied that the person's removal is necessary in their own interests or for preventing injury to the health of, or serious nuisance to, other persons.
Protecting the person's moveable property under the NAA 1948	• NAA 1948 s48 applies when a person is admitted to hospital, to accommodation provided under Part III of the NAA 1948, or is removed under section 47 of that Act. *continued*

Remedy	Possible relevance
	• It imposes a statutory duty on the relevant local authority to take reasonable steps to prevent or mitigate loss or damage to the person's movable property if the person is unable to protect or deal with it and no other suitable arrangements are in place. • A power is given to the local authority to enter the person's premises in order to take the steps necessary to protect their moveable property. Any reasonable expenses incurred in protecting the property are recoverable from the person concerned.
Emergency police powers to save life, limb, etc	Police and Criminal Evidence Act (PACE) 1984 s17(1)(e) authorises a police constable to enter and search any premises for the purpose of saving life or limb or preventing serious damage to property.
Public health remedies	• Public Health Act 1936 s83 allows the local authority to require the cleansing (by disinfecting and decorating) of any premises which are in such a filthy or unwholesome condition as to be prejudicial to health or are verminous. • Sections 84 and 85 contain supplementary provisions concerning the 'cleansing or destruction of filthy or verminous articles' and the 'cleansing of verminous persons and their clothing'. • Environmental Protection Act 1990 Part 3 provides local authorities with abatement powers in relation to 'premises in such a state as to be prejudicial to health or a nuisance'. • Powers of entry, if need be under warrant, are contained in Public Health Act 1936 s287 and Environmental Protection Act 1990 Sch 3. • Local authorities and social landlords may take action under the no-nuisance terms in tenancy agreements. • See *Professional Practice Note: Hoarding and how to approach it – Guidance for Environmental Health Officers and others*, Chartered Institute of Environmental Health, September 2012. (Available at: www.cieh.org/uploadedFiles/Core/Policy/Publications_and_information_services/Policy_publications/Publications/Hoarding_PPN_May09.pdf.)

Remedy	Possible relevance
Possible remedies for the incapacitated person	
Damages claim in the civil courts	Under English law, an individual may be entitled to compensation if they have been injured as a result of the negligence of another person. Other actionable civil wrongs include trespass to the person (assault, battery), nuisance, breach of privacy and breach of confidentiality.
HRA 1998 claim	The HRA 1998 makes it unlawful for a public authority to act incompatibly with the rights conferred by the European Convention on Human Rights. It allows a case to be brought in a UK court or tribunal against the authority if it does so. However, a public authority will not have acted unlawfully under the Act if as the result of another Act of Parliament it could not have acted differently. The Act extended the power to award damages for the breach of a convention right to any court that has the power to order payment of damages or compensation in a civil case.
Equality Act (EqA) 2010	• The EqA 2010 provides that a person is disabled if they have a physical or mental impairment which has a substantial and long-term adverse effect on their ability to carry out normal day-to-day activities. All employers and service providers in England, Wales and Scotland must follow the EqA 2010. • A person (A) discriminates against a disabled person (B) if: a) A treats B unfavourably because of something arising in consequence of B's disability, and b) A cannot show that the treatment is a proportionate means of achieving a legitimate aim. • This prohibition does not apply if A shows that A did not know, and could not reasonably have been expected to know, that B had the disability. EqA 2010 s19 deals with indirect discrimination, section 26 with the harassment of disabled people, section 27 with victimisation and Part 3 of the Act with the provision of services. • The EqA 2010 repealed and replaced the Disability Discrimination Act 1995.

Remedy	Possible relevance
Family law remedies	• The Family Law Act 1996 allows non-molestation orders and occupation orders to be made in respect of 'associated persons' such as married persons, civil partners, cohabitants, relatives, parties to family proceedings and persons who have or have had an intimate personal relationship. • A power of arrest may not be attached to a non-molestation order. However, breach of such an order without reasonable excuse is a criminal offence and also a contempt of court. • An occupation order is an order by which the court regulates occupation of the home by declaring a person's entitlement to occupy it, prohibiting someone's right to occupy it and so on. Such orders may be made in respect of associated persons who share, have shared or intend to share a dwelling house as their home. • It is often said that the Court of Protection cannot prohibit the rights of occupation of capacitated people and cannot therefore exclude a joint owner or spouse from a dwelling-house. However, there is no case in point. • A power of arrest may be attached to an occupation order and breach of such an order is also a contempt of court.
Anti-harassment injunction	• The High Court and the county court have jurisdiction to grant an injunction under the Protection from Harassment Act (PHA) 1997. • Section 1 provides that a person must not pursue a course of conduct: a) which amounts to harassment of another, and b) which the person knows or ought to know amounts to harassment of the other. • An actual or apprehended breach may be the subject of a claim in civil proceedings. An injunction may be made and the court may also award damages for (among other things) any anxiety caused by the harassment and any financial loss resulting from it. (A person who pursues a course of conduct in breach of section 1 also commits a criminal offence.)

Remedy	Possible relevance
Common law injunctions	It is still possible to obtain a common law injunction in the context of common law proceedings for torts such as assault, battery, trespass to the person and nuisance. However, it is relatively unusual for a situation not to be covered either by the Family Law Act 1996 or by the PHA 1997, eg where the behaviour complained of does not amount to a course of conduct involving associated persons.
Compensation for criminal injuries	Victims of violent crimes can apply to the Criminal Injuries Compensation Authority (CICA) for compensation. It does not matter that a prosecution was not brought or that the perpetrator could not be held responsible because they were suffering from a mental disorder. The claim must be brought within two years from the date of the incident. A responsible person can make a claim on behalf of an incapacitated victim.
Other kinds of legal proceedings (criminal)	
A remand in custody, bail conditions and/or term of imprisonment may serve to protect an incapacitated person.	
Offences relating to vulnerable or incapacitated persons	• MCA 2005 s44 created an (ambiguous) offence of ill-treatment or wilful neglect. It applies to deputies, donees (LPA or EPA) and anyone who has the care of a person who lacks capacity or whom the carer reasonably believes lacks capacity. • Domestic Violence, Crime and Victims Act 2004 s5 created a new offence of causing or allowing the death of a vulnerable adult. • MHA 1983 s127 makes it an offence for an officer or employee of an NHS hospital, independent hospital or care home to wilfully neglect or ill-treat a person who suffers from or appears to be suffering from a mental disorder. A like offence is committed if someone who has such a person in their custody or care ill-treats or wilfully neglects them. • The Sexual Offences Act 2003 includes various relevant offences such as sexual activity with a person with a mental disorder impeding choice and sexual activity by a care worker with a person with a mental disorder.

Remedy	Possible relevance
Standard offences	Incapacitated persons are also protected by the general criminal law (eg the Offences Against the Person Act 1861 and public order offences) but the likelihood of a successful prosecution may be affected by their inability to give evidence at trial.
Harassment and malicious communications, etc	• PHA 1997 s1 is dealt with above. • Criminal Justice and Police Act 2001 s42A makes it an offence to harass a person in their home. • The Malicious Communications Act 1988 provides that persons who send letters, electronic communications or make telephone calls with intent to cause distress or anxiety are guilty of a criminal offence. • Communications Act 2003 s127 makes it an offence to send a message which the perpetrator knows to be indecent, obscene, of a menacing character or grossly offensive for the purpose of causing annoyance, inconvenience or needless anxiety.

Funding and representation

How, why and when to get help or advice

6.1 The Court of Protection is a developing jurisdiction, hearing cases on a wide range of issues. This chapter looks at sources of advice, funding and representation.

6.2 As with the rest of this book, it is hoped that this chapter will be of use to those who take part in Court of Protection proceedings and for whatever reason do not obtain legal representation. This may be a matter of choice, or may result from lack of available funds. A person appearing in court proceedings without a legal representative is known as a 'litigant in person'.

6.3 Others will wish, and be able, to be represented. We suggest it is wise for anyone involved in Court of Protection proceedings at least to consider the possibility of obtaining legal advice. Court of Protection judges will sometimes make a specific recommendation to a litigant in person that he or she should seek legal advice. This should be followed up. Furthermore, legal advice is likely to be more effective if it is provided early on in the case.

6.4 The section below on funding for Court of Protection cases includes a guide to the legal aid scheme.

McKenzie friends

6.5 A 'McKenzie friend' is someone who provides reasonable assistance to a litigant in person. A McKenzie friend does not represent the litigant, but can sit beside them in court and 'quietly assist'. This can be a source of support.

6.6 In the light of an increase in the number of litigants in person, the Master of the Rolls and the President of the Family Division issued *Practice Guidance on McKenzie friends* on 12 July 2010.[1] The following key points should be noted:

- A McKenzie friend can only act on behalf of a person with litigation capacity.[2]
- Litigants in person can receive reasonable assistance from a McKenzie friend, subject to the discretion of the court. The court

---

1 *Practice Guidance: McKenzie friends (Civil and Family Courts)* ('Practice Guidance'), 12 July 2010; available at: www.familylaw.co.uk/system/uploads/attachments/0000/8125/McKenzie_Friends_Practice_Guidance_July_2010.pdf.
2 This is not stated in the Practice Guidance, but it is suggested from the scope of the role of such a friend as an assistant to the litigant.

may refuse to permit assistance by a McKenzie friend if satisfied that the interests of justice and fairness do not require it.[3]

- A litigant seeking assistance from a McKenzie friend should seek the court's permission as soon as possible and the McKenzie friend should submit a short CV and confirm their independence of the case and their understanding of their duty of confidentiality.[4]
- A McKenzie friend *may*: provide moral support; take notes; help with case papers; quietly give advice on any aspect of the conduct of the case.[5]
- A McKenzie friend may *not*: act as agent; manage the case outside court; address the court; or make submissions.[6]
- The right to a fair trial is engaged by the decision whether to permit a McKenzie friend, and the litigant should be given the chance to argue the point. Unless the proceedings are in private, the proposed McKenzie friend should be allowed in court to help the litigant. If (as is the case in most Court of Protection cases) the case is being heard in private, then it is for the litigant to justify the proposed McKenzie friend's presence in court.[7]
- Refusal would not be justified simply because the case is straightforward, or that the proposed McKenzie friend belongs to an organisation that promotes a particular cause, or that the proceedings are confidential. Refusal could be justified if the assistance was for an improper purpose; or the McKenzie friend was using the litigant as a 'puppet', or does not appear to understand the duty of confidentiality.[8]
- Rarely courts may grant rights of audience, or the right to conduct litigation, to McKenzie friends.[9]
- Litigants may agree to pay fees to McKenzie friends for the provision of reasonable assistance, and these costs cannot be recovered from the opponent. If the court has granted the McKenzie friend the right to conduct litigation or a right of audience, then costs incurred in these activities are in principle recoverable from the litigant, and may be recoverable from the opponent as a disbursement.[10]

3 Practice Guidance paras 2 and 5.
4 Practice Guidance para 6.
5 Practice Guidance para 3.
6 Practice Guidance para 4.
7 Practice Guidance paras 8 and 9.
8 Practice Guidance paras 12 and 13.
9 Practice Guidance paras 18–26.
10 Practice Guidance paras 27–30.

6.7   The role of the McKenzie friend in Court of Protection proceedings arose in *HBCC v LG*.[11] Eleanor King J had permitted P's daughter to receive assistance from CP, a McKenzie friend who was also a local councillor. The judge described the positive contribution that McKenzie friends can make:

> 141. This court is always keen to welcome McKenzie friends; they give time and support of inestimable value to the litigant they have agreed to assist. McKenzie friend[s] come from all walks of life: often they are personal friends or connections of the litigant; sometimes they are 'professional' McKenzie friends. Sometimes, as here they are respected members of the community who have been approached by a litigant for support and advice. Each has their place.

6.8   She gave C what she described as latitude, but considered that he had exceeded his role as McKenzie friend, not in his conduct during the trial itself, but in his behaviour outside court:

> 146. I am afraid that I regard CP's approach to the litigation as having been unhelpful and inflammatory; not it should be made clear during the trial itself, where his approach and behaviour as McKenzie friend were exemplary, but prior to the hearing (in particular in relation to the letters which I have already referred) and at his dogged maintenance of his stated position as to the behaviour of the local authority, after having heard the oral evidence.
> 147. CP undoubtedly went beyond what is proper in his role as McKenzie friend in his dealings with the local authority and the Official Solicitor outside the court proceedings prior to the hearing. I understand that democratically elected representatives be they Members of Parliament or local Councillors will often, appropriately, take up issues on behalf of their constituents. It follows that any elected representative must be cautious that in doing so they do not find themselves m conflict with their role as a McKenzie friend.

6.9   Given the informal nature of their role, McKenzie friends are not regulated.[12] McKenzie friends offering their services to support litigants can be found online. It may be useful to ask the following questions to anyone offering services as a McKenzie friend:

---

11   [2010] EWHC 1527 (Fam).

12   The Legal Services Consumer Panel (which provides independent advice to the Legal Services Board) produced a report on *Fee-charging McKenzie friends* in April 2014, recommending a greater acceptance of their role, and, in the first instance, self-regulation, but not recommending that they have an automatic right of audience. Available at: www.legalservicesconsumerpanel.org.uk/publications/research_and_reports/documents/2014%2004%2017%20MKF_Final.pdf.

- How are charges worked out, and what is the likely cost of support for the case in question?
- What is the professional background of the proposed McKenzie friend? They may be able to provide a CV.
- What experience does the McKenzie friend have? Are they able to supply references?
- Does the McKenzie friend hold a particular view about the issues involved in the case – for example, are they involved in relevant campaigns? This does not mean that they cannot act as McKenzie friend; but it may have a bearing on the advice they provide.

Independent mental capacity advocates

6.10   The functions of IMCAs are outside the scope of this book. The role of IMCAs as litigation friends is considered in chapter 12.

6.11   An IMCA (or an independent mental health advocate (IMHA), or a generic advocate) can play a very significant role in establishing P's wishes, and may be a valuable source of moral support to P during the court process, especially if P attends hearings. An IMCA should not be asked to provide advice or assistance to parties in the proceedings.

Litigation friends

6.12   The role of litigation friends is described in detail in chapter 12. For present purposes, it is important to recognise that the statutory role that they play is very different from that of a McKenzie friend or an advocate.

6.13   One point that should be noted here, however, is that a litigation friend (whether for P – if P is joined to the proceedings – or another party to the proceedings) will have to decide whether they wish to instruct legal representatives.

6.14   In the case of the Official Solicitor, who traditionally has been appointed to act on behalf of P where P has been joined to proceedings, the Official Solicitor will usually instruct legal representatives save in serious medical treatment cases, see chapter 23.

6.15   As set out in chapter 12, there has been an increasing trend for others to be appointed as litigation friends, in particular for P. In such cases, there is at present, a question mark as to whether such litigation friends must be *legally* entitled (ie authorised) in order to be appointed if they are not to *instruct* legal representatives to act for P.[13] In all cases, a litigation friend should consider very carefully whether they should instruct representatives in order to be able to conduct the litigation fairly and competently;[14] if a litigation friend is *not* so authorised but considers that they would wish to proceed without instructing solicitors, it is suggested that they seek confirmation from the court at the earliest possible opportunity that they *may* both conduct the litigation and provide P with advocacy services and discharge their role in this way.

Legal representation

Representatives

6.16   Unless the court gives permission for a McKenzie friend to conduct litigation, representation in the Court of Protection will be by a qualified lawyer.

6.17   As we have seen, cases in the Court of Protection may be heard by district judges, circuit judges or judges of the High Court. Most Court of Protection hearings will take place in private, sometimes referred to as 'in chambers'. Solicitors can appear in front of any hearing in private. If, however, for any reason the hearing takes place in public, then only barristers or solicitors with higher rights of audience may appear (represent a party).

6.18   Solicitors' firms are regulated by the Solicitors Regulation Authority (SRA) and barristers are regulated by the Bar Standards Board (BSB). Traditionally barristers are instructed by solicitors, but those who have been through suitable training can now receive instructions directly from members of the public (referred to as 'public access').

6.19   Fellows of the Chartered Institute of Legal Executives (CILEx) may appear at hearings in chambers before the district court, circuit court and High Court; and may address the court on unopposed applications for adjournment or to enter judgment by consent.

---

13   It is, in particular, not clear precisely how the provisions of the Legal Services Act 2007 (which makes specific provisions as to who can and cannot conduct litigation without the specific permission of the court) apply in relation to the discharge of the role of litigation friend. At the time of writing a judgment is expected from the President of the Court of Protection which will consider this question.

14   As they are required to by COPR r140(1).

Finding a lawyer

6.20 For members of the public seeking legal advice about Court of Protection cases, the following may be useful sources of information:

- The Law Society maintains a register of qualified solicitors and firms. This can be accessed through the 'Find a Solicitor' page in the Law Society's website.[15] The Law Society runs a number of accreditation schemes; however, at the time of writing there is no formal accreditation for Court of Protection work.
- The Law Society's LEXCEL accreditation scheme is a practice management standard.[16] Firms with LEXCEL accreditation have to show that they have met certain standards in client care, risk management and case management.
- The Bar Council maintains a list of all barristers, and a further list of those offering public access, on its website.[17] There is a dedicated telephone number for questions about public access: 020 7611 1472.
- Some publications provide information about solicitors and barristers practising in the Court of Protection, for example *Chambers and Partners* and the *Legal 500*.

See also appendix F below for further websites and useful addresses.

6.21 Solicitors and barristers acting on a public access basis are also obliged to provide information about their charges and the likely costs of the case at the outset of a case. Legal aid is available for certain cases in the Court of Protection, as is discussed further in the next section.

How are cases in the Court of Protection funded?

6.22 This section explains how cases in the Court of Protection can be funded. It is divided into the following sections:

- *Legal aid* – this section examines the legal aid scheme as it relates to Court of Protection cases.
- *Non-legal aid funding* – this section considers other funding options.

---

15 See: www.lawsociety.org.uk.
16 See: www.law.society.org.uk/accreditation/lexcel.
17 See: www.barcouncil.org.

Legal aid

6.23   Please note that the account which follows is not an exhaustive description of the legal aid scheme and readers are referred to the LAG *Legal aid handbook* for a comprehensive guide.[18] Regular updates appear on www.legalaidhandbook.com, which is an invaluable resource.

There is no single document which describes the legal aid scheme. Below is a list of the materials referred to, to which practitioners will need access from time to time:

Primary legislation
Legal Aid, Sentencing and Punishment of Offenders (LASPO) Act 2012 Schedule 1

Secondary legislation
Legal Aid, Sentencing and Punishment of Offenders Act 2012 (Amendment of Schedule 1) Order 2014
Civil Legal Aid (Merits Criteria) Regulations 2013 SI No 104
Civil Legal Aid (Financial Resources and Payment for Services) Regulations 2013 SI No 480
Civil Legal Aid (Statutory Charge) Regulations 2013 SI No 503
Civil Legal Aid (Procedure) Regulations 2012 SI No 3098

Guidance
Lord Chancellor's Guidance under section 4 of Legal Aid, Sentencing and Punishment of Offenders Act 2012
Costs Assessment Guidance 2013: for use with the 2013 Standard Civil Contract
Policy Statement on the intended evidence requirements in relation to the residence test for legal aid
VHCC: a solicitors' information pack (non-family) (2013)

LAA contracts
Standard Civil Contract 2010
2013 Individual Case Contract (High Costs Cases) Specification
Draft Standard Civil Contract 2014

Legal Aid, Sentencing and Punishment of Offenders Act 2012

6.24   Publicly funded advice and representation ('legal aid') is governed by the Legal Aid, Sentencing and Punishment of Offenders (LASPO)

---

18   V Ling and S Pugh (eds), *Legal aid handbook 2013/14*, LAG.

Act 2012, which came into force on 1 April 2013 and was the biggest reform of legal aid for a generation. The Act completely removed a number of areas of law out of scope of legal aid. The Legal Services Commission (LSC), which had previously administered legal aid in England and Wales, was replaced by the Legal Aid Agency (LAA) by the Act. The LAA is headed by the Director of Legal Aid Casework.

6.25   Before the LASPO Act 2012, legal aid was available for all cases unless it was expressly excluded. Now, unless a case is listed in one of the Schedules to the Act as being within scope, legal aid is not available.

6.26   Schedule 1 to the LASPO Act 2012 lists those areas of law where advice and/or representation can be provided under legal aid. If an area of law is not in Schedule 1, then no legal aid in any form may be provided to a client seeking help in this area of law unless it is necessary because to deny legal aid would be a breach of the European Convention on Human Rights (ECHR).[19]

6.27   Those areas of law listed in Schedule 1 are then subject to further exclusions and criteria which appear in the regulations. These will always need to be considered in order to ascertain whether a client presenting with a particular case is eligible to receive legal aid for their problem, and what form of legal aid should be provided.

The residence test for civil legal aid

6.28   From 4 August 2014, individuals seeking civil legal services must demonstrate that they have been lawfully resident in the UK, Channel Islands, the Isle of Man or British overseas territory for at least 12 months.[20] There are exceptions for asylum-seekers, re-settled refugees and members of the UK forces and their families.

6.29   The residence test does not apply to services in relation to deprivation of liberty authorised under:

- MCA 2005 s4B (deprivation of liberty necessary for life-sustaining treatment);
- MCA 2005 s16(2)(a) (a personal welfare order);

---

19 Under the LASPO Act 2012 s10, legal aid (Legal Help and certificates) may be made available on an 'exceptional' basis if it is necessary under the ECHR. The threshold for such exceptional funding is extremely high, requiring the applicant to show that to deny them legal aid would be a breach of the ECHR. Only a handful of the hundreds of applications under section 10 made since 1 April 2013 have been granted. There is no funding for making the application for exceptional funding unless it is actually granted.

20 Legal Aid, Sentencing and Punishment of Offenders Act 2012 (Amendment of Schedule 1) Order ('LASPO Sch 1 Amendment Order') 2014.

- MCA 2005 Sch A1 (deprivation of liberty safeguards (DOLS));[21] and
- those deprived of their liberty 'in exercise of the inherent jurisdiction of the High Court in relation to vulnerable adults'.[22]

6.30   In all other cases legal aid cannot be provided unless the residence requirement is satisfied.

6.31   The LAA has set out the approach it intends to take in relation to evidence in a Policy Statement[23] and this sets out the evidence that will be required. Providers must be familiar with this. The residence test must be carried out by the legal aid provider. People who fall into an excepted category – such as those detained under a standard authorisation – will need to provide documentary evidence that they are excepted from the residence test. The Policy Statement recognises that 'exceptionally the personal circumstances of the client may make it impracticable for evidence of the kind set out in the regulations and guidance to be supplied in whole or in part (for example because of their age, mental disability or because of being homeless)'. In these circumstances there will be 'some flexibility' over the evidential requirements, but the provider must still record why they are satisfied on a reasonable basis that the residence test is met.[24]

Legal aid contracts

6.32   All providers of legal aid must hold a contract with the LAA which covers the areas of law which they offer. The provider must at all times comply with the terms of the contract. Providers of legal aid who hold contracts in the areas of mental health and community care may also provide legal aid in cases arising under the MCA 2005. From August 2014 the position will be governed by the 2014 Standard Civil Contract and the associated category definitions.

The different levels of legal aid

6.33   Legal aid is provided at different levels. The usual first level of funding is Legal Help. This will cover an adviser taking instructions at the start of a case, writing letters and advising whether further action is required. It does not cover representing a client in court proceedings.

21 LASPO Sch 1 Amendment Order article 3 para 4.
22 LASPO Sch 1 Amendment Order article 3 para 6.
23 *Policy Statement on the intended evidence requirements in relation to the residence test for legal aid* ('Policy Statement') para 7.
24 Policy Statement para 7.

If the provider wishes to represent the client in the Court of Protection, a legal aid certificate must be obtained, which is linked to the specific proceedings.

Securing legal aid

6.34 In order to qualify for any form of legal aid at all, the following criteria have to be met. Each of these is addressed in more detail below:

1) The case must be within 'scope' of legal aid.
2) The client must meet the 'merits test' as to whether legal aid is warranted.
3) The client must meet the 'means test' and be financially eligible for legal aid.
4) The client must produce the relevant evidence of their means (benefits, bank statements etc) to satisfy the requirements of the LAA.

6.35 It is only once all four of the above are met that the client will be able to obtain advice or representation.

Scope of legal aid

6.36 The relevant paragraph of Schedule 1 to the LASPO Act 2012 for cases where the Court of Protection has jurisdiction is paragraph 5, which provides that civil legal services can be provided 'in relation to matters arising under the Mental Capacity Act 2005'.[25]

6.37 This means that legal aid can – provided all the other criteria are met – be provided in respect of legal issues arising under the MCA 2005.

6.38 However, this is subject to certain exclusions. First, no legal advice at all can be provided about:

a) the creation of lasting powers of attorney (LPAs) under the MCA 2005; or
b) the making of advance decisions under that Act.[26]

6.39 Therefore, practitioners may not provide any advice at all under legal aid to a client who wishes to prepare an LPA (whether financial or welfare) or an advance decision. Such clients will have to pay privately for advice. See below under 'Non-legal aid funding'. However, if a client requires advice or representation about a case before the Court of Protection which concerns determinations and declarations about the effect, meaning validity or applicability of a LPA or advance

---

25 LASPO Act 2012 Sch 1 Part 1 para 5(1).
26 LASPO Act 2012 Sch 1 Part 1 para 5(3).

decision, then it may be possible to provide legal aid, in some form, assuming that all other criteria are satisfied.[27]

6.40   Second, the legal services which can be provided exclude advocacy unless it is in the Supreme Court, the Court of Appeal, the High Court or the Court of Protection.[28]

6.41   If the case is in the Court of Protection, there is a further exclusion. Advocacy services can only be provided if the case concerns at least one of the following issues:

a) a person's right to life;
b) a person's liberty or physical safety;
c) a person's medical treatment (within the meaning of the Mental Health Act (MHA) 1983),
d) a person's capacity to marry, to enter into a civil partnership or to enter into sexual relations; or
e) a person's right to family life.[29]

The inherent jurisdiction

6.42   Civil legal services can be provided in relation to the 'inherent jurisdiction' of the High Court in relation to children (persons under the age of 18) and vulnerable adults (persons aged 18 and over).[30]

6.43   The advocacy exclusions set out above in relation to the Court of Protection do not apply in respect of the inherent jurisdiction.

Merits test

6.44   Once it has been established that the case is within the scope of legal aid, the next matter to be considered is whether the case meets the merits criteria. If it does not, legal aid will not be available for advice, or in the case of court proceedings, granted.

6.45   The relevant merits tests are set out in the Civil Legal Aid (Merits Criteria) Regulations 2013 SI No 104 and were made on 22 January 2013.

Legal Help

The criteria for qualification for Legal Help are set out at regulation 32 of the Merits Regulations. They are that it must be reasonable to provide Legal Help having regard to other potential sources of funding and that there will be sufficient benefit to justify the cost of Legal Help.

---

27 LASPO Act 2012 Sch 1 Part 1 para 5(4).
28 LASPO Act 2012 Sch 1 Part 3.
29 LASPO Act 2012 Sch 1 Part 3.
30 LASPO Act 2012 Sch 1 Part 1 para 9.

Legal Representation

6.46　There are general merits criteria, but in some cases these are displaced by specific criteria.

6.47　Note the definition of 'overwhelming importance to the client' in reg 2:

'A case with overwhelming importance to the individual' means a case which is not primarily a claim for damages or other sum of money and which relates to one or more of the following–

(a) the life, liberty or physical safety of the individual or a member of that individual's family (an individual is a member of another individual's family if the requirements of section 10(6) are met); or

(b) the immediate risk that the individual may become homeless ...

6.48　There are definitions of the tests of prospects of success (regs 4–5); public interest (reg 6); reasonable private paying individual (reg 7); and proportionality.

6.49　Legal aid may only be provided if the relevant merits test is met and it is reasonable in the light of the person's conduct (reg 11(7)).

6.50　The criteria for mental capacity cases are as follows.

Standard criteria

6.51　Does the case meet the standard criteria? These are set out in regulation 39 below. If they are not all satisfied, the individual will not get legal aid:

39. An individual may qualify for legal representation only if the Director is satisfied that the following criteria are met–

(a) the individual does not have access to other potential sources of funding (other than a conditional fee agreement) from which it would be reasonable to fund the case;

(b) the case is unsuitable for a conditional fee agreement;

(c) there is no person other than the individual, including a person who might benefit from the proceedings, who can reasonably be expected to bring the proceedings;

(d) the individual has exhausted all reasonable alternatives to bringing proceedings including any complaints system, ombudsman scheme or other form of alternative dispute resolution;

(e) there is a need for representation in all the circumstances of the case including–

(i)　the nature and complexity of the issues;

(ii)　the existence of other proceedings; and

(iii) the interests of other parties to the proceedings; and

(f) the proceedings are not likely to be allocated to the small claims track.

6.52   The impact of the test in regulation 39(c) was considered in *R (Moussa) v Legal Services Commission*.[31] This case was brought prior to the LASPO Act 2012, but the same test formed part of the previous merits criteria. The case concerned a dispute between a family and local authority as to where their son who had significant difficulties would live. The son was being cared for in residential care. The family wanted him to return home. The local authority commenced proceedings in the Court of Protection to determine P's best interests in terms of his residence. His mother was named as a respondent on the form COP1 and pursuant to Court of Protection Rules (COPR) SI No 1744 r73 she automatically became a party.

6.53   The court has the power to join other persons if 'desirable for the purpose of dealing with the application' (COPR r73(1)). The court may also remove parties: COPR r73(3). In this case the mother was financially ineligible. She had an amount of equity in her home that took her over the capital limits. In this particular case, the home was where the family wished to accommodate P. Mr Justice Charles agreed to join P's brother as a party. P's brother was a student and was financially eligible for legal aid. It was made clear to the Court of Protection that the reason for joining the brother was to ensure that there was one family member who was eligible for public funding. That member would then become the voice of the family. It was only ever anticipated that one party would be legally aided.

6.54   The LSC refused the brother funding on the basis that the mother could reasonably bring the case. It was argued that a refusal to fund the brother simply made it impossible for anyone to argue the family's position with the benefit of legal aid, because the mother could not access the equity in her home, and the home was the place where the family wished to accommodate their son. It was unrealistic to consider for example the sale of that property to allow the mother to realise some of her capital. While the judge expressed some sympathy to the family the application for judicial review was refused.

Cost-benefit and prospects of success criteria

6.55   The *cost-benefit* criteria and the *prospects of success* test must also be met (reg 41):

- The cost-benefit criteria require the Director to be satisfied that (assuming the case is not for damages, or of significant wider public interest) the reasonable private paying individual test is

---

31   [2013] EWHC 2804 (Admin).

met. If it is of significant wider public interest then the proportionality test must be met (reg 42).

- The prospects of success will be met if the Director is satisfied
  that the prospects of success are *either* very good, good or moderate. If the prospects of success are borderline or poor, funding will not be granted (Lord Chancellor's Guidance para 4.1.4,[32]
  which also provides that all the hurdles to a successful outcome
  must be considered).

Two further tests

6.56   If all the criteria above are met, a further test still needs to be carried
out if the case is being heard in the Court of Protection. This is set
out in regulation 52 and provides that full representation will only be
granted if two further tests are met (note that reg 52 does not apply to
cases heard under the 'inherent jurisdiction'):

- The *first test* is that the Court of Protection has ordered or is likely
  to order an oral hearing, *and* that it is necessary for the individual
  to be provided with full representation in the proceedings.[33] In the
  writers' experience, the court usually lists an attended hearing in
  almost all welfare cases, generally at the stage of granting permission. The test that an oral hearing is likely can therefore be satisfied relatively easily. (The Lord Chancellor's guidance on when it
  is 'necessary' to provide representation is considered below.)
- The *second test* is that the case relates to:
  (a) a person's right to life;
  (b) a person's liberty or physical safety;
  (c) a person's medical treatment (within the meaning of the Men-
      tal Health Act 1983);
  (d) a person's capacity to marry, to enter into a civil partnership or
      to enter into sexual relations; or
  (e) a person's right to family life.[34]

6.57   Note from the list above that the following types of cases may fall
outside the scope of legal aid:

- a person's right to psychological safety;
- a person's right to respect for their home or private life (ie the
  other limbs of article 8).

---

32 *Lord Chancellor's Guidance under section 4 of Legal Aid, Sentencing and Punishment
of Offenders Act 2012* ('Lord Chancellor's Guidance'), available at: www.justice.
gov.uk/downloads/legal-aid/funding-code/lord-chancellors-guidance.pdf.
33 Civil Legal Aid (Merits Criteria) Regulations 2013 reg 52(2).
34 Civil Legal Aid (Merits Criteria) Regulations 2013 reg 52(3).

6.58   To obtain legal aid for these cases, an application for exceptional funding would have to be made under LASPO Act 2012 s10. Such applications are rarely granted.

6.59   It is therefore important to consider carefully whether the case where funding is sought engages one of the factors in reg 52(3). An example is a case that primarily concerns P's accommodation, where P lives alone in his or her own home. The local authority or clinical commissioning group (CCG) may seek declarations that it is in P's best interests to move to residential or nursing care. Such a case is highly likely to concern P's right to liberty, as a forced move away from one's home will almost certainly engage ECHR article 5.

6.60   There is more information in the Lord Chancellor's Guidance, including looking at the approach that will be taken to the definition of 'overwhelming importance' to the individual (para 4.2.10 onwards); how the criteria for investigative representation as opposed to continuing on legal help will be considered (para 6.11); what 'other sources of funding' might be (para 7.14); when a case is unsuitable for a conditional fee agreement (CFA) (para 7.16).

6.61   Importantly, para 7.23 of the guidance deals with when it will be 'necessary' to represent the applicant for legal aid, and comments: 'It should not be necessary for there to be more parties legally represented than there are positions to be argued. This may be particularly relevant in a welfare case in the Court of Protection where an additional family member seeks representation ...'.

6.62   Section 9 of the Lord Chancellor's Guidance deals with mental health cases, which includes advice about the MCA 2005:

- Legal representation (ie a legal aid certificate) may be refused if it is premature or if legal help is more appropriate (para 9.5).
- For Court of Protection work, the expectation will be that 'support will be available through legal help' (para 9.8).
- A case will have overwhelming importance to P's family (ie could still be funded if the prospects of success are borderline) if they are of overwhelming importance to P.
- Accommodation cases will only be in scope if they affect P's family life.
- Although legal help is not available to create an advance decision or LPA, it is available to advise on potential or actual proceedings about the validity or applicability.

Financial eligibility (means test)

6.63 If the case is within the scope of legal aid and satisfies the merits criteria, the next step is to ascertain if the client is financially eligible for legal aid. This is governed by the Civil Legal Aid (Financial Resources and Payment for Services) Regulations 2013 SI No 480.

6.64 There is only one exception to the rule that the client must satisfy the means test before getting legal aid in the Court of Protection. This is where person is deprived of their liberty under a standard authorisation under MCA 2005 Sch A1 and there is an appeal against the authorisation under MCA 2005 s21A. In this case, the person under the authorisation can obtain legal aid without their means being assessed, and so can their 'relevant person's representative' (RPR).

6.65 The relevant regulation (reg 5(1)(g)) is below and shows when legal aid can be provided without the applicant satisfying the means test:

> (g) legal representation in relation to a matter described in paragraph 5(1)(c) (mental capacity) of Part 1 of Schedule 1 to the Act to the extent that—
> (i) the legal representation is in proceedings in the Court of Protection under section 21A of the Mental Capacity Act 2005; and
> (ii) the individual to whom legal representation may be provided is—
>> (aa) the individual in respect of whom an authorisation is in force under paragraph 2 of Schedule A1 to the Mental Capacity Act 2005; or
>> (bb) a representative of that individual appointed as such in accordance with Part 10 of that Schedule;

6.66 It is clear from the above that the intention is that non-means tested legal aid for DOLS appeals is only available while the authorisation is in force. This caused difficulties when courts themselves authorised the deprivation of P's liberty by making orders under MCA 2005 s16.

6.67 This practice was considered in *Re HA*,[35] a case determined before this regulation came into effect. Mr Justice Charles made the following comments in this case heard in February 2012:

> In a discussion with counsel for the Official Solicitor I have indicated that my present view is that in the context of an application under s21A the court should not, for example, extend a standard authorisation (even if it has the power to do so under s.21A), or somehow continue the statutory scheme, whilst it determines the application. Rather, my

---

35 [2012] EWHC 1068 (COP), [2012] COPLR 534.

present view is that the court should exercise its own powers to hold the ring whilst it determines the application and therefore give appropriate interim authorisations of any deprivation of liberty and make appropriate interim orders. If, when it determines the application, the court concludes that the relevant person should live in a care home, or be in a hospital, then, it seems to me, that it should generally direct that the statutory DOLS scheme should apply again to any deprivation of liberty. That regime has checks and balances that generally should be preferred to review by the court.

6.68   However, following the new regulations, which came into force in February 2013, the effect of a judge following the guidance in *Re HA* would be that P and the RPR would lose non-means tested legal aid.

6.69   This issue came to a head in the case of *UF v (1) A local authority (2) AS (3) Director of Legal Aid Casework (4) Ministry of Justice*.[36] UF appealed against a standard authorisation and HA-type directions were made by the district judge hearing the appeal. UF had non-means tested legal aid. On the expiry of the authorisation, UF was advised by the LAA that her means would now be assessed because she no longer came within regulation 5(1)(g)(ii)(aa) above. UF's means would have made her ineligible for legal aid. She applied to the court to vary the court's order so that the court's authorisation of her deprivation of liberty would be set aside. Charles J ruled that in addition to the power under MCA 2005 s16(2)(a) described in *Re HA*, in the vast majority of cases the court could:

a) exercise its powers under MCA 2005 s21A(3)(a) to vary the standard authorisation;

b) extend an extant authorisation pursuant to MCA 2005 s21A(2)(b).

6.70   The Director of Legal Aid Casework and Ministry of Justice assured Charles J that if a court adopted either of the courses in a) or b) or the course adopted in that of *UF*, it would not treat the orders as contrivances and refuse public funding for that reason when applying the merits test for public funding. The effect of these concessions is that it is clear that non-means tested legal aid should remain available on any application under MCA 2005 s21A for so long as P is deprived of his or her liberty, including under orders of the court which are framed as set out in *UF*. An example is set out below:

36 [2013] EWHC 4289 (COP), [2014] COPLR 93.

Example

P brings proceedings a) challenging a standard authorisation and b) seeking declarations that his article 5 rights have been breached by an act done in relation to the standard authorisation. At the first hearing the authorisation is about to expire but the judge varies the standard authorisation by extending it to the next hearing. P will continue to be eligible for non-means tested legal aid. At the second hearing the judge terminates the standard authorisation and P returns home. The proceedings continue while P seeks declarations about the lawfulness of the authorisation. P will no longer be eligible for non-means tested legal aid.

6.71 In *UF*, Charles J also indicated that, where the court varied the standard authorisation by extending it, the court may need to consider making an order under MCA 2005 s21A(6) exonerating the supervisory body from liability for the extended period as the court would have assumed the responsibility for the deprivation of liberty.

6.72 What if P is deprived of his or her liberty through the order of the court, because he or she lives in supported accommodation, and MCA 2005 Sch A1 (DOLS) cannot be used, because it only applies in hospitals or registered care homes?[37] In this case there is no non-means tested legal aid, so if P does not satisfy the means criteria then he or she will have to pay privately to be represented.

6.73 In some cases, if the applicant for legal aid is in receipt of certain benefits, then their income will not need to be further assessed.[38]

6.74 However, in all cases at all levels of legal aid, an applicant for legal aid must have their capital assessed (discussed in the next section).

Evidence of financial eligibility

6.75 All clients need to provide evidence of their capital, even if they are in receipt of 'passporting benefits' where the Department for Work and Pensions (DWP) has already undertaken an assessment of their capital in order to decide that they qualify for benefits.

6.76 Problems which can arise in securing evidence of means include:

- delay by the DWP in responding to requests for confirmation of benefits claims;

---

37 MCA 2005 Sch A1 para 1(2).
38 Civil Legal Aid (Financial Resources and Payments for Services) Regulations 2013 reg 6.

- banks asked to provide original bank statements citing data protection issues as a reason for not disclosing relevant information, leading to satellite disputes, all of which result in a delay in obtaining legal advice.

6.77 Where court proceedings are already in existence, it may be possible for an order to be obtained requiring disclosure of relevant financial information, however often this will not be possible. The LAA encourages practitioners having difficulty obtaining evidence of means in these cases to email: contactcivil@legalaid.gsi.gov.uk with the heading 'Vulnerable Client Means Assessment'.

Delegated functions

6.78 Practitioners holding contracts with the LAA are able to grant certificates for full representation in urgent cases. This is one of the 'delegated functions' (formerly known as 'devolved powers').

6.79 In granting a certificate under delegated functions, the practitioner will need to select the appropriate matter type code, identify the correct wording code, and apply a scope limitation and a costs limitation. The completed application must be received by the LAA within five working days of the grant of delegated functions.

Responsibilities to the LAA

6.80 In Court of Protection cases which are funded by legal aid, practitioners have the same responsibilities as in other civil legal aid cases. A full description of these is outside the scope of this book. Practitioners are referred to LAG's *Legal aid handbook* and to www.legalaidhandbook.com.

The statutory charge

6.81 This is governed by the Civil Legal Aid (Statutory Charge) Regulations 2013 SI No 503. In many welfare cases the question of the statutory charge will not arise.

6.82 It can arise where damages are awarded. An example is set out below:

Example

P obtains declarations in the Court of Protection that he has been unlawfully detained, pursuant to MCA 2005 s21A(6). P subsequently commences proceedings for damages in the county court, relying on the declarations that have been made in the Court of Protection. The defendant compromises the damages claim and agrees to pay P's costs for the county court claim. The statutory charge will apply to the costs incurred in the Court of Protection in securing the declarations. It will not apply if the defendant in the Court of Protection case pays P's costs in securing the declarations. For this reason it is important clearly to identify the costs that have been incurred in securing the finding that P was unlawfully detained (as opposed to dealing with other welfare issues, where it can be argued that the statutory charge should not attach).

6.83   The regulations give the Lord Chancellor discretion to waive all or part of the statutory charge in limited circumstances.[39]

Extensions

6.84   Once a certificate has been granted, it will have a financial limit and a scope limit, possibly limiting the legal aid to covering the next hearing and no further. Therefore at each stage in the case the provider needs to make an application to extend the certificate to cover each stage of the case. Applications to extend both the work covered and the overall costs limit have to be strictly justified.

Section 49 reports: note that section 49 reports cannot be claimed as a disbursement on legal help but may be an allowable disbursement on a legal aid certificate.[40]

Experts

6.85   This section should be read in conjunction with paras 13.68–13.75.

6.86   Experts' fees can be claimed as a disbursement on a party's legal aid certificate. The LAA sets rates which it will agree to pay experts. The current rates were set on 2 December 2013.[41] If a certain type of expert is not listed in the remuneration regulations, they will be

39   Civil Legal Aid (Statutory Charge) Regulations 2013 regs 8 and 9.
40   Costs Assessment Guidance 2013, paras 3.48–3.50.
41   Civil Legal Aid (Remuneration) (Amendment) Regulations 2013 Sch 2.

remunerated at a rate determined by the LAA, which will have regard to the codified rates in setting such a rate.

6.87 If an expert charges a rate in excess of the current codified rate, the LAA will only pay this if it considers it is reasonable to do so in exceptional circumstances *and* it has granted prior authority. The LAA considers the following to be exceptional circumstances:

- the expert's evidence is key to the client's case,

and either

- the complexity of the material is such that a high level of seniority is required, or
- the material is of such a specialised nature that only very few experts are available to provide the necessary evidence.[42]

6.88 Practitioners considering instructing an expert who charges above the codified rates must therefore obtain prior authority before instructing the expert. Practitioners will be expected strictly to demonstrate that the request for prior authority comes within the conditions set out above. It is often helpful to invite the court to approve the instructions of the particular expert when the court gives permission for the expert to be instructed.

6.89 A suitable form of words in a preamble would be:

AND UPON recording that the expert evidence provided for in this Order is reasonably required and necessary in order to resolve a significant issue in these proceedings and to safeguard [P's full name]'s rights under article[s 5 and[43]] 8 ECHR; and that the costs to be incurred in the preparation of such evidence are a wholly necessary, reasonable and proportionate disbursement on the funding certificate of [P]. Dr [Independent Psychiatrist]'s hourly rate of £... and the estimated costs of [his/her] report are reasonable in the light of [his/her] qualifications, experience and expertise and in the light of the issues that arise in this case; [Mr/Ms] [Independent Social Worker]'s hourly rate of £... and the estimated costs of [his/her] report are reasonable in the light of [his/her] qualifications, experience and expertise and in the light of the issues that arise in this case.[44]

6.90 This wording will not guarantee that the LAA will grant prior authority, but should be persuasive.

---

42 Standard Civil Contract 2010 para 6.62, Draft Standard Civil Contract 2014 para 6.61.

43 If the case involves a deprivation (or potential deprivation) of liberty.

44 For a precedent for an order giving the parties permission to instruct an expert, see appendix F below.

Case-law

6.91   Two applications for judicial review of the then-LSC's refusal to meet experts' payments in full in family cases have ramifications for Court of Protection practice: *JG v The Lord Chancellor and Others*[45] and *R (T) v LAA, LBE and others*.[46] Both highlight similarities and differences between the two jurisdictions.

6.92   *JG v The Lord Chancellor and others*[47] was brought by a child acting through her guardian. She appealed against a ruling in judicial review proceedings against the then Legal Services Commission. Her application was dismissed but Ryder J certified a point of general importance as to the approach to be taken when the family court considers expert evidence is necessary but the only means to pay for it was through the child's public funding certificate.

6.93   Ryder J had held that the LSC had acted lawfully. The Court's decision in 2009 as to how the report should be funded had been influenced by the fact that only the child had legal aid and thus the order had been in breach of AJA 1999 s22(4). This has been replaced by LASPO Act s30(1), which reads:

Position of other parties, courts and tribunals

30 (1) Except as expressly provided by regulations, any rights conferred by or under this Part on an individual for whom services are provided under this Part for the purposes of proceedings do not affect–
   (a) the rights or liabilities of other parties to the proceedings, or
   (b) the principles on which the discretion of a court or tribunal is normally exercised.

Black LJ said it was of central importance to the appeal to keep the paramount consideration of the child's welfare (CA 1989 s1(1)) 'well in mind'. Even if a child is not a party in family proceedings she is a 'powerful presence' whose welfare dictates the outcome and a welfare report is not sufficient to provide the information that the court needs. The LSC's initial approach – that if the father was not prepared to pay for the report then the status quo as to residence should continue – was 'extraordinary'.

6.94   A child will be made a party where this is in the best interests of the child (FPR r16.2) and this is likely to be in 'cases which involve an issue of significant difficulty' (FPR PD 16A). The default position was that a guardian would be appointed unless the child was competent

45 [2014] EWCA Civ 656.
46 [2013] EWHC 960 (Admin), [2013] 2 FLR 1315.
47 [2014] EWCA Civ 656.

to litigate without a guardian, whose responsibility was 'fairly and competently to conduct proceedings on behalf of the child', taking all decisions for the child's benefit. (PD 16A). This includes 'obtaining such professional assistance as is available which the children's guardian thinks appropriate or which the court directs be obtained'. (PD 16A para 6.3).

Clearly this is different from the position in the Court of Protection, where P is generally joined as a party. Therefore the mere fact in a Court of Protection case that P has been joined does not of itself signal that the case is of particular complexity.

6.95   The new requirement that expert evidence should be restricted to 'that which was necessary' was a high one. Again, this is a different test to that currently in the COPR, where expert evidence is restricted to that which is reasonably required to resolve the proceedings.[48]

6.96   FPR r25.12(6) provided that the 'relevant parties' would be responsible for the experts' fees jointly and the 'relevant parties' are 'the parties who wish to put expert evidence before the court' (FPR r25.11(2)).

AJA 1999 s22(4) and LASPO Act 2012 s10 (availability of exceptional funding) are also set out.

Black LJ expressed unease at the use of judicial review proceedings to determine a general question but because of its importance incorporated her thoughts into the judgment but stressed that these were not part of the ratio in an essentially fact-sensitive area where there are no universal answers.

6.97   The Law Society's position was that there was no point in funding representation for the child through the guardian but not allowing the guardian to obtain the evidence she needed. The Lord Chancellor argued that where the report was not genuinely required by the funded party alone, the cost should be equally apportioned, though there would be some exceptional cases where departure would be justified. The Lord Chancellor was described as 'wedded to the idea of a single joint expert'.

Black LJ noted that no party could be compelled to join instructions to an expert (this position also applies in the Court of Protection). The power to direct a SJE arises where there are two or more parties who wish to put expert evidence before the court (r25.11(1)). In the current case the guardian was the first to suggest a report, on the basis that she required it for the benefit of the child. On these

---

48 COPR r121.

facts the correct starting point was that the report was genuinely required for the child alone.

The involvement of the other parties in agreeing a letter of instruction will not necessarily 'convert' the child's expert into a SJE. The expert will only be a SJE if giving evidence on behalf of two or more parties. The rules permit a non-instructing party to communicate with or rely on another party's expert.

6.98   There are good practical reasons to be cautious about treating an expert as a SJE, as it would be undesirable for non-instructing parties to be deterred from contributing to an expert's instructions – and thus depriving the expert of useful information – because they were concerned about the expert being treated as a SJE.

It may therefore 'not be that infrequent' for an application by a child's guardian to be genuinely an expert for the child, even if the other parties have input into agreeing instructions.

If the expert genuinely is a SJE, what should the approach be? Even where resources are not a problem equal apportionment is not inevitable. The authorities (*Calderdale MBC v S and the LSC*,[49] *A Local Authority v DS*,[50] where the 'golden rule' was held to be that the instruction of an expert should not hold up the case, *London Borough of Lambeth v S*[51]) make it plain the court has a discretion as to apportionment, and this is to be exercised bearing in mind the circumstances of the case. Rule 25.12(6) provides that the parties are jointly and severally liable for the costs of an expert unless the court orders otherwise but that refers to the contractual relationship and does not guide the court as to how to exercise discretion. Thus AJA 1999 s22(4) (or LASPO Act 2012 s30 as it is now) does not prohibit departure from the principle of equal apportionment.

6.99   Black LJ went on to consider three conditions where the court might depart from equal apportionment: impecuniosity; breach of convention rights and 'a very exceptional case'.

Black LJ reminded herself that 'in discharging its obligation to provide parties to civil proceedings with legal aid ... the state must display diligence so as to secure ... the genuine and effective enjoyment of the rights guaranteed under Article 6' (*Muscat v Malta*[52])

6.100   A failure by the court to allow expert evidence can be a violation of article 8, depending on the circumstances (it was a factor in *Elsholz*

---

49 [2005] 1 FLR 751.
50 [2012] EWHC 1442 (Fam).
51 [2005] 2 FLR 1171.
52 App no 24197/10, 19 November 2012.

v Germany[53]). The Lord Chancellor's submissions were focused on the need to ensure the parents did not receive a benefit they were not entitled to as opposed to the welfare of the child. By the time the court has decided to join the child and the guardian has decided a report is needed there is the beginning of a 'strong foundation' for the argument that article 8 and article 6 rights are engaged.

6.101   There is no justification for an additional requirement of exceptionality once it is established that the lack of a report would breach an individual's convention rights.

6.102   When assessing impecuniosity the court cannot be expected to carry out the detailed level of enquiry that the LAA would do as that would delay the proceedings but financial eligibility for legal aid is relevant.

In the particular case, the original report was genuinely for the benefit of the child. The issue of the addendum sought by the father was no longer a live issue.

6.103   This case demonstrates the following points for the Court of Protection:

- The test of 'necessity' is a high one (and this is likely to become the test in the COP although it is not yet). The current test is that the evidence is reasonably required to resolve the proceedings.[54]
- Should the test of joining the child be reflected in the test for joining P ie only in a minority of cases? This would surely be undesirable. P is – rightly – a party in the majority of welfare cases in the COP. The mere fact that P is a party will probably not be as strong a factor in COP cases as in the Family Court.
- A report on P applied for by P's litigation friend (cf the child's guardian) may on the facts of the case genuinely be for P alone, even if the other parties have input into the instructions to allow the expert to discharge his responsibilities.
- No party can be compelled to join in the instructions of an expert.
- Where the expert is genuinely a SJE the court still has discretion as to apportionment and may depart from the usual rule if not to obtain the evidence would breach a party's convention rights and one or more of the parties cannot pay for the report.
- Convention rights under articles 6 and 8 may be engaged: legal aid in civil cases must be effective.

53 (2002) 34 EHRR 58.
54 COPR r121.

- There is no additional requirement of exceptionality if there will be a breach of the convention rights of a party if the evidence is not obtained.
- Financial eligibility for legal aid is relevant in assessing impecuniosity.

6.104 The second challenge to the then LSC arose in *R (T) v LAA, LBE and others*.[55] The district judge hearing a complex care case gave very detailed directions approving in full an estimate from a named expert agency, specifying the need for the evidence and the need for the hourly rate and number of hours. In short, the guidance set out in *A Local Authority v DS*[56] was followed. In the event that public funding was not granted, the LSC was to send a representative to court. The LSC granted prior authority for a lower figure, having failed to attend the court.

6.105 Collins J granted permission and allowed the application. He described as unrealistic the suggestion that the solicitors might accept the prior authority for the lower figure and argue for more on taxation. He noted that the President in the *DS* case had referred to the LSC's duty to give reasons if, following a judicial decision that expert evidence is necessary, and a particular expert at a specified figure is approved, the LSC refuses to agree to any or all of the application for prior authority. Collins J held that this guidance gave rise to a public law duty on the LSC. He further found that the fact that there had been a huge increase in applications for prior authority as a result of changes to the expert fees regime in October 2011 did not absolve the LSC from responsibility to deal with them properly. In this case, Collins J considered that the LSC had given no reasons for refusing the full figure and had not engaged with the district judge's attempts, by requiring the attendance of the LSC, to avoid the matter escalating to a judicial review. Collins J commented that even if the LSC merely confirmed its decision in its reasons, he found it difficult to see how it would have been reasonable not to comply with what the judge had found to be necessary, at least without engaging with her orally or in writing.

Very high costs cases

6.106 Very high costs cases (VHCCs) are defined in Civil Legal Aid (Procedure) Regulations 2012 SI No 3098 ('the Procedure Regs') reg 54(3). These cases are managed under an individual contract which

55 [2013] EWHC 960 (Admin), [2013] 2 FLR 1315.
56 [2012] EWHC 1442 (Fam), [2013] 1 FLR 1429.

is agreed between the practitioner and the Special Cases Unit and the LAA. For the purpose of Court of Protection cases, the VHCC provisions will apply when the Director of Legal Aid Casework has reason to believe that the actual or likely cost of the case exceed £25,000. Part 6 of the Procedure Regs governs VHCC cases.

6.107   Practitioners will keep the overall costs of any certificated case under careful review. If it appears that the likely costs of the case – taking into account counsel's fees and disbursements – are likely to exceed £25,000, then the practitioner must follow the steps set out in the LAA's information pack, *VHCC – A solicitors information pack (non-family)* ('Solicitors Information Pack').[57] It is not difficult for a contested Court of Protection case to become a VHCC, particularly if there are substantial interim hearings or experts are used.

6.108   It is essential to be familiar with the requirements of the LAA. The following documents must be considered:

- solicitors' and barristers' information packs;
- 2013 individual case contract (high costs cases) specification ('High Costs Case Specification');
- contract for signature.

These can all be downloaded from the LAA's website.[58]

6.109   This section summarises some of the key provisions relating to VHCCs and attempts to apply them to a Court of Protection context. Therefore it is not a substitute to reading the guidance in full.

6.110   It is possible but unlikely that a Court of Protection case will be identified as a VHCC at the outset. It is more likely that the practitioner will identify the case as a VHCC when considering applying to extend the costs limit in a given case. The guidance explains:

- Practitioners should apply to the regional office for the extension needed anyway, using form CIVAPP8 and providing estimates of the costs to settlement or other disposal. However, the guidance states that a fully costed case plan must be submitted with the CIVAPP8.[59] (This appears to be a change from the previous procedure, whereby the case plan could be submitted up to a month later.) If counsel is to be used, then they will need to be involved in the preparation of the case plan.[60]

---

57 Available at: www.justice.gov.uk/downloads/legal-aid/vhccs/solicitors-information-pack.pdf.
58 See: www.justice.gov.uk/legal-aid.
59 Solicitors Information Pack para 6.
60 Solicitors Information Pack para 15.

- The regional office will send the CIVAPP8 and case plan to the Special Cases Unit. The case manager can obtain independent counsel's opinion, can seek representation about funding from opponents and can require specific instructions to be given to experts. These powers are rarely used in Court of Protection cases. A case manager will consider whether the case justifies further funding, applying Procedure Regs regs 66 and 56.[61] If funding is refused, then there is a right of appeal.
- Assuming funding is to continue, the case manager will consider the case plan and seek to agree these with the practitioner.
- The VHCC contract starts when the case manager limits the certificate to the work in the key stage. Once that has happened work carried out prior to the contract can be claimed.[62] The LAA has expressed the wish to simplify this process and suggests that form CIVCLAIM1 is used, or alternatively the practitioner can submit a copy of their time recording records and an explanation of the work carried out. There is a right of appeal against the case manager's assessment to an independent cost assessor. Once the costs have been agreed the LAA will pay these within 28 days. These will be assessed at the usual remuneration rates, as if the contract had not been in force, with some exceptions[63] (see below under 'contract rates').
- If the case plan cannot be agreed there is a right to appeal by an Independent Funding Adjudicator.[64]
- Clients must be sent copies of the case plan because of the potential impact of the statutory charge.[65]
- Counsel is paid direct by the LAA, but must have signed the Counsel Acceptance Form and must have been provided with information set out in the specification.[66]
- The cost of a stage may be increased after the case plan is agreed, but only where work has to be done which could not reasonably have been foreseen, or in other exceptional circumstances. In both cases the extra work must be more than five per cent of the price of the stage.[67] Urgent work can be authorised by email exchange.[68]

---

61 Civil Legal Aid (Procedure) Regulations 2012.
62 High Cost Case Specification para 5.2.
63 Solicitors Information Pack para 12.
64 Solicitors Information Pack para 17.
65 High Cost Case Specification para 4.9.
66 High Cost Case Specification para 4.5.
67 Solicitors Information Pack para 18.
68 Solicitors Information Pack para 20.

The contract specification makes it plain that the additional work must be set out in a key stage and will not otherwise be paid.[69]

- Once a stage finishes, the practitioner reports to the case manager. If the cost of the stage is 95 per cent or above of the price, the full price agreed is payable. If the actual cost is between 50 per cent and 95 per cent, then the actual cost plus five per cent is paid. If the cost is under 50 per cent, then the actual cost only is paid.[70] If a key stage lasts for more than six months, a payment on account can be sought using form CIVCLAIM4. If any of the steps described in the key stage become unnecessary, the practitioner must ask the case manager to amend the key stage.[71]

- After each stage the case manager will consider whether further funding is justified, and will consider the next stage of the case plan.

Preparing the case plan

6.111   The LAA's information pack contains an example of a staged case plan for a clinical negligence case. Although the context is different, the example is useful in giving guidance as to the level of detail required and the type of information (for example, about experts) that should be provided.

6.112   A stage consists of a series of steps. In a Court of Protection case, a stage might be the work up to and including the next hearing; or up to and including the receipt and consideration of experts' reports; or up to and including a round table meeting or mediation. The possible variations at each stage need to be anticipated as far as possible to avoid having to amend the case plan.

The rates

6.113   In cases where it is likely that 'party and party' costs will be paid, payment is made at a lower, 'at risk' rate. Where it is not likely that 'party and party' costs will be paid, the LAA will pay at the usual remuneration rates. As the general rule in the Court of Protection is that the parties bear their own costs, a Court of Protection VHCC should be paid for at the usual civil rates. Practitioners seeking an enhancement will have to propose this with the case plan and justify it. The

---

69   High Cost Case Specification paras 4.3, 4.4.
70   Solicitors Information Pack para 21.
71   High Cost Case Specification para 4.3.

criteria for enhancement are set out in the Standard Civil Contract.[72] There is an initial threshold for any enhancement, namely that:

- the work was done with exceptional competence, skill or expertise;
- the work was done with exceptional speed; or
- the case involved exceptional circumstances or complexity.

6.114 Once the threshold is passed, the person assessing the costs shall have regard to the following factors in deciding what percentage of enhancement to allow:

- the degree of responsibility accepted by the fee earner;
- the care, speed and economy with which the case was prepared;
- the novelty, weight and complexity of the case.

6.115 The practitioner must claim their costs within three months of the conclusion of the case, unless otherwise agreed by the case manager.[73] There may be some cases where, unusually, a costs order is made for all or part of the work done. If another party has been ordered to pay all the costs of the legally aided party, then the practitioner can choose whether to take payment from the paying party or the LAA.[74] If the practitioner decides to takes payment from the LAA, then the LAA will instruct them to take reasonable enforcement steps against the paying party.[75]

6.116 Some cases may arise where some of the costs are payable by one of the parties but not all of them. For example, the court may consider the conduct of a party justifies departure from the general rule and may order that party to meet the cost of a particular hearing. If this happens, then the practitioner can ask to take payment both from the LAA and the paying party.[76] The information pack states that the statutory charge 'is likely to apply':[77] see para 6.107 above.

Non-legal aid funding

6.117 Where legal aid cannot be secured, clients will have to pay privately for legal representation. Providing privately funded representation in contested welfare cases brings many challenges, not least because of the difficulties in predicting the costs that will be incurred.

---

72 Standard Civil Contract 2014 paras 6.14, 6.16.
73 High Cost Case Specification para 5.3.
74 High Cost Case Specification para 5.3.
75 High Cost Case Specification para 5.5.
76 High Cost Case Specification paras 5.7–5.11.
77 Solicitors Information Pack para 25.

6.118   Providers may consider attempting to break down the case into stages. A 'window' of estimated costs can then be prepared for each stage. An example might be work conducted in the following stages:

- Stage 1: Up to and including an application for permission.
- Stage 2: From grant of permission up to and including the first attended hearing.
- Stage 3: From the first attended hearing up to but not including the final hearing. This is likely to be the largest stage, and may include, for example, the client's share of an expert report.
- Stage 4: The final hearing.

6.119   In some cases, practitioners may consider carrying out cases under a partial retainer – sometimes referred to as 'unbundling'. The Law Society has issued a practice note about partial retainer cases in family legal services.[78] Practitioners considering this option should consider the advice given in the practice note. The professional obligations of the solicitor on a partial retainer are onerous:

> Your client care obligations as outlined in the SRA Handbook apply as much to unbundled services as they do to a full retainer. In some ways, you may have greater responsibilities to clients of unbundled services to clearly set out your responsibilities and those of your client. For more information, see IB 1.2 and IB 1.5.
>
> You must also act in your client's best interests. In some circumstances unbundling may not be appropriate for your client such as in cases of great complexity or where you have concerns that the client does not have the intellectual or emotional capacity to carry out tasks that fall within their responsibility. In such cases you should carefully consider whether and to what extent it is in your client's interests to provide an unbundled service.[79]

6.120   There may, however, be some more straightforward cases which can benefit from providing legal services in this way.

---

78   *Unbundling family legal services*, 1 May 2013; available at: www.lawsociety.org.uk/advice/practice-notes/unbundling-family-legal-services/.

79   Para 4.31.

CHAPTER 7

Making an application: property and affairs cases

Introduction

7.1   The vast majority of the applications dealt with by the Court of Protection concern property and affairs. These make up in the region of 95 per cent of the work of the court.[1]

7.2   This chapter looks at the application process for a straightforward appointment of a deputy to manage P's property and affairs as well as a range of common applications concerning P's property and affairs such as authorising a statutory will. The very large majority of applications concerning P's property and affairs are not contested, and are necessary simply because court authority is needed lawfully to make the necessary decisions.

7.3   This chapter also looks as the role of the court in relation to lasting and enduring powers of attorney (LPAs and EPAs). It should be read in conjunction with chapters 4 and 5.

Deputyship applications

When is a deputy needed?

7.4   If a person loses their capacity to make some decisions about their finances and they have not planned for this eventuality by making an EPA (before 1 October 2007) or an LPA for property and affairs (from 1 October 2007 onwards) then it may be necessary for an application to be made to the court for the appointment of a property and affairs deputy. Without an attorney or deputy, the general rule is that no transactions can be validly undertaken on behalf of P.

7.5   When deciding if an application for the appointment of a deputy is necessary, the nature of P's assets and income should be considered. If the only income of the person concerned is state benefits then the appointment of a deputy may be disproportionate and costly, an application can be made an individual or an organisation (eg a council) to the Department for Work and Pensions (DWP) to be made their appointee to manage those benefits. This does not require an application to the court.[2]

7.6   If, however, there are other assets or income that needs to be managed, then it is likely that a deputy will need to be appointed.

---

1   In 2013, for instance, there were 24,923 property and affairs applications issued and 1,230 health and welfare applications (statistics provided by Senior Judge Lush).

2   See: https://www.gov.uk/become-appointee-for-someone-claiming-benefits.

This would include situations such as P owning a property or savings and investments that needed to be sold or accessed, for example to pay for the costs of a care home or to meet P's day-to-day expenses or regular payments.

7.7   It is important to keep in mind that under the Mental Capacity Act (MCA) 2005 capacity is 'decision-specific', there are no absolutes in terms of a person's decision-making capabilities (see paras 3.33– 3.64). There is no contradiction between having a deputy and retaining the ability to make some decisions. For example, a deputy may need to make decisions about investing a large sum of money while P retains the capacity to manage their weekly income to buy groceries and personal items.

Choice of deputy

7.8   The MCA 2005 does not set out any order for individuals to be considered for the role of deputy. The choice of suitable deputy will depend largely upon P's family and circumstances.

7.9   In *Re M; N v O and P*[3] Senior Judge Lush noted that pre-MCA 2005 authorities were still to be considered pertinent to the question of who to appoint as a deputy, and set out an 'order of preference' in which P's family was to be preferred by the court over strangers such as professional advisers or statutory bodies. Senior Judge Lush observed that:

> The court prefers to appoint a family member or close friend, if possible, as long as it is in P's best interests to do so. This is because a relative or friend will already be familiar with P's affairs, and wishes and methods of communication. Someone who already has a close personal knowledge of P is also likely to be better able to meet the obligation of a deputy to consult with P, and to permit and encourage him to participate, or to improve his ability to participate, as fully as possible in any act done for him and any decision affecting him. And, because professionals charge for their services, the appointment of a relative or friend is generally preferred for reasons of economy. There are, of course, cases in which the court would not countenance appointing a particular family member as deputy. For example, if there had been physical or financial abuse; if there is a conflict of interests; if the proposed deputy has an unsatisfactory track record in managing his own financial affairs; and if there is ongoing friction between various family members that is likely to interfere with the administration of P's affairs. This list is not exhaustive.[4]

3 [2013] COPLR 91.
4 Para 39.

7.10   In this case, in applying the balance-sheet approach, the various factors the court considered in assessing the merits of the two proposed deputies were:

a) ability to act;
b) willingness to act;
c) qualifications;
d) place of residence;
e) security;
f) conduct before and during the proceedings;
g) nature of relationship with M;
h) M's wishes and feelings;
i) views of others;
j) effect of hostility;
k) conflicts of interest;
l) remuneration; and
m) the terms of M's will.

7.11   Senior Judge Lush found that the two factors of 'magnetic importance' in deciding who the court should appoint as deputy for P, where there were competing candidates for the role were 'M's past and present wishes and feelings and the unanimous views of others, who are particularly close to him, as to what would be in his best interests'.[5] He went on to comment that there were also cases in which the court would not appoint a family member, such as where P has recovered damages in personal injury litigation specifically to fund a professional deputy appointment.

7.12   Some individuals will be considered as unsuitable to act as deputy, these include:

• current or former bankrupts;
• those with debt problems or who has entered into a debt-management plan or otherwise has a poor track record with handling finances;
• anyone who does not have their own UK bank account;
• non-UK residents.

7.13   Other factors that may influence the decision about who should be appointed as deputy include locality, health, family and work commitments.

7.14   It is possible for an application to be made for joint deputies to be appointed. This can help to share the burden but does require good communication to work efficiently. An appointment for joint

5 Para 78.

deputies is made in the same manner as for a sole deputy but with both prospective deputies detailed on the application forms, and an explanation as to why it is in P's best interests for two deputies to act for them.

7.15 Most deputies appointed are lay deputies, private individuals acting as deputy usually for a family member. There are, however, professionals who specialise in this area of work and whose appointment is appropriate in some circumstances. Many local authorities continue to have a deputyship department but they will often only act as deputies of last resort where a suitable relative can be traced to undertake the role. A professional deputy is usually appointed where P has received substantial funds in compensation for a personal injury, or where P has complex or very high value personal finances or if the court concludes that is in P's best interests for a neutral professional to undertake the role, usually where there is discord within a family. The Public Guardian also maintains a panel of deputies to whom cases can be referred to as a deputy of last resort (see also paras 21.41–21.42). Panel deputies are often appointed to act where there has been significant friction within the family about who should act as deputy for P. If the court believes that on-going family friction would impact upon the proper management of P's finances a panel deputy will be invited to take on the role.

7.16 Finally, it should be noted that a trust corporation can be appointed to be a property and affairs deputy (but not a health and welfare deputy).[6]

Application procedure

7.17 Having identified that P will need a deputy to manage their property and affairs, and decided upon an appropriate deputy or deputies to act, the next step is to prepare the application papers for submission to court. Permission is not required to make an application for the appointment of a property and affairs deputy.[7]

7.18 The documents needed to apply for the appointment of a property and affairs deputy are:

a) COP1 Application form;

b) COP1A Supporting evidence for property and affairs;

c) COP3 Assessment of capacity; COP4 Deputy's declaration.

6 MCA 2005 s19(1)(b).

7 COPR r51(2)(a)

7.19　Part 9 of the Court of Protection Rules (COPR) 2007 SI No 1744 deals with beginning proceedings. Practice Direction (PD) 9A provides guidance on completing the COP1, which is the main application form for starting proceedings. The COP1 form sets out the order or decision that the court is being asked to make, why the decision needs to be made and how it is in P's best interests to make the decision.

7.20　The COP1A form requires the provision of specific supporting information for property and affairs applications. All applications relating to property and affairs (unless made by an existing deputy or attorney under the procedure set out in PD 9D) require a COP1A form to provide the court with P's financial context. This information will be used by the court to set the appropriate guarantee bond and decide how much the deputy may access of P's funds in any given year without further authority or such other restrictions as it deems appropriate. It is important to give as much information as possible to ensure that the order ultimately made by the court does not unnecessarily curtail the deputy's authority or leave P exposed by the deputy being under-bonded.

7.21　The COP1A form also identifies who is a respondent to the application and who is to be notified. A respondent is 'any person (other than P) whom the applicant reasonably believes to have an interest which means he ought to be heard in relation to the application (as opposed to being notified of it)'.[8] The applicant should attempt to identify at least three people to notify of the application.[9] People to be notified are people who have a reasonable interest in being notified of the application. Those who are notified of an application may apply to be joined as parties.[10] There is a presumption (which can be displaced) that close members of P's family will have such an interest and PD 9B para 7 lists those who should ordinarily be notified, in descending order of closeness to P.[11] If someone in that list is not notified, then the application form then the reasons must be explained.

7.22　The COP3 form provides the court with an assessment of P's mental capacity in relation to the specific decision to be made by the court. It is usually completed by suitably qualified medical practitioner, social worker or other qualified professional. The Court of Protection's jurisdiction is only engaged where there is evidence

8　COPR r63(c)(iii).
9　COPR r70 and PD 9B para 4.
10　COPR r72(6) and (8); PD 9C para 4.
11　PD 9B para 7.

that on the balance of probabilities it is more likely than not that a person is not capable of making certain decisions for themselves because of a lack of capacity. When completing Part A of the form, advisers should ensure that they have correctly identified the issue or issues in respect of which P's decision making capabilities need to be assessed.

7.23 Occasionally there will be uncertainty as to a person's capacity or lack of capacity. If there is conflicting evidence all relevant evidence as to capacity should be put before the court for consideration.[12] The judge can then consider the evidence available and make a decision or give directions to resolve the issue of P's mental capacity. This may be by way of an oral hearing.

7.24 If the court is not satisfied with the medical evidence available, or if there has been some difficulty in having P's capacity assessed, the court is able to order under MCA 2005 s49 that a Special Visitor meets P to assess their capacity (see further in respect of section 49 reports, paras 13.42–13.49). A Special Visitor is a member of a panel appointed by the Lord Chancellor, with a medical qualification and special knowledge of and experience in cases of impairment of or disturbance in the functioning of the mind or brain;[13] one of their roles is to carry out assessments of capacity in these more difficult or unusual cases.

7.25 Medical evidence must be recent. If the court deems that the evidence is too old it may order that an updated assessment of capacity needs to be carried out which will delay the application. As a rule of thumb, the authors' experience is that if the COP3 form is dated more than six months before the application then the court is likely to ask for an updated assessment.

Process

7.26 The completed documents must be submitted (the address is in appendix F below) along with the appropriate application fee. In some circumstances a fee remission may be available. Details of fees and remissions are to be found in appendix G below.

7.27 For a straightforward application for the appointment of a deputy, the application from will usually be sealed and issued without the need for it to be referred for judicial scrutiny. To issue an application

---

12 See, by analogy, *Loughlin v Singh and others* [2013] EWHC 1641 (QB), [2013] COPLR 371.
13 MCA 2005 s61(2).

the court logs the details of the applicant and P on their system, allocates a case reference and makes up the court's paper file. A copy of the COP1 form, stamped with the date of issue and with the court reference number completed, will be returned to the applicant to carry out service.

7.28   In some cases the application will be referred to a judge before it is issued. This may be where there is conflicting evidence as to P's capacity, or if some information is incomplete for example. Depending upon the circumstances or the nature of the application the court may make enquiries or issue initial directions to obtain further information before issuing the requested application.

7.29   Once the applicant receives back the issued COP1 form, the next step is to deal with service. Service must be carried out within 21 days of the application being issued.[14] Those who have been identified on the application form at section 4A as respondents must be served with a copy of the application form as well as COP15 and a form COP5. Those who are treated as persons to be notified, and named in part 4B of the application, need not be provided with a copy of the issued COP1 but they must be provided by the applicant with a completed form COP15 along with a blank form COP5 to allow them to respond should they wish to. In a straightforward application for the appointment of a deputy, there will usually only be people to be notified rather than any respondents to be served.

7.30   When carrying out service, the applicant or their legal adviser should consider whether to include documents other than those required by the procedure. For instance, it is good practice to include information about the general rule as to costs should the party notified wish to take independent legal advice.

7.31   P is not automatically a party to proceedings, but must always be notified that proceedings have been issued. The rules for notifying P can be found in Part 7 of the COPR, and are discussed in paras 9.19–9.22. In summary, P must be notified that an application concerning them has been issued by the court. This must be done by personal service, rather than any other means. The applicant or their legal adviser should complete a COP14 notice of proceedings, setting out for P the nature of the application and details of who the applicant is and the effect on P of the requested order being made. Whoever notifies P of the application must also take steps to explain this notice to P using appropriate communication aids if necessary. P must also be handed a COP5 for them to respond to the application

14   COPR r66; see also paras 9.12–9.18.

if they wish. It is possible for notification to be dispensed with, either by the court on its own initiative, or upon an application.[15]

7.32   If at all possible, it is good practice for the deputy – especially one acting in a professional capacity without personal knowledge of P – to meet P and take steps to discuss the proposed application.

7.33   A COP5 must be provided to everyone who is notified of the application. See chapter 11 for details on responding to an application concerning property and affairs.

7.34   When service has been completed the applicant or their legal adviser confirms this to the court by submitting form COP20A and form COP20B. Unless a specific application has been made on the basis of particular urgency, the court will take no steps during the 21-day period during which those who have been notified must make their response.[16]

7.35   If no objections are received by the court during this period, the file will be referred back to the court for judicial consideration. If everything is in order at this stage, then the deputy order will usually be made. The applicant, or their legal adviser, will receive a letter notifying them that the court has made an order appointing them as deputy and advising them that the order will be released to them on the security bond has been put in place.

Security bond

7.36   The court has discretion to require a deputy to provide security for the discharge of the functions conferred upon them.[17] In the authors' experience, all deputies, whether lay or professional, are required to provide security by way of a bond, with the exception of local authority deputies. The level of the bond and the premium charged for it is determined by the court in reference to P's assets and the amount of money to which the deputy has access.[18] The security bond is to protect P from financial loss caused by the deputy, whether deliberately or by negligence. There is a bond arrangement in place which deputies can use or they may wish to try to obtain their own cover. Once the bond is in place, the court will be notified and sealed copies of the order will be sent out to the deputy.

---

15 COPR r40(3).
16 COPR r72 allows 21 days after service for acknowledgment of the application by the person upon whom the application is served.
17 MCA 2005 s19(9); see also COPR r200.
18 *Re H (a minor and incapacitated person); Baker v H and the Official Solicitor* [2009] COPLR Con Vol 606.

7.37   Deputies and their legal advisers should note that they may approach the court as circumstances change for the level of the security bond to be reviewed. During P's lifetime the nature and extent of their assets will alter and therefore the appropriate level of bond should be reviewed at regular intervals.

Supervision

7.38   When a new deputy is appointed the Office of the Public Guardian (OPG) will be notified by the court. The OPG will set a supervision level depending on P's circumstances and those of the deputy. The OPG requires that every deputy submit an annual report detailing how P's funds have been spent in the previous year and how any capital is invested. They check that the deputy obtains appropriate financial advice and acts upon it and they will schedule a visit by a court visitor to check that the deputy is coping with the new role. For more information on the role of the OPG, see chapter 21.

Restrictions

7.39   It is not uncommon for a deputy order to contain restrictions on what the deputy can do. When a new order is received, the deputy or their legal adviser should read it carefully and note any limits to their authority. Common restrictions include preventing the sale of a property without a further application to the court, or a limit to the amount of money that a deputy can spend in a year. If any of the restrictions are going to prove problematic, then so long as the application is made within 21 days of the order being served, a request can be made for a reconsideration under the provisions of COPR r89 (see further paras 19.3–19.6). Such a request can be made without incurring a further application fee.

7.40   A deputy order cannot be exhaustive in setting out what a deputy is and is not authorised to do; the new deputy, or their legal adviser, should ensure that they are aware of the limits to the scope of the powers that they may exercise without further authorisation of the court.

Powers and duties of a deputy

7.41   The order made by the court will set out the deputy's powers and their limits; typical orders are to be found in appendix C below.

7.42   A deputy has what is known as a fiduciary duty towards P, this means that there is a relationship of utmost trust and confidence between the deputy and P. Where a fiduciary relationship exists, money and property must be managed in P's best interests, without regard to any interest of the deputy. This means (among other things) that the deputy cannot profit personally by acting as P's deputy and the funds and assets of P must be kept entirely separate from those of P. In relation to property, the deputy cannot sanction a sale to him or herself, or a family member, particularly for less than full market value, without the additional approval of the court. It is also not appropriate for the deputy to receive any of P's funds into an account in their own name. All of P's assets and funds must remain be clearly in P's name at all times. Most bank accounts and other assets should be named 'A as deputy for Y' so that it is immediately clear who the asset belongs to.

7.43   A discussion of the full range of a deputy's powers and duties falls outside the scope of this chapter. However, any person considering putting themselves forward as a deputy would be well advised to familiarise themselves with the Code of Practice to the Mental Capacity Act, the principles of the MCA 2005 and the COPR. Recent cases[19] have demonstrated that the court will not be lenient on deputies, or attorneys, who simply do not understand the true nature and scope of the role.

7.44   We suggest the following by way of good practice upon the initial appointment of a deputy:

- The deputy should begin their task by circulating the deputy order to all of the financial institutions with whom P has a relationship. It is good practice to ask for an up-to-date statement or valuation and consider updating the court if it becomes clear once appointed that P had considerably more or fewer assets than were detailed in the COP1A. If P is living independently, the deputy should ensure as far as possible that their actions do not jeopardise P's day-to-day activities. If P relies upon a particular current account to access a pension to buy groceries, the deputy should make it clear to the bank and the DWP at the time of notifying them of the deputy order that they do not want any changes to the present arrangement.

- A deputy should ensure that P is receiving all the income to which they are entitled (but and none that they are not). This means that

---

19   See *Re GM* [2013] COPLR 290; and *Re Buckley* [2013] COPLR 39.

an early task for any deputy is to review P's benefits and make sure that claims are up-to-date.

- The deputy should check that insurance policies are updated and relevant to P's circumstances. If the deputy has been appointed because of an accident sustained by P, it may be, for instance, that P has a critical illness policy which would pay out a sum to P.

- If P lives in their own home, the deputy should visit and check how well-maintained it is. If repairs or adaptations are needed, the deputy should seek quotes and take professional advice about the suitability of any changes. If there is a property that needs to be sold, the deputy should check that the deputy order allows sale without further court approval, and if so, then approach estate agents to get a range of valuations before choosing whom to market a property with. If not, the deputy should seek specific approval from the court.

Investment

7.45   A deputy should take care to review P's finances and investments, preferably with the assistance of a suitably qualified Independent Financial Adviser. This is true not simply of new deputies but equally applies to long-standing appointments. P's needs and circumstances will alter over time and the deputy should be alive to these changes.

7.46   In *Re Buckley*[20] Senior Judge Lush took the opportunity to look at the investment responsibilities of an attorney, noting that:

> 20. There are two common misconceptions when it comes to investments. The first is that attorneys acting under an LPA can do whatever they like with the donors' funds. And the second is that attorneys can do whatever the donors could – or would – have done personally, if they had the capacity to manage their property and financial affairs.

> 21. Managing your own money is one thing. Managing someone else's money is an entirely different matter.

> 22. People who have the capacity to manage their own financial affairs are generally not accountable to anyone and don't need to keep accounts or records of their income and expenditure. They can do whatever they like with their money, and this includes doing nothing at all. They can stash their cash under the mattress, if they wish and, of course, they are entitled to make unwise decisions.

> 23. None of these options are open to an attorney acting for an incapacitated donor, partly because of their fiduciary obligations and partly because an attorney is required to act in the donor's best interests.

20 [2013] COPLR 39.

Section 1(5) of the Mental Capacity Act 2005 (the 2005 Act) states that, 'an act done, or decision made, under this Act for or on behalf of a person who lacks capacity must be done, or made, in his best interests'.

...

25. Attorneys hold a fiduciary position, which imposes a number of duties on them. Like trustees and other fiduciaries, they must exercise such care and skill as is reasonable in the circumstances when investing the donor's assets and this duty of care is even greater where attorneys hold themselves out as having specialist knowledge or experience.

26. Although it does not expressly apply to attorneys, s4 of the Trustee Act 2000 requires trustees to have regard to what are known as the 'standard investment criteria' when exercising any power of investment. [Senior Judge Lush then set out how these investment criteria apply]

7.47 This guidance was given in the context of a case concerning an LPA, but both the comments should be read as being equally applicable to a property and affairs deputy.

7.48 The investments made by the deputy (or attorney) on behalf of P must be in P's best interests, and in line with any other restrictions set out in the deputy order.

Deputyship in personal injury award cases

7.49 Many of the highest value deputyships arise from claims for personal injury where P has sustained a brain injury. As mentioned above, in these cases the court will often prefer a professional deputy. They raise specific considerations which merit brief highlighting here.

7.50 The deputy will usually become involved at a stage of the litigation where there has been an interim payment, or liability has been settled and an interim payment is anticipated. More rarely, a deputy is needed well before liability is established – for example, where P had an insurance policy that has paid out to a sole name account and their family need to access it to meet day-to-day bills.

7.51 If a referral is made before liability is established or any funds are available, the deputy must act cautiously; there is the possibility that the claim will fail and they should bear in mind how the court and other fees are to be funded. It may be necessary to advise the family of P on other options, eg appointeeship to claim benefits, local authority funding etc.

7.52   Once liability has been settled and an interim payment is made, the deputy should take steps to ensure that they know the terms of the payments made and the professional recommendations for P's care and case management. In cases of this sort, interim payments will be made for a particular purpose and a failure to manage funds in line with these purposes can have an adverse impact on the overall value of P's claim. The deputy needs to ensure that they have regular communication with the litigation team. The deputy should consider asking for certain litigation documents such as a copy of any order relating to interim payments as these are useful to have on the file to refer back to in the future.

7.53   Reports obtained in the course of litigation can also include valuable guidance as to how it is recommended that P's funds be applied, as well as how best to communicate with P to maximise their understanding and participate in decision-making. Professionals engaged to provide services to P such as case mangers, physiotherapists, occupational therapists and neuropsychologists will all provide costs estimates for their intervention. All this information can then be used by the deputy to formulate a proposed budget for the management of P's funds.

7.54   When establishing a budget, the deputy will typically communicate with family members or care-providers depending upon P's circumstances. Sadly it is often the case that a family will be under a huge amount of financial pressure if they have managed for some years without P's financial contribution or they have been frequently travelling to a distant hospital to visit P. The deputy may be able to consider alleviating some of this pressure by reimbursing some of these past losses. The legal team involved in running the personal injury claim will be able to guide on this point, and in some cases the order obtained in the personal injury claim approving the interim payment will make specific allowance for a sum to be paid to the family for these costs.

7.55   Clarity is important at this stage, first because whoever is paying sums out needs to be clear about the authority to make those payments; and second, because litigation can take many years to settle, it is important to make sure that everyone understands and records accurately what each payment is for.

7.56   In many personal injury cases insufficient funds are made available at the interim payment stage to implement all of the recommendations made to the claimant's litigation team. In an appropriate case, the deputy should consider exploring other funding avenues such as local authority funding in the form of direct payments.

7.57 The deputy is responsible for scrutinising the quality of the services they pay for on behalf of P. If a service or treatment provider is falling below an acceptable standard, or not providing what has been recommended for P, then there may be the risk that the cost of the service or treatment is disallowed when the damages are assessed.[21]

7.58 Occasionally the deputy may feel that they are being asked to perform a role outside that of simply managing P's property and affairs. If the deputy is being asked to make a decision that goes beyond the financial and budgetary, the authors would suggest that this is beyond the scope of the deputy's authority. For example, if P wants to go on holiday, the deputy would be expected to set a suitable budget and make sure that the costings include all the expected items; but it is not the deputy's role to decide if it is in P's best interests to go on that particular holiday at that particular time.

7.59 Depending upon the level of funds available and the expected expenditure where there is ongoing litigation, the deputy will usually want to consider putting in place regular budget updates. This allows the deputy to see if funds are being spent in accordance with recommendations and if budgets are being kept to. P's circumstances, and the recommendations for their care, can change rapidly; the deputy should keep pace with these changes.

7.60 Once a claim for compensation is settled the deputy will need to review the financial position P has been left in and begin to make plans for the longer term. Many cases settle for a lump sum plus periodical payments to meet P's care needs. The deputy will typically want to focus on investing the lump sum in such a way that P's needs are met now and in the future.

7.61 Other matters that the deputy should consider once any litigation has been finalised will include reviewing P's testamentary provision.

Statutory wills and gifting

7.62 The Court of Protection has the power under MCA 2005 s18 to authorise the execution of a will (or a codicil) on behalf of a person who lacks the relevant capacity, and also to authorise gifts on behalf of P that fall outside the very limited scope to gift that is enjoyed by deputies and attorneys alike. These applications raise particular

---

21 *Loughlin v Singh and others* [2013] EWHC 1641 (QB), [2013] COPLR 371.

issues which fall outside the scope of this book to discuss fully.[22] What follows is a summary of the key points that arise.

7.63   In each case the applicant should obtain specific medical evidence as to P's capacity in relation to the decision that the court will be invited to make. There are different tests for each decision.

1) In *A, B and C v X and Z*,[23] Hedley J held that the test of testamentary capacity before the Court of Protection is the common test formulated in *Banks v Goodfellow*,[24] ie that:

It is essential ... that a testator shall understand the nature of the act [of making a will] and its effects; shall understand the extent of the property of which he is disposing; shall be able to comprehend and appreciate the claims to which he ought to give effect, and ... that no disorder of mind shall poison their affections, pervert his sense of right, or prevent the exercise of his natural faculties – that no insane delusion shall influence his will in disposing of his property and bring about a disposal of it which, if his mind had been sound, would not have been made.

Note that the test in *Banks v Goodfellow* differs in some ways from the approach adopted under MCA 2005 ss2–3 (see further paras 3.33–3.64), in particular because it does not allow the reliance on supported decision making that applies to all other decisions under the MCA 2005.[25] It may well be that in due course there will be a case in which this question is revisited before the Court of Protection.

2) The test for the capacity to make a gift is – again – derived from the common law, this time from the test in *Re Beaney*.[26] The essence of this test is that it is calibrated to the circumstances of the gift, in particular the size of the gift in question in relation to the donor's assets.

7.64   The application for the court to approve a statutory will or gift is subject to the procedures outlined in PD 9F. In essence, it proceeds in the same fashion as outlined above for the basic application, with the

---

22 For more detail, readers are referred to Ashton et al, *Court of Protection Practice 2014*, Jordans, chapter 5, and D Lush and D Rees, consultant editors, *Heywood & Massey: Court of Protection Practice* (looseleaf), Sweet & Maxwell, chapters A20 (wills) and A21 (settlements and gifts).

23 [2012] EWHC 2400 (COP), [2013] COPLR 1.

24 (1870) LR 5 QB 549, [1861–1873] All ER 47.

25 See for further discussion Alex Ruck Keene and Annabel Lee, 'Testamentary capacity' [2013] Eld LJ 272.

26 [1978] 1 WLR 770; see also *Re P (capacity to tithe inheritance)* [2014] EWHC B14 (COP).

addition of a detailed witness statement on the part of the applicant setting out:

a) proposed draft will (for an application to approve a will) or details of the gift(s) proposed;

b) details of previous wills (if applicable);

c) schedule of capital;

d) schedule of income;

e) schedule of expenditure;

f) family tree;

g) schedule showing impact of inheritance tax and distribution of estate with and without proposed will or gift.

7.65   The applicant's witness statement needs to explain the reasoning behind the proposals and why it is in the best interests of P.

7.66   The case of *Re P*[27] sets out in some detail the relevant jurisprudence and the tests that will be applied by the court in deciding if a statutory will should be approved.

7.67   Careful consideration needs to be given to ensuring that the correct parties are identified and served as respondents in this type of application. If a person is named as a residuary beneficiary in an existing will of P they will need to be named as a respondent in any application to approve a statutory will. A pecuniary or specific legatee under P's will, whose entitlement would be unchanged by the proposed will, can be named as a person to be notified. If P is intestate (ie they have never made any testamentary provision) then the deputy will need to ascertain their family tree to establish who would inherit from P under the Intestacy Rules set out in the Administration of Estates Act 1925 ss46–47. Anyone who would inherit under P's intestacy should be notified as a respondent in any application to approve a statutory will.

7.68   Deputies have a very limited ability to make gifts on behalf of P. The standard wording of a deputy order gives the power to make gifts of 'a seasonal and customary nature' (see appendix C below). The case of *Re GM*[28] addressed the scope of a deputy's powers to make gifts from P's assets and Senior Judge Lush took the opportunity to provide some guidance on this topic. Having noted that the deputyship order permitted the deputies to make gifts 'on customary occasions to persons who are related to or connected with them, provided that the value of each such gift is not unreasonable having regard

---

27 [2009] EWHC 163 (COP), [2009] EWHC 163 (Ch), [2010] Ch 33.
28 [2013] COPLR 290.

to all the circumstances and, in particular, the size of their estate' and that 'a customary occasion is defined in MCA 2005 s12(3) as an anniversary of a birth, a marriage or a civil partnership, or any other occasion on which presents are customarily given within families or among friends or associates' and also that 'the value of the gift must be 'not unreasonable' (s12(2)). Senior Judge Lush set out very clearly the approach to be followed in determining what is reasonable in a given case:

> First, regard must be had to the totality of P's current and anticipated income and capital, expenditure and debts.
>
> Second, consideration must be given to P's best interests, including the following factors:
> • . the extent to which P was in the habit of making gifts or loans of a particular size or nature before the onset of incapacity;
> • P's anticipated life expectancy;
> • the possibility that P may require residential or nursing care and the projected cost of such care;
> • whether P is in receipt of aftercare pursuant to section 117 of the Mental Health Act 1983 or NHS Continuing Healthcare;
> • the extent to which any gifts may interfere with the devolution of P's estate under their or their will or intestacy; and
> • the impact of Inheritance Tax on P's death.
>
> Third, any gift that is not de minimis, must be approved in advance by the Court of Protection. A de minimis gift is to be construed as follows:
>> 'covering the annual IHT exemption of £3,000 and the annual small gifts exemption of £250 per person, up to a maximum of, say, ten people in the following circumstances:
>> (a) where P has a life expectancy of less than five years;
>> (b) their estate exceeds the nil rate band for Inheritance Tax ("IHT") purposes, currently £325,000;
>> (c) the gifts are affordable having regard to P's care costs and will not adversely affect P's standard of care and quality of life, and
>> (d) there is no evidence that P would be opposed to gifts of this magnitude being made on their behalf.'

7.69   Bearing this very clear guidance in mind, if a deputy thinks that a) a more significant gift should be made on behalf of P; b) that to do so would be in P's best interests; and c) the gift is affordable in P's circumstances, the deputy must apply to the court for approval *before* the gift is made.

7.70   In cases concerning the approval of a will or substantial gifting, P will usually be joined to proceedings as a party, and be represented by the Official Solicitor.

Powers of attorney

7.71 Prior to the implementation of the MCA 2005 on 1 October 2007, an EPA allowed a donor (the person who wishes to make arrangements for someone else to look after their finances if they are unable to do so in future) to appoint an attorney (or attorneys) to deal with their finances both immediately after the signing of the document and in the future, should the donor lose their capacity. An EPA could only be made to cover the donor's financial affairs; no power was conferred by it to allow decision-making with regard to health or welfare matters.[29]

7.72 To be valid, an EPA must be in the prescribed format and have been signed by all parties on or before 30 September 2007.[30] The attorneys named in an EPA are under a duty to register the document with the OPG when the donor has lost, or is losing their capacity.

7.73 LPAs were introduced by the MCA 2005 and come in two varieties: 1) health and welfare; and 2) property and affairs. The new property and affairs LPA is similar in function to the old EPA, but crucially it cannot be used until it has been registered with the OPG.

7.74 The special feature enjoyed by both the EPA and LPA is that the authority conferred by them continues even after the donor has lost their capacity. All other types of power of attorney (usually referred to as a 'general power of attorney') are automatically revoked by the donor's incapacity.

7.75 The OPG has a range of documents available to download[31] that can take the prospective donor through the process of making an LPA, and registering it. This is an administrative process, falling outside the scope of this book, with one important exception detailed in the bullet points below:

- The process of registration requires notification to any person named in the LPA for that purpose on a form LPA001.[32] If a person notified wishes to object to the registration of an LPA on a prescribed ground,[33] ie most obviously, that either fraud or undue pressure was used to execute an instrument for the purpose of

---

29 For more detail on EPAs and LPAs, see chapter 3 and D Lush, *Cretney & Lush on Lasting and Enduring Powers of Attorney*, 7th edn, Jordans, 2013.

30 Provisions relating to EPAs can now be found in MCA 2005 Sch 4.

31 See: www.justice.gov.uk/forms/opg.

32 MCA 2005 Sch 1 para 6.

33 MCA 2005 Sch 1 para 13(3), referring to MCA 2005 s22(3).

creating an LPA or to create a LPA,[34] then they must within three weeks from the date on which notice is given make an application to the Court of Protection in a form COP7 (not a COP1), and notify the OPG of their application in a form LPA008. There is no fee payable. The COP7 form will then be issued by the court; it must then be served as soon as practicable and in any event within 21 days; the COP7 form must be accompanied with a COP5 form for the person upon whom it is served to respond, and a certificate of service will be required under COP20. Taking these steps will have the effect of preventing the OPG from registering the LPA until the court has determined the application and directed the OPG to do so.[35]

- If the person who wishes to object to the registration was not a person notified on a LPA001 form, the application is made not on an COP7 form, but on a COP1 form; the OPG must also be notified. There is a fee payable in such case (see appendix G below). This will also apply if the LPA has already been registered, but the person wishes the power to be cancelled.

7.76   The Court of Protection has a range of powers in relation to determining both the validity of LPAs[36] and their operation.[37] The most relevant for present purposes are those related to the jurisdiction that the court exercises over the conduct of attorneys (which also extends to the conduct of attorneys under EPAs[38]); see further paras 7.83–7.92 below.

7.77   The court may determine the validity of an LPA[39] and if it finds that it was not properly created may order that the instrument is not registered. Other powers of the court include severing the appointment of an attorney under an LPA if there is more than one appointed. For example, if only one attorney were found to be in breach of their duties this would in itself not invalidate the appointment of any other attorney validly appointed in the same instrument.

7.78   The court also has powers to require attorneys to provide accounts or other information if the donor lacks the capacity to call for these themselves,[40] as well as giving directions about the remuneration of a

34 MCA 2005 s22(3)(a).
35 MCA 2005 Sch 1 para 13(4).
36 MCA 2005 s22.
37 MCA 2005 s23.
38 Under the – slightly different – provisions in MCA 2005 Sch 3 para 16.
39 MCA 2005 s22(2)(a).
40 MCA 2005 s23(3)(a).

donee[41] or alleviating them from liability for any breach of their duty as attorney.[42]

7.79 The court also has jurisdiction to authorise gifts that fall outside of the attorney's existing powers under the LPA, see para 7.62 above. The court's power to revoke an LPA is discussed below at para 7.83.

Jointly owned property and other trustee matters

7.80 In cases where P is a trustee, a deputy may not be given power to exercise P's functions as a trustee.[43] An application will need to be made to the court for the appointment of a new trustee to act in P's place.

7.81 This is most commonly found where P is the co-owner of real property as this is a form of trusteeship. P will usually need to be removed from the title to the land and a new trustee appointed in order for a sale of the land to take place.

7.82 An application to the court to appoint a trustee can be made by reference to PD 9G. This sets out the information that the court will require in order to consider the application.

Removal of attorney or deputy

7.83 A deputy or attorney may retire from their role and cease to act if circumstances change. They may do this by disclaiming the role. There are, however, occasions when another will apply to the court for the removal of a deputy or attorney. The MCA 2005 gives the court the power to revoke an LPA if P is unable to do so and the attorney:

a) has behaved, or is behaving, in a way that contravenes their authority or is not in P's best interests; or

b) proposes to behave in a way that would contravene their authority or would not be in P's best interests.[44]

The Court of Protection can also revoke the appointment of a deputy if it is satisfied that the deputy:

---

41 MCA 2005 s23(3)(c).
42 MCA 2005 s23(3)(d).
43 MCA 2005 s20(3).
44 MCA 2005 s22(3)(b).

a) has behaved, or is behaving, in a way that contravenes the authority conferred on them by the court or is not in P's best interests; or

b) proposes to behave in a way that would contravene that authority or would not be in P's best interests.[45]

7.84   An application may be made by the OPG (following an investigation – see chapter 25),[46] local authority safeguarding team if there are fears about financial abuse or by someone interested in P's welfare that has well-founded fears about the management of P's finances.

7.85   As more cases continue to be reported, there is more guidance emerging about what the court considers to be behaviour that justifies the removal of either an attorney or a deputy.

7.86   The cases of *Re J*[47] and *Re Harcourt*[48] both comment upon the relevant behaviour to be taken into account when considering applications of this type. In *Re J* HHJ Marshall QC considered the question of what conduct of the attorney would be of relevance to the question of revocation, holding that:

> ... on a proper construction of s22(3), the court can consider any past behaviour or apparent prospective behaviour by the attorney, [and], depending on the circumstances and apparent gravity of any offending behaviour found, it can then take whatever steps it regards as appropriate in P's best interests (this only arises if P lacks capacity), to deal with the situation, whether by revoking the power or by taking some other course.[49]

7.87   Senior Judge Lush commented in *Re Harcourt* that: 'Essentially, the Lasting Powers of Attorney scheme is based on trust and envisages minimal intervention by public authorities.'[50] He went on to note that: 'The factor of magnetic importance in determining what is in Mrs Harcourt's best interests is that her property and financial affairs should be managed competently, honestly and for her benefit.'[51]

7.88   The cases of *Re Buckley* and *Re GM* discussed above also resulted in the removal of the deputies involved. Finally, while *Re DB* (discussed below at paras 17.40ff) is a decision relating to costs, the case

---

45   MCA 2005 s16(8).
46   See, for instance, *Public Guardian v JM* [2014] EWHC B4 (COP).
47   [2011] COPLR Con Vol 716.
48   [2013] COPLR 69.
49   Para 13.
50   Para 39.
51   Para 60.

is also of note for the approach taken by the court to the suitability of a proposed deputy.

7.89   The process for making an application for the removal of an attorney or deputy follows that of all other applications relating to P's property and affairs. Firstly the applicant should obtain an assessment of capacity addressing the questions to be put before the court. Depending upon the situation the questions to be considered may include:

- whether P lacks the capacity to revoke their LPA;
- whether P can validly enter into a new LPA;
- whether P lacks capacity to request accounts from their attorney;
- whether P lacked the capacity to make a gift (or other relevant detrimental financial decision) at the relevant time.

7.90   The applicant would be wise to consider the outcome for P that would be achieved through making the application, if an LPA is to be revoked and P lacks capacity to enter into a new LPA, who will manage P's finances? It may be appropriate to ask the court, for example, not only to revoke the appointment of an attorney but to order the appointment of a neutral panel deputy.

7.91   The applicant may find that they do not have access to all the information that they need to support their application. P's financial documents are likely to be kept by the attorney or deputy. In these cases it may be preferable to approach the OPG to investigate and use its powers to obtain documents and to make any necessary application. If the applicant has access to sufficient evidence that the deputy or attorney may be acting in such a way that the court should consider their removal, then proceeding straight to apply to the court will be the quickest route to take.

7.92   The applicant may consider asking for immediate directions to protect P's position, but in the experience of the authors these are rarely granted in cases that solely concern P's property and affairs. During proceedings all parties can apply for directions following the process set out in chapter 11.

Redress

7.93   As mentioned earlier in this chapter, every deputy (with the exception of a local authority deputy) must purchase a security bond, which is in effect an insurance against them causing financial loss to P. If the court removes a deputy in circumstances in which their actions have caused loss to P, then it is possible to recover those funds for P, up to the value of the relevant security bond if the court orders it.

7.94   It may be possible to make an application for a security bond to be called in within the course of the proceedings to remove the deputy. If there is insufficient information at the time of the removal proceedings about the full scale of P's financial loss, a later application can be brought by the new deputy on behalf of P.

7.95   If P has suffered financial loss through the actions of their attorney or if this loss caused by his deputy exceeds the value of the security bond, the only remedy open is for the new deputy acting on behalf of P is to take civil action against the former attorney or deputy personally. Before considering this step (which would require the endorsement of the Court of Protection) the deputy would need to be sure that the removed attorney or deputy had sufficient resources to meet any liability.

Recovery of capacity

7.96   The Court of Protection's jurisdiction only extends to those who lack capacity to make certain decisions. It follows, therefore, that if P ceases to lack capacity in relation to their property and affairs, an application should be made for the discharge of the deputy.[52]

7.97   If a deputy believes that P has regained their capacity to manage their property and affairs, they should obtain updated medical evidence to this effect and then apply to the court, following the procedure described above, to approve the discharge of the deputyship.

7.98   The court will consider the evidence and if the application is approved will make an order for final accounts to be submitted, the ending of the security bond, the transfer of all assets to P's name and for final costs to be dealt with.[53]

Death of P

7.99   The death of P automatically ends both the valid appointment of a deputy and also that of an attorney. The deputy should liaise with the personal representatives of P's estate to make information available

52 See PD 23B para 5.
53 See PD 23B, COPR r167, and the Lasting Powers of Attorney, Enduring Powers of Attorney and Public Guardian Regulations 2007 SI No 1253 regs 37 and 40. See also paras 16.58ff.

to allow them to administer P's estate. A professional deputy will be entitled to final costs for winding up the deputyship. The deputy should notify the OPG of the death of P, by submitting a copy of the death certificate. Other matters for a deputy to deal with will include submitting a final report to the OPG and discharging the security.

Mixed applications

7.100 It is the experience of the authors that during the course of proceedings issues may arise that go beyond those concerning P's property and affairs, to touch on health and welfare issues as well. A common scenario is a dispute arising within a family about who should act as attorney or deputy for an incapacitated relative that also includes an aspect about where the individual should reside or the care they should receive.

7.101 In these cases, permission need only be sought for the part of the application where permission is required.[54] For the procedure for obtaining permission in relation to health and welfare decisions, see chapter 8.

7.102 Advisers should be aware of the differing costs regimes in property and affairs matters and health and welfare matters. Details on the appropriate treatment of costs in mixed applications can be found in chapter 17.

54 COPR r53(2).

CHAPTER 8

Making an application: health and welfare cases

Before making an application

8.1 In chapter 5 we consider how to decide when an application is appropriate. In chapter 22 we consider mediation and other forms of alternative dispute resolution (ADR). Advisers are referred to those chapters.

8.2 There is no formal pre-action protocol in the Court of Protection, but other than in cases of extreme urgency, the court will expect the parties to have made some attempt to resolve the issues between them through correspondence or discussions before seeking to issue an application. The Code of Practice anticipates that attempts will be made to resolve disputes outside the court arena in the first instance.[1]

8.3 There are broadly three types of case where an application to court will need to be made:

- First, *serious medical treatment cases* must be brought to court even if there is no dispute. The particular issues arising from medical treatment cases are considered in chapter 23.
- The second type concerns *potentially risky medical or welfare questions*, where even if there is no dispute, the implications of the decision are such that the court should be asked to authorise the proposed course of action.
- The third is where there is a *genuine dispute.*

8.4 The court will expect all such cases to be brought before the court. If one of the parties is a public body, then that body will be expected to take the initiative in bringing the matter before the court.[2] Parties should be aware that their conduct before proceedings start can be taken into account if the court is considering departing from the general rule in health and welfare cases that the parties should bear their own costs.[3]

Types of application

8.5 It is important to decide before making an application exactly what orders are to be sought. As set out in chapter 3, the court has the power

---

1 Mental Capacity Act 2005 Code of Practice chapter 15: www.justice.gov.uk/downloads/protecting-the-vulnerable/mca/mca-code-of-practice-0509.pdf.
2 *Hillingdon LBC v Neary* [2011] EWHC 1377 (COP), [2011] COPLR Con Vol 632; also *The local authority v Mrs D and another* [2013] EWHC B34.
3 Court of Protection Rules (COPR) 2007 SI No 1744 r159.

to make decisions on P's behalf[4] or appoint a deputy to make them for P.[5] However, a decision of the court is preferred to the appointment of a deputy[6] and the powers conveyed upon a deputy should be as limited as possible.[7] These powers are limited by Mental Capacity Act (MCA) 2005 s20. For example, a deputy cannot prohibit contact between P and a named person,[8] or refuse consent to life-sustaining treatment.[9] The Code of Practice indicates that the appointment of a health and welfare deputy would be appropriate where a series of linked decisions will be needed over time, or where someone with final authority to make decisions will be needed, or where there is a history of family disputes.[10] There is a difference of judicial opinion as to whether a health and welfare deputy should only be appointed in the most serious cases, but the statistics show that the courts are reluctant to appoint such deputies.[11]

8.6 A health and welfare deputyship should not be sought, therefore, if the underlying decision that the deputy wishes to make is a 'one off' decision, such as a change of residence. A welfare deputyship might be appropriate where there is a need to make decisions over time about the level and frequency of contact in P's best interests with a family member.

8.7 Finally, it should, be noted that in many cases, the issues that the court needs to address will relate both to P's health and welfare and to P's property and affairs. These 'mixed' applications are addressed in paras 7.100–7.102.

How to make an application

8.8 The majority of applications in health and welfare cases (including for the appointment of a deputy) will require permission from the court.[12] Permission for such cases is not required where an application is made by:

4 MCA 2005 s16(1).
5 MCA 2005 s16(2).
6 MCA 2005 s16(4)(a).
7 MCA 2005 s16(4)(b).
8 MCA 2005 s20(2).
9 MCA 2005 s20(5).
10 Code of Practice para 8.38.
11 In 2013, for instance, 205 health and welfare deputies were appointed. By contrast, 14,209 property and affairs deputies were appointed.
12 MCA 2005 s50.

- a person who lacks, or is alleged to lack, capacity;[13]
- a person with parental responsibility for someone under 18 who lacks or is alleged to lack capacity;[14]
- the donor or donee of a lasting power of attorney (LPA) to which the application relates;[15]
- a deputy appointed for P;[16]
- a person named in an existing order, where the application relates to that order;
- an application under MCA 2005 s21A by the relevant person's representative (RPR).[17]

8.9   Other exceptions may be provided for by the COPR. These exceptions include the Official Solicitor or Public Guardian;[18] applications under COPR Part 10 (ie an application within the course of proceedings);[19] or orders sought when filing an acknowledgment of service.[20] Other exceptions are listed in rule 51(2).

Forms

8.10   The following forms will be needed to commence an application for health and welfare declarations:

- COP1 – the application form;
- COP1B – supporting information for health and welfare applications;
- COP2 – permission application;
- COP3 – capacity assessment;
- supporting evidence either in form COP1, or in a statement in form COP24.

8.11   The following forms will be needed to commence an application for a health and welfare deputyship:

- COP1 – the application form;
- COP2 – permission application;

13 MCA 2005 s50(1)(a).
14 MCA 2005 s50(1)(b).
15 MCA 2005 s50(1)(c).
16 MCA 2005 s50(1)(a).
17 MCA 2005 s50(1A).
18 COPR r51(1)(a).
19 COPR r51(3).
20 COPR r51(4).

- COP1B – supporting information for health and welfare applications;
- COP3 – capacity assessment;
- COP4 – deputy's declaration;
- supporting evidence either in form COP1, or in a statement in form COP24.

8.12   Once these forms have been completed, they must be sent to the Court of Protection at First Avenue House, together with the appropriate fee (see para 8.34). The full address of the court appears at appendix F below, together with the telephone contact details. Details as to what will happen next appear in chapter 10.

Completing the forms, and guidance from the COPR and practice directions

8.13   COPR Part 9 deals with commencing proceedings. Practice Direction (PD) 9A provides guidance as to how to complete the application form (COP1). This form is not complex. However, the following issues need to be considered with particular care.

8.14   At section 4.1 of the form, respondents to the application need to be listed. Individuals listed here will automatically become parties[21] unless the court orders otherwise. PD 9A requires that the applicant must list as a respondent 'any person (other than P) whom the applicant reasonably believes to have an interest which means he ought to be heard in relation to the application (as opposed to being notified of it)'.

8.15   It may seem anomalous that P does not become a party automatically given that P's future is at stake in the application. However, rule 73(4) provides that P should not be named as a respondent to any proceedings without the leave of the court. The human rights implications of this are considered in paras 12.4–12.7. In practice, P is frequently joined by the court at an early stage. P is bound as if P were a party by orders of the court in any event.[22]

8.16   P can, however, make an application without permission, but must have a litigation friend[23] – see chapter 13 for a full discussion of the role of litigation friend; this is also considered in the context

---

21   COPR r73(1)(b).
22   COPR r74(2)(a).
23   COPR r141.

of applications under MCA 2005 s21A in chapter 24. Practical difficulties can arise if the adviser has represented P directly – perhaps in a forum such as a mental health tribunal where patients are represented without an intermediary – and an issue has arisen which the adviser reasonably believes requires resolution by the Court of Protection. The Official Solicitor will not normally accept an invitation to act unless proceedings have already started. If P has a family member or friend who might be willing to act as litigation friend, or an advocate who is willing to support P, that individual should be approached. In *Re UF*,[24] Charles J recognised that it may be necessary for pragmatic reasons for an interim litigation friend to be named in order to commence proceedings, but for the court at a later stage to invite the Official Solicitor to act.

8.17   There will be some cases where there is literally no individual who is willing to act as litigation friend, even for a limited period. In some cases this may mean that it is not possible to take the matter forward to the court, unless another party – for example, the relevant local authority – can be persuaded to issue proceedings. There may be some cases where the adviser reasonably considers that P's best interests will be seriously compromised if proceedings cannot be brought. In such cases we consider the adviser could act as litigation friend, solely in order to bring the case to court. The adviser should prepare a detailed witness statement in which the attempts to locate a suitable litigation friend are described. This is not entirely without precedent, as a solicitor was appointed litigation friend to a protected party whom he knew well.[25]

8.18   In addition to listing respondents, section 4.2 of form COP1 requires the applicant to list the people who will be notified of the application, once it has been issued by the court. PD 9B requires the applicant to try to identify at least three people who have an interest in being notified that the application has been issued.[26] Such individuals will have the opportunity of asking to be joined as parties.[27] They will be bound by the court's orders as if they were parties.[28] There is a presumption (which can be displaced) that close members of P's family will have such an interest and the Practice Direction lists those who should ordinarily be notified, in descending order of closeness

24 [2013] EWHC 4289 (COP), [2014] COPLR 93.
25 *Re RGS* [2013] EWHC 1417 (COP).
26 PD 9B para 4.
27 COPR r72(6), (8); PD 9C para 4.
28 COPR r74(2)(b).

to P.[29] If someone in that list is not notified, then the reasons must be explained. (For example, P may have several siblings, only one of whom has any contact or involvement with P. There might in that case be good reason not to notify the remaining three.)

8.19　　In addition to P's family, the following persons should generally be notified:[30]

- if P is under 18, anyone with parental responsibility for P;
- any person – including a legal entity such as a trust or local authority – likely to be affected by the outcome of the application;
- a deputy or attorney whose powers relate to the issue involved in the application.

8.20　　Section 5 of form COP1 repays careful drafting. This section asks three questions:

(1) What is the matter you want the court to decide?
(2) Please state the order you are asking the court to make?
(3) How would the order benefit the person to whom the application relates?

8.21　　These questions recur in form COP2. We consider there are real advantages to preparing a separate statement of facts and grounds, which can clearly set out in one place the factual background, the matter in dispute, the orders being sought and the likely benefit to P. Section 5 of form COP1 and section 2 of form COP2 can then simply refer to this document.

8.22　　It is of course essential to draft the form in a balanced manner and not to ask for inappropriately broad orders or powers.[31] The application form and the permission form contain a statement of truth, and proceedings for contempt of court may be brought if a person makes a false statement in a document verified by a statement of truth.[32] All litigants are 'required to help the court to further the overriding objective',[33] which is to deal with the case justly. Solicitors are further subject to the mandatory principles of the Solicitors Regulation Authority (SRA) Code of Conduct to act with integrity and maintain the trust of the public.[34] There is no requirement to send proposed respondents copies of the application before it is issued, but it is good

29　PB 9B para 7.
30　PB 9B para 10.
31　*Hillingdon LBC v Neary* [2011] EWHC 1377 (COP), [2011] COPLR Con Vol 632.
32　COPR r14.
33　COPR r4.
34　SRA Code of Conduct 2011, Principles 2 and 6.

practice to do so, especially if the proposed parties have been in correspondence before one of them decides to apply to the court.

8.23   Form COP1B requires some additional supporting information, but this form is largely self-explanatory.

8.24   Form COP2 is the permission form. When completing this form it is important to keep in mind the factors that the court will consider when deciding whether to grant permission. These include the applicant's connection with P, the reasons for the application, the benefit to P if the orders sought are made and whether the benefit can be achieved in any other way.[35] See further paras 9.1–9.7.

Evidence of capacity

8.25   Form COP3 is the assessment of capacity. It is important to note that this does not need to be completed by a medical practitioner – form COP3 was revised in 2013 to make expressly clear that it can be completed by a registered:

- medical practitioner, for example the GP of the person to whom the application relates;
- psychiatrist;
- approved mental health professional (AMHP);
- social worker;[36]
- psychologist;
- nurse; or
- occupational therapist.

8.26   The form also makes clear that in some circumstances it might also be appropriate for a registered therapist, such as a speech therapist or occupational therapist, to complete the form.

8.27   Some medical practitioners, in particular GPs, will charge to complete a COP3. There is a good argument that it should fall within the scope of the medical services that they provide to P, and advisers should always seek to query the basis upon which any charge is made before simply agreeing to pay.

---

35 *NK v VW and others* [2012] COPLR 105.

36 In *A Local Authority v SY* [2013] EWHC 3485 (COP), [2014] COPLR 1, decided before the change in the COP3, the COP3 had been completed by a social worker; Keehan J noted that: 'The assessment in this case demonstrates that an appropriately qualified social worker is eminently suited to undertake such capacity assessments. I commend the practice which I hope will be followed in appropriate future cases' (para 22).

8.28   Whoever completes the COP3 form, it is important that the practitioner completes the COP3 correctly and provides an appropriate level of detail. In particular, section 7.1 requires the practitioner to set out the areas of decision-making where P lacks capacity. These might, for example, be P's place of residence, P's care arrangements and contact with others. When the practitioner completes the rest of the form he or she must ensure that evidence of lack of capacity is set out in respect of all those three areas of decision-making.

8.29   A practical difficulty can arise if the applicant does not have access to P or P's records. A common scenario might concern estranged parents of an adult who lives with one parent and may lack capacity to make decisions about whether to see the other parent. The relationship between the parents is acrimonious and the parent with whom P lives will not allow the other parent to see P or be involved in P's life in any way. In that scenario, it may be possible for the estranged parent to invite P's GP or social worker to assess P's capacity and complete a COP3. However, this is not always realistic and in the event that the parent making an application to the court simply cannot provide a completed COP3, the applicant should prepare a witness statement which explains why he or she is not able to provide an assessment of capacity; what attempts have been made to obtain an assessment, and why he or she knows or believes that P lacks capacity to make a decision in relation to the matter the applicant wants the court to decide.[37]

8.30   A similar situation arose in *Re F*.[38] The solicitor advising P had concerns that she might lack capacity to make decisions about whether to accept or refuse care. P's GP refused to complete a COP3 because she felt that she lacked the necessary expertise. A COP3 was completed by a neuropsychologist who had met P once and tentatively considered that she had the requisite capacity. Proceedings were issued in the Court of Protection by P, with her father acting as her litigation friend. The court was provided with the COP3 form together with the views of the solicitor. The District Judge took the view that unless further evidence that P lacked capacity was provided, she did not have jurisdiction to hear the case. P appealed, and the appeal was upheld by HHJ Marshall. The decision is important because it sets out clearly how the court should approach the situation – which frequently arises in practice – where the applicant is unable to provide consistent evidence of lack of relevant capacity. HHJ Marshall said:

---

37 PD 8A(6).
38 [2009] EWHC B30 (Fam), [2009] COPLR Con Vol 390, (2009) 12 CCLR 530.

38. If the learned District Judge did not in fact ask herself whether the evidence before her was enough to rebut the presumption of capacity, but applied some lesser test, did she nonetheless apply too high a test? In my judgment she did, because it appears that she regarded nothing less than the positive opinion of a specialist medical practitioner to the effect that F did lack the relevant capacity as being sufficient to found her jurisdiction even to direct a psychiatric assessment of F.

39. This must, in my judgment, be setting too high a hurdle. The Act is meant to operate in a simple and practical way, and to facilitate any necessary determination about P's capacity if there is doubt. It is clearly intended at least that general medical practitioners and health professionals other than mental capacity specialists should be able to supply evidence which will enable the Court of Protection to decide whether it can or should intervene, and if so, how.

40. There is a danger, with the current spotlight on the new and more sophisticated approach to mental capacity contained in the Act and the very extensive Code of Practice, that general practitioners will think that that they cannot or should not complete such an assessment for the court because of lack of supposed expertise – as happened in this case. This would be likely to lead to their declining to do so in the very cases which are problematic, because there is doubt whether the borderline has been crossed between decisions which are the product of impaired powers of reasoning, or are merely eccentric unwise or unreasonable decisions in the opinion of others. It would be unfortunate if a conclusive specialist assessment came to be regarded as necessary before the court would accept jurisdiction at all.

41. At a minimum this would cause delay and expense. More seriously, it would risk leaving a vulnerable person to slip through the net of protection intended to be provided by the Act. This is especially so in the case of a person who, or whose family, could not readily afford the costs of a detailed psychiatric assessment, in which case it might then become very difficult or impossible to get the case before the court at all.

42. Second, it is in fact these very cases of difficulty, ie where lack of capacity is suspected but not clear, that the court needs to be called on to make an adjudication under s15 at all. An example is where professionals disagree about a person's capacity to make a particular type of decision: see paragraph 8.16 of the Code. If lack of capacity is clear, the point will never be debated. If it is not, but is genuinely in doubt, then that is just the case in which the court should be able to intervene promptly, to enable a fast and efficient determination of the issue.

43. A lower threshold for engagement of the court's powers under s48 is not at all inconsistent with the emphatic approach of the Mental Capacity Act 2005 that every adult is to be treated as entitled to make

his own decisions, and is not to be interfered with in that regard without good reason to suppose that he is vulnerable through lack of capacity. The jurisdiction under s48 has two stages, and, in my judgment, it is the second stage rather than the first which provides the real protection for P against undue interference with his affairs and his right to make his own decisions.

44. The proper test for the engagement of s48 in the first instance is whether there is evidence giving good cause for concern that P may lack capacity in some relevant regard. Once that is raised as a serious possibility, the court then moves on to the second stage to decide what action, if any, it is in P's best interests to take before a final determination of his capacity can be made. Such action can include not only taking immediate safeguarding steps (which may be positive or negative) with regard to P's affairs or life decisions, but it can also include giving directions to enable evidence to resolve the issue of capacity to be obtained quickly. Exactly what direction may be appropriate will depend on the individual facts of the case, the circumstances of P, and the momentousness of the urgent decisions in question, balanced against the principle that P's right to autonomy of decision-making for himself is to be restricted as little as is consistent with his best interests. Thus, where capacity itself is in issue, it may well be the case that the only proper direction in the first place should be as to obtaining appropriate specialist evidence to enable that issue to be reliably determined.

8.31   One last point to note in relation to the COP3 form is that it does not include a question specifically directed to the issue of whether P has capacity to conduct the litigation. If (as happens in most health and welfare cases involving P) P is to be joined as a party, then there will need to be evidence as to their capacity to litigate before the Official Solicitor will accept any invitation to act as their litigation friend; the same is also likely to apply in respect of any other person who might act as litigation friend (see further chapter 12). It is therefore necessary to make clear when inviting a practitioner to complete a COP3 form in a health and welfare case that they specifically direct their mind to the question of whether P has litigation capacity in order to avoid a delay in the progression of the proceedings thereafter.

Supporting evidence

8.32   COPR r64 provides that the evidence which supports the application should be filed at court with the application. PD 9A states that this can be provided in the form COP1, provided it is verified by a statement of truth, or by way of a witness statement in form COP24. It is suggested that in most cases it will be desirable for the applicant to provide a witness statement explaining the background to the case in appropriate detail. Questions of evidence are addressed in greater detail in chapter 13.

Human rights issues

8.33   Any claim for remedies under the Human Rights Act 1998 must be clearly pleaded and particularised. This issue is considered in chapter 26.

Fees

8.34   There is a fee for making an application. The current fees at the time of writing are set out in appendix G below.

Confidential matters

8.35   There may be cases where a party does not wish to reveal certain personal details to some or all of the other parties. The position is governed by COPR r15.[39] This provides that if a party does not wish to reveal his or her home or business address or telephone number, or P's address or telephone number, or details of a person with whom P is living, then those details must be provided to the court in any event. These details will, however, not be provided to any other party unless the court directs this. The party must provide an address for service that it within the jurisdiction of the court.

8.36   Anyone who does not wish to reveal the details set out above should explain their reasons in a witness statement. If the party wishes to withhold more details than this, then it will be necessary to follow the procedure discussed at paras 13.92–13.107 (withholding of disclosure).

---

39 COPR r15.

Applications relating to medical treatment

8.37 PD 9E provides guidance on applications relating to serious medical treatment. The court's jurisdiction in respect of medical treatment is considered in chapter 4. The practice direction includes details of:

- the types of cases regarded as serious medical treatment;[40]
- a list of cases which *must* always be brought before the court (cases involving withholding or withdrawing artificial nutrition and hydration from a person in a persistent vegetative state or minimally conscious state; cases involving organ or bone marrow donation by a person who lacks capacity to consent; non-therapeutic sterilisation of a person who lacks capacity to consent);[41]
- the allocation of serious medical treatment cases.

8.38 Medical treatment cases largely fall outside the scope of this work because they raise very specific issues that are unlikely to be encountered by the majority of those will have dealings with the Court of Protection. Chapter 23 below, however, summarises the particular issues arising in such cases.

Urgent applications

8.39 There will be some cases which are so urgent that it is not possible to carry out all the steps set out above or to wait for the court to grant permission. The majority, though not all, will be cases involving serious medical treatment. There is provision for urgent cases to be heard without notice, sometimes out of hours, where this is strictly necessary. PD 10B provides guidance as to how to contact the court to set up an urgent hearing (see section 13.58).

---

40 COPR PD 9E paras 3–5.
41 COPR PD 9E para 5.

CHAPTER 9

Permission, issue and service

Permission

9.1　Where permission is required (as to which, see paras 8.8 and 8.9), then within 14 days of the application for permission and supporting documents being filed at the court, the permission form will be issued. The court will then do one of three things:

1) grant the application for permission, in whole or part, or subject to conditions, without a hearing and may give directions;[1]
2) refuse the application for permission without a hearing,[2] in which case the applicant can invoke their right to a reconsideration of the decision (see further paras 19.3–19.6);
3) list the application for permission for a hearing.[3]

9.2　The test for the grant of permission is not set down either in the Mental Capacity Act (MCA) 2005 or in the Court of Protection (COP) Rules 2007 SI No 1744. However, in *NK v VW and others*,[4] Macur J held that in deciding whether to grant permission where such is required, the court must, in particular, have regard to:

a) the applicant's connection with the person to whom the application relates;
b) the reasons for the application;
c) the benefit to the person to whom the application relates or the proposed order or directions; and
d) whether the benefit can be achieved in any other way.

9.3　The court will send the applicant the order granting or refusing permission, together with reasons if permission has been refused.[5] This provision is only really of relevance where permission has been refused without a hearing. If permission has been refused following a hearing, the expectation would be that the reasons would be delivered at that hearing or in the judgment provided after the hearing. See further in relation to judgments, paras 16.49–16.51.

9.4　If a permission hearing is to take place, the court will notify the applicant and such other persons as it thinks fit to be notified of a permission hearing and will send those people the documents filed with the permission form and a form for acknowledging notification.[6] A

1　COPR r55(a).
2　COPR r55(b).
3　COPR r55(c).
4　[2012] COPLR 105.
5　COPR r59.
6　COPR r56.

person who is notified of a permission hearing and wishes to take part in it must file an acknowledgment of service (form COP5) within 21 days,[7] failing which he or she may not be allowed to take part in the hearing without permission of the court.[8] If the application is opposed, then a witness statement must be filed with the form COP5.[9]

9.5   If permission is refused after a hearing, then it is possible to seek to permission to appeal this decision in accordance with the rules for appeals discussed in chapter 21.[10]

9.6   If permission is granted without a hearing, then it would be possible for a respondent to seek reconsideration of the grant of permission by way of an application under rule 89. Such would be an unusual course of events, but might be appropriate if the respondent is possession of evidence that makes it clear that permission was, in effect, granted upon a false basis. It would also be possible for a respondent to seek permission to appeal a decision to grant permission reached after a contested hearing, but this would be a very unusual step.

9.7   In many cases where permission is granted the court will make initial directions. These may include: joinder of P; directions for the appointment of a litigation friend; requiring provision of further evidence; or fixing an attended hearing.[11] See further in this regard, chapter 12.

Disputing the court's jurisdiction

9.8   Disputes as to whether permission should be granted are rare. An – unusual, but important – example of where it is appropriate to contest permission is where a proposed party wishes to apply under COPR r87 for an order that either (a) the Court of Protection (COP) has no jurisdiction to hear an application; or (b) the COP will not exercise its jurisdiction. Such an application is governed by Practice Direction (PD) 12B: it should be made on a COP5 form and be accompanied by witness evidence.[12] One reported example of an application under

---

7   COPR r57(2).
8   COPR r58.
9   COPR r57(6).
10 COPR r60.
11 COPR r85(2).
12 PD 12B paras 2 and 8.

both of these grounds being made (and succeeding, in fact, on both of these grounds in relation to different aspects of the proceedings that the applicant wished to bring) is that of *Re PO*,[13] a cross-border case (discussed further in chapter 29) in which the local authority in the 'foreign' (Scottish) jurisdiction to which the person in question had been moved wished to dispute the jurisdiction of the Court of Protection on the basis that the person was no longer habitually resident in England and Wales.

9.9   It would be possible to make an application under rule 87 even after the grant of permission if this was done without a hearing; in this case, the party wishing to make the application would need also to seek a reconsideration of the order under rule 89 (see chapter 21).

9.10   It would be open to a party to seek to make an application under rule 87 later during the course of proceedings, but the court would wish to see clear evidence as to why the issue was not taken at the outset. An example of when this might be appropriate would be if P was moved abroad during the life of the proceedings. As discussed further in chapter 29, habitual residence (the primary basis upon which the COP has jurisdiction over P's health and welfare) is a question of fact, and can change during the lifetime of proceedings before the COP.[14] In an appropriate case, it might therefore be open to a party to submit that P's habitual residence had changed since the proceedings had begun such that the Court of Protection no longer had jurisdiction over P's welfare.

Issue of the proceedings

9.11   If permission is granted, the application form will be issued by the court. The court will seal the application form and stamp it with the date of issue. This is the date on which the proceedings formally commence.[15] This will be returned to the applicant for the applicant then to serve the proceedings in accordance with the procedure set out below.

13 [2013] EWHC 3932 (COP), [2014] COPLR 62.
14 *Re PO* at para 21.
15 COPR r62.

Service

Overview

9.12 The applicant is responsible for serving anyone named as a respondent or anyone who is to be notified of the proceedings.[16] The applicant must serve the respondents, and those to be notified of the issue of proceedings, within 21 days of the date of the issue of the application. The provisions as to service appear in Part 6 of the COPR, supported by PD 6A, which sets out how service should be effected (for example, by document exchange or electronically). Rule 32 explains the provisions for service on children or protected parties.

9.13 When serving respondents, or persons who are to be notified of an application,[17] the applicant must send each of them a copy of the following documents:

- COP15, in the case of those who are being notified of the issue of the application; respondents do not need to be sent COP15;
- COP5 for the individual to complete (see chapter 12);
- a copy of the issued application form;
- a copy of any documents filed with the application form (for example, the COP1B, COP3, COP4 if the application relates to a deputyship, any witness statements);
- a copy of any orders made by the court;
- notice of acting (if this has not been served) – COP30;
- notice of issue of legal aid certificate (if appropriate).

9.14 The applicant must then file a certificate of service or notification (COP20B).

Service – general

9.15 It should be noted that the court will serve documents in limited circumstances. The court will normally serve:

- an order or judgment of the court;
- an acknowledgement of service or notification; and
- a notice of hearing (other than an application for committal).[18]

---

16 COPR r66.
17 See chapter 8.
18 COPR r30.

9.16   In other cases the person relying on the document is responsible for serving it. For example, the person filing a witness statement with the court will also be responsible for serving it on the parties.

Dispensing with service

9.17   There are certain circumstances under which service can be dispensed with, either upon application to the court or of the court's own motion.[19] It has been held that a decision to dispense with service is not an act done or decision made on behalf of P, such that the principles of the MCA 2005 do not strictly apply to the decision: *Re AB*.[20] In the context of an application to dispense with service in the context of an application for the endorsement of a statutory will, District Judge Batten held that:

> 83. Each case must be dealt with in the light of its own particular facts and the judge will apply the overriding objective in the light of those facts ...

> 84. In my judgment permission to dispense with service or notification of an application altogether should only be made in exceptional circumstances, where there are compelling reasons for doing so. Otherwise the interests of justice will not be served and the court will not be seen to be acting fairly towards all parties.

> 85. The conduct of the Respondent may justify such an order: for example if he has been convicted of an offence of physical or sexual abuse of P, or if P's funds derive from a Criminal Injuries Compensation award where the Respondent was the assailant.

> 86. In matters concerning the Respondent's conduct, the court has to take a decision to dispense with service of the application while only having available evidence from the party seeking the order to dispense. The application is more likely to be successful if supported by objective evidence than unsupported allegations. The court is more likely to be persuaded of the strength of the case if there is independent and reliable corroborative evidence as to the past behaviour of the Respondent, whether in the form of criminal convictions, court orders, CAFCASS, or other reports by professionals, or other similar evidence.

> 87. The court may be willing to make an order to dispense with service of the application where the value of the financial benefit lost to the Respondent by the making of the order is not significant.

19 COPR r38.
20 [2013] EWHC B39 (COP). The judgment strictly has no precedent value, but District Judge Batten was asked to deliver a guideline judgment by the Official Solicitor.

Value should be considered both in absolute terms and relative to the Respondent's means. (A legacy of £10,000 may be of considerable significance to an elderly person on a low income but less important to a person of substantial wealth).

88. The court may also reach the conclusion, usually after enquiries have been made, that the cost to P's estate or to the parties, and the delay caused in concluding the application, of proceeding with service of an individual or class of Respondents (usually where tracing of potential Respondents will be necessary) is disproportionate relative to the value to the Respondents of the benefit they will lose by the proposed final order.

89. These examples are not intended to be exhaustive or to limit the circumstances in which judges may make an order to dispense with service of an application on a Respondent.

90. This judgment should also not be taken to apply to service of an application for a holding will, where there is acute urgency in the face of P's likely imminent death. The cases of *In re Davey* [1981] WLR p164 and In the matter of *R* [2003] WTLR 1051, although decided before the Mental Capacity Act 2005 came into force are of assistance as to service/notification of such applications.

9.18   It is suggested that District Judge Batten's observations apply more widely than to the context of statutory will applications alone, and rightly emphasise the exceptional nature of the decision to prevent an individual (or individuals) from being aware of and from participating in proceedings which may have an impact upon their financial or other interests.

Notifying P

9.19   The applicant is responsible for notifying P of the issue of an application, within 21 days of the issue of the application, unless P has already been made a party.

9.20   If P has been made a party, then COPR r141 provides that P must have a litigation friend and therefore the litigation friend or his or her solicitors will normally accept service on behalf of P (see further in respect of litigation friends, chapter 12).

9.21   If P has not been made a party, then P must be provided with the information personally, in a manner that is appropriate to P's circumstances, for example using simple language or visual aids.[21] P must be given a form COP14, which should explain clearly the matter which

21 COPR r46.

the court has been asked to decide, and a COP5 (acknowledgement of service).[22] Once this has been done, form COP20A must be filed.

9.22   Rule 49 allows an applicant or appellant or anyone directed to effect notification on P to apply to the court for an order dispensing with the requirement to comply with the provisions relating to the notification of P or requiring some other person to comply with those provisions. Moreover, the court can in any case, either on its own initiative or on application, direct that he must not be notified of any matter or document, or provided with any document.[23] The court might dispense with the requirement to notify P if P were in a permanent vegetative or minimally conscious state, or if notification by the applicant is likely to cause significant and disproportionate distress to P.[24]

22 PD 7 para 6.
23 COPR r40(3).
24 PD 7A para 9.

Responding to applications

Introduction

10.1   This chapter addresses the steps that should be taken to respond to an application, whether that application relates to property and affairs or to health and welfare. The same principles apply to both – perhaps the cardinal one being that it is always advisable to consider (where necessary with the benefit of legal advice) as soon as possible precisely what stance to take in relation to an application. The Court of Protection Rules (COPR) 2007 SI No 1744 provide for a number of variations, which will have different consequences for the shape of any proceedings.

Initial steps

10.2   Generally permission is not required prior to making an application to the court about a matter concerning P's property and affairs.[1] Service or notification that an application form has been issued will therefore usually be the first information that a respondent or a person notified will have of proceedings.

10.3   In proceedings relating to health and welfare, a respondent, or person notified of proceedings, may be notified of a permission hearing (discussed in chapter 9). However, it is more likely that the first contact with the proceedings will be the receipt of an issued application form, where permission will already have been granted. It is very important to consider carefully what other orders or directions have been made, as it is possible to seek reconsideration of these orders under the provisions of rule 89 (or, indeed, of the grant of permission itself: see paras 19.3–19.6).

10.4   In both cases:

- A respondent to an application will be served (by the applicant) with a copy of the COP1 as issued by the court as well as a COP5 acknowledgement of service or notification.
- A person notified will be served (by the applicant) with a COP15 notice of proceedings and a COP5.

10.5   Those who are served or notified of proceedings should consider taking appropriate legal advice about their response to the application as soon as possible. The sources of funding for such legal advice are discussed in chapter 6.

---

1   COPR r51(2)(a), although exceptions to this do appear in r52.

10.6   In our experience there can be significant variations in the amount of detail provided with an application. The receipt of the application will, however, offer the respondent an opportunity to consider the issues raised by the application and how he or she may be able to counter them. This is all part of the vital exercise of ensuring the actual issues in the case are identified as quickly and precisely as possible. The receipt of the application may be a useful time to consider not only the evidence that the respondent may be able to provide, but whether there are others in P's life who will be able to provide a helpful perspective as well. See further in this regard paras 10.21–10.23 below.

10.7   A point to which we return in the subsequent chapters but which needs emphasising here, however, is that it is vital that the matters are not set in stone at the outset. In other words, those served with the application as much as the person or body bringing the application keeps matters under review both as more evidence is gathered and (as often happens) P's circumstances themselves change during the currency of the proceedings.

Consenting to an application

10.8   If a person notified, or a respondent, considers that the application is one which is reasonable and that they support, then they can indicate this simply by completing and filing the COP5 to the effect that they agree with the application proposed. This response must be filed the court within 21 days of service.[2]

10.9   There is no obligation on the part of a person notified or a respondent to make any response to the application, but a failure to do so will not prevent the making of the order that is sought. Respondents or those notified who do not respond will still be bound be the decision of the court as if they had been a party.[3]

10.10   A person who has been notified will not become a party to the proceedings simply by filing a COP5 form consenting to the application. However, the authors would suggest that if a person notified has taken legal advice before reaching the conclusion that they wish to consent to the application as proposed, it would be appropriate to seek a direction that they be joined as a party to the proceedings only

---

2 COPR r72.
3 COPR r 74(2).

for purposes of seeking to recover their costs.[4] This is likely only to be of relevance in property and affairs case where the costs are in principle recoverable from the estate of P.[5]

10.11   Finally, it should perhaps be noted that, by contrast with proceedings in some other courts, there is no such category as 'interested party' in proceedings before the Court of Protection. A person (or body) is either a party or is not. Form DLA (Deprivation of Liberty Application Form) refers at section 2 to 'other interested parties', but it is suggested that this is an anomaly.

Becoming a party

10.12   A person who has been served as a respondent will automatically become a party to proceedings by filing a COP5 form.[6]

10.13   If a respondent wishes to oppose the application or to propose an alterative order, then the acknowledgement of service should be accompanied by a witness statement which contains any evidence upon which the respondent intends to rely.[7] In practice, however, it is not always appropriate or indeed possible to serve a witness statement along with COP5. The respondent may not have access to the full application papers, or to documents that would support his or her position. In these circumstances, directions should be sought for disclosure of the full application papers as well as for the provision of any information that the respondent requires, for example (for instance, in a financial case) bank statements or other financial information.

10.14   On receipt of a completed COP5 indicating that there is opposition to the order sought, the court will typically make a directions order for provision of information to all parties as well as the filing of any evidence on which each party wishes to rely, before any hearing is listed.

10.15   On receiving a completed COP5, and any witness statement, the court will serve this on the applicant. It is good practice, however, to serve the applicant and all other parties directly, as this will save time.

4 COPR r166.
5 COPR r156; see further chapter 17.
6 COPR r73(1)(b).
7 COPR r52(5).

10.16   If a person who is notified wishes to oppose the application, or to propose an alternative order, he must apply to be joined as a party to proceedings. The person does this by indicating his or her wish to be joined as a party on the COP5 and filing this response with the court within the appropriate timescale. The COP5 must set out the person's reasons for wishing to be a party and should be accompanied by a witness statement setting out his or her interest in the proceedings. The court will decide whether or not to join that person as a party.[8] The relevant test for whether a person should be joined as a party is whether the court considers it desirable for the purpose of deciding the application.[9]

10.17   A person who subsequently becomes aware of an application may apply to become a party. To do so, they must demonstrate 'sufficient interest' in the proceedings.[10] That interest must be a sufficient interest in the proceedings themselves – ie 'the ascertainment of the incapacitated person's best interests' – as opposed to any commercial (or other interest) of the applicant's own.[11] This approach was approved by the President in *Re G*.[12]

10.18   A person who wishes to be joined as a party must file an application notice (COP9) and a statement explaining his or her interest in the proceedings and – if he intends to ask the court to make an order that is different to the order sought by the applicant – the evidence on which he relies.[13] The person seeking to join should send enough copies of the application for all the parties and the court will serve it.[14] Again, the test will be whether it is desirable to join the person to the proceedings for the purpose of dealing with the application.[15]

8   COPR r72(8).
9   COPR r73(2).
10 COPR r75(1).
11 *Re SK* [2012] EWHC 1990 (COP), [2012] COPLR 712 at paras 41–43 per Bodey J (refusing application by defendant to personal injury proceedings brought by P to be joined to Court of Protection proceedings concerning P).
12 *Re G, London Borough of Redbridge v G (by her litigation friend the Official Solicitor), C and F* [2014] EWHC 1361 (COP).
13 COPR r75(3).
14 COPR r75(4).
15 COPR r73(2).

Contesting an application

10.19   Careful consideration should be given to the available evidence when considering whether to contest an application, or to suggest an alternative order.

10.20   The grounds on which an application may be contested will depend upon the facts of the case and the evidence available. The approaches to be taken may differ between property and affairs cases on the one hand, and health and welfare cases on the other.

10.21   In property and affairs cases, if there is a dispute, it is often likely to be between family members, rather than family members and a statutory body. In such cases – and especially given that the general rule as to costs is that the costs (of all parties) will be payable out of P's estate[16] – the temptation must be resisted for respondents to oppose applications on the basis of points that do not relate to the issues in the case and which will serve no purpose but to increase the cost to P. The court will primarily be concerned with P's present circumstances, and the resources of the court do not exist to allow the ventilation of unrelated allegations of the nature that can, sadly, often arise in the case of family disputes.

10.22   In welfare cases, costs will also be an issue – as the costs of any contested hearings will (most likely) be met out of the resources of the parties themselves.[17] This does not mean that genuinely contested applications should not be fully explored and prepared. Clearly, if after careful investigations and taking material from potential witnesses the adviser reaches the view that contesting an application will not succeed, then the adviser must give their client the appropriate advice. However, in welfare cases, families seeking to oppose the removal of P – or to seek P's return – must be given the opportunity fully to put their case to the court or their own rights under articles 8 (right to respect for private and family life) and indeed 6 (right to a fair trial) of the European Convention on Human Rights (ECHR) may be compromised. In deciding whether the case is one that should be contested, it is in the authors' experience often useful to look outside the areas of dispute between the applicant, often a statutory body, and the respondent(s), often family member(s) caring for P. In such a case, the following questions can usefully be considered at this very early stage:

---

16   COPR r156; see also chapter 17.
17   COPR r157; see also chapter 17.

- What were the care arrangements for P before the dispute arose? Has anything changed (for example, was additional support given by another carer who has died or moved away)?
- Has there been any change in the amount of support provided to P by the relevant statutory bodies?
- Who are the other important individuals in P's life apart from the respondent and members of the relevant statutory body? Can any of them provide evidence about positive aspects of P's care (past or current)? What, if anything, can they say about P's likes and dislikes and what is important to P?
- If the relationship between the respondent and the statutory body is currently poor, has this always been the case? Is the respondent in contact with any professionals with whom he or she has worked well in the past?
- Is evidence needed about any cultural issues or expectations? Who might be able to provide such evidence?
- Are there likely to be significant disputes of fact? If so, what evidence needs to be gathered to corroborate the respondent's case?
- Is it likely that expert evidence may be needed? It may not be possible on receipt of an application to make this judgment. However, once the need for an expert is identified by any party, they would be well advised to make enquiries as soon as possible about the costs and availability of suitable experts. This subject is discussed in detail in chapter 13.

10.23   In both cases, the relevance of the information put before the court both in the application and in any potential response should always be considered.

10.24   The authors further suggest that parties should maintain a flexible approach, focused on P's best interests and avoid entrenched positions as far as possible. This allows alternative options to be explored by way of mediation (see chapter 20), and may help to avoid incurring the expense of attended court hearing(s).

10.25   Advisers should, however, be alert to the danger of attempting to persuade parties to take an approach that fundamentally they do not agree with. In a welfare case, for instance, a family carer recently served with an application seeking a draconian step in relation to P should of course be given the opportunity to consider the benefits of consenting at an early stage. However, advisers will not at that stage have gathered all the available evidence that might point away from the application. It is important that advisers are scrupulous in following their client's instructions and gathering evidence that may support their position. In most cases, other than the most urgent, there will be time to undertake this task, which need not involve an adversarial stance while investigations are carrying on.

10.26   If the parties are able to reach a negotiated way forward that represents a compromise between the position advocated by the applicant and that desired by the respondent(s), the court should be notified and a consent order submitted, with each party or their legal representative confirming their consent to the order as agreed: see further in this regard para 11.43.

10.27   If the parties cannot agree a negotiated way forward, the court will proceed to determine how best to put itself in a position to reach a conclusion. This is discussed in chapter 11.

Being removed as a party

10.28   Finally, it is convenient to deal here with the position of a person (or body) who wishes to be *removed* as a party. They must apply using form COP9.[18] There is no guidance in either the COPR or the accompanying practice directions as to the test that the court will apply (nor are there any reported decisions on the point), but logic suggests that the application will be granted only if the court considers that the continued participation of the person as a party is no longer desirable for the purpose of dealing with the application. As a halfway house, and in line with the overriding objective in COPR r3, courts will sometimes allow parties to cease to play any active steps for certain stages in the proceedings where their contribution will not be required at all points (or will provide that the party in question only need file documentation or attend directions hearings 'if so advised').

18 COPR r76; see also paras 11.19ff.

CHAPTER 11

Preparing for and appearing at directions hearings and interim hearings

Introduction

11.1   In almost all disputed applications there will be at least one, and often several, hearings before a final decision is made. The purpose of such hearings will be:

- to set down the steps necessary for the determination of the central issues in the case; and/or
- to make such interim declarations and decisions under the provisions of Mental Capacity Act (MCA) 2005 s48[1] as are necessary to secure P's interests pending the final determination of those central issues.

11.2   Strictly, 'directions hearings' are only hearings listed for the first purpose, and hearings listed for the second purpose should be called 'interim hearings'. In practice, though, both types are regularly called directions hearings (or sometimes, especially after the first hearing, review hearings). The distinction is maintained in this chapter, though, so as to draw out the particular considerations relating to the two different purposes set out above.

11.3   This chapter addresses both proceedings relating to health and welfare and proceedings relating to property and affairs alike. This is because interim hearings take an essentially identical form regardless of the underlying nature of the proceedings.

11.4   This chapter addresses the steps necessary to prepare for interim hearings. It also sets out practical tips as to how effectively to maximise the efficiency of interim hearings, which can frequently be as important for what happens outside court as for what happens before the judge.

11.5   As a final preliminary point, it is important to note that in very many applications, especially in the health and welfare field, the distinction between the two types of hearing identified above collapses altogether and the court will be considering both case management and interim relief at the same hearing. Particularly in health and welfare proceedings, decisions and declarations will be made at directions and interim hearings which will be of very great day-to-day significance over an extended period of time, for instance by circumscribing contact as between P and P's family or authorising on an interim basis a deprivation of P's liberty.[2] In consequence, it is prudent always to prepare for all but the most limited of directions and

---

1   See para 11.8 below.
2   The particular factors that arise upon applications under MCA 2005 s21A relating to deprivation of liberty are considered further in chapter 22 below.

interim hearings upon the basis that they are, in essence, 'mini-final' hearings.

The jurisdiction of the court to make interim orders and give directions

11.6 Where an application has been made, the court has jurisdiction to exercise its powers on an interim basis to make orders and give directions where:

- there is reason to believe that P lacks capacity in relation to the matter;
- the matter is one to which its powers under the MCA 2005 extend; and
- it is in P's best interests to make the order, or give the directions, without delay.[3]

11.7 The first of these requirements was interpreted in *Re F*[4] as requiring no more than that there be sufficient evidence to justify a reasonable belief that P may lack capacity, or evidence which gives good cause for concern or raises a real possibility that P may lack capacity. This means, therefore, that the court does not need to make a decision as to whether P *in fact* lacks capacity in the material regard (which would often be impossible at the outset of the proceedings). The decision in *Re F* also makes it clear that the threshold that must be crossed is lower than that required (for instance) for the making of a final declaration under MCA 2005 s15.

11.8 While MCA 2005 s48 only talks of 'orders' and 'directions', this includes both decisions and declarations. In other words, assuming that the threshold is crossed, the court can – and will very often – make interim decisions and declarations to 'hold the ring' pending the final determination of the application before it. To emphasise the limited basis upon which they are made, interim declarations are very regularly phrased using wording such as: 'Pursuant to the provisions of section 48 of the Mental Capacity Act, in the interim and on the evidence currently before the Court it is declared that: ...'. (For precedent orders, see appendix C below.)

---

3 MCA 2005 s48(a)–(c).
4 [2009] EWHC B30 (COP), [2009] COPLR Con Vol 390, at para 36 per HHJ Marshall QC.

Case management

The powers of the court

11.9   Part 2 of the Court of Protection Rules (COPR) 2007 SI No 1744 (entitled 'The overriding objective') identifies two concurrent duties. The first is the duty of the parties under COPR r4 to help the court achieve the overriding objective of dealing with a case justly having regard to the principles contained in the MCA 2005. The second is the duty of the court under COPR r5 to manage cases.

11.10   The duty of the court under COPR r5 actively to manage cases includes:

- encouraging the parties to co-operate with each other in the conduct of the proceedings;
- identifying at an early stage the issues and who should be a party to the proceedings;
- deciding promptly which issues need a full investigation and hearing and which do not, and the procedure to be followed in the case;
- deciding the order in which issues are to be resolved;
- encouraging the parties to use an alternative dispute resolution procedure if the court considers that appropriate;
- fixing timetables or otherwise controlling the progress of the case;
- considering whether the likely benefits of taking a particular step justify the cost of taking it;
- dealing with as many aspects of the case as the court can on the same occasion;
- dealing with the case without the parties needing to attend at court;
- making use of technology; and
- giving directions to ensure that the case proceeds quickly and efficiently.

11.11   To enable it to further the overriding objective, the court is given general powers of case management by COPR r25, which details a wide-ranging suite of tools that judges can deploy, tools which (unsurprisingly) match closely the obligations imposed by rule 4. Judges are given added flexibility by COPR r26, which provides that, in addition to its general powers and those listed in COPR r25, the court may dispense with the requirement of any rule.

11.12 COPR r85 relates specifically to the making of directions by the court. In material part, it provides that:

85(1) The court may–
    (a) give directions in writing; or
    (b) get a date for a directions hearing; and
    (c) do anything else that may be set out in a practice direction.
(2) When giving directions, the court may do any of the following–
    (a) require a report under section 49 of the Act and give directions as to any such report;
    (b) give directions as to any requirements contained in these Rules or a practice direction for the giving of notification to any person or for that person to do anything in response to a notification;
    (c) if the court considers that P should be a party to the proceedings, give directions joining him as a party;
    (d) if P is joined as a party to proceedings, give directions as to the appointment of a litigation friend;
    (e) if the court considers that any other person or persons should be a party to the proceedings, give directions joining them as a party;
    (f) if the court considers that any party to the proceedings should not be a party, give directions for that person's removal as a party;
    (g) give directions for the management of the case and set a timetable for the steps to be taken between the giving of directions and the hearing;
    (h) subject to rule 86,[5] give directions as to the type of judge who is to hear the case;
    (i) give directions as to whether the proceedings or any part of them are to be heard in public, or as to whether any particular person should be permitted to attend the hearing, or as to whether any publication of the proceedings is to be permitted;
    (j) give directions as to the disclosure of documents, service of witness statements and any expert evidence;
    (k) give directions as to the attendance of witnesses and as to whether, and the extent to which, cross-examination will be permitted at any hearing; and
    (l) give such other directions as the court thinks fit.
(3) The court may give directions at any time–
    (a) on its own initiative; or
    (b) on the application of a party.

---

5 Which (amplified by Practice Direction (PD) 12A) sets out that certain categories of case must be heard by certain types of judge.

11.13   By a rule-change introduced with effect from 12 December 2011,[6] authorised officers of the court may exercise certain case management powers in (broadly) non-contentious applications relating to property and affairs. Authorised court officers may not conduct a hearing, and must refer to a judge any application or any question arising in any application which is contentious or which, in the opinion of the officer:

a) is complex;

b) requires a hearing; or

c) for any other reason ought to be considered by a judge.[7]

As this chapter is for the most part concerned with directions hearings, the powers of authorised officers are not addressed further here.

11.14   It can be seen that the powers of the court at a directions hearing are very wide. They extend as far as determining a case summarily upon its own motion, but that jurisdiction 'must be exercised appropriately and with a modicum of restraint': *KD and LD v Havering LBC*,[8] in which an appeal was allowed where the district judge brought proceedings to an end summarily before a best interests report (which the judge had previously directed be prepared) was filed.

Case management without a hearing

11.15   It is important to highlight that, in the majority of cases, judges will seek to make as many of the initial directions as possible upon consideration of the papers (and, where the grant of permission is required, often at the same time as granting permission).[9] Judges in the Court of Protection have a suite of template orders that they use, and precedent directions orders applying to the most common types of applications are included at appendix C below.

11.16   Examples of standard directions that are regularly made without a hearing at the first consideration by a judge of an application include:

---

6 Adding a new rule 7A to the COPR.

7 PD 3A para 2.2.

8 [2009] COPLR Con Vol 770 at para 28 per HHJ Horowitz QC.

9 The express power to do so is contained in COPR r85(1)(a).

- in health and welfare cases and in certain categories of property and affairs cases: adding P as a party and, where possible, appointing a litigation friend to act on behalf of P;[10]
- in certain categories of cases: allocation to a specific type of judge;
- identifying and joining relevant individuals/bodies as respondents to the application; and
- where appropriate, and usually at the specific request of the applicant: transferring further consideration of the case to one of the regional courts.

11.17 Those affected by orders made without a hearing have an automatic right to seek review of such orders by virtue of COPR r89 (see paras 19.3–19.6), but such review will inevitably add delay and expense. So as to avoid this, it is therefore important when making an application to ensure that in its face clear on the face either:

a) any of the 'standard' directions are inapplicable; or
b) any unusual directions are required at the outset.

Case management directions hearings

11.18 In most contested applications, at least one hearing will be convened at the instigation of the court to set directions going beyond the preliminary ones identified above. The hearing will usually be listed before the level of judge allocated to hear the final hearing: in other words, if the final hearing will be before a High Court judge, then directions hearings will take place before a High Court judge. If no specific allocation has been made by way of the preliminary directions outlined above, the directions hearings will take place before a district judge.

Directions sought during proceedings

11.19 In addition to directions hearings fixed by the court, directions hearings can also be listed in response to an application made by a party while the proceedings are on foot. The procedure for making an application within proceedings is set out in COPR Part 10, as well as in PD 10A. Part 10 of the rules also covers the position in respect of urgent applications (as to which, see further para 11.60 below). In short, when making an application, it is necessary to file an application

10 The question of litigation friends is addressed further at chapter 12 below.

notice (on a form COP9)[11] setting out the order or direction the applicant seeks and the grounds on which it is sought.[12] Where an unusually long or complex order is sought, an electronic copy should be provided; PD10 provides that this should be done on a disk[13] but increasingly the practice is for email to be used. The applicant should also file the evidence upon which they rely unless it is already before the court.[14] The court has the power to dispense with the need to file an application notice (for instance, by treating a letter sent during the currency of proceedings as if it were an application).[15]

11.20   A fee for issuing COP9 applications is to be introduced during 2014 (see appendix G below), although there will be some exemptions. Such fees will be disbursements for the purpose of any publicly funded party's legal aid certificate. Other litigants are unlikely to be able to recover the fees unless there is good reason for the court to depart from the general rule in welfare cases that the parties will bear their own costs.[16]

11.21   As a general rule, it is necessary for the applicant to serve a copy of the application notice on anyone named as a respondent in the application notice, every party to the proceedings and on any other person directed by the court, as soon as practicable and in any event within 21 days of service.[17] The application notice must be accompanied by a copy of the evidence filed in support,[18] and the applicant must file a COP20 certificate of service within 7 days of the date on which documents were served;[19] where a person has already been served with evidence, the applicant does not need to file a further copy of such evidence but should instead give notice of the evidence upon which they intend to rely.[20] The applicant can dispense with service only where there is exceptional urgency, where the overriding objective is best served by so doing, by consent of all the parties, with the permission of the court, or where a rule or other practice

---

11   COPR r78(1).
12   COPR r79. COPR r79(c) refers to information being required by a practice direction; PD 10A provides that certain basic information (for instance, the case number) is required, but does not materially add to the requirements.
13   PD 10A para 4.
14   COPR r78(2).
15   COPR r78(5).
16   COPR r157; also see chapter 19.
17   COPR r80(1).
18   COPR r80(2).
19   COPR r80(3).
20   COPR r80(4).

direction permits (the material practice direction here being PD 10B, discussed further at para 11.60 below).[21] Where the applicant has dispensed with service, the court can nonetheless still direct that service should be effected and specify who should be served with or notified of the application.[22]

11.22 Wherever possible, an application should be made so as that it can be considered at a hearing which is already listed.[23] If a hearing date has already been fixed and a party wishes to make an application at that hearing but does not have sufficient time in which to file an application notice, PD 10A provides that the applicant should inform the court (in writing if possible) and, if possible, the other parties as soon as they can of the nature of the application and the reason for it, and should then make the application orally at the hearing.[24]

11.23 Parties should also be aware of the power under COPR r85(4) to vary the time specified for a person to 'do any act' either by the rules or the practice directions or the court, by the written agreement of the parties. This cannot be used to vary the date of a final hearing or to vary the period within which a final hearing can take place. This will always require an application to the court.[25] Nor can it be used if the outcome of the variation would require variation of the date of the final hearing or the period in which the final hearing takes place.[26] However if – for example – it becomes clear that the timetable set by the court for the filing of evidence is unlikely to be me, and the parties agreed to vary it, a consent order minuting that agreement pursuant to COPR r85(4) could be filed at court, thus avoiding the need for an application.

Directions hearings: general provisions

11.24 However they have been listed, the general rule is that directions hearings take place in private (the exception is in the case of serious medical treatment cases, discussed in chapter 23).[27] They will usually be listed for between 30 minutes and one hour, and it is now very common for a direction to be made that parties are to attend one hour before for purposes of discussions. As set out further below,

21 PD 10A para 9.
22 PD 10A para 11.
23 PD 10A para 15.
24 PD 10A para 16.
25 COPR r85(5).
26 COPR r85(6).
27 See further chapter 14 below.

such discussions can be immensely productive, and every effort should be made to attend in good time for such discussions.

11.25   Directions hearings can also take place by telephone or video-link.[28] This can save time and expense in terms of travel, but frequently at the cost of additional expense before and after the hearing in terms of seeking to agree an order to put to the judge or to agree the terms of an order reflecting the directions made by the judge at the hearing. In anything other than a straightforward directions hearing, therefore, careful consideration needs to be given (both by the representatives and the court) to whether the cause of effective case management is not better served by personal attendance.

Practice Direction 13B

11.26   Whenever a hearing is listed for more than an hour before a district or circuit judge, and whenever it is listed before the President of the Family Division, the Chancellor or a High Court, PD 13B will apply. It applies to directions hearings, interim hearings and also final hearings, with the exception of any urgent application if and to the extent that it is impractical to comply with it. Even where the practice direction does not strictly apply (for instance, in relation to a 30-minute directions hearing before a district judge), the principles that it sets down should still be adhered to where possible so as to maximise the effectiveness of the hearing.

11.27   Where PD 13B does apply, paragraph 12 of the practice direction makes clear the penalty for failure to comply with any part of it may result in the judge removing the case from the list or moving it further back in the list, as well as adverse costs orders.

11.28   For present purposes, the two most important aspects of PD 13B are those relating to the preparation of the bundle, and the preparation of the so-called preliminary documents to accompany the bundle. Each of these is discussed in turn below.

Bundles

11.29   The general rule is that the party which is the applicant at the hearing (or the first applicant if there is more than one application) has the responsibility for producing the bundle for the use of the court

---

28   COPR r25(2)(d). See also PD 10A paras 18–21 in respect of applications made within proceedings.

at that hearing.[29] However, if that person is a litigant in person, then subject to any direction by the court, the responsibility falls upon the first listed respondent who is not a litigant in person or P.[30] If the first named respondent is P and he or she is represented by the Official Solicitor, the responsibility for preparing the bundle will fall to the next named respondent who is represented.[31] It is suggested that the same should apply if a litigation friend other than the Official Solicitor has been appointed to act on P's behalf.

11.30   If possible, the contents of the bundle must be agreed by all parties.[32] This can cause difficulties where one or more of the parties is a litigant in person (especially if they do not have access to a computer for purposes of reviewing and commenting upon a draft index). In such cases, while reasonable steps should be taken to try to agree the index with the litigant in person, a decision will need to be taken as to a cut-off point after which the process of agreement should be completed by the represented parties. PD 13B provides a timetable for the process of preparing and lodging the bundle, thus:

- The party preparing the bundle must (whether or not it has been agreed) provide a paginated index and, where practicable, paginated copies of material additional to that provided with the original application, to all other parties not less than five working days before the hearing.[33] It should be noted that this does not mean that a new, complete, bundle be supplied to each party in advance of a hearing, but experience has taught that it is much better for paginated copies of additional material to be supplied rather than relying upon parties to paginate their additional documents themselves. In such cases, it is almost invariably the case that at least one of the parties will end up operating from a differently paginated bundle at the hearing, with consequential delays and judicial frustration.

- Where counsel is to be instructed at any hearing, then if the bundle is not already in counsel's possession, the bundle must be provided to counsel by the person instructing that counsel not less than four working days before the hearing.[34]

29 PD 13B para 3.1.
30 PD 13B para 3.1.
31 PD 13B para 3.1.
32 PD 13B para 3.1.
33 PD 13B para 6.1.
34 PD 13B para 6.2.

- The bundle (with the exception of the preliminary documents if they are not then available) must be lodged with the court not less than three working days prior to the hearing, unless some other time has been specified by the judge.[35] Specific provisions are set out as to the appropriate office for lodging the bundle dependent on where the case is to be heard. It is always strongly advisable to confirm by telephone the day before the hearing with the relevant office whether the bundle has been received,[36] as it is sadly very common for bundles to go astray in the system.

11.31   Bundles should contain copies of all documents relevant to the hearing in chronological order, indexed and divided into separate sections.[37] They should also be paginated, either within the sections or separately – it is much better to paginate within sections because this allows for easier updating of the bundle. The sections required are as follows:

1) preliminary documents (discussed at para 11.34 below);
2) case management documents required by any other practice direction (in practice, at present, there are no such documents);
3) applications and orders including all Court of Protection forms filed with the application;
4) any registered, enduring or lasting power of attorney;
5) any urgent or standard authorisation given under MCA 2005 Sch A1 (ie authorising a deprivation of P's liberty in a hospital or care home);
6) statements and affidavits (which must state on the top right-hand corner of the front page the date when it was signed or sworn[38]);
7) care plans (where appropriate[39]);
8) experts' reports and other reports;[40]
9) other documents, divided into further sections as may be appropriate.

11.32   Bundles should be contained in one or more A4-size ring-binders or lever-arch files (each lever-arch file being limited to 350 pages), clearly marked on the front and the spine with the title and the number of the case, the court where the case has been listed, the hearing date

---

35   PD 13B para 6.3.
36   Useful telephone numbers are given in appendix F below.
37   PD 13B para 4.1.
38   See further para 13.13 onwards.
39   See further para 13.18 and appendix E.
40   See further para 13.50 onwards.

and time, (if known) the name of the judge hearing the case, and where there is more than one ring-binder or lever-arch file, a distinguishing letter or number and confirmation of the total number of binders or files (eg '1 of 3' etc).[41] It is *not* advisable to prepare even short bundles using treasury tags, because it makes it very difficult for the parties and the judge to take out or insert documents.

11.33   Perhaps the key principle to bear in mind in relation to the preparation of bundles is that they should contain those documents relevant to the specific hearing in question, but should not contain more than those documents. Especially where a matter has been ongoing for a considerable period of time, the documents generated in the proceedings can start to run to a (significant) number of lever-arch files: it may very well not be necessary for all of the documents in all of the files to be before the court on each occasion, and having too many before the court will slow the process down.

Preliminary documents and position statements

11.34   For directions and interim hearings to which PD 13B applies, each party (ie not just the applicant) *must* prepare a document (or documents) which sets out – either within the document(s) or by cross-reference to another document that will be in the bundle before the court:

- a case summary;
- a chronology of relevant events;
- the issues for determination at the hearing;
- an outline of the likely factual and legal issues at the trial of the case;
- the relief sought at the hearing; and
- a list of essential reading.[42]

11.35   In practice, this information is most usually set out in a 'position statement' (a term which does not appear in PD 13B, but which is common currency before the court and will be used here). Position statements are vital documents, and should be prepared even if PD 13B does not strictly apply.

11.36   Directions regularly provide that position statements should be limited, often to no more than a page. Especially in the case of a position statement prepared on behalf of the applicant at a hearing,

---

41 PD 13B paras 5.1–5.2.
42 PD 13B para 4.2.

it can, though, frequently be difficult properly to encapsulate the necessary information in so short a space. If the position statement runs to more than two or three pages, a clear introduction should be given which sets out a route map so that the judge can identify clearly where the necessary information will be found in the statement. A sample position statement is to be found at appendix D below.

11.37   PD 13B goes on to provide that 'where appropriate', the preliminary documents for a directions or interim hearing should include:

- a description of relevant family members and other persons who may be affected by or interested in the relief sought;
- a particularised account of the issues in the case;
- the legal propositions relied on, and in particular whether it is asserted that any issue is not governed by the MCA 2005;
- any directions sought concerning the identification and determination of the facts that are agreed, the facts the court will be invited to find and the factors it will be invited to take into account based on such agreed facts or findings of facts;
- any directions sought concerning the alternatives the court will be invited to consider in determining what is in P's best interests;
- any directions sought relating to expert evidence;
- any other directions sought; and
- a skeleton argument.[43]

11.38   These requirements stem from the judgment of Charles J in *LBL v PB and P*,[44] in which the judge made clear that the direction of preparation of position statements and skeleton arguments 'at an appropriate stage' containing this information will be necessary in most welfare cases.[45] The *LBL* case raised complex questions as to the scope of the jurisdiction of the Court of Protection, and the directions that were made in it therefore were arguably more extensive than will be required in many cases. Nonetheless, where PD 13B applies, it is incumbent upon the person preparing the preliminary document to consider whether it is appropriate to include each of the types of information set out above.

11.39   In almost all cases, and whether or not PD 13B strictly applies, it is advisable for the position statement to be accompanied by a draft of the directions that the court will be asked to make. This will be important not just so that the court can see precisely what is being

---

43 PD 13B para 4.3.
44 [2011] EWHC 502 (COP), [2011] COPLR Con Vol 166.
45 Para 46.

asked of it, but also so that the other parties can have sight in advance of the draft of the directions and – potentially – so that agreement can be reached upon the basis of one of the drafts.

11.40   Whenever a directions hearing has been listed, the directions will usually provide a specific point by which the preliminary documents should be filed (whether by reference to a specific date or the period before the hearing). It is always advisable, wherever possible, for the preliminary documents to be served upon the other parties in advance of this deadline so that the process of negotiation can begin quickly.

11.41   Where PD 13B applies, the preliminary documents (and any documents referred to in them which are not already in the bundle) must be lodged with the court no later than 11 am on the day before the hearing.[46] PD 13B provides that they should also be sent by email to the judge's clerk where the hearing is before a High Court judge and the judge's name is known;[47] most of the courts in which directions hearings are heard now also have dedicated email addresses for this purpose.[48] It is always better to err on the side of caution as regards lodging preliminary documents and to seek to ensure (for instance) that they have been sent both by fax and by email. Even where PD 13B does not apply, it is in any event *strongly* advisable that care is taken to make sure that the documents are with the court by 11 am the day before.

11.42   Questions of publicity, privacy and confidentiality are addressed further in chapter 15, but it should be noted that some judges have indicated that they are frustrated by the use of initials in position statements. In *J Council v GU and others*,[49] for instance, Mostyn J indicated that he considered that (as in proceedings before the Family Division) while the proceedings may be in private, all court documents should bear the parties' actual names.[50] Practice in this regard differs, but there is a great deal to be said for the use of parties' actual names; if they are to be used, however, proper precautions will need to be taken to ensure the security of the documents in which they are used. For instance, if a position statement is to be sent by email, it is advisable that it is password-protected.

---

46   PD 13B para 6.4.
47   PD 13B para 6.4.
48   Useful addresses are given in appendix F below.
49   [2012] EWHC 3531 (COP), [2013] COPLR 83.
50   Para 22.

Making effective use of court time

Before the directions hearing

11.43   In the run-up to a directions hearing, it is very sensible to seek to agree as many of the directions as possible or, at least, as many of the areas of agreement as possible. If complete agreement is reached, then a consent order should be submitted for endorsement. If PD 13B applies, then such a consent order *must* be submitted 'immediately', with an accompanying letter (jointly drafted if possible) outlining a short background summary of the case, the written details of each party who consents, and enough information to allow the court to decide whether to take the case out of the list and whether to make the proposed order.[51] The court should also be notified by telephone. PD 13B also envisages the situation where not all parties consent, because an order can still be submitted together with details of the steps taken to obtain that party's consent and, where known, an explanation of why that consent has not been given.[52] The likelihood of the court endorsing an order in such circumstances will depend greatly on whether: a) it has not been possible to contact the person to obtain their consent (for instance, because they are a litigant in person who has not given the proper contact details); or b) the person is actively objecting to all or part of the order. If the directions hearing is not going to be effective for any other reason, PD 13B (where it applies) mandates the same notification procedure, by telephone and letter. It is suggested that it is sensible to follow as much of PD 13B as is possible whether or not it strictly applies.

The day of the hearing

11.44   If the hearing is to take place in person, then (as noted above at para 11.24), it will often be the case that the parties are directed to attend one hour beforehand for discussions. It is in any event very sensible to try to agree with the other parties to attend (at least) one hour before. Depending on how busy their list is, judges are usually happy to give parties additional time to discuss matters, especially if this means that it is more likely that a consent order can be submitted for endorsement, but it is much better to start the discussion process sooner rather than later.

51   PD 13B para 11.
52   PD 13B para 11.

11.45   Finding suitable rooms for discussions at court can often be difficult, especially as it will usually be the case that more than one will be needed so that instructions can be taken in private away from the negotiations. This is another good reason to be at court earlier rather than later, as this will maximise the chances of obtaining suitable numbers of conference rooms.

11.46   Experience suggests that the most effective use of time before a directions hearing will be made if:

- one party's representative (often that instructed by the Official Solicitor if the Official Solicitor is acting on behalf of P) takes the lead in setting the agenda by identifying areas of agreement and disagreement;
- one party's representative takes the lead in taking a note of the order as it evolves. Some judges are in a position (and happy) to receive drafts of orders by email directly and/or it may be possible to persuade the court office to print off copies of the draft orders generated as a result of discussions. If it is possible for one of the parties' representatives to bring a laptop with internet access, therefore, it may well be possible for a draft order to be produced during the course of discussions and for it then to be given to the judge in type-written form. If this is not possible, then the choice of representative is likely to be dictated by the individual with the best handwriting;
- areas where agreement will not be reached are parked quickly, with an agreement to raise them before the judge;
- arrangements have been made in advance to make sure that, where information may be needed for (for instance) a social worker and that social worker cannot be at court, that social worker will be easily contactable during the period before the hearing so that information can be provided quickly;
- where interim relief is being negotiated (for instance, as to contact restrictions or the interim management of P's property and affairs: see further paras 11.53ff below), a clear distinction is drawn between discussions as to the progression of the case and negotiations as to such relief and sufficient time is allocated to both. In many cases, what (say) the family members will be most concerned about will be about the interim relief, whereas what will actually be most important for the speedy resolution of the application as a whole will be negotiations as to case management orders. If all parties are represented by solicitors and counsel, it can sometimes be possible for both sets of negotiations to be tak-

ing place simultaneously, but in such circumstances it is important that all those involved in one set of negotiations are clear as to what the other part of the legal team will be doing.

11.47   In many cases, especially those brought by public bodies concerning P's health and welfare, it is a productive use of staff resources for the relevant professionals to attend (at least the first) directions hearing. This is for two reasons: 1) because it will allow instructions to be received rapidly from the professionals involved; and 2) because of the importance of the interim declarations and decisions that are likely to be made at that hearing 'holding the ring' pending the final determination by the court of the application. Further, where (as is often the case) the underlying issues involve those of trust as between family members and the relevant public authorities, having the opportunity for the professionals to meet with the family members outside court can provide a surprisingly productive forum for discussions: if nothing else, knowing that a judge will be scrutinising whatever agreements are reached or reaching (interim) decisions upon any areas of disagreement serves very usefully to focus the minds of those attending.

The hearing

11.48   Directions hearings can take many forms, but in all cases the judge will want assistance in identifying what the key issues are in the case, and how the directions sought will bring about the speedy and proportionate determination of those issues. Especially before district judges, directions hearings can be relatively informal affairs.

11.49   It is unusual for evidence formally to be given in a directions hearing (as to the requirements in this regard, see para 13.13), but it is not uncommon for a judge to want to hear information directly from those with possession of it rather than through a legal representative. This is another reason why it makes sense in cases involving social services that the relevant social worker for the individual in question attends court.

After the hearing: the order

11.50   It is now very common for the judge to ask the representative for one of the parties (usually either the applicant, if legally represented, or the party represented by the Official Solicitor if the Official Solicitor is acting as litigation friend) to submit an order to the court reflecting the directions made during the hearing. Some judges will in essence dictate the order down to the last detail, such that the task of drawing together the order for submission is relatively straightforward. Some judges will identify the broad thrust of their directions and leave it to the parties to agree the details to be put into an order for endorsement.

11.51   It is clear that, if a party is charged with drawing up an order it is the duty of its solicitors and counsel to produce a draft that fairly reflects what they think the judge decided or directed.[53] Experience has shown that the more that details are left to be discussed by the parties after the hearing, the more room there can be for difficulties, in particular if one or more of the parties starts (in essence) re-running matters discussed during the hearing or (even worse) raising entirely new matters. While it is not always practical to do so, especially if the hearing has run late in the day, it is always a good idea to try to agree as many of the points in the order as possible before parties leave the court building because face-to-face discussion is almost invariably more effective in resolving debates than emails sent on the next or subsequent days. It is also likely to be more efficient in the majority of cases where disputes arise *not* to spend the subsequent days/weeks re-arguing the points between the parties, but rather to put two (or if necessary) more versions of the order to the judge by email so that the judge can decide. It is also suggested that unreasonable conduct in the post-hearing period is capable of attracting a costs sanction (ie it represents a basis under COPR r159 for departing from the normal costs rules set out in rules 156–157: see further, chapter 17 below).[54]

11.52   One specific wrinkle arises in respect of cases in which the Official Solicitor is instructed to act as litigation friend for P. The Official Solicitor's caseworker – ie the member of the Official Solicitor's office with delegated responsibility for giving instructions on behalf of the Official Solicitor – often requires sight of an order for purposes of giving approval. This can sometimes give rise to difficulties where matters have taken an unanticipated turn at the hearing and the Official Solicitor's caseworker (not having been present) takes the view that a different order to that set down by the judge should have been made. In such circumstances, and assuming that the provision in question reflects a direction made by the judge, the proper course

---

53 See, by analogy, *Webb Resolutions Ltd v JT Ltd* [2013] EWHC 509 (TCC), [2013] TCLR 6 at para 19 per Edwards-Stuart J.
54 See, by analogy, *Webb Resolutions* at para 23.

of action is for the Official Solicitor to seek leave to appeal the direction, rather than re-open matters in post-hearing correspondence.

Interim relief and interim hearings

11.53   On very many occasions that the court is considering making directions, it will also be considering what interim declarations or decisions are required to 'hold the ring' prior to the determination of the underlying application before it. For instance, in welfare cases, it will usually be necessary for the court to make interim declarations and decisions as to where P should live and with whom they should have contact prior to the final hearing. In property and affairs cases, it will very often be necessary to identify on an interim basis who should administer P's assets so as to secure them prior to a final determination of the application.

11.54   In some situations, especially those urgent ones discussed further at para 11.60 below, the primary focus of the hearing will be to consider the question of interim relief. As discussed at the outset, such hearings should technically be called interim hearings. Even in such hearings, though, the court is very likely to make directions as to the further consideration of the issues that have arisen or matters that flow in consequence of the decisions made.

11.55   Whenever interim relief is sought during the course of proceedings, the process for doing so is the same as set out above at paras 11.19–11.22 in relation to seeking directions.

11.56   The court has the power to enforce its interim decisions. Enforcement is dealt with at chapter 18 below, but in addition to the general powers granted the court under MCA 2005 s48, COPR r82 confirms that the court has the power to grant an interim injunction, an interim declaration or any other interim order it considers appropriate.

11.57   Any order for an interim injunction must set out clearly what the person to be subject to the injunction must or must not do. The courts have repeatedly emphasised the importance of clarity in this regard, together with the importance of ensuring that any injunction must not require the person subject to it to cross-refer to other material so as to understand their obligations: see, in particular, the comments of Munby LJ in *Re X and Y (children)*.[55]

---

55 [2012] EWCA Civ 1500, [2013] Fam Law 148 at paras 61–63. See also *Re Whiting* [2013] EWHC B27 (Fam), [2014] COPLR 107 at para 12(7).

11.58   In the authors' experience, judges will usually seek, at least at the outset of proceedings, not to make injunctions (for instance) restricting contact between P and family members, but rather to seek undertakings from the family members in question to abide by contact restrictions. Negotiating the terms of such undertakings will often represent some of the most important, if difficult, work done outside court at the hearing. It may not always be appropriate to proceed in such a way, most obviously if the proposed subject of the restriction is not present at the hearing; indeed, if they are represented but not actually present, some judges will not accept an undertaking because they consider it necessary to accept the undertaking personally from the individual and to explain its significance.

11.59   PD 10B provides that an interim injunction can be varied or discharged by any judge of the Court of Protection.[56] In other words, it is not necessary that the matter be brought back before the same judge, or even the same level of judge. It is important to note, however, that an appeal against a decision to grant an injunction must follow the usual appeal routes[57] – in other words, a district judge could consider an application to vary an injunction granted by a High Court judge, but could not consider the basis upon which it was granted in the first instance.

Urgent applications

11.60   While PD 10B emphasises[58] that applications that become urgent merely because steps were not taken sufficiently promptly at an earlier stage should be avoided, the court has the ability to deal with truly urgent applications 24 hours a day throughout the year. During court hours (ie between 10:30 and 16:30), it will usually be necessary for the application to be made before the judge at court, most frequently before the Urgent Applications judge in the Family Division.[59] Out of hours, or in the case of extreme urgency, applications can be made by telephone. Not all urgent applications will require a hearing, but in the majority of cases applications which are properly characterised as urgent will carry with an element of complexity which will necessitate one being arranged in short order.

56 PD 10B para 16.
57 See chapter 19 below.
58 PD 10B para 4.
59 Contact details are contained at appendix F below.

11.61   If sufficiently urgent, an application can be determined even though an application form has not been issued, or even filed;[60] in all circumstances, the defining characteristic of an urgent application will be that the respondent will not have been formally notified of it. It is always necessary to explain in the application form (or, if none is being filed, in clear terms to the court office or – if out of hours – the security office at the Royal Courts of Justice) precisely how urgent the application is, what level of judge is required to determine it and whether it requires a hearing.[61]

11.62   The guiding principle as regards urgent applications is that, as far as possible, the provisions relating to applications made on notice set out at paras 11.19ff above should be complied with.[62] In other words, the court and the respondent(s) should be provided with as much information as soon as possible (unless, in the respondent's case, to do so would be to defeat the purpose of the application), and that, as a minimum, steps should be taken to inform the respondent of the application by telephone or in writing.[63] The rationale for this is obvious, because it means that, even if the respondent cannot properly be said to have been notified of the application, the respondent may still be able to advance their views to the court at the hearing of the application, even only in writing.

11.63   The courts have repeatedly emphasised the stringency of the requirements upon those appearing before them on without notice applications and the care that must be exercised by judges in scrutinising them. In *KY v DD (without notice applications)*,[64] Theis J gave guidance applicable equally to applications regarding children in the Family Division of the High Court and applications in the Court of Protection. She emphasised the importance of the duty upon applicants to give full and frank disclosure,[65] including of matters that would suggest that the application should not be granted, and noted further that:

---

60 PD 10B paras 1 and 6–7.

61 PD 10B para 13; although this is in discretionary terms, the reality is that these obligations are mandatory.

62 PBD 10B para 7.

63 PD 10B para 5.

64 [2011] EWHC 1277 (Fam), [2012] 2 FLR 200.

65 Endorsing guidance previously given by Munby J (as he then was) in in *Re W (ex parte orders)* [2000] 2 FLR 927 and *Re S (ex parte orders)* [2001] 1 FLR 308 and by Charles J in *B Borough Council v S and another* [2006] EWHC 2584 (Fam). See also the comments of McFarlane J (as he then was) in *LLBC v TG, JG, and KR* [2007] EWHC 2640 (Fam), [2009] 1 FLR 414.

- If information is put before the court to substantiate a without notice order, it should be the subject of the closest scrutiny and, if the applicant is not present in person to verify it, be substantiated by production of a contemporaneous note of the instructions. If that is not available, there may need to be a short adjournment to enable steps to be taken to verify the information relied upon.
- If additional information is put before the court orally, there must be a direction for the filing of sworn evidence to confirm the information within a very short period of time.
- It is incumbent on those advising whether such an application is justified to consider rigorously whether an application is justified and be clear as to the evidential basis for it.

11.64 PD 10B provides that, where an order is made without notice to any party, the order should ordinarily contain:

a) an undertaking by the applicant to serve the application notice, evidence in support and any order made upon the affected parties as soon as possible or as ordered by the court; and

b) a return date for a further hearing at which the other parties can be present.[66]

COPR r81 further provides that a copy of the application notice, the order and the evidence in support is to be served by the applicant on anyone named as a respondent in the application notice (if not otherwise a party to the proceedings), every party to the proceedings and any other person directed by the court, such service to take place as soon as practicable or within such date as the court may direct. Where the application has been made in a situation of exceptional urgency and no application form has been issued, an undertaking will be required that the application form in the terms of the oral application be filed on the next working day, or as required by the court.[67]

11.65 While PD 10B is silent on the subject, it is at a minimum good practice, if not even obligatory, for a detailed note to be made of submissions made to the judge when the respondent is not present or represented, and of the reasons given by the judge for making (or not making) the order sought. The court will often order that such a note be filed in advance of the return date; in any event, without such a contemporaneous note it can be very difficult at any later date to

---

66 PD 10B para 6.
67 PD 10B para 9.

identify with clarity precisely how any without notice order came to be made.

11.66   Where a hearing of an urgent application takes place by telephone, PD 10B envisages that, where practicable, that hearing will take place by way of a conference call arranged (and in the first instance, paid for) by the applicant through a service provider (such as BT Connect), and that the service provider will record the call. In such situations, the applicant should order a transcript of the hearing from the service provider.[68] In the authors' experience, however, the majority of urgent telephone hearings in such cases (and especially those out of hours) take place by way of a direct telephone call between the applicant's representative and the judge and there is no possibility of recording the call for transcription. It is further not unheard of for the judge not to have all the papers before them, and for the judge then to be relying almost exclusively upon what they are being told by the applicant's representative. In such situations, the obligation to take a proper note of relevant matters is particularly onerous.

---

68 PD 10B para 12.

CHAPTER 12

Litigation friends[1]

continued

1   The comments upon this chapter of Alastair Pitblado, the Official Solicitor to the Senior Courts, and of Janet Ilett, Beverley Taylor and Helen Clift, all of the Office of the Official Solicitor and Public Trustee, are all gratefully acknowledged.

Introduction

12.1   It is a curious feature of the Mental Capacity Act (MCA) 2005 and the Court of Protection Rules (COPR) 2007 SI No 1744 that the person whom proceedings before the Court of Protection concern, P, need not be a party to those proceedings. Where P is a party, however, then the starting point is that they will require a litigation friend. Similarly, if any other party to the proceedings lacks litigation capacity or is a child, such a 'protected party' or the child will also require a litigation friend.

12.2   This chapter sets out the circumstances when a litigation friend will be required, who can act as a litigation friend, the duties of such a litigation friend, and how and when a litigation friend can be discharged. Before doing so, it discusses the circumstances under which P will be joined to proceedings.

12.3   It is important to note what this chapter is *not* about. It is not about the circumstances under which protected parties require litigation friends in proceedings before other courts. Space prevents a discussion of these questions, but in very summary form, although similar considerations arise, in particular as to the analysis of when a person has or lacks capacity to conduct litigation, the practical consequences of a lack of litigation capacity may well vary depending upon the setting.

Joining P to proceedings

12.4   As set out in more detail in chapter 9, it is necessary by virtue of the COPR[2] that P be notified when an application concerning them is brought before the Court of Protection. P is not, however, automatically made a party to proceedings by virtue of such notification: only the applicant and any party named as a respondent in the application form and who files a COP5 acknowledgement of service in respect of that form are parties as of right.[3] Indeed, P is specifically *not* to be named as a respondent to any proceedings unless the court orders otherwise.[4] P will, though, be bound as if a party.[5] Unless the court orders otherwise (for instance, on the ground that it would cause P

2   In particular COPR rr40 and 69.
3   COPR r73(1).
4   COPR r73(4).
5   COPR r74(2)(a).

distress), P must also be notified of the essential steps in the proceedings and be given appropriate explanations by the person effecting notification as to those steps.[6]

12.5   Although there is no specific guidance provided within the statutory framework, or by the case-law, there are now relatively well-established categories of case in which P will be joined. Indeed, the working presumption has developed that P will be joined in all serious medical treatment cases and in healthcare and welfare cases other than those concerning a very limited single decision to be taken on P's behalf. The position in relation to applications for authorisations for deprivation of liberty is, at the time of writing, under detailed scrutiny by the President of the Court of Protection.

12.6   Conversely, when it comes to the management of P's property and affairs, the practice (reflecting, perhaps, the practice prior to the coming into force of the MCA 2005) has been not to join P to proceedings, save in certain defined cases. The most important of these has been in relation to applications for a statutory will or a codicil to be made on P's behalf, or for the disposal of substantial amounts of P's property by way of settlement or gift.

12.7   Recent decisions of the European Court of Human Rights (ECtHR) can be read as suggesting that a judge should proceed with very considerable caution before concluding that P should not made a party to proceedings in any case in which the question of their capacity is in issue, especially if their decision-making capacity in more than one domain is in doubt.[7] The cases are not entirely easy to map across to the English and Welsh system, because they arise in the context of jurisdictions that retain a 'status'-based system, ie where a person can be deemed to be fully or partially incapacitated (and hence, in legal terms, a 'non-person'). However, at minimum, the decisions serve to emphasise the importance of participation of P in the proceedings (in which regard, see also the discussion of the circumstances under which judges will hear from P at paras 16.29ff).

---

6 COPR rr40–49.
7 *X and Y v Croatia* (App No 5193/90, decision of 3 November 2011), *Shtukaturov v Russia* (2012) 54 EHRR 27 and *Lashin v Russia* (App No 33117/02, decision of 22 January 2013).

When will a litigation friend be required?

Introduction

12.8　There are three distinct situations where a litigation friend will be required:[8]

- P, if a party to proceedings, must have a litigation friend, subject to one exception discussed further at paras 12.75ff below;
- any other 'protected party' who is a party to the proceedings must have a litigation friend, a 'protected party' being an adult other than P who lacks capacity to conduct the proceedings;[9]
- a child (ie a person under 18) must have a litigation friend, unless the court orders otherwise.

12.9　Each of these situations will be discussed in turn, after we have set out the core principles relating to capacity to litigate.

Capacity to litigate

12.10　As discussed in chapter 2 above, capacity is issue specific, and it is important (as the COPR do) to distinguish between the capacity to make a decision and the capacity to conduct proceedings in relation to that decision. The two are not synonymous.

12.11　　Questions of litigation capacity raise a number of complex issues outside the scope of this work.[10] In summary, however, whether a person has capacity to conduct proceedings is a test that must be answered by applying MCA 2005 ss2–3, but the courts have looked to cases decided under the common law to set out the relevant information that the person must be capable of understanding, using, weighing, retaining and/or communicating. In *A, B and C v X and Z*,[11] Hedley J considered that the 'heart of the test' were the observations of Chadwick LJ at para 75 of *Masterman-Lister*[12] that:

> [T]he test to be applied, as it seems to me, is whether the party to the legal proceedings is capable of understanding, with the assistance of

8　COPR r141(1)–(3).

9　COPR r6.

10　For a more detailed discussion, see chapter 8 of the Law Society/BMA's *Assessment of mental capacity: a guide for doctors and lawyers*, 3rd edn, 2009.

11　[2012] EWHC 2400 (COP), [2013] COPLR 1.

12　*Masterman-Lister v Brutton & Co, Masterman-Lister v Jewell and another* [2002] EWCA Civ 1889, [2003] 1 WLR 1511. The approach adopted in *Masterman-Lister* was recently endorsed by the Supreme Court in *Dunhill v Burgin (Nos 1 and 2)* [2014] UKSC 18, (2014) 17 CCLR 203.

proper explanation from legal advisers and experts in other disciplines as the case may require, the issues on which his consent or decision is likely to be necessary in the course of those proceedings. If he has capacity to understand that which he needs to understand in order to pursue or defend a claim, I can see no reason why the law – whether substantive or procedural – should require the interposition of a next friend.[13]

12.12   To this should perhaps also be added the important dicta of Munby J (as he then was) in *Sheffield City Council v E and another*[14] that:

> ... the question of capacity to litigate is not something to be determined in the abstract. One has to focus on the particular piece of litigation in relation to which the issue arises. The question is always whether the litigant has capacity to litigate in relation to the particular proceedings in which he is involved.[15]

12.13   In this regard, it should also be noted that it is possible that a person might have capacity to decide upon the matters raised in the application, but not have capacity to litigate upon those issues (and vice versa). In the *E* case Munby J commented, while he considered that:

> it was not difficult to think of situations where someone has subject-matter capacity whilst lacking litigation capacity, and such cases may not be that rare, I suspect that cases where someone has litigation capacity whilst lacking subject-matter capacity are likely to be very much more infrequent, indeed pretty rare. Indeed, I would go so far as to say that only in unusual circumstances will it be possible to conclude that someone who lacks subject-matter capacity can nonetheless have litigation capacity.[16]

12.14   The position where P, in fact, has capacity to conduct the litigation although they do not have the capacity to take the decisions in issue is discussed at paras 12.75ff.

When will P require a litigation friend?

12.15   The COPR are framed somewhat curiously in respect of P (and arguably reverse the presumption of capacity in MCA 2005 s1(2)), because they proceed on the basis that P necessarily lacks capacity to conduct proceedings, and will therefore require a litigation friend if he or

---

13   *A, B and C v X and Z* [2012] EWHC 2400 (COP), [2013] COPLR 1, para 42.
14   [2005] Fam 326.
15   Para 38.
16   Para 49.

she is joined as a party.[17] The starting point, therefore, is that P will *always* require a litigation friend if they are joined to proceedings. The procedure where P (or another person on their behalf) wishes to challenge this presumption is set out at paras 12.75ff below.

12.16 It should be noted that it is possible for P to be a child, as the MCA 2005 provides for the Court of Protection to make certain types of decision in respect of those between the age of 16 and 18 (and indeed, in respect of those below 18, to make any decision relating to P's property and affairs save for the making of a will, if the court considers it likely that P will still lack capacity to make decisions in respect of that matter when he reaches 18[18]).

12.17 It is important to note in such cases that the child in question may be unable to take a particular decision (and to litigate in respect of that decision) not because they suffer from a material impairment in the functioning of their mind or brain but because they are not 'competent': ie applying the test set down by the House of Lords in the case of *Gillick*,[19] they do not have sufficient maturity and intelligence to understand the nature and implications of the proposed decision.[20] In such a case, if relief is required from a court, then that court is not the Court of Protection, but, depending on the precise nature of the relief sought, then either the Family Court established by the Crime and Courts Act 2013[21] or the Family Division of the High Court.

12.18 If, however, the proceedings are properly before the Court of Protection, then, by definition, the child in question must be said to lack capacity to take the decisions in question by reference to the provisions of MCA 2005 ss2–3. In such a situation, then if the child is joined, it is suggested that the court should approach that child *as if* they were an adult P for the purposes of deciding questions relating to the appointment and termination of the appointment of a litigation friend.

---

17 COPR r141(1).
18 MCA 2005 ss2(5) and 18(3).
19 *Gillick v West Norfolk and Wisbech Area Health Authority* [1986] 1 AC 112.
20 [1986] 1 AC 112 at 189 per Lord Scarman. For a more detailed discussion of the position of children potentially subject to the MCA 2005, see Ashton et al, *Court of Protection Practice 2014*, Jordans, paras 2.91–2.94.
21 Section 31A and Schedule 10A, with effect from April 2014.

When will another adult party require a litigation friend?

12.19   The position in respect of adult parties other than P is in principle simpler: if they lack capacity to conduct the proceedings, then they require a litigation friend.[22] The same principles as set out above apply to the determination of litigation capacity.

12.20   One practical question that arises not infrequently is what the court is to do where it becomes apparent that an adult party lacks litigation capacity. In a sense, the question is somewhat simpler if the person has legal representation – it is clear that a responsible solicitor who has concerns as to the capacity of his or her client should take steps to obtain a medical opinion;[23] if that opinion suggests that the client lacks litigation capacity, then the solicitor should take steps to ensure that a litigation friend is appointed before proceeding further.[24]

12.21   If the person is acting for themselves, however, then a difficult question can arise. It is ultimately a judicial question whether an individual is or is not a protected party.[25] If the court is in possession of information raising a question as to capacity of a litigant in person to conduct the litigation, how is to satisfy itself as to whether the person has the requisite capacity? It may be that the litigant in person is prepared to agree to undergo a medical examination, but what if they refuse? A party to proceedings cannot be ordered to undergo a medical examination[26] and the court is therefore faced with a difficult dilemma. In *Baker Tilly (a firm) v Makar*,[27] Sir Raymond Jack made clear that:

> The absence of medical evidence cannot be a bar to a finding of lack of capacity but where most unusually circumstances arise in which medical evidence cannot be obtained, the court should be most cautious before concluding that the probability is that there is a disturbance of the mind. Section 2(3)(b) of the [Mental Capacity] Act must be kept in mind. A finding of lack of capacity is a serious matter for both parties. It takes away the protected party's right to conduct their

---

22   COPR rr141(2) and 6.

23   Whether that is from a GP, a psychiatrist or a psychologist will depend upon the circumstances of the case.

24   See *Masterman-Lister v Brutton & Co, Masterman-Lister v Jewell and another* [2002] EWCA Civ 1889, [2003] 1 WLR 1511 at para 30.

25   See *Carmathenshire CC v Lewis* [2010] EWCA Civ 1567 at para 8 per Rimer LJ.

26   See also para 4.59 of the Code of Practice accompanying the MCA 2005: 'Nobody can be forced to undergo an assessment of capacity.'

27   [2013] EWHC 759 (QB), [2013] COPLR 245.

litigation. It may constitute, and here would constitute, a serious disadvantage to the other party.

These comments were made in the context of adversarial civil proceedings, but it is suggested that they are equally applicable before the Court of Protection.

12.22 We suggest, however, that in appropriate cases the court can – and should – make findings as to litigation capacity even where a party refuses to attend a medical examination where there is sufficient evidence. Such evidence may emerge from a variety of sources. In *Re RGS*,[28] for instance, the court had limited medical information about RBS, P's son, who was known to have a history of contact with psychiatric services but who refused to attend a medical examination. The court found RBS to lack litigation capacity. The court found that such information as there was from the professional witnesses and RBS' own account founded the conclusion that RBS had an impairment or disturbance of the mind or brain. RBS' own conduct during the proceedings gave rise to the finding that the impairment/disturbance had compromised his ability to understand, retain and weigh the information relevant to the litigation.

12.23 In extreme cases, where a litigant in person refuses to take part in a medical examination, the court may be able to direct disclosure of the litigant's medical records to an independent medical examiner who could then prepare a report based on the clinical record. A party's medical records are confidential, but in *Bennett v Compass Group*[29] (a case relating to the disclosure of medical records in a personal injury case where the claimant's capacity was not in issue), comments made by both Chadwick LJ[30] and Pill LJ[31] would suggest that a (civil) court could make an order requiring a GP or hospital to disclose records direct to a party to the litigation without the consent of the person in question, although it is clear from the comments made in that case that such an order would be wholly exceptional. There is no reason in principle why such an approach could not be adopted by the Court of Protection, albeit after a very careful balancing exercise between the litigant's rights to maintaining the confidentiality of their medical records under article 8 (right to respect for private and family life) of the European Convention on Human Rights (ECHR)[32] and

28 [2012] EWHC 4162 (COP).
29 [2002] EWCA Civ 642, [2002] CP Rep 58.
30 At paras 67–68.
31 Para 88.
32 See in this regard *Z v Finland* (1997) 25 EHRR 371 at para 95.

the potential benefits to them of being represented by a litigation friend.

When will a child require a litigation friend?

12.24   A child – ie someone under 18[33] – who is party to proceedings but is not P, will require a litigation friend unless the court orders otherwise.[34] An application must be made for this dispensation; if the application is made by the child, then if a litigation friend has already been appointed to act on their behalf, it must be made on notice to that litigation friend.[35] It may otherwise be made without notice.[36] There is no guidance in the MCA 2005, the COPR or Practice Direction (PD) 17A as to the circumstances under which a court will permit a child to conduct proceedings without a litigation friend.

12.25   As discussed at para 12.16 above in relation to the position of 'child Ps', there are two potential bases upon which a child may lack capacity to conduct proceedings:

1) because they are not '*Gillick*-competent';[37] or
2) because they suffer from a material disturbance or impairment of the mind or brain.

12.26   If the concern in respect of the child arises not because of a suggestion that they are in some way suffering from a disability, but rather because of their age, then it is suggested that useful guidance can be found in the approach adopted the Family Procedure Rules (FPR) 2010,[38] which also contain a provision for the court to dispense with the requirement that a child be represented by a litigation friend (or a children's guardian) in certain circumstances. The FPR provide that an application by the child will be granted 'if [the court] considers that the child has sufficient understanding to conduct the proceedings concerned or proposed without a litigation friend or children's guardian'.[39] The FPR contain differences to the COPR, not least as they provide that the court can nonetheless require the litigation friend or guardian to continue to play a part in the proceedings, but

---

33   COPR r6.
34   COPR r141(3)–(4).
35   COPR r141(5)(b).
36   COPR r141(5)(c).
37   *Gillick v West Norfolk and Wisbech Area Health Authority* [1986] 1 AC 112.
38   SI No 2955, as amended.
39   FPR r16.6(6).

it is suggested that the approach set down in the FPR is likely to be adopted before the Court of Protection.

12.27   If the concern in respect of the child's ability to participate in the proceedings arises out of a concern that they are suffering from a disability affecting their capacity to conduct litigation, then while the guidance in the FPR does not cease entirely to be relevant, it is suggested that the primary considerations should be those set out at paras 12.19ff above in relation to adults.

12.28   Even where an order has been made permitting a child to act without a litigation friend, the court retains the power to appoint a litigation friend if it subsequently appears to the court that it would be desirable for such a litigation friend to conduct proceedings on the child's behalf. There is no guidance in the MCA 2005, the COPR or PD 17A as to when such a step would be desirable. At least where the appointment of a litigation friend for a child has taken place on the basis out of a concern that they are not sufficiently mature, then by analogy with the FPR[40] it is suggested that a court should be slow to re-appoint a litigation friend save where it has become clear that the child, in fact, lacks the understanding to conduct the proceedings. To do otherwise – for instance, on the basis that the child's conduct is disruptive – would be to risk depriving the child of a voice in the proceedings; the court has other mechanisms to control such disruptive conduct by way of its case management powers granted it under COPR rr3 and 5.

Appointment of litigation friends

12.29   There are two ways in which a litigation friend can be appointed: without a court order and with one.

Appointment without a court order

12.30   A deputy appointed with the specific power to conduct legal proceedings in the name of the protected party is entitled to act as litigation friend without a further order if their power extends to the proceedings in question.[41] Note in this regard that the conduct of legal proceedings is considered an aspect of the management of P's property

---

40 FPR r16.6(8).
41 COPR r142(2).

and affairs for purposes of the MCA 2005;[42] it would therefore be very unlikely that a deputy appointed to make decisions in relation to P's health and welfare would also be given the power by the court to make decisions in relation to the conduct of legal proceedings.

12.31   If a deputy is to act as litigation friend, the deputy must file and serve an official copy of the order on the other parties (or, if a party is represented by a litigation friend, upon that party's litigation friend).[43]

12.32   If there is no deputy, a person can become a litigation friend for a protected party or for a child (but not for P) without a court order if they file a certificate of suitability (with a statement of truth[44]) on a form COP22[45] stating (among other things) that:

- they can fairly and competently conduct proceedings on behalf of the individual in question;[46]
- they have no interests adverse to the individual in question;[47]
- that the litigation friend knows or believes that the child or protected party lacks capacity to conduct the proceedings themselves;[48]
- the grounds of the belief set out above (and, if the belief is based upon medical opinion, or the opinion of another suitably qualified expert, attach any relevant document to the certificate).[49] It is suggested that a court would wish to consider carefully any situation in which a litigation friend had been appointed pursuant to this process absent medical evidence.[50]

The first two bullet points are discussed further at paras 12.44ff below.

12.33   The proposed litigation friend must serve the certificate of suitability on the other parties (or, if a party is represented by a litigation friend, upon that party's litigation friend).[51] Unless the court directs otherwise, the proposed litigation friend does not need to serve any

---

42 MCA 2005 s18(1)(k).
43 COPR r142(4) and PD 17 para 5.
44 PD 17A para 8.
45 Which will serve as the requisite consent for purposes of PD 17A para 7(a).
46 COPR r142(3)(a) read together with COPR r140(1)(a).
47 COPR r142(3)(a) read together with COPR r140(1)(b).
48 PD 17A para 7(b).
49 PD 17A para 7(c).
50 Whether that is from a GP, a psychiatrist or a psychologist will depend upon the circumstances of the case. See *Masterman-Lister v Brutton & Co, Masterman-Lister v Jewell and Another* [2002] EWCA Civ 1889, [2003] 1 WLR 1511 at para 17.
51 COPR r142(3)(b) and PD17A para 9.

document relating to the medical or other opinion noted at the last bullet point above.

12.34 The proposed litigation friend must then file the certificate of suitability together with a certificate of service on a COP20 form when they first take a step in the proceedings.[52]

12.35 The procedure set out above cannot be used if the court has previously appointed a litigation friend.[53] Slightly curiously, it also cannot be used by the Official Solicitor[54] (the rationale for this is perhaps because the Official Solicitor is to be taken automatically to satisfy the suitability requirement and hence should not be required to file such a certificate).

Appointment with a court order

12.36 An order appointing a person as a litigation friend for a protected party, a child or – importantly – P (if P is joined to the proceedings) can be made either at the court's own initiative or upon application by any person (ie not just by the proposed litigation friend).[55] Any application must be supported by evidence[56] that will allow the court to be satisfied (as it must also be satisfied if it is contemplating making the order of its own initiative) that:

- the proposed litigation friend can fairly and competently conduct proceedings on behalf of the individual in question;[57]
- the proposed litigation friend has no interests adverse to the individual in question;[58]
- the proposed litigation friend consents to the appointment.[59]

The last of these criteria is self-evident; the first two are discussed at paras 12.44ff below.

12.37 As noted above, a court order is required in order to appoint the Official Solicitor as litigation friend for a protected party, a child or P.[60] Although the COPR are silent on this, it would seem that the Official Solicitor is automatically taken to meet the suitability criteria

---

52 PD17A para 11.
53 COPR r142(1)(b).
54 COPR r142(1)(c).
55 COPR r143(2).
56 COPR r143(1).
57 COPR r140(1)(a).
58 COPR r140(1)(b).
59 COPR r143(2).
60 COPR r142(1)(c).

and the Official Solicitor would never be required to file evidence to address these criteria.

12.38 Perhaps curiously, a person other than the Official Solicitor who either actively advances themselves to act as litigation friend for P or whom the court is contemplating of its own motion appointing to act for P does not, formally, need to file and serve a certificate of suitability, although (as set out above) the court will still need to be satisfied that they meet the criteria for appointment before making the order.

12.39 If the court considers that it requires further evidence before it can grant an application to be appointed as litigation friend, or if it appears to the judge during the course of proceedings that a person (other than P) may require a litigation friend, but that further evidence is required, directions can be made.[61] If P has previously made a successful application to be allowed to instruct representatives directly (see further paras 12.75ff below) but it then appears that the position has changed subsequently, then the same provisions will apply.

The further powers of the court upon the appointment of a litigation friend

12.40 The court has the power, exercisable on its own initiative or at the application of any person (whether or not that person is a party) to:

- prevent someone acting as a litigation friend (for any party);
- terminate their appointment; or
- appoint a new litigation friend in place of an existing one.[62]

12.41 Unsurprisingly, in light of the discussion above:

- any application for such an order must be supported by evidence;[63] and
- any proposed litigation friend must meet the criteria set out above.[64]

12.42 Termination of the appointment of a litigation friend in these circumstances is considered further at para 12.85 below.

---

61 COPR r143(5). The position where it appears that an adult party other than P may require a litigation friend is addressed at paras 12.19–12.23 above.
62 COPR r144.
63 COPR r144(2).
64 COPR r144(3).

Distinctions between Court of Protection proceedings and civil proceedings

12.43 While, as set out at the outset, space precludes a discussion of the position in relation to other types of proceedings, there are two points of distinction between proceedings before the Court of Protection and civil proceedings which are sufficiently important that mention of them should be made here:

- Unlike the position under the Civil Procedure Rules (CPR),[65] a person seeking to bring proceedings on behalf of someone lacking litigation capacity (whether that person would be 'P' or otherwise) is not required to undertake to pay any costs which the individual may be ordered to pay in relation to the proceedings, subject to any right he may have to be repaid from the assets of the child or protected party. This may well reflect the rather different position that prevails in respect of costs in the Court of Protection, discussed further in chapter 17 below; the specific risks that a litigation friend may face in respect of costs are discussed in para 12.88 below.

- Again unlike the position under the CPR,[66] the COPR are silent as to what the court may or may not do as regards the proceedings generally where a party who requires a litigation friend (including P) has not yet had one appointed. In particular, there is no equivalent to CPR 21.3(4), which expressly provides that a step taken before a child or a protected party has a litigation friend has no effect unless the court orders otherwise. The commentary in Jordan's *Court of Protection Practice* suggests, we consider correctly, that the silence of the COPR in this regards means that the court 'probably retains a discretion'[67] both to permit specified steps to be taken before a litigation friend is appointed or retrospectively to approve any steps to be taken without such an appointment. We note that it would also be open to a Court of Protection judge to apply CPR 21.3(4) through the (often overlooked) provisions of COPR r9.[68] No matter how it arises, however, we would suggest

---

65 CPR 21.4(c).

66 CPR 21.3.

67 Ashton et al, *Court of Protection Practice 2014*, Jordans, at p762, in the commentary to COPR r141.

68 Which provide that: 'In any case not expressly provided for by these Rules or the practice directions made under them, the Civil Procedure Rules 1998 (including any practice directions made under them) may be applied with any necessary modifications, insofar as is necessary to further the overriding objective.'

that the court should proceed with caution before retrospectively endorsing any steps that went beyond the merely procedural.[69] In terms of prospective steps, our experience is that the courts have shown themselves reluctant to take substantive steps in the proceedings where P is a party and where no litigation friend has yet been appointed to act on their behalf. In *WCC v AB and SB*,[70] for instance, a central reason that HHJ Cardinal appointed P's aunt to act as his litigation friend in the face of doubts raised as to her suitability was that she could be appointed immediately, and he considered that he could not delay before directions were made as to the instruction of an independent psychiatrist and independent social worker to provide reports upon P. He did not appear to have considered that he could simply rely upon the silence in the COPR to give him discretion to proceed.

Who may be appointed as a litigation friend?

Acting for P

12.44   When the Court of Protection was brought into being in 2007 in its new guise, the expectation among many was that the Official Solicitor would act as litigation friend for P *whenever* P was joined as a party to proceedings. It is now very clear that this assumption was inaccurate. While the exact basis upon which the Official Solicitor acts is a curious amalgam of statutory provisions, precedent and accidents of history which may well fall to be considered in due course by reference (for instance) to the extent to which it is consistent with P's rights under the ECHR and the UN Convention on the Rights of Persons with Disabilities (CRPD), the current position is that:

- The Official Solicitor is the litigation friend of last resort, such that he or she will only consider acting where no suitable and willing person can be identified to act. This is addressed further in the next paragraph.
- Save in the case of serious medical treatment cases (as to which, see chapter 23), even assuming that there is no other suitable and willing person, the Official Solicitor will only accept an appointment to act subject to being given suitable security for a)

---

69   By analogy with the position under the CPR: see *Dunhill v Burgin (Nos 1 and 2)* [2014] UKSC 18, [2014] 1 WLR 933, (2014) 17 CCLR 203.
70   [2013] COPLR 157.

the costs of any external solicitors he or she retains to act for P; or b) where he or she acts as solicitor and conducts the litigation, those costs of so acting. In other words, and while the Official Solicitor does not seek to recover his costs of acting as litigation friend, he or she must be satisfied that the costs incurred either by external solicitors or by his or her staff in acting as solicitors will be met, whether that be from P's own assets or by way of legal aid. The position in respect of costs is discussed further at paras 12.87ff below.

- Where the Official Solicitor is in a position to accept an appointment to act, then the order recording that fact will include detailed provisions relating to how he or she is to be provided for the security for the costs outlined above. A precedent order setting out these provisions can be found in appendix C, but in broad terms, it provides for third parties (including HM Revenue and Customs (HMRC)) to give financial information to the Official Solicitor for purposes of assessing P's finances, and also setting out how the costs in question will be met: whether by way of public funding, out of P's assets or otherwise. Such extensive orders are not normally required in cases concerning P's property and affairs as the issues at stake are financial and detailed financial information is provided in the application papers (form COP1A).

12.45   In deciding whether someone other than the Official Solicitor would be suitable to act as litigation friend for P, the following points are of importance:

- It is particularly important that the proposed litigation friend is clear as to the obligations that they would be under. These obligations are discussed further below in paras 12.49ff.
- The mere fact that a person (for instance, a family member) has strong views as to where P's best interests lie does not automatically disqualify them from acting as P's litigation friend, especially where competent legal representatives are instructed by that (proposed) litigation friend: *AVS v NHS Foundation Trust and P PCT*.[71]
- However, where there is a family dispute concerning P's best interests, it would be rare for it to be appropriate for a family member to be appointed as P's litigation friend in proceedings relating to that dispute. If they were to be so appointed, they would have 'to

71 [2011] EWCA Civ 7, [2011] COPLR Con Vol 219, at para 28 per Ward LJ (obiter). See also *WCC v AB and SB* [2013] COPLR 157 and *Westminster City Council v Manuela Sykes* [2014] EWHC B9 (COP), (2014) 17 CCLR 139.

demonstrate that he or she can, as P's litigation friend, take a balanced and even-handed approach to the relevant issues'.[72]

- In the case of those subject to the deprivation of liberty safeguards (DOLS) regime (see further chapter 24 below), the courts have specifically endorsed the appointment of P's relevant person's representative (RPR) as their litigation friend: see *AB v LCC (A Local Authority) and the Care Manager of BCH*.[73] In *Re UF*, Charles J, endorsing *AB*, suggested that the possibility of whether the RPR could act as a litigation friend should 'often' be investigated.[74]

- In *Re M*,[75] an application was brought under MCA 2005 s21A by P's Independent Mental Capacity Advocate (IMCA) as litigation friend; this was the first reported case in which an IMCA had so acted, but the authors are aware of a number of unreported cases where IMCAs have been appointed to act as P's litigation friend in proceedings brought by others, as well as bringing proceedings in P's name. It is clear that there is no reason in principle why they cannot do so.

- To act properly as a litigation friend can be an onerous undertaking. Where an RPR or an IMCA acts, it is important therefore that both they and – more importantly – their organisation are aware of the potentially significant amounts of time that may be required on their part properly to conduct litigation on P's behalf.

- It should be noted that there, is at present, a question mark as to whether a litigation friend (whether an RPR, and IMCA or a family member) must be *legally* entitled (ie authorised) in order to be appointed if they are not to *instruct* legal representatives to act for P.[76] In all cases, a litigation friend should consider very carefully whether they should instruct representatives in order to be able to conduct the litigation fairly and competently;[77] if a litigation friend is *not* so authorised but considers that they would wish to proceed without instructing solicitors, it is suggested that they seek confirmation from the court at the earliest possible opportunity that

---

72 *Re UF* [2013] EWHC 4289 (COP), [2014] COPLR 93 at para 23 per Charles J.

73 [2011] EWHC 3151 (COP), [2012] COPLR 314.

74 *Re UF* at para 19.

75 [2013] EHWC 3456 (COP), [2014] COPLR 93.

76 It is, in particular, not clear precisely how the provisions of the Legal Services Act 2007 (which makes specific provisions as to who can and cannot conduct litigation without the specific permission of the court) apply in relation to the discharge of the role of litigation friend.

77 As they are required to by COPR r140(1). This question was before the President of the Court of Protection at the time of writing.

they *may* both conduct the litigation and provide P with advocacy services and discharge their role in this way.

- In the case both of RPRs and IMCAs, specific arrangements will need to be made to ensure that their costs of acting as P's litigation friend (and, where appropriate, of instructing legal representatives) are met. The question of the basis upon which RPRs and IMCAs are entitled to reimbursement of their costs is addressed below at para 12.90, but for present purposes it is important to note that there is a difference between an entitlement to reimbursement and a guarantee that they will not be left out of pocket – ie security for their costs. It should be also remembered that when considering an application for legal aid it is P's means, and not those of the litigation friend, which will be assessed (see further, chapter 6). This is a separate issue to the question of the costs of the litigation friend in discharging his or her responsibilities.

- In very many cases, it is likely that the budgets of the bodies employing the RPRs and IMCAs will not extend to funding the (potentially significant) costs of litigation or (lesser, but still significant) time involved in discharging the role of litigation friend, ie the consideration of the materials received with a view to giving instructions to legal representatives. In such cases, it is suggested that there is nothing remotely improper in an RPR or an IMCA declining to act absent receiving appropriate security for their costs both of acting as litigation friend and, if necessary, instructing legal representatives. The terms of the orders that would then be made would be very similar to those made in cases where the Official Solicitor consents to act (although, to the extent that they made provision for the cost of acting as litigation friend, would go wider than those made in cases involving the Official Solicitor: see further para 12.44 above).

- Although it would be unusual for a solicitor to be appointed as litigation friend, this has happened in one publicly available case.[78]

12.46 Finally, it should be noted that the MCA 2005, the COPR and the practice directions are silent as to whether it must be an individual who acts as litigation friend, or whether the responsibility can be taken on by a body. This is of particular relevance in the context of the involvement of RPRs and IMCAs who may well – understandably – feel more comfortable (and more sure of themselves in demanding proper time to discharge their roles) if the formal responsibility for

---

78 *Re RGS* [2012] EWHC 4162 (COP), discussed further in chapter 24.

acting as litigation friend lies with their organisation, rather than resting solely upon their shoulders. The natural reading of the relevant provisions of the COPR would suggest that the draftsman had in mind the appointment of individuals, rather than organisations. We note, though, that:

- A trust corporation can be appointed as a deputy to manage P's property and affairs.[79] Management of property and affairs is specifically said to extend to the conduct of legal proceedings on P's behalf.[80] If appointed as deputy, therefore, and if the relevant order included specific provision relating to legal proceedings, a trust corporation could properly bring proceedings on P's behalf as P's litigation friend.
- We are, further, aware of unreported cases in which IMCA organisations have been appointed to act as litigation friend for P, although we do not understand that the matter has been the subject of argument.

12.47   Until such time as clarification as to whether a body can be appointed as a litigation friend is given either by the courts or by formal guidance/statutory amendment, the position is therefore unhelpfully unclear. We would strongly suggest that if any application to be appointed as a 'corporate' litigation friend is advanced, then it is made very clear in that application precisely who will have day-to-day responsibility for the conduct of the case on P's behalf and what arrangements are in place to ensure continuity of consideration in the event that that individual is unavailable.

Acting for a child or a protected party other than P

12.48   Essentially the same considerations as set out above in relation to P also apply in terms of the appointment of a suitable litigation friend to represent children or adult protected parties other than P. In particular, it should be noted that it is not unheard of for the Official Solicitor to act for other parties in addition to P: the authors have experience of one case in which the Official Solicitor was acting for two other family members as well as P. In such cases, where it is quite possible that it is necessary that different individuals have different cases advanced on their behalf, the Official Solicitor will put in place 'Chinese walls' to ensure that such can be carried out ie, strict rules

79 MCA 2005 s19(1)(b).
80 MCA 2005 s18(1)(k).

to ensure that each caseworker only sees the information relevant to their case.

Duties of the litigation friend

Preliminary

12.49 Save that it is clear from COPR r140(1) that a litigation friend must be able fairly and competently to conduct the proceedings, there is no guidance contained in the MCA 2005, the COPR or in any of the supporting materials as to how a litigation friend should discharge their duties. It is therefore necessary to look more widely for assistance.

12.50 It is perhaps easiest to start by identifying what a litigation friend is *not*. They are not:

- the advocate of the party on whose behalf they act, whether a) a lay advocate; b) a statutory advocate;[81] or c) a legally qualified advocate authorised to carry out the conduct of litigation – they are 'a great deal more';[82] or
- the equivalent of a children's guardian appointed in certain categories of family proceedings to represent the interests of a child.[83] The duties of such a guardian are wide-ranging[84] but, crucially, involve an investigatory and reporting role that is very different to that of a litigation friend; or
- a person discharging the function of a McKenzie friend. Such a friend (whose role is described in more detail at paras 6.5ff) can only assist a person who has litigation capacity.

12.51 Perhaps the most concise statement of the duties of the litigation friend – duties that are owed both to the party on whose behalf they act but also to the court – can be found in the judgment of Sir Robert Megarry V-C in *Re E (mental health patient)*:[85]

> The main function of a next friend [ie now, a litigation friend] appears to be to carry on the litigation on behalf of the plaintiff and in his best interests. For this purpose the next friend must make all the decisions

---

81 Such as an IMCA or an independent mental health advocate (IMHA) discharging functions under the MHA 1983.
82 *RP v Nottingham City Council and the Official Solicitor (mental capacity of parent)* [2008] EWCA Civ 462, [2008] 2 FLR 1516 at para 129 per Wall LJ.
83 Under Children Act (CA) 1989 s5; see also FPR Part 14 and rr16.3 and 16.4.
84 They are set out in PD 16A to the FPR.
85 [1984] 1 WLR 320. The judgment was reversed on appeal ([1985] 1 WLR 245), but these dicta were not questioned.

that the plaintiff would have made, had he been able. The next friend may, on behalf of the plaintiff, do anything which the Rules of the Supreme Court require or authorise the plaintiff to do ... It is the next friend who is responsible to the court for the propriety and the progress of the proceedings. The next friend does not, however, become a litigant himself: his functions are essentially vicarious.[86]

12.52   The Official Solicitor takes the view that:

... where I am acting in the family courts and the civil courts my duty is as set out in *Re E*. But in the Court of Protection the litigation concerns (1) whether P has or does not have capacity to make the relevant decisions; and (2) if not, what decisions are in P's best interests. It is therefore necessary for me to put a case as to both to the court without ... expecting to pre-empt the court's determination on either. In contradistinction, where I am acting as litigation friend for a protected party in the Court of Protection, my duty is to conduct the proceedings in the protected party's best interests but not to seek to advance a case about the protected party's best interests (as opposed to P's best interests). I conduct separate and distinct exercises when acting as litigation friend for both P and a protected party (or child).[87]

12.53   It is generally assumed – including in the passage set out immediately above[88] – that a litigation friend acting on behalf of P or a protected party is required to act in the best interests of that party within the meaning of the MCA 2005.[89] The decision of the ECtHR in *RP v UK*[90] would seem on its face to support this assumption (at least insofar as it relates to the discharge of the duties of a litigation friend acting on behalf of a protected party).

12.54   We suggest that there are grounds to doubt this assumption. However, the detail of these arguments are complex and beyond the

---

86 [1984] 1 WLR 320 at p324F–H. The passage continued with observations about the costs liability of a litigation friend that are discussed at para 12.92 below.

87 Extract reproduced, with the permission of the Official Solicitor and with acronyms expanded, from a statement he has made in an application for judicial review of the legal aid exceptional funding scheme, which he intends to publish in due course.

88 Echoing the approach set out in the witness statement appended to the decision of the Court of Appeal in *RP v Nottingham City Council and the Official Solicitor (mental capacity of parent)* [2008] EWCA Civ 462, [2008] 2 FLR 1516 (concerning his role as litigation friend for a protected party in care proceedings).

89 The position in relation to a litigation friend acting on behalf of a child is considered at paras 12.71–12.74 below.

90 *RP v UK* (App No 38245/08, decision of 9 October 2012), [2013] 1 FLR 744.

scope of this work. We therefore do not set them out here,[91] although we do suggest that the matter will, in due course, have to be examined by the Court of Protection, with specific reference to the particular procedures and processes of that court.[92] We further suggest that it will be necessary for the court to examine whether fidelity to the principles of the CRPD (as to which, see further chapter 28) require a litigation friend to act, in essence, as an advocate for the wishes and feelings of P (insofar as they can be ascertained).

The duties – litigation friend acting for P

12.55   The COPR draw no distinctions between the roles of a litigation friend depending upon whether they are acting on behalf of P or on behalf of a protected party (or, indeed, a child, a position addressed further at paras 12.71ff below).

12.56   However, it is suggested that there are, nonetheless, some important distinctions that apply depending upon whether the litigation friend is acting on behalf of P or on behalf of a protected party (or a child). As set out above (para 12.52), the Official Solicitor takes this view. We will consider the position of each category in turn, but we note as a preliminary point that the Department of Health has commissioned guidance for non-legal professionals such as IMCAs and RPRs, as well as family members, who are considering acting as litigation friends for P. Such guidance will be published during the course of 2014.

12.57   A litigation friend acting on behalf of P has a particularly important role to play, and they must be astute not inappropriately to interpose themselves as an additional decision-maker upon the issues in the case (be those of capacity or best interests). In order to discharge their functions and to give instructions to legal representatives (if they are instructed), such a litigation friend will have to form a view as to:

- whether P has capacity to take the decisions in issue (if they form the view that P has, in fact, got capacity to litigate, then, as discussed at paras 12.75ff below, they must bring that matter to the attention of the court as soon as possible); and

91 They will be discussed in greater detail in an article by Alex Ruck Keene and others to be published in due course.

92 The opportunity to examine the basis upon which the Official Solicitor acts in proceedings before the Court of Protection arose in a case called *TA v AA and others*, but the Court of Appeal determined the appeal upon an unrelated technicality: [2013] EWCA Civ 1661 (see further chapter 19).

- if P lacks capacity to take the decisions in issue, where P's best interests will lie.

12.58   However, while the litigation friend can – and should – proceed on the basis of the views concluded upon those issues, and (where appropriate) to put a case as to both to the court, it is vital that they a) do not thereby slip into a role akin to that of a children's guardian, a role that was specifically not provided for in the COPR; and (in turn or otherwise); (b) do not seek to pre-empt the court's determination upon the issues. This is particularly important where: i) where the assessment either of capacity or of best interests is finely balanced; or ii) P has very strong views which conflict with the litigation friend's assessment of the relevant issue.

12.59   In respect of this latter category of case (which is not unusual), as the law stands at present, it appears clear that a litigation friend is not bound to advance a case to the court that they properly consider – after suitably anxious consideration – to be unarguable.[93] However, it is important to recognise that, if P has a strong view as to what they wish the court to do but the litigation friend properly considers that such a view is unarguable, then there is a tension between the position of the litigation friend and P's rights under ECHR articles 6 (right to a fair trial) and 8 (right to respect for private and family life). This tension is particularly acute because – as set out above, and least as presently understood – the role of a litigation friend is not to act as advocate for P. This tension is likely to be examined in detail in due course within the context of the Court of Protection, but as Peter Jackson QC (as he then was) noted in advice given to the Official Solicitor and attached to the judgment of the Court of Appeal in *RP*:

> 15. ... This tension can however be avoided or diminished if the Official Solicitor does not positively support the making of the relevant order – indeed that the circumstances in which he would wish to do so should surely be rare.
>
> 16. There are several other possible reasons for taking this view:
> (i) The parent would not be obliged to make concessions if acting autonomously and there is no reason why they should be made on his/her behalf.
> (ii) It may be gratuitously distressing and offensive to (and thus not in the interests of) the parent to hear their representative making submissions that are flatly in opposed to their own views and feelings.

---

93 See in this regard *RP v UK* at para 76. See also note 90 above.

(iii) A decision of such gravity should be made by the court scrutinising the evidence, and not by concession.

(iv) Such concessionary submissions are almost always superfluous to the decision taken by the court.

17. I therefore believe that the role of litigation friend in these cases can properly be performed by making a positive case whenever this can properly be done without detriment to the parent, but where such a case cannot be made, to confine submissions to statements that (for example) the Official Solicitor does not wish to make submissions on this issue/makes no contrary submissions on that issue/does not oppose such-and-such a conclusion on another issue.

...

19. I reiterate that there may be cases in which it is in the parent's interests for a case contrary to his/her wishes to be actively pursued, or where the failure to concede an issue might appear unrealistic or fatuous, but these might be seen as exceptions.

12.60 This advice was given in the context of a litigation friend acting for a protected party, rather than on behalf of the subject of the proceedings. However, it is suggested that it holds equally good for litigation friends acting on behalf of P before the Court of Protection – where the tension between the duties owed by the litigation friend to the court and P's rights under ECHR articles 6 and 8 is arguably even starker.

12.61 In all cases where a litigation friend acts for P, it is clear from all that is set out above that, although they do not act as their advocate, it is vitally important that they take all necessary steps to relay P's wishes and feelings to the court upon the relevant issues in the case.

Litigation friend acting for P – deprivation of liberty cases

12.62 It is suggested that litigation friends should proceed with particular caution where P's right to liberty under ECHR article 5 (right to liberty and security) is engaged, and in particular in cases brought under MCA 2005 s21A in relation to authorisations granted under the DOLS regime (see further chapter 22). It is particularly unfortunate in this regard that the Court of Appeal in *TA v AA*[94] did not consider the substance of the appeal in that case, which was – in essence – against the decision of the Official Solicitor (substituted

94 [2013] EWCA Civ 1661.

– at his request – as litigation friend for *AA*) to seek permission to withdraw an application under MCA 2005 s21A challenging a standard authorisation. The questions that arose upon the appeal were of wider importance and it is therefore to be regretted that they remain unanswered.[95]

12.63   A person deprived of their liberty pursuant to an authorisation granted under the DOLS regime is – for purposes of ECHR article 5 – in the same position as a person detained under the provisions of the Mental Health Act (MHA) 1983. The statutory framework within which that deprivation of liberty is authorised are different, but both categories of person are subject to a deprivation of liberty falling within the scope of article 5(1) and therefore prima facie entitled to the same protections – and, in particular to the right under article 5(4) to take proceedings by which the lawfulness of their detention shall be decided speedily by a court and his release ordered if the detention is not lawful.

12.64   The ECtHR have laid down a number of important propositions in relation to ECHR article 5 in respect of deprivations of liberty in care homes and/or under the MHA 1983, of which the most relevant for present purposes are the following:

> In order to comply with art.5(1), the detention in issue must first of all be 'lawful', including the observance of a procedure prescribed by law; in this respect the Convention refers back essentially to national law and lays down the obligation to conform to the substantive and procedural rules thereof. It requires in addition, however, that any deprivation of liberty should be consistent with the purpose of art.5, namely to protect individuals from arbitrariness. Furthermore, the detention of an individual is such a serious measure that it is only justified where other, less severe measures have been considered and found to be insufficient to safeguard the individual or public interest which might require that the person concerned be detained. That means that it does not suffice that the deprivation of liberty is in conformity with national law; it must also be necessary in the circumstances.[96]

And:

> As the right set forth in Article 5 § 4 of the Convention is guaranteed to everyone, it is clear that special safeguards are called for in the case of detained mental patients who lack legal capacity to institute

---

95 See, for a discussion of the case and the issues that arise, Alastair Pitblado, 'An unanswered question: *TA v AA*' [2014] Eld LJ 98. It is clear from that article that not all of the propositions set down in the paragraphs that follow here would be agreed by the Official Solicitor.

96 *Stanev v Bulgaria* (2012) 55 EHRR 22 at para 143 (deprivation of liberty in a social care home).

proceedings before judicial bodies. However, it is not for this Court to dictate what form those special safeguards should take, provided that they make the right guaranteed by Article 5 § 4 as nearly as possible as practical and effective for this particular category of detainees as it is for other detainees.[97]

And:

Among the principles which can be found in the Court's case-law under Article 5 § 4 concerning 'persons of unsound mind' are the following:

...

(d) the judicial proceedings referred to in Article 5 § 4 need not always be attended by the same guarantees as those required under Article 6 § 1 for civil or criminal litigation. Nonetheless, it is essential that the person concerned should have access to a court and the opportunity to be heard either in person or, where necessary, through some form of representation.[98]

And (previously):

[Article 5(4)] is first and foremost a guarantee of fair procedure for reviewing the lawfulness of detention – an applicant is not required, as precondition for enjoying that protection, to show that on the facts of his case he stands any particular chance of success in obtaining his release.[99]

12.65 The analogy between patients detained under the MHA 1983 and those deprived of their liberty under DOLS authorisations is of particular importance given the regime that is in place to address the representation of patients without capacity in challenges to detention under the MHA 1983. Any unjustified difference in the regimes that apply would give rise to a clear breach of ECHR article 5 combined with article 14 (right not to be discriminated against in the enjoyment of the rights arising under the ECHR).

12.66 All patients detained under the MHA 1983 have a right to test the basis upon which they are detained at regular intervals;[100] if they do not seek to take up that right (including if they lack the capacity to instigate an application), then the relevant hospital managers must at appropriate intervals take steps to bring an application to the mental health tribunal to review whether the basis for continued detention is

---

97 *MH v UK* (App No 11577/06, decision of 22 October 2013), para 82. Note that a court must conduct a review that is wide enough to bear on all the conditions which are essential to the lawfulness of the detention: *MH* at para 74.

98 *MH* at para 77, citing *Megyeri v Germany* (1992) 15 EHRR 584 at para 22(c).

99 *Waite v UK* (2003) 36 EHRR 54 at para 59.

100 MHA 1983 s66.

made out.[101] In such applications, and if the patient lacks the capacity to give instructions, a legal representative can be appointed by the tribunal to act on their behalf.[102] While such a representative does not discharge precisely the same role as a litigation friend, we suggest that it is of some importance that the Law Society considers that, while a solicitor in such a case can – and indeed – must refuse to advance an argument which is not properly arguable, '[g]iven the "least restrictive alternative" principle in s1(6) of the Mental Capacity Act 2005 it would be in a rare case that to seek a client's discharge in accordance with his or her express wishes would not be "properly arguable", although it will be a matter for your judgment in each case'.[103]

12.67   The least restrictive principle noted above applies equally to circumstances where a person is deprived of their liberty subject to a DOLS authorisation,[104] and we also note the decision in *A v A Local Authority and others*[105] in which, despite there being no evidence to suggest that the deprivation of liberty was other than in A's best interests, the then-President, Sir Nicholas Wall, authorised the instruction of a visitor to report under the provisions of MCA 2005 s49. In so doing, Sir Nicholas Wall P noted that he was:

> [15] very conscious that the Act has laid down stringent conditions for the deprivation of liberty, and that the court cannot simply act as a rubber stamp, however beneficial the arrangements may appear to be for the individual concerned. In the instant case, A wishes to challenge the authorisation, which deprives him of his liberty.

---

101 MHA 1983 s68.
102 Under Tribunal Procedure (First-tier Tribunal) (Health, Education and Social Care Chamber) Rules 2008 SI No 2699 rule 11(7).
103 Practice note available at: www.lawsociety.org.uk/advice/practice-notes/ mental-health-tribunals/ at para 4.1, citing *AA v Cheshire and Wirral Partnership NHS Foundation Trust* [2009] UKUT 195 (AAC). Note that this practice note is at the time of writing under review.
104 The principles contained in MCA 2005 s1(6) apply equally in respect of the grant of authorisations under MCA 2005 Sch A1; para 5 of this Schedule also makes it a necessary condition to the grant of any authorisation that the deprivation of liberty is a proportionate response to the likelihood of the relevant person suffering harm and the seriousness of that harm.
105 [2011] EWHC 727 (COP), [2011] COPLR Con Vol 190. It should be noted that this was the course of action urged upon him by the Official Solicitor, acting on behalf of A, and in the face of submissions from the local authority (supported by A's son) that the case should be summarily determined.

Parliament has decreed that he should be entitled to do so,[106] and has created safeguards to protect those deprived of their liberty against arbitrary action.

12.68 In the circumstances, and taking into account, in particular, the case-law from the ECtHR, it is suggested that in a case involving a deprivation of liberty:

- a litigation friend for P must *always* consider testing whether it is correct that the assertion implicit in a request that the court uphold an authorisation or otherwise approve a deprivation of liberty that the regime in question is the least restrictive option. In other words, and to use the language of the ECtHR, the litigation friend must consider testing whether other, less severe measures have been considered and found to be insufficient to safeguard the individual or public interest which might require that the person concerned be detained;[107]
- where P wishes to challenge that deprivation, then we would suggest that the litigation friend is, in fact, *obliged* to do so unless satisfied, after the most careful deliberation, that there truly is no properly arguable case that the deprivation of liberty does not represent the least restrictive requirement. If this is the case, then we would further suggest that it would never be appropriate for the litigation friend actively to concede that the deprivation of liberty was in P's best interests. At most, we would suggest, the litigation friend could leave it to the judge to decide (having ensured that P's views were relayed to the court). This would still require an oral hearing.

The duties – litigation friend acting for a protected party

12.69 To some extent, the position of a litigation friend acting for a party other than P is easier. As the focus of the proceedings is not upon the best interests of the protected party, but rather upon the best

---

106 Note also in this regard the scope of duties imposed upon an IMCA appointed under MCA 2005 s39D (where the RPR is unpaid and, among other things, P requests an advocate be instructed), which include assisting P to exercise their right to apply to court if appears to the advocate that P wishes to exercise that right – there are no considerations as to whether such is in P's best interests.

107 As did the Official Solicitor in *Y County Council v ZZ* [2013] COPLR 463, in which ZZ vigorously disputed the necessity for the restrictions imposed upon him – primarily so as to secure against the risk that he would commit sexual offences against children.

interests of P, the potential risks of the litigation friend interposing themselves as decision-maker do not arise.

12.70   The main issue that is likely to arise is that which arose – by analogy – in the *RP* case – ie that the protected party will want to advance a positive case as to where P's best interests lie that the litigation friend considers after proper consideration not to be properly arguable. In such a case, it is suggested that the litigation friend is not required positively to advance that case to the court, albeit that it is vital that they put clearly the protected party's view to the court so as to secure their rights under ECHR article 6 (and arguably also article 8).

The duties – litigation friend acting for a child

12.71   Finally, we note the position of a litigation friend acting for a child. As set out at paras 12.24ff above, while a child must have a litigation friend unless the court orders otherwise,[108] there are – logically – two different reasons why this might be so: a) because their age and maturity means that they are not '*Gillick*-competent';[109] or b) because they suffer from a material disturbance or impairment of the mind or brain.

12.72   A litigation friend acting on behalf of a child over the age of 16 who suffers from a material disturbance of the mind of brain giving rise to a lack of litigation capacity is, we suggest, in the same position as a litigation friend acting on behalf of an adult protected party.

12.73   Strictly speaking, then assuming that litigation friends are, in general, bound to act pursuant to MCA 2005 s1(5),[110] the same does not go for:

- a litigation friend acting on behalf of a child under the age of 16 who suffers from a material disturbance or impairment of the mind or brain, as the MCA 2005 s1(5) could never apply to the litigation friend's actions given the wording of MCA 2005 s2(5);[111]
- a litigation friend acting on behalf of a child under 18 who requires a litigation friend because of their age and lack of maturity, MCA 2005 s1(5) not being capable of applying to them because there is no relevant impairment or disturbance of the mind or brain.

---

108 COPR r141(3)–(4).

109 *Gillick v West Norfolk and Wisbech Area Health Authority* [1986] 1 AC 112.

110 As to which, see further para 12.54 above.

111 Which provides that no power may be exercised by a person under the MCA 2005 in relation to a person who lacks capacity under the age of 16; the exception in section 18(3) would not apply.

12.74 In either of these circumstances, it is therefore suggested that a litigation friend acting for a child takes their duties from COPR r140, albeit (by analogy with the situation where a litigation friend is appointed for a child in family proceedings), all steps and decisions the litigation friend takes in the proceedings must be taken for the benefit of the child.[112]

Terminating the appointment of a litigation friend

Capacity regained

Litigation friend acting on behalf of P

12.75 P (or their litigation friend or any other party to the proceedings) can apply to discharge the appointment of P's litigation friend if P ceases to lack capacity to conduct the proceedings, but continues to lack capacity in relation to the matter or matters to which the application relates.[113] If P regains capacity in relation to the matter or matters to which the application relates, then the court will have no jurisdiction under the MCA 2005 and an application should be made (supported by evidence as to P's capacity in the relevant regard(s)) to bring the proceedings to come to an end[114] (see further paras 16.57ff).

12.76 An application to discharge a litigation friend acting on behalf of P must be supported by evidence.[115] Examples of applications made by or on behalf of P to discharge a litigation friend appointed to act on their behalf are rare. Indeed, the authors are aware of only one reported application, made in the medical treatment case of in *Re SB*,[116] where the Official Solicitor applied successfully to be discharged on the basis of expert evidence that P had litigation capacity.[117]

12.77 Save in a case where it is entirely clear that P can never have litigation capacity because of the severity of their underlying disability, the litigation friend acting on P's behalf should, nonetheless, be very astute to keep P's capacity to conduct the litigation under review and, if it appears that they may have regained litigation capacity, take immediate steps to bring matters before the court in short order.

---

112 FPR PD 16A para 2.1.
113 COPR r147(1).
114 COPR r148 and PD 23B.
115 PD 17A para 20.
116 [2013] EWHC 1417 (COP), [2013] COPLR 445.
117 See paras 27–30.

12.78   It should be noted that the COPR specifically provide that P *themselves* can make an application for an order discharging the litigation friend acting on their behalf.[118] It is suggested that this is an important safeguard for a P who wishes to dispute that they lack capacity to make the relevant decision(s) and/or to litigate. However, the structure of COPR rr141 and 147 can cause difficulty because they, in effect, require P to prove that he or she *does* have capacity (ie a reversal of the normal presumption of capacity). This is particularly so in the light of the requirement for evidence of capacity to be provided with the application.[119]

12.79   The Review Committee set up to consider the operation of the COPR recommended in 2010[120] that COPR r141 be reconsidered. Unfortunately, while the recommendation was accepted by the then-President of the Family Division, no further steps have been taken to implement it. Subsequent to the recommendation being made, the decision of the ECtHR in *RP*[121] emphasised the importance of steps being taken to make effective any right that exists to challenge the appointment of a litigation friend 'however effective in theory';[122] otherwise ECHR article 6(1) will not be complied with.

12.80   Pending any review of COPR r141, it is suggested that, in a case where P wishes to challenge the appointment of a litigation friend on the basis that they assert that they have litigation capacity, P can properly in their application for an order for discharge:

1) raise any difficulties that they have encountered in obtaining evidence in support of that assertion;
2) pray in aid the presumption of capacity; and
3) seek urgent directions from the court for the resolution of the question of their litigation capacity before any further steps are taken in the litigation.

---

118 COPR r147(3)(a).

119 PD 17A para 20.

120 *Report of the ad hoc Court of Protection Rules Committee*, available at: www.judiciary.gov.uk/Resources/JCO/Documents/Reports/committee-report-court-protection-29072010.pdf.

121 *RP v UK* (App No 38245/08, decision of 9 October 2012), [2013] 1 FLR 744.

122 *RP* at para 72, in the context of the right of a protected party in care proceedings to challenge the appointment of the Official Solicitor as litigation friend; the required steps in that case being as to the explanation in appropriate language of the fact of his appointment, the implications of his appointment, the existence of a means of challenging his appointment and the procedure for exercising it.

Litigation friend acting on behalf of an adult protected party

12.81 Where an adult protected party ceases to lack capacity to conduct the litigation, an application can be made for the litigation friend's order of appointment to be discharged akin to that discussed above in respect of P themselves[123] (para 12.75 above). Such application can be made by the protected party, their litigation friend or any other party to the proceedings.[124] Such application must be supported by evidence that the former protected party now has the requisite capacity.[125] The former protected party should also provide their address for service to all the other parties.[126]

Litigation friend acting on behalf of a child

12.82 When a child party to proceedings turns 18, then, if they are not a protected party (ie an adult without litigation capacity), the appointment of the litigation friend will come to an end automatically.[127] The child must, though, serve notice on every other party stating that they have reached full age, that the appointment of the litigation friend has ended, and providing their address for service.[128]

12.83 Although the COPR do not expressly contemplate it, it is suggested that there is nothing to prevent an application being made during the currency of proceedings that a child no longer requires a litigation friend to conduct the proceedings on their behalf.[129] This would be appropriate if, for instance, the litigation friend considers that a child not suffering from any disability but previously requiring a litigation friend because they were not *Gillick*-competent[130] has now matured sufficiently to understand and conduct their own litigation.

---

123 COPR r146(3).
124 COPR r146(4).
125 PD 17A para 20.
126 COPR r146(7).
127 COPR r146(1)(a) and (2).
128 COPR r146(6).
129 Ie for an order under COPR r141(4).
130 *Gillick v West Norfolk and Wisbech Area Health Authority* [1986] 1 AC 112.

Terminating the appointment of a litigation friend: other circumstances

12.84   Any litigation friend can also be removed by the court:

- on their own application (if, for instance, P is no longer eligible for public funding and the litigation friend cannot continue to discharge their functions without such funding to pay for legal advice and representation);[131]
- on the application of another party;[132] or
- of the court's own motion.[133]

12.85   COPR r144 does not place any limit on the power of the court to terminate the appointment of a litigation friend. In *Re A (conjoined twins: medical treatment) (No 2)*,[134] Ward LJ commented on the:

> ... particular situation in which the court is asked to replace a guardian ad litem because the guardian has in the conduct of litigation taken a course of action (in which we include an omission), or is about to take a course of action, which is manifestly contrary to the best interests of the child whose interests it is the guardian's duty to safeguard. If the guardian (or litigation friend) does act manifestly contrary to the child's best interests, the court will remove him even though neither his good faith nor his diligence is in issue.

It is suggested that a similar approach would be adopted in the Court of Protection (subject to the discussion at para 12.56 above as to the precise scope of the litigation friend's duties).

12.86   In any case where a litigation friend's appointment is terminated, the court will strive, if at all possible, to appoint a suitable person to act as replacement litigation friend[135] so that the proceedings can continue in an uninterrupted fashion.

---

131 COPR r144(1)(b). The application will be made under the Part 10 procedure described at paras 11.19–11.21.
132 COPR r144(1)(b).
133 COPR r144(1)(b).
134 [2001] 1 FLR 267.
135 COPR r144(1)(c).

Costs and the litigation friend

Costs incurred by the litigation friend

The Official Solicitor

12.87　The Official Solicitor is placed in a special position by virtue of COPR r163, which provides that his or her costs (if they are not met by payments made out of P's estate by P's deputy, donee or attorney) shall be paid by such person or out of such funds as the court may direct. As noted above, the Official Solicitor will not accept an invitation to act as litigation friend if he or she is not satisfied that there is provision for the (in-house or external) litigation costs to be met.

12.88　　Largely for historical reasons, the Official Solicitor receives sufficient central government funding to conduct (in-house) proceedings relating to serious medical treatment cases (as to which, see further chapter 23), and is also conventionally awarded half the costs of so doing against the relevant NHS body: see *An NHS Trust v D*.[136] The Official Solicitor will now frequently decline to act in such cases until an undertaking to meet half of his or her costs has been received from the NHS body in question.

Other litigation friends

12.89　There are no equivalent statutory provisions to those relating to the Official Solicitor to guarantee reimbursement for others who act as litigation friend (whether for P or another individual requiring such representation). In *B v B*,[137] a case concerned with the ability of the Official Solicitor to recover his costs of acting as the litigation friend of an adult in matrimonial proceedings, Bennett J held that a litigation friend acts as the agent of the protected party and is entitled to be reimbursed by the protected party for the properly incurred costs of so acting.[138]

12.90　　It is suggested that this principle holds true in Court of Protection proceedings for all litigation friends. There is, though, a difference between an entitlement to reimbursement and security for costs – ie a guarantee that the costs incurred (if properly incurred) will be repaid. As set out at para 12.45 above, it is suggested that – as with the Official Solicitor – it is entirely proper for a litigation friend such

---

as an IMCA or family member to decline an invitation to act without sufficient security for their costs of so doing.

Costs payable to other parties

12.91   As noted above (para 12.43), a curious feature of the COPR is that (unlike the CPR) they do not provide any circumstance under which the litigation friend is required personally to undertake to pay the costs incurred by other parties in proceedings before the Court of Protection. That most likely reflects the general rules on costs in such proceedings which are to the effect that either a) P is to pay the costs of proceedings relating to their property and affairs;[139] or b) there should be no order as to costs in proceedings relating to P's health and welfare[140] (see further chapter 17 below).

12.92   It is clear, however, that the party on whose behalf the litigation friend acts can be made the subject of a costs order – and, indeed, the general rule in property and affairs proceedings is that P will be required to pay the costs of those proceedings (including those costs incurred by others).[141] There is no reason in principle why a child or an adult protected party could not also be made the subject of a costs order. It would be the responsibility of the litigation friend to take appropriate steps to ensure that these costs are met (it is suggested as part of their duties to the court in the conduct of the litigation). It is not clear, however, that this would, formally give rise to a personal liability on the part of the litigation friend to meet the costs.[142] Even if it did, however, it is suggested that the litigation friend can look to the individual to reimburse them, at least if the proceedings have been properly conducted on the part of the litigation friend.[143]

12.93   Any litigation friend (theoretically including the Official Solicitor) is, however, potentially at risk of being ordered to pay costs *themselves*.[144] Even though they are not, themselves, a party to proceedings,

---

139   COPR r156.

140   COPR r157.

141   COPR r156.

142   Something which is unclear given that there is no equivalent in the COPR to the undertaking that a litigation friend must give in civil proceedings to pay such costs (required by CPR r21(4)(c)). It may be that the obligation arises at common law, see *ex p Brocklebank* (1877) 6 Ch D 358 at 360.

143   See, by analogy, *Re E (mental health patient)* [1984] 1 WLR 320 at p324H per Sir Robert Megarry V-C, and also *B v B* [2010] EWHC 453 (Fam), [2012] COPLR 450.

144   See para 12.46 above as to whether a litigation friend is required to be a natural person.

the COPR has provision for costs orders to be made against non-parties.[145] PD 17A para 22 also specifically notes that: 'The court has the power to make an order against a person who is not a party to proceedings (including a litigation friend).' In the absence of further guidance to clarify the scant provisions of the COPR as they relate to litigation friends other than the Official Solicitor, it has become an increasing practice for RPRs and IMCAs in welfare proceedings to make their agreement to act as litigation friend conditional on the giving of an undertaking on the part of the relevant public authority that they will not seek their costs against the RPR/IMCA. It is suggested that this is a useful mechanism by which RPRs/IMCAs can be given reassurance in the discharge of what is an important public function, although it cannot (and would not be seen by the court as) acting as a carte blanche to the RPR/IMCA acting as litigation friend to depart from the proper and proportionate conduct of litigation.

12.94   There are no reported cases in which a litigation friend has themselves been made the subject of a costs order in the Court of Protection, and it is suggested that such an order would only be made in the event of serious misconduct on the part of the litigation friend, especially if such misconduct had the consequence of increasing the costs of the proceedings. In the event of such misconduct, it is further suggested that a local authority that had given an undertaking of the nature described in the paragraph immediately above would readily be relieved of its obligation by a judge and given permission to seek their costs as against the litigation friend personally.

---

145 COPR r166.

Evidence and disclosure

Introduction

13.1   This chapter deals with the process by which sufficient evidence is obtained and put before a judge to enable him or her to decide upon the application before them. It deals, in particular, with the different categories of evidence that may be necessary, whether that be factual evidence or expert evidence. It addresses questions relating to hearsay evidence and – linked to this – hearing from P. It then turns, finally, to disclosure, in particular the questions of when and how disclosure is or should be withheld.

13.2   The matters covered in this chapter are very wide-ranging, and space precludes detailed discussion of the intricacies of such matters as the law relating to hearsay evidence. The reader is directed to such works as *Phipson on Evidence;*[1] there is also valuable commentary to be found about the application of the principles to public law proceedings relating to children (which bear certain analogies to proceedings relating to incapacitated adults) in works such as *Hershman and McFarlane: children law and practice.*[2]

Evidence

The powers of the court

13.3   The provisions of Part 14 of the Court of Protection Rules (COPR) 2007 SI No 1744, amplified by Practice Direction (PD) 14, set out a detailed framework by which the court can ensure that (ideally) it has before it that evidence, but only that evidence, which it needs to make the decision(s) it is asked to make. The heart of Part 14 is rule 95, which provides that:

>   **95**(1) The court may–
>   (a) control the evidence by giving directions as to:
>   (i)   the issues on which it requires evidence;
>   (ii) the nature of the evidence which it requires to give those issues; and
>   (iii) the way in which the evidence is to be placed before the court;
>   (b) use its power under this rule to exclude evidence that would otherwise be admissible;

---

1   Sweet & Maxwell, 18th edn, 2013.
2   Jordans, looseleaf, Section 7.

(c) allow or limit cross-examination; and

(d) admit such evidence, whether written or oral, as it thinks fit.

13.4   The powers granted to judges under this rule are in addition to the general case management powers granted them by rules 5 and 85 (as to which, see paras 11.9–11.11 above). They are very broad, and reflect the fact that a very wide range of cases come before the Court of Protection, requiring a carefully calibrated approach so as to ensure that (in line with the overriding objective set down in rule 4) evidence is obtained – and limited – in a proportional fashion.

What evidence is required?

13.5   The Mental Capacity Act (MCA) 2005 and COPR are silent as to the evidential requirements that must be satisfied before the court can decide the applications(s) before it. There are, though, two obligations of particular importance that are imposed upon the court:

1) to act in the best interests of the adult without capacity if the decision before it is one falling within the scope of MCA 2005 s1(5), which requires that an act done or decision made under the MCA 2005 for or on behalf of a person who lacks capacity 'must be done, or made, in his best interests';

2) to act compatibly with the rights under the European Convention on Human Rights (ECHR) of the adult without capacity (and, to the extent relevant, the rights of the other parties to the application or potentially affected by its decision)[3] (see further chapter 26).

13.6   Determining the nature and scope of the evidence required by the court is a matter that is complicated by the fact that:

> The processes of the Court of Protection are essentially inquisitorial rather than adversarial. In other words, the ambit of the litigation is determined, not by the parties, but by the court, because the function of the court is not to determine in a disinterested way a dispute brought to it by the parties, but rather, to engage in a process of assessing whether an adult is lacking in capacity, and if so, making decisions about his welfare that are in his best interests.[4]

---

3 Human Rights Act (HRA) 1998 s6(1), read together with s6(3).

4 *Cheshire West and Cheshire Council v P and M* [2011] EWHC 1330 (Fam), [2011] COPLR Con Vol 273 at para 52 per Baker J. This aspect of his decision was not the subject of challenge upon the Official Solicitor's appeal to the Court of Appeal or thereafter to the Supreme Court.

13.7   That having been said:

- In all cases, the burden lies upon the party asserting that P lacks capacity to take the material decisions in question to establish that this the case, on the balance of probabilities.[5]
- Further, it may be necessary that a party prove a particular fact or facts in a way akin to conventional civil litigation:
  - In *LBB v JM, BK and CM*[6] Hedley J held that, where the intervention of the court would engage a potential breach of rights under the ECHR, as is particularly likely in welfare cases, it is incumbent upon the applicant to establish a factual basis upon which the court can be satisfied that both that the jurisdiction should be exercised and that any interference is lawful.
  - Another (not uncommon) scenario is where it is said that a deputy or attorney has behaved in a way which justifies the intervention of the court; in such instance, it will fall to the party asserting such misconduct to establish it upon the basis of appropriate evidence.

13.8   Questions of the resolution of disputed facts are addressed further in chapter 16 below. The resolution of disputes as to capacity is addressed further in the context of the final determination of proceedings at chapter 17 below.

13.9   Further, even if a judge is presented with a consent order for approval by parties to an application, the judge is required to consider for themselves as an independent matter whether they can properly endorse that order, and must do so by reference to the evidence before them. In a contested application, one of the first questions for the court will be to determine as precisely as possible what evidence it will require before it can make any final decision(s) (see in this regard see also chapter 17, on directions hearings).

13.10   A failure to bring proceedings upon the basis of proper evidence can lead to substantial costs consequences. A good example of this is *A Local Authority v HS and others*,[7] in which the local authority maintained allegations that P's brother had sexually abused her but then withdrew them shortly before a hearing was to take place to determine them, on the basis that it accepted that it would not be able to establish them. The local authority applicant was ordered to pay all of the costs claimed by the Official Solicitor on behalf of P and

---

5   MCA 2005 ss1(2) and 2(4). See also *PH v A Local Authority and others* [2011] EWHC 1704 (Fam), [2012] COPLR 128 at para 16, per Baker J.

6   [2010] COPLR Con Vol 779.

7   [2013] EWHC 2410 (COP).

of P's brother in respect of the steps taken towards the determination of the allegation up to and including the point that the local authority withdrew the allegation. As the court noted: 'Cogent evidence never existed. It should have been obvious long before these proceedings were commenced ... that there was never any cogent evidence'.[8] Those costs amounted (together) to some £88,000.

Admissions

13.11   The COPR provide for the making of admissions by a party of the truth of the whole or another part of another party's case by giving notice in writing.[9] This provision is, in the authors' experience, rarely invoked, but it serves as a formal mechanism by which factual matters can be agreed between the parties and advanced to the court as an agreed basis upon which it can then be invited to take a decision. There is no necessary formality to the notice that is required (nor is it necessary that the notice be filed at court), but it is prudent to ensure that, where an admission is being made, express reference is made to the provisions of COPR r94(1) and care is taken to ensure that the precise scope of what is being admitted is defined.

Factual evidence

Overview

13.12   Very broadly, most evidence before the court will fall into one of two categories: factual evidence and expert evidence. The latter is discussed at paras 13.58ff below. The former constitutes a range of different types of material, the most obvious being evidence from witnesses as to facts relevant to the decision(s) that the court is being asked to take. The different categories of such evidence are discussed below.

Witness statements: formalities and contents

13.13   The general rule is that any fact that needs to be proved by the evidence of a witness must be proved by the oral evidence of that witness if there is a final hearing, and by their evidence in writing at

---

8   Para 185, per District Judge Eldergill.
9   COPR r94(1). The court may allow a party to amend or withdraw an admission: COPR r94(2).

any other hearing (or if there is no hearing).[10] It would appear that a permission form, an application form or an application notice can stand as evidence at a hearing other than a final hearing if verified by a statement of truth.[11]

13.14   Almost without exception, and in line with the position that prevails in civil litigation and proceedings involving children, a witness will be required to provide a witness statement in advance of the final hearing, which will stand (if they are to give oral evidence) as their evidence in chief.[12] In other words, the court will accept their statement (if it complies with the formal requirements discussed below) at a final hearing *as if* they had given its contents orally in response to questions from the representative of the party on whose behalf the witness has been called. The corollary of this is that a witness will only be allowed to amplify their statement and/or to give evidence relating to new matters if there is good reason to do so.[13] The latitude granted by judges to witnesses to go beyond the contents of their witness statement in oral evidence will depend greatly upon the circumstances of the case, but as a general rule it is prudent to proceed on the cautious basis that no amplification will be given, and the only opportunity that the witness will get to give oral evidence will be in response to questions asked in cross-examination by other parties or to questions asked by the judge.

13.15   While permission is not required to serve written evidence with an application (including an interim application) or in response to an application (and indeed, it is in some circumstances mandatory to file such evidence[14]), as a general rule it is only possible to rely upon written evidence filed subsequently if permission has been given by the court.[15] As noted above (and discussed further in chapter 11), one of the primary questions for the court as part of its case management functions will be to decide whether to grant such permission; indeed, it is required by the COPR to give directions as to the service

---

10   COPR r96(1).

11   COPR r11(3)(a).

12   COPR r96(2).

13   COPR r96(3)–(4).

14   For instance, a party served with an application who opposes it or seeks a different order must file a witness statement with their acknowledgment of service containing any evidence upon which they intend to rely: COPR r72(5); an interim application must also be accompanied by evidence if it the evidence not already before the court: COPR r78(2);

15   COPR r97(c).

of witness statements in advance of the final hearing.[16] Judges will be astute in deciding whether to grant permission to ensure – insofar as possible – that the written evidence filed only goes to the issues in question.

13.16　Witness statements to be used at a final hearing are the subject of particular requirements. They must contain a statement of truth and comply with the requirements of paras 33–50 of PD 14A.[17] While, strictly, witness evidence prepared for other purposes (for instance, at an interim hearing), does not need to comply with these requirements, it is advisable that, wherever practicable, witness evidence is put before the court in a form that can stand, if necessary, at the final hearing.

13.17　A sample witness statement is to be found in appendix D below. The most important points to emphasise in relation to the preparation of witness statements are as follows:

- Witness statements should be clearly headed so that it is immediately obvious who is giving the statement, on whose behalf they are giving it, whether it is the first statement that they are making (and, if not, which number it is), and the date upon which it was made.
- While witness statements must be attached to a COP24 form, it is not necessary that they are included in the form itself. The form is unwieldy; unless the statement is very short, it is often much better to prepare the statement as a stand-alone document and attach it to a COP24. If this is done, then it is advisable to include a statement of truth at the end of the stand-alone document as well as in the box contained in the COP24.
- Only evidence that is relevant to the issue(s) before the court should be included. Indeed evidence that is not relevant is strictly not admissible.[18] In this regard, it should also be noted that the Civil Procedure Rules (CPR) (from which the material provisions of the COPR were drawn) were themselves amended with effect from 1 April 2013 specifically to direct judges to consider making directions: 1) identifying or limiting the issues to which factual evidence may be directed; 2) identifying the witnesses who may be called or whose evidence may be read; or 3) limiting the length

---

16　COPR r99(2).

17　COPR r100 read together with PD 14A. PD 14B makes detailed provisions relating to statements of truth.

18　*Hollington v Hewthorn and Co Ltd* [1943] KB 587 at 594. For a detailed discussion of questions of relevance and admissibility, see *Phipson on Evidence* chapter 7.

or format of witness statements.[19] It is likely that in due course an equivalent provision will be incorporated into the COPR.

- It is important clearly to distinguish in the statement between facts that are directly within the knowledge of the person making the statement and those which are matters of information or belief (and, where the latter, the source for those matters). While it may be quite proper for a witness statement to contain hearsay evidence (ie evidence relating to matters that they have not witnessed directly, discussed further below at para 13.22 below), it is necessary that this is clearly identified.

- Any exhibits should be clearly referenced in the statement by the witness; where the witness gives more than one statement, the numbering of the exhibits should run consecutively throughout, rather than starting again with each statement. The mechanics of exhibiting documents (and other items) to a witness statement are set out at PD 14A paras 20–31.[20]

13.18   A common error in statements prepared by public bodies in welfare proceedings is that they do not set out in sufficient detail what is proposed for P, why the proposed option is considered to be in P's best interests and how, if there is to be a change in the arrangements for P (for instance a move) how any transition is to be managed. It is (often) the case that further investigation in fact reveals that the necessary issues have been considered, but that the analysis underpinning the conclusions set out in the statement is not set out in sufficient detail. A checklist for the preparation of such statements is to be found at appendix E but it will almost invariably be a useful exercise to include within any statement which sets out a proposal for P's future arrangements the balance sheet exercise of the nature identified by Thorpe LJ in the pre-MCA 2005 case of *Re A:*[21]

> There can be no doubt in my mind that the evaluation of best interests is akin to a welfare appraisal ... Pending the enactment of a checklist or other statutory direction it seems to me that the first instance judge with the responsibility to make an evaluation of the best interests of a claimant lacking capacity should draw up a balance sheet. The first entry should be of any factor or factors of actual benefit. In the present case the instance would be the acquisition of foolproof contraception. Then on the other sheet the judge should write any counterbalancing

---

19 CPR 32.2(3), as amended by Civil Procedure (Amendment) Rules 2013 SI No 262 r12.

20 Which apply not to just to affidavits, as suggested by their placement in the practice direction, but also to witness statements: see PD 14A para 39.

21 [2000] 1 FLR 549.

dis-benefits to the applicant. An obvious instance in this case would be the apprehension, the risk and the discomfort inherent in the operation. Then the judge should enter on each sheet the potential gains and losses in each instance making some estimate of the extent of the possibility that the gain or loss might accrue. At the end of that exercise the judge should be better placed to strike a balance between the sum of the certain and possible gains against the sum of the certain and possible losses. Obviously, only if the account is in relatively significant credit will the judge conclude that the application is likely to advance the best interests of the claimant.[22]

13.19   By the same token, if any other party wishes to advance an alternative suggestion as to what is in P's best interests in welfare proceedings (or, indeed, suggestions are being advanced as to P's best interests in proceedings relating to property and affairs), it is suggested that the maxim of 'show your workings' in terms of outlining the reasons why the course of action advanced is in P's best interests will always serve well.

Witness statements – timing

13.20   The court will usually consider, when giving directions as to service of witness statements, the order in which they are to be served.[23] Where P is a party to the proceedings, and the Official Solicitor acts their litigation friend, it is usual for the Official Solicitor to serve his evidence last. That evidence (save in the most straightforward of cases) takes a standard form and is not, formally, a witness statement, but simply a statement as the Official Solicitor does not have direct knowledge of the facts and matters in question. It is prepared by the solicitors instructed on the Official Solicitor's behalf (or by a lawyer or caseworker in the Official Solicitor's office if the matter is being handled in-house), but will be signed by the Official Solicitor or one of his or her deputies. It will set out the Official Solicitor's summary of the relevant background to and the procedural developments in the proceedings, and setting out the Official Solicitor's views as to P's best interests in the light of the evidence as it stands as at the time of the statement. Such views are almost invariably expressed as being subject to the caveat that they will be the subject of further consideration at the conclusion of the hearing, to cater for unanticipated developments at the hearing. It is suggested that a broadly similar approach

22 [2000] 1 FLR 549 at 560.
23 COPR r99(3).

should also be followed where another litigation friend is appointed to act on P's behalf.

13.21   In some circumstances, it is not possible for witness statements to be prepared and served in the way outlined above. There are two potential scenarios:

1) The party wishing to rely upon the evidence of the witness may not be able to take the formal steps required to enable the witness to give their statement (for instance, because the witness is unwell at the time). In such circumstances, the party can apply without notice to be permitted to file a witness summary, which is a summary of a) the evidence, if known, which would otherwise be included in a witness statement; or b) if the evidence is not known, the matters about which the party proposes to question the witness.[24] Unless the court directs otherwise, the summary must include the name and address of the intended witness, and the summary must be filed within the period in which the statement would have had to be filed.[25] The court will then apply, as far as practicable, the provisions relating to the amplification of witness statements discussed at para 13.14 above and also the provisions relating to the service of witness statements (for instance, as to the order in which the summary is to be served).[26]

2) It may become clear shortly before a hearing that a witness is able to give evidence necessary to the resolution of the matters before the court, but permission has not previously been granted to the relevant party to rely upon the evidence of the witness. In such circumstances, it is strongly advisable to notify the other parties and the court as soon as possible of the existence of the witness and the nature of the evidence that they will be able to give if permission is granted to rely upon their evidence at the hearing. Depending upon the timing, it may be possible for the question of permission to be determined in advance of the hearing; it may well, however, be necessary for the question to be decided at the outset of the hearing. If it will not be possible for the question of permission to be decided before the hearing, it is advisable that as full a statement as possible is obtained from the witness and served upon the other parties so as to reduce any element of surprise. The statement should also be filed with the court, but it is particularly important to flag up in any list of pre-reading

24 COPR r101(1)–(2).
25 COPR r101(3)–(4).
26 COPR r101(5).

prepared for the judge that permission has not been granted to rely upon the statement; if any party has indicated that they will object to the late service of the statement and/or the giving of evidence by the witness, the judge should not be invited to read the statement prior to the hearing.

Hearsay evidence

13.22 Space precludes a detailed discussion of the law relating to hearsay evidence, ie statements made otherwise than by a person while giving oral evidence in the proceedings which are tendered as evidence of the matters stated.[27] In contrast to the statutory schemes for both civil and family proceedings, the MCA 2005 and COPR make make no express reference to hearsay. However, in *Enfield LBC v SA and others*,[28] McFarlane J (as he then was) considered the position and held that:

- Court of Protection proceedings under the MCA 2005 fall within the very wide definition of 'civil proceedings' under the Civil Evidence Act (CEA) 1995. The CEA 1995 therefore applies to such proceedings, and hearsay evidence is admissible in accordance with the provisions of CEA 1995.[29]
- COPR r95(d) gives the Court of Protection power to admit hearsay evidence which originates from a person who is not competent as a witness and which would otherwise be inadmissible under CEA 1995 s5. This means that the court has the power to admit evidence from P who would, in many cases, not be competent as a witness and could not give admissible evidence. However, as McFarlane J noted: 'Admissibility is one thing, and the weight to be attached to any particular piece of hearsay evidence will be a matter for specific evaluation in each individual case. Within that evaluation, the fact that the individual from whom the evidence originates is not a competent witness will no doubt be an important factor, just as it is, in a different context, when the family court has to evaluate what has been said by a very young child.'[30]

---

27 The statutory definition contained in Civil Evidence Act (CEA) 1995 s1(2)(a). A detailed discussion can be found in chapter 29 of *Phipson on Evidence*.
28 [2010] EWHC 196 (Admin), [2010] COPLR Con Vol 362.
29 *SA* at paras 29–30.
30 *SA* at para 36.

13.23 In the light of the decision in *SA*, the formal position is that:

- If a party wishes to rely upon hearsay evidence, they must give to the other party or parties such formal notice of and (on request) such particulars of or relating to the evidence, as is required to enable them deal with any matters arising from its being hearsay.[31] It would appear that there is no requirement to give notice to rely upon a hearsay statement contained in a document within the agreed bundle (see paras 13.26–13.28 below).[32] In any event, in light of the flexibility granted by COPR r95(d), it is unlikely that a judge would decline to consider hearsay evidence in respect of which formal advance notice had not been given. The judge would, however, no doubt consider the extent to which the other party or parties had been disadvantaged by the fact that the maker of the original statement had not been produced for cross-examination.

- In estimating the weight (if any) to be given to the hearsay evidence the court shall have regard to any circumstances from which any inference can reasonably be drawn as to the reliability or otherwise of the evidence, and, in particular, may have regard to:

  a) whether it would have been reasonable and practicable for the party by whom the evidence was adduced to have produced the maker of the original statement as a witness;

  b) whether the original statement was made contemporaneously with the occurrence or existence of the matters stated;

  c) whether the evidence involves multiple hearsay;

  d) whether any person involved had any motive to conceal or misrepresent matters;

  e) whether the original statement was an edited account, or was made in collaboration with another or for a particular purpose;

  f) whether the circumstances in which the evidence is adduced as hearsay are such as to suggest an attempt to prevent proper evaluation of its weight.[33]

13.24 The position in respect of hearing from P is addressed at parsa 16.29–16.34.

---

31 CEA 1995 s2(1).
32 By analogy with *Charnock v Rowan* [2012] EWCA Civ 2, [2012] CP Rep 18.
33 CEA 1995 s4.

Affidavits

13.25 COPR and PD 14A both make reference to the giving of evidence by witnesses within the jurisdiction by way of affidavit instead of or in addition to a witness statement.[34] Save for the making of an application for an order for committal to prison for contempt of court,[35] there are no rules or practice directions (or other enactments) which require that evidence be given in such a form. A judge may require such to be given, but such is in practice unusual, especially given that proceedings for contempt of court can be brought against a person who makes or causes to be made a false statement in a witness statement verified by a statement of truth without an honest belief in its truth.[36]

Documentary evidence

13.26 PD14 provides both that a court may give directions requiring the parties to use their best endeavours to agree a bundle or bundles of documents for use at any hearing, and that all documents contained in such bundle(s) shall be admissible at that hearing as evidence of their contents unless a) the court orders otherwise; or b) a party gives written notice of objection to the admissibility of particular documents.

13.27 In practice, it is routine in welfare cases for a direction to be made at an early stage in the proceedings that social services and/or medical records relating to P be provided by the relevant public authorities to the litigation friend appointed to act on behalf of P, most usually the Official Solicitor. It is then not uncommon for parts of those records to be included (whether by the public authority or those acting on behalf of P) in the bundles before the court, and then to form a significant part of the evidence upon which the court will make its decision. It is therefore important that if a family member (say) wishes to object to the admissibility of any or all or those documents that this is made very clear in the preparation of the agreed bundles before the final hearing. Questions of the wider disclosure of such records during the currency of proceedings and (in particular) the circumstances under which such disclosure can be withheld raise difficult issues that are discussed further below at paras 13.99ff.

---

34 COPR rr102–103; PD 14A paras 1–19. The position of witnesses outside England and Wales is considered separately at paras 13.38–13.39 below.

35 COPR r186(1) and PD 21A.

36 COPR r14.

13.28 Another mechanism by which factual information can be put before the court is by the power granted under COPR r107 to the court to direct that a party with access to information which is not reasonably available to another party to direct the former to prepare and file a document recording the information and to serve it on the other party (or parties). Any document prepared pursuant to this rule must include sufficient details of all the facts, tests, experiments and assumptions which underlie any part of the information to enable the party on whom it is served to make, or to obtain, a proper interpretation of the information and an assessment of its significance.[37] This provision is rarely, if ever, invoked, but can serve a purpose if one party has information which is not reduced to documentary form which can and should properly be provided to the other parties to the court in a document which can be the subject of proper scrutiny. Rule 107 does not, itself, provide that a document produced under the provision is evidence of its contents, but if it is included within the agreed bundle for a hearing, the rule discussed at para 13.26 above will apply.

Notarial acts and instruments

13.29 A notarial act or instrument may, without further proof, be received in evidence as duly authenticated in accordance with the requirements of law unless the contrary is proved.[38] Such acts or instruments will, in most cases, originate from a foreign country in which notaries play an important role in authenticating documents.

Witness summons

13.30 A party can apply for the issue of a witness summons requiring a named individual to attend court and give oral evidence or to produce a document.[39] Permission to issue such a summons must be sought upon application using a COP9 form (see further paras 11.19ff), and the application notice must include particulars of the applicant, the proposed witness, any document which the proposed witness is required to produce, and the grounds upon which the application is made.[40] A summons to produce documents to the court must either identify the individual document(s) or by reference to a specific

---

37 PD 14A para 54.
38 COPR r105.
39 COPR r106(1).
40 COPR r106(2); PD 14D para 3.

category or event, but 'with sufficient certainty to leave no real doubt in the mind of the person to whom the summons is addressed about what they are required to do'.[41]

13.31 If the application is granted, the witness summons will then be prepared by the court[42] (PD 14D provides for the correction of errors in the name or address of the person to be summoned prior to service). The usual rule the party that made it must serve the summons; at the time of service, the party must be offered or paid a) a sum reasonably sufficient to cover his travelling expenses to and from court; and b) compensation for his loss of time.[43] Both of these sums are fixed by reference to those payable in criminal cases;[44] compensation for ordinary witnesses (ie those who are neither experts nor professionals) is capped at £33.50 for a period of absence not exceeding four hours and £67.00 for a longer period.[45] The court can also order that a witness be paid such general costs as it considers appropriate.[46] Although the COPR and the accompanying practice direction (PD 14D) are silent as to who should pay, the silence suggests that payment should be made by the party who sought the application.

13.32 In general, a witness summons is only binding if a) it is served more than seven days prior to the date on which the witness is required to attend court; and b) the requirements as to offering or paying compensation have been met.[47] It is possible, though, for the court to shorten the time period in an appropriate case (although not to dispense with the compensation requirements).[48]

13.33 Where the summons is issued solely so as to obtain documents and prove their authenticity, it is suggested that the same practice as is used in civil proceedings would be followed, ie that the summons specify a date for the production of the documents that is in advance

---

41 *Tajik Aluminium Plant v Hydo Aluminium AS* [2005] EWCA Civ 1218, [2006] 1 WLR 767 at para 28 per Moore-Bick LJ.

42 PD 14D para 4.

43 COPR r106(6)(a) and (b).

44 PD 14D para 10 and the Costs in Criminal Cases (General) Regulations 1986 SI No 1335 (made under the Prosecution of Offenders Act 1985 (as amended)).

45 Annex A to the *Guide to Allowances under Part V of the Costs in Criminal Cases (General) Regulations 1986*, 2007; available at: www.justice.gov.uk/downloads/information-access-rights/foi-disclosure-log/courts-tribunals/foi-76520-annex-a.pdf.

46 COPR r106(7).

47 COPR r106(3).

48 COPR r106(4).

of the substantive hearing.[49] This power is of little application in terms of documents held by the parties, because of the operation of COPR r107 (see above, para 13.28).

13.34 It should be noted, finally, that witness summons are not issued solely to comply reluctant witnesses to attend court, but also as a mechanism by which (for instance) an employer can be forced to allow an employee to attend to give evidence.

13.35 The COPR are silent as to the sanctions that follow a failure to comply with a witness summons. It is suggested, however, that, by analogy with the position that prevails in the High Court, such a failure can be punished as a contempt of court: see further chapter 18 below.

Depositions

13.36 It is possible for an order to be obtained for a person to be examined on oath before the relevant hearing takes place. Such an order must be sought upon application using a COP9 form (see further paras 11.19ff), although it is not necessary that it be made on notice to the other parties.[50] The deponent can be examined before a circuit judge or a district judge (whether or not nominated as a judge of the Court of Protection), an examiner of the court or such other person as the court appoints,[51] and the order can require the production of any document which the court considers is necessary for the purposes of the examination.[52] The court can also order that the party who obtained the order to file a witness statement or witness summary in relation to the evidence to be given by the person to be examined.[53]

13.37 A deposition that has been ordered under COPR r108 may be put in evidence at a hearing unless the court orders otherwise.[54] If a party intends to put such a deposition in evidence, they must file notice of their intention to do so with the court and serve it on every other party; absent order to the contrary, they must file such notice at least

---

49 See *Khanna v Lovell White Durrant* [1995] 1 WLR 121 and the *White Book 2014*, Sweet & Maxwell, at para 34.0.3.
50 COPR r108(1); PD 14B para 9.
51 COPR r108(3); 'examiners of the court' are appointed by the Lord Chancellor: see COPR r111.
52 COPR r108(4).
53 COPR r108(7).
54 COPR r113(1).

14 days before the hearing date.[55] The court can require the deponent to attend the hearing and give evidence orally.[56]

13.38　　Detailed provisions relating to the conduct of depositions to be taken in England and Wales are set out in PD 14B,[57] aimed primarily at ensuring the creation of an accurate record of the questions put and the answers given, and also at setting out the consequences of a failure of a deponent to attend the examination or a refusal to be sworn, answer any lawful question or produce any document. They are not addressed further here because the process is so rarely invoked before the Court of Protection.

Witnesses outside the jurisdiction

13.39　The COPR and PD 14A contain detailed provisions relating to the obtaining of evidence from witnesses outside England and Wales; they also (along with PD 14B) contain provisions relating to the taking of depositions outside England and Wales. In summary:

- a person may make an affidavit outside England and Wales in the same (limited) circumstances as provided for within England and Wales, or as in accordance with the law in the place where they make the affidavit;[58]
- the procedure for taking evidence outside the jurisdiction will vary depending upon whether or not the person in question is in an EU member state;[59]
- the same procedural requirements apply in relation to the putting before the court of evidence obtained outside the jurisdiction as do in relation to depositions taken from witnesses in England and Wales.[60]

13.40　Where a witness is outside the jurisdiction, it is more likely that steps will be taken to enable them to give any oral evidence required by way of video link, as provided for at COPR r98, and discussed further at chapter 16.

55　COPR r113(2)–(3).
56　COPR r113(4).
57　PD 14B paras 1–15.
58　COPR r104.
59　COPR rr115–116; PD 14B paras 16–33. If the person is within an EU member state, the Taking of Evidence Regulation (Council Regulation (EC) 1206/2001) applies.
60　COPR r113.

Documents held by the police

13.41　It should be noted that, where the police force of a particular area is not a party to the proceedings, but where the court agrees that documents are required from the police, the police normally require that any order be made in terms that a) are directed to the Chief Constable of the force in question; b) invite, rather than require, the production of documents; and c) include the full name and date of birth of the person to whom they relate. Many police forces have in place local protocols with local authorities for the disclosure of documents in proceedings relating to children; it is usually easiest if such protocols (modified as necessary) are adopted in proceedings relating to incapacitated adults. A model order is included in appendix C below.

Section 49 reports

13.42　The court has the power under MCA 2005 s49 to call for a report in respect of such matters relating to P as it may direct from:

- the Public Guardian;
- a Court of Protection Visitor, appointed by the Lord Chancellor to one of two panels, Special Visitors and General Visitors, the former requiring a medical qualification and special knowledge of and experience in cases of impairment of or disturbance in the functioning of the mind or brain;[61]
- a local authority or NHS body (such report to be produced by one of its officers or employees or such other person other than that the Public Guardian or a Court of Protection Visitor as the authority/NHS body considers appropriate).

13.43　There are specific provisions in MCA 2005 s49 and COPR r117 relating to the powers of those charged with producing such reports (which are normally, but not necessarily, provided in writing[62]). In summary:

- The Public Guardian or a Court of Protection Visitor is entitled, at all reasonable times, to examine and take copies of any health record, any record of or held by a local authority and compiled in connection with a social services function, and any record held by a person registered under Care Standards Act 2000 Part 2 or Health and Social Care Act 2008 Part 1 Chapter 2 (broadly, records

---

61　MCA 2005 s61(2).
62　MCA 2005 s49(6).

held by those managing private residential and nursing homes) relating to P.[63]

- Any person compiling a report can inspect and take copies of any document in the court records, unless the court orders to the contrary (or orders that they may only have access to the information on an edited basis).[64]
- A Public Guardian or Court of Protection Visitor can interview P in private for purposes of producing a report.[65]
- A Special Visitor can, if the court directs, carry out a private medical, psychiatric or psychological examination of P's capacity and condition.[66]
- An officer or an employee of a local authority or NHS body (or person reporting on their behalf) is expected to contact or seek to interview such persons as he thinks appropriate or the court directs, but is not granted any specific power to interview or examine P for purposes of producing a report.[67]

13.44 There are detailed provisions in COPR r117 and PD 14E relating to the contents of section 49 reports, which must (in general) be divided into four sections, namely the details of the person preparing the report, the details of P, the matters and materials considered in preparing the report, and the conclusions reached.[68] A precedent order for the obtaining of a section 49 report is contained as an annex to PD 14E, and an order based upon the authors' experience is to be found in appendix C below.[69]

13.45 A report made in response to an order under MCA 2005 s49 is made to the court, rather than to the parties. It will then be sent by the court to the parties; it can also be sent to such other persons as the court may direct.[70] A party (but not another person to whom the report has been sent) can apply for permission to put written questions to the maker of the report.[71] Such questions must be directed via the court, which will make such amendments as it sees fit; the

---

63 MCA 2005 s49(7).
64 COPR r117(5) and (7).
65 MCA 2005 s49(8).
66 MCA 2005 s49(9).
67 COPR r117(3)(a).
68 PD 14E paras 12–16.
69 In the precedent directions order made after the first attended hearing in welfare proceedings.
70 COPR r117(4).
71 COPR r118(1).

court will then send the replies received to the parties and such other person as it may direct.[72]

13.46   Section 49 reports, especially those produced by Court of Protection Visitors, bear a strong resemblance to expert reports, in that they will include both discussion of factual matters and also opinions reflecting the expertise of the maker of the reports. The provisions of PD 14E relating to the contents of the report bear a strong resemblance to those relating to the requirements imposed upon experts in PD 15A (discussed further at paras 13.76ff below). Further, both those providing reports under MCA 2005 s49 and experts reporting to the court owe a duty to the court (rather than to the parties) to assist on the matters within their expertise.[73] However, even though many section 49 reports are in substance identical to expert reports, they are treated distinctly to such reports for purposes of the COPR,[74] and therefore conceptually occupy a somewhat curious position in the conventional categorisation of evidence.

13.47   In many circumstances, however, the power exercisable under MCA 2005 s49 serves as an effective route by which the court can obtain independent evidence as to matters relevant to the application, and thus as an alternative to the grant of permission to the parties to instruct (jointly or separately) an expert to give evidence.

13.48   There is one substantial advantage to the parties in the obtaining of such a report, namely that the MCA 2005 and the COPR make no express provision for the payment of any fees. This is in contrast to the position in relation to experts where the default position is that the instructing parties are jointly and severally liable for the payment of the expert's fees and expenses[75] (see further para 13.69 below). In practice, this means that the costs fall upon the body required to produce the report (in the case of Special and General Visitors, they are remunerated for their work by Lord Chancellor, including for the provision of section 49 reports[76]). The authors are aware, anecdotally, of public bodies refusing to produce section 49 reports in the absence of payment (and, indeed, of provision for such payment being made

---

72 COPR r118(2)–(3).

73 COPR r117(2) (reports under MCA 2005 s49); COPR r122 (experts). The maker of a section 49 report must also give a statement of truth that relates both to the facts contained within their report and the expression of their professional opinions: PD 14E paras16(e).

74 By COPR r119(b), an expert does not include any person instructed to make a report under MCA 2005 s49.

75 COPR r131(5).

76 MCA 2005 s61(4).

in the order directing the production of such report). It is suggested that such a refusal is open to challenge on the basis that the production of the report forms part of the discharge of their general functions towards those to whom they owe statutory duties (whether in relation to their community care or their healthcare needs), but ultimately it is likely that this question will have to be the subject of judicial determination. In the interim, it is suggested that it is sensible to seek to include in any order directing a report under MCA 2005 s49 express provision that no fees are payable in respect of the order. See in this regard the model order provided at appendix C below.

13.49   There is, however, one important caveat that must be entered against the use of section 49 reports. The authors' experience is that their utility is directly proportional to the detail of the instructions given to the maker of the report in the order made by the court. By far the most useful reports are those which are produced in response to what are, to all intents and purposes, letters of instructions prepared as if to an independent expert (discussed further at paras 13.76ff below). In other words – and especially in the case of a report which goes beyond the relaying of mere factual information about P's circumstances and is intended to offer assistance to the court as to the resolution of questions regarding P's capacity and best interests – it is almost invariably necessary to proceed on the basis that the maker of the report is:

1) provided with:
   a) a summary of the relevant background matters (including, in many cases, relevant documentation); and
   b) a summary of the relevant legal tests to apply (including not just the provisions of the MCA 2005 but any relevant cases); and
2) asked detailed and specific questions.

This means, in practice, that it is advisable to invite the court to make an order providing that a letter of instruction be drafted and (if possible) agreed by the parties and submitted to the court for its endorsement and onward transmission.

Expert evidence

Overview

13.50   More than in many other types of proceedings, judges sitting in the Court of Protection will often require assistance from suitably qualified individuals as to such matters as:

- whether P has or lacks capacity to take the decision(s) in question; and
- what course of action is in P's physical and/or psychological best interests, especially if there are specific clinical or social work concerns.

13.51   That evidence will go beyond evidence of fact and, indeed, it will be of value to the court predominantly insofar as it constitutes evidence of opinion based upon the expertise of the individual in question. As such evidence would not otherwise be admissible, the MCA 2005 and COPR Part 15 contain provisions enabling such evidence can be put before the court in a proportionate fashion.[77] COPR Part 15 is accompanied by a practice direction (PD 15A); this is very much less detailed than the suite of practice directions that are now in force accompanying the Family Procedure Rules (FPR) 2010 SI No 2955 Part 25, the equivalent provisions in proceedings relating to children. The Rules Committee set up in December 2009 to undertake a review of the COPR recommended that an equivalent to a detailed practice direction issued by Sir Nicholas Wall P, the then President of the Family Division,[78] be issued for purposes of proceedings in the Court of Protection.[79] While these recommendations have not yet been implemented, the current President of the Family Division and of the Court of Protection, Sir James Munby, has indicated that he intends to take them forward, and it is likely that in due course a practice direction will be issued which gives detailed guidance as to matters such as the circumstances under which an expert should be instructed, the contents of letters of instructions, and the content of expert reports.

13.52   Slightly oddly, neither the Act MCA 2005 the COPR provide any definition of an 'expert',[80] but it is suggested that for these purposes an 'expert' is a person qualified to express an expert opinion upon a relevant matter by virtue of their qualifications or experience upon such matters. By analogy, Civil Evidence Act (CEA) 1972 s3 provides that where a person is called as a witness in any civil proceedings, the person's opinion on any relevant matter on which he or she is qualified to give expert evidence shall be admissible in evidence, and that

---

77   Space precludes a detailed discussion of the law relating to expert evidence; the reader is referred to *Phipson on Evidence* at para 33-09ff.
78   *Practice Direction (Family Proceedings: Experts)* [2008] 1 WLR 1027.
79   See: www.judiciary.gov.uk/media/media-releases/2010/news-release-2210.
80   Although, as noted above, it cannot be a person who gives a report under the provisions of MCA 2005 s49.

'a relevant matter' includes an issue in the proceedings in question. It is suggested that proceedings before the Court of Protection are 'civil proceedings' for these purposes (by analogy with *Enfield LBC v SA and others*[81]).

13.53 It is further suggested that an expert is a person who must have a degree of independence from P,[82] such that a family member could not properly qualify as an expert for these purposes. In the ordinary run of events, it would be unusual for a treating clinician (or a social worker involved with P's case) to be asked to provide expert evidence falling within the scope of COPR Part 15. However, in *O-M, GM (and KM) v The local authority, LO and EM*,[83] the Court of Appeal held that there is no blanket approach which prevents, in an appropriate case, a treating doctor becoming a jointly instructed expert in public law proceedings relating to children. It is suggested that there is no reason in principle why the same approach could not apply in proceedings in relation to adults.

13.54 In any event, 'specialist' professional witnesses employed or acting on behalf of a public body party to proceedings often give evidence that contains both evidence of fact and what would in layperson's terms be considered to be expert opinion evidence. For instance, a social worker will very often relate both events that that they have witnessed directly (or have knowledge of from their reading of social services records) and then also express their professional opinion as to where P's best interests may lie on the basis of their perception of those events. That opinion may well be due (and be given) significant weight by the court. As noted extra-judicially by Sir James Munby P (in comments relating to care proceedings but of equal relevance to proceedings under the MCA 2005):

> Social workers are experts. In just the same way, I might add, CAFCASS [Children and Family Court Advisory and Support Service] officers are experts. In every care case we have at least two experts – a social worker and a guardian – yet we have grown up with a culture of believing that they are not really experts and that we therefore need experts with a capital E. The plain fact is that much of the time we do not.

81 [2010] EWHC 196 (Admin), [2010] COPLR Con Vol 362, discussing the CEA 1995, which contains the same definition of 'civil proceedings'. See CEA 1972 s3; compare CEA 1995 s11.
82 See PD 15A paras 3–4, discussed further below, and also Ashton et al *Court of Protection Practice 2014*, Jordans, at p751.
83 [2009] EWCA Civ 1405, [2010] 2 FLR 58. See also *Hershman and McFarlane: children law and practice*, at para 3060-1.

Social workers may not be experts for the purposes of FPR Part 25 [the equivalent of COPR Part 15], but that does not mean that they are not experts in every other sense of the word. They are, and we must recognise them and treat them as such.[84]

13.55   As discussed below, therefore, where there is evidence before the court from a witness such as a social worker on behalf of a public authority, this will factor into the question of whether expert evidence falling within the scope of COPR Part 15 is in fact required.

13.56   It is also vital as a preliminary point to remember in respect of all expert evidence (both that falling within the scope of Part 15 and that of the quasi-expert nature discussed immediately above) that:

- where the opinion of an expert is based upon the report of facts, those facts, unless within the expert's own knowledge, must be proved independently;
- an expert may (in an appropriate case) give evidence upon 'ultimate questions' going to factual matters, for instance as to the accuracy or truthfulness of a witness, but the final decision remains that for the judge;[85]
- likewise, the 'ultimate' questions of whether P has capacity and as to what is in their best interests are matters for the court.[86]

13.57   In other words, and as Charles J observed in *A County Council v K, D and L*,[87] after a detailed review of the authorities:

... it is important to remember (i) that the roles of the court and the expert are distinct; and (ii) it is the court that is in the position to weigh the expert evidence against its findings on the other evidence ... the judge must always remember that he or she is the person who makes the final decision.

13.58   Allied to this is the fact that the judge is not limited in their determination even of questions upon which expert evidence might be

---

84 Sir James Munby P, 'View from the President's Chambers (3) The process of reform: expert evidence' [2013] Fam Law 816.

85 See, by analogy, *Re M and R* [1996] 2 FLR 195 at 205–213 per Butler-Sloss LJ and *Re M (sexual abuse allegations: interviewing techniques)* [1999] 2 FLR 92 per Sir Stephen Brown P. See also the discussion in *Hershman and McFarlane: children law and practice*, at para 3056.

86 *CC v KK and STCC* [2012] EWHC 2136 (COP), [2012] COPLR 627 at para 24 per Baker J.

87 [2005] EWHC 144 (Fam), [2005] 1 FLR 851, at paras 39 and 44. This case related to an application for a care order under the Children Act 1989, but its principles were held to be equally applicable to proceedings under the MCA 2005 by Baker J in *CC v KK and STCC* [2012] EWHC 2136 (COP), [2012] COPLR 627 at para 24.

thought to be of particular weight solely to consideration of that evidence. For instance:

> In assessing the question of capacity, the court must consider all the relevant evidence. Clearly, the opinion of an independently-instructed expert will be likely to be of very considerable importance, but in many cases the evidence of other clinicians and professionals who have experience of treating and working with P will be just as important and in some cases more important.[88]

13.59 To date, judges of the Court of Protection has not had regard to (or, at least, have not cited in its judgments) the decisions of the European Court of Human Rights (ECtHR) regarding determination of incapacity. As discussed also at para 12.7, the ECtHR has developed a consistent body of case-law to the effect that:

> ... it is the judge and not a physician, albeit a psychiatrist, who is to assess all relevant facts concerning the person in question and his or her personal circumstances. It is the function of the judge conducting the proceedings to decide whether such an extreme measure [as declaring a person lacks capacity] is necessary or whether a less stringent measure might suffice. When such an important interest for an individual's private life is at stake a judge has to balance carefully all relevant factors in order to assess the proportionality of the measure to be taken ... [i]t was for the judge to make any conclusions as regards the issue of divesting [an individual] of her legal capacity.[89]

13.60 This decision (and others to like effect) was given in the context of considering legal systems where capacity is a matter of status – ie a decision can be made that a person is to be either partially or totally 'incapacitated. However, too much can be made of the difference between 'status' based systems and that enshrined in the MCA 2005. After all, a decision that P lacks capacity in one or more respects gives the Court of Protection a wide-ranging jurisdiction to take decisions in P's best interests as regards those matters. Alternatively, in the case of (for instance) sexual relations, a decision by the Court of Protection that P lacks the capacity to consent to such relations, represents a significant – if no doubt justified – legal circumscription of P's autonomy. In the circumstances, the case-law of the ECtHR

---

88 *PH v A Local Authority and others* [2011] EWHC 1704 (Fam), [2012] COPLR 128 at para 16(xiii) per Baker J.

89 *X and Y v Croatia* (App No 5193/90, decision of 3 November 2011) at paras 103–104 (considered by reference to ECHR article 8). See also *Lashin v Russia* (App No 33117/02, decision of 22 January 2013) (considered by reference to ECHR article 8).

stands as a powerful reinforcement of the importance of the judge being the final decision-maker.

13.61   A corollary of the matters set out above is that the judge is entitled to depart from the expert evidence put before them, as happened in the *CC* case referred to above, where Baker J held in the face of all the professional and expert evidence before him that P had the capacity to decide where she wished to reside. By analogy with the position that prevails in relation to children, it is suggested that a departure where it concerns the potential level of risk to the welfare of P must be accompanied by appropriately detailed reasons.[90]

Permission

13.62   Although it is not necessary to obtain permission to file expert evidence as to capacity and/or best interests with the initial application to the court,[91] the court's permission must be obtained before filing any subsequent expert evidence[92] (and evidence filed with the application can only be relied upon to the extent and for the purposes that the court allows).[93]

13.63   The requirement to obtain permission is an important tool in the court's case management armoury. In addition to its general obligation to have regard to the general requirement to deal with cases in a proportionate fashion,[94] the court is also under a specific duty to limit expert evidence to that which is reasonably required to resolve the proceedings.[95] This duty extends not just to requiring careful consideration of whether expert evidence is required at all,[96] but also, where possible, requiring expert evidence upon a particular issue to be dealt with by a single expert.[97] In guidance sanctioned by the President of the Court of Protection, the provisions of the COPR and PD 15A were amplified to make clear that: 'Unnecessary expert assessments must be avoided. It will be rare indeed for the court to sanction the

---

90   See *Re B (care: expert witnesses)* [1996] 1 FLR 667 and *Hershman and McFarlane: children law and practice* at para 3056.

91   COPR r120(1)(a)–(b).

92   COPR r123(1).

93   COPR r120(2).

94   COPR r3(3)(c).

95   COPR r121.

96   See *City of Westminster v FS* (unreported, 9 September 2009) at paras 12–16, per HHJ Horowitz QC (consideration of whether first instance judge erred in refusing permission to the Official Solicitor to instruct an independent social work expert).

97   COPR r130(1) and PD 15A para 1.

instruction of more than one expert to advise in relation to the same issue.'[98]

13.64 It is perhaps worth noting that there are advantages to the instruction of single joint experts other than those of proportionality and cost-saving. As Ryder J (as he then was) noted after a review of the authorities in *JG (a child) v Legal Services Commission and others*[99] (in the context of a discussion of the principle of the equal apportionment of the costs of joint expert evidence (see further para 13.75 below)):

> 47. There are sound reasons, recognised in the decided cases, why there should be apportionment of costs in cases where there is joint expert evidence. Such evidence will:
> (a) be something which each party has an interest in making available to the court ...;
> (b) be something from which each party has the potential to benefit (whether or not they ultimately do so) ...; and
> (c) inform the positions of the parties ...
>
> 48. These points do not apply to evidence obtained, and paid for, on a single party's behalf. In *Lambeth*,[100] the court approved (at para [59](viii)) the comment of Bodey J in *Calderdale*[101] (at para [37](e)) in relation to the cost of a joint report prepared for care proceedings brought by a local authority that:
> '... there is much force in the Local Authority's point that parents need to know that reports which may prove to have a "preponderant influence" (per Munby J at paragraph 113(ii) of *Re L*) are not being prepared at the sole expense of the Local Authority – in which event they may feel that the Local Authority calls the tune.'

13.65 These comments were made in the context of a discussion of expert evidence in private law proceedings concerning a child, but it is suggested that they are equally applicable in proceedings under the MCA 2005.

13.66 The test in the COPR for the grant of permission to instruct an expert was taken from CPR.[102] The rules in family proceedings, which were likewise taken from the CPR, were tightened with effect

---

98 *Guidance in cases involving protected parties in which the Official Solicitor is being invited to act as guardian ad litem or litigation friend*, 2010, available at: www.familylaw.co.uk/system/uploads/attachments/0001/4515/Guidance_in_cases_involving_the_Official_Solicitor_-_December_2010.pdf.

99 [2013] EWHC 804 (Admin), [2013] 2 FLR 1174. This decision was reversed on appeal: [2014] EWCA Civ 656 but these dicta remain valid.

100 *Lambeth LBC v S, C, V and J (by his guardian); Legal Services Commission (intervening)* [2005] EWHC 776 (Fam), [2005] 2 FLR 1171.

101 *Calderdale MBC v S and the Legal Services Commission* [2004] EWHC 2529 (Fam), [2005] 1 FLR 751.

102 CPR 35.1.

from 31 January 2013 so as to impose a duty upon the court to limit expert evidence to 'that which in the opinion of the court is necessary to resolve the proceedings'.[103] That change raises the bar significantly: *Re TG (care proceedings: case management: expert evidence)*,[104] 'necessity' having 'the connotation of the imperative, what is demanded rather than what is merely optional or reasonable or desirable'.[105]

13.67   It is likely that this change will be introduced in due course in the Court of Protection, in line with the robust approach to the instruction of experts that the President of the Family Division (who is also the President of the Court of Protection), Sir James Munby strongly advocates.[106] It is therefore undoubtedly prudent to proceed on the basis that the party or parties who seek the instruction of an expert should be able to satisfy this higher hurdle.

13.68   A further hurdle to the obtaining of expert evidence in cases in which one or more parties are in receipt of public funding is the increasing reluctance of the Legal Aid Agency (LAA) to fund expert evidence (whether at the particular rate sought by the expert, or indeed at all). That the LAA has the power to refuse all or part of the instruction, even if permission has been granted by the court was confirmed by Collins J in *R (T) v Legal Aid Agency*[107] (and see further the discussion at paras 6.104ff).

13.69   The authors' experience is that it is strongly advisable that (in line with the approach that applies in family proceedings[108]):

- Where the court takes the view that the expert's report is required (under whatever test is ultimately applicable) for the resolution of the case, it should say so and should give reasons (and should do so even if the order is a consent order being endorsed by the court, as it is still a judicial decision).

- While the reasons need not be lengthy or elaborate, they must, however, explain to anyone reading them why the decision-

---

103   FPR r25.1 as amended by the Family Procedure (Amendment) (No 5) Rules 2012 SI No 3061.

104   [2013] EWCA Civ 5, [2013] 1 FLR 1250, at para 30 per Sir James Munby P; see also Sir James Munby P, 'View from the President's Chambers (3) The process of reform: expert evidence' [2013] Fam Law 816.

105   *Re HL (a child)* [2013] EWCA Civ 655 at paragraph 3, per Sir James Munby P.

106   See Sir James Munby P, 'View from the President's Chambers (3) The process of reform: expert evidence' [2013] Fam Law 816.

107   [2013] EWHC 960 (Admin), [2013] Fam Law 805.

108   *A Local Authority v S and others* [2012] EWHC 1442 (Fam), [2012] 1 WLR 3098 at para 45 per Sir Nicholas Wall P.

maker has reached the conclusion he or she has, particularly if the expert's rates exceed the maximum rates ordinarily allowable. This can be done by way of preamble to the order, or by a short judgment, delivered at dictation speed or inserted by the parties with the judge's approval. It is suggested that the preamble or judgment should include (and hence the material put to the court must indicate clearly):

- what relevant papers it has read;
- the reasons why it considers that the expert evidence is required to resolve proceedings, which should include the reasons why the evidence would not otherwise be available to it as part of the proceedings (for instance, from a social worker or a treating clinician who has given evidence on behalf of a public body);
- the reasons why the volume of work is required, if it is a particularly complex report;
- (if one or more parties is publicly funded) the reasons for why there is any need to exceed the maximum rates usually allowable by the LAA; and
- the reasons why there is any departure from: i) the principle that the costs of a single joint expert will be shared equally between the instructing parties, particularly if this has the effect of placing a disproportionately high cost burden on a party or parties in receipt of public funding (this should include a robust scrutiny of the means of any party claiming to be unable to afford the cost of the instruction); or ii) the principle that the instructing parties are to be jointly and severally liable for the costs of single joint expert.

13.70   The last point above requires some amplification because a question that arises relatively often is whether all the parties to proceedings *need* to join in the instruction of an expert and, if they do not, what, if any a) right do they have to have input into the instruction; and b) obligation do they have to pay the costs of the expert report?

13.71   The starting point in respect of both is simple: only a party who wishes to submit expert evidence is an 'instructing party';[109] only such a party has the right (but not the duty) to give instructions to the expert;[110] and the status of instructing party carries with it the obligation to meet jointly and severally the expert's fees and expenses.[111]

109 COPR r130(2).
110 COPR r131(1).
111 COPR r131(5).

The Court of Protection cannot force a party to join in the instructions; if a party refuses to do so, it is suggested that this should be recorded on the face of the directions giving permission to other party or parties to instruct the expert in question.

13.72   Conversely, especially where one party is a litigant in person and/ or is of limited means, the argument is often run that the letter of instruction should be circulated to the relevant party for their input and comment, but that they should not then be required to meet any part of the costs of the report. There is undoubtedly a pragmatic attraction to this, not least as written questions can be put to an expert by any party, not just an instructing party, and the presumption is that the costs of producing the replies will in the first instance be met by the instructing party or parties.[112] It may therefore be thought easier to ensure that the expert is asked to consider all matters compendiously, rather than having to respond to subsequent questions by a party who has not taken part in the instruction. Care needs to be exercised, however, both by the parties and the court, if this course is adopted. This is in part because it offends against the principle of the joint apportionment of costs which is enshrined in COPR r125(7). It is also, pragmatically, a course which is likely to lead to substantial problems if the LAA consider that there has been any degree of 'loading' of the costs of an expert report upon a public funding certificate for any party.

13.73   However, the position may now be somewhat more flexible at least where one (or more) parties is of limited means and one party is publicly funded following the decision in *JG v Lord Chancellor and others*.[113] This case was decided in the context of a private law dispute involving a child, but the central principles are equally applicable before the Court of Protection (see also the discussion of this case at paras 6.92ff). In this case, the Court of Appeal made a number of general observations, including that:

1) no party could be compelled to join in instructing an expert (under the FPR – this also applies to the COPR);
2) the involvement of other parties will not necessarily convert an expert instructed on behalf of one party into a single joint expert;
3) there are good practical reasons to be cautious about treating an expert as a joint expert, as it would be undesirable for non-instructing parties to be deterred from contributing to an expert's

---

112 COPR r125(1) and (7). See further para 13.85 below.
113 [2014] EWCA Civ 656.

instruction, and thus from providing useful information to an expert, for fear they will be treated as a joint expert;

4) if, on proper analysis, the expert is a joint expert, the possible grounds for departing from the principle of equal apportionment could be a) impecuniosity, b) the need to avoid a breach of the ECHR[114] and c) a 'very exceptional case'. If it is established that a lack of an expert report would breach an individual's rights under the ECHR, there was no need to consider exceptionality as an additional requirement.

13.74 It is important to remember that the pressure of work means that a judge at a case management hearing may not have time to master the details of the documents in the case. This means that it is particularly important to flag up all relevant matters clearly (and succinctly) for the judge, ideally in the position statement filed in advance of the hearing (discussed further at paras 11.34ff).

13.75 Wherever possible, the court being invited to grant permission to instruct an expert should be asked to give permission to instruct a specific expert, rather than a category of expert. In other words, the identity of the expert together with the professional qualifications should be made clear to the judge at the time that permission is sought, rather than permission being sought to rely upon (say) a consultant psychiatrist to report upon P's capacity in one or more domains. This has two advantages:

1) The court can make clear in its reasons for the grant of permission that it has considered the value that the specific expert proposed can add (assuming that such expert is endorsed by the court; if the expert is not, then appropriate steps can then be directed to put forward a suitable alternative for judicial endorsement).

2) Where more than one party is to be involved in the instruction of the expert, the order appointing that expert will name them. In the authors' experience, while there is a mechanism in the COPR for the resolution by the court of disputes as to the identity of the expert between joint instructing parties,[115] leaving matters open in the order can give rise to unhelpful and time-consuming debates subsequently that can be avoided by ensuring that any such discussions take place prior to the making of the order.

114 A failure by the court to allow expert evidence can be a violation of article 8 ECHR (see *Elsholz v Germany* (2002) 34 EHRR 58).

115 COPR r130(3), providing that the court can either select the expert from a list prepared or identified by the instructing parties or direct the manner by which the expert is to be selected.

Instructing the expert

13.76   An expert must be instructed before they can report. In other words, they must be provided with:

1) a summary of the background to the case;
2) a summary of the relevant legal provisions (and of any relevant case-law); and
3) relevant documentation.

13.77   The questions upon which their opinion is sought must also be set out with clarity. A sample letter of instruction is included at appendix D below, but particular points to emphasise are that:

- As noted above, the presumption is that expert evidence will be provided by way of an expert jointly instructed by all those parties who wish to submit expert evidence upon a particular issue or issues. In such circumstances, and while the COPR provide for separate instructions to be given by the instructing parties to the expert,[116] courts are in practice astute to seek to ensure that only one letter of instruction is sent, and will use their general case management powers to bring about (if all possible) one letter, agreed, if possible between the instructing parties. This means, in practice, that the solicitors for one of the parties should take the lead in drafting the letter and then circulate it to the other instructing parties for comment. Wherever the Official Solicitor is instructed as P's litigation friend and is participating in the instruction, it is conventional that the solicitors instructed by the Official Solicitor take on the task of producing the first draft. If agreement cannot be reached as to the terms of the letter, it is almost invariably quicker if rival drafts (with the differences clearly marked) are provided in writing along with submissions to the merits of the different drafts to the judge who made the original order granting permission for the judge to make the final decision as to the terms of the letter, rather that engaging in protracted rounds of correspondence.
- Where an expert is jointly instructed, the expert must be reminded that any communications that they have with one instructing party should be copied to the others; there is a real risk, otherwise, that the independence of the expert will (even if only apparently) be compromised.[117]

---

116 COPR r131(2).
117 See in this regard *SMBC v WMP* [2011] EWHC B13 (COP), (2011) 14 CCLR 413, [2011] COPLR Con Vol 1177 at para 57(vii) per HHJ Cardinal (discussions between the Official Solicitor's solicitor and the expert).

- Thought must be given as to the documentation that it is necessary that the expert reviews in order to give their report, and the mechanics by which the expert can review that documentation. In this regard two considerations arise, in particular:
  - The expert may well not need to see the entirety of files held upon P by relevant public bodies, but must be entitled to inspect and/or be provided with copies of sufficient documents in order to be able to reach their conclusions.
  - It is quite possible that the expert will need to see documents relating to P (for instance, their social services files) to which the other parties in the proceedings (most obviously family members) may well not have had sight of and which there are legitimate reasons to suggest the other parties should not see. In *Re L (care assessment: fair trial)*, Munby J (as he then was) held in relation to care proceedings that there might be a breach of ECHR article 6 (right to a fair trial) where a jointly instructed or other sole expert's report was 'likely to have a preponderant influence on the assessment of the facts' by the court, if a litigant were denied the opportunity, before the expert produced his report, a) to examine and comment on the documents being considered by the expert and b) to cross-examine witnesses interviewed by the expert and on whose evidence the report was based, and hence to participate effectively in the process by which the report was produced.[118] It is suggested that the same principle applies in relation to proceedings under the MCA 2005; this does not necessarily mean that an expert cannot have sight of documents withheld from other parties – rather, it means that consideration must be given to the basis upon which those documents are withheld both by the party wishing to withhold those documents and the court. These difficult issues are examined further at paras 13.99ff below.
- Arrangements must be made for the expert to be able to visit P (which will, in the majority of cases, be necessary for them to be able to form any proper conclusion as to their capacity and/or best interests[119]), and interview any individuals such as carers or

---

118 [2002] EWHC 1379 (Fam), at paras 113–118, applying *Mantovanelli v France* (App No 21497/93) (1997) 24 EHRR 370.

119 As an independent consultant neuro-psychiatric expert noted in *Wandsworth CCG v IA and TA* [2014] EWHC 990 (COP): 'assessment of capacity based on case notes is of necessity a relatively inadequate substitution for the complex assessments that occurs in a clinical interview' (*IA* at para 43).

family members whom the expert considers necessary in order to be able to produce a sufficiently rounded picture. If an expert is unable to obtain access to see P because of the actions of a family member, this is something that should be raised with the court at the earliest possible opportunity so that – if appropriate – steps can be taken to consider the making of injunctions (and, ultimately, initiating proceedings for contempt of court).

- While the court is likely to have indicated in the order granting permission the matters to be covered in the report,[120] it is unlikely that the order will set down the questions in detail (nor, in the ordinary run of events, is it likely that the judge making the order will have had sight of the letter of instruction before it is sent out). It is therefore important that care is taken to formulate the questions so as to direct the expert's attention to answering the issues that actually fall for consideration in the case. In the authors' experience, unclear reports are very frequently the result of unclear questions having been asked in the first place (and it is also difficult to 'salvage' such an unclear report by way of questions asked upon receipt of the report, discussed further at para 13.80 below).

- The expert should be reminded that they should exercise extreme care before expressing any provisional views to P: in *SC v BS and A Local Authority*,[121] the expert was criticised for having given an indication to P that he thought she had capacity in the material domains without having read the very extensive records. As Baker J noted: 'Although his comments to her were hedged with qualifications, it was highly probable that [P]'s hopes were raised that she would shortly be allowed to leave her current accommodation.'[122] No expert should give a patient a 'provisional' view of the patient's capacity without reading the patient's history.

- The expert should be reminded that they have the right to ask the court for directions to assist them in carrying out their functions as an expert.[123] While in the first instance, an expert would usually be expected to look to the representatives of the instructing parties to assist them to overcome any logistical difficulties, experts

120 COPR r126(1) provides that the court may give directions as to the matters to be covered in such a report.

121 [2012] COPLR 567.

122 Para 39.

123 COPR r129(1). Any such application must (in the absence of direction to the contrary) be provided in advance to the instructing party and to the other parties to the proceedings.

must, themselves, take responsibility for ensuring that they are satisfied that they have obtained the information necessary to report to the court. In *SMBC v WMP*, HHJ Cardinal indicated that, as a matter of good practice: 'An expert ... ought ... to seek clarifications and raise questions under r 129 Court of Protection Rules 2007 before completing a report referring to lacunae in the information before him.'[124]

- Instructions to an expert are not privileged against disclosure:[125] in other words, nothing should be put to an expert in a letter of instruction which cannot properly be seen by all the other parties to the proceedings.

The duties upon an expert

13.78 The expert must assist the court on the matters within his or her expertise.[126] This encompasses two equally important aspects:

1) No matter who the expert is instructed by or who pays them, the expert does not owe their duty to any party or parties, but to the court (and, to that end, their report is to be addressed to the court, rather than to any party from whom they have received their instructions[127]). An expert whose report lacks objectivity may themselves be at risk not just of having all or part of their fees disallowed, but may, themselves, be at risk of having to pay costs incurred by other parties in consequence of their report.[128]

2) The expert must only advise upon the matters within their expertise, and make clear if a matter upon which their opinion is sought lies outside their expertise.[129] While this is in large part, a matter for the expert, it also reflects the need to ensure that the right person is chosen by the instructing parties. In *SC v BS and A Local Authority*,[130] the court (in granting permission for another expert to be instructed to report upon capacity, where the first expert, although a nationally recognised expert on autism, had not demonstrated the requisite degree of knowledge of the MCA 2005 but

---

124 *SMBC v WMP* [2011] EWHC B13 (COP), [2011] COPLR Con Vol 1177, (2011) 14 CCLR 413, at para 57(i).
125 COPR r126(5).
126 COPR r122.
127 PD 15A para 8.
128 See, by analogy, *Phillips v Symes* [2004] EWHC 2330 (Ch), [2005] 1 WLR 2043. COPLR r166 provides for costs orders to be made against non-parties.
129 PD 15A para 6(a).
130 [2012] COPLR 567.

offered to undergo training) noted that: 'It cannot be satisfactory to seek the expert opinion from someone who perceives the need to undergo training before he can give that opinion.'[131]

The expert's report – content

13.79   PD 15A, amplifying COPR r126(2)–(4), sets out in some detail the requirements that apply both as to the form and the content of an expert's report, and they are not rehearsed here, save to emphasise that an expert report which does not comply with the requirements of paragraph 15 of PD 15A is unlikely to be accepted by the court, not just because of the formal defects, but more importantly because paragraph 15 sets out the 'route map' by which an expert can produce a report that establishes the proper building blocks by which reliable conclusions can be reached. As Henderson J put it in *Re S*: 'The rules are there for a good reason, and if they are not complied with a report, even from the most eminent of experts, is likely to lack the transparency and objectivity which the court rightly insists upon in expert evidence.'[132]

13.80   Further, and as set out above (para 13.56), an expert must be very careful in their report not to seek to determine factual issues that are outside their direct experience. If – as is regularly the case in reports relating to best interests – the view of the expert as to where P's interests will lie will vary depending upon which interpretation of the facts is preferred, the proper course of action is for the expert to set out both alternative chains of reasoning from factual scenario to opinion as to best interests. In other words, the expert should give their opinion as to where P's best interests will lie depending on whether the court accepts that the particular factual issue(s) is/are made out. The most obvious example is where the allegation is made that a named individual has abused or otherwise caused harm to come to P; in such a case, the expert should give their view as to (say) contact between P and that individual based upon either a) the allegation being established; or b) the allegation not being established (see chapter 15 below for further discussion of the resolution of factual disputes).

13.81   There are two particular risks that the courts have identified that experts must guard against in the assessment of capacity:

---

131 *SC* at para 37 per Baker J.
132 [2010] EWHC 2405 (COP), [2010] COPLR Con Vol 1112, at para 146.

1) The first, which applies equally (if not with greater force) to those involved in the ongoing care and treatment of P, is succumbing to the 'protection imperative', namely feeling 'drawn towards an outcome that is more protective of the adult and thus ... fail[ing] to carry out an assessment of capacity that is detached and objective';[133]

2) The second is not paying sufficient weight to the fact that (as necessarily occurs in most cases) the expert only has the benefit of a limited exposure to P by comparison with the more 'longitudinal' picture enjoyed by other professionals with longer-term contact with P. While on the one hand, this may make it easier to produce a detached report, the risk is that the resulting report will represent a snapshot alone.[134] There is, in reality, unlikely to be any way in which this risk can be entirely avoided; the best that can be done is to ensure that the expert is alive to its existence.

Once the report has been provided

13.82 An expert report disclosed by a party can be used by any party as evidence at any hearing in the proceedings. The report cannot be used by a party to whom it has been disclosed for any other purpose, unless:

1) the document has been read to or by the court or referred to at a public hearing (which will, at present be the minority of hearings in proceedings under the MCA 2005); or

2) the court otherwise permits.[135]

13.83 As noted above, any party (not just an instructing party) can put written questions to an expert.[136] That entitlement is limited in that (subject to a different order of the court or the agreement of all the relevant parties[137]):

1) the questions can only be put once;

---

133 *PH v A Local Authority and others* [2011] EWHC 1704 (Fam), [2012] COPLR 128 at para 16(xiii) per Baker J. See also *CC v KK and STCC* [2012] EWHC 2136 (COP), [2012] COPLR 627 and also *X and Y v Croatia* (App No 5193/90, decision of 3 January 2011) (criticism by the ECtHR of the fact that the psychiatrist charged with determining X's capacity saw her for only 20 minutes, at a time when she was 'tired and under the influence of medication' (para 87)).

134 *PH* at para 56.

135 COPR r18.

136 COPR r125(1).

137 COPR r125(3) also provides for a practice direction to make alternative provision; none at present does so.

2) must be put within 28 days beginning with the date upon which the report was served; and

3) can only be for purpose of clarification of the report.[138]

This last restriction is particularly important – courts take a very dim view of attempts to cross-examine experts in writing. Both to try to stop such questions being put and also so as to ensure that the expert is not bombarded with a sequence of questions from different parties, judges sometimes direct that any questions are to be put via the solicitors for one of the parties, most obviously those instructed on behalf of the Official Solicitor where P is a party and represented by the Official Solicitor.

13.84   If an expert fails to respond to a question put to them under the procedure put to them, then the court may order:

a) that the instructing party or parties may not rely on the evidence of the expert; and/or

b) that the party may not recover all or part the fees and expenses of the expert or part from any other party.[139]

13.85   Any answers given by the expert to questions put under the procedure set out above are treated as part of their report,[140] and subject to any different order of the court or final costs order, the instructing party or parties are responsible for meeting the costs both of the original report and of the answers.[141]

13.86   If permission has been granted to two (or more) experts to report upon an issue, then specific powers are granted to the court in addition to its general case management powers contained in COPR r5. The court may at any stage direct that the experts meet for purposes of identifying and discussing the expert issues in the proceedings and, where possible, reaching an agreed opinion on those issues.[142] The court can specify the issues the experts must discuss, and can direct that the experts prepare a joint statement for the court setting out issues upon which they agree and issues upon which they disagree (together with a summary of their reasons for disagreeing).[143] Whether contained in a statement or otherwise, the contents of the discussions may, absent order to the contrary, be referred to at any

---

138 COPR r125(2)–(3).
139 COPR r125(5)–(6).
140 COPR r125(4).
141 COPR r125(7).
142 COPR r128(1).
143 COPR r128(2)–(3).

hearing or at any stage in the proceedings (including, although the COPR do not say so expressly, for purposes of considering the conduct of any party for purposes of determining the final allocation of costs).[144]

13.87 The MCA 2005 and COPR are silent as to what should happen in the event that a party who has taken part in a joint instruction is dissatisfied with the expert report. By analogy with the position that prevails under the CPR, it is suggested that: 'If having obtained a joint expert's report, a party, for reasons which are not fanciful, wishes to obtain further information before making a decision as to whether or not there is a particular part (or indeed the whole) of the expert's report which he or she may wish to challenge, then they should, subject to the discretion of the court, be permitted to obtain that evidence.'[145] In the light of the statutory provisions and authorities discussed above, it is clear that the court will be astute to ensure that every other avenue is explored first before such permission is granted.

Disclosure

Overview

13.88 COPR Part 16 contains provisions relating to disclosure which are based upon those in CPR Part 31. In both, a party discloses a document by stating that it exists or has existed;[146] the CPR defines a 'document' broadly as 'anything in which information of any description is recorded',[147] while no equivalent description is given in the COPR it is suggested that the same definition should apply.

13.89 Because proceedings before the Court of Protection are, at heart, inquisitorial rather than adversarial,[148] it has become increasingly apparent that the provisions of COPR Part 16 are not altogether well-suited to the requirements of applications under the MCA 2005. In *Enfield LBC v SA and others*,[149] McFarlane J (as he then was)

---

144 COPR r128(4).

145 *Daniels v Walker (practice note)* [2000] 1 WLR 1382 at 1387 per Lord Woolf MR.

146 CPR 31.1; COPR r132.

147 CPR 31.4.

148 *Re G* [2014] EWCOP 1361 at para 26 per Sir James Munby P, endorsing *Cheshire West and Cheshire Council v P and M* [2011] EWHC 1330 (Fam), [2011] COPLR Con Vol 273 at para 52 per Baker J.

149 [2010] EWHC 196 (Admin), [2010] COPLR Con Vol 362.

commented adversely on the fact that the rules contained in COPR Part 16 were based upon:

> ... ordinary civil litigation with the expectation that disclosure will be based on whether documents 'adversely affect [a party's] own case' or 'support another party's case' (COPR r133(2)(b)) whereas the approach of the family court is that there is a duty to give *the court* all relevant material.[150]

He continued that there could be:

> ... no justification for there being a difference of this degree on the issue of disclosure between the family court and the Court of Protection in fact finding cases of this type where really the process and the issues are essentially identical whether the vulnerable complainant is a young child or an incapacitated adult. For the future in such cases in the Court of Protection it would seem to be justified for the court to make an order for 'specific disclosure' under COPR 2007 r133(3) requiring all parties to give 'full and frank disclosure' of all relevant material.[151]

See further in this regard, para 15.2 below.

13.90   To similar effect, the Rules Committee set up in December 2009 to undertake a review of the COPR and associated practice directions and forms noted that the provisions of COPR Part 16 'are based on the CPR when they might more usefully be based on family procedure with the emphasis on full and frank disclosure but with provisions for lists of documents by reference to defined issues and which cover the needs of a contentious property and affairs application as well as a health and welfare application'.[152] While these recommendations have not yet been implemented, the current President of the Family Division and of the Court of Protection, Sir James Munby, has indicated that he intends to take them forward, and it is therefore likely that the provisions of COPR Part 16 will be subject in due course to considerable modification.

13.91   In the light of the matters set out above, it will not be a surprise to learn that the majority of the provisions relating to disclosure in COPR Part 16 will not invoked in most applications. To that end, they are not discussed in detail in this chapter, the focus rather being upon the disclosure issues that arise most commonly in practice.

---

150 *SA* [2010] EWHC 196 (Admin) at para 57 (emphasis in original).

151 *SA* at para 58.

152 See: www.judiciary.gov.uk/media/media-releases/2010/news-release-2210.

Disclosure issues in practice

13.92 It is important to note that disclosure issues can arise at the very outset of proceedings in (at least) two ways.

13.93 First, if an application is brought on an ex parte basis (ie in the absence of the respondent) then, as discussed at para 11.60 above, there is a duty upon the advocate making that application to give full and frank disclosure of all relevant matters, including those tending to suggest that the application should not be brought.

13.94 Second, the decision in *Loughlin v Singh and others*[153] stands as a clear endorsement of the propositions:

1) that the rules that apply in civil proceedings as regards the privileged status of expert reports do not apply before the Court of Protection (see further para 13.112 below); and
2) (in consequence) that there is a duty to bring relevant material contained in expert evidence within the possession of the applicant to the attention of the court at the outset of proceedings.

In that case, an application had been made to the Court of Protection for a professional deputy to be appointed to manage the property and affairs of an adult who had suffered a number of serious injuries in a road traffic accident. The solicitors making the application were in possession of expert evidence which suggested that he *had* the requisite capacity, but did not bring this to the attention of the court. A district judge appointed the deputy without a hearing. In subsequent personal injury proceedings, the issue of the man's capacity to manage his property and affairs was hotly contested by the defendant. Kenneth Parker J found – on a fine balance[154] – that the claimant lacked capacity, such that there was ultimately no inconsistency between his decision and that which underpinned the appointment of the deputy. The judge was, however, highly critical of the actions of the solicitors, noting in an appendix to his judgment that:

> 14. In my view, this was a case where *all* available medical evidence relevant to the issue of capacity should have been disclosed to the court [of Protection] ... It is then almost certain that the court, faced with this welter of conflicting medical opinion and aware [of other unsatisfactory aspects of an expert's report] would have refused to determine the application on paper, but would have insisted on an oral hearing at which the issue could have been fully and properly considered. I am unwilling to speculate as to what the outcome might have been if a proper procedure had been followed at that time, but

153 [2013] EWHC 1641 (QB), [2013] COPLR 371.
154 Para 45.

the possibility cannot be ruled out that the court might at that time have found that the claimant had capacity. In the light of my own conclusion such a finding, although not unreasonable, would have been incorrect.

15. All I need add is that the lamentable failures that occurred here, and the invidious position in which the judge in the Court of Protection was unwittingly placed, must never be repeated. The issue of capacity is of very great importance, and all involved must ensure that the Court of Protection has all the material which, on proper reflection, is necessary for a just and accurate decision.

13.95   While the decision in *Loughlin v Singh* is not, strictly, binding on practitioners appearing before the Court of Protection, as it was a decision taken in the Queen's Bench Division, nor do these passages appear to reflect argument advanced to the court based upon analysis either of the MCA 2005 or of the COPR, it is suggested that the passages set out above are entirely correct in their approach and should be followed.

13.96   Once proceedings are under way, it would appear that the injunction given by McFarlane J in *SA* discussed at para 13.89 above is routinely ignored, orders for full and frank disclosure in welfare proceedings being made very rarely (if at all).

13.97   It is also at present unusual for the Court of Protection routinely to make an order for general disclosure, ie for each party to disclose those documents on which he relies, and documents which adversely affect his own case; adversely affect another party's case; or support another party's case. Indeed, in some cases, no disclosure orders will be made at all.

13.98   In welfare cases, however, orders are commonly made for the provision of specific categories of documents (for instance of medical or social services records), not to all the parties to the proceedings, but rather only to those with a specific need to have sight of them. This happens most obviously where P is a party to the proceedings and orders are made requiring (for instance) either all or part of the records held by the local authority's social services department relating to P to be provided to their litigation friend. The authors' experience is that these orders are made without judicial examination of the basis of the power under which they are made. It may, on a proper analysis, actually be that they are not specific disclosure orders[155] at all, but rather orders made under the provisions of COPR r107

155 Made under COPR r133(3).

(discussed at para 13.28 above) for the provision of information that one party has unique access to.

Withholding disclosure on confidentiality/welfare grounds

13.99   No matter the power under which such orders are made, one question arises with some regularity, namely the extent to which it is permissible for orders to be made allowing for documents to be seen by one party but not by others. Orders are regularly made providing (for instance) that social services records relating to P are to be provided to P's litigation friend (and can, in turn, be provided to any independent expert instructed to report to the court), but either making no provision for those records to be provided to other parties to the proceedings, or giving P's litigation friend a 'vetting' role so as to allow their litigation friend to determine which documents should be provided to other parties. The COPR do not contain any test or threshold for denying disclosure (whether to one or to more than one party), rule 138 merely providing in material part that:

> (1) A party who wishes to claim that he has a right or duty to withhold inspection of a document, or part of a document, must state in writing –
> (a) that he has such a right or duty; and
> (b) the grounds on which he claims that right of duty.

13.100   Moreover, as COPR r138 can only be invoked at the time that a disclosure list is provided,[156] and as such disclosure list are rarely, if ever, in fact used in the Court of Protection, it would appear that rule 138 does not, in fact, serve as the basis upon which disclosure of such materials as social work records is limited. The precise basis upon which such orders are made is therefore not entirely clear.

13.101   Following the decision of Sir James Munby P in *RC v CC and X Local Authority*,[157] it is, however, clear that the court does have the power to withhold disclosure of reports or records. *RC* did not spell out the basis upon which the power arose,[158] but it is suggested that it is perhaps most obviously under the court's general power to deal with a case justly under COPR r5(1).

13.102   The decision in *RC* also set out the test for the circumstances under which such orders can be made where a party wishes to withhold documents on the basis of their confidentiality and/or their

---

156 COPR r138(2).
157 [2014] EWHC 131 (COP), (2014) 17 CCLR 127.
158 See para 20.

adverse impact upon P (the position where disclosure is withheld on the basis of privilege is discussed at paras 13.108ff below).

13.103   Before addressing the decision in *RC*, it is worth noting the competing principles in play, in particular:

- P's right to the maintenance of confidentiality in relation to what will often be highly sensitive personal data (a right which is recognised at common law and by ECHR article 8 (right to respect for private and family life), and is enshrined in statutory provisions such as the Data Protection Act 1998). In the case of children, there has also been a historical acceptance that the particular circumstances in which social services records are created give rise to a presumption that they should be immune from disclosure on a public interest basis.[159]
- The rights of other parties to have sight of, and the ability to respond to, information contained in those documents if any reliance is to be placed by the court upon that information, whether that reliance is to be direct – ie the judge himself reading the documents – or indirect – ie an expert reporting to the court based upon the documents. The proper exercise of those rights are integral to enabling the fairness of the proceedings, a principle enshrined both at common law and in ECHR article 6.

13.104   In *RC*, Sir James Munby P drew direct analogies between the position that prevailed in proceedings in relation to children and those that should apply in the Court of Protection. He placed particular reliance upon three decisions,[160] and his conclusions can be summarised thus:

- It is a fundamental principle of fairness that a party is entitled to the disclosure of all materials which may be taken into account by the court when reaching a decision adverse to that party.
- When deciding whether to direct that a party referred to documentation should not be able to inspect the part which refers to them, the court should first consider whether disclosure of the material would involve a real possibility of significant harm to P.
- If it would, the court should next consider whether the overall interests of P would benefit from non-disclosure, weighing on the

159 *Re M (a minor) (disclosure of material)* [1990] 2 FLR 36. This case must now be treated with caution: *Dunn v Durham CC* [2012] EWCA Civ 1654, [2013] 1 WLR 2305 at para 45 per Munby LJ.

160 *In re D (minors) (adoption reports: confidentiality)* [1996] AC 593; *Re B (disclosure to other parties)* [2001] 2 FLR 1017; and *Dunn v Durham CC* [2012] EWCA Civ 1654, [2013] 1 WLR 2305.

one hand the interest of P in having the material properly tested, and on the other both the magnitude of the risk that harm will occur and the gravity of the harm if it does occur.

- If the court is satisfied that the interests of P point towards non-disclosure, the next and final step is for the court to weigh that consideration, and its strength in the circumstances of the case, against the interest of the parent or other party in having an opportunity to see and respond to the material. In the latter regard the court should take into account the importance of the material to the issues in the case.

- In all cases, the test for non-disclosure is whether it is strictly necessary to meet the risk identified by the court.[161]

13.105   Sir James Munby P also noted in *RC* that consideration should always be given to the fact that disclosure is never a binary exercise, and a proper evaluation and weighing of the various interests may lead to the conclusion that i) there should be disclosure but ii) the disclosure needs to be subject to safeguards such as limits to the use that may be made of the documents, in particular so as to limit the release into the public domain of intensely personal information about third parties. Further, the position initially arrived at is never set in stone and that it may be appropriate to proceed one step at a time.[162]

13.106   *RC* is of also significance because Sir James Munby P confirmed that the first instance judge had had the power to direct that some documents could be disclosed solely to the advocate for a party, with a direction that the representative could not disclose or discuss it with the client.[163] He made it clear that such limited disclosure can only be ordered if there is clear and express consent on the party of the affected party's legal representative, who should only give such consent if they are satisfied that they can do so without harming their client's case.[164]

13.107   Notwithstanding the endorsement by Sir James Munby P of 'confidentiality rings', it is suggested that any legal adviser should be very cautious before advancing or agreeing to one. The 'very serious problems' it creates between lawyer and client have led to doubts being placed upon the decision in *Mohammed* upon which Sir James

---

161 See paras 15–17.

162 See paras 18–19.

163 See paras 21–23. The appeal was allowed in this regard because of a doubt as to the basis upon which the power had been exercised.

164 *RC* at para 38, endorsing dicta of Moses LJ in *R(Mohammed) v Secretary of State for Defence* [2012] EWHC 3454 (Admin), [2014] 1 WLR 1071.

Munby P relied.[165] It is therefore likely that the decision in *RC* will not necessarily be the end of the story in this regard.

Privilege

13.108   Disclosure of documents can also be resisted on the basis that they are subject to legal professional privilege: ie that they represent 'protected' communications between lawyer and client (and, in certain circumstances, with third parties).

13.109   This is a very large topic. Space precludes a detailed discussion of it here,[166] but the position is set out in summary form in the paragraphs that follow. These paragraphs must be read subject to the caveat that, with the limited exception of the case of *Loughlin v Singh* discussed above (para 13.94), there has been no reported judicial consideration of the application of the law of privilege to proceedings before the Court of Protection. The paragraphs below therefore represent the authors' view that the closest analogy to such proceedings are those involving children, and that the principles derived in those proceedings can and should be applied before the Court of Protection.

13.110   There are two forms of legal professional privilege: legal advice privilege and litigation privilege.

- *Legal advice privilege* protects confidential communications between a client and their professional legal adviser that is made for purpose of seeking or giving any legal advice or related legal assistance. It is not necessary for it to apply that there is litigation in prospect.[167]
- *Litigation privilege* protects confidential communications between either the client or their legal adviser or their legal adviser and a third party (such as a factual or an expert witness), where such communications come into existence for the dominant purpose of being used in connection with actual, pending or contemplated litigation.[168]

13.111   Where a litigation friend has been appointed to act on behalf of a party (whether that be P or a protected party: see chapter 12), and whilst

---

165 *AHK, AM, AS, FM v Secretary of State for the Home Department* [2013] EWHC 1426 (Admin) at paras 20–28 per Ouseley J. The appeal against this decision to the Court of Appeal was stayed on 21 February 2014: [2014] EWCA Civ 151.

166 The reader is directed, in particular, to C Passmore *Privilege*, Sweet & Maxwell, 3rd edn, 2013.

167 Passmore, *Privilege*, para 1-002.

168 Passmore, *Privilege*, para 1-002.

there is no reported case from the Court of Protection on the point, it is suggested that for these purposes the litigation friend stands in the shoes of the client. By analogy, we note that the Court of Appeal accepted in *RP v Nottingham City Council* (it appears without argument) that the file maintained by a solicitor retained by the Official Solicitor where he was acting as litigation friend for a protected party in care proceedings contained privileged material.[169]

13.112   Litigation privilege is 'essentially a creature of adversarial proceedings'; it does not therefore extend to protect expert reports obtained in the context of care proceedings involving children.[170] It is suggested that this applies equally in the context of proceedings under the MCA 2005. Indeed, this would appear to be (albeit implicitly rather than expressly) the basis upon which Kenneth Parker J held in *Loughlin v Singh* (para 13.94 above) that all relevant expert reports in the possession of the claimant's solicitors should have been disclosed to the Court of Protection when making an application for the appointment of a deputy to manage his property and affairs. It should also be noted that it is clear from the COPR that *instructions* to an expert are not privileged against disclosure.[171]

13.113   It would, further, appear that it may well be the case that litigation privilege cannot be claimed in the context of other classes of documents or correspondence created in the context of proceedings before the Court of Protection.[172] Moreover, even if litigation privilege can be claimed, a number of family law cases have suggested this may be overridden by a duty to disclose documents where the court must determine what is in the best interests of the child.[173] It is suggested that such an approach would be likely also to be taken by the Court of Protection.

13.114   The position as regards legal advice privilege, however, is very different. Save for rare exceptions involving fraud or misconduct, the privilege has been held to be an absolute one even in respect of proceedings involving the determination of the best interests of children.[174] It is suggested that the same applies in proceedings under

169 [2008] EWCA Civ 462, (2008) 11 CCLR 316 at paras 34–35, per Wall LJ.
170 *Re L (a minor) (police investigation: privilege)* [1997] AC 16 at 27 per Lord Jauncey.
171 COPR r126(5).
172 Following the approach adopted by the House of Lords in *Three Rivers (No 6)* [2004] UKHL 48, [2005] 1 AC 610.
173 See, in particular, *Oxfordshire CC v M* [1994] 2 WLR 393.
174 *AB (care proceedings: disclosure of medical evidence to police)* [2002] EWHC 2198 (Fam), [2003] 1 FLR 579.

the MCA 2005 so as to protect lawyer-client communications, communications between a litigation friend appointed to act on behalf of P (or a protected party other than P) and the lawyers that that litigation friend has retained.

Publicity, privacy and confidentiality

Introduction

14.1   The approach to publication in the Court of Protection has changed significantly since the implementation of the Mental Capacity Act (MCA) 2005. This chapter looks at the legal and regulatory issues that surround the publication of information in the Court of Protection and considers how to work with the media in this context. This section includes a 'Question and Answer' section with Romana Canneti, in-house legal adviser to Independent Print Ltd.

The legal framework

14.2   The starting point is section 12 of the Administration of Justice Act (AJA) 1960, as amended by MCA 2005 Sch 6 para 10. The relevant part of section 12 reads:

> **Publication of information relating to proceedings in private**
>
> **12** (1) The publication of information relating to proceedings before any court sitting in private shall not of itself be contempt of court except in the following cases, that is to say–
>
> (a) where the proceedings–
>
>   (i) relate to the exercise of the inherent jurisdiction of the High Court with respect to minors;
>
>   (ii) are brought under the Children Act 1989; or
>
>   (iii) otherwise relate wholly or mainly to the maintenance or upbringing of a minor;
>
> (b) where the proceedings are brought under the Mental Capacity Act 2005 or under any provision of the Mental Health Act 1983 authorising an application or reference to be made to a Mental Health Review Tribunal or to a county court ...

Therefore it is generally a contempt of court to publish information relating to Court of Protection proceedings. This applies whether or not the court has made any order restricting publication of information about a specific case, and it is clearly essential that practitioners comply with the provisions of the AJA 1960.

14.3   The Court of Protection Rules (COPR) 2007 SI No 1744 provide exceptions to this where certain conditions apply. The relevant rules are COPR rr90–93. These are set out below for ease of reference:

Private hearings

General rule – hearing to be in private

90 (1) The general rule is that a hearing is to be held in private.

(2) A private hearing is a hearing which only the following persons are entitled to attend–

(a) the parties;

(b) P (whether or not a party);

(c) any person acting in the proceedings as a litigation friend;

(d) any legal representative of a person specified in any of sub-paragraphs (a) to (c); and

(e) any court officer.

(3) In relation to a private hearing, the court may make an order–

(a) authorising any person, or class of persons, to attend the hearing or a part of it; or

(b) excluding any person, or class of persons, from attending the hearing or a part of it.

Court's general power to authorise publication of information about proceedings

91 (1) For the purposes of the law relating to contempt of court, information relating to proceedings held in private may be published where the court makes an order under paragraph (2).

(2) The court may make an order authorising–

(a) the publication of such information relating to the proceedings as it may specify; or

(b) the publication of the text or a summary of the whole or part of a judgment or order made by the court.

(3) Where the court makes an order under paragraph (2) it may do so on such terms as it thinks fit, and in particular may–

(a) impose restrictions on the publication of the identity of–

(i) any party;

(ii) P (whether or not a party);

(iii) any witness; or

(iv) any other person;

(b) prohibit the publication of any information that may lead to any such person being identified;

(c) prohibit the further publication of any information relating to the proceedings from such date as the court may specify; or

(d) impose such other restrictions on the publication of information relating to the proceedings as the court may specify.

Power to order a public hearing

Court's power to order that a hearing be held in public

92 (1) The court may make an order–

(a) for a hearing to be held in public;

(b) for a part of a hearing to be held in public; or

(c) excluding any person, or class of persons, from attending a public hearing or a part of it.

(2) Where the court makes an order under paragraph (1), it may in the same order or by a subsequent order–
    (a) impose restrictions on the publication of the identity of–
        (i) any party;
        (ii) P (whether or not a party);
        (iii) any witness; or
        (iv) any other person;
    (b) prohibit the publication of any information that may lead to any such person being identified;
    (c) prohibit the further publication of any information relating to the proceedings from such date as the court may specify; or
    (d) impose such other restrictions on the publication of information relating to the proceedings as the court may specify.

Supplementary

Supplementary provisions relating to public or private hearings
93 (1) An order under rule 90, 91 or 92 may be made–
    (a) only where it appears to the court that there is good reason for making the order;
    (b) at any time; and
    (c) either on the court's own initiative or on an application made by any person in accordance with Part 10.
  (2) A practice direction may make further provision in connection with–
    (a) private hearings;
    (b) public hearings; or
    (c) the publication of information about any proceedings.

14.4   These COPR are supported by Practice Direction (PD) 13A. The impact of the rules is that hearings in the Court of Protection are generally in private, attended only by those persons listed in COPR r90(2). COPR r90(3) allows the court to authorise any person to attend all or part of a private hearing. Such an order may be made at any time under the court's initiative or at the request of a party and will be made where there is 'good reason' for making the order.[1]

14.5   The position is different if the case concerns serious medical treatment, as defined in PD 9E.[2] Paragraph 16 of PD 9E provides that in serious medical treatment cases the court will ordinarily make an order under COPR r92 that the hearing will be held in public with restrictions on reporting. For the wider issues arising in medical treatment cases, see chapter 23.[3]

---

1 COPR r93(1)(a).
2 PD 9E paras 5–7.
3 Where the Court of Protection directs a public hearing control over publicity is governed by the Contempt of Court Act 1981 ss1–4, 11, 19.

14.6   COPR r91 empowers the judge to authorise publication of information relating to private proceedings, or of all or part of a judgment
given in private proceedings.[4] Such an order will again be made when
there is good reason to make it.[5] COPR r91(3) provides that such an
order can be made in such terms as the court sees fit and gives examples of the types of restrictions the court may consider imposing (for
an example, given in proceedings where it is necessary for information contained in an order relating to P to be shared with others for
purposes of delivering care to them, see appendix C below[6]). Release
of information which complies with a direction under COPR r91 will
not be contempt of court.[7]

14.7   COPR r92 allows the court to direct that all or part of a hearing be
held in public. However this remains subject to the court's powers to
exclude persons or classes of persons from the hearing or part of it
and imposing restrictions on publication. Again the test is that there
is good reason for making such an order.

14.8   The relevant practice direction accompanying these rules (PD
13A) is in two parts. The first applies in all cases where an application is being made for orders under rules 91, 92 and 93 and provides
that such applications must be made by filing an application using
form COP9.[8] The court should then consider whether to deal with
the application as a discrete issue.[9]

14.9   If the court decides to authorise publication and at the same
time sets out restrictions as to what can or cannot be published
(for example, when a judge directs that a judgment should be published, but at the same time directs that the parties' names should be
anonymised), there is no need to give notice to the news media.[10]

14.10   Different considerations apply where the court has already made
an order authorising publication, or has agreed to sit in public, and
subsequently either an application is then made to restrict what
can be published, or the court is considering exercising its powers

---

4 COPR r91(2).

5 COPR r93(1)(a).

6 Paragraph 14 of the first directions order made in welfare proceedings after an
   attended hearing, which also provides for disclosure of information for purpose
   of communicating with a person exercising a relevant function authorised by
   statute or for the purpose of complying with an order of any court of competent
   jurisdiction.

7 COPR r91(1).

8 PD 13A Part 1 para 4.

9 PD 13A Part 1 para 6.

10 PD 13A Part 2 para 8.

to restrict the information.[11] In such cases, P's rights under the European Convention on Human Rights (ECHR) are engaged; but so are the ECHR article 10 rights to freedom of expression of the person seeking to publish the information.[12] Therefore, the practice direction draws attention to the requirement for notice to be given to the person whose article 10 rights would be affected (probably one of the media organisations) unless there are compelling reasons why that person should not be notified.[13]

14.11　The procedure which should then be followed is set out in paras 13–19, and it is important that this is followed. National newspapers and broadcasters subscribe to the Press Association's CopyDirect service. A list of the subscribing organisations is available online.[14] CopyDirect is responsible for notifying individual media organisations of an intended application, and notice of an application for an order that would affect the world at large can be given to CopyDirect.[15] However, the Copy-Direct service does not extend to regional or local media or magazines who would need to be served directly with notice of the application.[16]

14.12　The CopyDirect website makes it clear that CopyDirect will only notify organisations of applications and does not deal with service of orders once they are made.

14.13　Paragraphs 15–18 require the applicant to contact CopyDirect and sets out the information that is required. The court will also give advance notice if considering an order of its own initiative and will then provide such of the information listed in para 15 as it sees fit.[17] The court may also dispense with any of the requirements in paras 15–19.[18] An organisation which wishes to take part in any hearing must file an acknowledgement of service in form COP5 within 21 days of receipt of the notice from CopyDirect.[19] It is essential that the nature of the orders sought are clearly indicated and that anyone seeking restrictions on identifying or contacting individuals or classes of individuals should make this clear.[20]

11　PD 13A Part 2 para 12.
12　PD 13A Part 2 paras 10, 11.
13　PD 13A Part 2 para 10.
14　See: www.medialawyer.press.net/courtapplications.
15　PD 13A Part 2 para 14.
16　PD 13A Part 2 para 18.
17　PD 13A Part 2 para 20.
18　PD 13A Part 2 para 19.
19　PD 13A Part 2 paras 21, 22.
20　See also *W v M (reporting restriction order)* [2011] EWHC 1197 (COP), [2011] COPLR Con Vol 1226 discussed at para 14.24 below.

14.14   The practice direction gives guidance as to the approach to be taken when balancing P's ECHR rights under article 8 against the right under article 10 to freedom of expression. There is no precedence between the two and both are qualified. [21] The practice direction[22] draws attention to the need to have particular regard to:

i) the importance of freedom expression;
ii) the extent to which material has or is about to become public (orders will not usually be made prohibiting publication of material which is already in the public domain, apart from in exceptional cases);[23]
iii) the extent of the public interest in such material being published;
iv) the terms of any relevant privacy code.

14.15   The practice direction also notes that the aim of any restrictions should be to protect P rather than confer anonymity on others; but restrictions on identifying others could be justified if the absence of such restrictions might lead to the identification of P or restrict the ability of others to care for P. The identity of experts however is not usually subject to restrictions.[24]

14.16   Orders should last no longer than they are needed to achieve their purpose but may need to last until P's death, or indeed beyond.[25]

14.17   Special considerations arise in cases involving contempt of court. The following Practice Guidance was issued in June 2013 by the Lord Chief Justice and the President of the Court of Protection:

> 1. It is a fundamental principle of the administration of justice in England and Wales that applications for committal for contempt should be heard and decided in public, that is, in open court.
>
> 2. This principle applies as much to committal applications in the Court of Protection (rule 188(2) of the Court of Protection Rules 2007) and in the Family Division (rule 33.5(1) of the Family Procedure Rules 2010) as to committal applications in any other Division of the High Court.
>
> 3. The Court of Protection and, when the application arises out of proceedings relating to a child, the Family Division, is vested with a

---

21 PD 13A Part 2 para 24.
22 PD 13A Part 2 para 25.
23 PD 13A Part 2 para 28.
24 PD 13A Part 2 para 27.
25 PD 13A Part 2 para 28. See also *W v M and S (reporting restriction order)* [2011] EWHC 1197 (COP), [2011] COPLR Con Vol 1205 (injunctions were made in support of reporting restrictions that prevented contact being made with the laypeople at the heart of a high-profile medical treatment case were expressed so as to last for the lifetime of P).

discretionary power to hear a committal application in private. This discretion should be exercised only in exceptional cases where it is necessary in the interests of justice. The fact that the committal application is being made in the Court of Protection or in the Family Division in proceedings relating to a child does not of itself justify the application being heard in private. Moreover the fact that the hearing of the committal application may involve the disclosure of material which ought not to be published does not of itself justify hearing the application in private if such publication can be restrained by an appropriate order.

4. If, in an exceptional case, a committal application is heard in private and the court finds that a person has committed a contempt of court it must state in public (rule 188(3) of the Court of Protection Rules 2007; Order 52 rule 6(2) of the Rules of the Supreme Court 1965):

(a) the name of that person;

(b) in general terms the nature of the contempt of court in respect of which the committal order [committal order for this purpose includes a suspended committal order] is being made; and

(c) the punishment being imposed.

This is mandatory; there are no exceptions. There are never any circumstances in which any one may be committed to custody without these matters being publicly stated.

5. Committal applications in the Court of Protection or the Family Division should at the outset be listed and heard in public. Whenever the court decides to exercise its discretion to sit in private the judge should, before continuing the hearing in private, give a judgment in public setting out the reasons for doing so. At the conclusion of any hearing in private the judge should sit in public to comply with the requirements set out in paragraph 4.

6. In every case in which a committal order or a suspended committal order is made the judge should take appropriate steps to ensure that any judgment or statement complies with paragraphs 4 and 5 and that as soon as reasonably practicable:

(a) a transcript is prepared at public expense of the judgment (which includes for this purpose any judgment given in accordance with paragraph 5 and any statement given in accordance with paragraphs 4 and 5);

(b) every judgment as referred to in (a) is published on the BAILII website; and

(c) upon payment of any appropriate charge that may be required a copy of any such judgment is made available to any person who requests a copy.

Case-law

14.18   The tension between protecting P's ECHR rights and the freedom of the press has been considered in several judgments since the Court of Protection acquired its welfare jurisdiction. At the same time, the Court of Protection became the subject of a degree of criticism in the press, repeatedly being described as a 'secret court'. A detailed examination of these judgments is beyond the scope of this book and what follows is a summary of the approaches taken in the cases that have been brought in respect of this issue.[26]

14.19   In *Independent News and Media Ltd v A*,[27] the Court of Appeal approved the approach that Hedley J had taken at first instance. He had taken a two-stage approach to the application for an order under COPR r91. The first stage was to ascertain whether there was good reason to permit the application. If this is established, the court should proceed to weigh up the competing factors. The Court of Appeal noted the paradox whereby matters in respect of which adults with capacity would take their privacy for granted come before the Court of Protection: the incapacitated adult faces a risk to their privacy (because the relevant decisions are being taken by the court) that an adult with capacity would never face. The Court of Appeal noted the paradox whereby adults with capacity make decisions about their personal lives all the time, and take their privacy in doing so for granted, but that a person who needs the court to make these decisions, because he or she cannot, faces the potential loss of that privacy as a result:

> 29. As we have said, in broad general terms, the ways in which autonomous adults who are not disadvantaged by disability organise their lives are entirely private, and this is reflected by the presumption, or starting point in Rule 90(1). However, the public interest may, in exceptional cases, outweigh the privacy which those with a disability can normally expect in relation to hearings in the Court of Protection. In this context therefore, it seems to us that the provisions of article 8, while coinciding with the arrangements for privacy which are spelled out in the legislative structure, do not enhance their significance, but rather, repeat them.

---

26 It will be noted that initially Court of Protection judgments were reported with the citation 'Fam': it was some time before the court acquired its own citations and its separate place on the BAILII (British and Irish Legal Information Institute) website (www.bailii.org).

27 [2010] EWCA Civ 343, [2010] 1 WLR 2262.

14.20   In *G v E (anonymisation)*,[28] Baker J made an order identifying the local authority whose conduct towards the vulnerable adult in their care has been the subject of strong criticism. He considered this to be justified on the basis of accountability and transparency, though might have taken a different view had this risked the identification of the adult and his family.

14.21   In the first instance hearing at *Cheshire West and Chester Council v P and another*,[29] the local authority accepted that there was 'good reason' that they should be identified but argued that the risk of identifying P should tip the balance into withholding the local authority's name. Baker J commented that:

> ... the public interest in holding public authorities accountable for the actions of their employees manifestly amounts to a 'good reason' for publishing the judgment in an anonymised format but authorising the naming of the local authority in any published report of the judgment. I also endorse the submissions made by Mr. O'Brien that such publication will help to sustain public confidence that the Court of Protection is carrying out its functions in the public interest within the restrictions imposed by Parliament.[30]

He further did not consider the risk that this would identify P was significant.

14.22   In *Hillingdon LBC v Neary*,[31] Peter Jackson J again noted the salutary impact that publication of information could have, commenting that:

> There is a genuine public interest in the work of this court being understood. Not only is this healthy in itself – the presence of the media in appropriate cases has a bracing effect on all public servants, whether in the field of social services or the law – but it may also help to dispel misunderstandings. It is not in the interests of individual litigants, or of society at large, for a court that is by definition devoted to the *protection* of the welfare of disadvantaged people to be characterised (including in a report about this case, published as I write this judgment) as 'secretive'. It is part of our natural curiosity to want to know other people's secrets, and using pejorative descriptions of this kind may stimulate interest. The opportunity, in appropriate cases, to follow a process that has welfare, not secrecy, at its heart can only

---

28 [2010] EWHC 2042 (Fam), [2010] COPLR Con Vol 499.
29 [2011] EWHC 1330 (Fam), [2011] COPLR Con Vol 273. This aspect of the decision was not the subject of any further consideration on appeal.
30 Para 89.
31 [2011] EWHC 413 (COP), [2011] COPLR Con Vol 677.

help the media to produce balanced reporting, and not fall back on clichés.[32]

14.23　Steven Neary's name and circumstances had been in the public eye before proceedings had started – for example, his father's attempts to secure his return home had been covered in the BBC Radio 4 programme 'You and Yours'. The judge noted that there was no evidence that the publicity had or was likely to harm Steven. He further noted that stories about named individuals may hold more interest than those about unidentified people. Individuals should not be named at the outset of a case if there is a real possibility that at the end of the case the court would not allow publication; but it would be stultifying to withhold information when it was already in the public domain, as in this case.

14.24　*W v M (reporting restriction order)*[33] concerned the proposed withdrawal of artificial nutrition and hydration from a M, a minimally conscious patient. In accordance with PD 9E, Baker J directed that hearings should take place in open court. An application was then made for orders restraining publication of information likely to lead to the identification of M, family members and care staff. The application which was provided to the media through CopyDirect did not specify that an order would be sought preventing the media from contacting any person. In the event orders were granted restricting publication which could identify M, her family and care staff, but also restraining the media –who were not represented – from contacting anyone on a list of 65 persons involved in caring for M. Baker J agreed to reconsider the order on receipt of a letter from Times Newspapers Ltd expressing concern that the media had not been notified of the full nature of the orders to be sought and had therefore been unable to make representations.

14.25　Baker J held that:

- While PD 13A does not require the applicant to serve a draft order, it is essential for the applicant to give an outline of the orders sought and the applicant must indicate the categories of people whose identities it is proposed will be kept confidential.
- If the applicant seeks restrictions on contact by the media with individuals or categories of persons, the application must make this clear.

32　Para 15 (emphasis in original).
33　[2011] EWHC 1197 (COP), [2011] COPLR Con Vol 1205.

- There is no automatic precedence between the article 8 rights of P or P's family and the article 10 rights of the media organisations.
- There must be a proper evidential basis for concerns about the risk of harm from an interference with the article 8 rights of P or P's family.
- The public interest in freedom of expression in medical cases will usually lie in information being available about the general issues rather than the identity of individuals.
- There is a public interest in the practices of the Court of Protection being better understood and the urge to take an over-protective stance should be resisted.
- Celebrity cases and super-injunctions involve balancing the same convention rights, but the circumstances of the individuals concerned are so different that decisions in the two types of cases are unlikely to be relevant to each other.

14.26   In *Re RGS*,[34] DJ Eldergill found that RGS's son RBS lacked capacity to litigate the proceedings about his father. He refused an application for permission to report the proceedings. He noted that RBS had already criticised the judge and the court vociferously and made it clear he did not wish to restrict RBS's right to free speech more than was necessary. He invited RBS to reflect on the difference between secrecy and the right to privacy that RBS had himself claimed in the course of the proceedings, noting that the 'existence of a private sphere of action, free from public coercion and control, is indispensable to that independence which everyone needs to develop as an individual', and to deny the incapacitated the privacy or confidentiality that those with capacity claim is discriminatory.

14.27   In *Westminster City Council v Sykes*[35] DJ Eldergill decided to allow the publication of the names of Manuela Sykes and the local authority where she had once been a councillor and which was at the time depriving her of her liberty. DJ Eldergill commented that the general rule that a hearing is to be held in private and that this reflects the personal and private nature of the information the court considers. He commented:

> That is not the same as being secretive; a GP is not a 'secret doctor' because the press have no unqualified right to be present during patient consultations or to report what is said. All citizens have a right to expect that information about them will be held in confidence by their doctors and social workers, and to expect that any overriding,

34 [2012] EWHC 4162 (COP).
35 [2014] EWHC B9 (COP), (2014) 17 CCLR 139.

future, need to breach this right will go no further than necessary, and only exceptionally involve seeing it in national newspapers.

Everyone benefits from, and enjoys, this level of privacy and therefore there is a strong public interest in privacy. Not to allow an incapacitated person the same general right to privacy or confidentiality that we claim it for ourselves would be to discriminate against them because of their mental illness and vulnerability.

The one, highly important, difference is that whilst in an ideal world incapacitated people would have exactly the same right to privacy and confidentiality that the rest of us enjoy, when judges make decisions for them this brings into play the competing consideration that the public ought to know how courts of law function and administer justice: what kinds of decisions they are making, the quality of those decisions, and so forth.

While it is sometimes necessary to distinguish between 'the public interest' and 'matters which the public finds interesting,' there is a high public interest in seeing that hearings which determine the rights of incapacitated people, and their families, are fair and properly administered.

14.28　Ms Sykes had been a political campaigner all her life and had always wanted to he heard. On learning of her diagnosis of dementia she had shared her experiences on the internet, campaigning for the rights of those with the condition. Her personality and wishes were a magnetic factor in the balancing exercise, specifically the decision whether to name her or retain her anonymity.

14.29　The judge concluded:

> She has strong and clear views about the situation of women in society; and, in particular, older women; and, even more particularly, older women experiencing dementia. If she still had capacity, she would wish her own plight and personal story to be known in the hope that it will help people understand the difficulties faced by older women with dementia, and the resources available to them.

> She is a journalist herself. For 40 years, she wrote a paper called, 'Voice of the Unions'. Therefore, the court can be confident that her belief in and commitment to a free press and freedom of expression pre-dates any incapacity.

> She was also a member of the local authority's social services committee. She spent much of her free time discussing and decisions of the kind that her local authority faces in trying to provide social services to her.

> There is a clear and genuine private benefit, as well as a public benefit, to allowing her to be named in reports. It confers dignity, the dignity of being heard, rather than undermines her dignity, the indignity of being forgotten.

14.30   In *Re G*,[36] Sir James Munby, the President of the Court of Protection, considered an application by Associated Newspapers Ltd (ANL) to be joined as a party to various applications by the local authority in respect of G, an elderly woman. The applications included an order preventing C from taking G to any public protests, demonstrations or meetings with the press. The court had concluded at an earlier hearing that the consideration of this order required an assessment of G's capacity to communicate with and engage with the press. ANL sought to be joined as a party to the proceedings and to provide their own instructions to the expert, but subsequently refined the application and sought to be joined as an interested party in respect of certain issues.

14.31   The President held that that ANL were not ultimately seeking to publish material that was already in existence but material that might subsequently come into existence, namely that which ANL received from G. He further held that, if G lacked capacity to communicate with and engage with the Press, then the decision whether G should impart information to the Press was to be taken in G's best interests and that did not give rise to a justiciable issue between ANL and G. However, the President held, if the court made the decision that it was *not* in G's best interests to impart information to ANL, then G's best interests should be balanced against ANL's rights under ECHR article 10. The President therefore concluded that there was no need for ANL to be a party to the assessment either of G's capacity to communicate with the press or to her best interests in this regard (if she lacked capacity), nor was this desirable for the purpose of COPR r73.[37] Indeed, it was undesirable as this would extend the number of persons who would be entitled to the extensive access to documents relating to G.

The President's Guidance and the future

14.32   On 16 January 2014 Sir James Munby P issued guidance entitled *Transparency in the Court of Protection: publication of judgments*.[38] The President considered that too few judgments in the Court of Protection were made available to the public and that greater transparency

36   *Re G, Redbridge LBC v G (by her litigation friend the Official Solicitor) C and F* [2014] EWHC 1361 (COP).

37   As to which, see para 10.17.

38   Available at: www.judiciary.gov.uk/Resources/JCO/Documents/Guidance/transparency-in-the-cop.pdf.

was needed to build both understanding of and confidence in the court system. He made it clear that this was part of an incremental approach and that the guidance would be followed by further guidance, then practice directions and changes to the rules, with a view to harmonising practice in the Court of Protection with that in the Family Court.[39]

14.33 The President noted that when judgments are published the normal course of events is for the restrictions on publication to be set out in a rubric at the start of the judgment. These terms are a matter for the judge in each case and typically involve protecting the anonymity of the individuals involved,[40] but this may not be appropriate in all cases. Those who might wish to identify themselves with the individuals in the judgment could apply to the court.

14.34 The President's Guidance does not affect the approach of judges as to the degree of anonymity involved in published judgments but does affect the approach to be taken in deciding whether to permit publication in the first place. Paragraphs 16 and 17 set out classes of judgment which the judge must ordinarily allow to be published. First, where the judge concludes that publication would be in the public interest, whether or not any party or the media has asked for publication.[41] Second, where the judgment relates to one or more of a number of issues set out in the schedule below, and a written judgment exists or a transcription has been ordered, then the starting point is that the judgment should be published unless there are compelling reasons not to do so.

14.35 The schedule to para 17 lists issues that should give rise to publication, absent compelling reasons:

(i) any application for an order involving the giving or withholding of serious medical treatment and any other hearing held in public;
(ii) any application for a declaration or order involving a deprivation or possible deprivation of liberty;
(iii) any case where there is a dispute as to who should act as an attorney or a deputy;
(iv) any case where the issues include whether a person should be restrained from acting as an attorney or a deputy or that an appointment should be revoked or his or her powers should be reduced;
(v) any application for an order that an incapacitated adult (P) be moved into or out of a residential establishment or other institution;
(vi) any case where the sale of P's home is in issue;

---

39 *Transparency in the Court of Protection* [2014] EWCOP B2 paras 5, 6.
40 *Transparency in the Court of Protection* paras 9, 10.
41 *Transparency in the Court of Protection* para 16.

(vii) any case where a property and affairs application relates to assets (including P's home) of £1 million or more or to damages awarded by a court sitting in public;

(viii) any application for a declaration as to capacity to marry or to consent to sexual relations;

(ix) any application for an order involving a restraint on publication of information relating to the proceedings.

14.36   Judgments to be published pursuant to the provisions of the guidance described above should be placed on the BAILII website by the court as soon as possible.[42] Unless the judge orders otherwise, the cost of transcribing a judgment shall be at public expense.[43]

14.37   The second class of judgments are those published at the request of a party or accredited member of the media applies for an order permitting publication and the judge concludes permission should be given.[44] In such cases the judge should have regard to all the circumstances, any ECHR rights – including article 6 (right to a fair trial), article 8 (right to respect for private and family life) and article 10 (freedom of expression) – and the possible impact on any current or potential criminal proceedings.[45] The cost of transcribing judgments published on this basis will be at the expense of the party or person applying for the judgment[46] and it will be for the judge to decide if the court should place the judgment on BAILII.

14.38   In all cases where permission is given for publication the following guidance is given:[47]

(i) public authorities and expert witnesses should be named in the judgment approved for publication, unless there are compelling reasons why they should not be so named;

(ii) the person who is the subject of proceedings in the Court of Protection and other members of their family should not normally be named in the judgment approved for publication unless the judge otherwise orders

(iii) anonymity in the judgment as published should not normally extend beyond protecting the privacy of the adults who are the subject of the proceedings and other members of their families, unless there are compelling reasons to do so.

---

42 *Transparency in the Court of Protection* para 23.
43 *Transparency in the Court of Protection* para 22.
44 *Transparency in the Court of Protection* para 18.
45 *Transparency in the Court of Protection* para 19.
46 *Transparency in the Court of Protection* para 22.
47 *Transparency in the Court of Protection* para 20.

14.39   Unless the judgment expressly provides otherwise, the judgment should contain the following rubric:[48]

> 'This judgment was delivered in private. The judge has given leave for this version of the judgment to be published on condition that (irrespective of what is contained in the judgment) in any published version of the judgment the anonymity of the incapacitated person and members of their family must be strictly preserved. All persons, including representatives of the media, must ensure that this condition is strictly complied with. Failure to do so will be a contempt of court.'

The media and the court

14.40   This section considers how advisers can deal with the media. There are a number of scenarios which can arise in the Court of Protection context.

14.41   The first is where a client who is a party to the proceedings seeks advice as to whether they should involve the press in a particular case. In the authors' experience, this question often arises in highly charged cases where there is a poor relationship between the parties. A wish to involve the media can be born out of a sense of desperation to be heard. Advisers will have to be sensitive to this and at the same time give objective consideration to whether involving a wider audience is likely to be desirable. The first piece of advice should be that no contact should be made with the press about the particular case unless the court has made an order allowing that party to contact the press under COPR r91, because as set out above that would constitute contempt of court (see para 14.2).

14.42   The next question is whether the party should be advised to make an application under COPR r91. In considering this question solicitors are bound by their obligation to act in their clients' best interests.[49] There may well be some cases where involvement of the media is in the client's best interests. The client should be advised, however, that the court will need to conclude that the 'good reason' test is satisfied and if it is will make its decision by weighing up P's interests and ECHR rights as against the article 8 rights of any media organisation seeking to publish information about the case.

14.43   If the adviser concludes that it is in the best interests of the client to seek permission to involve the media, then a belt-and-braces

48   *Transparency in the Court of Protection* para 21.
49   Solicitors Regulation Authority (SRA) Code of Conduct 2011, Principle 4.

approach will be to make an application to the court for permission to contact media organisations and invite them in turn to make an application for permission to attend hearings with a view to making an application for permission to publish some of the information. As is clear from the interview with Romana Canneti that follows below, at least some highly regarded legal advisers to media organisations do not consider that this is necessary, but the authors' view is that the cumbersome process set out above is the only way to secure against the risk that parties or advisers will be alleged to be in contempt of court.

14.44   A situation can arise when the adviser is contacted by a journalist who has already learned about the case, possibly because a party to the case has already contacted them. The adviser is placed in a somewhat difficult position because the adviser cannot provide any information to the journalist – whatever their client's wishes – other than to suggest that the journalist's organisation make an application under the COPR. There is no reason why the journalist cannot be provided with the details of the court hearing the case, the case number, together with the relevant rules or a copy of the practice direction if they are unfamiliar with these. It will then be a matter for the court to decide on the application, if one is made.

14.45   If media organisations are given permission to attend court, advocates should be prepared to make submissions at the conclusion of hearings about whether permission to publish all or any of the material which has been aired during the hearing.

Question and Answer: Romana Canneti

14.46   Romana Canneti is an in-house legal adviser to Independent Print Ltd. She has been involved in several applications for permission to report Court of Protection cases including *Independent News Media v A* and *Hillingdon v Neary*.

Q. How do you become aware of cases which your paper may wish to report?

A. There are many ways, but a common way is that an adviser will contact either a journalist or the legal department at a paper, and explain that there is a potential story about an issue in a Court of Protection case which might be of public interest. The journalist would be given the case number, though no details about who is involved or the location of the parties. We would then contact the court. We would explain that we would like to file a COP9 to apply to attend a hearing and to do that we need the names of the parties. This information is given to us so we can make an application to attend the hearing and make representations about what we would like to report.

Q. Isn't the person who contacts the journalist committing contempt of court?

A. I don't think so. They are not disclosing anything other than the existence of the case, the number and the fact that it concerns a particular issue. I have never known that point to be taken.

Q. What is the distinction between an 'off the record' conversation and one that is on the record?

A. If you say something on the record it means that you expect to be quoted. If you say something is off the record you do not expect to be quoted. Journalists' duty to protect their sources of information is taken very seriously by newspapers and reflected in the Press Complaints Commission's Code of Conduct.[50]

Q. How does the CopyDirect process work?

A. This will normally only be used when a decision has already been made that a hearing is going to be heard in public, for example a serious medical treatment case, and one or more of the parties involved in the case applies for restrictions on what we can report.

Q. What changes have you noted in the approach to the press of the Court of Protection?

A. It has changed greatly. There seemed to be a generalised resistance to press scrutiny in the early days. We are now much less likely to face objections to attending hearings. The President's Guidance is helpful. I hope this will be followed up by further changes to the practice directions and the rules, so as to allow accredited reporters to attend hearings without the need to seek permission, which is the current position in cases involving children in the family courts.

Restrictions on disclosure of documents

14.47   A final, related, series of points should be noted as regards witness statements and/or other documents filed on behalf of a party:

---

50 See: www.pcc.org.uk/cop/practice.html.

- Where a document has been filed or disclosed, a party to whom it was provided may only use it for the purpose of the proceedings in which it was filed or disclosed, except where:
  1) the document has been read to or by the court or referred to at a public hearing (NB, which will, at present be the minority of hearings in proceedings under the MCA 2005); or
  2) the court otherwise permits.[51]
- A party to proceedings may (subject to any order to the contrary) inspect or obtain from the records of the court a copy of any document filed by a party to the proceedings.[52]
- Where the application has been for the appointment of a deputy or the variation of the order under which the deputy was appointed, the Public Guardian is entitled to be supplied with copies (among other things) of documents filed in the proceedings relevant to the decision to appoint the deputy, any powers conferred upon him, any duties imposed on him if the Public Guardian reasonably considers it necessary for him to have regard to them for purposes of the discharge of his statutory functions in relation to the supervision of deputies. The court can limit disclosure of particular documents or categories of documents or direct that the documents are provided on an edited basis.[53]
- Upon application, the court may authorise a person who is not a party to proceedings to inspect documents in the court records or to obtain a copy of any such documents or extracts from such documents.[54] The court must consider whether to provide any document on an edited basis.[55]

14.48   Sir James Munby P[56] has indicated that he is considering how best so as to allow accredited journalists appropriately controlled access to documents before the Court of Protection to allow them to report upon the proceedings in an informed fashion. It is likely that this will require a change to the COPR.

---

51 COPR r18.
52 COPR r16.
53 COPR r20(1)–(6).
54 COPR r17(2).
55 COPR r17(4).
56 See, for instance, the speech he gave to the Society of Editors at its annual conference in November 2013, 'Opening up the Family Courts: Transparency in the Family Court and the Court of Protection', available at: www.judiciary. gov.uk/Resources/JCO/Documents/Speeches/pfd-speech-society-editors-11112013.pdf.

Fact-finding

Introduction

15.1   Proceedings before the Court of Protection are primarily inquisitorial, not adversarial.[1] However, there will be circumstances in which it is necessary for the court to reach determinations upon contested facts before it is possible for it then to go on to consider where P's best interests lie (or to make other decisions/declarations open to it). It is open to a judge, in the exercise of their case management powers under rule 5 of the Court of Protection Rules (COPR) 2007 SI No 1744, to decide that it is necessary that such a determination of fact take place as a separate, stand-alone hearing – a fact-finding hearing.

15.2   This chapter discusses the question of when and how disputes of fact are resolved in the Court of Protection. It addresses, in particular, the circumstances under which a separate fact-finding hearing will be listed, and the particular steps required to prepare for such hearings. The issues that it raises are likely to be of most relevance in applications concerning P's welfare, and, in particular, in cases brought by local authorities in the discharge of their safeguarding obligations owed to adults at risk (as to which, see further, chapter 24 below).

When is fact-finding necessary?

15.3   Unlike in applications for care or supervision orders under Children Act (CA) 1989, the local authority (or other applicant) does not need to establish that the adult in question is suffering or is likely to suffer significant harm[2] before the court can move on to the second stage of considering whether making the order sought will promote the welfare of the adult. 'The Mental Capacity Act does not contain provisions equivalent to the threshold provisions under section 31(2) of the Children Act. Nor should any such provisions be imported in it as clearly Parliament intended that they should not be.'[3]

---

1   *Re G* [2014] EWCOP 1361 at para 52 per Sir James Munby P, endorsing *Cheshire West and Chester Council v P and M* [2011] EWHC 1330 (Fam), [2011] COPLR Con Vol 273 at para 52 per Baker J. This aspect of his decision was not the subject of challenge upon the Official Solicitor's appeal to the Court of Appeal or thereafter to the Supreme Court.

2   CA 1989 s31(2). The threshold criteria go further than this, but this requirement is at their core.

3   *LBB v JM, BK and CM* [2010] COPLR Con Vol 779 at para 8 per Hedley J.

15.4   However, that does not mean that the court can necessarily gloss over disputes of fact as to the conduct of those suspected of in some way acting in a way adverse to the adult in favour of a broader-brush analysis of where their best interests may lie. This is for several reasons, the most of important of which are that:

a) In order for any best interests decision to be made, the court needs to be satisfied as to 'all [of] the relevant circumstances' for purposes of the application of the checklist set down in Mental Capacity Act (MCA) 2005 s4. If those circumstances are disputed, it may well be necessary for the dispute to be resolved as a preliminary step to the determination of where the adult's best interests lie. For instance, if the allegation has been made that a family member has mistreated the adult, it is likely to be necessary for the court to determine whether that allegation is made out in order before it can make any best interests decision about contact with that family member.

b) Further, as Hedley J made clear in *LBB v JM, BK and CM*:[4] 'an intervention with parties' rights under Art 8 [of the European Convention on Human Rights (ECHR)] is a serious intervention by the State which requires to be justified under Art 8(2). If there is a contested factual basis it may often be right ... that that should be investigated and determined by the court'.[5]

15.5   The decision in *LBB* leaves open the question of when it is appropriate to dispense with a fact-finding exercise to resolve disputed factual matters. It also perhaps stands a little uncomfortably with the later decision of Charles J in *A Local Authority v PB and P*,[6] a case concerning the removal of an adult from his home in the context of allegations of inadequate care being given by his mother. There was no dispute that this involved the interference with a close relationship between mother and son, but Charles J noted that, in such cases, 'there are a number of ways in which the best interests issues can be put to the court. Some of them may well involve proceeding on the

---

4 [2010] COPLR Con Vol 779.

5 It is suggested that this approach holds good notwithstanding the subsequent decision of the Court of Appeal in *K v LBX and others* [2012] EWCA Civ 79, [2012] COPLR 411, (2012) 15 CCLR 112, that the consideration of article 8 rights follows on from the application of the MCA 2005 s4 checklist; the Court of Appeal was considering a different question: see para 2 of the judgment.

6 [2011] EWHC 502 (COP), [2011] COPLR Con Vol 166.

basis that history and historical disputes of fact can be left as that and as matters of disagreement. In other cases, that would not be so'.[7]

15.6   It is unfortunate that there are no reported cases from the Court of Protection in which clear guidance has been given as to *when* fact-finding is necessary (whether or not as a separate exercise). In the absence of such guidance – let alone guidance in the form of practice directions (PDs) or other statutory guidance – it is difficult not to escape the impression that decisions are reached on a somewhat ad hoc basis, driven, at least sometimes, by the knowledge that to engage upon a separate fact-finding exercise will inevitably give rise to delay and expense.[8]

15.7   It is, however, suggested that the proper approach to the question can be derived by analogy with the approach adopted by Wall J (as he then was) in the pre-MCA 2005 case of *Re S (adult's lack of capacity: carer and residence)*.[9] In this case, concerning a 33-year-old woman, S, the relevant local authority sought declarations as to S's capacity and best interests as regards her residence, care arrangements and contact with her father. The catalyst for the local authority's application was an alleged incident of assault by S's father upon her; it was also alleged that her father had on a number of occasions been drinking and had been unfit through drink to care for her. The father strongly denied both allegations. In a detailed discussion of the relevant legal principles, Wall J directed himself that:

> ... unlike care proceedings under the Children Act 1989, the exercise of the jurisdiction over mentally incapable adults is not dependent upon any threshold criteria apart from the fact of incapacity and the existence of what Dame Elizabeth Butler-Sloss P described in *Re F (No 2)*[10] at 47 and 521 respectively as 'a serious justiciable issue' which requires the court's adjudication.[11]

Applying *Re A (male sterilisation)*,[12] he further directed himself that the central question for the court was as to what outcome was in the best interests of the adult.[13] Pausing there, we note that both of these directions continue to hold good since the enactment of the MCA 2005.

---

7   Para 32.
8   See in this regard *WCC v GS, RS and JS* [2011] EWHC 2244 (COP) at paras 30–32 and the commentary to COPR r5(2)(b)(i) in Ashton et al, *Court of Protection Practice 2014*, Jordans, p687.
9   [2003] EWHC 1909 (Fam), [2003] 2 FLR 1235.
10 *Re F (adult: court's jurisdiction)* [2001] Fam 38.
11 Para 13.
12 [2000] 1 FLR 549.
13 Para 14.

15.8   Wall J then went on to note that both of the factors outlined immediately above, but in particular the absence of any threshold criteria,
raise 'the question as to the extent to which (if at all) it is necessary,
for the purposes of exercising the jurisdiction and deciding which
course of action is in the best interests of S, to make findings of fact
relating in particular to disputed historical issues'.[14]

15.9   Importantly, Wall J rejected the submission made on behalf of
the father to the effect that absent findings of fact which warranted
her removal from her father's care, the local authority would not have
made out a case for such removal, and that she should therefore be
returned, stating that:

> I do not accept that argument. I agree that there must be good reason
> for local authority intervention in a case such as the present. Equally,
> if there are disputed issues of fact which go to the question of Mr S's
> capacity and suitability to care for S, the court may need to resolve
> them if their resolution is necessary to the decision as to what is in S's
> best interests. Findings of fact against Mr S on the two issues identi-
> fied [above] would plainly reflect upon his capacity properly to care
> for S. But it does not follow, in my judgment, that the proceedings
> must be dismissed simply because the factual basis upon which the
> local authority instituted them turns out to be mistaken, or because
> it cannot be established on the balance of probabilities. What matters
> (assuming always that mental incapacity is made out) is which out-
> come will be in S's best interests. There will plainly be cases which are
> very fact specific. There will be others in which the principal concern
> is the future, and the relative suitability of the plans which each party
> can put forward for both the short and long-term care of the mentally
> incapable adult. The instant case, in my judgment, is one of the cases
> in the latter category.[15]

15.10   He continued:

> Whilst I acknowledge that in a relatively untried jurisdiction there are
> dangers in too relaxed an approach to historical issues, I am unable
> to accept the proposition that the approach to best interests is fettered
> in any way beyond that which applies to any judicial decision, namely
> that it has to be evidence based; that it excludes irrelevant material;
> and that it includes a consideration of all relevant material. In a field
> as complex as care for the mentally disabled, a high degree of prag-
> matism seems to me inevitable. But in each case it seems to me that
> the four essential building blocks are the same. First, is mental incap-
> acity established? Secondly, is there a serious, justiciable issue relat-
> ing to welfare? Thirdly, what is it? Fourthly, with the welfare of the

14 [2001] Fam 38 para 15.
15 Para 18.

incapable adult as the court's paramount consideration, what are the balance sheet factors which must be drawn up to decide which course of action is in his or her best interests?[16]

15.11   It is suggested that this approach holds equally true under the MCA 2005. The authors further suggest that it can usefully be amplified by reference (by analogy) to the guidance issued by the same judge several years later, by which stage he had been appointed President of the Family Division. In May 2010, he issued guidance in relation to split hearings in both public and private law family proceedings.[17] This guidance reminded the courts hearing family cases that 'a fact-finding hearing is a working tool designed to assist them to decide the case. Thus a fact-finding hearing should only be ordered if the court takes the view that the case cannot properly be decided without such a hearing', and that the court must have in mind the extent to which those allegations, if admitted or proved, 'would be relevant in deciding whether to make an order ... and, if so, in what terms'. 'Plainly', as the guidance continues, 'if the allegations are unlikely to have any impact on the court's order, there is no need for a separate fact-finding hearing'.

15.12   In this regard, it is, further, important to emphasise that the sole focus of proceedings under the MCA 2005 is (or should be) upon the interests of the adult lacking capacity. They do not exist as a forum to canvass allegations of misconduct save and to the extent it is necessary that such allegations are determined in order to allow the judge properly to determine the application before them. As has been said in the context of private law proceedings under the CA 1989: 'the finite resources of the court do not exist simply to provide a free-standing medium for one party to obtain, for no reason other than vindication, findings of matrimonial misconduct against the other'.[18] The same holds equally true of allegations of misconduct towards the adult without capacity.

15.13   In order to assist the court to determine whether a fact-finding exercise: a) will be necessary; and b) (if it is) should be listed as the first part of a split trial process, it is incumbent upon the parties to identify at an early stage precisely what the issues are and precisely what

16   Para 21.

17   *President's Guidance in relation to split hearings* [2010] 2 FLR 1897. See also *SW and another v Portsmouth City Council and others; Re W (children) (concurrent care and criminal proceedings)* [2009] EWCA Civ 644, [2009] 3 FCR 1; and *Re S (Children, W & T)* [2014] EWCA Civ 638 at 71 per Sir James Munby P.

18   *AA v NA (appeal: fact-finding)* [2010] EWHC 1282 (Fam), [2010] 2 FLR 1173 at para 18 per Mostyn J.

factual findings will be required from the court in order to ground the relief that is sought. This point was emphasised by Charles J in *PB*,[19] and is discussed further at chapter 11 above.

Preparing for a fact-finding hearing

15.14 As noted above, separate fact-finding hearings are most commonly directed by the court in what might be termed safeguarding cases brought by local authorities (see further chapter 24). In such cases, it is usually the case that the local authority will be seeking adverse findings against an individual or individuals to support its contention that (for instance) their contact with P should be limited, or that P should live other than in the family home.

15.15 In such cases, the practice has developed of requiring the local authority applicant to draw up a so-called '*Scott* schedule'[20] of allegations, in other words a table setting out:

a) the specific allegation made (for instance that 'X failed to provide adequate care to P');

b) the particulars of the allegation (for instance that 'On 9 September 2013 X failed to change P's incontinence pad for a period of 12 hours'); and

c) a cross-reference (or cross-references) to the evidence relied upon in support of the particulars of the allegation (for instance 'paragraph 9 of the witness statement of Ms Y, social worker, dated 20 October 2013').

15.16 It is conventional then for the subject of the allegation to be required to set out in the same table their response to the allegation and, if it is denied, cross-references to the evidence upon which they rely in support of their denial. The local authority is then usually permitted to reply to the response, again in the same format. A column can then be provided in which the court can in due course record its finding against each allegation. The end result is a table which (ideally) makes it easier for preparations to be made for the fact-finding hearing by bringing into sharp focus the allegations, whether the allegations are disputed (and, if so, whether in whole or in part) and the scope of the evidence that will be called by the parties.

19 [2011] EWHC 502 (COP), [2011] COPLR Con Vol 166 at paras 32–38.
20 So-called because the original schedule was devised by George Alexander Scott, who held the post of Official Referee (ie judge in what is now the Technology and Construction Court) in the 1920s.

15.17   Experience shows that the process of preparing and responding to *Scott* schedules serves significantly to focus the minds of both applicants and respondents as to the issues in the case and the strength of the evidence. Experience has also shown that it is very common for applicants to produce *Scott* schedules that run to many pages of allegations when, in reality, the court need only determine a limited number in order to be able to have a secure foundation upon which to determine where P's best interests lie. An important function of the final case management hearing prior to the fact-finding hearing will therefore to ensure that only those allegations that it is truly necessary for the court to determine are set down for resolution at that latter hearing.

15.18   PD 13B,[21] in turn, makes clear that at the start of any bundle prepared for the fact-finding hearing, there must be inserted a document or documents prepared by each party which should set out (either within the document(s) themselves or by cross-referring to another document that is, or will be, within the bundle):

a) the findings or fact that the court is being asked to make; and
b) cross-references to the evidence relied upon to found those findings,

(in other words, a *Scott* schedule).[22]

15.19   Where appropriate, the preliminary documents for a fact-finding should also include:

a) a chronology;
b) a skeleton argument; and
c) a description of relevant family members and other persons who may be affected by or interested in the relief sought.[23]

15.20   Where (as is often the case) the documents in the case run to several lever arch files, it is also strongly advisable for the applicant to prepare (on an agreed basis if possible) a core bundle which contains:

1) any relevant directions made by the court;
2) the completed *Scott* schedule;
3) a chronology of relevant dates;
4) the witness statements of the relevant witnesses; and
5) any documents to which those witnesses are likely to have to be taken for purposes of giving evidence.

---

21 Discussed in greater detail at paras 11.26ff.
22 PD 13B para 4.4.
23 PD 13B para 4.5.

15.21 One final point needs to be made in this regard. As discussed at paras 13.89ff, the provisions relating to disclosure in the COPR 2007 are not regularly applied. However, in *Enfield LBC v SA and others*,[24] McFarlane J (as he then was) considered a situation that had arisen where, during the course of a fact-finding hearing held to determine allegations of abusive parenting against a learning disabled woman, it emerged that the police had already conducted an 'achieving best evidence' (ABE) interview with the woman, in which the woman had denied that she had been abused, and had repeatedly asked to go home or to see her parents, and that the authority had a copy of this interview. The local authority had informed the Official Solicitor afterwards that the interview had taken place, but, having signed a police disclaimer, had not disclosed the interview, on the basis that it decided not to rely upon the content of the interview. McFarlane J was highly critical of the local authority, and his reasoning is sufficiently important to merit reproduction in this chapter almost in full:

> 55. ... [I]t would seem that in this case they have provided the disclosure that was required of them [under the directions made], yet the result, from the perspective of a judge who is embedded in the procedure and culture of child protection proceedings under the Children Act 1989, is totally unacceptable. In a fact-finding process, where the case is largely based upon what a vulnerable adult (P) has said and the aim of the court in due course is to make orders to meet P's best interests, how can it be appropriate, fair to the interests of all parties (but particularly P) or in any way acceptable for the applicant local authority to take part in arranging a formal ABE interview of P and subsequently take possession of a DVD recording of the interview yet be under no duty to inform the other parties or the court that that is the case?

> 56. The position in family proceedings is that 'it is a duty owed to the court both by the parties and by their legal representatives to give full and frank disclosure in ancillary relief applications and also in all matters in respect of children' [*Practice Direction (Family Proceedings: Case Management)* [1995] 1 WLR 332, [1995] 1 All ER 586, sub nom Practice Direction: Case Management (31 January 1995) [1995] 1 FLR 456]. If these were proceedings relating to children, then there is absolutely no doubt that the local authority, under the duty to give 'full and frank disclosure', would have been required to inform the parties and the court of the occurrence of the interview and to disclose the DVD record (subject to the court's power to limit or control disclosure on a case specific basis). Given that the aim of protection is common

24 [2010] EWHC 196 (Admin), [2010] COPLR Con Vol 362.

between child protection proceedings under the CA 1989, Part 4 and proceedings such as the present which aim to investigate allegations of harm to P and, if necessary, protect her, how can it be a requirement in one process for the applicant to disclose the existence of an ABE interview, yet not a requirement, absent of an express order from the court in the other process?

57. The apparent difference in the approach to disclosure as between the family courts and the Court of Protection may well arise from the fact that the rules for the latter are based upon ordinary civil litigation with the expectation that disclosure will be based on whether documents 'adversely affect [a party's] own case' or 'support another party's case' (COPR, r133(2)(b)) whereas the approach of the family court is that there is a duty to give *the court* all relevant material.

58. There can, in my view, be no justification for there being a difference of this degree on the issue of disclosure between the family court and the Court of Protection in fact-finding cases of this type where really the process and the issues are essentially identical whether the vulnerable complainant is a young child or an incapacitated adult. For the future in such cases in the Court of Protection it would seem to be justified for the court to make an order for 'specific disclosure' under COPR 2007, r133(3) requiring all parties to give 'full and frank disclosure' of all relevant material. If such a direction had been made in the present case, the local authority would have been under a duty to disclose the DVD of the ABE interview, and any other records relating to it, once they came into their possession.

The determination of contested facts

15.22   As noted at the outset to this chapter, the processes of the Court of Protection are essentially inquisitorial, which means that questions of the burden of proof are not relevant to some of its tasks. Questions of the burden of proof are, for instance, not relevant to the question of what is in P's best interests, which is 'primarily an inquiry by the courts, weighing into the balance various factors. No party is under a burden of proof; rather the court, after investigating best interests, decides that issue on a balance of probability'.[25]

---

25 *Cheshire West and Cheshire Council v P and M* [2011] EWHC 1330 (Fam), [2011] COPLR Con Vol 273 at paras 51–52 per Baker J, endorsing the submissions made by the mother of P, supported by the Official Solicitor. This aspect of his decision was not the subject of challenge upon the Official Solicitor's appeal to the Court of Appeal or thereafter to the Supreme Court. This approach was endorsed by Sir James Munby P in *Re G* [2014] EWCOP 1361 at para 52.

15.23   However, the court nonetheless proceeds on the basis of conventional civil principles when it comes to the determination of a fact or facts that one party must prove in order to obtain the relief that it seeks (properly called 'facts in issue'). These principles have been recently summarised thus:[26]

> i) The local authority [or, by the same token, any other party seeking to make good an allegation] must prove its allegations on the balance of probabilities, no more, no less: *Re B (Care Proceedings: Standard of Proof)*, [2009] 1 AC 11, [2008] 3 WLR 1, [2008] 2 FLR 141, at paras [2] and [70].
>
> ii) The law operates a binary system in which the only values are 0 and 1. The fact either happened or it did not. If the court is left in doubt, the doubt is resolved by a rule that one party or the other carries the burden of proof. If the party who bears the burden of proof fails to discharge it, a value of 0 is returned and the fact is treated as not having happened. If he does discharge it, a value of 1 is returned and the fact is treated as having happened: *Re B (Care Proceedings: Standard of Proof)*, at para [2] per Lord Hoffmann.
>
> iii) The more serious or improbable the allegation the greater the need for evidential 'cogency': *Re Dellow's Will Trusts; Lloyd's Bank v Institute of Cancer Research* [1964] 1 WLR 451 at 455; *Re H (Minors) (Sexual Abuse: Standard of Proof)* [1996] AC 563, [1996] 2 WLR 8, [1996] 1 FLR 80; *Re S-B (Children) (Care Proceedings: Standard of Proof)*, [2010] 1 AC 678, [2010] 2 WLR 238, [2010] 1 FLR 1161 at para [13]. Evidential cogency is obviously needed where the harmful event is itself disputed. However, where there is no dispute that it happened the improbability of the event is irrelevant: *Re B (Care Proceedings: Standard of Proof)*, at paras [72] and [73].
>
> iv) Sometimes the burden of proof will come to the judge's rescue: the party with the burden of showing that something took place will not have satisfied him that it did. But generally speaking a judge ought to be able to make up his mind where the truth lies without needing to rely upon the burden of proof: *Re B (Care Proceedings: Standard of Proof)* at paras [2] and [32]; *Rhesa Shipping Co SA v Edmond and Another: The Popi M* [1985] 1 WLR 948.
>
> v) It is impermissible for a judge to conclude in the case of a series of improbable causes that the least improbable or least unlikely is nonetheless the cause of the event: *Rhesa Shipping Co SA v Edmond and Another: The Popi M; Ide v ATB Sales Ltd; Lexus Financial Services t/a Toyota Financial Services (UK) plc v Russell* [2008] EWCA Civ 424 at para [4].

---

26 *Re D (a child)* [2014] EWHC 121 (Fam) at para 31 per Mostyn J. This was a care case, but the principles are of general application.

vi) There is no pseudo-burden or obligation cast on the respondents to come up with alternative explanations: *Lancashire County Council v D and E* [2010] 2 FLR 196 at paras [36] and [37]; *Re C and D (Photographs of Injuries)* [2011] 1 FLR 990, at para [203].

vii) The assessment of credibility generally involves wider problems than mere 'demeanour' which is mostly concerned with whether the witness appears to be telling the truth as he now believes it to be. With every day that passes the memory becomes fainter and the imagination becomes more active. The human capacity for honestly believing something which bears no relation to what actually happened is unlimited. Therefore, contemporary documents are always of the utmost importance: *Onassis and Calogeropoulos v Vergottis* [1968] 2 Lloyd's Rep 403, per Lord Pearce; *A County Council v M and F* [2011] EWHC 1804 (Fam) [2012] 2 FLR 939 at paras [29] and [30].

15.24   It is worth amplifying point ii): if a party decides not to advance an allegation (or withdraws it) because it does not consider that it can properly make it out the relevant facts supporting that allegation, for purposes of the court's determination of the issues to which the allegation goes, it must proceed on the basis that the facts did not happen.

15.25   Further, where the court is asked to determine allegations of harm it is suggested that, by analogy with the position that prevails in care proceedings relating to children, a conclusion that an adult has suffered from harm at the hands of another must be based upon facts, not just suspicion.[27] It is further suggested that a real possibility alone would not be sufficient.[28]

Fact-finding and future risk

15.26   'Safeguarding' cases are sometimes brought, not on the basis that an adult *has* suffered harm at the hands of another, but rather on the basis that they are *likely* to do so absent preventative action on the part of the court. In care proceedings, the approach that the court must take has been set down by the Supreme Court thus:

> 8. ... [I]f the case is based on the likelihood of future harm, the court must be satisfied on the balance of probabilities that the facts upon which that prediction was based did actually happen. It is not enough that they may have done so or that there was a real possibility that

27   *In re H (minors) (sexual abuse: standard of proof)* [1996] AC 563 at 591E per Lord Nicholls.

28   *In Re B* at para 70 per Baroness Hale.

they did ... [H]owever, if the case is based on the likelihood of future harm, the court does not have to be satisfied that such harm is more likely than not to happen. It is enough that there is 'a real possibility, a possibility that cannot sensibly be ignored having regard to the nature and gravity of the feared harm in the particular case', [*In re H (Minors) (Sexual Abuse: Standard of Proof)* [1996] AC 563] per Lord Nicholls of Birkenhead, at p 585f.

9. Thus the law has drawn a clear distinction between probability as it applies to past facts and probability as it applies to future predictions. Past facts must be proved to have happened on the balance of probabilities, that is, that it is more likely than not that they did happen. Predictions about future facts need only be based upon a degree of likelihood that they will happen which is sufficient to justify preventive action. This will depend upon the nature and gravity of the harm: a lesser degree of likelihood that the child will be killed will justify immediate preventive action than the degree of likelihood that the child will not be sent to school.[29]

15.27 This approach was also adopted prior to the coming into force of the MCA 2005 in the exercise of the inherent jurisdiction of the High Court to protect vulnerable adults,[30] and it is suggested that it remains equally applicable for judges of the Court of Protection.

Fact-finding: consequences

15.28 Although, as noted above, fact-finding can (and often will) take place at essentially the same time as the determination of the substantive best interests questions relating to P, where the fact-finding takes place separately it would be usual for the court to give a separate judgment in relation to the fact-finding hearing in order for the parties to take stock prior to the second stage. Part of this taking stock might well be to consider – in an appropriate case – the instruction of the relevant expert to report upon P's best interests. Experience has taught that it is frequently helpful to delay the instruction until this stage so that the expert can proceed upon the basis of clearly established facts, rather than having to give alternative conclusions upon the basis of what may be found in due course to have occurred (it being clear that an expert cannot seek to determine contested facts for themselves: see para 13.56).

29 *Re S-B (children)* [2009] UKSC 17, [2010] 1 AC 678 at para 8 per Baroness Hale.
30 *Re MM; local authority X v MM (by the Official Solicitor) and KM* [2007] EWHC 2003 (Fam), [2009] 1 FLR 443 at para 119 per Munby J (as he then was).

15.29   Importantly, as there is no difference in principle between the approach to be adopted to split hearings in the Court of Protection (at least in welfare cases) and public law child protection proceedings, the decision of the House of Lords in *Re B*[31] applies so as to require that once findings of fact have been made the case is part heard and the trial should not resume before a different judge.[32]

15.30   Finally, it should be noted that it is clear that a judge may subsequently revisit the conclusions reached at a fact-finding hearing if subsequent evidence warrants it.[33]

---

31 *In re B (children) (care proceedings: standard of proof) (CAFCASS intervening)* [2008] UKHL 35, [2009] 1 AC 11 at para 2 per Lord Hoffmann.

32 *Enfield LBC v SA and others* [2010] EWHC 196 (Admin), [2010] COPLR Con Vol 362 at para 113 per McFarlane J (as he then was).

33 *In re L and another (children) (preliminary finding: power to reverse)* [2013] 1 WLR 634 at para 34; see also *In re S-B (children) (care proceedings: standard of proof)* [2010] 1 AC 678 at para 46.

CHAPTER 16

The final determination of the application

Introduction

16.1   This chapter deals with how applications are finally disposed of by the court. After touching on the disposal of applications without a final hearing, the focus is on the steps required effectively to prepare and to conduct final hearings, as well as dealing with the subsequent steps of receiving the judgment and drawing up the final order. Because the issues of principle are the same, the chapter covers both proceedings relating to P's property and affairs, and P's health and welfare; many of the examples will, though, be drawn from applications relating to health and welfare because they form the bulk of the reported cases.

16.2   This chapter must be read alongside the preceding chapters, and in particular those relating to directions hearings (chapter 11), evidence and disclosure (chapter 13) and (in an appropriate case) fact-finding (chapter 15). It is clear from the reported cases, and in particular that of *A Local Authority v PB and P*,[1] that matters will very rapidly go awry in a contested case unless a proper focus is maintained by all parties – and the court – upon the final destination of the proceedings and of the steps required along the route.

Determining an application without a final hearing

16.3   The vast majority of applications to the Court of Protection are disposed of without any hearing at all. By way of example, of the 26,153 applications received by the court in 2013, 24,923 (95.3 per cent) concerned property and affairs and only 1,230 (4.7 per cent) concerned health and welfare.[2] Of the applications relating to property and affairs, the vast majority (well over 90 per cent) were non-contentious and were dealt without a hearing. There were, in total, 1,460 hearings in London and in the regional courts in which Court of Protection judges sit, a very significant proportion of which would have been directions/interim hearings rather than final hearings.

16.4   Moreover, many applications which start out hotly contested end up being resolved by consent without the need for a final hearing. This can be, for instance, because an independent expert has provided a report making entirely clear where P's interests lie which is accepted by all parties and encapsulated in a proposal put to the

---

1 [2011] EWHC 502 (COP), [2011] COPLR Con Vol 166.
2 These statistics are provided by Senior Judge Lush.

court to be endorsed as a consent order. In other cases, mediation or some other form of alternative dispute resolution (discussed further in chapter 20) can achieve a resolution to the issues dividing the parties that they consider that they can properly put to the court as being in P's best interests.

16.5　　As discussed above (para 11.43), where parties have reached agreement, they are required to notify the court as soon as possible. Where a consent order has been submitted for approval which finally disposes of all the issues in the case, the starting position will be that the court will only convene a hearing a) if insufficient notice has been given; or b) there is some specific feature which the court considers it must deal with at an attended hearing. One (extreme) example of the latter would be in an application for withdrawal of artificial nutrition and hydration from a person in a permanent vegetative state; it is often the case that such applications are ultimately agreed by all the parties, but judges will always convene a hearing and deliver a judgment recording their determination (see further in relation to serious medical treatment cases, chapter 23).[3] Another less extreme, but probably – and sadly – more common example, is where the information provided with the consent order is not sufficient to satisfy the judge that they can endorse it without further clarification that the decisions/declarations set out are properly in P's best interests.

16.6　　It should be remembered that wherever the court makes an order without a hearing, Court of Protection Rules (COPR) 2007 SI No 1744 r89 applies so as to allow P, any party to the proceedings, or any person affected by the order to apply for reconsideration. Reconsideration is addressed further in chapter 19, but is unlikely to be relevant where the court is endorsing a consent order submitted by the parties for approval.

16.7　　The balance of this chapter is concerned with the position where the issue(s) in the application are not resolved by the time that matter is listed for a final hearing.

Finalising the issues and the evidence; timetabling

16.8　　As discussed in detail in chapter 11 above, one of the key case management tasks of the court is to ensure that the issues in the case are identified at an early stage, in large part so that directions can be made to ensure that the evidence (but only the evidence) necessary

---

3　See, for instance, *Re D* [2012] EWHC 885 (COP), [2012] COPLR 493.

to resolve those issues will be before the court. It is worth emphasising, however, that the issues can – and frequently do – evolve during the currency of proceedings. For instance, if P is elderly, their health may deteriorate and different priorities may assert themselves when it comes to their best interests. A case brought before the court on an urgent basis arising out of a safeguarding concern may evolve dramatically if further investigation reveals that the concern is in part not borne out. If a separate fact-finding hearing has been listed (see chapter 15 above), the court may in giving its judgment upon the matters considered at that hearing make findings which require one or other party to take stock of how it wishes to present its case at the subsequent hearing to determine the substantive best interests questions. Alternatively, expert evidence may be directed following such a fact-finding hearing which puts a different complexion upon the best interests exercise. It can also be the case that trial periods of contact (for instance) directed at an interim hearing have proceeded sufficiently successfully that a local authority applicant decides that it can adopt a more 'relaxed' position at the final hearing.

16.9   By the same token, it can also frequently be necessary for provision to be made for the filing of updating evidence relating to P's circumstances: the court will be determining what is in P's best interests *as at* the time of the final hearing, so it is necessary that it is provided with the most up-to-date evidence possible. While witnesses can amplify their written evidence in the witness box (see further para 16.23 below), it is desirable to ensure that that written evidence is as current as possible.

16.10   In any case of any complexity, therefore, it is likely that the court will conduct a pre-hearing review relatively shortly (in the order of a month or so) prior to the final hearing. Such a hearing will follow the pattern of directions hearing discussed in chapter 11, but with a particular focus on ensuring that both the issues and the evidence have been finalised insofar as possible in advance of the final hearing. The judge at the hearing will also be astute to ensure that the time estimate for the final hearing remains realistic, and will frequently seek to set a time-table for the hearing. In this regard, the following points are of particular importance:

- Paragraph 10.1 of Practice Direction (PD) 13B (which will almost invariably apply to a final hearing)[4] makes clear that time estimates should be prepared – and, so far as practicable – agreed by the parties on the basis of separate provision being made for 1)

4   PD 13B para 2.1.

judicial pre-reading; 2) hearing all the evidence and submissions; and 3) preparation and delivery of judgment. Experience suggests that estimates given by legal representatives often underestimate the time for 2) and almost invariably do not give sufficient time for either 1) or 3);

- While PD 13B suggests that time estimates should be prepared on the basis that all witnesses will have in advance of giving evidence read all relevant filed statements and reports,[5] judges conducting pre-hearing reviews will be very likely to test with the legal representatives whether adequate time has, in fact, been allocated to each witness. This is particularly so if any of the witnesses needs the services of an interpreter or is giving evidence by way of video-link (see further paras 16.36ff below).

Bundle preparation

16.11   The preparation of bundles for directions hearings is discussed in detail at paras 11.29ff above. The same practical requirements set out in PD 13B will apply to almost all final hearings as they do to interim hearings (including as to the timing for lodging them), and they are not repeated here. There are, though, specific requirements that apply to the preliminary documents that must appear in the bundle, addressed in the paragraphs which follow.

16.12   At the start of the bundle there must be inserted a document or documents prepared by each party ('the preliminary documents for a final hearing') which should set out (either within the preliminary documents themselves, or by cross-reference to what is set out in another document that is in, or is to be put in the bundle):

a) the relief sought;
b) a skeleton argument.[6]

16.13   Where appropriate, the preliminary documents for a final hearing should include:

a) a chronology;
b) the findings of fact that the court is being invited to make and the factors based on such findings or agreed facts that the court is being invited to take into account;
c) an appropriately particularised description of the alternatives the court is being invited to consider; and

5   PD 13B para 10.2.
6   PD 13B para 4.6.

d) a description of relevant family members and other persons who may be affected by or interested in the relief sought.[7]

16.14   Each of the preliminary documents must state on the front page immediately below the heading the date when it was prepared and the date of the hearing for which it was prepared.[8] All case summaries, chronologies and skeleton arguments contained in the preliminary documents must be cross-referenced to the relevant pages of the bundle.[9]

16.15   Where the nature of the hearing is such that a complete bundle of all documents is unnecessary – for instance, because the relief now being sought by the applicant has been refined significantly – the bundle (which need not be repaginated) may comprise only those documents necessary for the hearing, but i) the preliminary documents must state that the bundle is limited or incomplete; and ii) the bundle must if reasonably practicable be in a form agreed by all parties.[10]

16.16   One injunction which is regularly honoured more in the breach, but which is actually of some importance, is that, where a bundle has been taken away after a directions hearing and is then re-lodged, the bundle must be updated and superseded documents must be *removed*.[11] Judges – understandably – become very impatient with bundles that contain numerous iterations of documents: it is very rarely necessary for any but (for instance) the most recent version of the care plan for P to be contained in the bundle.

16.17   Where witnesses are to give evidence at the final hearing, it is important that a separate bundle is provided which can be put into the witness box for them to use during the course of the hearing. It is equally important (but sadly not always the case) that this bundle matches the pagination of the bundles being used by the parties and the judge to avoid unnecessary delays during the hearing.

Skeleton arguments

16.18   As noted above (para 16.12), PD 13B envisages that the parties will each provide skeleton arguments in advance of the final hearing. The

---

7   PD 13B para 4.7.
8   PD 13B para 4.8.
9   PD 13B para 4.9.
10   PD 13B para 4.10.
11   PD 13B para 4.11.

courts have repeatedly emphasised that skeleton arguments should be just that – ie skeletal. In the course of a judgment given in the Court of Appeal, but of equal relevance to proceedings before the Court of Protection, Mummery LJ emphasised that:

> ... skeleton arguments should not be prepared as verbatim scripts to be read out in public or as footnoted theses to be read in private. Good skeleton arguments are tools with practical uses: an agenda for the hearing, a summary of the main points, propositions and arguments to be developed orally, a useful way of noting citations and references, a convenient place for making cross references, a time-saving means of avoiding unnecessary dictation to the court and laborious and pointless note-taking by the court.[12]

The hearing

The day of the hearing

16.19 Even more than is the case with directions hearing, it is important to get to court early on the day of the final hearing. This will allow for any last-minute discussions to take place and for steps to be taken in the event of any logistical problems (a common one being that the bundle provided for the witnesses has not found its way into the witness box). If witnesses are to give evidence, it will also allow time to take their details and give them to court staff – who need to know, in particular, whether the witness will swear on the Bible or other Holy Book, or affirm.

Private or public?

16.20 As discussed in greater detail in chapter 14, in the majority of cases, final hearings at present take place in private. The main exception is in in relation to serious medical treatment cases, where PD 9E provides that the court will ordinarily make an order that any hearing shall be held in public subject to reporting restrictions[13] (see further chapter 23). Sir James Munby P has also expressed his clear intention to align the rules in proceedings before the Court of Protection with family cases such that accredited journalists will have the right to attend most hearings unless proper grounds for excluding them

---

12 See *Raja v Van Hoogstraten (No 9)* [2009] 1 WLR 1143 at para 126 per Mummery LJ.

13 PD 9E para 16.

can be established on narrowly defined grounds.[14] This is therefore an area which is likely to be subject to some considerable change in the short to medium term.

Opening speeches

16.21   Especially where full skeleton arguments have been provided, it is unlikely that the judge will want to hear lengthy opening speeches from any of the legal representatives; the usual practice is to proceed very rapidly (often within a matter of minutes) to the calling of the first witness for the applicant.

Witness evidence

16.22   Proceedings before the Court of Protection are formal proceedings, such that witnesses will be required to swear on the Bible or other Holy Book, or affirm as to the truth of their evidence.

16.23   As discussed at para 13.14 above, a witness statement will stand as the evidence-in-chief of a witness, such that they will only be permitted to give supplementary evidence in answer to questions from the party on whose behalf they appear with the permission of the court. How readily this will be granted will depend upon the nature of the case; it can, though, be the case that a witness will have done no more than confirm their name and address and that the contents of their statement are true before they are answering questions put by the other parties.

16.24   A witness called on behalf of a party will then be cross-examined by the other parties, and can then be re-examined by the party on whose behalf they have given evidence. They can also be asked questions by the judge: especially given the inquisitorial nature of the Court of Protection's processes, it is quite frequently the case that many of the questions that are put to the witness in the court are, in fact, asked by the judge. The judge should then give the chance to the parties to ask any further questions of the witness arising out of their questions.

16.25   The usual practice is for all the witnesses of fact to give their evidence, first those called on behalf of the applicant, then those called on behalf of the first respondent, and so forth, before any expert witness

---

14   Sir James Munby P, 'Opening up the Family Courts: Transparency in the Family Court and the Court of Protection', speech given to the Society of Editors on 11 November 2013. Available at www.judiciary.gov.uk/Resources/ JCO/Documents/Speeches/pfd-speech-society-editors-11112013.pdf.

gives their evidence. Ideally, an expert witness such as an independent social worker will have had the chance to hear the evidence of the witnesses of fact so that they are able to consider this evidence when giving their opinion to the court; if the hearing is lengthy, however, it may well be too expensive and/or logistically impracticable for the expert to attend all the days of the hearing. In such a case, then the party calling the expert (which will, if the Official Solicitor has been instructed on behalf of P, almost invariably be the Official Solicitor) should make sure that they give a summary to the expert of any relevant evidence given in their absence.

16.26   Space precludes a detailed discussion of the principles of witness handling, the principles of which are the same before the Court of Protection as they are before any other court or tribunal. In very brief summary, *preparation* and *politeness* are the two watchwords that will perhaps most usefully serve. What the judge wants is to have brought out before them the evidence upon which they can:

a) determine any facts in issue; and
b) determine whether
    i) P has or lacks the requisite decision-making capacity; and
    ii) (if P lacks capacity), where P's best interests lie.

It is only by being clear as to what submissions will be made in closing arguments as to the evidence going to a) and b) that proper lines of questioning can be developed. Further, while it can frequently be necessary to be robust in cross-examination, and it is important that particular points of contention are put to the witnesses so that they can properly respond, judges respond very negatively to discourtesy in questioning. This is particularly so when it comes to the cross-examination of independent experts, whose duty it is to assist the court rather than one of the parties (see paras 13.50ff). Moreover, experience teaches that it is generally extremely unlikely that 'badgering' an expert under cross-examination will lead them to recant their opinions. It is generally far more productive for an advocate to treat the expert as a fellow professional and, in essence, to engage with them upon their own terms so as to tease out the nuances in their views.

16.27   One point cannot be emphasised enough. As obvious as it seems, it is vital to recall that the focus of the hearing will be upon P's capacity and best interests. The court will therefore be very impatient with questions that are directed to the canvassing of allegations of misconduct or poor practice save and to the extent necessary for the court to be able to determine where the interests of P lie (see also para 15.12). This can place advocates in particular difficulties where they are being pressured by their lay clients to put questions to others because they want grievances aired. Those grievances – for instance as to how another family member or a local authority social worker has conducted themselves – may well be very deeply felt, but unless they relate to the issues actually before the court they should not be advanced by way of questioning. In this regard, it is useful to recall the strong guidance given by the Court of Appeal that:

> Something of a myth about the meaning of the client's 'instructions' has developed. ... the client does not conduct the case. The advocate is not the client's mouthpiece, obliged to conduct the case in accordance with whatever the client, or when the advocate is a barrister, the solicitor 'instructs' him. In short, the advocate is bound to advance the defendant's case on the basis that what his client tells him is the truth, but save for well-established principles [relating specifically to criminal cases] the advocate, and the advocate alone remains responsible for the forensic decisions and strategy. That is the foundation for the right to appear as an advocate, with the privileges and responsibilities of advocates and as an advocate, burdened with twin responsibilities, both to the client and to the court.[15]

This guidance was given in the context of criminal proceedings, but in its general thrust it is suggested that it is equally applicable to proceedings before the Court of Protection.

16.28   Finally, it should be noted that it is very important to keep a proper note of the evidence given by witnesses; while proceedings before the Court of Protection are recorded, such recordings a) can sometimes contain gaps at the vital moments; b) can take some time to transcribe; and c) will usually only be transcribed upon payment of a fee by the party requesting the transcription.

Witnesses: special cases (1) hearing from P

16.29   Recent decisions of the European Court of Human Rights (ECtHR) can be read as suggesting there should be a presumption that judges should hear from P.[16] In *Shtukaturov v Russia*, for instance, the ECtHR decided that the decision of the judge to decide the application for incapacitation[17] on the basis of documentary evidence, without seeing or hearing from the applicant, who was both an interested

---

15 *Farooqi and others v R* [2013] EWCA Crim 1649 at para 108.

16 *X and Y v Croatia* (App No 5193/90, decision of 3 November 2011); *Shtukaturov v Russia* (2012) 54 EHRR 27; and *Lashin v Russia* (App No 33117/02, decision of 22 January 2013).

17 The legal process in Russia by which a person is declared to lack capacity in all domains. See the next paragraph.

party and 'at the same time, the main object of the court's examination',[18] breached his rights under article 6 (right to a fair trial) of the European Convention on Human Rights (ECHR). To similar end, but considering the question by reference to article 8 (right to respect for private and family life), the ECtHR in *X and Y v Croatia*, concluded that 'judges adopting decisions with serious consequences for a person's private life, such as those entailed by divesting someone of legal capacity, should in principle also have personal contact with those persons'.[19]

16.30   The cases are not entirely easy to map across to the English and Welsh system, because they arise in the context of jurisdictions that retain a 'status'-based system, ie where a person can be deemed to be fully or partially incapacitated (and hence, in legal terms, a 'non-person'). The difference can, though, be over-emphasised because the practical effect of declaration that P lacks decision-making capacity in multiple domains is to open the door to potentially draconian decisions that made that may strongly conflict with P's wishes and feelings.

16.31   There is, therefore, in the authors' view, a strong argument that the presumption should be that the judge determining any case in which either capacity or best interests is in issue should take steps to ensure that they have had personal contact with P.[20] It is of note in this regard one of the very few cases in which P has been found to have capacity (in that case to decide where she wished to live) in the face of all the professional evidence was where the judge heard directly from her: see *CC v KK and STCC*.[21]

16.32   Where P is present in the court, then the judge will usually make a point – if possible – of seeking to hear directly from P. This would not necessarily take the form of hearing from P as a witness, as P may well not be competent to give evidence. In this regard, though, it is important to note that the test for competence to give evidence is different to (say) the test for whether P has capacity to conduct the litigation. The test is whether the witness is capable of understanding the nature of an oath and of giving rational testimony.[22] If P is not

18 *Shtukaturov* at paras 72–73.

19 *X and Y v Croatia* at para 84.

20 This argument is reinforced by considerations arising out of the Convention on the Rights of Persons with Disabilities: see chapter 26. COPR r88(1) provides that the court may hear P on the question of whether or not an order should be made, whether or not he is a party to proceedings.

21 [2012] EWHC 2136 (COP), [2012] COPLR 627. See also *Re SB; A patient; capacity to consent to termination* [2013] EWHC 1417 (COP), [2013] COPLR 445.

22 *Phipson on Evidence*, Sweet & Maxwell, 12th edn, 2012, para 9-08.

competent to give evidence as a witness, then, formally, the judge will not take their evidence, and whatever information P relays (say, as to their wishes and feelings) will stand as hearsay evidence.[23] The process of obtaining information from P by the judge may well be done in a very informal fashion. It can, on occasion, take place outside the court – including, for instance, at P's bedside – and in the presence of only a limited number of representatives so as to minimise any pressure upon P. A proper record should, though, be kept of any such discussion, usually by the representative of the Official Solicitor if instructed on P's behalf.

16.33   In this regard, note should also be taken of the comments of Peter Jackson J in *Re M*,[24] a case concerning a challenge under MCA 2005 s21A to a standard authorisation under the deprivation of liberty safeguards (DOLS) regime, in which a District Judge visited P in the care home a month before the final hearing:

> A careful written record was made and placed with the papers. The visit has therefore had the dual purpose of informing the court of M's views and of making M feel connected to the proceedings without putting her into the stressful position of having to come to court in person. I commend this as an approach that may be of value in other cases of this kind.

16.34   It is suggested that this approach is one that is likely to be of value not just in cases concerning deprivation of liberty but across a considerably broader spectrum of cases involving both health and welfare and property and affairs.

Witnesses: special cases (2) vulnerable witnesses

16.35   Although it is likely to be rare that the court will need to hear from a witness who themselves is vulnerable (by reason of age, disability or otherwise), the possibility cannot be ruled out. There are no specific provisions in the COPR to cater for the putting in place of special measures to cater for vulnerable witnesses; however, there are a suite of such measures that are regularly deployed in family proceedings that can be pressed into service by the court.[25] These include such measures as the use of a video-link or an intermediary.[26] A particularly

---

23 See *Enfield LBC v SA and others*, [2010] EWHC 196 (Admin), [2010] COPLR Con Vol 362 at paras 29–36.

24 [2013] EWHC 3456 (COP).

25 Using, in particular, COPR rr3 and 95(a)(iii).

26 See, by analogy, *Re A (a child) (vulnerable witness)* [2013] EWHC 1694 (Fam), [2013] Fam Law 1134.

useful recourse in this regard is the Advocate's Gateway, a free resource designed to assist in the questioning of particularly vulnerable witnesses, including specific resources to assist in (for instance) the questioning of those suffering from learning disability.[27]

Witnesses: special cases (3) interpreters

16.36 Her Majesty's Courts and Tribunals Service (HMCTS) will meet the reasonable costs of interpreters for deaf and hearing-impaired litigants for hearings in civil proceedings, including those before the Court of Protection.[28] If an interpreter is needed, the court will make arrangements for an interpreter to attend. Many people have a friend or relative who usually interpret for them. Permission will be required from the judge before such a friend or relative can translate, and the judge must be satisfied that the friend or relative can exactly interpret what is being said to the court and what the court is saying to the individual in question.

16.37 Unless the relative or friend has a recognised qualification in relaying information between deaf and hearing people, it may be better to use a qualified interpreter. The friend or relative may still be able to attend and provide support, but permission should be sought from the judge first.

16.38 Language interpreters will be arranged at public expense in certain limited circumstances:

a) proceedings for committal for contempt of court (see further chapter 18), where the subject of the application cannot understand or speak the language used in court;

b) where it is the only way in which a litigant can take part in proceedings, ie where the person:
   i) cannot speak or understand the language of the court well enough to take part in the hearing;
   ii) cannot get public funding;
   iii) cannot afford to fund an interpreter privately; and
   iv) has no family member, or friend, who can attend to interpret for them and who is acceptable to the court.

16.39 It is vital to give as much notice as possible wherever an interpreter will have to be arranged by the Courts Service, especially where the services are required for interpretation to and from an unusual language.

---

27 See: www.theadvocatesgateway.org/.
28 See: www.justice.gov.uk/courts/interpreter-guidance.

16.40   It will also be necessary to factor in extra time for the giving of evidence whenever the services of an interpreter is required – a rough rule of thumb is that it is sensible to double the time-estimate for any given witness because of the inevitable impact upon the speed at which questions can be put and answered.

Witnesses: special cases (4) 'remote' evidence giving

16.41   COPR r98 provides that the court can allow a witness to give evidence through a video-link or other communication technology.

16.42   Increasing number of court centres are now equipped to receive evidence from witnesses by video.

> It is, however, inevitably not as ideal as having the witness physically present in court. Its convenience should not therefore be allowed to dictate its use. Consideration should be given in each case as to whether its use is likely to be beneficial to the efficient, fair and economic disposal of the proceedings.[29]

16.43   It is necessary to make an application for a video-link to be used in good time, not least as most court centres will only have a limited number of court rooms in which it is possible to use the necessary equipment. The application must be made on a COP9[30] form by the party wishing to call the relevant witness by video. Detailed guidance as to the process that should be followed is set out in annex 2 to PD 14A. This annex also set out in some detail the practical considerations that arise when taking evidence by video, in particular given the 'lag' that can arise between receipt of the picture and accompanying sound, and also as to how to ensure that the person giving evidence has access to the same documents as those in the courtroom with the judge.

16.44   In urgent medical treatment cases (see further chapter 23), it is not uncommon for evidence to be given by the treating clinicians by telephone; the courts discourage the use of telephone evidence in final hearings in other cases, and it would be very unusual indeed for it to be acceptable for a witness giving evidence as to contested facts to give telephone evidence because of the difficulties to which this gives rise in terms of assessing their credibility absent the ability to see their face and body language. If it is proposed that evidence should be taken from a witness by telephone in anything other than the most urgent hearing, a detailed application for permission should

29   PD 14A annex 2 para 2.
30   See further paras 11.19ff.

be submitted on a COP9 form in good time. Wherever telephone evidence is taken, particular care must be taken to ensure that the loudspeaker on the telephone in the court room is set to a sufficiently loud volume to be able to be picked up by the tape transcription of the proceedings.

16.45   Finally, it should be noted that the courts have been prepared, in cases involving children, to accept evidence by Skype, but only with a considerable degree of caution:

> The technology can be very effective for informal use, but does not lend itself to the court environment. There are problems in everyone seeing and hearing the picture and in the evidence being recorded. There are also issues about security. I would not be willing to use this method if there was any alternative.[31]

16.46   It is possible, however, for a specialist service to be employed to provide a bridge between the witness using Skype and the ISDN system in place at court. This technology mediates between the systems and provides some protection against hacking. The Skype user is provided with a download allowing them to connect to the court's system. In addition to the program, the witness requires a PC, an internet connection, a webcam, a microphone and a mobile or landline number with which to contact the company for instructions. Again, if there is a suggestion that Skype should be used, this is something that should be raised as early as possible and by way of a detailed COP9 application.

Closing arguments

16.47   The normal practice is that the applicant will make their closing submissions first, followed by the respondent(s), and then the applicant will have the last word by way of a reply. Where P is a party, the court will usually wish to hear from the Official Solicitor (if he is acting as P's litigation friend) after all of the other respondents. As noted at para 13.20 above, the Official Solicitor will usually have filed a statement in advance of the final hearing setting out a summary of the relevant background to and the procedural developments in the proceedings, and setting out the Official Solicitor's views as to P's best interests in the light of the evidence as it stands as at the time of the statement. Such views are usually expressed as being subject

---

31   *Re ML (Use of Skype Technology)* [2013] EWHC 2091 (Fam), per Peter Jackson J at para 13.

to the caveat that they will be the subject of further consideration at the conclusion of the hearing, to cater for unanticipated developments at the hearing. The court will therefore be particularly astute to glean from the Official Solicitor what his final position is as to P's best interests in light of all the evidence heard. It is suggested, again, that broadly the same procedure should be followed if a litigation friend other than the Official Solicitor has been appointed to act on P's behalf.

Negotiations during the hearing

16.48   It is very common for the positions of parties to shift during the course of a final hearing, especially if it lasts any length of time. This is particularly so if the evidence given by a witness (or witnesses) is either particularly compelling or is demonstrated to be particularly weak by way of cross-examination. It is important always to keep in mind that there is no reason why agreement in such circumstances cannot be reached upon part (or even the whole) of the application. While judges are reluctant to risk letting a case overrun by granting too many adjournments, it is usually the case that a judge will be happy to retire to allow discussions to take place during the time set aside for the final hearing if they can be satisfied that constructive progress is being made.

Judgment

16.49   In some cases, the judge will be in a position to give an oral judgment immediately following the close of oral arguments or after a short period of reflection. Judgments given orally (known as ex tempore judgments) are recorded; again, though, it is important for as full as possible a note to be taken. If permission to appeal the judgment is to be sought from a higher court (as to which, see chapter 19 below), the time limits are sufficiently short that it can frequently be necessary to seek permission from that higher court before a transcription can be prepared. This makes it particularly important that a proper note be taken of the judgment so that, if necessary, it can be filed with the application for permission to appeal.[32]

---

32   Note also that there can be a duty upon an advocate for the respondent to any application to appeal to provide their note promptly and free of charge to an unrepresented appellant: see para 19.26 below.

16.50   In cases of any complexity, it is likely that the judgment will be 'reserved:' in other words, the judge will take a longer period of time to deliberate and will then, most often, prepare their judgment in written form. Where judgments are given in writing, the practice increasingly is for a draft to be circulated to the legal representatives in advance. The purpose of so doing 'is to introduce an orderly procedure for the delivery of reserved judgments, whereby the parties' lawyers can have time to consider and agree the terms of any consequential orders they may invite the court to make and the process of delivering judgment can be abbreviated by avoiding the need for the judge to read the judgment orally in court'.[33] Such draft judgments must be kept strictly confidential to the parties' lawyers. While judges will normally invite the submission of corrections of typographical errors, the circulation of a draft judgment is not intended to afford an opportunity to the parties to re-argue their case.[34] Where a party or parties are not legally represented, the practice commonly adopted is not to circulate a draft judgment for correction, but rather to hand down a draft judgment 'subject to editorial corrections', allowing for any revisions to be incorporated before a final approved version is handed down.[35]

16.51   One matter that will usually have to be resolved after judgment has been given is as to costs. This is addressed further at chapter 17 below.

Final orders

16.52   The decision of the court, whatever it may be, must be recorded in an order. If the judgment has been circulated in draft ahead of it being handed down, the judge will expect that the parties will have tried to agree the terms of that order. If the judgment has been given orally, and if the order records anything more than a simple decision/declaration, then it may well prove difficult for all the details of the order made to be finalised at the end of what is likely to have been a long court day. For similar reasons as discussed at para 11.50 above in

---

33 *Prudential Assurance Company v McBains Cooper and others* [2000] 1 WLR 2000 at 2008E–F per Brooke LJ. See also Civil Procedure Rules (CPR) PD 40E (Reserved judgments).

34 See *Egan v Motor Services (Bath) Ltd* [2007] EWCA Civ 1002, [2008] 1 All ER 1156 and *G v A* [2009] EWHC 11 (Fam).

35 See, by analogy, *R (S) v General Teaching Council for England* [2013] EWHC 2779 (Admin) at para 5.

relation to directions hearings, however, every effort should be made to ensure that the broad outlines of the order have been agreed and (if possible) endorsed by the judge before the parties leave for the day to avoid lengthy – and expensive – debates in the ensuing days via correspondence as to the terms of the order.

16.53 One oddity of proceedings under the MCA 2005 is that is far from unusual that an order made at what all parties and the court treat as final hearing will not, in fact, be a final order. A good example of this is where the court has, itself, authorised the deprivation of P's liberty (for instance, because P is deprived of their liberty in supported accommodation, so cannot be made the subject of the DOLS regime discussed in chapter 22 below). In such a case, it is necessary in order to secure P's rights under ECHR article 5 (right to liberty) that the court undertakes regular reviews of that deprivation.[36] In such cases, particular care needs to be paid to the way in which the order made at the hearing provides for the payment of the costs of any publicly funded party so as to ensure that such funding is readily available for purposes of any further review by the court.

16.54 A final point should be made here. In many cases, the court will be asked to take a decision on P's behalf. In other cases, though, the court will be asked to make a declaration under MCA 2005 s15 as to where P's best interests lie in a specific regard. It is quite possible that circumstances will change after the hearing, however, such that P's best interests may dictate a different course of action. The question that arises immediately in this regard is whether it is necessary to return the matter to court, or whether the parties to the proceedings are bound by the declaration(s) contained in the final order.

16.55 Although the question has not yet come before the courts to be determined (at least in any recorded cases), it is suggested that, by analogy with the position that prevails in respect of decisions taken by mental health tribunals, the parties must consider themselves bound by the decision unless they reasonably and in good faith consider that they have information unknown to the court 'which put a significantly differently complexion on the case as compared

---

36 *Cheshire West and Chester Council v P* [2011] EWCA Civ 1257, [2012] COPLR 37, (2012) 15 CCLR 48 at para 4 per Munby LJ. This aspect of the judgment of the Court of Appeal was not contested before the Supreme Court on the Official Solicitor's (successful) appeal against the decision. The question of court reviews in such circumstances was at the time of writing before the President of the Court of Protection in cases involving consideration of the procedures for the authorisation of deprivation of liberty by the court.

with that before the [court]'.[37] If there has not been such a material change of circumstances, but the circumstances are such that they nonetheless require revisiting by the court then, depending upon the length of time since the original proceedings were concluded (and especially if all questions relating to costs have been resolved), it may be necessary for a fresh application to be made. If a fresh application has to be made, then it would be prudent for the applicant to make clear that the proceedings were previously before the court and to seek an order at the first directions hearing that (if the court bundle from the previous proceedings is still in readily accessible form and remains relevant) that the documents contained in the bundle stand as evidence in the new proceedings, so as to ensure that all relevant materials are before the court in the new proceedings.

16.56   The position where P regains capacity after the proceedings have come to an end is covered by PD 23B. Where P ceases to lack capacity after proceedings have concluded, an application may be made to the court to discharge any orders made (including an order appointing a deputy or an order in relation to a security bond) by filing a COP9 application notice, together with any evidence in support of the application. The application notice should set out details of the order or orders the applicant seeks to have discharged, and should in particular be supported by evidence that P no longer lacks capacity to make decisions in relation to the matter or matters to which the proceedings relate.[38] Note that if the Court Funds Office is holding funds or assets on behalf of P, it will require an order of the court to the effect that P no longer lacks capacity to make decisions with regard to the use and disposition of those funds or assets before any funds or assets can be transferred to him.[39]

P regains capacity or dies

16.57   There are two other events that will bring about a final determination of the proceedings in a way other than provided for in the balance of this chapter, namely P regaining the relevant capacity to take the decision(s) in question or P dying. What should happen in these circumstances is, in part, set out in PD 23B.

---

37 *R (von Brandenburg) v East London and City NHS Trust* [2004] 2 AC 280 at para 10 per Lord Bingham.

38 PD 23B para 5.

39 PD 23B para 6.

16.58   If P regains capacity (or, to use the terminology of PD23B, 'ceases to lack capacity'), then steps should be taken forthwith to end the proceedings and discharge any orders made in respect of P. Such an application can be made by P, their litigation friend or any other person who is party to the proceedings, and should be made on a COP9 form together with, in particular, evidence that P no longer lacks capacity to make decisions in relation to the matter or matters to which the proceedings relate.[40] It should be noted that COPR r148 (which PD 23B amplifies) governs the procedure where P ceases to lack both litigation capacity (see further para 12.75) and subject-matter capacity. It is suggested, though, that as a matter of logic, if P regains subject-matter capacity then even if (which is unlikely, but not actually impossible) they continue to lack litigation capacity, the proceedings should come to an end because the Court of Protection would have no jurisdiction to take decisions on their behalf.

16.59   If P dies during the currency of proceedings (which is, sadly, not an altogether unusual experience), then this should be brought to the attention of the court as soon as practicable. At that point, proceedings will come to an effective halt,[41] although the court retains a residual jurisdiction in respect of matters such as:

1) costs;[42]
2) the remuneration of a deputy, donee or attorney;[43]
3) fees;
4) the discharge of security;[44]
5) (if a deputy has been appointed), the deputy's final report on the termination of his appointment;[45] and
6) the transfer and delivery of funds.[46]

---

40 PD 23B paras 3–4.
41 See *Re RC (deceased)* [2010] COPLR Con Vol 1022 at paras 50–54 per Senior Judge Lush.
42 COPR r165 and PD 23B para 10.
43 COPR r167.
44 Lasting Powers of Attorney, Enduring Powers of Attorney and Public Guardian Regulations 2007 SI No 1253 reg 37.
45 Lasting Powers of Attorney, Enduring Powers of Attorney and Public Guardian Regulations 2007 reg 40.
46 PD 23B para 11.

CHAPTER 17

Costs

Introduction

17.1   This chapter sets out how costs are dealt with in the Court of Protection. The costs rules that apply are unique to the court, balancing as they do a number of interests that are not necessarily in play in other forms of litigation. They also make different provisions for applications involving property and affairs on the one hand, and health and welfare on the other. This chapter addresses both categories of application, together with the (common) scenario where the two are mixed.

The statutory provisions

Mental Capacity 2005

17.2   Mental Capacity (MCA) 2005 s55 provides that:

(1) Subject to Court of Protection Rules, the costs of and incidental to all proceedings in the court are in its discretion.

(2) The rules may in particular make provision for regulating matters relating to the costs of those proceedings, including prescribing scales of costs to be paid to legal or other representatives.

(3) The court has full power to determine by whom and to what extent the costs are to be paid.

(4) The court may, in any proceedings-

(a) disallow, or

(b) order the legal or other representatives concerned to meet,

the whole of any wasted costs or such part of them as may be determined in accordance with the rules.

(5) 'Legal or other representative', in relation to a party to proceedings, means any person exercising a right of audience or right to conduct litigation on his behalf.

(6) 'Wasted costs' means any costs incurred by a party—

(a) as a result of any improper, unreasonable or negligent act or omission on the part of any legal or other representative or any employee of such a representative, or

(b) which, in the light of any such act or omission occurring after they were incurred, the court considers it is unreasonable to expect that party to pay.

17.3   Practitioners should be aware of the powers in MCA 2005 s55(3)–(6) to use costs sanctions against legal representatives when the court considers this to be justified. These powers replicate the powers in Senior Courts Act 1981 s51(6), and will be deployed according to the same criteria.[1]

---

1   *Sharma and Judkins v Hunters* [2011] EWHC 2546 (COP), [2012] COPLR 166.

Court of Protection Rules

17.4 Part 19 of the Court of Protection Rules (COPR) 2007 SI No 1744 sets out the general provisions dealing with costs. We set out the key provisions below.

Application of other statutes and the Civil Procedure Rules

17.5 Some of the provisions in the Civil Procedure Rules (CPR) 1998 apply to Court of Protection cases, with modifications.[2] The relevant provisions in the COPR importing specific rules from the CPR were drafted prior to the re-writing of the CPR in 2013. Prior to April 2013, the provisions incorporated included:

- Parts of the former CPR 44.3, which set out the nature of the costs orders that the court could make as between one party and another, such as proportions of costs or costs covering particular stages in the proceedings.
- Former CPR 44.4, which allowed the court to assess costs on either the standard or indemnity basis. The principal difference is that in when costs are assessed on the standard basis, the court will resolve a doubt as to whether costs are reasonably incurred, or reasonable and proportionate in amount, in favour of the party who is paying the costs. When costs are assessed on the indemnity basis, such doubts are resolved in favour of the party being paid.
- Former CPR 44.5, which set out the factors to be taken into account in deciding the amount of costs.
- Former CPR 44.8, which provides when costs orders should be complied with.

17.6 Confusingly for practitioners, the COPR have not been updated to take account of changes in the CPR. Therefore, the numbering set out in COPR r160 no longer corresponds with the CPR as they now stand. The anomalies are obvious – for instance, on its face, the COPR now incorporate the entirety of CPR 44.2 as it now stands, which provides (inter alia) that the general rules in civil litigation, namely that the unsuccessful party will be ordered to pay the costs of the successful party.[3]

---

2 COPR r160; Practice Direction (PD) 19A.
3 CPR 44.2(2)(a).

17.7   The current situation is entirely unsatisfactory, because it is unclear whether parliament can be taken to have intended that the COPR were intended to cross-refer to the CPR as they stood at the time that the COPR were enacted, or whether they were intended to cross-refer to them on a 'rolling' basis, ie subject to any continuing amendment process. There are equally valid arguments either way. Moreover, COPR r9 provides that in cases not expressly provided for by the COPR, the CPR are to apply, with any necessary modification necessary to further the over-riding objective. So even if the intention was that the cross-references were to be the CPR in their pre-April 2013 state, it would always be open to a judge to apply the current provisions subject to any necessary modifications – including, most obviously, disapplying CPR 44.2 in favour of the rules contained in COPR rr156 and 157 (setting out the general rules in relation to property and affairs and welfare cases respectively, discussed further at paras 17.10–17.14 below).

17.8   Until such time as the COPR are amended (or practice guidance or a practice direction is issued), we would strongly advise that judges are expressly asked to consider making directions identifying precisely which versions of the CPR they are applying. This is particularly relevant in relation to (new) CPR 44.3 and 4 dealing with the basis of the assessment of costs. The assessment of costs is a specialist area outside the scope of this work,[4] but it is important for present purposes to note that the CPR as they stand after 1 April 2013 contain a new definition of proportionality. If the final order made in the proceedings makes clear which version of the CPR are to apply for the purposes of the assessment of costs, this will remove any subsequent ambiguity and additional expense in the assessment process.

17.9   By virtue of provisions contained in the Legal Aid, Sentencing and Punishment of Offenders (LASPO) Act 2012, a costs order can be made against a party who holds a legal aid certificate, but these cannot exceed the amount which it is reasonable for that party to pay, having regard to the circumstances including the conduct and financial resources of all the parties. If a legally aided party is ordered to pay an amount of costs which is less than the costs incurred by the receiving party, then the receiving party may apply for an order that the shortfall is met by the Lord Chancellor. There is no reason why,

---

4 Readers are referred, in particular, to Simon Middleton and Jason Rowley, *Cook on Costs 2014*, LexisNexis.

in principle, such an order could not be made in favour of a public body.[5]

The general rule

17.10   The COPR set out two very different general rules:

1) The general rule in cases concerning P's welfare is that there will be no order as to the costs of the proceedings, or of that part of the proceedings that concerns P's welfare.[6] This means that in 'pure' welfare cases, the parties should expect to bear their own costs. Clients who are not legally aided therefore need to be advised that they cannot expect to recover costs they incur in those proceedings.

2) In respect of cases concerning P's property and affairs, the general rule is that the costs will be met from P's estate.[7]

17.11   Special provisions apply in relation to the appointment of deputies:

- An order appointing a property and affairs deputy will deal with both with any legal costs incurred by the deputy in making the application and the expenses incurred by the deputy in the discharge of their functions. Where a lay deputy is appointed, the costs will be limited to reasonable out-of-pocket expenses.[8] Where a professional is appointed, either as a sole appointment or jointly with a lay deputy, a clause will be included to permit fixed costs to be taken,[9] or for the costs to be assessed by the Supreme Court Costs Office. The rates that can be charged by a professional deputy are subject to the Guideline Hourly Rates.[10]

- Health and welfare deputies will not usually be allowed to recover either the legal costs of making the application or of the expenses incurred in discharging their functions. Professional deputies are – rarely – appointed to act as health and welfare deputies, and it is suggested that the same approach would be adopted as if they were a property and affairs deputy.

---

5   See LASPO Act 2012 s26; Civil Legal Aid (Costs) Regulations 2013; and the detailed Guidance Notes on the application of LASPO Act 2012 s26(1), issued by the Senior Costs Judge.

6   COPR r157.

7   COPR r156.

8   MCA 2005 s19(7).

9   COPR r164; PD 19B.

10 See http://www.judiciary.gov.uk/guideline-hourly-rates-2011.

17.12   Many cases involve a mixture of welfare and property and affairs issues. It is important to differentiate between the different elements of the case to ensure that there is clarity as to who is responsible for what. The court will, insofar as possible, apportion the costs between the issues.[11]

17.13   The following is an example of mixed applications and how the costs implications could be approached.

> **Example**
>
> Anita has a daughter, Bernice, who has severe physical and learning disabilities following birth injuries. Some years ago, Bernice secured an award from the NHS Trust whose negligence caused her injuries. Anita acted as Bernice's litigation friend in the personal injury proceedings and was appointed Bernice's property and affairs deputy.
>
> The responsible local authority makes an application for declarations that Bernice lacks capacity to make decisions about her residence and care; and that it is in Bernice's best interests to move to supported living rather than continue to live with Anita. Anita has legal aid to be represented in the proceedings. The local authority has concerns about how Anita is managing Bernice's money and applies to become Bernice's property and affairs deputy in place of Anita. The two applications are be dealt with together.
>
> Anita's solicitor informs the Legal Aid Agency (LAA) of the deputyship application immediately. There are two potential solutions in this scenario.
>
> i)   The first is that the LAA may be willing to agree that the property and affairs element to the case is ancillary to the main issue in the proceedings. If this happens, then Anita's solicitor can claim for work carried out to deal with both the welfare and property and affairs aspects of the case.
>
> ii)   However, if this is not agreed by the LAA, then Anita's solicitor should ensure that the court and parties are aware that Anita is not an assisted party for the purpose of the deputyship application. It would be prudent to secure a direction allowing Anita to claim her costs for that part of the case from Bernice's estate. Anita's solicitor would then open a separate file for the deputyship application and apportion the work carried out on the deputyship and welfare elements in the case between the two files as accurately as possible.

11   COPR r158.

Serious medical treatment cases

17.14   While the general rule in health and welfare cases is as set out above, it is important to note that the courts have recognised what amounts to one further general rule in cases relating to serious medical treatment (see further in respect of such cases, chapter 23). Reflecting the position that prevailed before the MCA 2005 came into force, the invariable practice is for the NHS Trust that made the application to pay half of the costs of the Official Solicitor (who will, in all cases where P is made a party – ie almost all[12] – act as P's litigation friend).[13]

Departing from the general rule

17.15   As COPR r159 makes clear, the court can depart from rules set out above (rules 156–157) if the circumstances so justify. Rule 159 provides that:

> (1) The court may depart from rules 156 to 158 if the circumstances so justify, and in deciding whether departure is justified the court will have regard to all the circumstances, including–
>   (a) the conduct of the parties;
>   (b) whether a party has succeeded on part of his case, even if he has not been wholly successful; and
>   (c) the role of any public body involved in the proceedings.
> (2) The conduct of the parties includes–
>   (a) conduct before, as well as during, the proceedings;
>   (b) whether it was reasonable for a party to raise, pursue or contest a particular issue;
>   (c) the manner in which a party has made or responded to an application or a particular issue; and
>   (d) whether a party who has succeeded in his application or response to an application, in whole or in part, exaggerated any matter contained in his application or response.
> (3) Without prejudice to rules 156 to 158 and the foregoing provisions of this rule, the court may permit a party to recover their fixed costs in accordance with the relevant practice direction.

17.16   It will be seen that the court retains a broad discretion to award costs and to take into account the parties' behaviour before and during

---

12   Essentially the only exception being where urgency makes this impossible: for an example, see *Newcastle-upon-Tyne Foundation Trust v LM* [2014] EWHC 454 (COP).
13   *Re D (costs)* [2012] EWHC 886 (COP), [2012] COPLR 499.

the proceedings. Advisers need to be alert to this issue which should be drawn to clients' attention in the appropriate client care letter and/or terms and conditions. Examples as to how the courts have approached this appear below.

Case-law: welfare

17.17   We summarise below the significant cases where the Court of Protection has considered departing from the general rule, although we note that the courts have repeatedly stated that the starting point must always remain the general rules contained in COPR rr156 and 157.

SC v LBH

17.18   *SC v LBH*[14] was an appeal heard by Senior Judge Lush against an order against a litigant in person who was a relative of P, in a welfare dispute. The trial judge was critical of the relative's conduct and concluded there were exceptional cases where a party 'behaves so badly and fails to see reason and commonsense that it would be offensive to allow that party to rely on rule 157'.

17.19   On appeal Senior Judge Lush said that:

> The purpose of a general rule is that it should apply in a typical case. SC is not untypical of many of the litigants in person who appear on a regular basis in health and welfare proceedings in the Court of Protection and, despite what [the District Judge] and [counsel for the local authority] have said about this being an exceptional case, it is not. It could almost be said that this aspect of the court's jurisdiction was created to deal with situations of this kind, where a local authority, NHS Trust or private care home is experiencing problems with a particularly difficult and vociferous relative.
>
> Accordingly, the general rule (rule 157) should apply, and the court should only depart from the general rule where the circumstances so justify. Without being prescriptive, such circumstances would include conduct where the person against whom it is proposed to award costs is clearly acting in bad faith. Even then, there should be a carefully worded warning that costs could be awarded against them, and a consideration of their ability to pay. If one were to depart from rule 157 in all the cases involving litigants whom [the expert witness] has described as 'extreme product champions', the court would be

14   [2010] EWHC B29 COP; sub nom *Re RC (deceased)* [2010] COPLR Con Vol 1022.

overwhelmed by satellite litigation on costs, enforcement orders, and committal proceedings.

G v E (costs)

17.20   In *G v E (costs)*[15] an order for costs against a local authority was made by Baker J. Baker J had made findings that the local authority had breached E's rights under article 5 (right to liberty) of the European Convention on Human Rights (ECHR) by depriving him of his liberty and two placements without seeking either a standard authorisation or an order of the court; and had breached his rights under article 8 (right to respect for private and family life) by removing him from the care of his foster mother and carer of many years without proper authority. Baker J had strongly criticised the local authority's errors. He had concluded that the case justified departure from the general rule and ordered that the local authority pay the costs of G, E and F in full, including pre-litigation costs, up to and including the first day of the eight-day interim hearing on an indemnity basis (see above).

17.21   Baker J ordered the local authority to pay a third of the other parties' costs on a standard basis from 14 January 2010 until the final hearing on 6 May 2010. Baker J concluded that the local authority's conduct amounted to a significant degree of unreasonableness and rejected the suggestion that costs should not have been ordered because the legislation was new and complex, or that costs orders should not be made because of the impact on the local authority's social care budget. He commented:[16]

> Of course, it is right that the Court should follow the general rule where appropriate. Parties should be free to bring personal welfare issues to the Court of Protection without fear of a costs sanction. Local authorities and others who carry out their work professionally have no reason to fear that a costs order will be made. The submission that local authorities will be discouraged from making applications to the Court of Protection if a costs order is made in this case is a thoroughly bad argument. The opposite is, in fact, the truth. It is only local authorities who break the law, or who are guilty of misconduct that falls within the meaning of rule 159, that have reason to fear a costs order. Local authorities who do their job properly and abide by the law have nothing to fear. In particular, the Court of Protection recognises that professional work in this very difficult field often involves very

15   *G v E (by his litigation friend the Official Solicitor) and F* [2010] EWHC 3385 (Fam), (2011) 14 CCLR 140, [2010] COPLR Con Vol 454.

16   Para 40.

difficult judgments and decisions. The Court is not going to impose a costs burden on a local authority simply because hindsight demonstrates that it got those judgments wrong.

17.22   Baker J accepted that there would have been the need for some kind of court process but found that the hearing would have been significantly less lengthy and complex had the matter been brought to court in a timely fashion by the local authority and E's sister G who initiated the proceedings would have played a smaller role.

17.23   The local authority appealed. On appeal it was argued that no order should be made because Baker J concluded it was not in G's best interests to return home and therefore the local authority had 'won' the case. This argument was rejected. The Court of Appeal dismissed the appeal, agreeing with Baker J's reasoning.[17] The Court of Appeal noted it had been a finely balanced judgment. Moreover, the court found, many of the factors which swayed the judge had arisen because of the failure of the local authority to bring the matter to court. The local authority could not therefore benefit from the fact that a status quo had developed if this resulted from its own misconduct.

Hillingdon LBC v Neary

17.24   In *Hillingdon LBC v Neary*, Hillingdon was found to have breached the ECHR articles 5 and 8 rights of Steven Neary.[18] Peter Jackson J reviewed the existing judgments and concluded that:

> 7. ... [T]hese decisions do not purport to give guidance over and above the words of the Rules themselves – had such guidance been needed the Court of Appeal would no doubt have given it in *Manchester City Council v G*. Where there is a general rule from which one can depart where the circumstances justify, it adds nothing definitional to describe a case as exceptional or atypical. Instead, the decisions represent useful examples of the manner in which the court has exercised its powers.

> 8. Each application for costs must therefore be considered on its own merit or lack of merit with the clear appreciation that there must be a good reason before the court will contemplate departure from the general rule. Beyond that, as MCA 2005 s55(3) – cited above – makes plain, the court has 'full power' to make the appropriate order.

---

17   *Manchester City Council v G and others* [2011] EWCA Civ 939, (2011) 14 CCLR 725, [2012] COPLR 95.

18   [2011] EWHC 3522 (COP), [2011] COPLR Con Vol 632. See chapters 2 and 22 for a fuller account of this case.

17.25　The approach taken by Hillingdon was significantly unreasonable in each of those respects. This was anything but a typical case and an award of costs was 'plainly justified'.

17.26　Hillingdon was ordered to pay Steven's costs on the standard basis from the date of the issue of proceedings (28 October 2010) to the conclusion of the main hearing (27 May 2011), except insofar as those costs are attributable to the press issues.

17.27　The judge explained the apportionment below:

(1) I favour an approach that is as simple as possible.

(2) I do not see why Hillingdon should not pay the full costs from the date of issue to the date of the December hearing. Having finally issued proceedings, it asked for inappropriately wide powers and it then took a court order to get Steven home.

(3) Thereafter, it is true that Hillingdon accepted the conclusions of the joint experts on Steven's future placement, but those conclusions echoed ones reached by the IMCA, which Hillingdon could itself have arrived at months earlier. Hindsight was not required. Again there is no reason for anything less than full costs to be paid for the period between December and May.

(4) The nature of the findings at the May hearing make the argument for payment of that component of the costs unanswerable.

(5) In contrast, the period between May and July was spent in coopera-tive efforts to secure successful future arrangements for Steven, and should not attract a costs award.

(6) As to the costs of the press issues, no order is appropriate. As it happens, the Official Solicitor's submissions about publicity failed, but a stronger reason for making no order is that the press application raised issues of general public importance.

(7) As to the basis of assessment, there are some aspects of Hillingdon's conduct that make the application for indemnity costs a respectable one, but overall I consider an award on the standard basis to be suf-ficient in the circumstances of the case.

(8) Stepping back, I do not know whether my order is more favourable to Steven than the application as presented by the Official Solicitor. In some respects the award is more generous than the application, and in others less so. Faced with disagreement between the parties, the court is not constrained by the way in which the parties themselves frame the issue, but has to deal with the matter on its merits.

(9) Finally, there is nothing in this decision to deter public authorities or others from issuing proceedings in a timely way in appropriate cases. Far from increasing the risk of costs orders being made, or their being made with effect from an earlier date, the greater likeli-hood is that matters would not reach the stage where such orders were in prospect at all.

AH v (1) Hertfordshire Partnership NHS Trust, (2) Ealing Primary Care Trust

17.28   In *AH v (1) Hertfordshire Partnership NHS Trust, (2) Ealing Primary Care Trust*,[19] applications for declarations were made by 12 adults all of whom had lifelong disabilities, in most cases as a result of childhood autism and learning disabilities. Most had spent years in long-stay hospitals but over the past ten years they had lived in a purpose-built resource, SRS, a 'campus' type facility in the grounds of Harperbury Hospital. In the period leading up to the litigation the local and health bodies had reviewed the placements of the residents who brought the claim and were proposing alternatives, which it was considered would offer greater independence.

17.29   The court noted at the outset that it was not intended to discontinue providing services at SRS. Had this been the case, the appropriate remedy would have been judicial review.[20] Instead the issue for the court to determine was the best interests of each resident, using the principles of the MCA 2005.

17.30   The judgment deals in detail with the circumstances of 'Alan', and gave a 'firm provisional judgment' in the hope that this would encourage settlement of the remaining cases. In Alan's case it became clear that the proposed move had been influenced by the national context of the move towards closure of hospital campus facilities and the belief that in general small domestic settings would best suit those with severe learning disabilities. The local authority had never carried out a balance sheet 'best interests' exercise in respect of 'Alan' but its assessments had been either 'conducted on the assumption that he would one day have to move, or took the form of arguments justifying a decision already taken'. Two independent experts instructed to assist the court took the firm view that there was no discernible benefit in a move.

17.31   The court found no dependable benefit in a move and given Alan's complex needs and the fact that they were presently well met, described the prospect of greater independence and fulfilment as 'a chimera'. Compromise on the remaining cases was subsequently reached.

17.32   The residents – some of whom had been legally aided – sought 50 per cent of their costs. They relied on the pre-action conduct of

19   [2011] EWHC 3524 (COP), [2012] COPLR 327.
20   See also in this regard the discussion in chapter 25 in relation to the dividing line between the Court of Protection and the Administrative Court.

the respondents, who were significantly unwilling to provide even incomplete information; the respondents failed to place the dispute before the court; the respondents persisted in the face of clear expert evidence.

17.33   Peter Jackson J noted that there was no suggestion of bad faith in this case. It was a major piece of litigation, involving the future of around 30 residents. The origin of the litigation in respect of all the cases was the same, namely, the voluntary plans of the commissioners to move the residents from SRS to other placements.

17.34   The judge looked at the circumstances of the lead case and then considered the remainder of the cases, which raised identical issues. The respondents had made it very difficult for those representing the residents to obtain information. The burden on the residents was increased by the failure of the public bodies to bring what was clearly a dispute to the court so that the residents had to make the applications. Departure from the normal rule was based upon poor compliance with the *Practice Direction on pre-action conduct*, the fact that the residents were left to bring proceedings, the absence of any proper best interests assessment, lack of proper planning, and a successful outcome for the residents.

WBC v CP and others

17.35   In *WBC v CP and others*[21] Ryder J (as he then was) considered an application from LPM, a legally aided party, and brother of CP, for his costs to be paid by the local authority, WBC. Ryder J had previously given a judgment in proceedings brought by LPM initially in the Administrative Court but then linked to proceedings in the Court of Protection.[22] In that judgment, the judge had been critical of the conduct of the local authority and had found serious shortcomings in the management of CP's care, including breaches of the processes of the MCA 2005 and the Children Act 1989, breaches of WBC's statutory responsibilities to CP, breaches of CP's rights under article 5 and a failure to follow relevant guidance (the Code of Practice to the Mental Health Act 1983). Ryder J re-stated the comments of the Court of Appeal in the *G v E* case[23] that the court should follow the general rule where it is appropriate and it is only local authorities

---

21 [2012] EWHC 1944 (COP).

22 [2011] EWHC 1539 (Admin).

23 *Manchester City Council v G and others* [2011] EWCA Civ 939, (2011) 14 CCLR 725, [2012] COPLR 95.

who have broken the law or who are guilty of misconduct who should fear a costs order.

17.36   Ryder J said that the fact that LPM received public funding was irrelevant to the exercise of the court's discretion. Despite having made some appropriate concessions during the proceedings, and having engaged positively in the 'best interests' element of the case, WBC's misconduct justified departure from the general rule, and there was no need to show that WBC had acted in bad faith. Ryder J concluded that the local authority's actions were 'tainted with illegality' and its decision-making was 'impoverished and disorganized'. It was responsible for the delay in referring CP's circumstances to the appropriate court and could have arrived at the position reached by the court many months earlier. WBC was ordered to pay LPM's costs, to be assessed if not agreed.

A Local Authority v HS

17.37   In *A Local Authority v HS* (discussed also in para 24.15 (safeguarding)),[24] District Judge Eldergill referred back to the statement of principle in *VA v Hertfordshire PCT and others* to the effect that a costs order may be justified where there has been 'substandard practice and a failure by the public bodies to recognise the weakness of their own cases and the strength of the cases against them'.

17.38   The case concerned an allegation, based on very flimsy evidence, that HS's brother had sexually abused her. The judge accepted that 'there has been substandard practice and a failure by the local authority in this case to recognise the weakness of its own case. In my opinion, this has been proved'.

17.39   In a critical judgment, DJ Eldergill said that:

> In order to make good such serious allegations, cogent evidence would be required bearing in mind the guidance given by the House of Lords in *Re H (Minors) (Sexual Abuse: Standard of Proof)* [1996] AC 563, D–H.[25]

He continued:

> 185. Cogent evidence never existed. It should have been obvious long before these proceedings were commenced – the allegations had been made in 2009 and 2010, giving plenty of time for analysis of whether they were likely to stand up – that there was never any cogent evidence.

24   [2013] EWHC 2410 (COP).
25   Para 184.

186. The local authority's solicitor and the senior social workers ought to have been aware of the flaws and the fact that any case based on that evidence would not get anywhere near the threshold required by the court. The local authority's case was never there.

187. This is not a case of the local authority being 'damned if it does and damned if it doesn't' or of it being on the horns of a dilemma. The local authority was not expected to investigate and analyse the allegation and evidence to the same high standard later demonstrated by Mr McGuire QC. However, It had plenty of time, and took plenty of time and resources, before proceedings were commenced to come to and defend a position: this was not a case of having urgently to remove someone following an allegation of abuse at home, where a difficult and immediate decision has to be made as to what weight to give a yet-to-be investigated allegation.

188. There was a prolonged failure on the local authority's part to recognise the weakness of its case. The allegations were vague and insufficiently particularised. The 'evidence' in support was manifestly inadequate. It was internally inconsistent and unreliable. The truth of what was alleged was assumed without any proper, critical, analysis.

Case-law: property and affairs

17.40   Costs in these cases start from a very different assumption than those in welfare cases, and in the experience of one of the authors the court has been extremely reluctant to depart from the general rule. The decision of Cobb J in *JS v KB and MP (property and affairs deputy for DB)*,[26] gives some limited guidance as to when the court will depart from the general rule.

17.41   The facts of this case are a case-study in the consequences of the assumption of authority over the property and affairs by a family member without the proper legal authority. JS is the daughter of DB, and with the acquiescence of her brother KB she made a number of financial and legal arrangements concerning their mother DB. These included selling DB's property and using the proceeds to purchase an alternative property in the names of JS and her husband MS. The matter came to the court's attention when JS sought to be appointed as property and affairs deputy for DB. The application was dismissed by District Judge Ralton on the papers and a panel deputy, MP, was appointed. Despite this appointment, JS continue to pursue her own appointment as her mother's deputy as well as asserting a number of

26   [2014] EWHC 483 (COP).

other financial claims concerning the ownership of the property. The substantive elements of the litigation were resolved by consent and the costs issue was referred to Cobb J for consideration.

17.42   In making a costs order against JS, Cobb J took into account that her application to be appointed as deputy for DB was 'doomed to failure' and she had not been prudent to pursue it, particularly past the point at which she obtained legal advice. He also commented upon the manner in which she had previously dealt with her mother's finances, before the application was made.

17.43   This case is an important reminder for parties engaging in litigation about P's property and affairs that when it comes to matters of costs that their behaviour and the reasonableness of their continuing with the litigation will be taken into account when a judge is invited to depart from the general rule. Feelings can run extremely high in these cases, and advisers should be careful to ensure that their client is advised as to the possible outcome of refusing to reach a reasonable and timely resolution.

17.44   We note, finally, the comments made by Cobb J in this case about the approach that the court should take to the determination of costs where proceedings have settled. He specifically endorsed comments in a case called *Boxall*[27] that:

> ... at each end of the spectrum there will be cases where it is obvious which side would have won had the substantive issues been fought to a conclusion. In between, the position will, in differing degrees, be less clear. How far the court will be prepared to look into the previously unresolved substantive issues will depend on the circumstances of the particular case, not least the amount of costs at stake and the conduct of the parties.

While his comments were made in the context of a case decided under COPR r156, they are of equal application to cases where the court is assessing whether a departure from the general rule in a health and welfare case.

---

27   *R (Boxall) v Waltham Forest LBC* (2001) 4 CCLR 258, QBD. This case is no longer good law – see *M v Croydon LBC* [2012] EWCA Civ 595, but the guidance that is now to be followed is to similar effect as that cited by Cobb J.

Alternative dispute resolution/mediation – costs consequences

17.45   There is an increasing emphasis upon forms of alternative dispute resolution (ADR) including mediation as a way both to prevent disputes reaching the Court of Protection and to bring about a speedier resolution to proceedings if they do. This is discussed in more detail in chapter 20. As noted in that chapter, the court has no power to require parties to engage in a form of ADR. We suggest, however, that, by analogy with the approach adopted in family proceedings,[28] an unreasonable failure to engage in ADR might give a basis for departure from the general rule.

Summary

17.46   Drawing the threads of this chapter together, the following practice points can be made by way of summary:

- It is essential for anyone embarking on litigation, however it is to be funded, to be properly advised about the likely costs risks at the start of the case and throughout it.
- A costs order can, in a suitable case, be made against a legally aided party and ultimately against the Lord Chancellor.
- The fact that a party seeking costs is legally aided is not relevant.[29]
- Costs do not necessarily follow the outcome of the case, although they may do.[30]
- Bad faith is not necessary to establish a reason to depart from the general rule.[31]
- Refusal to co-operate prior to the issue of proceedings may be relevant to costs at the conclusion of the case.[32]
- A failure to comply with the provisions of the MCA 2005 or other statutes or guidance may be relevant to the question of costs.[33]

---

28   Eg *Mann v Mann* [2014] EWHC 537 (Fam).
29   *WBC v CP.*
30   *G v E; Hillingdon v Neary; AH and others.*
31   *G v E; AH and others.*
32   *AH and others.*
33   *AH and others; WBC v CP.*

- A party that refuses to modify its position in the face of the evidence may be vulnerable to a costs order.[34]
- Public bodies can be expected to know the risks of litigation and warnings are not pre-conditions for costs orders against public bodies, though warnings may be appropriate before costs are awarded against private individuals, especially those acting in person.[35]
- The risk of a costs order should not deter applicants from bringing disputes to the court for resolution.[36] Failure to bring a dispute to court in a timely fashion may be a relevant factor leading to a costs order.[37]
- An unreasonable refusal to engage in ADR may leave a party vulnerable to a costs order.[38]

---

34 *AH and others; Re HS.*
35 *AH and others; SC v LBH.*
36 *G v E; AH and others; Re HS.*
37 *Hillingdon v Neary; AH and others.*
38 *Mann v Mann.*

Enforcement

Introduction

18.1   Previous chapters in this book have set out the steps by which a judge can be placed in a position to determine applications relating to P (and to grant interim relief pending such final determination). Sometimes, all the court will be required to do is to grant a declaration,[1] and no substantive decisions will be taken by the court that will require enforcement. For instance, a declaration that undertaking a particular course of serious medical treatment is not in P's best interests would itself stand as sufficient protection for the clinicians and nursing staff involved that no further decisions would necessarily be required from the court.[2] In such situations, there would be no need for the judgment and the accompanying order of the court to be enforced.

18.2   However, on other occasions, one (or more) of the parties to the proceedings may be required either to take or to refrain from taking specific actions. This requirement can arise in three main ways:

1) by way of case management directions made so as to secure the effective resolution of the application;
2) as a necessary consequence of a decision (for instance, that P is to be moved from their home into a care home), which can only be given effect by one or more of the parties;
3) by the court making an injunction specifically requiring one of the parties to do something or not to do something (for instance, not to have contact with P save under specified circumstances).

18.3   Absent the ability to enforce decisions falling into the categories set out above, the Court of Protection would be toothless. This chapter discusses the mechanisms by which the court can enforce its judgments and its orders.

The powers of the Court of Protection

Powers drawn from those of the High Court

18.4   Before turning to the detail of the enforcement mechanisms set out in Part 21 of the Court of Protection Rules (COPR) 2007 SI No 1744, it is necessary first to discuss the more general powers of the

---

1   Under Mental Capacity Act (MCA) 2005 s15.
2   See *Aintree University Hospitals NHS Foundation Trust v James* [2013] UKSC 67, [2013] COPLR 492, (2013) 16 CCLR 554 at para 22 per Baroness Hale.

Court of Protection. The Court of Protection is a superior court of record,[3] which has 'in connection with its jurisdiction the same powers, rights, privileges and authority as the High Court'.[4] This has the following consequences:

- A judge sitting in the Court of Protection can grant an injunction so as to give effect to their decision and to secure the best interests of the adult. Senior Courts Act 1981 s37 provides that 'the High Court may by order (whether interlocutory or final) grant an injunction ... in all cases in which it appears to the court to be just and convenient to do so'. The Court of Protection is, by MCA 2005 s47(1), given these same powers.[5] Such an injunction will either require a person to do a specified act or (more usually) not to do a specified act or acts. Its terms must be clear and unambiguous in order for it to be effective,[6] and the person to whom it is addressed must have proper notice of its terms.[7]

- That the High Court would use its powers to grant an injunction so as to secure the interests of an adult without capacity (at least pending the final resolution of the application) had been established prior to the coming into the force of the MCA 2005.[8] The power to grant an interim injunction has now been codified in the Court of Protection Rules 2007,[9] and is regularly exercised so as to 'hold the ring' pending the determination of an application.

- It is also possible to grant an injunction that will continue in force after the end of proceedings. In *W v M*, a high-profile case regarding the withdrawal of treatment from M, a person in a minimally conscious state, injunctions were made in support of reporting restrictions that prevented contact being made with the lay people at the heart of the case; those injunctions were expressed so as to

3 MCA 2005 s45(1).
4 MCA 2005 s47(1).
5 *W v M and S (reporting restriction order)* [2011] EWHC 1197 (COP), [2011] COPLR Con Vol 1205 at para 21 per Baker J.
6 *Iberian Trust Ltd v Founders Trust and Investment Co Ltd* [1932] 2 KB 87; *R v City of London Magistrates' Court, ex p Green* [1997] 3 All ER 551. See also the commentary in *Halsbury's Laws* Volume 22 (5th edn, 2012), at para 75, and *Re Whiting* [2013] EWHC B27 (Fam), [2014] COPLR 107 at para 12.
7 *R v City of London Magistrates' Court ex p Green* [1997] 3 All ER 551. See also the commentary in *Halsbury's Laws*, Volume 22, 5th edn, LexisNexis, 2012, at para 75.
8 See, for example, *Re S (hospital patient: court's jurisdiction)* [1996] Fam 1, [1995] 1 FLR 1075 and the commentary in Ashton et al *Court of Protection Practice 2014*, Jordans, at para 1.40.
9 COPR r82(1)(a). See further paras 11.53ff above.

last for M's lifetime.[10] An analogy can also be drawn with the circumstances of *Re SA (vulnerable adult with capacity: marriage)*,[11] a case decided under the inherent jurisdiction of the High Court. In this case,[12] Munby J (as he then was) made final orders prohibiting the family members of a vulnerable adult from either themselves or by others removing her from the jurisdiction and/ or arranging for her marriage save in very clearly defined circumstances. A time-limited power of arrest was attached to one provision (relating to the use of violence), but the remainder of the injunctions were expressed to run on an indefinite basis.[13]

• An order made by a Court of Protection judge (of no matter what level) has the same status as that made by a High Court judge.

• A breach of an order made by a Court of Protection judge, whether for purposes of case management or for purposes of giving effect to a judgment, can amount to a contempt of court and the court has the power to punish such contempt.[14] There are detailed provisions in COPR Part 21 relating to the procedural steps for applications for committal to prison for contempt of court, addressed further at paras 18.10ff below. It is suggested that the underlying power to commit a person to prison (or to fine them) does not derive from the COPR, but rather, from MCA 2005 s47(1) and, in turn, the inherent, common law power of the High Court both to control its own processes[15] and to enforce compliance with its decisions.[16]

---

10 *W v M* at para 70. It may be possible for reporting restrictions to continue after P's death: *Newcastle upon Tyne Hospitals Foundation Trust v LM* [2014] EWCOP 454.

11 [2005] EWHC 2942 (Fam), [2006] 1 FLR 867.

12 Which pre-dated the MCA 2005 and concerned an adult with capacity, but who was vulnerable to coercion.

13 Paras 136–137.

14 See, for a discussion of the relevant powers of the High Court, *Halsbury's Laws*, Volume 22 (5th edn, 2012), at paras 66ff, and the commentary in the *White Book 2014* at section 3C.

15 See *Days Healthcare UK Ltd (formerly known as Days Medical AIDS Ltd) v Pihsiang Machinery Manufacturing Co Ltd* [2006] EWHC 1444, [2007] CP Rep 1 at paras 20–23 per Langley J.

16 See *Griffin v Griffin* [2000] 2 FLR 44, CA at para 21 per Hale LJ.

Specific powers contained in the COPR

18.5 In addition to the procedural matters discussed in the next section, the COPR[17] contains specific provisions relating to the enforcement powers of the Court of Protection. In particular:

- The court is given a specific power to direct that a penal notice be attached to any order. Such a notice makes clear that any person upon whom a copy of the order is served that disobedience would be a contempt of court punishable by imprisonment or a fine.[18] It should be made in the following terms: 'You must obey this order. If you do not, you may be sent to prison for contempt of court.'[19] In practice, such penal notices – which are not infrequently used in welfare cases – usually also specify the precise paragraphs of the order which contain the particular act(s) that the person in question must do or not do.
- If the court does not make a penal notice direction, then a penal notice may not be attached to the order.[20] It should be noted, however, that this does not mean that – in a suitable case – the court cannot consider whether disobedience of the order represents a contempt of court: this flows both from the provisions of the COPR themselves[21] and also from the wide powers granted to the court by MCA 2005 s47.

Enforcement of judgments and orders

18.6 COPR r184 imports into the COPR the material provisions of the Civil Procedure Rules (CPR) and the Rules of the Supreme Court (RSC) Orders 45–47 (which now form part of Schedule 1 to the CPR). These provide a suite of tools which are, in practice, relatively infrequently used by the Court of Protection. They enable the party entitled to enforce a judgment or order ('the judgment creditor') to enforce such a judgment or order against another party ('the judgment debtor'). As the use of the terms 'creditor' and 'debtor' suggest, these tools are primarily directed to the enforcement of judgments or orders in relation to property and affairs. They are applicable also to

---

17 See also MCA 2005 s51(2)(j), providing specific authority for rules to be made for the enforcement of orders made and directions given in proceedings.
18 COPR r192(1).
19 COPR r192(3).
20 COPR r192(2).
21 In particular the 'saving' provision in COPR r194.

enforce undertakings given to the court. The CPR has been amended since the COPR were made, and the two sets of statutory provisions do not, as matters stand, sit entirely easily together; it is, however, suggested that until the COPR are amended, judges are likely to seek to use their discretionary powers under the COPR[22] to comply, so far as possible, with the provisions of the CPR as they now stand.

18.7　　In summary, these tools (all of which are only applicable at the instigation of the judgment creditor, and in some cases only with the permission of the court) are as follows:

- The Court of Protection can transfer enforcement proceedings to the county court,[23] although certain forms of writ (such as a writ of sequestration) can only be issued by the Court of Protection.
- The court may make an order requiring the judgment debtor to provide specific information to court about such matters as their means.[24]
- The court may make an order requiring a third party to pay a judgment creditor a specified sum.[25]
- The court may make a charging order (which is the equivalent of a mortgage) in favour of the judgment creditor over land or other property owned by the judgment debtor.[26]
- The court may prevent certain steps being taken (by way of a stop order and stop notice) in relation to securities and funds held by the judgment debtor.[27]
- So as to enforce a judgment or order for the giving of the possession of land, the court may: (1) issue a writ of possession against that land; (2) or, where the judgment or order in question required the judgment debtor to do or abstain from doing a particular act, either (a) commit the person to prison; or (b) issue a writ of sequestration against the person's property (ie, authorise an enforcement officer to take control of the person's property and the benefits accruing from it).[28]
- So as to enforce a judgment or order for the delivery of goods which does not give the judgment debtor the alternative of paying the assessed value of the goods, the court may 1) issue a writ of

---

22　In particular COPR rr9 and 26.
23　COPR r184(a); CPR Part 70; CPR 70.3.
24　COPR r184(a); CPR Part 71.
25　COPR r184(a); CPR Part 72.
26　COPR r184(a); CPR Part 73.
27　COPR r184(a); CPR Part 73.
28　COPR r184(b); RSC Ord 45 para 3.

delivery to recover the goods without alternative provision for recovery of the assessed value of those goods; 2) or, where the judgment or order in question required the judgment debtor to do or abstain from doing a particular act, either a) commit the person to prison; or b) issue a writ of sequestration against the person's property (ie authorise an enforcement officer to take control of and manage the person's property and the benefits accruing from it).[29]

- So as to enforce a judgment or order for the delivery of goods which gives the judgment debtor the alternative of paying the assessed value of the goods, the court may: (1) issue a writ of delivery to recover the goods or their assessed value; (2) issue a writ of delivery to recover the goods without alternative provision for recovery of the assessed value of those goods; or (3) where the judgment or order in question required the judgment debtor to do or abstain from doing a particular act, a writ of sequestration against the person's property.[30]

- Where a specific act is required by the court, the court may (in addition to the exercise of its powers to punish the disobedient party for contempt) direct that the act be done, so far as practicable, either by the party by whom the judgment or order was obtained, or by some other person appointed by the court, at the cost of the disobedient party. In such cases, there is then power to recover those costs from the disobedient party; [31]

- Where a sum of money is due under a judgment or order, the court may issue a writ of fieri facias (usually abbreviated to 'fi fa'), by which an enforcement officer is directed to seize and sell a debtor's goods for the purpose of recovering the sum due.[32]

18.8 The wording of COPR r184 is ambiguous in that it imports Part 70 of the CPR, which, in turn, makes reference to certain forms of order that can be made by the county court (such as an attachment of earnings order); however, such orders are, in fact, made under various provisions of the County Court Rules (CCR) 1981 (rather than the RSC).[33] Whereas the material provisions of the RSC are incorporated into the COPR; the material provisions of the CCR are not. It is suggested that the Court of Protection, being equivalent in status to the

---

29 COPR r184(b); RSC Ord 45 para 4(1).
30 COPR r184(b); RSC Ord 45 para 4(2).
31 COPR r184(b); RSC Ord 45 para 8.
32 COPR r184(b); RSC Ord 46.
33 In the case of an attachment of earnings order, CCR Order 27.

High Court,[34] has as its disposal the same enforcement tools as does the High Court. This means that, if consideration is being given to making an order that falls within the scope of the CCR, then the proper course of action would be for the proceedings to be transferred to the county court.

18.9   Space precludes a discussion of the procedural steps required to invoke enforcement proceedings, but the central steps are set out clearly in CPR Practice Direction (PD) 70 (Enforcement of judgments and orders). They are, in the authors' experience, rarely invoked.

Committal proceedings

Bringing proceedings

18.10   The COPR contains detailed provisions[35] (accompanied by a practice direction[36]) relating to the procedure that applies when an application is made to a Court of Protection judge to commit a person for contempt of court. Such an application can be made in a range of circumstances, including where the person has: a) refused or neglected to do an act required by a judgment or an order within the specified time; b) disobeyed a judgment or order requiring them to abstain from doing a specific act; and c) breached the terms of an undertaking given to the court.[37] With one exception, no permission is required to bring such an application. That exception is where the application is brought on the basis that made or caused to be made a false statement in a document verified by a statement of truth (such as a witness statement). Such an application can only be brought by the Attorney-General and with the permission of the court.[38]

18.11   The provisions of the COPR do not govern the *power* to commit a contemnor to prison which, as discussed at para 18.4 above, is derived (via MCA 2005 s47(1)) from the High Court's common law powers in this regard. Rather, they govern the *procedure* for such applications.

18.12   The provisions of the COPR rr185–191 are largely self-explanatory, requiring as they do the filing of an application notice on a COP9, accompanied (unusually) by an affidavit containing specific

---

34   MCA 2005 s47(1).
35   COPR rr185–191.
36   PD 21A.
37   PD 21A para 6.
38   COPR r14(2)(a).

details set out in PD 21A, most importantly of the alleged act(s) of contempt.[39]

18.13   In *Re Whiting*,[40] an application for committal for alleged breaches of orders made by the Court of Protection, Hayden J emphasised some crucial features of the committal process:

> (1) the procedure has an essentially criminal law complexion. That is to say, contempt of court must be proved to the criminal standard, i.e. so that the judge is sure. The burden of proof rests throughout on the applicant (see: *Mubarak v Mubarak* [2001] 1 FLR 698);
>
> (2) contempt of court involves a deliberate contumelious disobedience to the court (see: *Re A (A Child)* [2008] EWCA Civ 1138);
>
> (3) it is not enough to suspect recalcitrance; it must be proved (see: *London Borough of Southwark v B* [1993] 2 FLR 559);
>
> (4) committal is not the automatic consequence of a contempt, though the options before the court are limited – for example: (a) do nothing; (b) adjourn where appropriate; (c) levy a fine; (d) sequester assets; (e) where relevant, make orders under the Mental Health Act (see: *Jamie Malcolm Hale v Rachel Tanner* [2000] 2 FLR 879);
>
> (5) the objectives of the application are usually dual, ie to punish for the breach and to ensure future compliance;
>
> (6) bearing in mind the dual purpose of many committal proceedings, they should be brought expeditiously, whilst primary evidence is available and the incidents are fresh in the mind of the relevant witness. This is particularly important in the Court of Protection where there may be reliance on a vulnerable witness and where capacity might have to be assessed.
>
> (7) It follows, therefore, that where injunctive orders are made, they should be clear, un-ambivalent and drafted with care. In my judgment, simplicity should be the guide.[41] Similarly, where breaches are alleged, they should be particularised with care, both so that the alleged contemnor knows exactly what, where, when and how it is contended that he is in breach, so as to be able to marshal his defence, but also to help the applicant focus on what evidence is likely to be required to establish the breach to the requisite standard of proof.[42]

18.14   In the same case, and criticising the vagueness of the evidence advanced by the local authority which brought the application for committal for contempt, Hayden J, further, emphasised that:

---

39   COPR r186(1).

40   [2013] EWHC B27 (Fam), [2014] COPLR 107.

41   See also the comments of Munby LJ (as he then was) in *Re X and Y (children)* [2012] EWCA Civ 1500, [2013] Fam Law 148 at paras 61–63.

42   Para 12.

What is required ... is an intellectually rigorous relationship between the lawyers and the social workers in every aspect of the Court of Protection, of course, but particularly on an application of this kind. The lawyers preparing the case must realise that establishing breaches to the criminal standard of proof requires forensic precision and the careful identification of evidence to support each of the particulars of the breach ... The process requires the lawyer and the social worker to work closely together to look at the order, to identify the breach and to marshal the material as if proving the constituent parts on a count on an indictment. Nothing less will do where the liberty of the individual is at stake.[43]

The hearing

18.15   COPR r188(2) makes clear that, even if the underlying proceedings are (or were) taking place in private, applications for committal are to be heard in public unless the court directs otherwise. Following significant (and often erroneous) press coverage of the circumstances of the committal to prison of Wanda Maddocks by a judge of the Court of Protection,[44] Practice Guidance was issued in May 2013 by the Lord Chief Justice and the President of the Family Division (who is also the President of the Court of Protection).[45] It is sufficiently important (and short) to merit reproduction in full:

1. It is a fundamental principle of the administration of justice in England and Wales that applications for committal for contempt should be heard and decided in public, that is, in open court.

2. This principle applies as much to committal applications in the Court of Protection (rule 188(2) of the Court of Protection Rules 2007) and in the Family Division (rule 33.5(1) of the Family Procedure Rules 2010) as to committal applications in any other Division of the High Court.

3. The Court of Protection and, when the application arises out of proceedings relating to a child, the Family Division, is vested with a discretionary power to hear a committal application in private. This discretion should be exercised only in exceptional cases where it is necessary in the interests of justice. The fact that the committal application is being made in the Court of Protection or in the Family Division in proceedings relating to a child does not of itself justify the application being heard in private. Moreover the fact that the hearing of the committal application may involve the disclosure of material

---

43   Para 15.
44   [2013] EWHC 1137 (COP).
45   *Committal for Contempt of Court: Practice Guidance* (issued on 3 May 2013), available at: www.bailii.org/ew/cases/EWHC/COP/2013/B4.html.

which ought not to be published does not of itself justify hearing the application in private if such publication can be restrained by an appropriate order.

4. If, in an exceptional case, a committal application is heard in private and the court finds that a person has committed a contempt of court it must state in public (rule 188(3) of the Court of Protection Rules 2007; Order 52 rule 6(2) of the Rules of the Supreme Court 1965):

    (a) the name of that person;

    (b) in general terms the nature of the contempt of court in respect of which the committal order [committal order for this purpose includes a suspended committal order] is being made; and

    (c) the punishment being imposed.

This is mandatory; there are no exceptions. There are never any circumstances in which any one may be committed to custody without these matters being publicly stated.

5. Committal applications in the Court of Protection or the Family Division should at the outset be listed and heard in public. Whenever the court decides to exercise its discretion to sit in private the judge should, before continuing the hearing in private, give a judgment in public setting out the reasons for doing so. At the conclusion of any hearing in private the judge should sit in public to comply with the requirements set out in paragraph 4.

6. In every case in which a committal order or a suspended committal order is made the judge should take appropriate steps to ensure that any judgment or statement complies with paragraphs 4 and 5 and that as soon as reasonably practicable:

    (a) a transcript is prepared at public expense of the judgment (which includes for this purpose any judgment given in accordance with paragraph 5 and any statement given in accordance with paragraphs 4 and 5);

    (b) every judgment as referred to in (a) is published on the BAILII website; and

    (c) upon payment of any appropriate charge that may be required a copy of any such judgment is made available to any person who requests a copy.

18.16 Supplemental guidance was issued in June 2013[46] by the President of the Family Division (and of the Court of Protection) detailing the way in which committal applications should be referred to in the court lists, and also providing that in any committal application heard in public the judge and the advocates should be robed.

---

46 *Committal for contempt of court: Practice Guidance* (issued on 4 June 2013), available at www.bailii.org/ew/cases/EWHC/COP/2013/B7.html.

18.17   If a person wishes at the hearing of the committal application to give oral evidence, they must be allowed to do so,[47] as well as to obtain legal advice if they are not represented.[48]

18.18   The court, when determining an application for contempt, may, in an appropriate case, commit the person to prison. COPR r193, however, also makes clear that the powers granted to the court under MCA 2005 s47 in respect of the punishment of contempt are not limited solely to committal to prison, but that the court can also require a person guilty of contempt of court to pay a fine or give security for his good behaviour: see also the passages from *Re Whiting* set out at para 22.13.

Continuing contempt

18.19   In *A Local Authority v B, F and G*,[49] HHJ Cardinal confirmed that the Court of Protection has the power to make a *Hadkinson* order[50] – ie an order refusing to hear further representations in the proceedings from a person who has been found to be in contempt of court in those proceedings until such point as they have 'purged' their contempt and acceded to the court's powers. Such an order can be made in respect of any party to the proceedings who has been held in contempt. The question for the court upon such an application is:

> ... whether, taking into account all the circumstances of the case, it is in the interests of justice not to hear the contemnor. Refusing to hear a contemnor is a step that the court will only take where the contempt itself impedes the course of justice. What is meant by impeding the course of justice in this context comes from the judgment of Lord Justice Denning in *Hadkinson v Hadkinson* [1952] P 285 and means making it more difficult for the court to ascertain the truth or to enforce the orders which it may make.[51]

---

47 COPR r187.
48 See, by analogy, *Hammerton v Hammerton* [2007] EWCA Civ 248 at para 52 per Wall LJ.
49 [2014] EWCOP B18.
50 Named after *Hadkinson v Hadkinson* [1952] P 285.
51 *JSC BTA Bank v Mukhtar Ablyazov* [2013] EWHC 1979 (Comm) at para 13 per Popplewell J.

Reconsideration and appeals

Introduction

19.1   This chapter sets out how when decisions can be reconsidered; how they can be appealed; and the basis upon which appeals will be considered by the higher courts.

19.2   The framework for such appeals is set down in Part 20 of the Court of Protection Rules (COPR) 2007 SI No 1744,[1] amplified by Practice Direction (PD) 20A. It is important to note, however, that the COPR do not apply to applications for permission to appeal to, or hearings before, the Court of Appeal or the Supreme Court.[2]

Reconsideration

19.3   P, or any party or person affected by an order made without a hearing or without notice to them, has an automatic right to seek a reconsideration of that order.[3] An application should be made within 21 days of the date of the order being served (or such other period as the court may direct).[4]

19.4   Reconsideration may be undertaken on the papers or at an oral hearing.[5] The reconsideration can be by any judge of the Court of the Protection (including the one who made the decision in respect of which reconsideration),[6] except by a judge who is higher up in the appellate structure than the original judge.[7] Decisions taken by court officer authorised to exercise the jurisdiction of the Court of Protection[8] will always be reconsidered by a judge.[9]

19.5   The COPR are silent as to whether it is possible to appeal a decision made upon without a hearing (or without notice to the party in question) if reconsideration has not been sought.[10] However, given

---

1 Special provisions in COPR Part 20 apply to appeals made in relation to transitory and transitional provisions; they are not addressed here given the passage of time since the Mental Capacity Act (MCA) 2005 came into force.
2 *Cheshire West and Chester Council v P (No 2)* [2011] EWCA Civ 1333, [2012] COPLR 76 at para 3 per Munby LJ.
3 COPR r89(2).
4 COPR r89(3)(a).
5 COPR r89(4). An oral hearing can be requested: COPR r89(10).
6 COPR r89(6)(a).
7 COPR r89(6)(b).
8 Ie under COPR r7A.
9 PD 3A paras 4.1 and 4.2.
10 They do, though make clear that a decision made after reconsideration has to be appealed – it cannot be further reconsidered: COPR r89(7).

that reconsideration is not an appeal but is, instead, an opportunity for the court to look at matters again afresh, it will therefore usually be better to seek reconsideration where possible. If there are proper grounds to do so, there is nothing inappropriate in asking in the application notice that the reconsideration should be undertaken by a different judge to the one who made the first order.

19.6 The purpose of COPR r89 and the way in which it operates were described by Her Honour Judge Hazel Marshall QC in *Re S and S*[11] in the following terms:

[61] ... Such a reconsideration is not an appeal. The processes in the Court of Protection are intended to give the court wide flexibility to reach a decision quickly, conveniently and cost effectively where it can, whilst preserving a proper opportunity for those affected by its orders to have their views taken into account in full argument if necessary. To that end, on receiving an application, the court can make a decision on the papers, or direct a full hearing, or make any order as to how the application can best be dealt with. This will often lead to a speedy decision made solely on paper which everyone is content to accept, but any party still has the right to ask for a reconsideration.

[62] If this occurs, the court should approach the matter as if making the decision afresh, not on the basis that the question is whether there is a justifiable attack on the first order. The party making the application has not had a proper opportunity to be heard, and should be allowed one without feeling that s/he suffers from the disadvantage of having been placed in the position of an appellant by an order made without full consideration of his points or his views.

What can be appealed?

19.7 Any decision of the court can be appealed.[12] This means any judicial decision can be appealed, including case management decisions, the grant or refusal of an interim application or a final decision. Somewhat curiously, there is no mention in COPR Part 20 or the associated practice direction of appeals against a decision of an authorised court officer exercising the jurisdiction of the Court of Protection. This would constitute a 'decision of the court' for purposes of MCA 2005 s53 and COPR Part 20, and would, on its face, be capable of being appealed directly to the Court of Appeal (as the default appellate court). It is suggested that this is an oversight: in any event, as

11 [2008] COPLR Con Vol 1074.
12 COPR r169.

there is an automatic right of reconsideration by a judge,[13] any person aggrieved by a decision of an authorised court officer would be well advised to seek such reconsideration in the first instance. Any decision taken thereafter would then slot into the conventional appellate structure described below.

Who can appeal?

19.8   Any person bound by the order of the court by virtue of operation of COPR r74 is, in principle, entitled to seek to appeal that order.[14] This has two consequences:

a) P is entitled to seek to appeal, even where they were not joined to the proceedings (as will frequently be the case in property and affairs cases: see paras 12.4ff);

b) a person who has been served with or notified of an application form but who has not been joined as a party will also be entitled to seek to appeal.

Appellate structure

19.9   The default provision in the Mental Capacity Act (MCA) 2005 is that an appeal lies to the Court of Appeal against any decision of the Court of Protection.[15] This default provision is, however, modified by operation of Part 20 of the COPR,[16] and the appeal routes are, in practice, as follows:

1) A decision of a district judge is appealed to a circuit judge.[17] Any second appeal from the decision of that circuit judge will be to the Court of Appeal.[18]

2) A first instance decision of a circuit judge is appealed to a High Court judge nominated to sit in the Court of Protection,[19] the

---

13 PD 3A paras 4.1 and 4.2.
14 COPR r172(2).
15 MCA 2005 s53.
16 By virtue of MCA 2005 s53(2)–(3).
17 COPR r180(b).
18 COPR r182(1).
19 Technically, a puisne judge of the High Court, ie a 'full' High Court judge as opposed to – for instance – a deputy.

President of the Family Division or the Chancellor of the Chancery Division.[20]

3) A decision of a High Court judge will be appealed to the Court of Appeal.[21]

4) A decision of the Court of Appeal will be appealed to the Supreme Court.

Permission

19.10   With the exception of an appeal against an order for committal to prison, an appeal against a decision of the Court of Protection requires permission.[22]

19.11   Unless the decision under challenge is, itself, one made on appeal (in which case, see paras 19.49–19.51 below), an application for permission to appeal can be made either to the judge who made the decision in question ('the first instance judge') or to a judge of the court to whom the appeal is made ('the appeal judge').[23] There is, in other words, no requirement that the application is made to the first instance judge first. There are five reasons, though, why it is prudent to apply to the first instance at the time of judgment:

1) the judge is fully seized of the matter and so the application will take less time;

2) an application at this stage involves neither party in additional costs;

3) no harm is done if the application fails – the party enjoys two bites at the cherry;

4) if the application succeeds and the party subsequently decides to appeal, they avoid the permission stage in the appeal court;

5) no harm is done if the application succeeds but the litigant subsequently decides not to appeal.[24]

19.12   The default position is that the application will be considered by the first instance judge. If the appellant wishes to seek permission

---

20   COPR r180(a) and MCA 2005 s46(2)(a)–(c).

21   COPR r181(1).

22   MCA 2005 s53(4) read together with COPR r172(1) and (8).

23   COPR r172(1).

24   See *T (a child)* [2002] EWCA Civ 1736 at paras 12–13, see also the commentary in the *White Book 2014* at para 52.3.4 Jackson LJ, editor-in-chief, Sweet & Maxwell, 2014.

directly from the appeal judge, the appellant must spell this out in their appellant's notice (see further para 19.24 below).[25]

19.13   In some circumstances, it may be possible (and appropriate) to seek permission from the first instance judge at the hearing at which the decision is given. This could either be at the end of an interim hearing or at a hearing at which a reserved judgment (see paras 16.49–16.50) is handed down. In such a case, then it is suggested that there is no need to file an appellant's notice in advance: it will, though, be necessary to file an appellant's notice subsequently within the requisite time frame: ie within 21 days of the decision being appealed subject to any different order being made by the first instance judge.[26]

19.14   Note that, if a ground of appeal is that the judge has failed to deal with a particular point, the judge should be given an opportunity to deal with that point at the hearing before the application for permission is made.[27]

19.15   If no application for permission is made to the first instance judge at the relevant hearing, then it will be necessary to file an appellant's notice, a COP35 form.[28] Again, subject to any different order being made by the first instance judge, this notice must be filed within 21 days of the decision being appealed. If the first instance judge announces their decision and reserves their reasons for their judgment, then the date for filing the appellant's notice should be varied so as to take this into account.[29] The COPR suggest that an application for an extension of time for filing an appellant's notice must be made to the appeal judge.[30] If, however, the appellant wishes to seek permission to appeal from the first instance judge and the time for doing so has not yet extended, it is suggested that it would be possible to make an application (on a COP9 form) to that judge for an extension of the time.[31]

19.16   If the time for seeking to appeal has expired, it would appear that any application for permission to appeal must be made to an appeal

---

25   COPR r175(1).

26   COPR r175(2)(b).

27   *English v Emery Reimbold and Strick Ltd* [2002] EWCA Civ 605, [2002] 1 WLR 2409 at para 25 and *In the matter of S (children)* [2007] EWCA Civ 694 at paras 23–25.

28   COPR r175(1).

29   PD 20A para 5, read together with COPR r175(2)(a).

30   COPR r177(1).

31   Ie for the judge to exercise their power under COPR r175(2)(a) to set a period for the filing of the appellant's notice.

judge, rather than to the first instance judge.[32] This must be done in an appellant's notice, which should include in it a formal application for an extension of time stating the reason(s) for the delay and the steps taken prior to the application being made.[33]

19.17 Respondents are not generally expected to file any submissions at the permission stage unless they are addressed to the point that the appeal would not meet the relevant threshold test or tests or there is some material inaccuracy in the papers placed before the court. In general, respondents should not make submissions on the merits at the permission stage.[34]

19.18 Permission applications are usually determined by the first instance (or where appropriate) appeal judge without a hearing. If there is an attended hearing, then it is likely to be given only a short time-listing. There is no expectation that a respondent attend a permission hearing; by analogy with the position that prevails under the Civil Procedure Rules (CPR) (which may not be exact because of the specific rules as to costs that prevail at all stages prior to the Court of Appeal[35]), it is likely that a respondent would be in difficulty seeking their costs of doing so unless their attendance has specifically been requested.[36]

19.19 Permission to appeal will granted only where:

1) the court considers that the appeal would have a real prospect of success (ie a realistic, as opposed to a fanciful, prospect of success[37]); or

2) there is some other compelling reason why the appeal should be heard.[38]

19.20 If the first instance judge refuses permission, a further application for permission can be made:

1) where permission was refused by a district judge, to:
   a) the President or Vice-President of the Court of Protection;

---

32 COPR r177(1) read together with PD 20A paras 8–9.
33 PD 20A paras 8–9. A respondent has the right to be heard on an application for an extension of time where permission to appeal has been given or is not required: PD 20A para 10.
34 By analogy with the position under the CPR: *Jolly v Jay* [2002] EWCA Civ 277.
35 See chapter 17.
36 See *Jolly v Jay* [2002] EWCA Civ 277 and PD 52C.
37 By analogy with the equivalent provision in the CPR: see *Tanfern Ltd v Cameron-MacDonald (Practice Note)* [2000] 1 WLR 1311 at para 21 per Brooke LJ, citing *Swain v Hillman* [2001] 1 All ER 91.
38 COPR r173(1)(a) and (b).

    b) a High Court judge nominated to sit in the Court of Protection, the President of the Family Division[39] or the Chancellor of the Chancery Division; or

    c) a circuit judge;[40]

2) where permission was refused by a circuit judge, to:

    a) the President or Vice-President of the Court of Protection; or

    b) a High Court judge nominated to sit in the Court of Protection, the President of the Family Division or the Chancellor of the Chancery Division.

19.21 It should be noted that the provisions of CPR r173 provide for permission to be granted by a judge who is two rungs above the first instance judge in the appellate structure – ie a nominated High Court judge can grant permission to appeal the decision of a district judge. In such a case, the substantive appeal will be heard by the appropriate judge – ie even if a nominated High Court judge has granted permission to appeal a decision of a district judge, the substantive appeal will still fall to be heard by a circuit judge (see para 19.19 above).

19.22 An order giving permission may limit the issues to be heard, and be made subject to conditions. If a first instance judge makes an order limiting permission, then it would be open to the appellant to seek permission from an appeal judge in respect of those matters where permission was refused. If the order limiting permission was made by the appeal judge without a hearing, then it is suggested that it would be open to the appellant to seek a reconsideration of this decision at an oral hearing under the provisions of COPR r89. However, if the appeal judge refuses permission to appeal on the remaining issues at or after an oral hearing, it is suggested that the appellant cannot then renew their application for permission in respect of those issues at the hearing of the appeal.[41]

19.23 It is not possible to appeal a refusal by an appeal judge of permission to appeal from the first instance judge (see further paras 19.49–19.51 below).[42]

---

39 Who will normally also be the President of the Family Division.

40 COPR r173(5) and (6).

41 See, by analogy, *Fieldman v Markovic* [2001] CP Rep 119 and *James v Baily Gibson & Co* [2002] EWCA Civ 1690.

42 *TA v AA and another* [2013] EWCA Civ 1661 (concerning refusal of permission to appeal by judge of the High Court sitting as a judge of the Court of Protection; the same would also apply by analogy, it is suggested, with a refusal of permission to appeal by a circuit judge).

The appellant's notice and skeleton argument

19.24 In all cases where an appellant's notice is required, PD 20A sets out in some detail what must be included.[43] The documents that are required[44] are:

a) one additional copy of the appellant's notice for the court;

b) one copy of a skeleton argument using, or attached to, a COP37 form, either be filed with the appellant's notice or within 21 days of filing the notice;[45]

c) a sealed copy of the order being appealed;

d) a copy of any order giving or refusing permission to appeal, together with a copy of the judge's reasons for allowing or refusing permission to appeal;

e) any witness statements or affidavits in support of any application included in the appellant's notice;

f) the application form and any application notice or response (where relevant to the subject of the appeal);

g) any other documents which the appellant reasonably considers necessary to enable the court to reach its decision on the hearing of the application or appeal. PD 20A suggests – correctly – that in almost all cases this will include a chronology;[46]

h) a suitable record of the judgment of the first instance judge; and

i) such other documents as the court may direct.

19.25 A 'suitable record' of the judgment of the first instance judge will be:

a) where the judgment has been officially recorded by the court, an approved transcript (not a photocopy);[47]

b) where the judgment has been given in writing, a copy of that judgment endorsed with the judge's signature;[48]

c) where the judgment was not officially recorded or given in writing, a note prepared by the advocate for the appellant. For purposes of an application for permission to appeal, a note would suffice; where permission to appeal has been granted, the note should be agreed (if possible) with the advocate for the respondent and approved by the first instance judge (or, in the absence of

---

43 Which must either accompany the notice or be filed and served on all respondents within 21 days of filing the appellant's notice.

44 PD 20A para 11.

45 PD 20A paras 16–17.

46 PD 20A para 14.

47 PD 20A para 22.

48 PD 20A para 23.

agreement), the judge should be invited in writing to approve one of the two rival versions.[49]

19.26   Where an appellant is unrepresented before the first instance judge, it is the duty of any advocate for the respondent to make their note of the judgment promptly available – free of charge – where there is no officially recorded judgment or the court directs; similarly, if the appellant was but is no longer represented, it is the duty of their former advocate to make their note available. The appellant should, in turn, submit the note to the appeal judge.[50]

19.27   In some circumstances, the evidence given during the hearing may be of relevance to the appeal. If so, then an official transcript must be obtained or, if the evidence was not officially recorded, a typed version of the judge's notes of evidence.[51] Where the appellant is unrepresented, or represented on a pro bono basis, an application can be made (wherever possible to the first instance judge at the time of seeking permission to appeal) for a transcript of the evidence or the proceedings to be obtained at public expense.[52] Such a transcript will only ordered if the court is satisfied that the cost of such a transcript would be an excessive burden on the appellant and there are reasonable grounds for appeal.[53] PD 20A suggests that transcripts or notes of evidence are generally not needed for purposes of seeking permission to appeal,[54] although in a case where the evidence will be of relevance if permission is granted, steps should be put in place as quickly as possible to obtain a transcript of the evidence because it can take some time to obtain.

19.28   Where it is not possible to provide a document or documents required by PD 20A with the appellant's notice, the appellant should indicate what documents have not yet been filed, why they have not been filed and when they estimate that they can be filed (and then file and serve them as soon as reasonably practicable thereafter).[55]

19.29   In completing the appellant's notice and the accompanying skeleton argument it is necessary to be clear as to the distinction between:

---

49 PD 20A para 24.
50 PD 20A para 25.
51 PD 20A para 26.
52 PD 20A paras 28–29.
53 PD 20A paras 28–29.
54 PD 20A para 26.
55 PD 20A para 12.

a) the grounds of appeal: ie what it said that the judge did wrong, which can – and should – be summarised shortly (ie 'the judge was wrong to find that P was not deprived of his liberty'), which should be set out in box 5 of the COP35 form; and

b) the arguments advanced in support of those grounds of appeal: these will be set out in the skeleton argument and will be longer in form, although (as discussed at para 16.18) they should still be concise and to the point.[56]

19.30 The court will issue the appellant's notice upon it being filed; unless the court orders otherwise, the appellant must serve the appellant's notice upon each respondent and upon such other persons as the court may direct as soon as practicable and in any event within 21 days of the date on which it was issued.[57] The appellant must file a certificate of service within seven days of the date on which the notice was served.[58]

19.31 It should be noted, finally, that it is possible to apply in an appellant's notice either for a remedy incidental to the appeal or for an interim remedy, either by including the application in the notice itself or by attaching a COP9 application form to the appellant's notice (see further paras 11.19ff in relation to interim remedies).

The respondent's notice and skeleton argument

19.32 Unless the court directs otherwise, or unless they, too, wish to appeal, a respondent need not take any action when served with an appellant's notice until they are notified that permission to appeal has been granted (see paras 19.17–19.18 above in relation to the role of respondents pre-permission).[59]

19.33 Where the respondent has been notified that the permission has been granted (or that the application for permission to appeal has been listed to be heard together with the appeal itself), what they should then do will depend upon what they wish to request of the appeal judge:

---

56 See also PD 20A paras 18–21 in relation to the contents of skeleton arguments accompanying appellants' notices.

57 COPR r175(3).

58 COPR r175(4).

59 PD 20A para 32.

a) if the respondent wishes to request that the decision of the first instance judge be upheld for the reasons given by that judge, they do not need to file a respondent's notice;

b) if the respondent wishes to request that the decision of the first instance judge be upheld for reasons different to or additional to those given by the first instance judge, they need to file a respondent's notice (on a COP36 form), otherwise they will not be able to rely upon such reasons except with the permission of the court.[60]

19.34   If a respondent also wishes to seek permission to appeal, the respondent should file a respondent's notice.[61]

19.35   Where a respondent's notice is necessary, then (unless the first instance judge makes an order to different effect) it must be served within 21 days of whichever is the soonest of:

a) the date on which the respondent was served with the appellant's notice (ie where permission to appeal was given by the first instance judge or permission was not required);

b) the date on which the respondent was served with notification that an appeal judge has given the appellant permission to appeal; or

c) the date on which the respondent was served with notification that the application for permission to appeal and the appeal itself are to be heard together.[62]

19.36   The same requirements as to service of the respondent's notice and the filing of a certificate of service apply to respondent's notices as to appellant's notices.[63] A respondent who wishes to apply out of time for permission to appeal must include that application in their respondent's notice.[64] While, formally, the same requirements do not apply to respondents as to applicants in respect of the giving of reasons, it is suggested that it would be prudent to ensure that the respondent's notice details the reason(s) for the delay and the steps taken prior to the application being made.

19.37   Unsurprisingly, what a respondent must provide in and with a respondent's notice[65] is very similar to what an appellant must

---

60   COPR r176(1)(b) and PD 20A paras 33–34.

61   COPR r176(1)(a); PD 20A para 31. Permission, where necessary, must be sought in the respondent's notice: COPR r176(2).

62   COPR r176(4).

63   COPR r176(5)–(6).

64   COPR r177(1).

65   Set out in PD 20A para 40. A respondent can also apply for incidental relief: PD 20A para 41.

provide in and with an appellant's notice, save that the respondent is not under the same obligation as the appellant to provide such documents as a suitable record of the judgment.

19.38 In any case where the respondent wishes to address arguments to the court (ie whether or not they have filed a respondent's notice), they must file and serve a skeleton argument.[66] If the respondent files a respondent's notice, then the skeleton argument must either accompany that notice or be filed and served within 21 days of filing that notice.[67] If the respondent does not file a respondent's notice, then any skeleton argument must be filed and served at least seven days before the appeal hearing.[68]

19.39 The same requirements apply to the contents of the respondent's skeleton argument as to those of an appellant, with the added – unsurprising – requirement that it should, where appropriate, answer the arguments set out in the appellant's skeleton argument.[69]

The position between the grant of permission and the determination of the appeal

19.40 It is not unknown for the appellant's case to change after the grant of permission. In such a case, the appellant's representatives should write to the appeal court and to the other party, indicating the proposed nature of the changed case. The court should be asked to indicate whether it will deal with the matter at the beginning of the hearing of the appeal or whether it will give directions on an earlier date. After being informed of the respondent's attitude, the court can decide whether to shut out the new grounds or allow them to be argued.[70] Similarly, if there has been a material change in circumstances after the grant of permission, which would affect the question of whether permission should have been given, the applicant should inform the

---

66 PD 20A para 44.
67 PD 20A paras 45–46. A certificate of service is required: PD 20A para 49.
68 PD 20A para 47.
69 PD 20A para 48.
70 See by analogy, *Shire v Secretary of State for Work and Pensions* [2003] EWCA Civ 1465 at paras 6–7 and the commentary in the *White Book 2014* at paras 52.3.20 and 52.8.

court in writing.[71] A failure to take either step will waste money and court time, and may have adverse cost consequences.[72]

Determination of appeals

19.41   It is, in principle, open to the appeal judge to deal with all or part of an appeal without a hearing.[73] However, as reconsideration can be sought of an order made without a hearing (see above paras 19.3–19.6), appeal judges will often err on the side of ordering a hearing, especially where they have gleaned from the prior history that the appellant will be likely to seek reconsideration.

19.42   An appeal judge has all the powers of the first instance judge whose decision is under appeal.[74] The appeal judge can in particular, if they allow the appeal, decide the issue in question themselves, rather than sending it back to the first instance judge (or ordering a new hearing before a first instance judge). Appeal judges will, however, be cautious about deciding cases themselves unless there is plainly only one answer: wherever it is a question of evaluation, it is more usual for the matter to be remitted to a first instance judge (whether that be the one who initially heard the case or another judge) to consider it in the light of the judgment of the appeal court.

19.43   The starting point in relation to appeals is that they are reviews, rather than re-hearings.[75] It would only be in very unusual circumstances that the appeal court will undertake a re-hearing; the appeal court will therefore not usually receive either oral evidence or evidence that was not before the first instance judge, although the appeal court has the power to do all three.[76] While the MCA 2005 and COPR are silent as to the circumstances under which fresh evidence will be admitted, it is suggested that the appropriate test to apply is that which applies in civil proceedings, namely consideration of whether:

1) the evidence could have been obtained with reasonable diligence for use at the trial;

---

71   See, by analogy, *Walbrook Trustee (Jersey) Ltd v Fattal* [2008] EWCA Civ 427 at para 49.
72   See, by analogy, *R (a child)* [2010] EWCA Civ 303 at paras 14–16.
73   COPR r171(2), having regard to the factors set out in COPR r84(3).
74   COPR r178(1).
75   COPR r179(1).
76   COPR r179(1)(b) and (2)(a) and (b) respectively.

2) the evidence is such that, if given, it would probably have an important influence on the result of the case, though it need not be decisive; and

3) the evidence is such as is presumably to be believed; ie whether it is apparently credible, though it need not be incontrovertible.[77]

19.44   By way of an example of a circumstance in which was appropriate to receive fresh evidence, we note the case of *Aintree University Hospitals NHS Foundation Trust v James*,[78] concerned with whether life-sustaining treatment should be withheld from a critically ill patient in a minimally conscious patient. Here, the Court of Appeal received fresh evidence as to the deterioration in the patient's condition between the time of the hearing before the first instance judge and the date of the hearing before the Court of Appeal. The Supreme Court ultimately found that the Court of Appeal had been right to determine that – at that point the case was before the Court of Appeal, and on the basis of that fresh evidence – it was in the man's best interests not to receive life-sustaining treatment.[79]

19.45   The COPR provides that an appeal will be allowed where the decision of the first instance judge is (a) wrong; or (b) unjust, because of a serious procedural or other irregularity in the proceedings before the first instance judge.[80] In the Supreme Court decision in *Aintree University Hospitals NHS Foundation Trust v James*, Baroness Hale, relying upon *Re B (a child) (care proceedings: appeal)*,[81] held that, where a judge of the Court of Protection had correctly directed themselves as to the law, an appellate court could only interfere with their decision as to the evaluation of best interests if satisfied that it was wrong.[82] Strictly, this decision only relates to the power of the Supreme Court upon an appeal, but it is – at the very least – powerful guidance as to how lower courts should interpret the provisions of the COPR.

---

77 See *Ladd v Marshall* [1954] 1 WLR 1489, *Terluk v Berezovsky* [2011] EWCA Civ 1534 and the commentary in the *White Book 2014* at para 52.11.2.

78 *Aintree University Hospitals NHS Foundation Trust v DJ* [2013] EWCA Civ 65, [2013] COPLR 217.

79 *Aintree University Hospitals NHS Foundation Trust v James* [2013] UKSC 67, [2013] 3 WLR 1299, (2013) 16 CCLR 554. It also found that the Court of Appeal had misdirected itself as to the relevant legal principles and the first instance judge had got the law correct and reached the right decision at the point that he was considering the matter.

80 COPR r179(3).

81 [2013] UKSC 33, [2013] 1 WLR 1911.

82 At para 42.

19.46 The decision in *Aintree* and the application of *Re B* gives rise to two important, related, points:

1) The majority of the Supreme Court in *Re B* (albeit not Baroness Hale herself) had held in the context of proceedings relating to children that it is not for an appellate court itself to conduct a 'de novo' assessment of the proportionality of any interference with rights enjoyed by parties under the European Convention on Human Rights (ECHR). In other words, unless – exceptionally – it considers that it is necessary to conduct a re-hearing, the appellate court is confined to reviewing the decision of the first instance judge as to the proportionality of the interference. Given that almost every best interests decision taken by the Court of Protection will engage one or more rights under the ECHR, this suggests strongly that the same approach will apply in the context of almost all appeals against best interests decisions.

2) While the majority of the Supreme Court in *Re B* rejected the addition of any gloss to the word 'wrong' (such as 'plainly'), Baroness Hale made clear in *Aintree* that in sensitive and difficult cases (which will, by definition, be those most likely to attract appeals), appellate courts should be very slow to find that a first instance judge's evaluation of best interests is wrong. The threshold for intervention by the appellate courts is therefore a high one.

19.47 Where the appeal lies not against an evaluative decision but against the exercise of a discretion (most obviously in the context of case management decisions), then the test is subtly different: the appellate court should only interfere if 'satisfied that the judge erred in principle, took into account irrelevant matters, failed to take into account relevant matters, or came to a decision so plainly wrong that it must be regarded as outside the generous ambit of the discretion entrusted to the judge': *Re TG (children) (care proceedings: case management: expert evidence)*.[83]

19.48 It should be noted that where an appeal is to a circuit judge (against a decision of district judge) or to a High Court judge (against the decision of a circuit judge), then the normal costs rules contained in the COPR apply (see chapter 20).

---

83 [2013] EWCA Civ 5, [2013] 1 FLR 1250 per Munby LJ (as he then was) at para 35.

Second appeals

19.49 A decision which was, itself, made on appeal, can only be appealed to the Court of Appeal.[84] Permission must be sought from the Court of Appeal for such an appeal, and the test is stricter; the Court of Appeal will only grant permission where:

a) the appeal would raise an important point of principle or practice; or

b) there is some other compelling reason for the Court of Appeal to hear it.[85]

19.50 This rule does *not* apply if the appeal is against a decision of a High Court judge sitting in the Court of Protection as a first instance judge.[86]

19.51 It is important to note that a decision from an appeal court refusing permission to appeal to that court from a lower court is not a 'decision' for these purposes: it is not possible to appeal such a refusal.[87]

Appeals to the Court of Appeal and Supreme Court

19.52 As noted at the outset of this chapter, appeals to the Court of Appeal and Supreme Court fall outside the scope of the COPR (except that, as set out at para 19.49 above, the COPR set out a specific test that the Court of Appeal will apply where it is considering an application for permission to appeal in relation to a second appeal).

19.53 If, therefore, an appeal is being considered against a decision of a High Court judge sitting in the Court of Protection as a first instance judge,[88] then the relevant rules to apply are not the COPR but rather those set out in Part 52 of the Civil Procedure Rules (CPR) 1998, as amplified by PDs 52A and 52C. CPR Part 52 and PDs 52A and 52C can be found in the supporting materials section. They are, in most

---

84 COPR r182(1).

85 COPR r182(2).

86 Or the President of the Family Division or the Chancellor of the Chancery Division: ie any of the judges nominated under MCA 2005 s46(2)(a)–(c).

87 *TA v AA and another* [2013] EWCA Civ 1661 (concerning refusal of permission to appeal by judge of the High Court sitting as a judge of the Court of Protection; the same would also apply by analogy, it is suggested, with a refusal of permission to appeal by a circuit judge).

88 Or the President of the Family Division or the Chancellor of the Chancery Division: ie any of the judges nominated under MCA 2005 s46(2)(a)–(c).

respects, very similar to the rules set out in the COPR and discussed above, and are not rehearsed here.

19.54   If an appeal lies from a decision of the Court of Appeal to the Supreme Court in relation to a matter that was originally determined by a judge of the Court of Protection, the relevant procedural rules are set out in the Supreme Court Rules 2009 SI No 1603 and the associated practice directions. These can be found on the Supreme Court website;[89] they are not addressed here because they are beyond the scope of this work. The only point that should be noted it does not appear that there is a possibility for a 'leapfrog' appeal to be made directly to the Supreme Court from a decision of a High Court judge sitting in the Court of Protection. The relevant provisions of the Administration of Justice Act (AJA) 1969 allow such a 'leapfrog' appeal in respect of 'civil proceedings in the High Court'.[90] It is, however, suggested that a judge of the High Court sitting as a Court of Protection judge is not hearing civil proceedings in the High Court.[91]

19.55   In any appeal to the Court of Appeal the costs rules set out in the COPR do not apply. Unless an application is made under CPR 52.9A (as to which, see para 19.56 below), the normal costs rules set out in the CPR will apply, and the unsuccessful party will be ordered to pay the costs.[92] In *Cheshire West and Chester Council v P (No 2)*,[93] Munby LJ rejected an argument made on behalf of the unsuccessful party, P, that there should be no order as to costs because proceedings in the Court of Protection were analogous to public law family proceedings (and appeals therefrom) which are exempt from the material provisions of the CPR.[94] Munby LJ held:[95]

> I cannot accept Mr Gordon's argument of principle. It comes perilously close to an impermissible invitation to us to re-write [CPR 44.2], whether by incorporating within it the principle in r157 of the Court of Protection Rules or by adjusting CPR r[44.2(3)] to include a

89 See: www.supremecourt.uk/procedures/rules-of-the-court.html.

90 AJA 1969 s12(2).

91 See, by analogy, *TA v AA and another* [2013] EWCA Civ 1661 and the discussion at para 55 of that case of the earlier decision in *Re B (a patient) (Court of Protection – appeal)* [2006] 1 WLR 278,

92 This is now contained in CPR 44.2(a); prior to 1 April 2013, this was contained in CPR 44.3(a).

93 [2011] EWCA Civ 1333, [2012] COPLR 76.

94 These are now contained in CPR 44.2(3)(a); prior to 1 April 2013 they were contained in CPR 44.3(3)(a).

95 Para 6. The references to the CPR have been amended to reflect the position that prevails post 1 April 2013.

reference to the Court of Protection. Our task is to apply CPR r[44.2]. I accept, of course, that we can properly have regard to the fact that the appeal concerns a vulnerable adult in the context of the court's protective functions and not, for example, a valuable cargo in the context of a commercial dispute, but this is not because of some supposed analogy with either [CPR r44.2] or r157 of the Court of Protection Rules. It is simply because it is one of the 'circumstances' – and, it may be, one of the more important of the circumstances – to which CPR r44.3(4) bids us have regard.

19.56   With effect from 1 April 2013, a new provision was introduced into the CPR to cater for appeals from 'no costs' or 'low costs' jurisdiction. It is suggested that the Court of Protection is such a jurisdiction because of the specific rules in COPR rr156 and 157. It is therefore possible for an application to be made by either party for an order under CPR 52.9A limiting the recoverable costs of an appeal to the extent that the court specifies. In making such an order, the Court of Appeal will have regard to:

1) the means of both parties;
2) the circumstances of the case; and
3) the need to facilitate access to justice.

As the Court of Appeal explained in *JE (Jamaica) v Secretary of State for the Home Department*:[96] 'The rule deals with appeals coming up from a "no costs" or a "low costs" jurisdiction. It enables the appeal court to put in place a similar regime to that which applied in the court or tribunal below.'[97] The Court of Appeal in the same case noted the importance of any application being made at any early stage, so that both parties know the costs regime under which they are proceeding; if the appellant is seeking the order, it may be 'convenient and economic' to include such an application in the appellant's notice, but that is not required by the rule. The application will then be determined in writing unless the court orders otherwise.[98]

19.57   The costs rules that apply in relation to appeals to the Supreme Court are contained in Part 7 of the Supreme Court Rules; they are beyond the scope of this work.

---

96 [2014] EWCA Civ 14.
97 Para 8, per Jackson LJ.
98 CPR 52.9A(4).

PART 3

Specific issues

Alternative dispute resolution

Introduction

20.1   In common with the expectations in other forms of civil and family litigation, advisers are expected to discuss the possibility of mediation or other forms of alternative dispute resolution (ADR) before litigating and to keep this decision under review. A wide range of methods of ADR may be used in the life of a Court of Protection case, ranging from informal discussions outside court, to formal mediation processes that are independently facilitated and may run into several days.

Code, rules and case-law

Code of Practice

20.2   The Code of Practice[1] to the Mental Capacity Act (MCA) 2005 provides guidance to decision-makers about managing 'conflicting concerns' when establishing the best interests of a person who lacks capacity. Paragraph 5.64 reads:

> The decision-maker will need to find a way of balancing these concerns or deciding between them. The first approach should be to review all elements of the best interests checklist with everyone involved. They should include the person who lacks capacity (as much as they are able to take part) ... It may be possible to reach agreement at a meeting to air everyone's concerns. But an agreement in itself might not be in the person's best interests. Ultimate responsibility for working out best interests lies with the decision-maker.

20.3   Chapter 15 of the code concerns settling disagreements. The code stresses again the importance of the person without capacity having support and representation,[2] including during mediation.[3]

20.4   The code advocates mediation as a means of solving a problem at an early stage. The code makes a number of claims for mediation, which it describes as offering a wider range of solutions than court proceedings as well as having the potential to be 'less stressful, more cost-effective and quicker. People who come to an agreement through mediation are more likely to keep to it, because they have taken part in mediation'.[4]

---

1   Available at: www.legislation.gov.uk/ukpga/2005/9/pdfs/ukpgacop_20050009_en.pdf.
2   Code of Practice para 15.3.
3   Code of Practice para 15.6; see also the scenarios at the end of this chapter.
4   Code of Practice para 15.7.

20.5   The code refers to the availability of legal aid funding for mediation but states this is available mainly for family mediation.[5] This is not entirely correct: see para 20.26, 'Practicalities'.

20.6   The emphasis in the code on co-operation does not detract from the need to refer matters to the court where it is not possible to reach agreement. In *G v E (deputyship and litigation friend)*[6] Baker J commented:

> The Act and Code are ... constructed on the basis that the vast majority of decisions concerning incapacitated adults are taken informally and collaboratively by individuals or groups of people consulting and working together. It is emphatically not part of the scheme underpinning the Act that there should be one individual who as a matter of course is given a special legal status to make decisions about incapacitated persons. Experience has shown that working together is the best policy to ensure that incapacitated adults such as E receive the highest quality of care. This case is an example of what can go wrong when people do not work together. Where there is disagreement about the appropriate care and treatment, (which cannot be resolved by the methods suggested in Chapter 15) or the issue is a matter of particular gravity or difficulty, the Act and Code provide that the issue should usually be determined by the court. The complexity and/or seriousness of such issues are likely to require a forensic process and formal adjudication by an experienced tribunal.

20.7   This point was emphasised by Peter Jackson J in *Hillingdon LBC v Neary*:[7]

> 196. Lastly, I have already indicated that the protracted delay in applying to court in this case was highly unfortunate. There are repeated references, particularly by the service manager, to the burden being on Mr Neary to take the matter to court if he wished to challenge what was happening. That approach cannot be right. I have already referred to the decision in *Re S*, which rightly observes that the practical and evidential burden is on a local authority to demonstrate that its arrangements are better than those that can be achieved within the family. It will discharge the practical burden by ensuring that there is a proper forum for decision. It will not do so by allowing the situation it has brought about to continue by default. Nor is it an answer to say, as Hillingdon has done, that Mr Neary could always have gone to court himself, and that it had told him so. It was Steven's rights, and not those of his father, that were in issue. Moreover, local authorities have the advantage over individuals both in terms of experience and, even nowadays, depth of pocket. The fact that an individual does not

---

5 Code of Practice para 15.13.

6 [2010] EWHC 2512 (COP), [2010] COPLR Con Vol 470.

7 [2011] EWHC 1377 (COP), [2011] COPLR Con Vol 632.

bring a matter to court does not relieve the local authority of the obligation to act, it redoubles it.

Court of Protection Rules

20.8   The Court of Protection Rules (COPR) 2007 SI No 1744 require parties to help the court in furthering the overriding objective of dealing with cases justly.[8] Judges are required to further the overriding objective by 'active case management', described in COPR r5 as including:

(a) encouraging the parties to co-operate with each other ...

(e) encouraging the parties to use an alternative dispute resolution procedure if the court considers that appropriate ...

20.9   As discussed in more detail in chapter 13, this is often reflected in practice. For example, judges may routinely include in standard directions a requirement that the parties should take steps to seek to narrow the disputes between them. This may be expressed simply as a requirement to attend court an hour before the hearing takes place, in order to have discussions. Sometimes the Court of Protection may make a direction requiring the parties to make contact with each other before the day of the hearing.

Case-law

20.10   There are no reported cases that give specific guidance as to mediation or ADR in this jurisdiction. In *A Local Authority v PB and P,*[9] Charles J was invited to comment on the issue of mediation or ADR but declined on the basis that this had not arisen in the facts of the case that he was considering.

20.11   Some assistance can be found by analogy in the case of *AI v MT (alternative dispute resolution)*[10] Baker J approved a consent order which had been reached after a lengthy arbitration process by a separating couple overseen by the New York Beth Din. The principles he identified in the context of the family courts are of relevance in the Court of Protection:

• the court's jurisdiction cannot be ousted by agreement between the parties;

---

8 COPR rr3, 4.

9 [2011] EWHC 502 (COP), [2011] COPLR Con Vol 166.

10 [2013] EWHC 100 (Fam), [2013] 2 FLR 371.

- unless statute provides otherwise, the child's welfare is the para-mount consideration;
- respect for the practice and beliefs of all faiths and cultures does not oblige the court to depart from the welfare principle because this principle is 'sufficiently broad and flexible to accommodate many cultural and religious practices';
- it is always in the interests of the parties to try to resolve disputes by agreement if possible and the courts will encourage this but will be cautious not to endorse a process which might oust the jurisdiction of the court.

20.12 In *Mann v Mann*,[11] again in the family sphere, Mostyn J concluded that:

- if parties have made a written agreement to engage in ADR before going ahead with an application, the court could adjourn to allow this to take place even if one party was seeking to back out of the agreement;
- this could be coupled with an order to make clear that an unreason-able refusal to participate in ADR could attract a costs sanction;
- the adjournment could not be open-ended because that would operate as a restriction on the right to apply to the court.

20.13 The Select Committee of the House of Lords conducting post-legislative scrutiny of the MCA 2005[12] considered the role of medi-ation. It noted a limited pilot scheme proposed by the Office of the Public Guardian (OPG), though was disappointed by the limited terms of the pilot and the fact that mediation would be conducted by telephone, in an area where building relationship and trust is crucial. It concluded that:

- mediation in the Court of Protection must comply with the deci-sion-making framework of the MCA 2005 and provision must be made to ensure representation of P's views and interests;
- mediation would be beneficial in many cases prior to issue and consideration should be given to making it a pre-requisite for launching proceedings, especially financial proceedings where the costs will fall to P's estate.

---

11 [2014] EWHC 537 (Fam).
12 *Mental Capacity Act 2005:post-legislative scrutiny*, HL Paper 139, March 2013, paras 224–232; available at: www.publications.parliament.uk/pa/ld201314/ldselect/ldmentalcap/139/139.pdf.

In its response ('Valuing every voice, respecting every right'[13]) the government agreed mediation would be suitable in some property and affairs cases, but less so in health and welfare cases. The government did not consider mediation should be a prerequisite to issuing as this would detract from its voluntary nature.

Mediation and ADR in practice – types of ADR and how to decide between them

Round table meetings

What they are and how they work

20.14   Round table meetings (RTMs) are often suggested by parties, or sometimes by judges of their own motion. An RTM is a meeting which would usually take place away from a court setting. RTMs are sometimes hosted by legal advisers or barristers' chambers. They may take place in local authority offices.

20.15   The difference between an RTM and a mediation is that an RTM is not facilitated by an external mediator. In welfare cases, an RTM is often chaired by the solicitor or barrister acting for P. The rationale behind this is that they are more likely to be seen as neutral than the other parties and to ensure that P's interests are central.

20.16   An RTM will usually involve the parties and their legal advisers. In some cases independent experts attend as well. In most cases solicitors rather than barristers will attend the meeting with their clients, and everyone attending will be present during the meeting. It is often prudent to ascertain if, in addition to the room where the meeting is taking place, any other rooms are available so that confidential discussions between lawyers and their clients can take place and to provide some space if any participant needs a break from the meeting. These rooms are sometimes described as 'breakout rooms'.

20.17   There are no rules governing the conduct of RTMs, so it is essential before such a meeting starts for the participants to address their minds to the following questions:

---

13 'Valuing every voice, respecting every right: Making the case for the Mental Capacity Act – The Government's response to the House of Lords Select Committee Report on the Mental Capacity Act 2005 (June 2014)': https://www. gov.uk/government/uploads/system/uploads/attachment_data/file/318730/ cm8884-valuing-every-voice.pdf.

- Will the discussions be confidential, or can they be referred to in the litigation? If the latter, how will the contents of the meeting be recorded?
- What is the status of any agreement reached at the RTM?
- Who is going to attend the meeting?
- Who is going to chair the meeting?
- What will be on the agenda?
- At what point will the RTM be abandoned?
- Will the venue be suitable? Will there be enough space and is there a 'breakout room' for confidential discussions?

Advantages and disadvantages

20.18 RTMs can be arranged more quickly than formal mediation. They are cheaper as there are no mediation fees. It can often be productive to suggest an RTM at the every early stages of a dispute, perhaps in pre-action correspondence. A dispute between a family member and social work staff may have become entrenched. Sometimes the involvement of lawyers, both for the family member and the statutory body, can help the clients narrow the issues and an RTM at this stage may obviate the need for litigation at all.

20.19 As with all forms of ADR, one advantage of an RTM is it can allow the parties to reach an outcome which could not be achieved through litigation alone – for example, an apology.

20.20 The potential disadvantage at this early stage may be that it is unlikely that P will be represented, and thus it will be difficult to ensure P's effective participation. As we have seen above, the code suggests that P might be supported by an advocate during mediation, and the same solution might then be used. This may, however, result in two parties to a dispute – for example, the local authority and statutory services – being legally represented at an RTM, while P remains without legal advice.

20.21 RTMs will be challenging if there is a particularly difficult relationship between two or more parties, as they tend to involve the participation of all the parties. Not all lawyers feel comfortable chairing RTMs, and the lawyer may be seen as less objective than an external mediator because the lawyer may already have had to express a view on important issues on an interim basis which may have been unpopular with one or more of the parties.

Mediation

20.22   This section provides a very basic summary of what mediation is, and then looks at the issues arising when mediating Court of Protection cases. Readers interested in learning more about mediation are recommended to read *Making mediation work for you*,[14] on which this section draws.

What mediation is

20.23   Mediation can take various different forms, but all mediations share the following characteristics:

- An independent mediator is used to facilitate the process.
- Mediation is confidential (though there are some exceptions) – the aim is that this encourages parties to be open and flexible. What one party says to the mediator will not be disclosed to the other without permission.
- Mediation is 'without prejudice' – the discussions which take place cannot be referred to in litigation.
- Mediation is a voluntary process – parties cannot be forced to mediate.
- Mediation is non-binding in that the parties are not obliged to reach agreement.
- If the mediation results in agreement, this can be recorded in the form of a legally binding agreement.

20.24   The involvement of an independent trained mediator can bring benefits to a case where the parties may find it difficult to see solutions. A skilled mediator will try to identify the parties' real interests in the case, which may involve going behind the parties' stated positions. The mediator will try to identify areas of common interest between the parties.

Practicalities

20.25   Although mediation may obviate the need for a contested hearing if it is successful and may therefore save money, it is not a cheap option, and it is important to anticipate the likely cost and make arrangements about how this is to be met. A mediator will require the parties and/or their representatives to sign and agreement to mediate, and this will include details as to how the mediator's costs will be met.

14 Kate Aubrey-Johnson with Helen Curtis, *Making mediation work for you*, LAG, 2012.

20.26 The mediator's fees are usually shared by the parties who are mediating. If any of the parties are legally aided, then the mediator's fees will be a disbursement on the certificate or Legal Help form. Prior authority should be sought from the Legal Aid Authority (LAA) (see chapter 6). Advisers should ensure that they have identified all the potential costs of the mediation. These may, for example, include room hire; or it may have been suggested that any experts who have reported should also attend the mediation.

20.27 The Ministry of Justice comments on its website, alongside the directory of accredited mediators:[15]

> Courts should be the last resort for people involved in civil or family disputes unless there are issues around urgency and safety, eg in relation to child abuse or domestic violence.
>
> Mediation, in particular, can be a flexible, speedy and cost effective way to resolve disputes. It is a confidential process that enables both parties to explain and then discuss what their needs and concerns are to each other in the presence of an independent third party – the mediator – so that they reach an agreement between themselves.
>
> The individuals concerned have greater control and responsibility in resolving disagreements than if they went to court. Mediation empowers parties to control the length of the process, the issues they would like to discuss, and the outcome. Mediation can also be less stressful, particularly for any children involved, and in the long run, can be cheaper than going to court.

20.28 While therefore the LAA would be expected broadly to support attempts to mediate a dispute, the costs can be considerable and it is essential to ensure that these are identified before an application for prior authority is made.

Finding a mediator

20.29 Finding a mediator who will be able to conduct an effective mediation in a Court of Protection case can be daunting. There are different types of mediator, reflecting the different specialist areas of mediation – civil, family, workplace and community mediators. There is no single body which regulates mediators. Family mediators are accredited by organisations which belong to the Family Mediation Council. The Civil Mediation Council (CMC) accredits mediation providers, who must have a panel of at least six mediation providers who can show that they meet the CMC's accreditation standards. Thus, individual mediators will not themselves be accredited by the

---

15 See: www.justice.gov.uk/courts/mediation.

CMC. The Ministry of Justice maintains a directory of mediators accredited by the CMC which can be searched by geographical area. Individual mediators will be accredited if they have been trained by a body recognised by the CMC. The Law Society has an accreditation scheme for civil and commercial mediators.[16]

20.30   In addition to checking the mediator's accreditation, it is advisable to ask to see their CV and ask about the cases they have taken on.

Preparation for the mediation

20.31 For those who have proposed mediation or responded to a suggestion by the court or another party, it is essential to consider what to expect from the mediation. Advisers will need to have a clear grasp of the strengths and weaknesses of the client's case. Perhaps for this reason, many Court of Protection mediations take place after the receipt of experts' reports, if these are being used. This is an ideal time to take stock of the evidence as it now stands, in as objective a way as possible. This may be difficult because of the highly charged atmosphere that can develop in Court of Protection disputes, especially in cases involving a relationship between family carers and statutory bodies, which may have been deteriorating over a number of years before matters come to a head and proceedings are issued. Advisers may find it helpful to underline to their clients the benefit of the fresh perspective on a case that the mediator should bring.

20.32   In anticipation of the mediation the following issues should be considered:

- Assuming that new evidence in the form of expert reports has been received, what if any impact have these had on the views and positions of the parties?
- Advisers should explore with their clients as neutrally as possible whether there are any concessions which the client feels they could offer, which might promote an agreement. These might be matters that could not be achieved through litigation alone. This could include eg an apology; an agreement to make a gift in kind; or an agreement to work with the other parties in a different manner in the future. Possible concessions that might be sought from the other parties should also be considered.
- It is important to evaluate in the light of the evidence what the client can realistically achieve in the litigation. If mediation fails to deliver an agreement, what is the likely outcome of a contested hearing? If an adviser's client is legally aided, is there any risk that

16 See: www.lawsociety.org.uk.

the client's legal aid will be not be extended to cover a contested hearing if mediation fails?

- Is there any reason (on an objective evaluation) to believe that any of the other parties have not agreed to mediate in good faith?
- The potential benefits to mediation should be weighed, even if it is unlikely to deliver a full resolution: might it narrow the issues or at least improve the parties' ability to communicate?
- With this point in mind, advisers are encouraged to manage their clients' expectations.
- Practicalities – will the parties agree to sit in the same room for all or any of the process?
- In the civil sphere, an unreasonable refusal to mediate can give rise to costs sanctions: see *Halsey v Milton Keynes NHS Trust.*[17] The costs implication of a refusal to mediate in the Court of Protection sphere is considered in more detail at para 17.45.

20.33   It is not always necessary for the mediator to be provided with all the papers filed in a given case. However the mediator may need to see at least some of the documents from the Court of Protection proceedings. Before mediating the parties will need to agree the contents of a bundle of core documents for the mediator. The court will need to give permission to disclose this information to the mediator. This could be the subject of an application on COP9, usually by consent.

20.34   The mediator may wish to speak to the parties or their legal advisers in advance of the mediation. This can be a useful opportunity to agree the procedure to be followed and can make attending the mediation itself less daunting. Some mediators invite the parties to prepare a short position statement or make a short opening statement.

20.35   It is highly likely that the mediator will ask the parties to sign an agreement to mediate. The contents of this will vary but the agreement will probably contain the following provisions:

- who is responsible for the mediator's fees and when these will be paid;
- confirmation that the parties have agreed to mediate voluntarily;
- confidentiality, perhaps with a provision that nothing said during the mediation will be referred to in the litigation;
- any ground rules the mediator considers necessary, including the discretion to end the mediation;
- a requirement that whoever attends on behalf of the parties has authority to settle.

17 [2004] EWCA Civ 576, [2004] 1 WLR 3002.

The mediation process

20.36   Mediation is a flexible process which can be designed to fit the needs of the parties involved. Many mediations will commence with a plenary meeting, where all the parties gather in one room and where the mediator will introduce him or herself and explain the procedure to be followed. Opening statements may be made during this session. Typically, after this the parties will then retreat to separate rooms, while the mediator speaks to them in turn. This can take time, and mediation can often seem to involve a considerable amount of waiting.

20.37   The mediator will seek to establish the parties' core interests to explore potential common ground which may provide an opening for agreement. The mediator may want to explore how one party would react in the event that a particular concession is made by one of the parties.

20.38   Court of Protection cases can pose particular challenges. P's interests need to remain central to the process. If P is a party, he or she will have a litigation friend who is likely to be present (or be represented) at the mediation. The litigation friend should make every attempt to ascertain P's wishes and feelings on the issues which are being mediated. By definition, P is unlikely to be able to take part in the process of compromise and give-and-take that may be involved in mediation. This in turn runs the risk that the focus of the mediation could be drawn entirely to the minutiae of the dispute between the other parties.

20.39   The second difficulty is that Court of Protection cases will frequently involve an imbalance of power between the parties, as they may typically involve a dispute between a statutory body and one or more individuals. It is suggested that this requires the mediator to satisfy him or herself that even though one party may be in a much stronger position, that party remains willing genuinely to consider an element of compromise.

20.40   An experienced mediator should be alert to both these issues.

20.41   If agreement is reached, the agreement should be put in writing. In the authors' experience, this is usually done by the legal advisers. This needs to be done with care. Once proceedings have started, the court will need to approve any agreement before it is fully binding. However, it is undesirable to be in the position of resiling from a signed mediation agreement. It is absolutely essential that there is sufficient time, even at the end of what may have been a long day, for advisers to satisfy themselves that their client fully understands, and is willing to comply with, the mediation agreement. If a party needs, for example, to consider their position overnight, see if this can be agreed.

20.42   If the mediation is successful, then the mediation agreement should be approved by the judge, who will need to be satisfied that the outcome is one that can properly be said to be in the best interests of P.

What kind of Court of Protection cases are suitable for mediation?

20.43   While mediation is not a panacea, an attempt at mediation can be beneficial even in intractable cases. The following scenarios describe how mediation might affect the outcome in some of the types of disputes which come before the Court of Protection.

Scenario 1

20.44   Janet and John are separating after 25 years of marriage. John has moved out of the family home. They have one child, Janice, who is 20 and has a severe learning disability. Janice has always lived at home. Janice lacks capacity to make decisions about where she should live and how she should be cared for. Janet and John's separation is acrimonious. Janet refuses to allow John to visit Janice, and John issues an application in the Court of Protection seeking declarations that it is in Janice's best interests to live with him. Janice is represented by the Official Solicitor. All the parties agree to mediate. The mediator enables Janet and John to focus on their areas of agreement and on Janice's own feelings during the separation. They are able to agree that Janice is happy at home but misses her father. They agree a formula which allows John to see Janice regularly.

Scenario 2

20.45   Bernice has cared for her learning disabled son Alan all his life. Alan is 25. The local authority has in recent years held concerns about Bernice's ability to care for Alan and ensure his access to the community. Matters reach a head when Bernice goes away to stay with a sick relative leaving Alan alone in their home. Alan is placed in respite by the local authority. When Bernice returns home she wants Alan to move back with her. The local authority refuses. The local authority agrees to issue proceedings in the

Court of Protection, but there is some delay in this. Once proceedings are issued, an independent social work report finds that Alan is thriving in his placement and enjoying spending time with Bernice at weekends. Bernice has developed a good relationship with the placement. The expert recommends mediation. At mediation it becomes clear that Bernice accepts that Alan is happy in his new placement but is angry that the case was not brought to court more quickly and strongly feels this was deliberate. The local authority accepts that it should have brought the dispute to the court more quickly and agrees to write a letter of apology to Bernice. Bernice withdraws her opposition to declarations that it is in Alan's best interests to remain in his current placement.

Scenario 3

20.46   X local authority has been supporting Susan, an elderly woman with dementia who lives with Jim, her husband. Their relationship has always been volatile and Susan's social worker is concerned that Susan is at risk from Jim. Following some unexplained bruising on Susan's back which was noticed at a day centre, the local authority carries out a safeguarding investigation and concludes that they cannot protect Susan from Jim if she remains at home with him. The local authority obtains urgent declarations and orders from the court and Susan is removed to a nearby care home. Jim's visits to the care home cause concern: he is aggressive and staff members complain that he is bullying Susan and other staff. Jim denies this and all other allegations point-blank. He insists Susan should come home. Susan settles well at the home and tells an advocate who is appointed litigation friend that she prefers to remain at home. Mediation is attempted but fails to result in an agreement on any issues. Jim refuses to discuss anything other than an immediate return home by Susan. The local authority do not agree to this nor does the litigation friend consider it to be in Susan's best interests. The case is therefore restored to the court so a decision can be taken in Susan's best interests.

Office of the Public Guardian

Introduction

21.1   The role of Public Guardian and the creation of the Office of the Public Guardian (OPG), in its present format, were established by Mental Capacity Act (MCA) 2005 ss57–61. The present Public Guardian is Alan Eccles, who has been in post since 2012. Full contact details for the OPG can be found in appendix F below.

21.2   The OPG is an executive agency of the Ministry of Justice through which the Public Guardian caries out his statutory functions.

Responsibilities

21.3   Under MCA 2005 s58(1), the Public Guardian is responsible for:

(a) establishing and maintaining a register of lasting powers of attorney,

(b) establishing and maintaining a register of orders appointing deputies,

(c) supervising deputies appointed by the court,

(d) directing a Court of Protection Visitor to visit–
  (i)   a donee of a lasting power of attorney,
  (ii) a deputy appointed by the court, or
  (iii) the person granting the power of attorney or for whom the deputy is appointed ('P'),
  and to make a report to the Public Guardian on such matters as he may direct,

(e) receiving security which the court requires a person to give for the discharge of his functions,

(f) receiving reports from donees of lasting powers of attorney and deputies appointed by the court,

(g) reporting to the court on such matters relating to proceedings under this Act as the court requires,

(h) dealing with representations (including complaints) about the way in which a donee of a lasting power of attorney or a deputy appointed by the court is exercising his powers,

(i) publishing, in any manner the Public Guardian thinks appropriate, any information he thinks appropriate about the discharge of his functions.

Register of lasting powers of attorney and deputies

21.4   The MCA 2005 updated the law with regard to the provisions that can be made by an individual to appoint a decision maker (attorney) to make certain decisions on their behalf should they lose the capacity in the future.[1]

21.5　Prior to 1 October 2007 an enduring power of attorney (EPA) allowed a donor (the person who wishes to make arrangements for someone else to look after their finances if they are unable to do so in future) to appoint an attorney (or attorneys) to deal with their finances both immediately after the signing of the document and in the future, should the donor lose their capacity. The scope of an EPA was limited to financial affairs. To be valid the EPA must be in the prescribed format and have been signed by all parties on or before 30 September 2007.

21.6　An EPA does not need to be registered to be used, although the attorneys named in the document are under a duty to register the document with the OPG when they believe that the donor has lost, or is losing their capacity[2].

21.7　Properly created EPAs are still valid, although the authors are aware of considerable anecdotal evidence that banks and other financial institutions refuse to acknowledge these documents unless they are now registered.

21.8　From 1 October 2007 the MCA 2005 replaced EPAs with lasting powers of attorney (LPAs), of which there are two varieties:

- property and affairs – which covers the donor's financial matters; and
- health and welfare – which allows a donor to nominate attorney(s) to take decisions about their future medical treatment, care and other related matters if they lost the capacity to do so themselves.

21.9　A property and affairs LPA is similar in function to the old EPA but crucially it cannot be used until it has been registered with the OPG. The special feature enjoyed by both EPA and LPA is that the authority conferred by them continues after the donor has lost their capacity. All other types of power of attorney are automatically revoked by the donor's incapacity.

21.10　The process for validly entering into an LPA lies outside the scope of this work, but is the subject of detailed guidance and commentary[3] (see also chapter 7). The OPG has a range of documents available

---

1　See also chapter 7.
2　Enduring Powers of Attorney Act 1985 s4(2).
3　See in particular Denzil Lush, *Cretney & Lush on Lasting and Enduring Powers of Attorney*, 7th edn, Jordans, 2013.

to download that take the prospective donor through the process of making an LPA, registering it and acting as an attorney.[4]

21.11   The range of options for entering into an LPA now includes an online tool[5] for generating a document to be printed off, signed and submitted for registration. It is hoped that innovations like this will help donors to ensure that the document they create is valid and complete and thereby reduce the number of applications for registration that are returned by the OPG each year for the rectification of minor errors or omissions.

21.12   LPAs are more detailed than the EPAs they replaced, and allow more scope for a donor to give specific advice to their chosen attorneys about how they want decisions to be made on their behalf. Restrictions can be placed upon the powers of the attorneys both in relation to finance and welfare and the donor may set out guidance for her attorneys to follow when discharging their duties. The nature of this guidance will depend upon the wishes and circumstances of the donor, but may include religious or ethical considerations, or stipulations as to specific decisions that attorneys may not take without further authority of the court (for example, to sell a property or valuable artefact). There are also specific requirements that must be followed if a donor of an LPA wishes to grant the power to their attorneys to refuse life-sustaining treatment. Those who are advising a donor entering into an LPA should ensure that they make the donor aware of these options and requirements.

21.13   Advisers to both donors entering into LPAs and attorneys acting under an LPA should ensure that their clients are aware of the limits to the scope of their powers under LPAs. In the authors' experience the extent of an attorney's authority is frequently misunderstood. There would seem to be common misunderstandings and assumptions in relation to powers to gift and invest money, as well as their options when deciding on care arrangements under a health and welfare LPA. Ensuring that all parties have clarity at the time that arrangements are made will help to avoid problems, including possibly interventions by the court, in future. Details about the court's powers in relation to EPAs and LPAs can be found in chapter 7 (it should be noted that the OPG has the power to – and regularly does

---

4   See: https://www.gov.uk/government/publications/make-a-lasting-power-of-attorney.

5   See: https://www.gov.uk/lasting-power-of-attorney.

– apply to the Court of Protection to sever ineffective provisions in LPAs under provisions of MCA 2005 Sch 2 para 11[6]).

21.14 It is also worth noting that the OPG only maintains a register of instruments for England and Wales. Arrangements for decision-making for those who lack capacity will vary significantly in jurisdictions outside England and Wales (including Northern Ireland and Scotland). For further information please see chapter 27.

Searching the registers

21.15 Anyone may apply to search the registers of EPAs, LPAs and deputyships maintained by the OPG.[7] A standard 'first-tier' search is made by completing an OPG100 form[8] and sending it to the OPG. There is no charge for making an application.

21.16 There were 8,778 first-tier searches made between May 2012 and April 2013.[9]

21.17 Information that may be revealed by this search includes:

- the allocated case number;
- known other names of the donor/person the order is about;
- date of birth of the donor/person the order is about;
- name(s) of any deputy/deputies;
- name(s) of any attorney(s);
- whether the LPA, EPA or deputyship order relates to 'property and affairs' or 'personal welfare';
- the date the LPA, EPA or deputyship order was made;
- the date the LPA, EPA or deputyship order was registered;
- the date the LPA or EPA was revoked (if applicable);
- the date the deputyship order expires (if applicable);
- the date the deputyship order was cancelled (if applicable);
- name(s) of any replacement deputy/deputies/attorney(s);

---

6 For examples of orders made in this regard, see: www.justice.gov.uk/ protecting-the-vulnerable/mental-capacity-act/orders-made-by-the-court-of-protection/lasting-powers-of-attorney.

7 Under Lasting Powers of Attorney, Enduring Powers of Attorney and Public Guardian Regulations 2007 SI No 1253 reg 31. See also the *Office of the Public Guardian Registers guidance*, LPA 109, available at: https://www.gov.uk/ government/publications/search-public-guardian-registers.

8 Available at the website in the footnote above.

9 *Enabling digital by default – impact assessment*, available at: https://consult. justice.gov.uk/digital-communications/opg-enabling-digital-default/ supporting_documents/iaopgdigitaldefault.pdf.

- whether any replacement deputy/deputies/attorney(s) are active;
- whether the deputies/attorneys are appointed jointly;
- whether deputies/attorneys are appointed jointly and severally; and
- whether there are conditions or restrictions on the LPA, EPA or deputyship order (but not details about the conditions or restrictions).

21.18   Information will only be provided if there is an exact match between the details provided on the application form and those held on the registers. If there is a close but not exact match the OPG may contact the applicant for more information.

21.19   A first-tier search will not reveal any details about EPAs/LPAs that have not yet been registered, or any applications for the appointment of a deputy that are pending with the court. It also does not include details of any other types of order made by the court, for example those authorising a statutory will. If this information is sought, then an application must be made to the court and the usual rules of disclosure under the Court of Procedure Rules (COPR) 2007 SI No 1744 will apply (for more on disclosure, see paras 13.88ff).

21.20   Additional information about the donor/P may be sought by requesting a 'second-tier' search.[10] This is done by making an application in writing to the OPG setting out the name of the donor/P, the applicant's relationship to them, why the applicant needs the information requested and why the applicant has been unable to obtain it by any other route. The OPG considers such applications on their merit and any information provided is at the discretion of the OPG, if he considers that there is 'good reason' to provide the information.[11]

21.21   As part of an ongoing government-wide project to improve transparency and access to information, the OPG has proposed digital searches for tier-one requests. It is hoped that this will be available sometime in 2014 or 2015.[12]

---

10 Under Lasting Powers of Attorney, Enduring Powers of Attorney and Public Guardian Regulations reg 32.

11 Lasting Powers of Attorney, Enduring Powers of Attorney and Public Guardian Regulations reg 32(2).

12 See: https://www.gov.uk/government/consultations/transforming-the-services-of-the-office-of-the-public-guardian-enabling-digital-by-default.

Supervision

21.22   When a new deputyship order is made, the court will notify the OPG which will then allocate a supervision level to that particular matter. Each new deputyship is assessed by the OPG to decide on the most suitable supervision regime, depending upon factors such as the level of assets involved; the deputy's experience and P's circumstances.

21.23   There are four levels of supervision:

- Type 1 – close supervision for complex cases, where there has been a dispute or the deputy is under investigation.
- Type 2A – intermediate supervision, usually appropriate for a new lay deputyship when more support is needed in the first year.
- Type 2 – light supervision, usually where the deputy is a close relative and the case is straightforward.
- Type 3 – minimal supervision – where there are less than £18,000 worth of assets to be managed.

21.24   The appropriate level of supervision may be revised by the OPG if circumstances change for example once a lay deputy is familiar with the role or if an investigation is begun.

Annual reports

21.25   Deputies are required by the OPG to produce a report each year detailing how they have managed P's funds.[13] These reports may be audited and the OPG may require that invoices, receipts or other evidence of expenditure is submitted.

21.26   The annual reports are straightforward for most deputies, but lay deputies may wish to instruct an accountant or solicitor to prepare them if P's finances are more complicated. The costs of professional advice can be met from P's funds.

Court Visitors

21.27   One of the most important ways in which the OPG keeps in touch with deputies and provides ongoing supervision and support is through the network of Court of Protection Visitors.

---

13   MCA 2005 s19(9)(b).

21.28   The OPG maintains two panels of experts or Visitors on behalf of the Lord Chancellor. MCA 2005 s61 provides that:

61(1) A Court of Protection Visitor is a person who is appointed by the Lord Chancellor to–
    (a) a panel of Special Visitors, or
    (b) a panel of General Visitors.

(2) A person is not qualified to be a Special Visitor unless he–
    (a) is a registered medical practitioner or appears to the Lord Chancellor to have other suitable qualifications or training, and
    (b) appears to the Lord Chancellor to have special knowledge of and experience in cases of impairment of or disturbance in the functioning of the mind or brain.

(3) A General Visitor need not have a medical qualification.

(4) A Court of Protection Visitor–
    (a) may be appointed for such term and subject to such conditions, and
    (b) may be paid such remuneration and allowances,
    as the Lord Chancellor may determine.

(5) For the purpose of carrying out his functions under this Act in relation to a person who lacks capacity ('P'), a Court of Protection Visitor may, at all reasonable times, examine and take copies of–
    (a) any health record,
    (b) any record of, or held by, a local authority and compiled in connection with a social services function, and
    (c) any record held by a person registered under Part 2 of the Care Standards Act 2000
    so far as the record relates to P.

(6) A Court of Protection Visitor may also for that purpose interview P in private.

21.29   Generally a lay deputy can expect to have a visit from a General Visitor within the first 12 months of their appointment. This will usually take the format of a meeting with the deputy, and P, face-to-face to discuss how the deputy is managing in their role.

21.30   As well as routine visits as part of the ongoing supervision regime, the OPG can request a general visit for many reasons, for example:

- when a deputy is new to the role;
- to answer questions and make sure the deputy understands and can meet their responsibilities;
- if the OPG need reassurance that the deputy is acting in accordance with the terms of order and in P's best interests;
- for access to paperwork, for example bank statements, receipts etc; and
- when the OPG is carrying out an investigation.

21.31 The Visitor will contact the deputy in advance to arrange a suitable time for the meeting and to provide details of what information and paperwork they need access to.[14] They will usually wish to meet with the deputy and P separately; they may also wish to meet with third parties such as a care manger, social worker etc. Court Visitors carry identification and will show this when they visit.

21.32 After a visit, a report will be prepared for the OPG, making recommendations – for example, about issues that need to be monitored or the appropriate time before a follow-up visit needs to be scheduled.

21.33 Deputies may request a visit if they feel that the OPG can provide support with a particular issue.

21.34 The court has wide-ranging powers to call for reports.[15] Where a medical report is required, the OPG Special Visitors can be commissioned to undertake this role. This can be useful, for example when P does not wish to co-operate with an assessment of capacity, or if there is a dispute as to P's capacity. See further for the role of Visitors in this regard paras 13.42ff.

Investigations

21.35 The Public Guardian has the power to conduct investigations into the conduct of attorneys and deputies. The Court of Protection can order that a report be made to the Public Guardian by a deputy.[16]

21.36 Anyone who has concerns about the conduct of an attorney or deputy may raise these concerns with the OPG Compliance Unit. Investigations will usually centre on the attorney or deputy's management of P's finances, and allegations of suspected financial abuse, but may encompass other aspects of the attorney or deputy's behaviour in relation to P.

21.37 Following an investigation, the OPG will produce a report which will make recommendations. In the event that the OPG concludes that it is in P's best interests to do so an application can be made to the Court of Protection. The OPG does not require permission to make such an application.[17]

21.38 In the financial year 2012/13 the Public Guardian received a total of 2,982 safeguarding referrals. Of these, 728 (24 per cent) were

14 Lasting Powers of Attorney, Enduring Powers of Attorney and Public Guardian Regulations 2007 reg 44.
15 MCA 2005 s49.
16 MCA 2005 s19(9)(b).
17 COPR r51(1)(b).

referred for full investigation and the Public Guardian approved 480 investigation case recommendations. Of the recommendations made, only 136 resulted in an application to the Court of Protection for the removal of an attorney or deputy.[18]

21.39   The case of *The Public Guardian v JM*[19] looked at the interface between a police investigation into the conduct of an attorney and an investigation by the OPG. In his judgment, Senior Judge Lush noted that:

> 44. There are significant differences between a police investigation and an investigation conducted by the OPG. When the police investigate an alleged crime, they need to consider whether there is sufficient evidence to present to the Crown Prosecution Service ('CPS') to guarantee a realistic prospect of conviction ...
>
> 45. By contrast, an investigation by the OPG is concerned primarily with establishing whether an attorney or deputy has contravened his authority under the Mental Capacity Act 2005, or has acted in breach of his fiduciary duties under the common law of agency, or has behaved in a way that is not in the best interests of the person who lacks capacity. The standard of proof, 'on the balance of probabilities', is lower than the criminal standard.

21.40   This case is a reminder to attorneys, as well as deputies, and their advisers that the Court of Protection will still act to remove an individual who it believes has not acted in P's best interests, despite that individual not facing prosecution for their actions.

Panel deputies

21.41   The OPG maintains a panel of professional deputies who can be appointed as property and affairs deputy for P where there is no other suitable person to take on the role. Panel deputies are 'deputies of last resort' as in most cases the deputy will be a member of P's family or a legal professional who is already familiar with P.

21.42   The court will often order the appointment of a panel deputy in cases where there has been a dispute within the family as to who should be a property and affairs deputy or where there has been abuse. For further details about disputed applications for the appointment of a property and affairs deputy and the revocation of EPAs, LPAs and deputyships, see chapter 7 above.

18 *Office of the Public Guardian Annual Report and Accounts 2012–2013*, available at: www.justice.gov.uk/downloads/publications/corporate-reports/OPG/opg-annual-report-2012-13.pdf.

19 [2014] EWHC B4 (COP).

CHAPTER 22

Applications under Mental Capacity Act 2005 s21A

Introduction

22.1   One of the most important tasks of the Court of Protection was given to it after the Mental Capacity Act (MCA) 2005 came into force. By amendments to the MCA 2005 made by the Mental Health Act (MHA) 2007, the Court of Protection was given the task of considering applications under MCA 2005 s21A in respect of authorisations granted under the deprivation of liberty safeguards (DOLS) regime introduced by the MHA 2007 in the form of Schedule A1 to the MCA 2005. These safeguards were introduced to seek to fill the legislative lacuna (known as the 'Bournewood gap') which was exposed in the important case of *HL v UK*.[1]

22.2   The jurisdiction of the Court of Protection under MCA 2005 s21A overlaps with its jurisdiction to make declarations and decisions regarding P's health and welfare under MCA 2005 ss15–16, but it is essentially a standalone jurisdiction. It can only be understood by reference to the – complex – provisions of Schedule A1. This chapter therefore sets out the background to the provisions of Schedule A1 and highlights the key features of that schedule (including its interaction with the MHA 1983) before turning to the operation of MCA 2005 s21A.

This chapter should be reaad in conjunction with paras 3.166– 3.229.

Background: *HL v UK*

22.3   Mr L was a man in his 40s with severe autism, who could only communicate non-verbally. He had spent many years in Bournewood Hospital, but was then placed with paid carers, Mr and Mrs E. He lived with them for around four years, although his care continued to be managed by Bournewood Hospital rather than the community team. Having become disturbed at his day centre one day in July 1997, Mr L was taken to Bournewood Hospital. He was considered to need inpatient treatment and was admitted as an informal patient as he was making no attempt to leave. A decision was taken that Mr and Mrs E should not be allowed to visit as it was considered that this might cause agitation. Mr L was given medication and had he attempted to leave he would have been prevented from doing so, by

1   *HL v UK* (App No 45508/99), [2004] ECHR 471, (2004) 7 CCLR 498.

use of the MHA 2005. Mr L did not have the capacity to consent to admission to hospital.

22.4   Mr and Mrs E applied for judicial review and habeas corpus on HL's behalf. Having been unsuccessful at first instance he was successful at the Court of Appeal. The hospital appealed to the House of Lords where the Court of Appeal's decision was overturned (with a strong dissenting judgment from Lord Steyn).

22.5   Following the decision of the Court of Appeal, HL was detained under the MHA 1983 but was discharged in December 1997 and returned to live with Mr and Mrs E.

22.6   HL appealed to the European Court of Human Rights (ECtHR) in 1998, asserting that his rights under article 5 (right to liberty) of the European Convention on Human Rights (ECHR) had been violated. The ECtHR found that HL had been deprived of his liberty for the purpose of article 5 and that this was not in accordance with a procedure prescribed by law.

22.7   In making this finding the court commented:

> ... the key factor [is] that the health care professionals treating and managing the applicant exercised complete and effective control over his care and movement ... any suggestion to the contrary is ... fairly described ... as 'stretching credulity to breaking point' and as a 'fairy tale'.[2]

22.8   This case demonstrated the need for legal safeguards that would allow incapacitated compliant patients to be deprived of their liberty in order to be provided with care and treatment when this was in their best interests, without infringing their rights under article 5. By analogy, the case also demonstrated the need for equivalent protections to those who were to be deprived of their liberty by the state in residential care homes.

22.9   The government decided to fill the lacuna by amending the MCA 2005. Through the MHA 2007, amendments were made to sections 4, 16, 21 and 39; and two schedules were added, Schedule A1 and Schedule 1A. The amendments created the Deprivation of Liberty Safeguards (DOLS).

22.10   A second Code of Practice (*Mental Capacity Act 2005: Deprivation of liberty safeguards Code of Practice,*[3] referred to as the 'DOLS Code of Practice') was produced at the same time.

---

2 Para 91.

3 Available at: http://webarchive.nationalarchives.gov.uk/20130107105354/
http://www.dh.gov.uk/prod_consum_dh/groups/dh_digitalassets/@dh/@en/
documents/digitalasset/dh_087309.pdf.

What is a deprivation of liberty?

22.11   The DOLS Code of Practice provides guidance on identifying deprivation of liberty. This must now be considered in the light of the Supreme Court's decision in the linked appeals of *P (by his litigation friend the Official Solicitor) v Cheshire West and Chester Council and another*, and *P and Q (by their litigation friend the Official Solicitor) v Surrey County Council.*[4]

22.12   This landmark case concerned the living arrangements of three disabled people: P, a man with cerebral palsy and two sisters, referred to as MIG and MEG in the Court of Protection, P and Q in the Court of Appeal, and then MIG and MEG in the Supreme Court. There was no dispute that the arrangements were in the best interests of P, MIG and MEG. The Supreme Court had to determine whether these arrangements amounted to a deprivation of their liberty.

a)   MIG and MEG were from a chaotic and abusive background and had been taken into care. MIG had moderate to severe learning disability (mental age 2.5); impaired sight and hearing, communication difficulties. She lived with her foster mother who provided intensive support to her. MEG had mild/moderate learning disability (mental age 4); her behaviour was more challenging than her sister's and she required medication and sometimes restraint. She lived in a small group home. Both sisters had access to education, family contact and social lives; Parker J held that neither MIG nor MEG was deprived of her liberty and that their lives were 'dictated by their own cognitive limitations ... they are there to receive care'.[5] This finding was upheld by Court of Appeal.[6]

b)   P had cerebral palsy and Down's syndrome. He needed 24-hour care, including prompting with activities of daily living including hygiene and continence. He wore a 'bodysuit' and required invasive interventions including 'fingersweep' to mouth to stop him ingesting harmful substances, such as his incontinence pads. Baker J held that the care arrangements amounted to a deprivation of his liberty. The Court of Appeal decided, however, that P's circumstances did not amount to a deprivation of liberty. Giving the lead judgment, Munby LJ was concerned that the need to identify the concrete situation of the person concerned could lead to the 'worrying and ultimately stultifying conclusion that the detail in

4   [2014] UKSC 19, [2014] 2 WLR 642, (2014) 17 CCLR 5.
5   [2010] EWHC 785 (Fam).
6   *Re P and Q* [2011] EWCA Civ 190.

every case can be safely arrived at only after a minute examination of all the facts in enormous detail'.[7] He concluded that the answer lay with the question of the relevant comparator: who should you compare P with? The relevant comparator was 'the kind of lives that people like X would normally expect to lead'.

22.13   All seven Supreme Court justices upheld P's appeal; and a majority of four upheld MIG's and MEG's appeal. In the lead judgment for the majority on the points of principle, Lady Hale stressed the universal nature of human rights and said:

> It is axiomatic that people with disabilities ... have the same human rights as the rest of the human race ... This flows inexorably from the universal charter of human rights ... and is confirmed in the UNCRPD. Far from disability entitling the state to deny such people human rights: rather it places on the state (and on others) the duty to make reasonable accommodation to cater for the special needs of those with disabilities.[8]

22.14   Lady Hale identified[9] as an 'acid test' for deprivation of liberty the question of whether P was under continuous supervision and control and not free to leave. This had been a key feature in recent Strasbourg cases.[10] She identified as irrelevant factors:

- P's compliance or lack of objections;
- the relative normality of the placement;
- the reasons/purpose behind the placement.[11]

22.15   Three of the judges did not agree with the 'acid test' approach, commenting that no one would describe 'people living happily in a domestic setting as deprived of their liberty'.[12]

Overview of DOLS

22.16   DOLS can be used to authorise the detention of incapacitated patients in hospitals and care homes, if the requirements are complied

---

7   *Cheshire West and Chester Council v P* [2011] EWCA Civ 1257, (2012) 15 CCLR 48, [2012] COPLR 37 at para 38.

8   *Cheshire West* at para 45.

9   At para 48.

10   *HL v UK* (2004) 40 EHRR 761, *Stanev v Bulgaria* (2012) 55 EHRR 696, *DD v Lithuania* (App No 13469/06, 12 February 2012); *Kedzior v Poland* (App No 45026/07, 16 October 2012), *Mihailovs v Latvia* (App No 35939/10).

11   *Cheshire West* at para 50.

12   *Cheshire West* at para 108 per Lord Clarke.

with. DOLS cannot be used in supported living or educational establishments.

22.17   The following amendments were made to the body of the MCA 2005:

- Section 4A(3) provides that D may deprive P of his liberty if in doing so, D is giving effect to 'a relevant decision of the Court'. This means an order by the Court of Protection which expressly permits P to be deprived of his liberty and might be used for example in supported living settings where the DOLS procedure cannot be used.

- Section 4A(5) provides that D may deprive P of his liberty if this is authorised by Schedule A1 (ie if an standard or urgent authorisation under DOLS is in place).

- Section 4B permits D to deprive P of their liberty to enable P to receive vital or life-sustaining treatment while a decision on a relevant matter is sought from the court.

- Section 16A makes it clear that if a person is ineligible for a standard or urgent authorisation under DOLS, then this cannot be rectified by the Court of Protection making an order which purports to deprive P of their liberty. (However, following the decision in Dr A, it appears that such an order could be made by the Court using its inherent jurisdiction.)

- Section 21A gives the Court of Protection to determine a range of issues arising from challenges to DOLS authorisations.

22.18   The MHA 2007 introduced the concept of standard and urgent authorisations. Such authorisations allow a 'managing authority' (which will be a hospital or care home) lawfully to deprive P of their liberty, if all the requirements contained in the authorisation procedure are complied with.

22.19   An urgent authorisation can be self-granted up to seven days (MCA 2005 Sch A1 para 78). A standard authorisation can be granted by the supervisory body (now always local authority) up to maximum of one year (para 42(2)(b)).

22.20   A standard authorisation must be requested by the managing authority when it appears to the managing authority that P is accommodated in relevant care home or hospital or will be within 28 days; and is or is likely to be a detained resident; and meets or is likely to meet all the qualifying requirements (MCA 2005 Sch A1 para 24). This requires the managing authority to identify correctly when a deprivation of liberty is occurring.

22.21   An application for an authorisation must be made where it appears to the managing authority that (P is or will be a detained resident, ie will be deprived of their liberty for the purpose of article 5 (MCA 2005 s64(5));

22.22   The six requirements for a standard authorisation are set out below:

1) Age requirement: ie P must be over 18 (MCA 2005 Sch A1 para 13).
2) Mental health requirement: ie P must have a mental disorder for the purpose of the MHA 1983. If this is a learning disability it need not be associated with abnormally aggressive or seriously irresponsible behaviour (para 14).
3) Mental capacity requirement: ie P must lack capacity to decide whether or not he should be accommodated in the relevant hospital or care home for the purpose of being given the relevant care or treatment (para 15).
4) Best interests requirement: ie it is in P's best interests to be a detained resident and it is necessary and proportionate to the risk of harm to P (para 16).
5) Eligibility requirement: ie P is not ineligible by virtue of Schedule 1A, which deals with the interface with the MHA 2005 (para 17). This is explained further at paras 22.35–22.51 below.
6) No refusals requirement: ie there must be no valid advance decision that applies to some or all of the relevant treatment; or the proposed treatment must not be in conflict with a valid decision (ie a decision within the scope of their authority) of a donee of a lasting power of attorney (LPA) or a deputy (paras 18–20).

22.23   All the requirements must be assessed. The mental health assessment and best interests assessment must be done by different people: MCA 2005 Sch A1 para 129(5). 'Best interests assessors' are required to carry out the best interests requirement.

22.24   Paragraph 50 provides that the supervisory body must give a standard authorisation if all assessments are positive ie conclude P meets relevant requirement. However, this should not be regarded merely as a need for the supervisory body to tick the boxes. This was considered in *Hillingdon LBC v Neary*:[13]

> The granting of DOL standard authorisations is a matter for the local authority in its role as a supervisory body. The responsibilities of a supervisory body, correctly understood, require it to scrutinise the

13 [2011] EWHC 1377, [2011] COPLR Con Vol 623 para 33.

assessment it receives with independence and a degree of care that is appropriate to the seriousness of the decision and to the circumstances of the individual case that are or should be known to it. Where, as here, a supervisory body grants authorisations on the basis of perfunctory scrutiny of superficial best interests assessments, it cannot expect the authorisations to be legally valid.

22.25   Paragraph 139 provides that the supervisory body must appoint a 'relevant person's representative' (RPR) as soon as possible after an authorisation is granted. (P must also be represented during the assessment process by an independent mental capacity advocate (IMCA) if no other appropriate person, MCA 2005 s39A.)

22.26   This important task should be carried out in accordance with the regulations which govern it.[14] Regulation 3 excludes certain persons from appointment as an RPR (for example, those under 18 or with financial interests in the managing authority. If the best interests assessor considers that P has capacity to choose an RPR, P should be allowed to do so.[15] If P lacks capacity to select an RPR, but has a deputy or donee with appropriate authority to select an RPR, then the donee or deputy may select the RPR (and can select himself or herself).[16] If P lacks capacity to select an RPR, or chooses not to do so, and either has no deputy or donee, or has a deputy or donee who chooses not to appoint an RPR, then the best interests assessor may select one of P's family members, friends or carers provided that there is no objection to this from P or from any donee or deputy and the person is eligible to be an RPR.[17] The supervisory body must follow the best interests assessor's recommendations.[18] If the best interests assessor does not represent an RPR, then the supervisory body must select a professional RPR who fulfils criteria set out in regulation 9.[19] It should be

---

14 Mental Capacity (Deprivation of Liberty: Appointment of Relevant Person's Representative) Regulations 2008 SI No 1315 (England).

15 Mental Capacity (Deprivation of Liberty: Appointment of Relevant Person's Representative) Regulations 2008 regs 4 and 5.

16 Mental Capacity (Deprivation of Liberty: Appointment of Relevant Person's Representative) Regulations 2008 reg 6.

17 Mental Capacity (Deprivation of Liberty: Appointment of Relevant Person's Representative) Regulations 2008 regs 6 and 7.

18 Mental Capacity (Deprivation of Liberty: Appointment of Relevant Person's Representative) Regulations 2008 reg 11.

19 In Wales, the procedure is governed by the Mental Capacity (Deprivation of Liberty: Appointment of Relevant Person's Representative) (Wales) Regulations 2009 SI No 266.

noted that that the Code of Practice makes it clear that the RPR need not support the deprivation of liberty.[20]

22.27   MCA 2005 Sch A1 para 140 sets out the role of the RPR which is to maintain contact with relevant person, represent and support them in matters related to or connected with this schedule.

22.28   A managing authority can grant an urgent authorisation when it is required to make a request for a standard authorisation but there is an urgent need for the person to be a detained resident: para 76.

22.29   It is important to recognise that an authorisation merely regulates the care and treatment of a person lacking capacity where they are deprived of their liberty in a placement. It does not do anything else, and in particular it cannot be used to resolve disputes about P's residence, as the cases below demonstrate.

22.30   In *Hillingdon LBC v Neary*[21] Mr Justice Peter Jackson commented that DOLS 'not to be used by a local authority as a means of getting its own way on the question of whether it is in the person's best interests to be in the place at all' (para 33).

22.31   In *C v Blackburn with Darwen Borough Council*[22] the same judge said that it was: 'not appropriate for genuinely contested issues about residence of a resisting incapacitated person' to be dealt with via DOLS or guardianship regime.

22.32   The impact of these two cases is that if a local authority or a trust consider that a change in residence is in the best interests of a person who lacks capacity to decide where to live ('P'), then they cannot simply rely on DOLS to override objections either by P or P's family or carers. The question of the person's residence must be determined by the Court of Protection. If the court determines that the change in residence is in P's best interests, then an authorisation under DOLS may be used to authorise any deprivation of P's liberty that may result.

22.33   As we have seen DOLS can only be used in hospitals or registered care homes. If it is necessary to deprive a person lacking capacity to make decisions about residence of their liberty in their best interests another setting such as supported living an application must be made to the Court of Protection by the care provider or the relevant public body (local authority or Trust). As long as the person concerned is not ineligible then the Court can make an order under MCA 2005 s16(2)(a) which can specifically authorise the deprivation

20 DOLS Code of Practice para 7.17.
21 [2011] EWHC 1377 (COP), [2011] COPLR Con Vol 632.
22 [2011] EWHC 3321 (COP), [2012] COPLR 350.

of P's liberty. Such orders should be reviewed by the Court, usually annually. See *Salford City Council v GJ, NJ and BJ*.[23] Echoing a recommendation made by the House of Lords Select Committee that conducted post-legislative scrutiny of the MCA 2005,[24] Lady Hale noted in *Cheshire West* that the DOLS regime 'could in due course be simplified and extended to placements outside hospitals and care homes'.[25] In its response to the House of Lords Select Committee Report[26] the government said it had asked the Law Commission to consider both issues.

22.34   Non-secure children's homes and residential special schools are not entitled to deprive children or young people of their liberty as this would conflict with their governing regulations. The Court of Protection has no power to authorise breaches of the regulations and therefore such establishments may not apply to the court for authority to deprive child residents of their liberty.[27] For the same reasons, orders and declarations under the inherent jurisdiction could not be made either.

The interface between MHA 1983 and DOLS

22.35   One of the mandatory requirements for a standard authorisation is that the patient is not 'ineligible' to be detained under DOLS. MCA 2005 Sch 1A aims to explain this criteria and how the MCA 2005 and the MHA 1983 work together. A detailed description of this topic is outside the scope of this work. It is important to be aware, however, that if P is ineligible for detention under DOLS, the Court of Protection cannot make an order depriving P of their liberty. In such cases it may be possible for the court to deprive P of their liberty using the inherent jurisdiction: see *An NHS Trust v Dr A*.[28]

22.36   The table below is the starting point for considering whether P is ineligible or not.

23 [2008] EWHC 1097 Fam, [2008] 2 FLR 1295.

24 *Mental Capacity Act 2005: post-legislative scrutiny* HL Paper 139, March 2014; available at: www.publications.parliament.uk/pa/ld201314/ldselect/ldmentalcap/139/139.pdf.

25 *Cheshire West* at para 57.

26 'Valuing every voice, respecting every right', June 2014, Cm 8884.

27 *Deprivation of liberty – guidance for providers of children's homes and residential special schools*, President of the Court of Protection and Ofsted, February 2014; available at: www.ofsted.gov.uk/resources/deprivation-of-liberty-guidance-for-providers-of-childrens-homes-and-residential-special-schools.

28 [2013] EWHC 2442 (COP), [2013] COPLR 605.

MCA 2005 Sch 1A para 2		
	Status of P	**Determination of ineligibility**
Case A	P is– (a) subject to the hospital treatment regime, and (b) detained in a hospital under that regime.	P is ineligible.
Case B	P is– (a) subject to the hospital treatment regime, but (b) not detained in a hospital under that regime.	See paragraphs 3 and 4.
Case C	P is subject to the community treatment regime.	See paragraphs 3 and 4.
Case D	P is subject to the guardianship regime.	See paragraphs 3 and 5.
Case E	P is– (a) within the scope of the Mental Health Act, but (b) not subject to any of the mental health regimes.	See paragraph 5.

22.37   Case A is on the face of it, straightforward. Being 'subject to the hospital regime' means that P is the subject of an order any of the following sections of the MHA: ss2, 3, 4, 35, 36, 37, 38, 44, 45A, 47, 48 or 51. It does not therefore include patients subject to community treatment orders (CTOs) or guardianship. To fall within case A, P must also be detained under that regime.

22.38   Case B applies to those who are subject to the hospital regime. As with case A it applies to those in respect of whom an order has been made under any of the following sections of the MHA: ss2, 3, 4, 35, 36, 37, 38, 44, 45A, 47, 48 or 51. As with case those under CTOS or guardianship are excluded. However, case B applies to those who are not detained under that regime. So it would apply to those who are on section 17 leave or section 73 conditional discharges.

22.39   Schedule 1A does not provide that all those on section 17 leave or conditional discharges are ineligible to be deprived of their liberty. There are two further points to be considered, both of these are linked to the reason for the proposed authorisation.

- The first is whether the 'authorised course of action' conflicts with a requirement that P is already subject to, because of the relevant 'mental health regime'.
- The second is whether the relevant treatment consists in whole or in part of medical treatment for mental disorder.

22.40   These two concepts recur in other cases within the schedule. The authorised course of action means, in essence, the proposed plan for P which will involve deprivation of their liberty. This could be declarations about where P should live and about how their care will be delivered, which have been made by the court. Or it could mean accommodation of P in a care home under Schedule A1, if the authorisation is granted.

22.41   The 'mental health regime' means either the hospital, guardianship or community treatment regime which P is subject to. A requirement under this regime could include a condition as to where P is to reside.

22.42   The relevant care or treatment needs to be considered. P will be ineligible to be detained using DOLS if the care and treatment that the DOLS would authorise is in whole or in part medical treatment for mental disorder in hospital.

22.43   Case C concerns patients described as 'subject to the community treatment regime'. A patient who is under a CTO pursuant to MHA s17A (or any other England and Wales enactment which has the same effect) is 'subject to the community treatment regime'. As with Case B, it is necessary to consider the 'authorised course of action' and whether it conflicts with any conditions attached to the CTO. If there is a conflict, then P is ineligible to be deprived of their liberty using DOLS of an order of the Court of Protection. P would also be ineligible if either the standard authorisation or the Court order would authorise – in whole or in part – medical treatment in hospital for mental disorder.

22.44   Case D applies to patients who are 'subject to the guardianship regime' which means that they are under a guardianship order pursuant to MHA s7 or s37. They can be subject to both a guardianship order and a DOLS authorisation, provided the requirements of each do not conflict with each other . However, they will be ineligible if all of the following further conditions apply:

- The first condition is that the standard authorisation (or the order of the court) authorises P to be a 'mental health patient', defined as 'a person being accommodated in hospital for the purpose of being given medical treatment for mental disorder'.

- The second condition is that P objects to being a mental health patient, or to some or all of the mental health treatment. This is ascertained by having regard to all the circumstances including P's behaviour, wishes and feelings, and views, beliefs and values.
- The third condition is that no donee or deputy has made a valid decision to consent to each matter to which P objects.

22.45   This places patients under guardianship in a different position to those on CTOs, section 17 leave or conditional discharges. We have seen that DOLS cannot be used to administer inpatient treatment for mental disorder for the latter three categories. But a patient who is under a guardianship could be admitted to hospital for medical treatment for mental disorder as long as P does not object or, if they do object, a deputy or donee of an LPA has agreed on P's behalf.

22.46   Case E relates to patients who are not subject to any orders of any sort under the MHA, but is 'within the scope of the Mental Health Act'. This is one of the most troublesome definitions in MCA 2005 Sch 1A.

22.47   It is useful to consider the purpose of Case E, and this was set out by the Department of Health in a letter referred to in *DN v Northumberland and Wear NHS Foundation Trust*.[29] The following passage is relevant:

> The Government's policy intention was that people who lack capacity to consent to being admitted to hospital, but who are clearly objecting to it, should generally be treated like people who have capacity and are refusing to consent to mental health treatment. If it is considered necessary to detain them in hospital, and they would have been detained under the MHA if they had the capacity to refuse treatment, then as a matter of policy it was thought right that the MHA should be used in preference to the MCA

22.48   The question of how decision-makers should approach the possibility of treatment under the MCA 2005 or MHA 1983 was considered by the Upper Tribunal in a judgment by Charles J in *AM v South London and the Maudsley NHS Foundation Trust and the Secretary of State for Health*.[30]

22.49   AM argued that she should be discharged from detention under section 2 by a Tribunal and her treatment in hospital should be continued using the Deprivation of Liberty Safeguards.

22.50   The judge noted that in bringing in the DOLS, Parliament must have intended to provide an alternative to the MHA to authorise the

29   [2011] UKUT 327 (AAC), [2011] MHLR 249.
30   [2013] UKUT 365 (AAC), [2013] COPLR 510.

detention of an incapacitated person, and that this must have been intended to include occasions where such a person would be detained using DOLS in hospital for mental disorder. Decision-makers under the MHA 1983 (which would include approved mental health professionals (AMHPs) and also tribunals) therefore needed to consider the availability of treatment authorised by DOLS.

22.51   In essence, the process of reasoning which the judge considered to be required was:

- Is admission to hospital required?
- Will P be a mental health patient, and if so does P object to all or part of the relevant treatment? If so, P is ineligible for DOLS, and the MHA 1983 must be used.
- Does the relevant person have capacity to consent to admission to hospital?
- Can the hospital rely on the provisions of the MCA 2005 to assess and treat the person lawfully? This requires consideration of the likelihood of the person remaining compliant with their treatment (and therefore remain eligible to be deprived of their liberty using DOLS); and also whether there is a risk that cannot sensibly be ignored that the treatment regime will amount to a deprivation of liberty.
- How should the existence of a choice between reliance on the MHA and the MCA/DOLS be taken into account? This involves the relevant decision-maker taking a fact-sensitive approach to try to identify the least restrictive way of best achieving the proposed assessment or treatment. DOLS will not always be less restrictive than the MHA 1983, but may carry less stigma in the eyes of some. An AMHP or a tribunal cannot compel a managing authority to apply for an authorisation or a supervisory body to grant one, so the AMHP or tribunal needs to know whether those who could implement the MCA/DOLS regime are in fact prepared to do so. Charles J was at pains to emphasise that the two schemes (MHA 1983 and MCA/DOLS) are not mutually exclusive. The question of which regime has primacy over the other in a given case will depend on the circumstances of that case.

Challenging an authorisation

22.52 The supervisory body may carry out a review of a standard authorisation at any time. The supervisory body must carry out a review of a standard authorisation if requested by an eligible person.[31] An 'eligible person' means P, the RPR or the managing authority.[32] There is no equivalent procedure for urgent authorisations.

22.53 There is no procedure for an automatic referral to the court but an application to the Court of Protection can be made and MCA 2005 s21A gives the court wide powers including terminating or varying an authorisation if an application is made.

MCA 2005 s21A

22.54 It is important to be aware of the breadth of the jurisdiction of s21A. The section is set out in full below.

> 21A(1) This section applies if either of the following has been given under Schedule A1–
>   (a) a standard authorisation;
>   (b) an urgent authorisation.
>   (2) Where a standard authorisation has been given, the court may determine any question relating to any of the following matters–
>   (a) whether the relevant person meets one or more of the qualifying requirements;
>   (b) the period during which the standard authorisation is to be in force;
>   (c) the purpose for which the standard authorisation is given;
>   (d) the conditions subject to which the standard authorisation is given.
>   (3) If the court determines any question under subsection (2), the court may make an order–
>   (a) varying or terminating the standard authorisation, or
>   (b) directing the supervisory body to vary or terminate the standard authorisation.
>   (4) Where an urgent authorisation has been given, the court may determine any question relating to any of the following matters–
>   (a) whether the urgent authorisation should have been given;
>   (b) the period during which the urgent authorisation is to be in force;
>   (c) the purpose for which the urgent authorisation is given.
>   (5) Where the court determines any question under subsection (4), the court may make an order–

31 MCA 2005 Sch A1 para 102.
32 MCA 2005 Sch A1 para 102.

(a) varying or terminating the urgent authorisation, or

(b) directing the managing authority of the relevant hospital or care home to vary or terminate the urgent authorisation.

(6) Where the court makes an order under subsection (3) or (5), the court may make an order about a person's liability for any act done in connection with the standard or urgent authorisation before its variation or termination.

(7) An order under subsection (6) may, in particular, exclude a person from liability.

22.55   From this it will be seen that section 21A fulfils the role required by ECHR article 5(4) in providing review of the lawfulness of P's detention by a court. As such, the Court is able to bring an authorisation to an end.[33] However, it goes further by allowing the court to:

- vary an urgent or standard authorisation or direct that such authorisations are varied;

- direct that the relevant authority terminate a standard or urgent authorisation;[34]

- make an order about a person's liability 'for any act done in connection with the standard or urgent authorisation' which can include excluding a person from liability.[35] This power only arises when the court either varies, or terminates an authorisation, or directs that it is varied or terminated.[36]

22.56   These powers are in contrast with the more limited powers available to Mental Health Tribunals, and it is important to consider all the potential remedies available under section 21A before making an application. All the remedies sought ideally should be pleaded in the application; but there is no bar on making a further application during the course of the proceedings if grounds for further challenges emerge during the course of the proceedings.

22.57   Any person can apply for permission to bring an application under MCA 2005 s21A, as is the case with any other application. However P does not need to apply for permission to bring an application and nor does P's RPR.[37] It is important not to lose sight of the distinction. P has a right to apply to the court under section 21A in their own right, irrespective of whether the RPR supports P's application. Practical questions may arise if P wishes to challenge the authorisation and

33 MCA 2005 s21A(3)(a), (5)(a) (standard and urgent authorisations respectively).

34 MCA 2005 s21A(3)(b), (5)(b) (standard and urgent authorisations respectively).

35 MCA 2005 ss21A (6), (7).

36 MCA 2005 s21A(6).

37 MCA 2005 s50(1), (1A).

the RPR is reluctant to do so and these are considered in para 22.75 below.

Application or review?

22.58   Paragraph 3 above briefly describes the process of a review under Part 8 of Schedule A1 to the MCA 2005. There is no requirement to request a review before making an application to the court under MCA 2005 s21A. The Part 8 review process is internal and does not provide P with independent scrutiny of whether the criteria for the authorisation are met. Nor does the review process include the considerations of liability available under section 21A(6) and (7) (see above para 22.55). The review process does not and is not intended to meet the requirements of ECHR article 5(4), namely the entitlement of a detained person 'to take proceedings by which the lawfulness of his detention shall be decided speedily by a court and his release ordered if the detention is not lawful'.

22.59   Practitioners should seek to resolve issues without litigation if at all possible. This stems from the overriding objective and the parties' duty to assist the court in furthering the overriding objective.[38] It would usually be appropriate to advise the supervisory body of the issues taken with the authorisation before making an application under section 21A. But applicants are not required to seek a review before commencing proceedings under section 21A and in our view a decision to proceed directly to an application under section 21A, without requesting a review first, should not attract criticism.

22.60   There will, however, be some cases where practitioners may wish to advise requesting a review before proceeding to court. In the authors' view, the factors below point to the use of the review process first:

- There is reason to believe, from correspondence or initial discussion with the supervisory body or their advisers, that there is a realistic possibility that agreement to terminate or vary the authorisation will be reached.
- The practitioner is advising a third party who is not P's RPR and is unlikely to be appointed as P's litigation friend, and that third party is not financially eligible for legal aid.
- In both cases, there is no risk that P will suffer serious distress and/or harm if the status quo continues pending the review.

38 COPR rr3 and 4.

Making an application

22.61 The procedure for making an application is not complex. Guidance is provided in Practice Direction (PD) 10AA. It is essential for practitioners to be familiar with this practice direction and to follow the procedure it sets out to ensure that the application is treated with the appropriate urgency.

22.62 There is a designated team to deal with DOLS applications. The team is also known as the Technical Specialist Team. Initial telephone contact with the court is made via a single telephone number, which will be answered by a member of the Court Enquiries Service. The court advises that practitioners should then ask for the Technical Team (rather than the DOLS team) to assist in ensuring the call is directed to the right people straightaway. The details set out in the practice direction at paras 4–6 precede the move by the Court of Protection to First Avenue House, and these paragraphs now should read as follows:

> 4. Contact details for the DoLs team are:
>
> Urgent Attn of the Technical Specialists Team
> Court of Protection
> PO Box 70185
> First Avenue House
> 42–49 High Holborn
> London WC1A 9JA
>
> DX 160013 Kingsway 7
>
> Tel: 0300 456 4600
> Fax: 020 7071 5718
> E-mail: courtofprotectionenquiries@hmcts.gsi.gov.uk
>
> 5. The court office is open for personal attendance between the hours of 10 a.m. to 4.00 p.m. on working days. The DoL team can receive telephone calls and faxes between the same hours. Faxes transmitted after 4.00 p.m. will be dealt with the next working day.
>
> 6. When in an emergency it is necessary to make a telephone application to a judge outside normal court hours, the security office at the Royal Courts of Justice should be contacted on 020 7947 6000. The security officer should be informed of the nature of the case. In the Family Division, the out-of-hours application procedure involves the judge being contacted through a Family Division duty officer, and the RCJ security officer will need to contact the duty officer and not the judge's clerk or the judge.

22.63 There is more information about urgent applications in chapter 13 above.

22.64   Practitioners will see from the practice direction that they are asked to contact the Technical Specialists Team as soon as they know that an application is likely to be issued.[39] It is important for practitioners to note that they can and should alert the Technical Specialists Team in the event of other very urgent matters, that are not applications under section 21A but which may relate to deprivation of liberty and require urgent attention.

22.65   Applications made under section 21A should be made on the forms that have been specially designed for this purpose, and the benefit of these is that they are easily distinguished from other applications and can be dealt with by the right team urgently. If at all possible, it is very helpful to have electronic copies as part of a case management system allowing details to be inputted electronically. The forms are:

- Form DLA – Deprivation of Liberty Application form. This provides a comprehensive 'prompt' to the practitioner to ensure that all the relevant issues are addressed. Section 2 allows information to be added about interested parties. This term is not used in the rules (see further para 12.13). Inclusion in this section does not result automatically in the person or body named as interested party being joined as a party, as they have not been named as a respondent. If served with the application, however, the proposed interested party will be bound by orders of the court as it they were a party.[40] Section 3 requires consideration of whether an interim application is being made and asks whether other applications are to be made. Section 4 asks for a detailed statement of grounds and in most cases it will be advisable to prepare this – or instruct counsel or a Higher Rights Advocate – as a separate document. It should be noted that that section requires a statement of facts relied on. It is suggested that Sections 8 and 5 could conveniently be combined in the same document. Section 5 asks the applicant to identify other 'issues that will arise for determination in respect of the relevant person' and any other applications that have been made or that the applicant intends to make. These might include broader welfare questions such as an application for a declaration as to P's best interests in terms of residence or contact. Section 6 seeks information about other pending applications, so that the court can consider whether these should be linked. In addition to outstanding welfare applications, practitioners should check

---

39   PD 10AA paras 2–3.
40   COPR rr73(1), 74. See also chapter 8.

whether they are aware of any outstanding property and affairs applications. Section 10 provides a helpful checklist.

- Form DLB is a declaration of exceptional urgency to be used to explain if it is necessary for the court's usual timetable to be abridged.
- Form DLC is to be used when the applicant requires permission from the court. This form will therefore be used for anyone other than P or P's RPR (or lawyers instructed by them). Practitioners should address the factors set out in MCA 2005 s50 which the court will consider when deciding whether to grant permission. These are briefly: the applicant's connection with P, the reasons for the application; the potential benefit to P and whether this could be achieved in any other way.[41]

22.66   It should be noted that the practice direction anticipates that the above forms will be served at the same time that they are lodged with the court.[42] In addition to the forms a fee of £410 is payable (see appendix G below). This can be claimed as a disbursement on the applicant's legal aid certificate.

22.67   In addition to the forms which must be completed, it will be seen that form DLA lists a number of supporting documents which might be filed at court with the forms. These include copies of the author-isation and assessments, a witness statement on form COP24, a copy of the legal aid certificate if any, copies of relevant statutory mate-rial, and a draft order which if possible should also be provided elec-tronically on disk.[43] It is our advice to provide as much information as possible, given that the first order will be made on the basis of the information in the papers alone.[44] Witness statements should be carefully prepared. Although significant information can be provided by means of the statement of facts and grounds, this is no substitute for witness evidence in which the applicant is able to set out in full their perspective as well as state the relevant facts. Considerable time will be saved if the documents are paginated and indexed. A pagin-ated indexed bundle is required for the first hearing in any event.[45]

22.68   Once the documents are received by the court, the practice direc-tion provides that steps will immediately be taken to ensure the papers are considered by a judge who will make a first order. The

---

41 MCA 2005 s50(3).
42 PD 10AA para 9.
43 PD 10AA para 14.
44 PD 10AA para 19.
45 PD 10AA para 25.

applicant is responsible for following up any directions made and is also responsible for service of the order and any other relevant papers that have not already been served, together with form DLE (acknowledgement of service). The applicant must file form DLD (certificate of service).

22.69 The first attended hearing should be listed within five working days of the judge's first order (ie, the date of issue of the application).[46] If the applicant considers this will be too late, this should be made clear on form DLB (see para 22.65 above). Consideration should be given to the directions which will be sought at that hearing. For example, are there any outstanding issues about the appointment of a litigation friend?[47] Is expert evidence required? Given the pressure of time in section 21A appeals, an application for permission to instruct an expert is more likely to be granted if an expert has already been identified and his or her timetable ascertained in advance of the hearing.

22.70 There will be some cases where it is possible to determine the challenge to the authorisation at the first hearing. However, in the majority of cases further evidence will be needed and therefore the court will consider how to regulate the intervening period, if P is to continue to be deprived of their liberty while the case continues In *Re HA*[48] Charles J indicated that, rather than allow the standard authorisation to continue, the court should 'hold the ring' and authorise the continued deprivation of liberty itself by making orders under MCA 2005 s16. Charles J reiterated this approach in *Re UF*[49] and the funding implications of that case are discussed in chapter 6. The solution Charles J arrived at in *UF* was to exercise his powers under section 21A(3) to vary the standard authorisation by extending it for a period of six months, and to exclude the supervisory body from liability during that period. The rationale behind taking this course rather than allowing the standard authorisation to run its usual course was that it is the court's role to take control of the interim position and thus avoid unnecessary responsibilities for the decision-makers and assessors of the supervisory body. The Ministry of Justice and Legal Aid Agency (LAA) agreed that the approach above would not be seen as a contrivance and that non-means-tested legal aid should continue to be available to P and the RPR. The position would be different

---

46 PD 10AA para 23.

47 See chapter 12 on litigation friends.

48 [2012] EWHC 1068 (COP), [2012] COPLR 534.

49 [2013] EWHC 4289 (COP), [2014] COPLR 93; see also chapter 5.

however were the standard authorisation to be terminated at the first hearing, on the basis that P will no longer be deprived of their liberty (for example, because they are going to their home for a trial period) and the proceedings to continue either to consider liability for the earlier deprivation of liberty, or to consider P's best interests under MCA 2005 s16.

Particular issues arising in DOLS cases

Getting the case to court

22.71   *UF* (discussed above) highlighted a problem which is often experienced in Court of Protection cases generally, namely the difficulties that can arise in simply getting the case before the court in the first place. In this case, UF had been deprived of her liberty at a care home under a standard authorisation, and an RPR had been appointed. UF's RPR supported the deprivation of liberty, as did all her family save AF, one of UF's daughters, who considered her mother to be very unhappy at the care home, to the point that AF felt her mother's life was endangered.

22.72   AF could have made the application herself, but as Charles J noted there was 'force in seeing whether an application should be made by or on behalf of P'.[50] It was clear that the RPR was unlikely to agree to commence proceedings. The advice given to AF by her 'experienced solicitor'[51] was for AF to apply under MCA 2005 s21A as UF's litigation friend. This was a pragmatic solution which ensured that the case was brought before the court, although Charles J ultimately concluded that AF's understandable emotional involvement in the case made it inappropriate for her to continue as litigation friend.

22.73   Practitioners advising family members or carers concerned about a standard authorisation may wish to check that an RPR has been appointed (as this is sometimes overlooked) and whether the guidance in the DOLS Code of Practice and the requirements of the regulations as set out in para 22.26 have been followed. Practitioners should also seek to ascertain whether the RPR is willing to challenge the authorisation. If they are not, however they and the family member or carer are able to provide evidence suggesting that P objects to their placement, then the best solution may be for the

---

50   *Re UF* para 13.
51   Richard Charlton, Chair of the Mental Health Lawyers Association.

family member or carer to facilitate an application by acting as P's litigation friend. If this happens, the proposed litigation friend can apply for non-means tested legal aid on P's behalf. If this course of action is adopted, it must be borne in mind that the court may well consider at a later date that an alternative litigation friend should be appointed.[52]

22.74   In *MH v UK*[53] the ECtHR held that MH's article 5 rights had been breached by her detention under MHA 1983 s2. MH lacked capacity to apply to the tribunal and, following a barring order, her mother and nearest relative could not apply to the tribunal. There was no mechanism whereby MH could exercise her article 5(4) rights. In a passage that has significance for applications under section 21A the court commented:[54]

> That being said, the Court has accepted that with regard to persons who, on account of their mental disabilities, are not fully capable of acting for themselves, there is no doubt that special procedural safeguards may be called for (see, among other authorities, *Winterwerp*, cited above, § 60; see also the United Nations Convention on the Rights of Persons with Disabilities, cited at paragraphs 49–50 above). When a mental patient is not fully capable of acting for herself on account of her mental disabilities, by definition the compensatory safeguards to which the State might have recourse in order to remove the legal or practical obstacles barring such a person from being able to benefit from the procedural guarantee afforded by Article 5 § 4 may well include empowering or even requiring some other person or authority to act on the patient's behalf in that regard.

22.75   In the context of MCA 2005 s21A the 'other person or body' could be either the RPR or another person with a relationship with P who could obtain advice and take steps to bring the matter before the court on P's behalf. The Care Quality Commission's (CQC) report on DOLS in 2012/13 found evidence that some people were not able to exercise their legal rights or challenge their detention.[55]

52 See also chapter 12.

53 *MH v UK* (App No 1157/06).

54 At para 93.

55 *Monitoring the use of the Mental Capacity Act deprivation of liberty safeguards in 2012/13*, available at: www.cqc.org.uk/sites/default/files/media/documents/ dols_2014.pdf.

How are P's views to be put before the court?

22.76   The vital importance of ensuring that P's views are put before the court is discussed in chapter 12. In a number of recent cases, judges in the Court of Protection have heard directly from P: see, for example, *KK v STCC*,[56] *Re SB*,[57] *Re M*[58] and *Westminster City Council v Sykes*.[59] In these cases, hearing P's views directly has been of significant assistance to the court. In some of these cases, P's circumstances have necessitated the judge visiting P. All cases in the Court of Protection are fact-sensitive, but DOLS cases perhaps particularly turn on P's perception of his or her circumstances. The more direct the judge's knowledge of these circumstances and their impact on P, the better equipped the judge may be in carrying out the delicate balance required to decide these cases. Consideration should therefore be given at an early stage either to arranging for P to attend court, or requesting that the trial judge visit P.

The development of the case

22.77   While some DOLS cases will turn on the level of restrictions to which P is subject, the majority will also involve a dispute about P's best interests as regards residence. The decision in *Hillingdon LBC v Neary*[60] makes it clear that a supervisory body has the responsibility of bringing genuine residence disputes before the court by making an application under MCA 2005 s16. In such cases, as we have seen in chapter 5, any party applying for legal aid will need to satisfy the means test. Similarly if – for example – P is placed in a care setting and is made subject to a standard authorisation, appeals against it, successfully secures the termination of the authorisation at an interim hearing and then goes home on a trial basis, the case will no longer be considered a section 21A appeal for the purpose of legal aid. If this happens, then practitioners have a responsibility to inform the LAA of the change in circumstances and need to have advised their clients that there cannot be a guarantee that non-means tested legal aid will remain available for the duration of the case.

56 [2012] EWHC 2136 (COP), [2012] COPLR 627.
57 *Re SB (a patient: capacity to consent to termination)* [2013] EWHC 1417 (COP), [2013] COPLR 445.
58 *Re M (best interests: deprivation of liberty)* [2013] EWHC 3456 (COP), [2014] COPLR 35.
59 [2014] EWHC B9 (COP).
60 [2011] EWHC 1377 (COP), [2011] COPLR Con Vol 632.

22.78   In *Re HA*[61] Charles J provided guidance as to how the key issue of contested residence which underpinned the section 21A appeal he was hearing should be resolved speedily. He considered that the key to this was an investigation of the 'pragmatically available options' which would be achieved in that case through the local authority identifying the potential alternatives (for example, maintaining the status quo, a move to another provider or a home placement) and informing the court and parties how these could be provided and funded.

The future

22.79 In January 2014 Sir James Munby, President of the Court of Protection, provided guidance on the publication of judgments[62] and set out types of cases where judges should normally permit anonymised judgments to be published. These include 'any application for a declaration or order involving a deprivation or possible deprivation of liberty' (para 17(ii)). It is therefore likely that there will be an increasing number of reported judgments.

22.80   Some recent judgments have been striking in their willingness to promote P's autonomy over safety – see, in particular, *Re M*[63] and *Westminster City Council v Sykes*.[64]

22.81   It should be noted that the House of Lords Select Committee that conducted post-legislative scrutiny of the MCA 2005,[65] responding to almost unanimous evidence to it as to the difficulties experienced with the operation of MCA 2005 Sch A1, was extremely critical of the DOLS regime and recommended 'a comprehensive review of the Deprivation of Liberty Safeguards with a view to replacing them with provisions that are compatible in style and ethos to the rest of the Mental Capacity Act'.[66]

22.82   The government responded to the Select Committee's report on 10 June 2014, with 'Valuing every voice, respecting every right'.[67] By this point some of the implications of the judgment of the Supreme

---

61 [2012] EWHC 1068, [2012] COPLR 534.
62 *Practice Guidance (Transparency in the Court Of Protection)* [2014] EWHC B2 (COP), discussed further in chapter 16.
63 [2013] EWHC 3456 (COP), [2014] COPLR 35.
64 [2014] EWHC B9 (COP), (2014) 17 CCLR 139.
65 *Mental Capacity Act 2005: post-legislative scrutiny* HL Paper 139.
66 Summary, p2.
67 'Valuing every voice, respecting every right', June 2014, Cm 8884.

Court in *Cheshire West* were being felt with an exponential increase in DOLS applications and applications under MCA 2005 s16 to authorise deprivations of liberty in supported living placements and other settings where DOLS did not apply. The government agreed that the implementation had not been at the expected level but did not accept that the legislation was fundamentally flawed.

22.83   The government has asked the Law Commission to undertake a review to consult on and potentially draft a new legal framework to authorise 'best interests deprivation of liberty in supported living arrangements', which would be 'firmly rooted in the MCA 2005' and would include wide consultation. At the same time the Law Commission would be asked to consider improvements to the DOLS, with the intention that these are in keeping with the ethos of the MCA 2005, clearly drafted and easily understood, and that they consider how to strengthen the role of the RPR.

Medical treatment cases

Introduction

23.1   Cases involving medical treatment form a distinct sub-set of the cases that are decided by the Court of Protection, and cases involving serious medical treatment have their own dedicated practice direction. This chapter highlights some of the key features of such cases, but it is likely that in such cases specialist advice and representation will be required going beyond the scope of this work.[1]

The scope of the court's jurisdiction

23.2   As set out in chapter 4, the Court of Protection has jurisdiction regarding (among other matters) medical treatment in relation to those aged 16 and above who lack the material decision-capacity. Conventionally, medical treatment cases involving those below the age of 18 have been brought before the High Court for relief under its inherent jurisdiction; however, where a 16- or 17-year-old is considered to lack decision-making capacity, it would be equally possible to bring the case to the Court of Protection. If the concern on the part of the treating clinicians is not that the individual (aged 16 or over) lacks capacity but that they are vulnerable and under the influence of another, then the appropriate route would be, again, to seek relief from the High Court under the inherent jurisdiction.

Serious medical treatment cases: definition

23.3   Practice Direction (PD) 9E makes specific provision for cases involving 'serious medical treatment', defined for this purpose as treatment which involves providing, withdrawing or withholding treatment in circumstances where:

- (if a single treatment is proposed) there is a fine balance between its benefits and burdens and risks;
- (if there is a choice) a decision as to which treatment is finely balanced; or

---

1   More detail about the Mental Capacity Act (MCA) 2005 and the role of the Court of Protection in medical treatment cases can be found in Christopher Johnston et al, *Medical treatment*, 2nd edn, Bloomsbury, 2010.

- the treatment, procedure or investigation would be likely to involve serious consequences for the patient.[2]

23.4 'Serious consequences' are, in turn, defined, as those which could have a serious impact on P, either from the effects of the treatment, procedure or investigation itself or its wider implications. This may include treatments, procedures or investigations which:

- cause, or may cause, serious and prolonged pain, distress or side-effects;
- have potentially major consequences for P; or
- have a serious impact on P's future life choices.

23.5 There is a degree of ambiguity as to whether a treatment itself must be serious, or whether seriousness can emerge solely from the consequences. For instance, there may be some drug treatments which would not, in and of themselves, be regarded as 'serious' but where either administering or withholding them to the particular P in question could give rise to serious consequences. The Rules Review Committee recommended that consideration be given to amending this practice direction so as to make it clear that serious medical treatment can encompass treatment which is not in and of itself serious, but where the consequence of administering/not administering it would be serious.[3] To date, no progress has been made in this regard, but the current President of the Court of Protection, Sir James Munby, has indicated his intention to press ahead with implementing in full the recommendations of the Committee.

23.6 PD 9E sets[4] out certain decisions which should be regarded as serious medical treatment decisions and should be brought to the court. These are:

- decisions about the proposed withholding or withdrawal of artificial nutrition and hydration from a person in a permanent vegetative state or a minimally conscious state;[5]
- cases involving organ or bone marrow donation by a person who lacks capacity to consent; and

---

2 PD 9E para 3.

3 Available at: www.judiciary.gov.uk/Resources/JCO/Documents/Reports/committee-report-court-protection-29072010.pdf.

4 PD 9E para 5.

5 NB, in all such cases, reference must now be made to the guidelines issued by the Royal College of Physicians in December 2013 on *Prolonged disorders of consciousness*, available at: www.rcplondon.ac.uk/prolonged-disorders-consciousness-national-clinical-guidelines.

- cases involving non-therapeutic sterilisation of a person who lacks capacity to consent.[6]

23.7   The word 'should' in PD 9E might on its face appear ambiguous; it is, though, clear that cases in these three categories *must* be brought to court.[7]

23.8   PD 9E also gives a non-exhaustive list of examples of other decisions which should be considered serious medical treatment.[8] It does not state expressly that such decisions should be brought to court. However, case-law makes clear that at least two categories of case must come to court:

- In respect of a proposed termination of a pregnancy in relation to a person who lacks capacity to consent to such a procedure, an application must be made where:
  a) there is dispute over capacity;
  b) the patient may regain capacity during her pregnancy;
  c) there is any lack of unanimity;
  d) the procedures under Abortion Act 1967 s1 have not been followed;
  e) the patient or members of her immediate family have opposed a termination; or
  f) there are other exceptional circumstances, including that this may be the patient's last chance to bear a child.[9]
- (It appears) the carrying out of Caesarean section operations on incapacitated patients where any degree of force of restraint is contemplated. This follows the media outcry in the case of the Italian national, Ms Pacchieri, who was detained under the Mental Health Act (MHA) 1983 while temporarily present in England and in respect of whom such an operation was authorised.[10]

23.9   That a case falls within the category of serious medical treatment does not itself mean that it *has* to be brought to court, unless it is one of those falling with the categories set out in the paragraphs above. In some cases, the treatment could potentially be provided in reliance

---

6   See also in this regard *A Local Authority v K and others* [2013] EWHC 242 (COP), [2013] COPLR 194.

7   *W v M and others* [2011] EWHC 2443 (Fam), [2012] COPLR 222 at para 257 per Baker J (in relation to the proposed withdrawing of artificial nutrition and hydration from a person in a minimally conscious state).

8   PD 9E para 6.

9   *D v An NHS Trust (medical treatment: consent)* [2004] 1 FLR 1110; see also *Re P (abortion)* [2013] EWHC 50 (COP), [2013] COPLR 405.

10   *Re AA* [2012] EWHC 4378 (COP).

upon the defence in MCA 2005 s5 on the basis that it is reasonably considered to be in the best interests of the patient. However, the treating NHS trust must, at the very least, consider whether an application to court is necessary if the treatment in question falls within the scope of 'serious medical treatment' as defined in PD 9E, and – we suggest – *must* bring the matter to court in the event of dispute either between the treating clinicians as to either P's capacity or best interests or between the treating clinicians and P's family members,

23.10   The expectation in serious medical treatment cases is that the application will be brought by the organisation providing the treatment to P. If they are not the applicant (which would be unusual), then they should be a respondent.[11] If the question is whether P should be admitted to hospital for purposes of being provided with medical treatment, then one would expect to see the relevant clinical commissioning group (CCG) (as the funding body) making the application, and that the treating hospital would either be a joint applicant or joined as a respondent.

Other medical treatment cases

23.11   Merely because a case involving medical treatment does not fall within the categories of serious medical treatment as defined in PD 9E does not mean that it should not be brought to court if – for instance – there is a serious dispute between those properly concerned with P's wellbeing as to whether the medical treatment should be administered or withheld. An example would be a dispute about the withholding of antibiotics. Such an application would, though, fall to be considered for purposes of case management as akin to a 'standard' welfare application. They are not therefore discussed separately in the majority of the balance of this chapter.

Pre-action steps

23.12   A particular feature of serious medical treatment cases is that P will almost invariably be joined as a party, and the Official Solicitor will almost invariably be invited to and will accept the invitation to act as P's litigation friend (see further para 23.18 below). The Official Solicitor will also almost invariably act both as litigation friend

11 PD 9E para 9.

and solicitor for P – in other words, external solicitors will not be instructed and the Official Solicitor's own lawyers will handle the case from start to finish, instructing counsel if needs be. This means that, wherever possible, it is sensible to ensure that contact is made with the Official Solicitor's office before an application is issued (the contact details are in appendix F below[12]), both to discuss the case in outline and to ensure that the Official Solicitor is in a position to respond quickly when the application is issued. The pressure of work upon the Official Solicitor, however, is that the authors' experience is that the Official Solicitor is increasingly reluctant to become formally involved before an application is lodged.

Urgent applications

23.13   The courts are well used to dealing with urgent medical treatment applications, including those that arise out of normal court hours. The procedures in relation to urgent applications are discussed at paras 11.60ff, and they will apply equally in medical treatment cases. It is particularly important in such cases that the treating clinicians are available by telephone so that the judge is able to hear from them directly if needs be – which may well entail setting up a conference call if the matter is being heard out of normal court hours.

23.14   It should be noted the Official Solicitor does not operate an out of hours service, so on any application brought out of normal court hours the court will normally strive to make the most limited order possible until such point as the matter can be brought back with the Official Solicitor present. The same will also generally apply if the urgency of the application has meant that the Official Solicitor has been unable to attend,[13] although in the case of a decision that simply cannot wait, the court will make the decision on the spot.[14]

23.15   The general rule in medical treatment cases is that it is better to bring the application sooner rather than later so that all the necessary inquiries can be made and information obtained to allow the court to reach a proper conclusion as to where P's best interests lie. It should be noted, however, that a somewhat unfortunate consequence of

---

12   The address details in PD 9E para 8 are incorrect – in particular, the telephone number is now 020 3681 2751.

13   For a good example, see *Nottinghamshire Healthcare NHS Trust v RC* [2014] EWHC 1136 (COP).

14   See *Newcastle-upon-Tyne Hospitals Foundation Trust v LM* [2014] EWHC 454 (COP).

the decision in *Aintree University Hospitals NHS Trust v James*[15] is a lack of clarity as to exactly when applications should be brought in respect of the withholding of life-sustaining treatment. Lady Hale, giving the judgment of the Supreme Court noted that, if an application is brought too early, then there is a risk that that the court may be unable to say that when the treatments are needed that they will not be in the best interests of the patient.[16] The logical corollary of this is that some decisions may be delayed – and that a sudden clinical deterioration may then require an urgent application to be brought.[17]

Allocation

23.16   Where the application relates to the lawfulness of withholding or withdrawing artificial nutrition and hydration from a person in a permanent vegetative state or a minimally conscious state or a minimally conscious state, or it is a case involving an ethical dilemma in an untested area, then the whole proceedings (including the permission stage and the giving of any directions) must be conducted by the President or a judge nominated by the President.[18]

23.17   All other serious medical treatment cases or cases in which a declaration of incompatibility is sought pursuant to Human Rights Act (HRA) 1998 s4 must be conducted by the President, the Chancellor or a High Court judge nominated to sit as a Court of Protection judge.[19]

Case management

23.18   Serious medical treatment cases will be managed according to the same principles as other cases before the Court of Protection, but the following distinctive features should be noted:

- As noted above, P will almost invariably be joined as a party and the Official Solicitor be appointed to act as P's litigation friend.

15 [2013] UKSC 67, (2013) 16 CCLR 554, [2013] COPLR 492.
16 Para 47.
17 See further in this regard the article by Vikram Sachdeva, Alex Ruck Keene and Victoria Butler-Cole entitled 'The MCA in the Supreme Court – Reflections on *Aintree v James*' [2014] Eld LJ 54.
18 PD 9E para 11.
19 PD 9E para 12.

The Official Solicitor receives sufficient central government funding to conduct (in-house) such proceedings, and is also conventionally awarded half the costs of doing so against the relevant NHS body.[20] The Official Solicitor will often decline to act until an undertaking is given by the relevant NHS body to meet half of his costs.

- Unlike the position that prevails in other proceedings before the Court of Protection, the presumption is that the application will be heard in public with suitable reporting restrictions imposed.[21] This means that it is very likely that the applicant NHS trust will need to apply for a reporting restrictions order under the provisions of Court of Protection Rules (COPR) 2007 SI No 1744 r92(2): see in this regard paras 14.10ff. The courts are increasingly reluctant to grant anonymity to NHS trusts and the treating clinicians, save where this is necessary to protect the identity of P and their place of treatment (it is therefore likely that an NHS trust responsible for more than one hospital will be named as the chances of P being identified would be materially reduced in such a case).

- Unless the urgency of the case makes it impossible, the Official Solicitor will usually wish to obtain independent expert evidence (and will usually seek to do so a joint basis). Questions of expert evidence are addressed further in chapter 13. The courts will place considerable weight upon the evidence of any expert(s) instructed, but – as in all other cases – will exercise independent judgment upon the questions both of P's capacity and best interests. A good example of the latter is *An NHS trust v (1) K (2) Another foundation trust*[22] in which Holman J declined to follow the 'unduly pessimistic' evidence of the independent expert as to the risks to the patient surrounding the operation in question.

- Any decision in a serious medical treatment case (whether or not held in public) will prima facie fall to be published (subject to suitable anonymisation) in line with the President's guidance on *Transparency in the Court of Protection: publication of judgments*.[23]

---

20 *An NHS Trust v D* [2012] EWHC 886 (COP), [2012] COPLR 499.

21 PD 9E para 16; see also *W v M and others (reporting restrictions order)* [2011] EWHC 1197 (COP), [2011] COPLR Con Vol 1206.

22 [2012] EWHC 2292 (COP), [2012] COPLR 694.

23 [2014] EWHC B2 (COP), [2014] COPLR 78. See also paras 14.32ff.

Declarations

23.19   Serious medical treatment cases are unusual in that the applicant
(usually the treating NHS Trust) does not generally seek decisions
from the court,[24] but rather declarations as to whether a proposed
course of action is lawful.[25] PD 9E gives examples of the wording
that should be adopted in respect of particular categories of cases.[26]
It is particularly important to be precise. In *Aintree*, for instance, the
NHS trust in question made an application for a declaration that it
would be lawful to withhold three types of life-sustaining treatment
from Mr James 'in the event of a clinical deterioration'. As Lady Hale
noted, this actually meant 'should his condition deteriorate that they
[ie the treatments] become necessary', and that it would have been
helpful to say so.

23.20   The courts have also shown themselves to be careful to maintain
a distinct line between matters in respect of which they can properly
make declarations under the MCA 2005 and those matters which
fall within the scope of the ethical and clinical obligations owed by
the treating doctors. In *A NHS Trust v (1) K (2) Another Foundation
Trust*,[27] for instance, Holman J authorised the sedation of a woman
who needed a hysterectomy before she was to be informed that it was
proposed to carry out the proposed surgery so as to reduce the risk
that she would be non-compliant.[28] Holman J noted, however, that
'an ethical issue may arise as to the degree of sedation and whether
the surgeon can ethically proceed to operate unless he has given to
the patient an adequate account of what he proposes to do while she
retains sufficient awareness to hear it and take it in. But that is an
ethical matter for him'.[29]

Is there really a best interests decision to be taken?

23.21   We conclude this chapter by raising a question that is starkly posed
by the decision of the Supreme Court in *Aintree University Hospitals*

---

24   Ie under MCA 2005 s16.
25   Under MCA 2005 s15.
26   PD 9E paras 17 and 18.
27   [2012] EWHC 2292 (COP), [2012] COPLR 694.
28   Relying on *DH NHS Foundation Trust v PS* [2010] EWHC 1217 (Fam), [2010]
COPLR Con Vol 346. Holman J did not authorise restraint to be used on the
patient because of the risk to her given her other medical difficulties.
29   Para 44.

NHS Foundation Trust v James,[30] but which has yet fully to be grappled with by the courts. The Supreme Court emphasised – in our view correctly – that the MCA 2005 is concerned with 'enabling the court to do for the patient what he could do for himself if of full capacity, but it goes no further. On an application under this Act, therefore, the court has no greater powers than the patient would have if he were of full capacity'.[31] The Court of Protection cannot therefore order a doctor to provide a particular treatment to a patient; rather, its task is to 'decide whether a particular treatment is in the best interests of a patient who is incapable of making the decision for himself'.[32]

23.22   In some cases, therefore, the treating clinicians will have concluded that they will not offer specific treatment(s) to the patient (or would wish to withdraw such treatment) because they consider that either offering or continue to offer it would be clinically inappropriate or futile. In such a case, it would be irrelevant that the patient lacks the capacity to consent to the treatment because it would not be offered to them even if they had capacity and were requesting it. In this situation then, assuming (as is not unknown) that no other treating clinician would offer (or continue to offer) such treatment, then there is a good argument that there is, in fact, no best interests decision for the court to take.

23.23   This situation arose in the pre-*Aintree* case of *An NHS Trust v L, FL and TL*[33] in which Moylan J was of the view that there were no treatment options available. He was, however, constrained (with evident unhappiness) to make a best interests decision because none of the parties before him were prepared to submit that such was the case. In a future case, it is quite possible, we suggest, to imagine a situation in which a judge would decline to make a best interests decision.

23.24   We would suggest that, if – on a proper analysis – there is no best interests decision for the Court of Protection to take, then if the NHS trust wishes (quite properly) to have legal 'cover' for its actions, then the proper course of action may well not to be to make an application to the Court of Protection but rather to issue an application in the Queen's Bench Division under Part 8 of the Civil Procedure Rules (CPR) for a declaration that their actions (or potentially proposed

---

30 [2013] UKSC 67, (2013) 16 CCLR 554, [2013] COPLR 492.
31 *Aintree* at para 18 per Lady Hale.
32 *Aintree* at para 18 per Lady Hale.
33 [2013] EWHC 4313 (Fam), [2013] COPLR 558.

omissions) are lawful.[34] There would in such a case be a potential tension with the requirements in PD 9E regarding bringing serious medical treatment cases to the Court of Protection; that having been said, the spirit of the practice direction would be complied with in that the matter would be before a court (even if not the Court of Protection). We anticipate that the implications of PD 9E in this regard will be the subject of further consideration in due course when the COPR and associated practice directions are reviewed. In the meantime, especially in any case where there is a dispute between the treating clinicians and the family members of P in respect of the withholding or withdrawing of the treatment in question, the prudent course of action remains to bring an application for a declaration that it is lawful as being in P's best interests not to (continue) provide the treatment in question because it is futile or not clinically indicated.

---

34 See further Vikram Sachdeva, Alex Ruck Keene and Victoria Butler-Cole, 'The MCA in the Supreme Court – Reflections on *Aintree v James*' [2014] Eld LJ 54.

Safeguarding and the Court of Protection

Introduction[1]

24.1   A significant proportion of the welfare applications made to the Court of Protection are made by local authorities on the basis of concerns that an adult lacking decision-making capacity in one or more domains, either has been subjected to or is at risk of harm. Such applications frequently arise, therefore, in the context of the discharge by the local authority of the obligations that are imposed upon it by various routes to safeguard adults at risk within their area. The overlap between actions taken on the basis of safeguarding obligations and applications before the Court of Protection is one that justifies a specific chapter of its own because of the difficulties that can arise where local authorities are not sufficiently clear as to the specific requirements that arise when matters move from investigation to proceedings before the court.

24.2   This chapter therefore outlines briefly what is meant by safeguarding, by specific reference to the changes to the law in England and Wales in the Care Act 2014. It then highlights how Court of Protection proceedings form an aspect of safeguarding, before making clear the specific steps required when an adult's circumstances move from being the subject of a safeguarding investigation to an application before the Court of Protection. It, finally, notes what should happen while Court of Protection proceedings are ongoing and further safeguarding concerns arise.

24.3   It should, perhaps, also be noted that it is not solely local authorities who have safeguarding obligations: other bodies, most obviously NHS bodies, will have responsibilities toward adults at risk, and may find that those responsibilities give rise to a need to bring proceedings before the Court of Protection. While the changes set out in the Care Act 2014 will not apply to such bodies, the principles set out in the subsequent parts of the chapter apply with equal force to them.

---

1   Parts of this chapter originally appeared, in different form, in an article by Alex Ruck Keene entitled 'Safeguarding and the Court of Protection,' in November 2013 *Encyclopedia of Local Government Law Bulletin*, Sweet & Maxwell.

What is safeguarding?

24.4   Safeguarding has both a broad and a narrow definition.[2] The broader definition encompasses the prevention of abuse, and can encompass consideration of all aspects of a person's general welfare. As such, it forms part of the general approach to be taken to the assessment and delivery of services to adults by local social services authorities. The narrow definition – perhaps more accurately called 'adult protection' – refers to investigation and intervention where it is suspected that abuse may have occurred. In neither case was there traditionally a single legal framework setting out either the responsibilities of local authorities. Their duties arose from a mixture of statutory obligations (in particular, the duty to undertake community care assessments); statutory guidance in the form of the *No Secrets* guidance issued by the Department of Health and Home Office in 2000;[3] and public law requirements, in particular those imposed under articles 2, 3, 5 and 8 of the European Convention on Human Rights (ECHR).

24.5   The Care Act 2014 changes the law in this area by imposing two duties upon local authorities.

24.6   First, implementing one of the main recommendations of the Law Commission in its review of adult social care, the Care Act 2014 introduces an overarching principle in section 1 to the effect that the general duty of a local authority in the discharge of its functions relating to care and support of specific individual is to promote the well-being of that individual. 'Well-being,' in turn, is defined as including protection from an abuse and neglect.[4]

24.7   Second, and again implementing one of the main recommendations of the Law Commission, the Care Act 2014 introduces[5] a statutory duty of enquiry upon a local authority wherever it has reasonable cause to suspect that an adult in its area (whether or not ordinarily resident there):

---

2   See the Law Commission's report *Adult social care*, Law Com No 326, May 2011, para 9.2; available at: http://lawcommission.justice.gov.uk/docs/lc326_adult_social_care.pdf.

3   *No Secrets: guidance on developing and implementing multi-agency policies and procedures to protect vulnerable adults from abuse*, Department of Health/Home Office, 2000; available at: https://www.gov.uk/government/publications/no-secrets-guidance-on-protecting-vulnerable-adults-in-care.

4   Care Act 2014 s1(2)(c).

5   Care Act 2014 s42.

a) has needs for care and support (whether or not the authority is meeting any of those needs) (ie whether or not the adult is eligible for community care services provided by the local authority);
b) is experiencing, or is at risk of, abuse or neglect; and
c) as a result of those needs is unable to protect himself or herself against the abuse or neglect or the risk of it.

24.8   While 'abuse' is not given a specific definition, the Care Act makes clear[6] that it includes financial abuse, financial abuse being defined, in turn, as including:

- having money or other property stolen;
- being defrauded;
- being put under pressure in relation to money or other property; and
- having money or other property misused.

It is suggested that it would also encompass physical, sexual, psychological, or discriminatory abuse.[7] 'Neglect' is not defined in the Care Act, but is conventionally understood as including the failure to respond to medical or physical care needs, the failure to provide to provide access to appropriate health, social care or educational services and the withholding of the necessities of life, such as medication, adequate nutrition and heating.[8]

24.9   Where the duty of enquiry arises, the local authority must make or cause to be made whatever enquiries it thinks necessary to enable it to decide whether any action should be taken in the adult's care and, if so, what and by whom.[9]

24.10   The Care Act 2014 does not, however, introduce any additional *powers* for local authorities in respect of either the prevention or the investigation of abuse or neglect. In particular, the government declined on several occasions during the passage of the bill through parliament to amend it to introduce a power of entry by which a local authority would be able to seek a judicial warrant to enter a property and speak to an adult at risk. An equivalent power – and indeed, more extensive powers including a power of removal – is to be found in the Adult Support and Protection (Scotland) Act 2007, but the

---

6 Care Act 2014 s42(3).
7 The categories set out in *No secrets* para 2.7.
8 See *No Secrets* para 2.7.
9 Care Act 2014 s42(2).

government considered[10] that there was insufficient support to be found from a consultation exercise carried out to warrant the introduction of such a power.

24.11   Local authorities will therefore continue to utilise a range of pre-existing powers and/or draw upon cooperation from other authorities with responsibilities and powers in relation to adults at risk (most obviously, police forces). Space prevents a detailed discussion of these powers,[11] but for purposes of this book, the most relevant is the ability of a local authority – where the adult lacks decision-making capacity in the relevant domains – to bring proceedings before the Court of Protection for declarations and decisions as to such matters as to where they should live and with whom they should have contact.

24.12   It is stressed that local authorities or other public bodies must obtain the authority of the court if they consider it necessary to remove a person lacking capacity to consent from their home or restrict their contact with others.[12]

The overlap between safeguarding and the Court of Protection

24.13   It can be seen from the very brief review above that what might be entitled adult protection proceedings before the Court of Protection sit within the broader safeguarding context. It is, however, vitally important to recognise that a decision to instigate proceedings before the Court of Protection is a decision that gives rise to a specific set of obligations upon the applicant – be that a local authority or NHS body – arising from the demands of the court process. These obligations are discussed in greater detail in the main part of this work; of particular relevance is chapter 15, because fact-finding will – often – form an important part of adult protection proceedings.

---

10   *Government Response to the Safeguarding Power of Entry Consultation*, May 2013; available at: https://www.gov.uk/government/uploads/system/uploads/attachment_data/file/197739/Gov_Response_to_PoE.pdf.

11   A comprehensive discussion is to be found in the Social Care Institute for Excellence guidance, *Safeguarding adults at risk of harm: a legal guide for practitioners*, 2011; available at: www.scie.org.uk/publications/reports/report50.pdf.

12   *Re A and C (Equality and Human Rights Commission intervening)*, [2010] EWHC 978 (Fam), [2010] COPLR Con Vol 10; *Hillingdon LBC v Neary* [2011] EWHC 1377 (COP), [2011] COPLR Con Vol 632.

24.14   Perhaps the most important point to emphasise here is that it is inappropriate for Court of Protection proceedings to be used as a 'voyage of discovery',[13] such that it is important that the applicant is satisfied at the outset that it has a satisfactory evidential basis for the allegations that it advances against those whom it contends have harmed the adult or from whom the adult is at risk. That evidential basis may, in a very urgent case, be limited, but as a general rule, it is clear that a local authority should not embark upon Court of Protection proceedings except on the basis that it is satisfied that it has the evidence that it will need at the final hearing to support factual allegations made against any individuals.

24.15   This means that a decision to bring proceedings has to be taken after as rigorous a process as possible in the time allowed (involving senior members of the social work management team and the legal department) so as to ensure that:

a) a considered decision is taken as to whether evidence being put before the Court is sufficiently cogent. While the standard of proof before the Court of Protection is the civil standard (see further para 15.22), it is axiomatic that a serious allegation should not be advanced absent proper evidence;[14]

b) the sources of information forming the foundation of the decisions being made are checked so as to allow an assessment to be made about its reliability. 'The fact that a piece of information has been repeated many times does not enhance its reliability';[15]

c) where orders are being sought that interfere with rights under ECHR article 8, the picture being put to the court is a balanced one, rather than one presenting solely the negative information or the facts cast only in a negative light;[16] and

d) proper consideration has been given to whether it is necessary to put the allegations to the alleged abuser before taking steps upon the basis of those allegations. The obligation upon public bodies to treat parties affected by their actions in a just manner is capable

---

13 *A Local Authority v PB and P* [2011] EWHC 502 (COP), [2011] COPLR Con Vol 166 at para 38, per Charles J.

14 *A Local Authority v HS and others* [2013] EWHC 2410 (COP) at paras 184–186, per District Judge Eldergill. This decision does not have precedent value but is cited here as it contains a very detailed discussion of the consequences of a failure to analyse the evidential basis upon which an adult protection application is brought.

15 *Surrey CC v M and others* [2013] EWHC 2400 (Fam), (2013) 157(32) SJLB 31 at para 77 per Theis J (the comments relate to care proceedings, but are of wider application).

16 *Surrey CC v M and others* at para 78.

of being overridden by the obligation to protect an adult at risk, but a failure to recognise that obligation can, itself, give rise to flawed decision-making.[17]

24.16 The courts are alive to the fact that, on occasion, local authorities are on the horns of a dilemma, and that it may be necessary urgently to invoke the jurisdiction of the Court of Protection before it has been possible properly to investigate an allegation of abuse.[18] However, in such a case, it is all the more important that stock is taken as soon as possible thereafter of matters. A failure to do so leads to (at least) two adverse consequences:

a) leaving allegations '[hanging] like a cloud' over family members or other individuals can act as a substantial distraction to the real welfare issues, by placing those individuals in an unnecessarily adversarial position vis-à-vis the local authority;[19]

b) in the worst case scenario, it can lead to very substantial costs being incurred unnecessarily by other parties which fall to be paid by the local authority. By way of example, a local authority was ordered to pay the full costs of the Official Solicitor and of P's brother (agreed in the total sum of £88,000) after it withdrew allegations of sexual abuse against the brother almost two years after the proceedings were brought in the Court of Protection. District Judge Eldergill held that:

> There was a prolonged failure on the local authority's part to recognise the weakness of its case. The allegations were vague and insufficiently particularized. The 'evidence' in support was manifestly inadequate. It was internally inconsistent and unreliable. The truth of what was alleged was assumed without any proper, critical, analysis.[20]

24.17 The propositions set out above do not affect the general duty to place before the court disputes where the best outcome may not be immediately clear. Court of Protection proceedings need not be adversarial and may be the best forum for resolving finely-balanced questions as to what may constitute the best and least restrictive alternative for P. In all cases, however, it is essential to show that available evidence

---

17 *R (Davis and Davis) v West Sussex CC* [2012] EWHC 2152 (Admin), [2013] PTSR 494.

18 *HS* at para 187.

19 *A London Borough v (1) BB (by her litigation friend the Official Solicitor) (2) AM (3) SB (4) EL Trust* [2011] EWHC 2853 (Fam), [2012] COPLR 16 at para 18 per Ryder J (as he then was).

20 Para 188.

has been properly evaluated and that it is openly shared with the court and the parties.

24.18   One particular feature of adult protection proceedings before the Court of Protection is that they may well require the involvement of the police to implement the decisions and declarations of the court. This is especially so if the judge determines that it is necessary that P be removed from a place that they have been residing with family members or carers whom it is thought will seek to frustrate the process. In such a case, the courts have set down guidance as to the steps should be followed:

> In the event that it is expected that the assistance of the Police may be required to effect or assist with the removal of a vulnerable/ incapacitated adult ('P') which the Court is being asked to authorise, the following steps should generally be taken:
>
> (1) the Local Authority/NHS body/other organisation/person (the Applicant) applying to the Court for an authorisation to remove P should, in advance of the hearing of the Application, discuss and, where possible, agree with the Police the way in which it is intended that the removal will be effected, to include, where applicable, the extent to which it is expected that restraint and/or force may be used and the nature of any restraint (for example, handcuffs) that may be used;
>
> (2) the Applicant should ensure that information about the way in which it is intended that removal will be effected is provided to the Court and to the litigation friend (in cases where a person has been invited and/or appointed to act as P's litigation friend) before the Court authorises removal. In particular, the Court and the litigation friend should be informed whether there is agreement between the Applicant and the Police and, if there is not, about the nature and extent of any disagreement;
>
> (3) where the Applicant and the Police do not agree about how removal should be effected, the Court should give consideration to inviting/ directing the Police to attend the hearing of the Application so that the Court can, where appropriate, determine how it considers removal should be effected and/or ensure that any authorisation for removal is given on a fully informed basis.[21]

---

21 *LBH v GP and MP* (unreported, 8 April 2009), at para 31 per Coleridge J.

Safeguarding during the currency of Court of Protection proceedings

24.19 In the authors' experience, there can sometimes be confusion on the part of public authorities as to what it is that they are required to do during the currency of Court of Protection proceedings if a further safeguarding concern arises in relation to P. They can, in particular, sometimes be unclear as to whether they can take any steps without the authorisation of the court.

24.20 The short answer is that the fact that Court of Protection proceedings are on foot does not alleviate the obligations upon the local authority (or NHS body) where they have reason to believe that P has suffered harm or is at risk of harm. However, while they should take such steps as are immediately necessary to meet the situation, it is likely always to be necessary to bring the matter back to court if they will involve a substantial change in P's circumstances (for instance, where they are living).

24.21 One specific requirement in such case was identified by McFarlane J (as he then was) in *Enfield LBC v SA and others.*[22] Where there are extant Court of Protection proceedings, then in the absence of an absolutely pressing emergency (using that phrase in an extreme sense), McFarlane J held that any question of whether or not P was to be the subject of an 'achieving best evidence' interview[23] must be raised with the court and be subject to a direction from the judge. He noted that where the substance of the interview might relate to allegations that another party to the proceedings (or someone closely connected to a party) had harmed P then there would be good grounds for the matter being raised, at least initially, without notice to that party. However, in every case, he held, notice should be given to the Official Solicitor or any other person who acted as P's litigation friend. [24]

---

22 [2010] EWHC 196 (Admin), [2010] COPLR Con Vol 362.

23 Ie an interview carried out by police officers with a possible view to criminal proceedings, complying with the guidance set down in *Achieving best evidence in criminal proceedings: guidance on interviewing victims and witnesses, and guidance on using special measures*, Ministry of Justice, (now) 3rd revision, 2011; available at: www.justice.gov.uk/downloads/victims-and-witnesses/vulnerable-witnesses/achieving-best-evidence-criminal-proceedings.pdf.

24 *Enfield LBC v SA* at para 46.

CHAPTER 25

The Court of Protection and the Administrative Court

Introduction

25.1   For some years after the coming into force of the Mental Capacity Act (MCA) 2005, it was not entirely clear how far the Court of Protection could go in deciding where P's best interests lay. In particular, where P's care was provided by a public body (whether a local authority or a health body), it was not entirely clear whether the Court of Protection was entitled to decide – in the abstract – where (for instance) it was in P's best interests for them to live, or whether the Court of Protection was limited to choosing between the options put on the table by the public body. It is now, however, clear that, save in exceptional cases, a refusal by a public body to advance an option for consideration by the court can only be challenged by way of judicial review in the Administrative Court.

25.2   This chapter outlines briefly the dividing lines between the jurisdiction of the Court of Protection and that of the Administrative Court, before addressing the practical questions that arise where parallel proceedings are likely to be necessary and, finally, the approach that the Administrative Court is likely to take in any challenge arising out of a case before the Court of Protection.

The limits of the Court of Protection's jurisdiction

25.3   In *ACCG and another v MN and another*,[1] Eleanor King J was faced with a position where the clinical commissioning group (CCG) funding the care of a young man made it clear that it was not prepared to fund contact between the man and his family at the parents' home. The CCG therefore submitted that this was not an option for the court to consider when making best interests decisions; Counsel for the parents submitted that the court should embark upon a trial in relation to home contact (and to the delivery of personal care by the man's mother). In declining to embark upon a consideration of a hypothetical option, Eleanor King J conducted an extensive review of the authorities concluding with the dicta of Baroness Hale in the Supreme Court case of *Aintree v James*[2] to the effect that the Court of Protection has no greater powers than P would have if they had full capacity. Eleanor King J noted that:

---

1   [2013] EWHC 3859 (COP).
2   *Aintree University Hospitals NHS Foundation Trust v James* [2013] UKSC 67, (2013) 16 CCLR 554, [2013] COPLR 492.

An inevitable consequence of a person lacking capacity is that a public authority will often be providing services to that incapacitated person pursuant to various statutory duties. There is a danger of a blurring of the distinction as between the Court of Protection's statutory duties in a private law context, (namely to consider the best interests of an incapacitated adult), with public law challenges in relation to the willingness, unwillingness, reasonableness or rationality of the services a public authority is willing or able to provide.[3]

25.4 She further noted that considering where the man's best interests lay prior to considering questions of funding

... would potentially be using a best interests decision as a means of putting pressure upon the ACCG to allocate their resources in a particular way and in doing so would be going against the first principle now enshrined in *Aintree* that this Act is concerned with enabling the court to do for the patient what he could do for himself if of full capacity, but it goes no further.[4]

25.5 Eleanor King J further noted that:

There will undoubtedly be cases where courts wish to explore with providers the possibility of funding being made available for packages of care which may, for example, have been identified by independent social workers. In my judgment such discussions and judicial encouragement for flexibility and negotiation in respect of a care package are actively to be encouraged. Such negotiations are however a far cry from the court embarking on a 'best interests' trial with a view to determining whether or not an option which has been said by care provider (in the exercise of their statutory duties) not to be available, is nevertheless in the patient's best interest.[5]

25.6 Consistent with the approach that had been adopted prior to the coming into force of the MCA 2005,[6] she therefore held that the Court of Protection is, save in exceptional cases,[7] constrained to choosing between the options available to P and that judicial review remained the proper vehicle through which to challenge unreasonable or irrational decisions made by care providers and other public authorities.

---

3 Para 34.
4 Para 52.
5 Para 57.
6 See, in particular, *A v A Health Authority and another* [2002] Fam 213 and *Re S (vulnerable adult)* [2007] 2 FLR 1095.
7 Which might include where there was a possibility of a third party providing funds additional to those made available by public authorities: see *Re SK* [2012] EWHC 1990 (COP), [2012] COPLR 712 and *Re SK (impact of best interests decision on Queen's Bench Proceedings)* [2013] COPLR 458.

25.7   As discussed further at paras 26.10ff, there is one important caveat to this proposition that arises in cases where a proper claim can be framed based upon the Human Rights Act (HRA) 1998 that a public authority in declining to fund a particular form of care package is acting in a way incompatible with rights under the European Convention on Human Rights (ECHR).

Parallel proceedings

25.8   Parallel proceedings will be unusual,[8] not least because it is not easy to mount a judicial review challenge (in particular given the ever more limited scope of public funding available). The Administrative Court also applies a permission filter significantly more stringently than does the Court of Protection (the filter not even applying in all cases before the latter: see chapter 10). Administrative Court judges will, further, be astute to ensure that cases that should properly be determined within the four walls of the Court of Protection remain there. In *R (DO) v LBH*,[9] for instance, permission was refused to the sister of P in concurrent Court of Protection proceedings to bring judicial review applications against decisions of the local authority which had the effect of removing her from caring for her brother and making decisions as to his care arrangements. HHJ Jarman QC (sitting as a Deputy High Court Judge) noted that such questions were ones which the Court of Protection with its expertise was particularly suited to deal with and that judicial review was a remedy of last resort which should only be deployed where (for instance) an application or appeal within Court of Protection proceedings was not available.

25.9   However, where a party or parties wish to challenge a failure by a public body to put a particular option on the table, by way of judicial review proceedings, then, as identified in *ACCG*, any delay or increased expense of litigation can be ameliorated to a considerable extent by an early identification of the issues and, if needs be, the matter being listed before a High Court judge who sits both in the Court of Protection and the Administrative Court.[10] If the application

---

8   An example of a combined judicial review and Court of Protection application (albeit not arising out of a refusal to put an option on the table) is *R (C) v A Local Authority and others* [2011] EWHC 1539 (Admin), [2011] COPLR Con Vol 972.

9   [2012] EWHC 4044 (Admin).

10 All High Court judges who sit in the Family Division are entitled to sit in the Court of Protection. Some also hold a 'ticket' to sit in the Administrative Court.

was being heard by a district or a circuit judge, therefore, it will be necessary to apply to have the matter transferred to be heard before a High Court judge with the relevant 'tickets'. Detailed directions will also be required to ensure that matters are considered in the right sequence – ie broadly, all the stages of the judicial review first so as to ensure that there is clarity as to exactly what options are before the Court of Protection when it comes to consider where P's best interests will lie.

25.10 Finally, we should emphasise (as did Eleanor King J in *ACCG*) that it is vital that there is clarity in respect of the available options as early as can reasonably be achieved (see also paras 11.38ff). A failure to identify which options are actually on the table and which are not can lead to a party told at the last minute that an option is not available feeling – quite understandably – that the 'ground has been cut from under their feet by ... the public authorities' "knock out blow"'.[11] It may well be the case that the public authority, for good reason, may well not wish to commit itself to a stark statement that 'option A is not available' so as to allow room for discussion and the maintenance of a working relationship. However, if the reality is that it is not, it is likely to be better for this to be established sooner rather than later, if for no other reason that a failure to do so will inevitably lead to a prolonging of proceedings – and of consequent expense – which are, on a proper analysis, futile.

The approach of the Administrative Court

25.11 As touched upon in *ACCG*, it is of considerable importance to remember that the fact that a person lacks the capacity to decide (for instance) where they should live:

> ... does not import the test of 'what is in her best interests?' as the yardstick by which all care decisions are to be made ... Section 1(5) of the Act applies to 'an act done, or decision made ... for or on behalf of a person who lacks capacity'. Its decision-making criteria and procedures are designed to be a substitute for the lack of independent capacity of the person to act or take decisions for him or herself. They come into play in circumstances where a person with capacity would take, or participate in the taking of, a decision.[12]

11 *ACCG* at para 46.
12 *R (Chatting) v (1) Viridian Housing (2) Wandsworth LBC* [2012] EWHC 3595 (Admin), [2013] COPLR 108 at paras 99–100 per Nicholas Paines QC sitting as a Deputy High Court Judge.

25.12   In other words, very many decisions relating to the provision of care by public bodies to adults lacking capacity to take material decisions are not, on a proper analysis, best interests decisions falling within the scope of the MCA 2005. Rather, they are decisions taken as to (1) what the adult's needs are; and (2) how those needs are to be met. They are decisions taken by reference to substantial bodies of legislation and of case-law that apply to all adults, not just those who lack capacity in one or more regards;[13] they are therefore precisely the sort of decisions that have conventionally fallen – and continue to fall – to be decided in the Administrative Court by reference to the well-developed tests that apply when that court is considering whether the public bodies in question have erred in their decision-making.

25.13   Space precludes a detailed discussion here of the tests that apply in judicial review proceedings,[14] but it is important to note that the crucial distinction between the approach of the Administrative Court and the approach of the Court of Protection is that the former is (broadly) focused upon the process by which the public body has taken the decision in question; the latter is, itself, the decision-maker and will therefore engage in a detailed examination of the merits of the various options before it. This hard-edged distinction can be appear to be blurred in certain categories of cases, in particular those requiring the assessment by the Administrative Court of the proportionality of any interference with rights under the ECHR, but even in such cases the Administrative Court will not, formally, be conducting a review of the merits of the decision and will not therefore be standing in the shoes of the decision-maker.[15]

---

13 See Luke Clements and Pauline Thompson, *Community care and the law*, LAG, 5th edn, 2011. The law in relation to community care has been substantially recast by the Care Act 2014 but the core principles remain largely unchanged.
14 See, in this regard, in particular, Jonathan Manning, Sarah Salmon and Robert Brown, *Judicial review proceedings: a practitioner's guide*, LAG, 3rd edn, 2013.
15 See *R (A) v Chief Constable of Kent* [2013] EWCA Civ 1706.

Human rights and the Court of Protection

Introduction

26.1   The Court of Protection is, almost by definition, a court whose every substantive decision will be taken after balancing different rights arising under the European Convention on Human Rights (ECHR), both those of P and – frequently – those third parties (most often family members) upon whom the court's decisions in relation to P will impact. In this chapter, we outline briefly some of the key points that advisers need to consider in relation to the ECHR. We also touch upon the impact of the Convention on the Rights of Persons with Disabilities (CRPD).

Human Rights Act 1998 declarations and damages

26.2   The Court of Protection has a jurisdiction to grant:

- a declaration that the ECHR rights of P have been breached;[1]
- a declaration that the ECHR rights of another person who can claim to be a victim have been breached;[2]
- damages under Human Rights Act (HRA) 1998 s8 where such are required to afford just satisfaction for either category of breach;[3]
- a declaration under HRA 1998 s4 that a provision of the Mental Capacity Act (MCA) 2005 is incompatible with the ECHR.[4] To date, no declarations have been granted (or, indeed, sought, at least in any reported case).

26.3   If a declaration or damages for a breach of rights under the ECHR is sought, it is necessary that the precise basis for this claim be set out. Practice Direction (PD) 11A, dealing with HRA claims, outlines the relevant procedure at paras 1–3 for making a claim, but in summary the most important requirement is that it is set out as soon as practicable so that the other parties and the court are aware that a specific claim in this regard is being made.

26.4   A specific procedure must be followed if a declaration of incompatibility is sought, including notice to and the joining of the Crown.[5] The entirety of a case from the permission stage onwards in which

---

1   *YA(F) v A local authority and others* [2010] EWHC 2770, [2010] COPLR Con Vol 1226.
2   *YA(F)*. See also *City of Sunderland v MM and others* [2009] COPLR Con Vol 881.
3   *YA(F)*.
4   COPR r83(1) and HRA 1998 s4(5)(f).
5   PD 11A paras 4–8.

a declaration of incompatibility is sought must be heard before the President of the Family Division, the Chancellor or by a High Court judge nominated to sit in the Court of Protection.[6]

26.5   It should be noted that PD 11A also suggests that the entirety of *any* claim in which reliance is placed upon any provision of or right arising out of the HRA 1998 must be heard before the same level of senior judge as set out above.[7] It is unclear whether this practice direction is actually complied with in practice.[8]

26.6   Claims for declarations/damages under the HRA 1998 that follow on the substantive determination by the Court of Protection of questions of P's best interests have sometimes been brought either in the county court (or, if it is a high value claim) in the Queen's Bench Division of the High Court. There is no reason in principle why this aspect of the claim cannot be heard before the Court of Protection and, as suggested above, this has the advantage that the judge in question will be familiar with all of the surrounding issues. At present, however, thanks to the wording of PD 11A, unless the whole case has been before a suitably senior judge from the outset, the specifically HRA 1998 aspects of the claim would have to be 'hived off' and dealt with separately by such a judge at the conclusion of the proceedings. This is not a satisfactory situation, and the authors suspect that the practice direction may be honoured as much in the breach here.

26.7   Some Court of Protection judges are reluctant to address 'historic' breaches of rights under the ECHR, preferring to focus upon P's best interests now and for the future. In such circumstances, it may be necessary for any such breaches to be addressed by way of a separate claim in the county court or the Queen's Bench Division of the High Court. One further important reason why it may make sense to hive off any HRA 1998 aspects is that the standard costs rules in civil proceedings will apply, by contrast to the specific rules that apply in the Court of Protection (as to which, see chapter 17). If it appears that the defendant public authority is likely to contest the HRA 1998 claim, then it may be prudent to proceed before the civil courts so that a full award of costs can be sought against the public authority. If P is publicly funded then if this civil claim is, in turn, compromised, care will need to be taken to ensure that the costs consequences are

---

6   PD 11A para 9.

7   PD 11A para 9.

8   On its face, for instance, the decision in *City of Sunderland* would appear not to be compliant because HHJ Moir was not a so-called puisne judge of the High Court.

considered both by reference to the costs in the civil proceedings and before the Court of Protection so as to ensure that, insofar as possible, any damages awarded to P are not then swallowed up by the statutory charge imposed by the Legal Aid Agency (LAA). This is addressed at paras 6.81–6.83.

26.8   However, if it is anticipated that the substantive proceedings will (and should) be heard before a District or Circuit Judge, but there will also be a claim for HRA 1998 declarations or damages which the party bringing the claim would wish to be heard before that judge, then pending any review of PD 11A, it is suggested that:

- paragraph 9 of PD 11A should be highlighted in the COP1 application form (or, if the issue arises during the course of proceedings, the COP10 form in which the application is made);
- the court be asked specifically to consider the question of the allocation of that part of the claim falling within the scope of PD 11A separately to the allocation of the 'substantive' aspect of the claim. It may very well be that appropriate course of action is to defer consideration of the HRA aspects of the claim until the substantive elements are decided, at which point questions of permission and allocation can then be considered. A technical point will then potentially arise as to whether the HRA 1998 claim has been 'brought' within the requisite one year of the act complained of,[9] but is suggested that even if it has not formally been brought prior to the grant of permission, this would be a circumstance in which the court's discretion to extend time under HRA 1998 s7(5)(b) would invariably be exercised if the steps set out above have been taken and subject to judicial endorsement at an early stage.

Human Rights Act 1998 – procedural aspects

26.9   The ECHR permeates all aspects of the decision-making of the Court of Protection, and we have touched upon specific considerations at relevant points in the balance of this book. For instance, questions of disclosure (and withholding of disclosure) engage difficult balancing exercises between the different ECHR rights of the parties involved (see paras 13.99ff).

26.10   A fundamental – and distinct – procedural aspect engaging the HRA 1998 was addressed for the first time in *ACCG and another v*

9   HRA 1998 s7(5)(a).

MN and others.[10] In this case, considered in paras 25.3–25.6, Eleanor King J held that, in principle, the Court of Protection is constrained to choosing between the options available to P and that judicial review remained the proper vehicle through which to challenge unreasonable or irrational decisions made by care providers and other public authorities. Importantly, however, Eleanor King J recognised that:

> There may be rare cases where it appears to those representing a party that a public authority, in failing to agree to provide funding for or a particular form of care package, is acting in a way which is incompatible with Convention rights. In those circumstances, notwithstanding the fact that such an option is not available and before the court, the court may exceptionally, pursuant to a formal application made under s7(1)(b) HRA, conduct an assessment of the person's best interests beyond the scope of the available options, in order to determine whether the public authority has acted in a way which is disproportionate and incompatible with a convention right.[11]

26.11   Eleanor King J, however, emphasised that this course of action would only be adopted exceptionally by the Court of Protection, and it did not follow that in every case where a provider has declined to fund a package, or limited the available options, that there should thereafter routinely be an assessment of whether such an option would be in the best interests of the patient in order to ascertain whether there has been a breach of their rights under the ECHR. Applying *K v LBX*,[12] Eleanor King J held that, in the ordinary course of events, protection of the ECHR article 8 rights of the parties (the right which will most often be engaged) will be guaranteed by a consideration of them by the court as part of all the relevant circumstances required by the carrying out of MCA 2005 s4 best interests assessment.

26.12   If a party wishes the court to carry out the 'exceptional' assessment of a hypothetical option on the basis set out in the paragraphs immediately above, then the following will apply:

- the claim must be formulated and pleaded properly by reference to HRA 1998 s7(1)(b);
- the claim will then be dealt with by the Court of Protection as part of the main proceedings: it will not be treated as a discrete issue separated from the rest of the case.[13]

---

10 [2013] EWHC 3859 (COP).

11 Para 86(iii).

12 [2012] EWCA Civ 79, [2012] COPLR 411.

13 *ACCG* at para 79, applying *Re L (care proceedings: human rights claims)* [2003] 2 FLR 160 and *Re V* [2004] 1 FLR 944.

26.13   In line with the discussion set out in the section above, the wording of PD 11A would suggest that a case of the nature envisaged by Eleanor King J would have to be heard before a High Court judge sitting in the Court of Protection (or the President or Chancellor).

Convention on the Rights of Persons with Disabilities

26.14   The CRPD was concluded in 2006. The convention seeks to bring about a radical change in the approach adopted in the social, political and legal arenas to those suffering from disabilities (and, indeed, to the very concept of disability). Among other provisions, it seeks to bring about a fundamental shift away from the taking of decisions on behalf of individuals on the basis of an asserted lack of capacity. The CPRD has been very widely ratified, including by the UK. A good guide to the CRPD and its implications for English law can be found in Lucy Series, 'Comparing old and new paradigms of legal capacity'.[14]

26.15   At least as interpreted by the Committee on the Rights of Persons with Disabilities, compliance with article 12 of the CPRD (which provides for equal recognition before the law) means that states party to the CPRD should replace legislation providing for substitute decision-making for incapacitated adults based 'on what is believed to be in the objective 'best interests' of the person concerned, as opposed to being based on the person's own will and preferences'.[15]

26.16   There is a very live academic debate as to the precise meaning of article 12 and its implications for national legislatures, in particular those of the countries which are also bound by obligations under the ECHR.[16] However, on its face, the MCA 2005 is not compatible with article 12 not least because, no matter how important a role P's wishes and feelings play in the consideration of where their best interests lie under MCA 2005 s4, the test is ultimately one that is predicated

---

14   [2014] Eld LJ 62. See also the discussion paper on the CRPD available at www.39essex.com/newsletters.

15   Committee on the Rights of Persons with Disabilities, 'General Comment on Article 12: Equal Recognition before the law', para 23; available at: www.ohchr. org/EN/HRBodies/CRPD/Pages/GC.aspx.

16   See, for instance, Philip Fennell and Urfan Khaliq, 'Conflicting or complementary obligations? The UN Disability Rights Convention, the European Convention on Human Rights and English law', *European Human Rights Law Review*, No 6 (2011): pp662–674.

upon a determination of the objective best interests of P.[17] There are other articles of the CRPD with which the compatibility of the MCA 2005 is doubtful,[18] but article 12 poses the most direct challenge to the MCA 2005 as currently drafted.

26.17   While the CRPD has not been incorporated into domestic law, the Court of Appeal has endorsed it as having persuasive authority as an aid to interpretation.[19] It was referred to by the Supreme Court in the seminal decision upon deprivation of liberty under the MCA 2005, *Cheshire West*[20] (discussed in more detail in chapter 24), and has been referred to, essentially in passing, in a number of cases before the Court of Protection[21] and it is now regularly referred to by the European Court of Human Rights, it has yet to be the subject of any detailed consideration by the Court of Protection. This may, in part, be because the obligations that it imposes are at the state level, rather than (for instance) at the level of the discharge by either public authorities or courts of their respective functions under domestic legislation. It is also likely, however, that this is as much a function of the fact that the CRPD is – as yet – remarkably little known by practitioners.

26.18   The Committee on the Rights of Persons with Disabilities is due to consider the UK's compliance with the CRPD (both in respect of England and Wales and the very different regimes in Northern Ireland and Scotland) in the course of 2015; what will happen in this regard (and what the government will do in response) is not clear at the time of writing. In the interim, however, it is suggested that it is entirely in order for practitioners to rely upon the provisions of the CRPD to support arguments that:

- In deciding whether all practicable steps have been taken without success before concluding that P lacks capacity (MCA 2005 s1(3)), the Court of Protection must be astute to examine precisely what support mechanisms have been put in place to enable P to

---

17 *Aintree University Hospitals NHS Foundation Trust v James* [2013] UKSC 67, [2013] 3 WLR 1299, (2013) 16 CCLR 554 at para 24 per Lady Hale.

18 Most obviously article 14, which on its face cannot be squared with ECHR article 5 (right to liberty).

19 *Burnip v Birmingham City Council and another* [2012] EWCA Civ 629, [2013] PTSR 117 (obiter, in the context of interpretation of ECHR article 14).

20 *P (by his litigation friend the Official Solicitor) v Cheshire West and Chester Council and another, and P and Q (by their litigation friend the Official Solicitor) v Surrey CC* [2014] UKSC 19, [2014] 2 WLR 642, (2014) 17 CCLR 5.

21 The first being *An NHS Trust v DE* [2013] EWHC 2562 (Fam), [2013] COPLR 531.

participate in the decision in respect of which their capacity is questioned and – where necessary – to direct that such support mechanisms be provided. An example of such support – directed during the currency of proceedings – would be that given to DE[22] by way of education, which allowed him to attain capacity to consent to sexual relations.

- P must be supported to participate as fully as possible in the proceedings before the Court of Protection (consistent with the emphasis also placed by the European Court of Human Rights of the importance of such participation by reference to the provisions of the ECHR: see paras 16.29ff);
- Particular weight must be placed upon P's wishes and feelings in the determination of where their best interests may lie. Indeed, it can be suggested that, where it is possible to identify which of the available options P would have chosen then then that gives the answer as to where their best interests will lie for purposes of MCA 2005 s4, regardless of whether this is an option that the professionals (or indeed the court) consider to be 'wise.' A very good example of such a decision (albeit one that was reached without citation of the CRPD) would be *Re M (Best Interests: Deprivation of Liberty)*,[23] in which Peter Jackson J endorsed the return home of a woman with severe diabetes in circumstances in which it was clear that there was a strong likelihood that she would not comply with her medication with potentially fatal consequences. In reaching this decision, Peter Jackson J expressly took into account the extent to which M was deeply unhappy at the care home where she was being provided with accommodation and being kept 'safe' by the public authorities in question, and her very strong desire to return home.

---

22 *An NHS Trust v DE* [2013] EWHC 2562 (Fam), [2013] COPLR 531.
23 [2013] EWHC 3456 (COP), [2014] COPLR 35, [2014] COPLR 35.

CHAPTER 27

Cross-border matters

Introduction

27.1   The majority of cases before the Court of Protection concern the property or personal welfare of people who are habitually resident in England and Wales. However, the Mental Capacity Act (MCA) 2005 also includes detailed provisions relating to the powers of the court over people who are habitually resident other than in England but in respect of whom, for whatever reason, declarations or decisions are sought. This might be, for instance, because an incapacitated adult has been kidnapped from their home country and brought to England and Wales. In such a case, an order may well be sought in their home country seeking their return; Schedule 3 to the MCA 2005 contains provisions detailing when and how such an order would be given effect by the Court of Protection. Alternatively, a question might arise as to the proper disposal of property in England belonging to someone habitually resident abroad upon whose behalf decisions are now being taken by a guardian appointed under the laws of that country.

27.2   The private international law rules governing decision-making for incapacitated adults with a foreign connection is a complex topic, a full discussion of which lies outside the scope of this book.[1] The complications are only increased by the fact that MCA 2005 Sch 3 implements – as the law of Wales – many of the provisions of the Hague Convention on the International Protection of Adults 2000, but the UK has not, to date, ratified the convention as regards England and Wales.[2]

27.3   This chapter limits itself to highlighting those jurisdictional questions that are most likely to arise in the court setting before noting the position in relation to foreign lasting powers of attorney (LPAs) (ie powers made under other legal systems which have a similar effect to LPAs).

What counts as a foreign jurisdiction?

27.4   It is important to realise that, for purposes of proceedings before the Court of Protection, both Scotland and Northern Ireland count

---

1   Readers are directed, in particular, to Part X of Ashton et al, *Court of Protection Practice 2014*, Jordans; and also, for a fuller discussion, to Frimston et al, *International Protection of Adults* (forthcoming, OUP, 2014).

2   It has done so in respect of Scotland.

as foreign jurisdictions.[3] This means, therefore, that a move of an incapacitated adult from England to Scotland would give rise to a cross-border jurisdictional question; as would questions concerning the exercise of a Scottish power of attorney in England.

The basis of jurisdiction of the Court of Protection

27.5 The Court of Protection has jurisdiction to make declarations and decisions under MCA 2005 ss15–16 in relation to:

a) an adult habitually resident in England and Wales;
b) an adult's property in England and Wales;
c) an adult present in England and Wales or who has property there, if the matter is urgent; or
d) an adult present in England and Wales, if a protective measure which is temporary and limited in its effect to England and Wales is proposed in relation to him.[4]

27.6 'Habitual residence' is not defined in the MCA 2005, but the phrase has been the subject of judicial consideration. Above all, it is 'a question of fact to be determined in the individual circumstances of the case'.[5] In the case of an adult who lacks the capacity to decide where to live, habitual residence can in principle be lost and another habitual residence acquired without the need for any court order or other formal process, such as the appointment of an attorney or deputy.[6] If an adult has been moved across borders, then a central question in deciding whether their habitual residence has changed will be whether there has been any element of wrongfulness in the move.[7] Habitual residence can in principle be lost and another habitual residence acquired on the same day.[8]

27.7 An adult is deemed to be habitually resident in England and Wales if:

---

3 MCA 2005 Sch 3 para 1.
4 MCA 2005 Sch 3 para 7(1).
5 *Re MN (recognition and enforcement of foreign protective measures)* [2010] EWHC 1926 (Fam), [2010] COPLR Con Vol 893 at para 22 per Hedley J.
6 *Re PO* [2013] EWHC 3932 (COP), [2013] WLR (D) 495, per Sir James Munby P at para 18.
7 *Re MN* (move in apparent breach of instruction in Californian Advance Healthcare Directive); or *Re HM (vulnerable adult: abduction)* [2010] EWHC 870 (Fam), [2010] 2 FLR 1057 (move in breach of a court order).
8 *Re PO* [2013] EWHC 3932 (COP), [2013] WLR (D) 495 at para 17.

1) their habitual residence cannot be determined;
2) they are a refugee; or
3) they have been displaced as a result of disturbance in the country of their habitual residence.[9]

Recognition and enforcement of foreign protective measures

27.8   Perhaps the most important function of the provisions of MCA 2005 Sch 3 is to put in place a mechanism for declarations to be obtained that foreign 'protective measures' be recognised and enforced in England and Wales. Such 'protective measures' will include any measure directed to the protection of the person or property of an adult, who for these purposes is any person over 16[10] who, as a result of an impairment or insufficiency of his personal faculties, cannot protect their interests.[11] The MCA 2005 gives examples of such protective measures;[12] examples that have come before the Court of Protection include:

- an order made by a Californian court requiring the return of an adult to California after her removal from the jurisdiction to England in questionable circumstances;[13] and
- the placement of an Irish national in an English psychiatric institution by way of an order made in the High Court in the Republic of Ireland.[14]

It is important to note that, for these purposes, a protective measure includes not just single court orders but also the appointment of a guardian or equivalent by the relevant authorities in the foreign jurisdiction.

27.9   Where a measure has been taken on the ground that an adult is habitually resident in any foreign jurisdiction (including, for these

---

9 MCA 2005 Sch 3 para 7(2).
10 Except if they are aged 16 or 17 and subject to the provisions either of the 1996 Convention on the Jurisdiction, Applicable Law, Recognition, Enforcement and Co-operation in respect of Parental Responsibility and Measures for the Protection of Children or Council Regulation (2201/2003) concerning jurisdiction and the recognition and enforcement of judgments in matrimonial matters and the matters of parental responsibility.
11 MCA 2005 Sch 3 para 4.
12 MCA 2005 Sch 3 para 5.
13 *Re MN.*
14 *Re M* [2012] COPLR 430 (COP).

purposes, Scotland and Northern Ireland[15]), any interested person can apply to the Court of Protection for a declaration that it is to be recognised in England and Wales.[16] Such an application will almost invariably be accompanied by an application that the measure be declared enforceable here as well.[17] Although neither the MCA 2005 nor the Court of Protection Rules (COPR) 2007 SI No 1744 set down any formal procedure by which applications for recognition and enforcement are to be made, they should be made by way of a standard COP1 application,[18] and do not require permission.[19] They should be accompanied by full details and – where relevant – a certified translation of the relevant order(s).

27.10   A judge of the Court of Protection asked to recognise and/or declare enforceable a foreign protective measure operates within strict limits. Their role is confined, in essence, to scrutinising whether core procedural and substantive rights have been complied with. They cannot, in particular, conduct their own analysis of where the adult's best interests may lie, although they can – and must – consider the adult's best interests in deciding how the measure is to be implemented.[20]

Foreign lasting powers of attorney

27.11   An adult who is habitually resident other than in England and Wales at the point of making an LPA[21] can specify that they want English law to apply to questions of existence, extent, modification or extinction, if:

a) they do so in writing; and
b) they are:
   i) a UK national;
   ii) they have previously been habitually resident in England and Wales; or

---

15   By virtue of the definition of 'country' given in MCA 2005 Sch 3 para 1.
16   MCA 2005 Sch 3 para 20(1).
17   MCA 2005 Sch 3 para 22(1).
18   As happened in *Re MN*.
19   MCA 2005 Sch 3 para 20(2).
20   *Re MN* at paras 29 and 31; and MCA 2005 Sch 3 para 12.
21   Which will include a power of like effect to an English LPA: MCA 2005 Sch 6 para 6(c).

iii) they have property here (subject to the limitation that they are only entitled to specify that English law applies in relation to the property here).[22]

c) If they do not make any such specification, then the law of the country in which they were habitually resident at the point of making the power will apply.

27.12   A foreign LPA – ie made by someone habitually resident other than in England and Wales at the point of making it – is automatically effective in England and Wales if it satisfies the requirements of the law that applies under the test set out in the paragraph immediately above.[23] If, though, the foreign power is not exercised in a manner sufficient to guarantee the protection of the person or property of the donor, the Court of Protection can – if it has jurisdiction over the person or their property (applying the tests set out in para 27.5 above) disapply or modify the power.[24]

27.13   It should be noted that – as matters stand – the Office of the Public Guardian does not register foreign LPAs alongside those of English powers. If a bank or other institution is not willing to accept that a foreign LPA is effective, then, assuming that the jurisdictional test set out in para 27.5 above is met, it may be necessary to bring an application to the Court of Protection for a declaration that – for instance – the attorney is acting lawfully in exercising the foreign power in England and Wales. Such an application is not an application for recognition and enforcement;[25] it would appear, further, that permission would be required.[26]

27.14   The situation described immediately above is not satisfactory; in due course, if ratification of the 2000 convention is extended to England and Wales, then the situation will improve – at least between contracting states to the 2000 convention. Under article 38 of the 2000 convention, authorities of a contracting state to the Convention where a measure of protection has been taken or a power of representation confirmed can issue to the person entrusted with the protection of the adult's person or property a certificate indicating

---

22 MCA 2005 Sch 3 para 12(2)(b).

23 This flows from MCA 2005 Sch 3 para 13(1)–(2).

24 MCA 2005 Sch 3 para 14(1).

25 See Frimston et al, *International protection of adults*, chapter 9. This is by contrast with an application by a guardian appointed by a foreign court for recognition and enforcement of their appointment, which would be such an application.

26 MCA 2005 s51(2); the attorney would not be the donee of an LPA falling within the provisions of the MCA 2005.

the capacity in which the person is entitled to act and the powers conferred. Under a provision of the MCA 2005 which will come into force upon ratification with effect to England and Wales,[27] such a certificate would stand – unless the contrary is shown – as proof of the capacity in which the representative acts and the powers conferred upon them by the power of representation.

---

27 They are not currently in force: *Re PO* at para 9.

CHAPTER 28

Instructing psychiatrists in Court of Protection cases[1]

---

1 By Dr Ian Hall, Consultant Psychiatrist for People with Learning Disability,
East London NHS Foundation Trust; Chair, Faculty of Psychiatry of Intellectual
Disability, Royal College of Psychiatrists.

This chapter is written by Dr Ian Hall, Consultant Psychiatrist for People with Learning Disability, East London NHS Foundation Trust; Chair, Faculty of Psychiatry of Intellectual Disability, Royal College of Psychiatrists.

Introduction

28.1   This chapter is concerned with instructing psychiatrists in Court of Protection cases. After briefly considering why psychiatrists would want to do such work, and therefore how lawyers can successfully engage them in it, consideration is given to the essential aspects that psychiatrists look for in their instructions from lawyers that facilitate a proper assessment of issues such as capacity and best interests. Finally, the support psychiatrists might look for in court is discussed.

Persuading psychiatrists to get involved in a case

28.2   Psychiatrists are medically qualified doctors that specialise in helping people with mental disorders. The vast majority of consultant psychiatrists in the UK do most or all of their clinical work in the NHS, and therefore lead busy professional lives. Why would anyone with such commitments be interested in taking on the additional role of being an expert witness for the Court of Protection?

28.3   The simple answer might be because of the fee, or because it is a fairly local case and therefore easy to arrange. But there are other motivators instructing lawyers can appeal to. Psychiatrists working in psychiatric specialties where mental capacity is often an issue – such as psychiatry of learning disability or psychiatry of old age – may have developed a particular interest in Court of Protection work. For any psychiatrist, doing such work gives the opportunity to do a very thorough and detailed assessment of a case, and particularly in cases where an opinion about best interests is sought, it can be very appealing to be essentially speaking up for the person with a mental disorder. Those that are highly experienced in court work may relish particularly interesting cases where new case-law may be made. Others may welcome the whole court experience as something they can use to train junior doctors or other team members.

Instructions

Expertise

28.4   The letter of instruction is obviously crucial to getting a report that addresses the issues you want. It is helpful to be explicit about the role of the expert in the case, and particularly which parties are instructing the expert. Questions need to be as clear as possible, and within the expertise of the psychiatrist. If you are not sure about what might be within their expertise, then it can be helpful to discuss this with the psychiatrist before the letter of instruction is finalised. Having said that, the diagnosis and treatment of mental disorder, and the assessment of capacity are core skills. Commenting on best interests can be, particularly when it concerns directly, or has some bearing on medical or psychiatric assessment and treatment. Because of this concern about appropriate expertise, it is important to instruct a psychiatrist from the right subspeciality. As well as General Adult Psychiatrists, there are specialist psychiatrists for Older Adults; for Children and Adolescents; and for People with Learning (Intellectual) Disability. There are also Forensic Psychiatrists for people with mental disorder who are involved in criminal proceedings.

28.5   Some psychiatrists focus almost exclusively on medico-legal work, and have developed great expertise in the technical aspects of report writing and giving evidence. However, if they have not been in clinical practice for some time, then their knowledge and skills about current psychiatric practice may be more limited, and their expertise brought into question.

Evidence of mental disorder

28.6   When outlining the circumstances of the case, the medical and psychiatric history is highly relevant and any psychiatrist would be grateful for as much detail as possible in this area, and permission to access medical records is usually very helpful.

28.7   An essential element to assessing capacity is determining whether there is a mental disorder present, and assessing the nature and severity of that disorder. Therefore any evidence of mental disorder is really helpful. Obviously this may include previous psychiatric assessments, but psychology assessments, especially psychometric assessments (eg IQ assessments), occupational therapy assessments (eg standardised assessments of skills) and speech and language therapy assessments (eg of communication skills) can all be very valuable. It is also helpful to have detailed descriptions of any recent events or behaviour that have led to concerns about the person being mentally unwell. Previous assessments of capacity are also essential material to include, as are details of any particular attempts that have been made to support decision making in the past.

Assessment of capacity

28.8   Assessment of capacity requires a determination of the information needed to make the decision. It is therefore important to have all the background information relevant to the decision, such as social work reports or statements for welfare decisions, and medical reports for medical decisions. It is of course very helpful if the court has made a determination of the information needed to make the decision in the particular case or if there is any relevant case law about the type of decision in question (eg capacity to consent to sex, capacity to decide residence).

28.9   In cases where there are disputes about capacity or best interests, there are often others involved who have a powerful influence on the person. Because this can substantially affect the ability to weigh information up in the process of making a decision (especially where capacity is borderline) it is important to know as much as possible about this. Sometimes where there are disputes about best interests, there can be significant mental health issues in the family (whether diagnosed or not) and it is very helpful to have full details of such concerns.

Practicalities

28.10   It is important to give contact details for people the psychiatrist need to get history from, or will need to discuss best interests with, or who can assist in setting up the assessment. In order to maximise decision-making ability, it is often helpful to see the person in an environment with which they are familiar, and multiple visits may be required, depending on the complexity of the questions, and how the person is able to engage in the assessment.

28.11   Having described above the sort of information that is very helpful to the assessment, this does not mean that the psychiatrist needs to see the whole court bundle, and judicious limiting of the reading is helpful, especially if opinions about best interests decisions are not required.

28.12   Because the psychiatrist is likely to have many other commitments, it is important to set a realistic timetable for the assessment of at least a few weeks unless the clinical or social situation is very urgent.

Supporting the expert in court

28.13   Many psychiatrists can be anxious about giving oral evidence in court, so it is very helpful if a clear idea of issues to be discussed can be given in advance so that they can prepare properly. Often psychiatrists will be asked questions in court that stray outside their area of expertise, and it is of course for the expert witness to point this out. However, it also helps not to be asked the question in the first place. Psychiatrists are usually happy to participate in meetings of experts, as this is more akin to clinical practice than the more adversarial court process. Finally, on a practical note, it is of course very helpful to fix dates and times as far in advance as possible, bearing in mind that if a case is listed for several days, psychiatrists in clinical practice are unlikely to be able to keep the whole period free, so guidance should be given about when their evidence is likely to be required.

APPENDICES

continued

Primary legislation[1]

MENTAL CAPACITY ACT 2005

Part 1: Persons who lack capacity

The principles

The principles

1 (1) The following principles apply for the purposes of this Act.

(2) A person must be assumed to have capacity unless it is established that he lacks capacity.

(3) A person is not to be treated as unable to make a decision unless all practicable steps to help him to do so have been taken without success.

(4) A person is not to be treated as unable to make a decision merely because he makes an unwise decision.

(5) An act done, or decision made, under this Act for or on behalf of a person who lacks capacity must be done, or made, in his best interests.

(6) Before the act is done, or the decision is made, regard must be had to whether the purpose for which it is needed can be as effectively achieved in a way that is less restrictive of the person's rights and freedom of action.

Preliminary

People who lack capacity

2 (1) For the purposes of this Act, a person lacks capacity in relation to a matter if at the material time he is unable to make a decision for himself in relation to the matter because of an impairment of, or a disturbance in the functioning of, the mind or brain.

(2) It does not matter whether the impairment or disturbance is permanent or temporary.

(3) A lack of capacity cannot be established merely by reference to–

(a) a person's age or appearance, or

(b) a condition of his, or an aspect of his behaviour, which might lead others to make unjustified assumptions about his capacity.

(4) In proceedings under this Act or any other enactment, any question whether a person lacks capacity within the meaning of this Act must be decided on the balance of probabilities.

(5) No power which a person ('D') may exercise under this Act–

(a) in relation to a person who lacks capacity, or

(b) where D reasonably thinks that a person lacks capacity,

is exercisable in relation to a person under 16.

(6) Subsection (5) is subject to section 18(3).

Inability to make decisions

3 (1) For the purposes of section 2, a person is unable to make a decision for himself if he is unable–

(a) to understand the information relevant to the decision,

(b) to retain that information,

(c) to use or weigh that information as part of the process of making the decision, or

(d) to communicate his decision (whether by talking, using sign language or any other means).

(2) A person is not to be regarded as unable to understand the information relevant to a decision if he is able to understand an explanation of it given to him in a way that is appropriate to his circumstances (using simple language, visual aids or any other means).

(3) The fact that a person is able to retain the information relevant to a decision for a short period only does not prevent him from being regarded as able to make the decision.

(4) The information relevant to a decision includes information about the reasonably foreseeable consequences of–

(a) deciding one way or another, or

(b) failing to make the decision.

Best interests

4 (1) In determining for the purposes of this Act what is in a person's best interests, the person making the determination must not make it merely on the basis of–

(a) the person's age or appearance, or

(b) a condition of his, or an aspect of his behaviour, which might lead others to make unjustified assumptions about what might be in his best interests.

(2) The person making the determination must consider all the relevant circumstances and, in particular, take the following steps.

(3) He must consider–

(a) whether it is likely that the person will at some time have capacity in relation to the matter in question, and

(b) if it appears likely that he will, when that is likely to be.

(4) He must, so far as reasonably practicable, permit and encourage the person to participate, or to improve his ability to participate, as fully as possible in any act done for him and any decision affecting him.

(5) Where the determination relates to life-sustaining treatment he must not, in considering whether the treatment is in the best interests of the person concerned, be motivated by a desire to bring about his death.

(6) He must consider, so far as is reasonably ascertainable–

(a) the person's past and present wishes and feelings (and, in particular, any relevant written statement made by him when he had capacity),

(b) the beliefs and values that would be likely to influence his decision if he had capacity, and

(c) the other factors that he would be likely to consider if he were able to do so.

(7) He must take into account, if it is practicable and appropriate to consult them, the views of–

(a) anyone named by the person as someone to be consulted on the matter in question or on matters of that kind,

(b) anyone engaged in caring for the person or interested in his welfare,

(c) any donee of a lasting power of attorney granted by the person, and

(d) any deputy appointed for the person by the court,

as to what would be in the person's best interests and, in particular, as to the matters mentioned in subsection (6).

(8) The duties imposed by subsections (1) to (7) also apply in relation to the exercise of any powers which–

(a) are exercisable under a lasting power of attorney, or

(b) are exercisable by a person under this Act where he reasonably believes that another person lacks capacity.

(9) In the case of an act done, or a decision made, by a person other than the court, there is sufficient compliance with this section if (having complied with the requirements of subsections (1) to (7)) he reasonably believes that what he does or decides is in the best interests of the person concerned.

(10) 'Life-sustaining treatment' means treatment which in the view of a person providing health care for the person concerned is necessary to sustain life.

(11) 'Relevant circumstances' are those–

(a) of which the person making the determination is aware, and

(b) which it would be reasonable to regard as relevant.

Restriction on deprivation of liberty

4A(1) This Act does not authorise any person ('D') to deprive any other person ('P') of his liberty.

(2) But that is subject to–

(a) the following provisions of this section, and

(b) section 4B.

(3) D may deprive P of his liberty if, by doing so, D is giving effect to a relevant decision of the court.

(4) A relevant decision of the court is a decision made by an order under section 16(2)(a) in relation to a matter concerning P's personal welfare.

(5) D may deprive P of his liberty if the deprivation is authorised by Schedule A1 (hospital and care home residents: deprivation of liberty).

Deprivation of liberty necessary for life-sustaining treatment etc

4B(1) If the following conditions are met, D is authorised to deprive P of his liberty while a decision as respects any relevant issue is sought from the court.

(2) The first condition is that there is a question about whether D is authorised to deprive P of his liberty under section 4A.

(3) The second condition is that the deprivation of liberty–

(a) is wholly or partly for the purpose of–

(i) giving P life-sustaining treatment, or

(ii) doing any vital act, or

(b) consists wholly or partly of–

(i) giving P life-sustaining treatment, or

(ii) doing any vital act.

(4) The third condition is that the deprivation of liberty is necessary in order to–

(a) give the life-sustaining treatment, or

(b) do the vital act.

(5) A vital act is any act which the person doing it reasonably believes to be necessary to prevent a serious deterioration in P's condition.

Acts in connection with care or treatment

5(1) If a person ('D') does an act in connection with the care or treatment of another person ('P'), the act is one to which this section applies if–

    (a) before doing the act, D takes reasonable steps to establish whether P lacks capacity in relation to the matter in question, and

    (b) when doing the act, D reasonably believes–

        (i) that P lacks capacity in relation to the matter, and

        (ii) that it will be in P's best interests for the act to be done.

(2) D does not incur any liability in relation to the act that he would not have incurred if P–

    (a) had had capacity to consent in relation to the matter, and

    (b) had consented to D's doing the act.

(3) Nothing in this section excludes a person's civil liability for loss or damage, or his criminal liability, resulting from his negligence in doing the act.

(4) Nothing in this section affects the operation of sections 24 to 26 (advance decisions to refuse treatment).

Section 5 acts: limitations

6 (1) If D does an act that is intended to restrain P, it is not an act to which section 5 applies unless two further conditions are satisfied.

(2) The first condition is that D reasonably believes that it is necessary to do the act in order to prevent harm to P.

(3) The second is that the act is a proportionate response to–

    (a) the likelihood of P's suffering harm, and

    (b) the seriousness of that harm.

(4) For the purposes of this section D restrains P if he–

    (a) uses, or threatens to use, force to secure the doing of an act which P resists, or

    (b) restricts P's liberty of movement, whether or not P resists.

(5) [Repealed.]

(6) Section 5 does not authorise a person to do an act which conflicts with a decision made, within the scope of his authority and in accordance with this Part, by–

    (a) a donee of a lasting power of attorney granted by P, or

    (b) a deputy appointed for P by the court.

(7) But nothing in subsection (6) stops a person–

    (a) providing life-sustaining treatment, or

    (b) doing any act which he reasonably believes to be necessary to prevent a serious deterioration in P's condition,

while a decision as respects any relevant issue is sought from the court.

Payment for necessary goods and services

7 (1) If necessary goods or services are supplied to a person who lacks capacity to contract for the supply, he must pay a reasonable price for them.

(2) 'Necessary' means suitable to a person's condition in life and to his actual requirements at the time when the goods or services are supplied.

Expenditure

8 (1) If an act to which section 5 applies involves expenditure, it is lawful for D–

    (a) to pledge P's credit for the purpose of the expenditure, and

    (b) to apply money in P's possession for meeting the expenditure.

(2) If the expenditure is borne for P by D, it is lawful for D–

    (a) to reimburse himself out of money in P's possession, or

(b) to be otherwise indemnified by P.

(3) Subsections (1) and (2) do not affect any power under which (apart from those subsections) a person–

(a) has lawful control of P's money or other property, and

(b) has power to spend money for P's benefit.

Lasting powers of attorney

Lasting powers of attorney

9 (1) A lasting power of attorney is a power of attorney under which the donor ('P') confers on the donee (or donees) authority to make decisions about all or any of the following–

(a) P's personal welfare or specified matters concerning P's personal welfare, and

(b) P's property and affairs or specified matters concerning P's property and affairs,

and which includes authority to make such decisions in circumstances where P no longer has capacity.

(2) A lasting power of attorney is not created unless–

(a) section 10 is complied with,

(b) an instrument conferring authority of the kind mentioned in subsection (1) is made and registered in accordance with Schedule 1, and

(c) at the time when P executes the instrument, P has reached 18 and has capacity to execute it.

(3) An instrument which–

(a) purports to create a lasting power of attorney, but

(b) does not comply with this section, section 10 or Schedule 1,

confers no authority.

(4) The authority conferred by a lasting power of attorney is subject to–

(a) the provisions of this Act and, in particular, sections 1 (the principles) and 4 (best interests), and

(b) any conditions or restrictions specified in the instrument.

Appointment of donees

10 (1) A donee of a lasting power of attorney must be–

(a) an individual who has reached 18, or

(b) if the power relates only to P's property and affairs, either such an individual or a trust corporation.

(2) An individual who is bankrupt or is a person in relation to whom a debt relief order is made may not be appointed as donee of a lasting power of attorney in relation to P's property and affairs.

(3) Subsections (4) to (7) apply in relation to an instrument under which two or more persons are to act as donees of a lasting power of attorney.

(4) The instrument may appoint them to act–

(a) jointly,

(b) jointly and severally, or

(c) jointly in respect of some matters and jointly and severally in respect of others.

(5) To the extent to which it does not specify whether they are to act jointly or

jointly and severally, the instrument is to be assumed to appoint them to act jointly.

(6) If they are to act jointly, a failure, as respects one of them, to comply with the requirements of subsection (1) or (2) or Part 1 or 2 of Schedule 1 prevents a lasting power of attorney from being created.

(7) If they are to act jointly and severally, a failure, as respects one of them, to comply with the requirements of subsection (1) or (2) or Part 1 or 2 of Schedule 1–

    (a) prevents the appointment taking effect in his case, but

    (b) does not prevent a lasting power of attorney from being created in the case of the other or others.

(8) An instrument used to create a lasting power of attorney–

    (a) cannot give the donee (or, if more than one, any of them) power to appoint a substitute or successor, but

    (b) may itself appoint a person to replace the donee (or, if more than one, any of them) on the occurrence of an event mentioned in section 13(6)(a) to (d) which has the effect of terminating the donee's appointment.

Lasting powers of attorney: restrictions

11 (1) A lasting power of attorney does not authorise the donee (or, if more than one, any of them) to do an act that is intended to restrain P, unless three conditions are satisfied.

(2) The first condition is that P lacks, or the donee reasonably believes that P lacks, capacity in relation to the matter in question.

(3) The second is that the donee reasonably believes that it is necessary to do the act in order to prevent harm to P.

(4) The third is that the act is a proportionate response to–

    (a) the likelihood of P's suffering harm, and

    (b) the seriousness of that harm.

(5) For the purposes of this section, the donee restrains P if he–

    (a) uses, or threatens to use, force to secure the doing of an act which P resists, or

    (b) restricts P's liberty of movement, whether or not P resists,

or if he authorises another person to do any of those things.

(6) [Repealed.]

(7) Where a lasting power of attorney authorises the donee (or, if more than one, any of them) to make decisions about P's personal welfare, the authority–

    (a) does not extend to making such decisions in circumstances other than those where P lacks, or the donee reasonably believes that P lacks, capacity,

    (b) is subject to sections 24 to 26 (advance decisions to refuse treatment), and

    (c) extends to giving or refusing consent to the carrying out or continuation of a treatment by a person providing health care for P.

(8) But subsection (7)(c)–

    (a) does not authorise the giving or refusing of consent to the carrying out or continuation of life-sustaining treatment, unless the instrument contains express provision to that effect, and

    (b) is subject to any conditions or restrictions in the instrument.

Scope of lasting powers of attorney: gifts

12 (1) Where a lasting power of attorney confers authority to make decisions about P's property and affairs, it does not authorise a donee (or, if more than one, any of them) to dispose of the donor's property by making gifts except to the extent permitted by subsection (2).

(2) The donee may make gifts–

(a) on customary occasions to persons (including himself) who are related to or connected with the donor, or

(b) to any charity to whom the donor made or might have been expected to make gifts,

if the value of each such gift is not unreasonable having regard to all the circumstances and, in particular, the size of the donor's estate.

(3) 'Customary occasion' means–

(a) the occasion or anniversary of a birth, a marriage or the formation of a civil partnership, or

(b) any other occasion on which presents are customarily given within families or among friends or associates.

(4) Subsection (2) is subject to any conditions or restrictions in the instrument.

Revocation of lasting powers of attorney etc

13 (1) This section applies if–

(a) P has executed an instrument with a view to creating a lasting power of attorney, or

(b) a lasting power of attorney is registered as having been conferred by P, and in this section references to revoking the power include revoking the instrument.

(2) P may, at any time when he has capacity to do so, revoke the power.

(3) P's bankruptcy, or the making of a debt relief order (under Part 7A of the Insolvency Act 1986) in respect of P, revokes the power so far as it relates to P's property and affairs.

(4) But where P is bankrupt merely because an interim bankruptcy restrictions order has effect in respect of him or where P is subject to an interim debt relief restrictions order (under Schedule 4ZB of the Insolvency Act 1986), the power is suspended, so far as it relates to P's property and affairs, for so long as the order has effect.

(5) The occurrence in relation to a donee of an event mentioned in subsection (6)–

(a) terminates his appointment, and

(b) except in the cases given in subsection (7), revokes the power.

(6) The events are–

(a) the disclaimer of the appointment by the donee in accordance with such requirements as may be prescribed for the purposes of this section in regulations made by the Lord Chancellor,

(b) subject to subsections (8) and (9), the death or bankruptcy of the donee or the making of a debt relief order (under Part 7A of the Insolvency Act 1986) in respect of the donee or, if the donee is a trust corporation, its winding-up or dissolution,

(c) subject to subsection (11), the dissolution or annulment of a marriage or civil partnership between the donor and the donee,

     (d) the lack of capacity of the donee.

(7) The cases are–
     (a) the donee is replaced under the terms of the instrument,
     (b) he is one of two or more persons appointed to act as donees jointly and severally in respect of any matter and, after the event, there is at least one remaining donee.

(8) The bankruptcy of a donee or the making of a debt relief order (under Part 7A of the Insolvency Act 1986) in respect of a donee does not terminate his appointment, or revoke the power, in so far as his authority relates to P's personal welfare.

(9) Where the donee is bankrupt merely because an interim bankruptcy restrictions order has effect in respect of him, or where the donee is subject to an interim debt relief restrictions order (under Schedule 4ZB of the Insolvency Act 1986), his appointment and the power are suspended, so far as they relate to P's property and affairs, for so long as the order has effect.

(10) Where the donee is one of two or more appointed to act jointly and severally under the power in respect of any matter, the reference in subsection (9) to the suspension of the power is to its suspension in so far as it relates to that donee.

(11) The dissolution or annulment of a marriage or civil partnership does not terminate the appointment of a donee, or revoke the power, if the instrument provided that it was not to do so.

Protection of donee and others if no power created or power revoked

14 (1) Subsections (2) and (3) apply if–
     (a) an instrument has been registered under Schedule 1 as a lasting power of attorney, but
     (b) a lasting power of attorney was not created,
     whether or not the registration has been cancelled at the time of the act or transaction in question.

(2) A donee who acts in purported exercise of the power does not incur any liability (to P or any other person) because of the non-existence of the power unless at the time of acting he–
     (a) knows that a lasting power of attorney was not created, or
     (b) is aware of circumstances which, if a lasting power of attorney had been created, would have terminated his authority to act as a donee.

(3) Any transaction between the donee and another person is, in favour of that person, as valid as if the power had been in existence, unless at the time of the transaction that person has knowledge of a matter referred to in subsection (2).

(4) If the interest of a purchaser depends on whether a transaction between the donee and the other person was valid by virtue of subsection (3), it is conclusively presumed in favour of the purchaser that the transaction was valid if–
     (a) the transaction was completed within 12 months of the date on which the instrument was registered, or
     (b) the other person makes a statutory declaration, before or within 3 months after the completion of the purchase, that he had no reason at the time of the transaction to doubt that the donee had authority to dispose of the property which was the subject of the transaction.

(5) In its application to a lasting power of attorney which relates to matters in addition to P's property and affairs, section 5 of the Powers of Attorney Act 1971 (c 27) (protection where power is revoked) has effect as if references to revocation included the cessation of the power in relation to P's property and affairs.

(6) Where two or more donees are appointed under a lasting power of attorney, this section applies as if references to the donee were to all or any of them.

General powers of the court and appointment of deputies

Power to make declarations

15 (1) The court may make declarations as to–

    (a) whether a person has or lacks capacity to make a decision specified in the declaration;

    (b) whether a person has or lacks capacity to make decisions on such matters as are described in the declaration;

    (c) the lawfulness or otherwise of any act done, or yet to be done, in relation to that person.

(2) 'Act' includes an omission and a course of conduct.

Powers to make decisions and appoint deputies: general

16 (1) This section applies if a person ('P') lacks capacity in relation to a matter or matters concerning–

    (a) P's personal welfare, or

    (b) P's property and affairs.

(2) The court may–

    (a) by making an order, make the decision or decisions on P's behalf in relation to the matter or matters, or

    (b) appoint a person (a 'deputy') to make decisions on P's behalf in relation to the matter or matters.

(3) The powers of the court under this section are subject to the provisions of this Act and, in particular, to sections 1 (the principles) and 4 (best interests).

(4) When deciding whether it is in P's best interests to appoint a deputy, the court must have regard (in addition to the matters mentioned in section 4) to the principles that–

    (a) a decision by the court is to be preferred to the appointment of a deputy to make a decision, and

    (b) the powers conferred on a deputy should be as limited in scope and duration as is reasonably practicable in the circumstances.

(5) The court may make such further orders or give such directions, and confer on a deputy such powers or impose on him such duties, as it thinks necessary or expedient for giving effect to, or otherwise in connection with, an order or appointment made by it under subsection (2).

(6) Without prejudice to section 4, the court may make the order, give the directions or make the appointment on such terms as it considers are in P's best interests, even though no application is before the court for an order, directions or an appointment on those terms.

(7) An order of the court may be varied or discharged by a subsequent order.

(8) The court may, in particular, revoke the appointment of a deputy or vary the powers conferred on him if it is satisfied that the deputy–

(a) has behaved, or is behaving, in a way that contravenes the authority conferred on him by the court or is not in P's best interests, or

(b) proposes to behave in a way that would contravene that authority or would not be in P's best interests.

Section 16 powers: Mental Health Act patients etc

16A(1) If a person is ineligible to be deprived of liberty by this Act, the court may not include in a welfare order provision which authorises the person to be deprived of his liberty.

(2) If—

(a) a welfare order includes provision which authorises a person to be deprived of his liberty, and

(b) that person becomes ineligible to be deprived of liberty by this Act,

the provision ceases to have effect for as long as the person remains ineligible.

(3) Nothing in subsection (2) affects the power of the court under section 16(7) to vary or discharge the welfare order.

(4) For the purposes of this section—

(a) Schedule 1A applies for determining whether or not P is ineligible to be deprived of liberty by this Act;

(b) 'welfare order' means an order under section 16(2)(a).

Section 16 powers: personal welfare

17 (1) The powers under section 16 as respects P's personal welfare extend in particular to—

(a) deciding where P is to live;

(b) deciding what contact, if any, P is to have with any specified persons;

(c) making an order prohibiting a named person from having contact with P;

(d) giving or refusing consent to the carrying out or continuation of a treatment by a person providing health care for P;

(e) giving a direction that a person responsible for P's health care allow a different person to take over that responsibility.

(2) Subsection (1) is subject to section 20 (restrictions on deputies).

Section 16 powers: property and affairs

18 (1) The powers under section 16 as respects P's property and affairs extend in particular to—

(a) the control and management of P's property;

(b) the sale, exchange, charging, gift or other disposition of P's property;

(c) the acquisition of property in P's name or on P's behalf;

(d) the carrying on, on P's behalf, of any profession, trade or business;

(e) the taking of a decision which will have the effect of dissolving a partnership of which P is a member;

(f) the carrying out of any contract entered into by P;

(g) the discharge of P's debts and of any of P's obligations, whether legally enforceable or not;

(h) the settlement of any of P's property, whether for P's benefit or for the benefit of others;

(i) the execution for P of a will;

(j) the exercise of any power (including a power to consent) vested in P whether beneficially or as trustee or otherwise;

(k) the conduct of legal proceedings in P's name or on P's behalf.

(2) No will may be made under subsection (1)(i) at a time when P has not reached 18.

(3) The powers under section 16 as respects any other matter relating to P's property and affairs may be exercised even though P has not reached 16, if the court considers it likely that P will still lack capacity to make decisions in respect of that matter when he reaches 18.

(4) Schedule 2 supplements the provisions of this section.

(5) Section 16(7) (variation and discharge of court orders) is subject to paragraph 6 of Schedule 2.

(6) Subsection (1) is subject to section 20 (restrictions on deputies).

Appointment of deputies

19 (1) A deputy appointed by the court must be–

(a) an individual who has reached 18, or

(b) as respects powers in relation to property and affairs, an individual who has reached 18 or a trust corporation.

(2) The court may appoint an individual by appointing the holder for the time being of a specified office or position.

(3) A person may not be appointed as a deputy without his consent.

(4) The court may appoint two or more deputies to act–

(a) jointly,

(b) jointly and severally, or

(c) jointly in respect of some matters and jointly and severally in respect of others.

(5) When appointing a deputy or deputies, the court may at the same time appoint one or more other persons to succeed the existing deputy or those deputies–

(a) in such circumstances, or on the happening of such events, as may be specified by the court;

(b) for such period as may be so specified.

(6) A deputy is to be treated as P's agent in relation to anything done or decided by him within the scope of his appointment and in accordance with this Part.

(7) The deputy is entitled–

(a) to be reimbursed out of P's property for his reasonable expenses in discharging his functions, and

(b) if the court so directs when appointing him, to remuneration out of P's property for discharging them.

(8) The court may confer on a deputy powers to–

(a) take possession or control of all or any specified part of P's property;

(b) exercise all or any specified powers in respect of it, including such powers of investment as the court may determine.

(9) The court may require a deputy–

(a) to give to the Public Guardian such security as the court thinks fit for the due discharge of his functions, and

(b) to submit to the Public Guardian such reports at such times or at such intervals as the court may direct.

Restrictions on deputies

20 (1) A deputy does not have power to make a decision on behalf of P in relation to a matter if he knows or has reasonable grounds for believing that P has capacity in relation to the matter.

(2) Nothing in section 16(5) or 17 permits a deputy to be given power—
   (a) to prohibit a named person from having contact with P;
   (b) to direct a person responsible for P's health care to allow a different person to take over that responsibility.

(3) A deputy may not be given powers with respect to—
   (a) the settlement of any of P's property, whether for P's benefit or for the benefit of others,
   (b) the execution for P of a will, or
   (c) the exercise of any power (including a power to consent) vested in P whether beneficially or as trustee or otherwise.

(4) A deputy may not be given power to make a decision on behalf of P which is inconsistent with a decision made, within the scope of his authority and in accordance with this Act, by the donee of a lasting power of attorney granted by P (or, if there is more than one donee, by any of them).

(5) A deputy may not refuse consent to the carrying out or continuation of life-sustaining treatment in relation to P.

(6) The authority conferred on a deputy is subject to the provisions of this Act and, in particular, sections 1 (the principles) and 4 (best interests).

(7) A deputy may not do an act that is intended to restrain P unless four conditions are satisfied.

(8) The first condition is that, in doing the act, the deputy is acting within the scope of an authority expressly conferred on him by the court.

(9) The second is that P lacks, or the deputy reasonably believes that P lacks, capacity in relation to the matter in question.

(10) The third is that the deputy reasonably believes that it is necessary to do the act in order to prevent harm to P.

(11) The fourth is that the act is a proportionate response to—
   (a) the likelihood of P's suffering harm, and
   (b) the seriousness of that harm.

(12) For the purposes of this section, a deputy restrains P if he—
   (a) uses, or threatens to use, force to secure the doing of an act which P resists, or
   (b) restricts P's liberty of movement, whether or not P resists,
   or if he authorises another person to do any of those things.

(13) [Repealed.]

Transfer of proceedings relating to people under 18

21 (1) The Lord Chief Justice, with the concurrence of the Lord Chancellor, may by order make provision as to the transfer of proceedings relating to a person under 18, in such circumstances as are specified in the order—
   (a) from the Court of Protection to a court having jurisdiction under the Children Act 1989, or

(b) from a court having jurisdiction under that Act to the Court of Protection.

(2) The Lord Chief Justice may nominate any of the following to exercise his functions under this section—

(a) the President of the Court of Protection;

(b) a judicial office holder (as defined in section 109(4) of the Constitutional Reform Act 2005).

Powers of the court in relation to Schedule A1

Powers of court in relation to Schedule A1

21A(1) This section applies if either of the following has been given under Schedule A1—

(a) a standard authorisation;

(b) an urgent authorisation.

(2) Where a standard authorisation has been given, the court may determine any question relating to any of the following matters—

(a) whether the relevant person meets one or more of the qualifying requirements;

(b) the period during which the standard authorisation is to be in force;

(c) the purpose for which the standard authorisation is given;

(d) the conditions subject to which the standard authorisation is given.

(3) If the court determines any question under subsection (2), the court may make an order—

(a) varying or terminating the standard authorisation, or

(b) directing the supervisory body to vary or terminate the standard authorisation.

(4) Where an urgent authorisation has been given, the court may determine any question relating to any of the following matters—

(a) whether the urgent authorisation should have been given;

(b) the period during which the urgent authorisation is to be in force;

(c) the purpose for which the urgent authorisation is given.

(5) Where the court determines any question under subsection (4), the court may make an order—

(a) varying or terminating the urgent authorisation, or

(b) directing the managing authority of the relevant hospital or care home to vary or terminate the urgent authorisation.

(6) Where the court makes an order under subsection (3) or (5), the court may make an order about a person's liability for any act done in connection with the standard or urgent authorisation before its variation or termination.

(7) An order under subsection (6) may, in particular, exclude a person from liability.

Powers of the court in relation to lasting powers of attorney

Powers of court in relation to validity of lasting powers of attorney

22 (1) This section and section 23 apply if—

(a) a person ('P') has executed or purported to execute an instrument with a view to creating a lasting power of attorney, or

(b) an instrument has been registered as a lasting power of attorney conferred by P.

(2) The court may determine any question relating to–
  (a) whether one or more of the requirements for the creation of a lasting power of attorney have been met;
  (b) whether the power has been revoked or has otherwise come to an end.

(3) Subsection (4) applies if the court is satisfied–
  (a) that fraud or undue pressure was used to induce P–
    (i) to execute an instrument for the purpose of creating a lasting power of attorney, or
    (ii) to create a lasting power of attorney, or
  (b) that the donee (or, if more than one, any of them) of a lasting power of attorney–
    (i) has behaved, or is behaving, in a way that contravenes his authority or is not in P's best interests, or
    (ii) proposes to behave in a way that would contravene his authority or would not be in P's best interests.

(4) The court may–
  (a) direct that an instrument purporting to create the lasting power of attorney is not to be registered, or
  (b) if P lacks capacity to do so, revoke the instrument or the lasting power of attorney.

(5) If there is more than one donee, the court may under subsection (4)(b) revoke the instrument or the lasting power of attorney so far as it relates to any of them.

(6) 'Donee' includes an intended donee.

Powers of court in relation to operation of lasting powers of attorney

23 (1) The court may determine any question as to the meaning or effect of a lasting power of attorney or an instrument purporting to create one.

(2) The court may–
  (a) give directions with respect to decisions–
    (i) which the donee of a lasting power of attorney has authority to make, and
    (ii) which P lacks capacity to make;
  (b) give any consent or authorisation to act which the donee would have to obtain from P if P had capacity to give it.

(3) The court may, if P lacks capacity to do so–
  (a) give directions to the donee with respect to the rendering by him of reports or accounts and the production of records kept by him for that purpose;
  (b) require the donee to supply information or produce documents or things in his possession as donee;
  (c) give directions with respect to the remuneration or expenses of the donee;
  (d) relieve the donee wholly or partly from any liability which he has or may have incurred on account of a breach of his duties as donee.

(4) The court may authorise the making of gifts which are not within section 12(2) (permitted gifts).

(5) Where two or more donees are appointed under a lasting power of attorney, this section applies as if references to the donee were to all or any of them.

Advance decisions to refuse treatment

Advance decisions to refuse treatment: general

24 (1) 'Advance decision' means a decision made by a person ('P'), after he has reached 18 and when he has capacity to do so, that if–
  (a) at a later time and in such circumstances as he may specify, a specified treatment is proposed to be carried out or continued by a person providing health care for him, and
  (b) at that time he lacks capacity to consent to the carrying out or continuation of the treatment,
  the specified treatment is not to be carried out or continued.
  (2) For the purposes of subsection (1)(a), a decision may be regarded as specifying a treatment or circumstances even though expressed in layman's terms.
  (3) P may withdraw or alter an advance decision at any time when he has capacity to do so.
  (4) A withdrawal (including a partial withdrawal) need not be in writing.
  (5) An alteration of an advance decision need not be in writing (unless section 25(5) applies in relation to the decision resulting from the alteration).

Validity and applicability of advance decisions

25 (1) An advance decision does not affect the liability which a person may incur for carrying out or continuing a treatment in relation to P unless the decision is at the material time–
  (a) valid, and
  (b) applicable to the treatment.
  (2) An advance decision is not valid if P–
  (a) has withdrawn the decision at a time when he had capacity to do so,
  (b) has, under a lasting power of attorney created after the advance decision was made, conferred authority on the donee (or, if more than one, any of them) to give or refuse consent to the treatment to which the advance decision relates, or
  (c) has done anything else clearly inconsistent with the advance decision remaining his fixed decision.
  (3) An advance decision is not applicable to the treatment in question if at the material time P has capacity to give or refuse consent to it.
  (4) An advance decision is not applicable to the treatment in question if–
  (a) that treatment is not the treatment specified in the advance decision,
  (b) any circumstances specified in the advance decision are absent, or
  (c) there are reasonable grounds for believing that circumstances exist which P did not anticipate at the time of the advance decision and which would have affected his decision had he anticipated them.
  (5) An advance decision is not applicable to life-sustaining treatment unless–
  (a) the decision is verified by a statement by P to the effect that it is to apply to that treatment even if life is at risk, and
  (b) the decision and statement comply with subsection (6).
  (6) A decision or statement complies with this subsection only if–
  (a) it is in writing,
  (b) it is signed by P or by another person in P's presence and by P's direction,

    (c) the signature is made or acknowledged by P in the presence of a witness, and

    (d) the witness signs it, or acknowledges his signature, in P's presence.

(7) The existence of any lasting power of attorney other than one of a description mentioned in subsection (2)(b) does not prevent the advance decision from being regarded as valid and applicable.

Effect of advance decisions

26 (1) If P has made an advance decision which is—

    (a) valid, and

    (b) applicable to a treatment,

the decision has effect as if he had made it, and had had capacity to make it, at the time when the question arises whether the treatment should be carried out or continued.

(2) A person does not incur liability for carrying out or continuing the treatment unless, at the time, he is satisfied that an advance decision exists which is valid and applicable to the treatment.

(3) A person does not incur liability for the consequences of withholding or withdrawing a treatment from P if, at the time, he reasonably believes that an advance decision exists which is valid and applicable to the treatment.

(4) The court may make a declaration as to whether an advance decision—

    (a) exists;

    (b) is valid;

    (c) is applicable to a treatment.

(5) Nothing in an apparent advance decision stops a person—

    (a) providing life-sustaining treatment, or

    (b) doing any act he reasonably believes to be necessary to prevent a serious deterioration in P's condition,

while a decision as respects any relevant issue is sought from the court.

Excluded decisions

Family relationships etc

27 (1) Nothing in this Act permits a decision on any of the following matters to be made on behalf of a person—

    (a) consenting to marriage or a civil partnership,

    (b) consenting to have sexual relations,

    (c) consenting to a decree of divorce being granted on the basis of two years' separation,

    (d) consenting to a dissolution order being made in relation to a civil partnership on the basis of two years' separation,

    (e) consenting to a child's being placed for adoption by an adoption agency,

    (f) consenting to the making of an adoption order,

    (g) discharging parental responsibilities in matters not relating to a child's property,

    (h) giving a consent under the Human Fertilisation and Embryology Act 1990 (c 37)

    (i) giving a consent under the Human Fertilisation and Embryology Act 2008.

(2) 'Adoption order' means—

(a) an adoption order within the meaning of the Adoption and Children Act 2002 (c 38) (including a future adoption order), and

(b) an order under section 84 of that Act (parental responsibility prior to adoption abroad).

Mental Health Act matters

28 (1) Nothing in this Act authorises anyone–

(a) to give a patient medical treatment for mental disorder, or

(b) to consent to a patient's being given medical treatment for mental disorder,

if, at the time when it is proposed to treat the patient, his treatment is regulated by Part 4 of the Mental Health Act.

(1A) Subsection (1) does not apply in relation to any form of treatment to which section 58A of that Act (electro-convulsive therapy, etc) applies if the patient comes within subsection (7) of that section (informal patient under 18 who cannot give consent).

(1B) Section 5 does not apply to an act to which section 64B of the Mental Health Act applies (treatment of community patients not recalled to hospital).

(2) 'Medical treatment', 'mental disorder' and 'patient' have the same meaning as in that Act.

Voting rights

29 (1) Nothing in this Act permits a decision on voting at an election for any public office, or at a referendum, to be made on behalf of a person.

(2) 'Referendum' has the same meaning as in section 101 of the Political Parties, Elections and Referendums Act 2000 (c 41).

Research

Research

30 (1) Intrusive research carried out on, or in relation to, a person who lacks capacity to consent to it is unlawful unless it is carried out–

(a) as part of a research project which is for the time being approved by the appropriate body for the purposes of this Act in accordance with section 31, and

(b) in accordance with sections 32 and 33.

(2) Research is intrusive if it is of a kind that would be unlawful if it was carried out–

(a) on or in relation to a person who had capacity to consent to it, but

(b) without his consent.

(3) A clinical trial which is subject to the provisions of clinical trials regulations is not to be treated as research for the purposes of this section.

(3A) Research is not intrusive to the extent that it consists of the use of a person's human cells to bring about the creation *in vitro* of an embryo or human admixed embryo, or the subsequent storage or use of an embryo or human admixed embryo so created.

(3B) Expressions used in subsection (3A) and in Schedule 3 to the Human Fertilisation and Embryology Act 1990 (consents to use or storage of gametes, embryos or human admixed embryos etc) have the same meaning in that subsection as in that Schedule.

(4) 'Appropriate body', in relation to a research project, means the person, committee or other body specified in regulations made by the appropriate authority as the appropriate body in relation to a project of the kind in question.

(5) 'Clinical trials regulations' means–

(a) the Medicines for Human Use (Clinical Trials) Regulations 2004 (SI No 1031) and any other regulations replacing those regulations or amending them, and

(b) any other regulations relating to clinical trials and designated by the Secretary of State as clinical trials regulations for the purposes of this section.

(6) In this section, section 32 and section 34, 'appropriate authority' means–

(a) in relation to the carrying out of research in England, the Secretary of State, and

(b) in relation to the carrying out of research in Wales, the National Assembly for Wales.

Requirements for approval

31 (1) The appropriate body may not approve a research project for the purposes of this Act unless satisfied that the following requirements will be met in relation to research carried out as part of the project on, or in relation to, a person who lacks capacity to consent to taking part in the project ('P').

(2) The research must be connected with–

(a) an impairing condition affecting P, or

(b) its treatment.

(3) 'Impairing condition' means a condition which is (or may be) attributable to, or which causes or contributes to (or may cause or contribute to), the impairment of, or disturbance in the functioning of, the mind or brain.

(4) There must be reasonable grounds for believing that research of comparable effectiveness cannot be carried out if the project has to be confined to, or relate only to, persons who have capacity to consent to taking part in it.

(5) The research must–

(a) have the potential to benefit P without imposing on P a burden that is disproportionate to the potential benefit to P, or

(b) be intended to provide knowledge of the causes or treatment of, or of the care of persons affected by, the same or a similar condition.

(6) If the research falls within paragraph (b) of subsection (5) but not within paragraph (a), there must be reasonable grounds for believing–

(a) that the risk to P from taking part in the project is likely to be negligible, and

(b) that anything done to, or in relation to, P will not–

(i) interfere with P's freedom of action or privacy in a significant way, or

(ii) be unduly invasive or restrictive.

(7) There must be reasonable arrangements in place for ensuring that the requirements of sections 32 and 33 will be met.

Consulting carers etc

32 (1) This section applies if a person ('R')–

(a) is conducting an approved research project, and

    (b) wishes to carry out research, as part of the project, on or in relation to a person ('P') who lacks capacity to consent to taking part in the project.

(2) R must take reasonable steps to identify a person who–

    (a) otherwise than in a professional capacity or for remuneration, is engaged in caring for P or is interested in P's welfare, and

    (b) is prepared to be consulted by R under this section.

(3) If R is unable to identify such a person he must, in accordance with guidance issued by the appropriate authority, nominate a person who–

    (a) is prepared to be consulted by R under this section, but

    (b) has no connection with the project.

(4) R must provide the person identified under subsection (2), or nominated under subsection (3), with information about the project and ask him–

    (a) for advice as to whether P should take part in the project, and

    (b) what, in his opinion, P's wishes and feelings about taking part in the project would be likely to be if P had capacity in relation to the matter.

(5) If, at any time, the person consulted advises R that in his opinion P's wishes and feelings would be likely to lead him to decline to take part in the project (or to wish to withdraw from it) if he had capacity in relation to the matter, R must ensure–

    (a) if P is not already taking part in the project, that he does not take part in it;

    (b) if P is taking part in the project, that he is withdrawn from it.

(6) But subsection (5)(b) does not require treatment that P has been receiving as part of the project to be discontinued if R has reasonable grounds for believing that there would be a significant risk to P's health if it were discontinued.

(7) The fact that a person is the donee of a lasting power of attorney given by P, or is P's deputy, does not prevent him from being the person consulted under this section.

(8) Subsection (9) applies if treatment is being, or is about to be, provided for P as a matter of urgency and R considers that, having regard to the nature of the research and of the particular circumstances of the case–

    (a) it is also necessary to take action for the purposes of the research as a matter of urgency, but

    (b) it is not reasonably practicable to consult under the previous provisions of this section.

(9) R may take the action if–

    (a) he has the agreement of a registered medical practitioner who is not involved in the organisation or conduct of the research project, or

    (b) where it is not reasonably practicable in the time available to obtain that agreement, he acts in accordance with a procedure approved by the appropriate body at the time when the research project was approved under section 31.

(10) But R may not continue to act in reliance on subsection (9) if he has reasonable grounds for believing that it is no longer necessary to take the action as a matter of urgency.

Additional safeguards

33 (1) This section applies in relation to a person who is taking part in an approved research project even though he lacks capacity to consent to taking part.

(2) Nothing may be done to, or in relation to, him in the course of the research–

   (a) to which he appears to object (whether by showing signs of resistance or otherwise) except where what is being done is intended to protect him from harm or to reduce or prevent pain or discomfort, or

   (b) which would be contrary to–

      (i) an advance decision of his which has effect, or

      (ii) any other form of statement made by him and not subsequently withdrawn,

of which R is aware.

(3) The interests of the person must be assumed to outweigh those of science and society.

(4) If he indicates (in any way) that he wishes to be withdrawn from the project he must be withdrawn without delay.

(5) P must be withdrawn from the project, without delay, if at any time the person conducting the research has reasonable grounds for believing that one or more of the requirements set out in section 31(2) to (7) is no longer met in relation to research being carried out on, or in relation to, P.

(6) But neither subsection (4) nor subsection (5) requires treatment that P has been receiving as part of the project to be discontinued if R has reasonable grounds for believing that there would be a significant risk to P's health if it were discontinued.

Loss of capacity during research project

34 (1) This section applies where a person ('P')–

   (a) has consented to take part in a research project begun before the commencement of section 30, but

   (b) before the conclusion of the project, loses capacity to consent to continue to take part in it.

(2) The appropriate authority may by regulations provide that, despite P's loss of capacity, research of a prescribed kind may be carried out on, or in relation to, P if–

   (a) the project satisfies prescribed requirements,

   (b) any information or material relating to P which is used in the research is of a prescribed description and was obtained before P's loss of capacity, and

   (c) the person conducting the project takes in relation to P such steps as may be prescribed for the purpose of protecting him.

(3) The regulations may, in particular,–

   (a) make provision about when, for the purposes of the regulations, a project is to be treated as having begun;

   (b) include provision similar to any made by section 31, 32 or 33.

Independent mental capacity advocate service

Appointment of independent mental capacity advocates

35 (1) The responsible authority must make such arrangements as it considers reasonable to enable persons ('independent mental capacity advocates') to be available to represent and support persons to whom acts or decisions proposed under sections 37, 38 and 39 relate or persons who fall within section 39A, 39C or 39D.

(2) The appropriate authority may make regulations as to the appointment of independent mental capacity advocates.

(3) The regulations may, in particular, provide–

  (a) that a person may act as an independent mental capacity advocate only in such circumstances, or only subject to such conditions, as may be prescribed;

  (b) for the appointment of a person as an independent mental capacity advocate to be subject to approval in accordance with the regulations.

(4) In making arrangements under subsection (1), the responsible authority must have regard to the principle that a person to whom a proposed act or decision relates should, so far as practicable, be represented and supported by a person who is independent of any person who will be responsible for the act or decision.

(5) The arrangements may include provision for payments to be made to, or in relation to, persons carrying out functions in accordance with the arrangements.

(6) For the purpose of enabling him to carry out his functions, an independent mental capacity advocate–

  (a) may interview in private the person whom he has been instructed to represent, and

  (b) may, at all reasonable times, examine and take copies of–

    (i)   any health record,

    (ii) any record of, or held by, a local authority and compiled in connection with a social services function, and

    (iii) any record held by a person registered under Part 2 of the Care Standards Act 2000 or Chapter 2 of Part 1 of the Health and Social Care Act 2008,

  which the person holding the record considers may be relevant to the independent mental capacity advocate's investigation.

(6A) In subsections (1) and (4), 'the responsible authority' means–

  (a) in relation to the provision of the services of independent mental capacity advocates in the area of a local authority in England, that local authority, and

  (b) in relation to the provision of the services of independent mental capacity advocates in Wales, the Welsh Ministers.

(6B) In subsection (6A)(a), 'local authority' has the meaning given in section 64(1) except that it does not include the council of a county or county borough in Wales.

(7) In this section, section 36 and section 37, 'the appropriate authority' means–

  (a) in relation to the provision of the services of independent mental capacity advocates in England, the Secretary of State, and

  (b) in relation to the provision of the services of independent mental capacity advocates in Wales, the National Assembly for Wales.

Functions of independent mental capacity advocates

36 (1) The appropriate authority may make regulations as to the functions of independent mental capacity advocates.

(2) The regulations may, in particular, make provision requiring an advocate to take such steps as may be prescribed for the purpose of–

(a) providing support to the person whom he has been instructed to represent ('P') so that P may participate as fully as possible in any relevant decision;

(b) obtaining and evaluating relevant information;

(c) ascertaining what P's wishes and feelings would be likely to be, and the beliefs and values that would be likely to influence P, if he had capacity;

(d) ascertaining what alternative courses of action are available in relation to P;

(e) obtaining a further medical opinion where treatment is proposed and the advocate thinks that one should be obtained.

(3) The regulations may also make provision as to circumstances in which the advocate may challenge, or provide assistance for the purpose of challenging, any relevant decision.

Provision of serious medical treatment by NHS body

37 (1) This section applies if an NHS body–

(a) is proposing to provide, or secure the provision of, serious medical treatment for a person ('P') who lacks capacity to consent to the treatment, and

(b) is satisfied that there is no person, other than one engaged in providing care or treatment for P in a professional capacity or for remuneration, whom it would be appropriate to consult in determining what would be in P's best interests.

(2) But this section does not apply if P's treatment is regulated by Part 4 or 4A of the Mental Health Act.

(3) Before the treatment is provided, the NHS body must instruct an independent mental capacity advocate to represent P.

(4) If the treatment needs to be provided as a matter of urgency, it may be provided even though the NHS body has not been able to comply with subsection (3).

(5) The NHS body must, in providing or securing the provision of treatment for P, take into account any information given, or submissions made, by the independent mental capacity advocate.

(6) 'Serious medical treatment' means treatment which involves providing, withholding or withdrawing treatment of a kind prescribed by regulations made by the appropriate authority.

(7) 'NHS body' has such meaning as may be prescribed by regulations made for the purposes of this section by–

(a) the Secretary of State, in relation to bodies in England, or

(b) the National Assembly for Wales, in relation to bodies in Wales.

Provision of accommodation by NHS body

38 (1) This section applies if an NHS body proposes to make arrangements–

(a) for the provision of accommodation in a hospital or care home for a person ('P') who lacks capacity to agree to the arrangements, or

(b) for a change in P's accommodation to another hospital or care home,
and is satisfied that there is no person, other than one engaged in providing
care or treatment for P in a professional capacity or for remuneration, whom
it would be appropriate for it to consult in determining what would be in P's
best interests.

(2) But this section does not apply if P is accommodated as a result of an obligation imposed on him under the Mental Health Act.

(2A) And this section does not apply if–

    (a) an independent mental capacity advocate must be appointed under sec-
tion 39A or 39C (whether or not by the NHS body) to represent P, and

    (b) the hospital or care home in which P is to be accommodated under the
arrangements referred to in this section is the relevant hospital or care
home under the authorisation referred to in that section.

(3) Before making the arrangements, the NHS body must instruct an independent mental capacity advocate to represent P unless it is satisfied that–

    (a) the accommodation is likely to be provided for a continuous period which
is less than the applicable period, or

    (b) the arrangements need to be made as a matter of urgency.

(4) If the NHS body–

    (a) did not instruct an independent mental capacity advocate to represent P
before making the arrangements because it was satisfied that subsection
(3)(a) or (b) applied, but

    (b) subsequently has reason to believe that the accommodation is likely to be
provided for a continuous period–

        (i) beginning with the day on which accommodation was first provided
in accordance with the arrangements, and

        (ii) ending on or after the expiry of the applicable period,

it must instruct an independent mental capacity advocate to represent P.

(5) The NHS body must, in deciding what arrangements to make for P, take into
account any information given, or submissions made, by the independent
mental capacity advocate.

(6) 'Care home' has the meaning given in section 3 of the Care Standards Act
2000.

(7) 'Hospital' means–

    (a) in relation to England, a hospital as defined by section 275 of the National
Health Service Act 2006; and

    (b) in relation to Wales, a health service hospital as defined by section 206 of
the National Health Service (Wales) Act 2006 or an independent hospital
as defined by section 2 of the Care Standards Act 2000.

(8) 'NHS body' has such meaning as may be prescribed by regulations made for
the purposes of this section by–

    (a) the Secretary of State, in relation to bodies in England, or

    (b) the National Assembly for Wales, in relation to bodies in Wales.

(9) 'Applicable period' means–

    (a) in relation to accommodation in a hospital, 28 days, and

    (b) in relation to accommodation in a care home, 8 weeks.

(10) For the purposes of subsection (1), a person appointed under Part 10 of
Schedule A1 to be P's representative is not, by virtue of that appointment,

engaged in providing care or treatment for P in a professional capacity or for remuneration.

Provision of accommodation by local authority

39 (1) This section applies if a local authority propose to make arrangements–
    (a) for the provision of residential accommodation for a person ('P') who lacks capacity to agree to the arrangements, or
    (b) for a change in P's residential accommodation,
and are satisfied that there is no person, other than one engaged in providing care or treatment for P in a professional capacity or for remuneration, whom it would be appropriate for them to consult in determining what would be in P's best interests.

(2) But this section applies only if the accommodation is to be provided in accordance with–
    (a) section 21 or 29 of the National Assistance Act 1948, or
    (b) section 117 of the Mental Health Act,
as the result of a decision taken by the local authority under section 47 of the National Health Service and Community Care Act 1990.

(3) This section does not apply if P is accommodated as a result of an obligation imposed on him under the Mental Health Act.

(3A) And this section does not apply if–
    (a) an independent mental capacity advocate must be appointed under section 39A or 39C (whether or not by the local authority) to represent P, and
    (b) the place in which P is to be accommodated under the arrangements referred to in this section is the relevant hospital or care home under the authorisation referred to in that section.

(4) Before making the arrangements, the local authority must instruct an independent mental capacity advocate to represent P unless they are satisfied that–
    (a) the accommodation is likely to be provided for a continuous period of less than 8 weeks, or
    (b) the arrangements need to be made as a matter of urgency.

(5) If the local authority–
    (a) did not instruct an independent mental capacity advocate to represent P before making the arrangements because they were satisfied that subsection (4)(a) or (b) applied, but
    (b) subsequently have reason to believe that the accommodation is likely to be provided for a continuous period that will end 8 weeks or more after the day on which accommodation was first provided in accordance with the arrangements,
they must instruct an independent mental capacity advocate to represent P.

(6) The local authority must, in deciding what arrangements to make for P, take into account any information given, or submissions made, by the independent mental capacity advocate.

(7) For the purposes of subsection (1), a person appointed under Part 10 of Schedule A1 to be P's representative is not, by virtue of that appointment, engaged in providing care or treatment for P in a professional capacity or for remuneration.

Person becomes subject to Schedule A1

39A(1) This section applies if–

    (a) a person ('P') becomes subject to Schedule A1, and

    (b) the managing authority of the relevant hospital or care home are satisfied that there is no person, other than one engaged in providing care or treatment for P in a professional capacity or for remuneration, whom it would be appropriate to consult in determining what would be in P's best interests.

  (2) The managing authority must notify the supervisory body that this section applies.

  (3) The supervisory body must instruct an independent mental capacity advocate to represent P.

  (4) Schedule A1 makes provision about the role of an independent mental capacity advocate appointed under this section.

  (5) This section is subject to paragraph 161 of Schedule A1.

  (6) For the purposes of subsection (1), a person appointed under Part 10 of Schedule A1 to be P's representative is not, by virtue of that appointment, engaged in providing care or treatment for P in a professional capacity or for remuneration.

Section 39A: supplementary provision

39B(1) This section applies for the purposes of section 39A.

  (2) P becomes subject to Schedule A1 in any of the following cases.

  (3) The first case is where an urgent authorisation is given in relation to P under paragraph 76(2) of Schedule A1 (urgent authorisation given before request made for standard authorisation).

  (4) The second case is where the following conditions are met.

  (5) The first condition is that a request is made under Schedule A1 for a standard authorisation to be given in relation to P ('the requested authorisation').

  (6) The second condition is that no urgent authorisation was given under paragraph 76(2) of Schedule A1 before that request was made.

  (7) The third condition is that the requested authorisation will not be in force on or before, or immediately after, the expiry of an existing standard authorisation.

  (8) The expiry of a standard authorisation is the date when the authorisation is expected to cease to be in force.

  (9) The third case is where, under paragraph 69 of Schedule A1, the supervisory body select a person to carry out an assessment of whether or not the relevant person is a detained resident.

Person unrepresented whilst subject to Schedule A1

39C(1) This section applies if–

    (a) an authorisation under Schedule A1 is in force in relation to a person ('P'),

    (b) the appointment of a person as P's representative ends in accordance with regulations made under Part 10 of Schedule A1, and

    (c) the managing authority of the relevant hospital or care home are satisfied that there is no person, other than one engaged in providing care or treatment for P in a professional capacity or for remuneration, whom it would be appropriate to consult in determining what would be in P's best interests.

(2) The managing authority must notify the supervisory body that this section applies.

(3) The supervisory body must instruct an independent mental capacity advocate to represent P.

(4) Paragraph 159 of Schedule A1 makes provision about the role of an independent mental capacity advocate appointed under this section.

(5) The appointment of an independent mental capacity advocate under this section ends when a new appointment of a person as P's representative is made in accordance with Part 10 of Schedule A1.

(6) For the purposes of subsection (1), a person appointed under Part 10 of Schedule A1 to be P's representative is not, by virtue of that appointment, engaged in providing care or treatment for P in a professional capacity or for remuneration.

Person subject to Schedule A1 without paid representative

39D(1) This section applies if–

(a) an authorisation under Schedule A1 is in force in relation to a person ('P'),

(b) P has a representative ('R') appointed under Part 10 of Schedule A1, and

(c) R is not being paid under regulations under Part 10 of Schedule A1 for acting as P's representative.

(2) The supervisory body must instruct an independent mental capacity advocate to represent P in any of the following cases.

(3) The first case is where P makes a request to the supervisory body to instruct an advocate.

(4) The second case is where R makes a request to the supervisory body to instruct an advocate.

(5) The third case is where the supervisory body have reason to believe one or more of the following–

(a) that, without the help of an advocate, P and R would be unable to exercise one or both of the relevant rights;

(b) that P and R have each failed to exercise a relevant right when it would have been reasonable to exercise it;

(c) that P and R are each unlikely to exercise a relevant right when it would be reasonable to exercise it.

(6) The duty in subsection (2) is subject to section 39E.

(7) If an advocate is appointed under this section, the advocate is, in particular, to take such steps as are practicable to help P and R to understand the following matters–

(a) the effect of the authorisation;

(b) the purpose of the authorisation;

(c) the duration of the authorisation;

(d) any conditions to which the authorisation is subject;

(e) the reasons why each assessor who carried out an assessment in connection with the request for the authorisation, or in connection with a review of the authorisation, decided that P met the qualifying requirement in question;

(f) the relevant rights;

(g) how to exercise the relevant rights.

(8) The advocate is, in particular, to take such steps as are practicable to help P or R–

(a) to exercise the right to apply to court, if it appears to the advocate that P or R wishes to exercise that right, or

(b) to exercise the right of review, if it appears to the advocate that P or R wishes to exercise that right.

(9) If the advocate helps P or R to exercise the right of review–

(a) the advocate may make submissions to the supervisory body on the question of whether a qualifying requirement is reviewable;

(b) the advocate may give information, or make submissions, to any assessor carrying out a review assessment.

(10) In this section–

'relevant rights' means–

(a) the right to apply to court, and

(b) the right of review;

'right to apply to court' means the right to make an application to the court to exercise its jurisdiction under section 21A;

'right of review' means the right under Part 8 of Schedule A1 to request a review.

Limitation on duty to instruct advocate under section 39D

39E (1) This section applies if an advocate is already representing P in accordance with an instruction under section 39D.

(2) Section 39D(2) does not require another advocate to be instructed, unless the following conditions are met.

(3) The first condition is that the existing advocate was instructed–

(a) because of a request by R, or

(b) because the supervisory body had reason to believe one or more of the things in section 39D(5).

(4) The second condition is that the other advocate would be instructed because of a request by P.

Exceptions

40 (1) The duty imposed by section 37(3), 38(3) or (4), 39(4) or (5), 39A(3), 39C(3) or 39D(2) does not apply where there is–

(a) a person nominated by P (in whatever manner) as a person to be consulted on matters to which that duty relates,

(b) a donee of a lasting power of attorney created by P who is authorised to make decisions in relation to those matters, or

(c) a deputy appointed by the court for P with power to make decisions in relation to those matters.

(2) A person appointed under Part 10 of Schedule A1 to be P's representative is not, by virtue of that appointment, a person nominated by P as a person to be consulted in matters to which a duty mentioned in subsection (1) relates.

Power to adjust role of independent mental capacity advocate

41 (1) The appropriate authority may make regulations–

(a) expanding the role of independent mental capacity advocates in relation to persons who lack capacity, and

(b) adjusting the obligation to make arrangements imposed by section 35.

(2) The regulations may, in particular–

(a) prescribe circumstances (different to those set out in sections 37, 38 and 39) in which an independent mental capacity advocate must, or circumstances in which one may, be instructed by a person of a prescribed description to represent a person who lacks capacity, and

(b) include provision similar to any made by section 37, 38, 39 or 40.

(3) 'Appropriate authority' has the same meaning as in section 35.

Miscellaneous and supplementary

Codes of practice

42 (1) The Lord Chancellor must prepare and issue one or more codes of practice–

(a) for the guidance of persons assessing whether a person has capacity in relation to any matter,

(b) for the guidance of persons acting in connection with the care or treatment of another person (see section 5),

(c) for the guidance of donees of lasting powers of attorney,

(d) for the guidance of deputies appointed by the court,

(e) for the guidance of persons carrying out research in reliance on any provision made by or under this Act (and otherwise with respect to sections 30 to 34),

(f) for the guidance of independent mental capacity advocates,

(fa) for the guidance of persons exercising functions under Schedule A1,

(fb) for the guidance of representatives appointed under Part 10 of Schedule A1,

(g) with respect to the provisions of sections 24 to 26 (advance decisions and apparent advance decisions), and

(h) with respect to such other matters concerned with this Act as he thinks fit.

(2) The Lord Chancellor may from time to time revise a code.

(3) The Lord Chancellor may delegate the preparation or revision of the whole or any part of a code so far as he considers expedient.

(4) It is the duty of a person to have regard to any relevant code if he is acting in relation to a person who lacks capacity and is doing so in one or more of the following ways–

(a) as the donee of a lasting power of attorney,

(b) as a deputy appointed by the court,

(c) as a person carrying out research in reliance on any provision made by or under this Act (see sections 30 to 34),

(d) as an independent mental capacity advocate,

(da) in the exercise of functions under Schedule A1,

(db) as a representative appointed under Part 10 of Schedule A1,

(e) in a professional capacity,

(f) for remuneration.

(5) If it appears to a court or tribunal conducting any criminal or civil proceedings that–

(a) a provision of a code, or

(b) a failure to comply with a code,

is relevant to a question arising in the proceedings, the provision or failure must be taken into account in deciding the question.

(6) A code under subsection (1)(d) may contain separate guidance for deputies appointed by virtue of paragraph 1(2) of Schedule 5 (functions of deputy conferred on receiver appointed under the Mental Health Act).

(7) In this section and in section 43, 'code' means a code prepared or revised under this section.

Codes of practice: procedure

43 (1) Before preparing or revising a code, the Lord Chancellor must consult–

(a) the National Assembly for Wales, and

(b) such other persons as he considers appropriate.

(2) The Lord Chancellor may not issue a code unless–

(a) a draft of the code has been laid by him before both Houses of Parliament, and

(b) the 40 day period has elapsed without either House resolving not to approve the draft.

(3) The Lord Chancellor must arrange for any code that he has issued to be published in such a way as he considers appropriate for bringing it to the attention of persons likely to be concerned with its provisions.

(4) '40 day period', in relation to the draft of a proposed code, means–

(a) if the draft is laid before one House on a day later than the day on which it is laid before the other House, the period of 40 days beginning with the later of the two days;

(b) in any other case, the period of 40 days beginning with the day on which it is laid before each House.

(5) In calculating the period of 40 days, no account is to be taken of any period during which Parliament is dissolved or prorogued or during which both Houses are adjourned for more than 4 days.

Ill-treatment or neglect

44 (1) Subsection (2) applies if a person ('D')–

(a) has the care of a person ('P') who lacks, or whom D reasonably believes to lack, capacity,

(b) is the donee of a lasting power of attorney, or an enduring power of attorney (within the meaning of Schedule 4), created by P, or

(c) is a deputy appointed by the court for P.

(2) D is guilty of an offence if he ill-treats or wilfully neglects P.

(3) A person guilty of an offence under this section is liable–

(a) on summary conviction, to imprisonment for a term not exceeding 12 months or a fine not exceeding the statutory maximum or both;

(b) on conviction on indictment, to imprisonment for a term not exceeding 5 years or a fine or both.

Part 2: The Court of Protection and the Public Guardian

The Court of Protection

The Court of Protection

45 (1) There is to be a superior court of record known as the Court of Protection.

(2) The court is to have an official seal.

(3) The court may sit at any place in England and Wales, on any day and at any time.

(4) The court is to have a central office and registry at a place appointed by the Lord Chancellor, after consulting the Lord Chief Justice.

(5) The Lord Chancellor may, after consulting the Lord Chief Justice, designate as additional registries of the court any district registry of the High Court and any county court office.

(5A) The Lord Chief Justice may nominate any of the following to exercise his functions under this section–

   (a) the President of the Court of Protection;

   (b) a judicial office holder (as defined in section 109(4) of the Constitutional Reform Act 2005).

(6) The office of the Supreme Court called the Court of Protection ceases to exist.

The judges of the Court of Protection

46 (1) Subject to Court of Protection Rules under section 51(2)(d), the jurisdiction of the court is exercisable by a judge nominated for that purpose by–

   (a) the Lord Chief Justice, or

   (b) where nominated by the Lord Chief Justice to act on his behalf under this subsection–

      (i) the President of the Court of Protection; or

      (ii) a judicial office holder (as defined in section 109(4) of the Constitutional Reform Act 2005).

(2) To be nominated, a judge must be–

   (a) the President of the Family Division,

   (b) the Chancellor of the High Court,

   (c) a puisne judge of the High Court,

   (d) a circuit judge,

   (e) a district judge,

   (f) a District Judge (Magistrates' Courts),

   (g) a judge of the First-tier Tribunal, or of the Upper Tribunal, by virtue of appointment under paragraph 1(1) of Schedule 2 or 3 to the Tribunals, Courts and Enforcement Act 2007,

   (h) a transferred-in judge of the First-tier Tribunal or of the Upper Tribunal (see section 31(2) of that Act),

   (i) a deputy judge of the Upper Tribunal (whether under paragraph 7 of Schedule 3 to, or section 31(2) of, that Act),

   (j) the Chamber President, or Deputy Chamber President, of a chamber of the First-tier Tribunal or of a chamber of the Upper Tribunal,

   (k) the Judge Advocate General,

   (l) a Recorder,

(m) the holder of an office listed in the first column of the table in section 89(3C) of the Senior Courts Act 1981 (senior High Court Masters etc),
(n) a holder of an office listed in column 1 of Part 2 of Schedule 2 to that Act (High Court Masters etc),
(o) a deputy district judge appointed under section 102 of that Act or under section 8 of the County Courts Act 1984,
(p) a member of a panel of Employment Judges established for England and Wales or for Scotland,
(q) a person appointed under section 30(1)(a) or (b) of the Courts-Martial (Appeals) Act 1951 (assistants to the Judge Advocate General),
(r) a deputy judge of the High Court,
(s) the Senior President of Tribunals,
(t) an ordinary judge of the Court of Appeal (including the vice-president, if any, of either division of that court),
(u) the President of the Queen's Bench Division,
(v) the Master of the Rolls, or
(w) the Lord Chief Justice.
(3) The Lord Chief Justice, after consulting the Lord Chancellor, must–
(a) appoint one of the judges nominated by virtue of subsection (2)(a) to (c) to be President of the Court of Protection, and
(b) appoint another of those judges to be Vice-President of the Court of Protection.
(4) The Lord Chief Justice, after consulting the Lord Chancellor, must appoint one of the judges nominated by virtue of subsection (2)(d) to (q) to be Senior Judge of the Court of Protection, having such administrative functions in relation to the court as the Lord Chancellor, after consulting the Lord Chief Justice, may direct.

Supplementary powers

General powers and effect of orders etc
47 (1) The court has in connection with its jurisdiction the same powers, rights, privileges and authority as the High Court.
(2) Section 204 of the Law of Property Act 1925 (orders of High Court conclusive in favour of purchasers) applies in relation to orders and directions of the court as it applies to orders of the High Court.
(3) Office copies of orders made, directions given or other instruments issued by the court and sealed with its official seal are admissible in all legal proceedings as evidence of the originals without any further proof.

Interim orders and directions
48   The court may, pending the determination of an application to it in relation to a person ('P'), make an order or give directions in respect of any matter if–
(a) there is reason to believe that P lacks capacity in relation to the matter,
(b) the matter is one to which its powers under this Act extend, and
(c) it is in P's best interests to make the order, or give the directions, without delay.

Power to call for reports

49 (1) This section applies where, in proceedings brought in respect of a person ('P') under Part 1, the court is considering a question relating to P.

(2) The court may require a report to be made to it by the Public Guardian or by a Court of Protection Visitor.

(3) The court may require a local authority, or an NHS body, to arrange for a report to be made–

(a) by one of its officers or employees, or

(b) by such other person (other than the Public Guardian or a Court of Protection Visitor) as the authority, or the NHS body, considers appropriate.

(4) The report must deal with such matters relating to P as the court may direct.

(5) Court of Protection Rules may specify matters which, unless the court directs otherwise, must also be dealt with in the report.

(6) The report may be made in writing or orally, as the court may direct.

(7) In complying with a requirement, the Public Guardian or a Court of Protection Visitor may, at all reasonable times, examine and take copies of–

(a) any health record,

(b) any record of, or held by, a local authority and compiled in connection with a social services function, and

(c) any record held by a person registered under Part 2 of the Care Standards Act 2000 or Chapter 2 of Part 1 of the Health and Social Care Act 2008, so far as the record relates to P.

(8) If the Public Guardian or a Court of Protection Visitor is making a visit in the course of complying with a requirement, he may interview P in private.

(9) If a Court of Protection Visitor who is a Special Visitor is making a visit in the course of complying with a requirement, he may if the court so directs carry out in private a medical, psychiatric or psychological examination of P's capacity and condition.

(10) 'NHS body' has the meaning given in section 148 of the Health and Social Care (Community Health and Standards) Act 2003.

(11) 'Requirement' means a requirement imposed under subsection (2) or (3).

Practice and procedure

Applications to the Court of Protection

50 (1) No permission is required for an application to the court for the exercise of any of its powers under this Act–

(a) by a person who lacks, or is alleged to lack, capacity,

(b) if such a person has not reached 18, by anyone with parental responsibility for him,

(c) by the donor or a donee of a lasting power of attorney to which the application relates,

(d) by a deputy appointed by the court for a person to whom the application relates, or

(e) by a person named in an existing order of the court, if the application relates to the order.

(1A) Nor is permission required for an application to the court under section 21A by the relevant person's representative.

(2) But, subject to Court of Protection Rules and to paragraph 20(2) of Schedule

3 (declarations relating to private international law), permission is required for any other application to the court.

(3) In deciding whether to grant permission the court must, in particular, have regard to–

(a) the applicant's connection with the person to whom the application relates,

(b) the reasons for the application,

(c) the benefit to the person to whom the application relates of a proposed order or directions, and

(d) whether the benefit can be achieved in any other way.

(4) 'Parental responsibility' has the same meaning as in the Children Act 1989.

Court of Protection Rules

51 (1) Rules of court with respect to the practice and procedure of the court (to be called 'Court of Protection Rules') may be made in accordance with Part 1 of Schedule 1 to the Constitutional Reform Act 2005.

(2) Court of Protection Rules may, in particular, make provision–

(a) as to the manner and form in which proceedings are to be commenced;

(b) as to the persons entitled to be notified of, and be made parties to, the proceedings;

(c) for the allocation, in such circumstances as may be specified, of any specified description of proceedings to a specified judge or to specified descriptions of judges;

(d) for the exercise of the jurisdiction of the court, in such circumstances as may be specified, by its officers or other staff;

(e) for enabling the court to appoint a suitable person (who may, with his consent, be the Official Solicitor) to act in the name of, or on behalf of, or to represent the person to whom the proceedings relate;

(f) for enabling an application to the court to be disposed of without a hearing;

(g) for enabling the court to proceed with, or with any part of, a hearing in the absence of the person to whom the proceedings relate;

(h) for enabling or requiring the proceedings or any part of them to be conducted in private and for enabling the court to determine who is to be admitted when the court sits in private and to exclude specified persons when it sits in public;

(i) as to what may be received as evidence (whether or not admissible apart from the rules) and the manner in which it is to be presented;

(j) for the enforcement of orders made and directions given in the proceedings.

(3) Court of Protection Rules may, instead of providing for any matter, refer to provision made or to be made about that matter by directions.

(4) Court of Protection Rules may make different provision for different areas.

Practice directions

52 (1) Directions as to the practice and procedure of the court may be given in accordance with Part 1 of Schedule 2 to the Constitutional Reform Act 2005.

(2) Practice directions given otherwise than under subsection (1) may not be given without the approval of–

(a) the Lord Chancellor, and

(b) the Lord Chief Justice.

(3) The Lord Chief Justice may nominate any of the following to exercise his functions under this section–

    (a) the President of the Court of Protection;

    (b) a judicial office holder (as defined in section 109(4) of the Constitutional Reform Act 2005).

Rights of appeal

53 (1) Subject to the provisions of this section, an appeal lies to the Court of Appeal from any decision of the court.

(2) Court of Protection Rules may provide that where a decision of the court is made by–

    (a) a person exercising the jurisdiction of the court by virtue of rules made under section 51(2)(d),

    (b) a district judge, or

    (c) a circuit judge,

an appeal from that decision lies to a prescribed higher judge of the court and not to the Court of Appeal.

(3) For the purposes of this section the higher judges of the court are–

    (a) in relation to a person mentioned in subsection (2)(a), a circuit judge or a district judge;

    (b) in relation to a person mentioned in subsection (2)(b), a circuit judge;

    (c) in relation to any person mentioned in subsection (2), one of the judges nominated by virtue of section 46(2)(a) to (c).

(4) Court of Protection Rules may make provision–

    (a) that, in such cases as may be specified, an appeal from a decision of the court may not be made without permission;

    (b) as to the person or persons entitled to grant permission to appeal;

    (c) as to any requirements to be satisfied before permission is granted;

    (d) that where a higher judge of the court makes a decision on an appeal, no appeal may be made to the Court of Appeal from that decision unless the Court of Appeal considers that–

        (i) the appeal would raise an important point of principle or practice, or

        (ii) there is some other compelling reason for the Court of Appeal to hear it;

    (e) as to any considerations to be taken into account in relation to granting or refusing permission to appeal.

Fees and costs

Fees

54 (1) The Lord Chancellor may with the consent of the Treasury by order prescribe fees payable in respect of anything dealt with by the court.

(2) An order under this section may in particular contain provision as to–

    (a) scales or rates of fees;

    (b) exemptions from and reductions in fees;

    (c) remission of fees in whole or in part.

(3) Before making an order under this section, the Lord Chancellor must consult–

    (a) the President of the Court of Protection,

    (b) the Vice-President of the Court of Protection, and

    (c) the Senior Judge of the Court of Protection.

(4) The Lord Chancellor must take such steps as are reasonably practicable to bring information about fees to the attention of persons likely to have to pay them.

(5) Fees payable under this section are recoverable summarily as a civil debt.

Costs

55 (1) Subject to Court of Protection Rules, the costs of and incidental to all proceedings in the court are in its discretion.

(2) The rules may in particular make provision for regulating matters relating to the costs of those proceedings, including prescribing scales of costs to be paid to legal or other representatives.

(3) The court has full power to determine by whom and to what extent the costs are to be paid.

(4) The court may, in any proceedings–

    (a) disallow, or

    (b) order the legal or other representatives concerned to meet,

    the whole of any wasted costs or such part of them as may be determined in accordance with the rules.

(5) 'Legal or other representative', in relation to a party to proceedings, means any person exercising a right of audience or right to conduct litigation on his behalf.

(6) 'Wasted costs' means any costs incurred by a party–

    (a) as a result of any improper, unreasonable or negligent act or omission on the part of any legal or other representative or any employee of such a representative, or

    (b) which, in the light of any such act or omission occurring after they were incurred, the court considers it is unreasonable to expect that party to pay.

Fees and costs: supplementary

56 (1) Court of Protection Rules may make provision–

    (a) as to the way in which, and funds from which, fees and costs are to be paid;

    (b) for charging fees and costs upon the estate of the person to whom the proceedings relate;

    (c) for the payment of fees and costs within a specified time of the death of the person to whom the proceedings relate or the conclusion of the proceedings.

(2) A charge on the estate of a person created by virtue of subsection (1)(b) does not cause any interest of the person in any property to fail or determine or to be prevented from recommencing.

The Public Guardian

The Public Guardian

57 (1) For the purposes of this Act, there is to be an officer, to be known as the Public Guardian.

(2) The Public Guardian is to be appointed by the Lord Chancellor.

(3) There is to be paid to the Public Guardian out of money provided by Parliament such salary as the Lord Chancellor may determine.

(4) The Lord Chancellor may, after consulting the Public Guardian–
  (a) provide him with such officers and staff, or
  (b) enter into such contracts with other persons for the provision (by them or their sub-contractors) of officers, staff or services,

  as the Lord Chancellor thinks necessary for the proper discharge of the Public Guardian's functions.

(5) Any functions of the Public Guardian may, to the extent authorised by him, be performed by any of his officers.

Functions of the Public Guardian

58 (1) The Public Guardian has the following functions–
  (a) establishing and maintaining a register of lasting powers of attorney,
  (b) establishing and maintaining a register of orders appointing deputies,
  (c) supervising deputies appointed by the court,
  (d) directing a Court of Protection Visitor to visit–
     (i)   a donee of a lasting power of attorney,
     (ii) a deputy appointed by the court, or
     (iii) the person granting the power of attorney or for whom the deputy is appointed ('P'),
     and to make a report to the Public Guardian on such matters as he may direct,
  (e) receiving security which the court requires a person to give for the discharge of his functions,
  (f) receiving reports from donees of lasting powers of attorney and deputies appointed by the court,
  (g) reporting to the court on such matters relating to proceedings under this Act as the court requires,
  (h) dealing with representations (including complaints) about the way in which a donee of a lasting power of attorney or a deputy appointed by the court is exercising his powers,
  (i) publishing, in any manner the Public Guardian thinks appropriate, any information he thinks appropriate about the discharge of his functions.

(2) The functions conferred by subsection (1)(c) and (h) may be discharged in co-operation with any other person who has functions in relation to the care or treatment of P.

(3) The Lord Chancellor may by regulations make provision–
  (a) conferring on the Public Guardian other functions in connection with this Act;
  (b) in connection with the discharge by the Public Guardian of his functions.

(4) Regulations made under subsection (3)(b) may in particular make provision as to–
  (a) the giving of security by deputies appointed by the court and the enforcement and discharge of security so given;
  (b) the fees which may be charged by the Public Guardian;
  (c) the way in which, and funds from which, such fees are to be paid;
  (d) exemptions from and reductions in such fees;

(e) remission of such fees in whole or in part;

(f) the making of reports to the Public Guardian by deputies appointed by the court and others who are directed by the court to carry out any transaction for a person who lacks capacity.

(5) For the purpose of enabling him to carry out his functions, the Public Guardian may, at all reasonable times, examine and take copies of–

(a) any health record,

(b) any record of, or held by, a local authority and compiled in connection with a social services function, and

(c) any record held by a person registered under Part 2 of the Care Standards Act 2000 or Chapter 2 of Part 1 of the Health and Social Care Act 2008,

so far as the record relates to P.

(6) The Public Guardian may also for that purpose interview P in private.

59   Repealed.

Annual report

60 (1) The Public Guardian must make an annual report to the Lord Chancellor about the discharge of his functions.

(2) The Lord Chancellor must, within one month of receiving the report, lay a copy of it before Parliament.

Court of Protection Visitors

Court of Protection Visitors

61 (1) A Court of Protection Visitor is a person who is appointed by the Lord Chancellor to–

(a) a panel of Special Visitors, or

(b) a panel of General Visitors.

(2) A person is not qualified to be a Special Visitor unless he–

(a) is a registered medical practitioner or appears to the Lord Chancellor to have other suitable qualifications or training, and

(b) appears to the Lord Chancellor to have special knowledge of and experience in cases of impairment of or disturbance in the functioning of the mind or brain.

(3) A General Visitor need not have a medical qualification.

(4) A Court of Protection Visitor–

(a) may be appointed for such term and subject to such conditions, and

(b) may be paid such remuneration and allowances,

as the Lord Chancellor may determine.

(5) For the purpose of carrying out his functions under this Act in relation to a person who lacks capacity ('P'), a Court of Protection Visitor may, at all reasonable times, examine and take copies of–

(a) any health record,

(b) any record of, or held by, a local authority and compiled in connection with a social services function, and

(c) any record held by a person registered under Part 2 of the Care Standards Act 2000 (c 14) or Chapter 2 of Part 1 of the Health and Social Care Act 2008,

so far as the record relates to P.

(6) A Court of Protection Visitor may also for that purpose interview P in private.

Part 3: Miscellaneous and General

Declaratory provision

Scope of the Act

62　For the avoidance of doubt, it is hereby declared that nothing in this Act is to be taken to affect the law relating to murder or manslaughter or the operation of section 2 of the Suicide Act 1961 (assisting suicide).

Private international law

International protection of adults

63　Schedule 3–
(a) gives effect in England and Wales to the Convention on the International Protection of Adults signed at the Hague on 13th January 2000 (Cm 5881) (in so far as this Act does not otherwise do so), and
(b) makes related provision as to the private international law of England and Wales.

General

Interpretation

64 (1) In this Act–
'the 1985 Act' means the Enduring Powers of Attorney Act 1985,
'advance decision' has the meaning given in section 24(1),
'authorisation under Schedule A1' means either–
(a) a standard authorisation under that Schedule, or
(b) an urgent authorisation under that Schedule;
'the court' means the Court of Protection established by section 45,
'Court of Protection Rules' has the meaning given in section 51(1),
'Court of Protection Visitor' has the meaning given in section 61,
'deputy' has the meaning given in section 16(2)(b),
'enactment' includes a provision of subordinate legislation (within the meaning of the Interpretation Act 1978),
'health record' has the meaning given in section 68 of the Data Protection Act 1998 (as read with section 69 of that Act),
'the Human Rights Convention' has the same meaning as 'the Convention' in the Human Rights Act 1998,
'independent mental capacity advocate' has the meaning given in section 35(1),
'lasting power of attorney' has the meaning given in section 9,
'life-sustaining treatment' has the meaning given in section 4(10),
'local authority', except in section 35(6A)(a) and Schedule A1, means–
(a) the council of a county in England in which there are no district councils,
(b) the council of a district in England,
(c) the council of a county or county borough in Wales,
(d) the council of a London borough,
(e) the Common Council of the City of London, or
(f) the Council of the Isles of Scilly,
'Mental Health Act' means the Mental Health Act 1983,

'prescribed', in relation to regulations made under this Act, means prescribed by those regulations,

'property' includes any thing in action and any interest in real or personal property,

'public authority' has the same meaning as in the Human Rights Act 1998,

'Public Guardian' has the meaning given in section 57,

'purchaser' and 'purchase' have the meaning given in section 205(1) of the Law of Property Act 1925,

'social services function' has the meaning given in section 1A of the Local Authority Social Services Act 1970,

'treatment' includes a diagnostic or other procedure,

'trust corporation' has the meaning given in section 68(1) of the Trustee Act 1925, and

'will' includes codicil.

(2) In this Act, references to making decisions, in relation to a donee of a lasting power of attorney or a deputy appointed by the court, include, where appropriate, acting on decisions made.

(3) In this Act, references to the bankruptcy of an individual include a case where a bankruptcy restrictions order under the Insolvency Act 1986 has effect in respect of him.

(3A) In this Act references to a debt relief order (under Part 7A of the Insolvency Act 1986) being made in relation to an individual include a case where a debt relief restrictions order under the Insolvency Act 1986 has effect in respect of him.

(4) 'Bankruptcy restrictions order' includes an interim bankruptcy restrictions order.

(4A) 'Debt relief restrictions order' includes an interim debt relief restrictions order.

(5) In this Act, references to deprivation of a person's liberty have the same meaning as in Article 5(1) of the Human Rights Convention.

(6) For the purposes of such references, it does not matter whether a person is deprived of his liberty by a public authority or not.

Rules, regulations and orders

65 (1) Any power to make rules, regulations or orders under this Act, other than the power in section 21–

(a) is exercisable by statutory instrument;

(b) includes power to make supplementary, incidental, consequential, transitional or saving provision;

(c) includes power to make different provision for different cases.

(2) Any statutory instrument containing rules, regulations or orders made by the Lord Chancellor or the Secretary of State under this Act, other than–

(a) regulations under section 34 (loss of capacity during research project),

(b) regulations under section 41 (adjusting role of independent mental capacity advocacy service),

(c) regulations under paragraph 32(1)(b) of Schedule 3 (private international law relating to the protection of adults),

(d) an order of the kind mentioned in section 67(6) (consequential amendments of primary legislation), or

(e) an order under section 68 (commencement),

is subject to annulment in pursuance of a resolution of either House of Parliament.

(3) A statutory instrument containing an Order in Council under paragraph 31 of Schedule 3 (provision to give further effect to Hague Convention) is subject to annulment in pursuance of a resolution of either House of Parliament.

(4) A statutory instrument containing regulations made by the Secretary of State under section 34 or 41 or by the Lord Chancellor under paragraph 32(1)(b) of Schedule 3 may not be made unless a draft has been laid before and approved by resolution of each House of Parliament.

(4A) Subsection (2) does not apply to a statutory instrument containing regulations made by the Secretary of State under Schedule A1.

(4B) If such a statutory instrument contains regulations under paragraph 42(2)(b), 129, 162 or 164 of Schedule A1 (whether or not it also contains other regulations), the instrument may not be made unless a draft has been laid before and approved by resolution of each House of Parliament.

(4C) Subject to that, such a statutory instrument is subject to annulment in pursuance of a resolution of either House of Parliament.

(5) An order under section 21–

(a) may include supplementary, incidental, consequential, transitional or saving provision;

(b) may make different provision for different cases;

(c) is to be made in the form of a statutory instrument to which the Statutory Instruments Act 1946 applies as if the order were made by a Minister of the Crown; and

(d) is subject to annulment in pursuance of a resolution of either House of Parliament.

Existing receivers and enduring powers of attorney etc

66 (1) The following provisions cease to have effect–

(a) Part 7 of the Mental Health Act,

(b) the Enduring Powers of Attorney Act 1985 (c 29).

(2) No enduring power of attorney within the meaning of the 1985 Act is to be created after the commencement of subsection (1)(b).

(3) Schedule 4 has effect in place of the 1985 Act in relation to any enduring power of attorney created before the commencement of subsection (1)(b).

(4) Schedule 5 contains transitional provisions and savings in relation to Part 7 of the Mental Health Act and the 1985 Act.

Minor and consequential amendments and repeals

67 (1) Schedule 6 contains minor and consequential amendments.

(2) Schedule 7 contains repeals.

(3) The Lord Chancellor may by order make supplementary, incidental, consequential, transitional or saving provision for the purposes of, in consequence of, or for giving full effect to a provision of this Act.

(4) An order under subsection (3) may, in particular–

(a) provide for a provision of this Act which comes into force before another provision of this Act has come into force to have effect, until the other provision has come into force, with specified modifications;

(b) amend, repeal or revoke an enactment, other than one contained in an

Act or Measure passed in a Session after the one in which this Act is passed.

(5) The amendments that may be made under subsection (4)(b) are in addition to those made by or under any other provision of this Act.

(6) An order under subsection (3) which amends or repeals a provision of an Act or Measure may not be made unless a draft has been laid before and approved by resolution of each House of Parliament.

Commencement and extent

68 (1) This Act, other than sections 30 to 41, comes into force in accordance with provision made by order by the Lord Chancellor.

(2) Sections 30 to 41 come into force in accordance with provision made by order by–
   (a) the Secretary of State, in relation to England, and
   (b) the National Assembly for Wales, in relation to Wales.

(3) An order under this section may appoint different days for different provisions and different purposes.

(4) Subject to subsections (5) and (6), this Act extends to England and Wales only.

(5) The following provisions extend to the United Kingdom–
   (a) paragraph 16(1) of Schedule 1 (evidence of instruments and of registration of lasting powers of attorney),
   (b) paragraph 15(3) of Schedule 4 (evidence of instruments and of registration of enduring powers of attorney).

(6) Subject to any provision made in Schedule 6, the amendments and repeals made by Schedules 6 and 7 have the same extent as the enactments to which they relate.

Short title

69 This Act may be cited as the Mental Capacity Act 2005.

SCHEDULE A1: HOSPITAL AND CARE HOME RESIDENTS: DEPRIVATION OF LIBERTY

Part 1: Authorisation to Deprive Residents of Liberty etc

Application of Part

1 (1) This Part applies if the following conditions are met.

(2) The first condition is that a person ('P') is detained in a hospital or care home–for the purpose of being given care or treatment–in circumstances which amount to deprivation of the person's liberty.

(3) The second condition is that a standard or urgent authorisation is in force.

(4) The third condition is that the standard or urgent authorisation relates–
   (a) to P, and
   (b) to the hospital or care home in which P is detained.

Authorisation to deprive P of liberty

2 The managing authority of the hospital or care home may deprive P of his liberty by detaining him as mentioned in paragraph 1(2).

No liability for acts done for purpose of depriving P of liberty

3 (1) This paragraph applies to any act which a person ('D') does for the purpose of detaining P as mentioned in paragraph 1(2).

(2) D does not incur any liability in relation to the act that he would not have incurred if P–

(a) had had capacity to consent in relation to D's doing the act, and

(b) had consented to D's doing the act.

No protection for negligent acts etc

4 (1) Paragraphs 2 and 3 do not exclude a person's civil liability for loss or damage, or his criminal liability, resulting from his negligence in doing any thing.

(2) Paragraphs 2 and 3 do not authorise a person to do anything otherwise than for the purpose of the standard or urgent authorisation that is in force.

(3) In a case where a standard authorisation is in force, paragraphs 2 and 3 do not authorise a person to do anything which does not comply with the conditions (if any) included in the authorisation.

Part 2: Interpretation: Main Terms

Introduction

5 This Part applies for the purposes of this Schedule.

Detained resident

6 'Detained resident' means a person detained in a hospital or care home– for the purpose of being given care or treatment–in circumstances which amount to deprivation of the person's liberty.

Relevant person etc

7 In relation to a person who is, or is to be, a detained resident–

'relevant person' means the person in question;

'relevant hospital or care home' means the hospital or care home in question;

'relevant care or treatment' means the care or treatment in question.

Authorisations

8 'Standard authorisation' means an authorisation given under Part 4.

9 'Urgent authorisation' means an authorisation given under Part 5.

10 'Authorisation under this Schedule' means either of the following–

(a) a standard authorisation;

(b) an urgent authorisation.

11 (1) The purpose of a standard authorisation is the purpose which is stated in the authorisation in accordance with paragraph 55(1)(d).

(2) The purpose of an urgent authorisation is the purpose which is stated in the authorisation in accordance with paragraph 80(d).

Part 3: The Qualifying Requirements

The qualifying requirements

12 (1) These are the qualifying requirements referred to in this Schedule–

(a) the age requirement;

(b) the mental health requirement;

(c) the mental capacity requirement;

(d) the best interests requirement;
(e) the eligibility requirement;
(f) the no refusals requirement.

(2) Any question of whether a person who is, or is to be, a detained resident meets the qualifying requirements is to be determined in accordance with this Part.

(3) In a case where–
   (a) the question of whether a person meets a particular qualifying requirement arises in relation to the giving of a standard authorisation, and
   (b) any circumstances relevant to determining that question are expected to change between the time when the determination is made and the time when the authorisation is expected to come into force,
   those circumstances are to be taken into account as they are expected to be at the later time.

The age requirement

13   The relevant person meets the age requirement if he has reached 18.

The mental health requirement

14 (1) The relevant person meets the mental health requirement if he is suffering from mental disorder (within the meaning of the Mental Health Act, but disregarding any exclusion for persons with learning disability).

(2) An exclusion for persons with learning disability is any provision of the Mental Health Act which provides for a person with learning disability not to be regarded as suffering from mental disorder for one or more purposes of that Act.

The mental capacity requirement

15   The relevant person meets the mental capacity requirement if he lacks capacity in relation to the question whether or not he should be accommodated in the relevant hospital or care home for the purpose of being given the relevant care or treatment.

The best interests requirement

16 (1) The relevant person meets the best interests requirement if all of the following conditions are met.

(2) The first condition is that the relevant person is, or is to be, a detained resident.

(3) The second condition is that it is in the best interests of the relevant person for him to be a detained resident.

(4) The third condition is that, in order to prevent harm to the relevant person, it is necessary for him to be a detained resident.

(5) The fourth condition is that it is a proportionate response to–
   (a) the likelihood of the relevant person suffering harm, and
   (b) the seriousness of that harm,
   for him to be a detained resident.

The eligibility requirement

17 (1) The relevant person meets the eligibility requirement unless he is ineligible to be deprived of liberty by this Act.

(2) Schedule 1A applies for the purpose of determining whether or not P is ineligible to be deprived of liberty by this Act.

The no refusals requirement

18   The relevant person meets the no refusals requirement unless there is a refusal within the meaning of paragraph 19 or 20.

19 (1) There is a refusal if these conditions are met–
   (a) the relevant person has made an advance decision;
   (b) the advance decision is valid;
   (c) the advance decision is applicable to some or all of the relevant treatment.
   (2) Expressions used in this paragraph and any of sections 24, 25 or 26 have the same meaning in this paragraph as in that section.

20 (1) There is a refusal if it would be in conflict with a valid decision of a donee or deputy for the relevant person to be accommodated in the relevant hospital or care home for the purpose of receiving some or all of the relevant care or treatment–
   (a) in circumstances which amount to deprivation of the person's liberty, or
   (b) at all.
   (2) A donee is a donee of a lasting power of attorney granted by the relevant person.
   (3) A decision of a donee or deputy is valid if it is made–
   (a) within the scope of his authority as donee or deputy, and
   (b) in accordance with Part 1 of this Act.

Part 4: Standard Authorisations

Supervisory body to give authorisation

21   Only the supervisory body may give a standard authorisation.

22   The supervisory body may not give a standard authorisation unless–
   (a) the managing authority of the relevant hospital or care home have requested it, or
   (b) paragraph 71 applies (right of third party to require consideration of whether authorisation needed).

23   The managing authority may not make a request for a standard authorisation unless–
   (a) they are required to do so by paragraph 24 (as read with paragraphs 27 to 29),
   (b) they are required to do so by paragraph 25 (as read with paragraph 28), or
   (c) they are permitted to do so by paragraph 30.

Duty to request authorisation: basic cases

24 (1) The managing authority must request a standard authorisation in any of the following cases.
   (2) The first case is where it appears to the managing authority that the relevant person–
   (a) is not yet accommodated in the relevant hospital or care home,
   (b) is likely–at some time within the next 28 days–to be a detained resident in the relevant hospital or care home, and
   (c) is likely–

(i) at that time, or

(ii) at some later time within the next 28 days,

to meet all of the qualifying requirements.

(3) The second case is where it appears to the managing authority that the relevant person–

(a) is already accommodated in the relevant hospital or care home,

(b) is likely–at some time within the next 28 days–to be a detained resident in the relevant hospital or care home, and

(c) is likely–

(i) at that time, or

(ii) at some later time within the next 28 days,

to meet all of the qualifying requirements.

(4) The third case is where it appears to the managing authority that the relevant person–

(a) is a detained resident in the relevant hospital or care home, and

(b) meets all of the qualifying requirements, or is likely to do so at some time within the next 28 days.

(5) This paragraph is subject to paragraphs 27 to 29.

Duty to request authorisation: change in place of detention

25 (1) The relevant managing authority must request a standard authorisation if it appears to them that these conditions are met.

(2) The first condition is that a standard authorisation–

(a) has been given, and

(b) has not ceased to be in force.

(3) The second condition is that there is, or is to be, a change in the place of detention.

(4) This paragraph is subject to paragraph 28.

26 (1) This paragraph applies for the purposes of paragraph 25.

(2) There is a change in the place of detention if the relevant person–

(a) ceases to be a detained resident in the stated hospital or care home, and

(b) becomes a detained resident in a different hospital or care home ('the new hospital or care home').

(3) The stated hospital or care home is the hospital or care home to which the standard authorisation relates.

(4) The relevant managing authority are the managing authority of the new hospital or care home.

Other authority for detention: request for authorisation

27 (1) This paragraph applies if, by virtue of section 4A(3), a decision of the court authorises the relevant person to be a detained resident.

(2) Paragraph 24 does not require a request for a standard authorisation to be made in relation to that detention unless these conditions are met.

(3) The first condition is that the standard authorisation would be in force at a time immediately after the expiry of the other authority.

(4) The second condition is that the standard authorisation would not be in force at any time on or before the expiry of the other authority.

(5) The third condition is that it would, in the managing authority's view, be unreasonable to delay making the request until a time nearer the expiry of the other authority.

(6) In this paragraph–
  (a) the other authority is–
    (i) the decision mentioned in sub-paragraph (1), or
    (ii) any further decision of the court which, by virtue of section 4A(3), authorises, or is expected to authorise, the relevant person to be a detained resident;
  (b) the expiry of the other authority is the time when the other authority is expected to cease to authorise the relevant person to be a detained resident.

Request refused: no further request unless change of circumstances

28 (1) This paragraph applies if–
  (a) a managing authority request a standard authorisation under paragraph 24 or 25, and
  (b) the supervisory body are prohibited by paragraph 50(2) from giving the authorisation.

(2) Paragraph 24 or 25 does not require that managing authority to make a new request for a standard authorisation unless it appears to the managing authority that–
  (a) there has been a change in the relevant person's case, and
  (b) because of that change, the supervisory body are likely to give a standard authorisation if requested.

Authorisation given: request for further authorisation

29 (1) This paragraph applies if a standard authorisation–
  (a) has been given in relation to the detention of the relevant person, and
  (b) that authorisation ('the existing authorisation') has not ceased to be in force.

(2) Paragraph 24 does not require a new request for a standard authorisation ('the new authorisation') to be made unless these conditions are met.

(3) The first condition is that the new authorisation would be in force at a time immediately after the expiry of the existing authorisation.

(4) The second condition is that the new authorisation would not be in force at any time on or before the expiry of the existing authorisation.

(5) The third condition is that it would, in the managing authority's view, be unreasonable to delay making the request until a time nearer the expiry of the existing authorisation.

(6) The expiry of the existing authorisation is the time when it is expected to cease to be in force.

Power to request authorisation

30 (1) This paragraph applies if–
  (a) a standard authorisation has been given in relation to the detention of the relevant person,
  (b) that authorisation ('the existing authorisation') has not ceased to be in force,
  (c) the requirement under paragraph 24 to make a request for a new standard authorisation does not apply, because of paragraph 29, and
  (d) a review of the existing authorisation has been requested, or is being carried out, in accordance with Part 8.

(2) The managing authority may request a new standard authorisation which would be in force on or before the expiry of the existing authorisation; but only if it would also be in force immediately after that expiry.

(3) The expiry of the existing authorisation is the time when it is expected to cease to be in force.

(4) Further provision relating to cases where a request is made under this paragraph can be found in–

    (a) paragraph 62 (effect of decision about request), and

    (b) paragraph 124 (effect of request on Part 8 review).

Information included in request

31   A request for a standard authorisation must include the information (if any) required by regulations.

Records of requests

32 (1) The managing authority of a hospital or care home must keep a written record of–

    (a) each request that they make for a standard authorisation, and

    (b) the reasons for making each request.

(2) A supervisory body must keep a written record of each request for a standard authorisation that is made to them.

Relevant person must be assessed

33 (1) This paragraph applies if the supervisory body are requested to give a standard authorisation.

(2) The supervisory body must secure that all of these assessments are carried out in relation to the relevant person–

    (a) an age assessment;

    (b) a mental health assessment;

    (c) a mental capacity assessment;

    (d) a best interests assessment;

    (e) an eligibility assessment;

    (f) a no refusals assessment.

(3) The person who carries out any such assessment is referred to as the assessor.

(4) Regulations may be made about the period (or periods) within which assessors must carry out assessments.

(5) This paragraph is subject to paragraphs 49 and 133.

Age assessment

34   An age assessment is an assessment of whether the relevant person meets the age requirement.

Mental health assessment

35   A mental health assessment is an assessment of whether the relevant person meets the mental health requirement.

36   When carrying out a mental health assessment, the assessor must also–

    (a) consider how (if at all) the relevant person's mental health is likely to be affected by his being a detained resident, and

    (b) notify the best interests assessor of his conclusions.

Mental capacity assessment

37 A mental capacity assessment is an assessment of whether the relevant person meets the mental capacity requirement.

Best interests assessment

38 A best interests assessment is an assessment of whether the relevant person meets the best interests requirement.

39 (1) In carrying out a best interests assessment, the assessor must comply with the duties in sub-paragraphs (2) and (3).

(2) The assessor must consult the managing authority of the relevant hospital or care home.

(3) The assessor must have regard to all of the following–
   (a) the conclusions which the mental health assessor has notified to the best interests assessor in accordance with paragraph 36(b);
   (b) any relevant needs assessment;
   (c) any relevant care plan.

(4) A relevant needs assessment is an assessment of the relevant person's needs which–
   (a) was carried out in connection with the relevant person being accommodated in the relevant hospital or care home, and
   (b) was carried out by or on behalf of–
       (i) the managing authority of the relevant hospital or care home, or
       (ii) the supervisory body.

(5) A relevant care plan is a care plan which–
   (a) sets out how the relevant person's needs are to be met whilst he is accommodated in the relevant hospital or care home, and
   (b) was drawn up by or on behalf of–
       (i) the managing authority of the relevant hospital or care home, or
       (ii) the supervisory body.

(6) The managing authority must give the assessor a copy of–
   (a) any relevant needs assessment carried out by them or on their behalf, or
   (b) any relevant care plan drawn up by them or on their behalf.

(7) The supervisory body must give the assessor a copy of–
   (a) any relevant needs assessment carried out by them or on their behalf, or
   (b) any relevant care plan drawn up by them or on their behalf.

(8) The duties in sub-paragraphs (2) and (3) do not affect any other duty to consult or to take the views of others into account.

40 (1) This paragraph applies whatever conclusion the best interests assessment comes to.

(2) The assessor must state in the best interests assessment the name and address of every interested person whom he has consulted in carrying out the assessment.

41 Paragraphs 42 and 43 apply if the best interests assessment comes to the conclusion that the relevant person meets the best interests requirement.

42 (1) The assessor must state in the assessment the maximum authorisation period.

(2) The maximum authorisation period is the shorter of these periods–
   (a) the period which, in the assessor's opinion, would be the appropriate

maximum period for the relevant person to be a detained resident under the standard authorisation that has been requested;

(b) 1 year, or such shorter period as may be prescribed in regulations.

(3) Regulations under sub-paragraph (2)(b)–

    (a) need not provide for a shorter period to apply in relation to all standard authorisations;

    (b) may provide for different periods to apply in relation to different kinds of standard authorisations.

(4) Before making regulations under sub-paragraph (2)(b) the Secretary of State must consult all of the following–

    (a) each body required by regulations under paragraph 162 to monitor and report on the operation of this Schedule in relation to England;

    (b) such other persons as the Secretary of State considers it appropriate to consult.

(5) Before making regulations under sub-paragraph (2)(b) the National Assembly for Wales must consult all of the following–

    (a) each person or body directed under paragraph 163(2) to carry out any function of the Assembly of monitoring and reporting on the operation of this Schedule in relation to Wales;

    (b) such other persons as the Assembly considers it appropriate to consult.

43 The assessor may include in the assessment recommendations about conditions to which the standard authorisation is, or is not, to be subject in accordance with paragraph 53.

44 (1) This paragraph applies if the best interests assessment comes to the conclusion that the relevant person does not meet the best interests requirement.

(2) If, on the basis of the information taken into account in carrying out the assessment, it appears to the assessor that there is an unauthorised deprivation of liberty, he must include a statement to that effect in the assessment.

(3) There is an unauthorised deprivation of liberty if the managing authority of the relevant hospital or care home are already depriving the relevant person of his liberty without authority of the kind mentioned in section 4A.

45 The duties with which the best interests assessor must comply are subject to the provision included in appointment regulations under Part 10 (in particular, provision made under paragraph 146).

Eligibility assessment

46 An eligibility assessment is an assessment of whether the relevant person meets the eligibility requirement.

47 (1) Regulations may–

    (a) require an eligibility assessor to request a best interests assessor to provide relevant eligibility information, and

    (b) require the best interests assessor, if such a request is made, to provide such relevant eligibility information as he may have.

(2) In this paragraph–

    'best interests assessor' means any person who is carrying out, or has carried out, a best interests assessment in relation to the relevant person;

    'eligibility assessor' means a person carrying out an eligibility assessment in relation to the relevant person;

    'relevant eligibility information' is information relevant to assessing whether or not the relevant person is ineligible by virtue of paragraph 5 of Schedule 1A.

No refusals assessment

48 A no refusals assessment is an assessment of whether the relevant person meets the no refusals requirement.

Equivalent assessment already carried out

49 (1) The supervisory body are not required by paragraph 33 to secure that a particular kind of assessment ('the required assessment') is carried out in relation to the relevant person if the following conditions are met.

(2) The first condition is that the supervisory body have a written copy of an assessment of the relevant person ('the existing assessment') that has already been carried out.

(3) The second condition is that the existing assessment complies with all requirements under this Schedule with which the required assessment would have to comply (if it were carried out).

(4) The third condition is that the existing assessment was carried out within the previous 12 months; but this condition need not be met if the required assessment is an age assessment.

(5) The fourth condition is that the supervisory body are satisfied that there is no reason why the existing assessment may no longer be accurate.

(6) If the required assessment is a best interests assessment, in satisfying themselves as mentioned in sub-paragraph (5), the supervisory body must take into account any information given, or submissions made, by–

(a) the relevant person's representative,

(b) any section 39C IMCA, or

(c) any section 39D IMCA.

(7) It does not matter whether the existing assessment was carried out in connection with a request for a standard authorisation or for some other purpose.

(8) If, because of this paragraph, the supervisory body are not required by paragraph 33 to secure that the required assessment is carried out, the existing assessment is to be treated for the purposes of this Schedule–

(a) as an assessment of the same kind as the required assessment, and

(b) as having been carried out under paragraph 33 in connection with the request for the standard authorisation.

Duty to give authorisation

50 (1) The supervisory body must give a standard authorisation if–

(a) all assessments are positive, and

(b) the supervisory body have written copies of all those assessments.

(2) The supervisory body must not give a standard authorisation except in accordance with sub-paragraph (1).

(3) All assessments are positive if each assessment carried out under paragraph 33 has come to the conclusion that the relevant person meets the qualifying requirement to which the assessment relates.

Terms of authorisation

51 (1) If the supervisory body are required to give a standard authorisation, they must decide the period during which the authorisation is to be in force.

(2) That period must not exceed the maximum authorisation period stated in the best interests assessment.

52   A standard authorisation may provide for the authorisation to come into force at a time after it is given.

53 (1) A standard authorisation may be given subject to conditions.

(2) Before deciding whether to give the authorisation subject to conditions, the supervisory body must have regard to any recommendations in the best interests assessment about such conditions.

(3) The managing authority of the relevant hospital or care home must ensure that any conditions are complied with.

Form of authorisation

54   A standard authorisation must be in writing.

55 (1) A standard authorisation must state the following things–

(a) the name of the relevant person;

(b) the name of the relevant hospital or care home;

(c) the period during which the authorisation is to be in force;

(d) the purpose for which the authorisation is given;

(e) any conditions subject to which the authorisation is given;

(f) the reason why each qualifying requirement is met.

(2) The statement of the reason why the eligibility requirement is met must be framed by reference to the cases in the table in paragraph 2 of Schedule 1A.

56 (1) If the name of the relevant hospital or care home changes, the standard authorisation is to be read as if it stated the current name of the hospital or care home.

(2) But sub-paragraph (1) is subject to any provision relating to the change of name which is made in any enactment or in any instrument made under an enactment.

Duty to give information about decision

57 (1) This paragraph applies if–

(a) a request is made for a standard authorisation, and

(b) the supervisory body are required by paragraph 50(1) to give the standard authorisation.

(2) The supervisory body must give a copy of the authorisation to each of the following–

(a) the relevant person's representative;

(b) the managing authority of the relevant hospital or care home;

(c) the relevant person;

(d) any section 39A IMCA;

(e) every interested person consulted by the best interests assessor.

(3) The supervisory body must comply with this paragraph as soon as practicable after they give the standard authorisation.

58 (1) This paragraph applies if–

(a) a request is made for a standard authorisation, and

(b) the supervisory body are prohibited by paragraph 50(2) from giving the standard authorisation.

(2) The supervisory body must give notice, stating that they are prohibited from giving the authorisation, to each of the following–

(a) the managing authority of the relevant hospital or care home;

(b) the relevant person;

(c) any section 39A IMCA;

(d) every interested person consulted by the best interests assessor.

(3) The supervisory body must comply with this paragraph as soon as practicable after it becomes apparent to them that they are prohibited from giving the authorisation.

Duty to give information about effect of authorisation

59 (1) This paragraph applies if a standard authorisation is given.

(2) The managing authority of the relevant hospital or care home must take such steps as are practicable to ensure that the relevant person understands all of the following–

(a) the effect of the authorisation;

(b) the right to make an application to the court to exercise its jurisdiction under section 21A;

(c) the right under Part 8 to request a review;

(d) the right to have a section 39D IMCA appointed;

(e) how to have a section 39D IMCA appointed.

(3) Those steps must be taken as soon as is practicable after the authorisation is given.

(4) Those steps must include the giving of appropriate information both orally and in writing.

(5) Any written information given to the relevant person must also be given by the managing authority to the relevant person's representative.

(6) They must give the information to the representative as soon as is practicable after it is given to the relevant person.

(7) Sub-paragraph (8) applies if the managing authority is notified that a section 39D IMCA has been appointed.

(8) As soon as is practicable after being notified, the managing authority must give the section 39D IMCA a copy of the written information given in accordance with sub-paragraph (4).

Records of authorisations

60 A supervisory body must keep a written record of all of the following information–

(a) the standard authorisations that they have given;

(b) the requests for standard authorisations in response to which they have not given an authorisation;

(c) in relation to each standard authorisation given: the matters stated in the authorisation in accordance with paragraph 55.

Variation of an authorisation

61 (1) A standard authorisation may not be varied except in accordance with Part 7 or 8.

(2) This paragraph does not affect the powers of the Court of Protection or of any other court.

Effect of decision about request made under paragraph 25 or 30

62 (1) This paragraph applies where the managing authority request a new standard authorisation under either of the following–

(a) paragraph 25 (change in place of detention);

(b) paragraph 30 (existing authorisation subject to review).

(2) If the supervisory body are required by paragraph 50(1) to give the new authorisation, the existing authorisation terminates at the time when the new authorisation comes into force.

(3) If the supervisory body are prohibited by paragraph 50(2) from giving the new authorisation, there is no effect on the existing authorisation's continuation in force.

When an authorisation is in force

63 (1) A standard authorisation comes into force when it is given.

(2) But if the authorisation provides for it to come into force at a later time, it comes into force at that time.

64 (1) A standard authorisation ceases to be in force at the end of the period stated in the authorisation in accordance with paragraph 55(1)(c).

(2) But if the authorisation terminates before then in accordance with paragraph 62(2) or any other provision of this Schedule, it ceases to be in force when the termination takes effect.

(3) This paragraph does not affect the powers of the Court of Protection or of any other court.

65 (1) This paragraph applies if a standard authorisation ceases to be in force.

(2) The supervisory body must give notice that the authorisation has ceased to be in force.

(3) The supervisory body must give that notice to all of the following–
   (a) the managing authority of the relevant hospital or care home;
   (b) the relevant person;
   (c) the relevant person's representative;
   (d) every interested person consulted by the best interests assessor.

(4) The supervisory body must give that notice as soon as practicable after the authorisation ceases to be in force.

When a request for a standard authorisation is 'disposed of'

66 A request for a standard authorisation is to be regarded for the purposes of this Schedule as disposed of if the supervisory body have given–
   (a) a copy of the authorisation in accordance with paragraph 57, or
   (b) notice in accordance with paragraph 58.

Right of third party to require consideration of whether authorisation needed

67 For the purposes of paragraphs 68 to 73 there is an unauthorised deprivation of liberty if–
   (a) a person is already a detained resident in a hospital or care home, and
   (b) the detention of the person is not authorised as mentioned in section 4A.

68 (1) If the following conditions are met, an eligible person may request the supervisory body to decide whether or not there is an unauthorised deprivation of liberty.

(2) The first condition is that the eligible person has notified the managing authority of the relevant hospital or care home that it appears to the eligible person that there is an unauthorised deprivation of liberty.

(3) The second condition is that the eligible person has asked the managing

authority to request a standard authorisation in relation to the detention of the relevant person.

(4) The third condition is that the managing authority has not requested a standard authorisation within a reasonable period after the eligible person asks it to do so.

(5) In this paragraph 'eligible person' means any person other than the managing authority of the relevant hospital or care home.

69 (1) This paragraph applies if an eligible person requests the supervisory body to decide whether or not there is an unauthorised deprivation of liberty.

(2) The supervisory body must select and appoint a person to carry out an assessment of whether or not the relevant person is a detained resident.

(3) But the supervisory body need not select and appoint a person to carry out such an assessment in either of these cases.

(4) The first case is where it appears to the supervisory body that the request by the eligible person is frivolous or vexatious.

(5) The second case is where it appears to the supervisory body that–
   (a) the question of whether or not there is an unauthorised deprivation of liberty has already been decided, and
   (b) since that decision, there has been no change of circumstances which would merit the question being decided again.

(6) The supervisory body must not select and appoint a person to carry out an assessment under this paragraph unless it appears to the supervisory body that the person would be–
   (a) suitable to carry out a best interests assessment (if one were obtained in connection with a request for a standard authorisation relating to the relevant person), and
   (b) eligible to carry out such a best interests assessment.

(7) The supervisory body must notify the persons specified in sub-paragraph (8)–
   (a) that the supervisory body have been requested to decide whether or not there is an unauthorised deprivation of liberty;
   (b) of their decision whether or not to select and appoint a person to carry out an assessment under this paragraph;
   (c) if their decision is to select and appoint a person, of the person appointed.

(8) The persons referred to in sub-paragraph (7) are–
   (a) the eligible person who made the request under paragraph 68;
   (b) the person to whom the request relates;
   (c) the managing authority of the relevant hospital or care home;
   (d) any section 39A IMCA.

70 (1) Regulations may be made about the period within which an assessment under paragraph 69 must be carried out.

(2) Regulations made under paragraph 129(3) apply in relation to the selection and appointment of a person under paragraph 69 as they apply to the selection of a person under paragraph 129 to carry out a best interests assessment.

(3) The following provisions apply to an assessment under paragraph 69 as they apply to an assessment carried out in connection with a request for a standard authorisation–
   (a) paragraph 131 (examination and copying of records);

(b) paragraph 132 (representations);

(c) paragraphs 134 and 135(1) and (2) (duty to keep records and give copies).

(4) The copies of the assessment which the supervisory body are required to give under paragraph 135(2) must be given as soon as practicable after the supervisory body are themselves given a copy of the assessment.

71 (1) This paragraph applies if–

(a) the supervisory body obtain an assessment under paragraph 69,

(b) the assessment comes to the conclusion that the relevant person is a detained resident, and

(c) it appears to the supervisory body that the detention of the person is not authorised as mentioned in section 4A.

(2) This Schedule (including Part 5) applies as if the managing authority of the relevant hospital or care home had, in accordance with Part 4, requested the supervisory body to give a standard authorisation in relation to the relevant person.

(3) The managing authority of the relevant hospital or care home must supply the supervisory body with the information (if any) which the managing authority would, by virtue of paragraph 31, have had to include in a request for a standard authorisation.

(4) The supervisory body must notify the persons specified in paragraph 69(8)–

(a) of the outcome of the assessment obtained under paragraph 69, and

(b) that this Schedule applies as mentioned in sub-paragraph (2).

72 (1) This paragraph applies if–

(a) the supervisory body obtain an assessment under paragraph 69, and

(b) the assessment comes to the conclusion that the relevant person is not a detained resident.

(2) The supervisory body must notify the persons specified in paragraph 69(8) of the outcome of the assessment.

73 (1) This paragraph applies if–

(a) the supervisory body obtain an assessment under paragraph 69,

(b) the assessment comes to the conclusion that the relevant person is a detained resident, and

(c) it appears to the supervisory body that the detention of the person is authorised as mentioned in section 4A.

(2) The supervisory body must notify the persons specified in paragraph 69(8)–

(a) of the outcome of the assessment, and

(b) that it appears to the supervisory body that the detention is authorised.

Part 5: Urgent Authorisations

Managing authority to give authorisation

74 Only the managing authority of the relevant hospital or care home may give an urgent authorisation.

75 The managing authority may give an urgent authorisation only if they are required to do so by paragraph 76 (as read with paragraph 77).

Duty to give authorisation

76 (1) The managing authority must give an urgent authorisation in either of the following cases.

(2) The first case is where–

    (a) the managing authority are required to make a request under paragraph 24 or 25 for a standard authorisation, and

    (b) they believe that the need for the relevant person to be a detained resident is so urgent that it is appropriate for the detention to begin before they make the request.

(3) The second case is where–

    (a) the managing authority have made a request under paragraph 24 or 25 for a standard authorisation, and

    (b) they believe that the need for the relevant person to be a detained resident is so urgent that it is appropriate for the detention to begin before the request is disposed of.

(4) References in this paragraph to the detention of the relevant person are references to the detention to which paragraph 24 or 25 relates.

(5) This paragraph is subject to paragraph 77.

77 (1) This paragraph applies where the managing authority have given an urgent authorisation ('the original authorisation') in connection with a case where a person is, or is to be, a detained resident ('the existing detention').

(2) No new urgent authorisation is to be given under paragraph 76 in connection with the existing detention.

(3) But the managing authority may request the supervisory body to extend the duration of the original authorisation.

(4) Only one request under sub-paragraph (3) may be made in relation to the original authorisation.

(5) Paragraphs 84 to 86 apply to any request made under sub-paragraph (3).

Terms of authorisation

78 (1) If the managing authority decide to give an urgent authorisation, they must decide the period during which the authorisation is to be in force.

(2) That period must not exceed 7 days.

Form of authorisation

79   An urgent authorisation must be in writing.

80   An urgent authorisation must state the following things–

    (a) the name of the relevant person;

    (b) the name of the relevant hospital or care home;

    (c) the period during which the authorisation is to be in force;

    (d) the purpose for which the authorisation is given.

81 (1) If the name of the relevant hospital or care home changes, the urgent authorisation is to be read as if it stated the current name of the hospital or care home.

(2) But sub-paragraph (1) is subject to any provision relating to the change of name which is made in any enactment or in any instrument made under an enactment.

Duty to keep records and give copies

82 (1) This paragraph applies if an urgent authorisation is given.

(2) The managing authority must keep a written record of why they have given the urgent authorisation.

(3) As soon as practicable after giving the authorisation, the managing authority must give a copy of the authorisation to all of the following–
   (a) the relevant person;
   (b) any section 39A IMCA.

Duty to give information about authorisation

83 (1) This paragraph applies if an urgent authorisation is given.
   (2) The managing authority of the relevant hospital or care home must take such steps as are practicable to ensure that the relevant person understands all of the following–
   (a) the effect of the authorisation;
   (b) the right to make an application to the court to exercise its jurisdiction under section 21A.
   (3) Those steps must be taken as soon as is practicable after the authorisation is given.
   (4) Those steps must include the giving of appropriate information both orally and in writing.

Request for extension of duration

84 (1) This paragraph applies if the managing authority make a request under paragraph 77 for the supervisory body to extend the duration of the original authorisation.
   (2) The managing authority must keep a written record of why they have made the request.
   (3) The managing authority must give the relevant person notice that they have made the request.
   (4) The supervisory body may extend the duration of the original authorisation if it appears to them that–
   (a) the managing authority have made the required request for a standard authorisation,
   (b) there are exceptional reasons why it has not yet been possible for that request to be disposed of, and
   (c) it is essential for the existing detention to continue until the request is disposed of.
   (5) The supervisory body must keep a written record that the request has been made to them.
   (6) In this paragraph and paragraphs 85 and 86–
   (a) 'original authorisation' and 'existing detention' have the same meaning as in paragraph 77;
   (b) the required request for a standard authorisation is the request that is referred to in paragraph 76(2) or (3).

85 (1) This paragraph applies if, under paragraph 84, the supervisory body decide to extend the duration of the original authorisation.
   (2) The supervisory body must decide the period of the extension.
   (3) That period must not exceed 7 days.
   (4) The supervisory body must give the managing authority notice stating the period of the extension.
   (5) The managing authority must then vary the original authorisation so that it states the extended duration.
   (6) Paragraphs 82(3) and 83 apply (with the necessary modifications) to the

variation of the original authorisation as they apply to the giving of an urgent authorisation.

(7) The supervisory body must keep a written record of–

(a) the outcome of the request, and

(b) the period of the extension.

86 (1) This paragraph applies if, under paragraph 84, the supervisory body decide not to extend the duration of the original authorisation.

(2) The supervisory body must give the managing authority notice stating–

(a) the decision, and

(b) their reasons for making it.

(3) The managing authority must give a copy of that notice to all of the following–

(a) the relevant person;

(b) any section 39A IMCA.

(4) The supervisory body must keep a written record of the outcome of the request.

No variation

87 (1) An urgent authorisation may not be varied except in accordance with paragraph 85.

(2) This paragraph does not affect the powers of the Court of Protection or of any other court.

When an authorisation is in force

88 An urgent authorisation comes into force when it is given.

89 (1) An urgent authorisation ceases to be in force at the end of the period stated in the authorisation in accordance with paragraph 80(c) (subject to any variation in accordance with paragraph 85).

(2) But if the required request is disposed of before the end of that period, the urgent authorisation ceases to be in force as follows.

(3) If the supervisory body are required by paragraph 50(1) to give the requested authorisation, the urgent authorisation ceases to be in force when the requested authorisation comes into force.

(4) If the supervisory body are prohibited by paragraph 50(2) from giving the requested authorisation, the urgent authorisation ceases to be in force when the managing authority receive notice under paragraph 58.

(5) In this paragraph–

'required request' means the request referred to in paragraph 76(2) or (3);

'requested authorisation' means the standard authorisation to which the required request relates.

(6) This paragraph does not affect the powers of the Court of Protection or of any other court.

90 (1) This paragraph applies if an urgent authorisation ceases to be in force.

(2) The supervisory body must give notice that the authorisation has ceased to be in force.

(3) The supervisory body must give that notice to all of the following–

(a) the relevant person;

(b) any section 39A IMCA.

(4) The supervisory body must give that notice as soon as practicable after the authorisation ceases to be in force.

Part 6: Eligibility Requirement not Met: Suspension of Standard Authorisation

91 (1) This Part applies if the following conditions are met.

(2) The first condition is that a standard authorisation–

(a) has been given, and

(b) has not ceased to be in force.

(3) The second condition is that the managing authority of the relevant hospital or care home are satisfied that the relevant person has ceased to meet the eligibility requirement.

(4) But this Part does not apply if the relevant person is ineligible by virtue of paragraph 5 of Schedule 1A (in which case see Part 8).

92   The managing authority of the relevant hospital or care home must give the supervisory body notice that the relevant person has ceased to meet the eligibility requirement.

93 (1) This paragraph applies if the managing authority give the supervisory body notice under paragraph 92.

(2) The standard authorisation is suspended from the time when the notice is given.

(3) The supervisory body must give notice that the standard authorisation has been suspended to the following persons–

(a) the relevant person;

(b) the relevant person's representative;

(c) the managing authority of the relevant hospital or care home.

94 (1) This paragraph applies if, whilst the standard authorisation is suspended, the managing authority are satisfied that the relevant person meets the eligibility requirement again.

(2) The managing authority must give the supervisory body notice that the relevant person meets the eligibility requirement again.

95 (1) This paragraph applies if the managing authority give the supervisory body notice under paragraph 94.

(2) The standard authorisation ceases to be suspended from the time when the notice is given.

(3) The supervisory body must give notice that the standard authorisation has ceased to be suspended to the following persons–

(a) the relevant person;

(b) the relevant person's representative;

(c) any section 39D IMCA;

(d) the managing authority of the relevant hospital or care home.

(4) The supervisory body must give notice under this paragraph as soon as practicable after they are given notice under paragraph 94.

96 (1) This paragraph applies if no notice is given under paragraph 94 before the end of the relevant 28 day period.

(2) The standard authorisation ceases to have effect at the end of the relevant 28 day period.

(3) The relevant 28 day period is the period of 28 days beginning with the day on which the standard authorisation is suspended under paragraph 93.

97   The effect of suspending the standard authorisation is that Part 1 ceases to apply for as long as the authorisation is suspended.

Part 7: Standard Authorisations: Change in Supervisory Responsibility

Application of this Part

98 (1) This Part applies if these conditions are met.

(2) The first condition is that a standard authorisation–

(a) has been given, and

(b) has not ceased to be in force.

(3) The second condition is that there is a change in supervisory responsibility.

(4) The third condition is that there is not a change in the place of detention (within the meaning of paragraph 25).

99   For the purposes of this Part there is a change in supervisory responsibility if–

(a) one body ('the old supervisory body') have ceased to be supervisory body in relation to the standard authorisation, and

(b) a different body ('the new supervisory body') have become supervisory body in relation to the standard authorisation.

Effect of change in supervisory responsibility

100 (1) The new supervisory body becomes the supervisory body in relation to the authorisation.

(2) Anything done by or in relation to the old supervisory body in connection with the authorisation has effect, so far as is necessary for continuing its effect after the change, as if done by or in relation to the new supervisory body.

(3) Anything which relates to the authorisation and which is in the process of being done by or in relation to the old supervisory body at the time of the change may be continued by or in relation to the new supervisory body.

(4) But–

(a) the old supervisory body do not, by virtue of this paragraph, cease to be liable for anything done by them in connection with the authorisation before the change; and

(b) the new supervisory body do not, by virtue of this paragraph, become liable for any such thing.

Part 8: Standard Authorisations: Review

Application of this Part

101 (1) This Part applies if a standard authorisation–

(a) has been given, and

(b) has not ceased to be in force.

(2) Paragraphs 102 to 122 are subject to paragraphs 123 to 125.

Review by supervisory body

102 (1) The supervisory body may at any time carry out a review of the standard authorisation in accordance with this Part.

(2) The supervisory body must carry out such a review if they are requested to do so by an eligible person.

(3) Each of the following is an eligible person–

(a) the relevant person;

(b) the relevant person's representative;

(c) the managing authority of the relevant hospital or care home.

Request for review

103 (1) An eligible person may, at any time, request the supervisory body to carry out a review of the standard authorisation in accordance with this Part.

(2) The managing authority of the relevant hospital or care home must make such a request if one or more of the qualifying requirements appear to them to be reviewable.

Grounds for review

104 (1) Paragraphs 105 to 107 set out the grounds on which the qualifying requirements are reviewable.

(2) A qualifying requirement is not reviewable on any other ground.

Non-qualification ground

105 (1) Any of the following qualifying requirements is reviewable on the ground that the relevant person does not meet the requirement–

(a) the age requirement;

(b) the mental health requirement;

(c) the mental capacity requirement;

(d) the best interests requirement;

(e) the no refusals requirement.

(2) The eligibility requirement is reviewable on the ground that the relevant person is ineligible by virtue of paragraph 5 of Schedule 1A.

(3) The ground in sub-paragraph (1) and the ground in sub-paragraph (2) are referred to as the non-qualification ground.

Change of reason ground

106 (1) Any of the following qualifying requirements is reviewable on the ground set out in sub-paragraph (2)–

(a) the mental health requirement;

(b) the mental capacity requirement;

(c) the best interests requirement;

(d) the eligibility requirement;

(e) the no refusals requirement.

(2) The ground is that the reason why the relevant person meets the requirement is not the reason stated in the standard authorisation.

(3) This ground is referred to as the change of reason ground.

Variation of conditions ground

107 (1) The best interests requirement is reviewable on the ground that–

(a) there has been a change in the relevant person's case, and

(b) because of that change, it would be appropriate to vary the conditions to which the standard authorisation is subject.

(2) This ground is referred to as the variation of conditions ground.

(3) A reference to varying the conditions to which the standard authorisation is subject is a reference to–

(a) amendment of an existing condition,

(b) omission of an existing condition, or

(c) inclusion of a new condition (whether or not there are already any existing conditions).

Notice that review to be carried out

108 (1) If the supervisory body are to carry out a review of the standard authorisation, they must give notice of the review to the following persons–
  (a) the relevant person;
  (b) the relevant person's representative;
  (c) the managing authority of the relevant hospital or care home.

(2) The supervisory body must give the notice–
  (a) before they begin the review, or
  (b) if that is not practicable, as soon as practicable after they have begun it.

(3) This paragraph does not require the supervisory body to give notice to any person who has requested the review.

Starting a review

109 To start a review of the standard authorisation, the supervisory body must decide which, if any, of the qualifying requirements appear to be reviewable.

No reviewable qualifying requirements

110 (1) This paragraph applies if no qualifying requirements appear to be reviewable.

(2) This Part does not require the supervisory body to take any action in respect of the standard authorisation.

One or more reviewable qualifying requirements

111 (1) This paragraph applies if one or more qualifying requirements appear to be reviewable.

(2) The supervisory body must secure that a separate review assessment is carried out in relation to each qualifying requirement which appears to be reviewable.

(3) But sub-paragraph (2) does not require the supervisory body to secure that a best interests review assessment is carried out in a case where the best interests requirement appears to the supervisory body to be non-assessable.

(4) The best interests requirement is non-assessable if–
  (a) the requirement is reviewable only on the variation of conditions ground, and
  (b) the change in the relevant person's case is not significant.

(5) In making any decision whether the change in the relevant person's case is significant, regard must be had to–
  (a) the nature of the change, and
  (b) the period that the change is likely to last for.

Review assessments

112 (1) A review assessment is an assessment of whether the relevant person meets a qualifying requirement.

(2) In relation to a review assessment–
  (a) a negative conclusion is a conclusion that the relevant person does not meet the qualifying requirement to which the assessment relates;
  (b) a positive conclusion is a conclusion that the relevant person meets the qualifying requirement to which the assessment relates.

(3) An age review assessment is a review assessment carried out in relation to the age requirement.

(4) A mental health review assessment is a review assessment carried out in relation to the mental health requirement.

(5) A mental capacity review assessment is a review assessment carried out in relation to the mental capacity requirement.

(6) A best interests review assessment is a review assessment carried out in relation to the best interests requirement.

(7) An eligibility review assessment is a review assessment carried out in relation to the eligibility requirement.

(8) A no refusals review assessment is a review assessment carried out in relation to the no refusals requirement.

113 (1) In carrying out a review assessment, the assessor must comply with any duties which would be imposed upon him under Part 4 if the assessment were being carried out in connection with a request for a standard authorisation.

(2) But in the case of a best interests review assessment, paragraphs 43 and 44 do not apply.

(3) Instead of what is required by paragraph 43, the best interests review assessment must include recommendations about whether–and, if so, how–it would be appropriate to vary the conditions to which the standard authorisation is subject.

Best interests requirement reviewable but non-assessable

114 (1) This paragraph applies in a case where–

(a) the best interests requirement appears to be reviewable, but

(b) in accordance with paragraph 111(3), the supervisory body are not required to secure that a best interests review assessment is carried out.

(2) The supervisory body may vary the conditions to which the standard authorisation is subject in such ways (if any) as the supervisory body think are appropriate in the circumstances.

Best interests review assessment positive

115 (1) This paragraph applies in a case where–

(a) a best interests review assessment is carried out, and

(b) the assessment comes to a positive conclusion.

(2) The supervisory body must decide the following questions–

(a) whether or not the best interests requirement is reviewable on the change of reason ground;

(b) whether or not the best interests requirement is reviewable on the variation of conditions ground;

(c) if so, whether or not the change in the person's case is significant.

(3) If the supervisory body decide that the best interests requirement is reviewable on the change of reason ground, they must vary the standard authorisation so that it states the reason why the relevant person now meets that requirement.

(4) If the supervisory body decide that–

(a) the best interests requirement is reviewable on the variation of conditions ground, and

(b) the change in the relevant person's case is not significant,

they may vary the conditions to which the standard authorisation is subject in such ways (if any) as they think are appropriate in the circumstances.

(5) If the supervisory body decide that–

(a) the best interests requirement is reviewable on the variation of conditions ground, and
(b) the change in the relevant person's case is significant,
they must vary the conditions to which the standard authorisation is subject in such ways as they think are appropriate in the circumstances.
(6) If the supervisory body decide that the best interests requirement is not reviewable on–
(a) the change of reason ground, or
(b) the variation of conditions ground,
this Part does not require the supervisory body to take any action in respect of the standard authorisation so far as the best interests requirement relates to it.

Mental health, mental capacity, eligibility or no refusals review assessment positive

116 (1) This paragraph applies if the following conditions are met.
(2) The first condition is that one or more of the following are carried out–
(a) a mental health review assessment;
(b) a mental capacity review assessment;
(c) an eligibility review assessment;
(d) a no refusals review assessment.
(3) The second condition is that each assessment carried out comes to a positive conclusion.
(4) The supervisory body must decide whether or not each of the assessed qualifying requirements is reviewable on the change of reason ground.
(5) If the supervisory body decide that any of the assessed qualifying requirements is reviewable on the change of reason ground, they must vary the standard authorisation so that it states the reason why the relevant person now meets the requirement or requirements in question.
(6) If the supervisory body decide that none of the assessed qualifying requirements are reviewable on the change of reason ground, this Part does not require the supervisory body to take any action in respect of the standard authorisation so far as those requirements relate to it.
(7) An assessed qualifying requirement is a qualifying requirement in relation to which a review assessment is carried out.

One or more review assessments negative

117 (1) This paragraph applies if one or more of the review assessments carried out comes to a negative conclusion.
(2) The supervisory body must terminate the standard authorisation with immediate effect.

Completion of a review

118 (1) The review of the standard authorisation is complete in any of the following cases.
(2) The first case is where paragraph 110 applies.
(3) The second case is where–
(a) paragraph 111 applies, and
(b) paragraph 117 requires the supervisory body to terminate the standard authorisation.

(4) In such a case, the supervisory body need not comply with any of the other provisions of paragraphs 114 to 116 which would be applicable to the review (were it not for this sub-paragraph).

(5) The third case is where–
  (a) paragraph 111 applies,
  (b) paragraph 117 does not require the supervisory body to terminate the standard authorisation, and
  (c) the supervisory body comply with all of the provisions of paragraphs 114 to 116 (so far as they are applicable to the review).

Variations under this Part

119 Any variation of the standard authorisation made under this Part must be in writing.

Notice of outcome of review

120 (1) When the review of the standard authorisation is complete, the supervisory body must give notice to all of the following–
  (a) the managing authority of the relevant hospital or care home;
  (b) the relevant person;
  (c) the relevant person's representative;
  (d) any section 39D IMCA.

(2) That notice must state–
  (a) the outcome of the review, and
  (b) what variation (if any) has been made to the authorisation under this Part.

Records

121 A supervisory body must keep a written record of the following information–
  (a) each request for a review that is made to them;
  (b) the outcome of each request;
  (c) each review which they carry out;
  (d) the outcome of each review which they carry out;
  (e) any variation of an authorisation made in consequence of a review.

Relationship between review and suspension under Part 6

122 (1) This paragraph applies if a standard authorisation is suspended in accordance with Part 6.

(2) No review may be requested under this Part whilst the standard authorisation is suspended.

(3) If a review has already been requested, or is being carried out, when the standard authorisation is suspended, no steps are to be taken in connection with that review whilst the authorisation is suspended.

Relationship between review and request for new authorisation

123 (1) This paragraph applies if, in accordance with paragraph 24 (as read with paragraph 29), the managing authority of the relevant hospital or care home make a request for a new standard authorisation which would be in force after the expiry of the existing authorisation.

(2) No review may be requested under this Part until the request for the new standard authorisation has been disposed of.

(3) If a review has already been requested, or is being carried out, when the new

standard authorisation is requested, no steps are to be taken in connection with that review until the request for the new standard authorisation has been disposed of.

124(1) This paragraph applies if–

(a) a review under this Part has been requested, or is being carried out, and

(b) the managing authority of the relevant hospital or care home make a request under paragraph 30 for a new standard authorisation which would be in force on or before, and after, the expiry of the existing authorisation.

(2) No steps are to be taken in connection with the review under this Part until the request for the new standard authorisation has been disposed of.

125   In paragraphs 123 and 124–

(a) the existing authorisation is the authorisation referred to in paragraph 101;

(b) the expiry of the existing authorisation is the time when it is expected to cease to be in force.

Part 9: Assessments under this Schedule

Introduction

126   This Part contains provision about assessments under this Schedule.

127   An assessment under this Schedule is either of the following–

(a) an assessment carried out in connection with a request for a standard authorisation under Part 4;

(b) a review assessment carried out in connection with a review of a standard authorisation under Part 8.

128   In this Part, in relation to an assessment under this Schedule–

'assessor' means the person carrying out the assessment;

'relevant procedure' means–

(a) the request for the standard authorisation, or

(b) the review of the standard authorisation;

'supervisory body' means the supervisory body responsible for securing that the assessment is carried out.

Supervisory body to select assessor

129(1) It is for the supervisory body to select a person to carry out an assessment under this Schedule.

(2) The supervisory body must not select a person to carry out an assessment unless the person–

(a) appears to the supervisory body to be suitable to carry out the assessment (having regard, in particular, to the type of assessment and the person to be assessed), and

(b) is eligible to carry out the assessment.

(3) Regulations may make provision about the selection, and eligibility, of persons to carry out assessments under this Schedule.

(4) Sub-paragraphs (5) and (6) apply if two or more assessments are to be obtained for the purposes of the relevant procedure.

(5) In a case where the assessments to be obtained include a mental health assessment and a best interests assessment, the supervisory body must not select the same person to carry out both assessments.

(6) Except as prohibited by sub-paragraph (5), the supervisory body may select the same person to carry out any number of the assessments which the person appears to be suitable, and is eligible, to carry out.

130 (1) This paragraph applies to regulations under paragraph 129(3).

(2) The regulations may make provision relating to a person's–
  (a) qualifications,
  (b) skills,
  (c) training,
  (d) experience,
  (e) relationship to, or connection with, the relevant person or any other person,
  (f) involvement in the care or treatment of the relevant person,
  (g) connection with the supervisory body, or
  (h) connection with the relevant hospital or care home, or with any other establishment or undertaking.

(3) The provision that the regulations may make in relation to a person's training may provide for particular training to be specified by the appropriate authority otherwise than in the regulations.

(4) In sub-paragraph (3) the 'appropriate authority' means–
  (a) in relation to England: the Secretary of State;
  (b) in relation to Wales: the National Assembly for Wales.

(5) The regulations may make provision requiring a person to be insured in respect of liabilities that may arise in connection with the carrying out of an assessment.

(6) In relation to cases where two or more assessments are to be obtained for the purposes of the relevant procedure, the regulations may limit the number, kind or combination of assessments which a particular person is eligible to carry out.

(7) Sub-paragraphs (2) to (6) do not limit the generality of the provision that may be made in the regulations.

Examination and copying of records

131   An assessor may, at all reasonable times, examine and take copies of–
  (a) any health record,
  (b) any record of, or held by, a local authority and compiled in accordance with a social services function, and
  (c) any record held by a person registered under Part 2 of the Care Standards Act 2000 or Chapter 2 of Part 1 of the Health and Social Care Act 2008,
  which the assessor considers may be relevant to the assessment which is being carried out.

Representations

132   In carrying out an assessment under this Schedule, the assessor must take into account any information given, or submissions made, by any of the following–
  (a) the relevant person's representative;
  (b) any section 39A IMCA;
  (c) any section 39C IMCA;
  (d) any section 39D IMCA.

Assessments to stop if any comes to negative conclusion

133 (1) This paragraph applies if an assessment under this Schedule comes to the conclusion that the relevant person does not meet one of the qualifying requirements.

(2) This Schedule does not require the supervisory body to secure that any other assessments under this Schedule are carried out in relation to the relevant procedure.

(3) The supervisory body must give notice to any assessor who is carrying out another assessment in connection with the relevant procedure that they are to cease carrying out that assessment.

(4) If an assessor receives such notice, this Schedule does not require the assessor to continue carrying out that assessment.

Duty to keep records and give copies

134 (1) This paragraph applies if an assessor has carried out an assessment under this Schedule (whatever conclusions the assessment has come to).

(2) The assessor must keep a written record of the assessment.

(3) As soon as practicable after carrying out the assessment, the assessor must give copies of the assessment to the supervisory body.

135 (1) This paragraph applies to the supervisory body if they are given a copy of an assessment under this Schedule.

(2) The supervisory body must give copies of the assessment to all of the following–

(a) the managing authority of the relevant hospital or care home;

(b) the relevant person;

(c) any section 39A IMCA;

(d) the relevant person's representative.

(3) If–

(a) the assessment is obtained in relation to a request for a standard authorisation, and

(b) the supervisory body are required by paragraph 50(1) to give the standard authorisation,

the supervisory body must give the copies of the assessment when they give copies of the authorisation in accordance with paragraph 57.

(4) If–

(a) the assessment is obtained in relation to a request for a standard authorisation, and

(b) the supervisory body are prohibited by paragraph 50(2) from giving the standard authorisation,

the supervisory body must give the copies of the assessment when they give notice in accordance with paragraph 58.

(5) If the assessment is obtained in connection with the review of a standard authorisation, the supervisory body must give the copies of the assessment when they give notice in accordance with paragraph 120.

136 (1) This paragraph applies to the supervisory body if–

(a) they are given a copy of a best interests assessment, and

(b) the assessment includes, in accordance with paragraph 44(2), a statement that it appears to the assessor that there is an unauthorised deprivation of liberty.

(2) The supervisory body must notify all of the persons listed in sub-paragraph (3) that the assessment includes such a statement.

(3) Those persons are–

(a) the managing authority of the relevant hospital or care home;

(b) the relevant person;

(c) any section 39A IMCA;

(d) any interested person consulted by the best interests assessor.

(4) The supervisory body must comply with this paragraph when (or at some time before) they comply with paragraph 135.

Part 10: Relevant Person's Representative

The representative

137   In this Schedule the relevant person's representative is the person appointed as such in accordance with this Part.

138 (1) Regulations may make provision about the selection and appointment of representatives.

(2) In this Part such regulations are referred to as 'appointment regulations'.

Supervisory body to appoint representative

139 (1) The supervisory body must appoint a person to be the relevant person's representative as soon as practicable after a standard authorisation is given.

(2) The supervisory body must appoint a person to be the relevant person's representative if a vacancy arises whilst a standard authorisation is in force.

(3) Where a vacancy arises, the appointment under sub-paragraph (2) is to be made as soon as practicable after the supervisory body becomes aware of the vacancy.

140 (1) The selection of a person for appointment under paragraph 139 must not be made unless it appears to the person making the selection that the prospective representative would, if appointed–

(a) maintain contact with the relevant person,

(b) represent the relevant person in matters relating to or connected with this Schedule, and

(c) support the relevant person in matters relating to or connected with this Schedule.

141 (1) Any appointment of a representative for a relevant person is in addition to, and does not affect, any appointment of a donee or deputy.

(2) The functions of any representative are in addition to, and do not affect–

(a) the authority of any donee,

(b) the powers of any deputy, or

(c) any powers of the court.

Appointment regulations

142   Appointment regulations may provide that the procedure for appointing a representative may begin at any time after a request for a standard authorisation is made (including a time before the request has been disposed of).

143 (1) Appointment regulations may make provision about who is to select a person for appointment as a representative.

(2) But regulations under this paragraph may only provide for the following to make a selection–

(a) the relevant person, if he has capacity in relation to the question of which person should be his representative;

(b) a donee of a lasting power of attorney granted by the relevant person, if it is within the scope of his authority to select a person;

(c) a deputy, if it is within the scope of his authority to select a person;

(d) a best interests assessor;

(e) the supervisory body.

(3) Regulations under this paragraph may provide that a selection by the relevant person, a donee or a deputy is subject to approval by a best interests assessor or the supervisory body.

(4) Regulations under this paragraph may provide that, if more than one selection is necessary in connection with the appointment of a particular representative–

(a) the same person may make more than one selection;

(b) different persons may make different selections.

(5) For the purposes of this paragraph a best interests assessor is a person carrying out a best interests assessment in connection with the standard authorisation in question (including the giving of that authorisation).

144(1) Appointment regulations may make provision about who may, or may not, be–

(a) selected for appointment as a representative, or

(b) appointed as a representative.

(2) Regulations under this paragraph may relate to any of the following matters–

(a) a person's age;

(b) a person's suitability;

(c) a person's independence;

(d) a person's willingness;

(e) a person's qualifications.

145 Appointment regulations may make provision about the formalities of appointing a person as a representative.

146 In a case where a best interests assessor is to select a person to be appointed as a representative, appointment regulations may provide for the variation of the assessor's duties in relation to the assessment which he is carrying out.

Monitoring of representatives

147 Regulations may make provision requiring the managing authority of the relevant hospital or care home to–

(a) monitor, and

(b) report to the supervisory body on,

the extent to which a representative is maintaining contact with the relevant person.

Termination

148 Regulations may make provision about the circumstances in which the appointment of a person as the relevant person's representative ends or may be ended.

149 Regulations may make provision about the formalities of ending the appointment of a person as a representative.

Suspension of representative's functions

150(1) Regulations may make provision about the circumstances in which functions exercisable by, or in relation to, the relevant person's representative (whether under this Schedule or not) may be–
(a) suspended, and
(b) if suspended, revived.

(2) The regulations may make provision about the formalities for giving effect to the suspension or revival of a function.

(3) The regulations may make provision about the effect of the suspension or revival of a function.

Payment of representative

151   Regulations may make provision for payments to be made to, or in relation to, persons exercising functions as the relevant person's representative.

Regulations under this Part

152   The provisions of this Part which specify provision that may be made in regulations under this Part do not affect the generality of the power to make such regulations.

Effect of appointment of section 39C IMCA

153   Paragraphs 159 and 160 make provision about the exercise of functions by, or towards, the relevant person's representative during periods when–
(a) no person is appointed as the relevant person's representative, but
(b) a person is appointed as a section 39C IMCA.

Part 11: IMCAs

Application of Part

154   This Part applies for the purposes of this Schedule.

The IMCAs

155   A section 39A IMCA is an independent mental capacity advocate appointed under section 39A.

156   A section 39C IMCA is an independent mental capacity advocate appointed under section 39C

157   A section 39D IMCA is an independent mental capacity advocate appointed under section 39D.

158   An IMCA is a section 39A IMCA or a section 39C IMCA or a section 39D IMCA.

Section 39C IMCA: functions

159(1) This paragraph applies if, and for as long as, there is a section 39C IMCA.

(2) In the application of the relevant provisions, references to the relevant person's representative are to be read as references to the section 39C IMCA.

(3) But sub-paragraph (2) does not apply to any function under the relevant provisions for as long as the function is suspended in accordance with provision made under Part 10.

(4) In this paragraph and paragraph 160 the relevant provisions are–
(a) paragraph 102(3)(b) (request for review under Part 8);
(b) paragraph 108(1)(b) (notice of review under Part 8);
(c) paragraph 120(1)(c) (notice of outcome of review under Part 8).

160 (1) This paragraph applies if–

    (a) a person is appointed as the relevant person's representative, and

    (b) a person accordingly ceases to hold an appointment as a section 39C IMCA.

(2) Where a function under a relevant provision has been exercised by, or towards, the section 39C IMCA, there is no requirement for that function to be exercised again by, or towards, the relevant person's representative.

Section 39A IMCA: restriction of functions

161 (1) This paragraph applies if–

    (a) there is a section 39A IMCA, and

    (b) a person is appointed under Part 10 to be the relevant person's representative (whether or not that person, or any person subsequently appointed, is currently the relevant person's representative).

(2) The duties imposed on, and the powers exercisable by, the section 39A IMCA do not apply.

(3) The duties imposed on, and the powers exercisable by, any other person do not apply, so far as they fall to be performed or exercised towards the section 39A IMCA.

(4) But sub-paragraph (2) does not apply to any power of challenge exercisable by the section 39A IMCA.

(5) And sub-paragraph (3) does not apply to any duty or power of any other person so far as it relates to any power of challenge exercisable by the section 39A IMCA.

(6) Before exercising any power of challenge, the section 39A IMCA must take the views of the relevant person's representative into account.

(7) A power of challenge is a power to make an application to the court to exercise its jurisdiction under section 21A in connection with the giving of the standard authorisation.

Part 12: Miscellaneous

Monitoring of operation of Schedule

162 (1) Regulations may make provision for, and in connection with, requiring one or more prescribed bodies to monitor, and report on, the operation of this Schedule in relation to England.

(2) The regulations may, in particular, give a prescribed body authority to do one or more of the following things–

    (a) to visit hospitals and care homes;

    (b) to visit and interview persons accommodated in hospitals and care homes;

    (c) to require the production of, and to inspect, records relating to the care or treatment of persons.

(3) 'Prescribed' means prescribed in regulations under this paragraph.

163 (1) Regulations may make provision for, and in connection with, enabling the National Assembly for Wales to monitor, and report on, the operation of this Schedule in relation to Wales.

(2) The National Assembly may direct one or more persons or bodies to carry out the Assembly's functions under regulations under this paragraph.

Disclosure of information

164 (1) Regulations may require either or both of the following to disclose prescribed information to prescribed bodies–

(a) supervisory bodies;

(b) managing authorities of hospitals or care homes.

(2) 'Prescribed' means prescribed in regulations under this paragraph.

(3) Regulations under this paragraph may only prescribe information relating to matters with which this Schedule is concerned.

Directions by National Assembly in relation to supervisory functions

165 (1) The National Assembly for Wales may direct a Local Health Board to exercise in relation to its area any supervisory functions which are specified in the direction.

(2) Directions under this paragraph must not preclude the National Assembly from exercising the functions specified in the directions.

(3) In this paragraph 'supervisory functions' means functions which the National Assembly have as supervisory body, so far as they are exercisable in relation to hospitals (whether NHS or independent hospitals, and whether in Wales or England).

166 (1) This paragraph applies where, under paragraph 165, a Local Health Board ('the specified LHB') is directed to exercise supervisory functions ('delegated functions').

(2) The National Assembly for Wales may give directions to the specified LHB about the Board's exercise of delegated functions.

(3) The National Assembly may give directions for any delegated functions to be exercised, on behalf of the specified LHB, by a committee, sub-committee or officer of that Board.

(4) The National Assembly may give directions providing for any delegated functions to be exercised by the specified LHB jointly with one or more other Local Health Boards.

(5) Where, under sub-paragraph (4), delegated functions are exercisable jointly, the National Assembly may give directions providing for the functions to be exercised, on behalf of the Local Health Boards in question, by a joint committee or joint sub-committee.

167 (1) Directions under paragraph 165 must be given in regulations.

(2) Directions under paragraph 166 may be given–

(a) in regulations, or

(b) by instrument in writing.

168 The power under paragraph 165 or paragraph 166 to give directions includes power to vary or revoke directions given under that paragraph.

Notices

169 Any notice under this Schedule must be in writing.

Regulations

170 (1) This paragraph applies to all regulations under this Schedule, except regulations under paragraph 162, 163, 167 or 183.

(2) It is for the Secretary of State to make such regulations in relation to authorisations under this Schedule which relate to hospitals and care homes situated in England.

(3) It is for the National Assembly for Wales to make such regulations in relation to authorisations under this Schedule which relate to hospitals and care homes situated in Wales.

171   It is for the Secretary of State to make regulations under paragraph 162.

172   It is for the National Assembly for Wales to make regulations under paragraph 163 or 167.

173 (1) This paragraph applies to regulations under paragraph 183.

(2) It is for the Secretary of State to make such regulations in relation to cases where a question as to the ordinary residence of a person is to be determined by the Secretary of State.

(3) It is for the National Assembly for Wales to make such regulations in relation to cases where a question as to the ordinary residence of a person is to be determined by the National Assembly.

Part 13: Interpretation

Introduction

174   This Part applies for the purposes of this Schedule.

Hospitals and their managing authorities

175 (1) 'Hospital' means–

(a) an NHS hospital, or

(b) an independent hospital.

(2) 'NHS hospital' means–

(a) a health service hospital as defined by section 275 of the National Health Service Act 2006 or section 206 of the National Health Service (Wales) Act 2006, or

(b) a hospital as defined by section 206 of the National Health Service (Wales) Act 2006 vested in a Local Health Board.

(3) Independent hospital'–

(a) in relation to England, means a hospital as defined by section 275 of the National Health Service Act 2006 that is not an NHS hospital; and

(b) in relation to Wales, means a hospital as defined by section 2 of the Care Standards Act 2000 that is not an NHS hospital.

176 (1) 'Managing authority', in relation to an NHS hospital, means–

(a) if the hospital–

(i) is vested in the appropriate national authority for the purposes of its functions under the National Health Service Act 2006 or of the National Health Service (Wales) Act 2006, or

(ii) consists of any accommodation provided by a local authority and used as a hospital by or on behalf of the appropriate national authority under either of those Acts,

the Local Health Board or Special Health Authority responsible for the administration of the hospital;

(aa) in relation to England, if the hospital falls within paragraph (a)(i) or (ii) and no Special Health Authority has responsibility for its administration, the Secretary of State;

(b) if the hospital is vested in a . . . National Health Service trust or NHS foundation trust, that trust;

(c) if the hospital is vested in a Local Health Board, that Board.

(2) For this purpose the appropriate national authority is—
  (a) in relation to England: the Secretary of State;
  (b) in relation to Wales: the National Assembly for Wales;
  (c) in relation to England and Wales: the Secretary of State and the National Assembly acting jointly.

177 'Managing authority', in relation to an independent hospital, means—
  (a) in relation to England, the person registered, or required to be registered, under Chapter 2 of Part 1 of the Health and Social Care Act 2008 in respect of regulated activities (within the meaning of that Part) carried on in the hospital, and
  (b) in relation to Wales, the person registered, or required to be registered, under Part 2 of the Care Standards Act 2000 in respect of the hospital.

Care homes and their managing authorities

178 'Care home' has the meaning given by section 3 of the Care Standards Act 2000.

179 'Managing authority', in relation to a care home, means—
  (a) in relation to England, the person registered, or required to be registered, under Chapter 2 of Part 1 of the Health and Social Care Act 2008 in respect of the provision of residential accommodation, together with nursing or personal care, in the care home, and
  (b) in relation to Wales, the person registered, or required to be registered, under Part 2 of the Care Standards Act 2000 in respect of the care home.

Supervisory bodies: hospitals

180 (1) The identity of the supervisory body is determined under this paragraph in cases where the relevant hospital is situated in England.

  (2) If the relevant person is ordinarily resident in the area of a local authority in England, the supervisory body are that local authority.

  (3) If the relevant person is not ordinarily resident in England and the National Assembly for Wales or a Local Health Board commission the relevant care or treatment, the National Assembly are the supervisory body.

  (4) In any other case, the supervisory body are the local authority for the area in which the relevant hospital is situated.

  (4A) Local authority' means—
  (a) the council of a county;
  (b) the council of a district for which there is no county council;
  (c) the council of a London borough;
  (d) the Common Council of the City of London;
  (e) the Council of the Isles of Scilly.

  (5) If a hospital is situated in the areas of two (or more) local authorities, it is to be regarded for the purposes of sub-paragraph (4) as situated in whichever of the areas the greater (or greatest) part of the hospital is situated.

181 (1) The identity of the supervisory body is determined under this paragraph in cases where the relevant hospital is situated in Wales.

  (2) The National Assembly for Wales are the supervisory body.

  (3) But if the relevant person is ordinarily resident in the area of a local authority in England, the supervisory body are that local authority.

  (4) 'Local authority' means—
  (a) the council of a county;

(b) the council of a district for which there is no county council;
(c) the council of a London borough;
(d) the Common Council of the City of London;
(e) the Council of the Isles of Scilly.

Supervisory bodies: care homes

182 (1) The identity of the supervisory body is determined under this paragraph in cases where the relevant care home is situated in England or in Wales.

(2) The supervisory body are the local authority for the area in which the relevant person is ordinarily resident.

(3) But if the relevant person is not ordinarily resident in the area of a local authority, the supervisory body are the local authority for the area in which the care home is situated.

(4) In relation to England 'local authority' means–
  (a) the council of a county;
  (b) the council of a district for which there is no county council;
  (c) the council of a London borough;
  (d) the Common Council of the City of London;
  (e) the Council of the Isles of Scilly.

(5) In relation to Wales 'local authority' means the council of a county or county borough.

(6) If a care home is situated in the areas of two (or more) local authorities, it is to be regarded for the purposes of sub-paragraph (3) as situated in whichever of the areas the greater (or greatest) part of the care home is situated.

Supervisory bodies: determination of place of ordinary residence

183 (1) Subsections (5) and (6) of section 24 of the National Assistance Act 1948 (deemed place of ordinary residence) apply to any determination of where a person is ordinarily resident for the purposes of paragraphs 180, 181 and 182 as those subsections apply to such a determination for the purposes specified in those subsections.

(2) In the application of section 24(6) of the 1948 Act by virtue of subsection (1) to any determination of where a person is ordinarily resident for the purposes of paragraph 182, section 24(6) is to be read as if it referred to a hospital vested in a Local Health Board as well as to hospitals vested in the Secretary of State and the other bodies mentioned in section 24(6).

(3) Any question arising as to the ordinary residence of a person is to be determined by the Secretary of State or by the National Assembly for Wales.

(4) The Secretary of State and the National Assembly must make and publish arrangements for determining which cases are to be dealt with by the Secretary of State and which are to be dealt with by the National Assembly.

(5) Those arrangements may include provision for the Secretary of State and the National Assembly to agree, in relation to any question that has arisen, which of them is to deal with the case.

(6) Regulations may make provision about arrangements that are to have effect before, upon, or after the determination of any question as to the ordinary residence of a person.

(7) The regulations may, in particular, authorise or require a local authority to do any or all of the following things–

(a) to act as supervisory body even though it may wish to dispute that it is the supervisory body;
(b) to become the supervisory body in place of another local authority;
(c) to recover from another local authority expenditure incurred in exercising functions as the supervisory body.

Same body managing authority and supervisory body

184(1) This paragraph applies if, in connection with a particular person's detention as a resident in a hospital or care home, the same body are both–
(a) the managing authority of the relevant hospital or care home, and
(b) the supervisory body.
(2) The fact that a single body are acting in both capacities does not prevent the body from carrying out functions under this Schedule in each capacity.
(3) But, in such a case, this Schedule has effect subject to any modifications contained in regulations that may be made for this purpose.

Interested persons

185   Each of the following is an interested person–
(a) the relevant person's spouse or civil partner;
(b) where the relevant person and another person are not married to each other, nor in a civil partnership with each other, but are living together as if they were a married couple: that other person;
(d) the relevant person's children and step-children;
(e) the relevant person's parents and step-parents;
(f) the relevant person's brothers and sisters, half-brothers and half-sisters, and stepbrothers and stepsisters;
(g) the relevant person's grandparents;
(h) a deputy appointed for the relevant person by the court;
(i) a donee of a lasting power of attorney granted by the relevant person.

186(1) An interested person consulted by the best interests assessor is any person whose name is stated in the relevant best interests assessment in accordance with paragraph 40 (interested persons whom the assessor consulted in carrying out the assessment).
(2) The relevant best interests assessment is the most recent best interests assessment carried out in connection with the standard authorisation in question (whether the assessment was carried out under Part 4 or Part 8).

187   Where this Schedule imposes on a person a duty towards an interested person, the duty does not apply if the person on whom the duty is imposed–
(a) is not aware of the interested person's identity or of a way of contacting him, and
(b) cannot reasonably ascertain it.

188   The following table contains an index of provisions defining or otherwise explaining expressions used in this Schedule–

age assessment	paragraph 34
age requirement	paragraph 13
age review assessment	paragraph 112(3)
appointment regulations	paragraph 138
assessment under this Schedule	paragraph 127

negative conclusion	paragraph 112(2)(a)
new supervisory body	paragraph 99(b)
no refusals assessment	paragraph 48
no refusals requirement	paragraph 18
no refusals review assessment	paragraph 112(8)
non-qualification ground	paragraph 105
old supervisory body	paragraph 99(a)
positive conclusion	paragraph 112(2)(b)
purpose of a standard authorisation	paragraph 11(1)
purpose of an urgent authorisation	paragraph 11(2)
qualifying requirements	paragraph 12
refusal (for the purposes of the no refusals requirement)	paragraphs 19 and 20
relevant care or treatment	paragraph 7
relevant hospital or care home	paragraph 7
relevant managing authority	paragraph 26(4)
relevant person	paragraph 7
relevant person's representative	paragraph 137
relevant procedure	paragraph 128
review assessment	paragraph 112(1)
reviewable	paragraph 104
section 39A IMCA	paragraph 155
section 39C IMCA	paragraph 156
section 39D IMCA	paragraph 157
standard authorisation	paragraph 8
supervisory body (except in Part 8)	paragraph 180, 181 or 182
supervisory body (in Part 8)	paragraph 128 and paragraph 180, 181 or 182
unauthorised deprivation of liberty (in relation to paragraphs 68 to 73)	paragraph 67
urgent authorisation	paragraph 9
variation of conditions ground	paragraph 107

SCHEDULE 1: LASTING POWERS OF ATTORNEY: FORMALITIES

Section 9

Part 1: Making Instruments

General requirements as to making instruments

1 (1) An instrument is not made in accordance with this Schedule unless–
   (a) it is in the prescribed form,
   (b) it complies with paragraph 2, and

(c) any prescribed requirements in connection with its execution are satisfied.

(2) Regulations may make different provision according to whether–

(a) the instrument relates to personal welfare or to property and affairs (or to both);

(b) only one or more than one donee is to be appointed (and if more than one, whether jointly or jointly and severally).

(3) In this Schedule–

(a) 'prescribed' means prescribed by regulations, and

(b) 'regulations' means regulations made for the purposes of this Schedule by the Lord Chancellor.

Requirements as to content of instruments

2 (1) The instrument must include–

(a) the prescribed information about the purpose of the instrument and the effect of a lasting power of attorney,

(b) a statement by the donor to the effect that he–

(i) has read the prescribed information or a prescribed part of it (or has had it read to him), and

(ii) intends the authority conferred under the instrument to include authority to make decisions on his behalf in circumstances where he no longer has capacity,

(c) a statement by the donor–

(i) naming a person or persons whom the donor wishes to be notified of any application for the registration of the instrument, or

(ii) stating that there are no persons whom he wishes to be notified of any such application,

(d) a statement by the donee (or, if more than one, each of them) to the effect that he–

(i) has read the prescribed information or a prescribed part of it (or has had it read to him), and

(ii) understands the duties imposed on a donee of a lasting power of attorney under sections 1 (the principles) and 4 (best interests), and

(e) a certificate by a person of a prescribed description that, in his opinion, at the time when the donor executes the instrument–

(i) the donor understands the purpose of the instrument and the scope of the authority conferred under it,

(ii) no fraud or undue pressure is being used to induce the donor to create a lasting power of attorney, and

(iii) there is nothing else which would prevent a lasting power of attorney from being created by the instrument.

(2) Regulations may–

(a) prescribe a maximum number of named persons;

(b) provide that, where the instrument includes a statement under sub-paragraph (1)(c)(ii), two persons of a prescribed description must each give a certificate under sub-paragraph (1)(e).

(3) The persons who may be named persons do not include a person who is appointed as donee under the instrument.

(4) In this Schedule, 'named person' means a person named under sub-paragraph (1)(c).

(5) A certificate under sub-paragraph (1)(e)–
   (a) must be made in the prescribed form, and
   (b) must include any prescribed information.

(6) The certificate may not be given by a person appointed as donee under the instrument.

Failure to comply with prescribed form

3 (1) If an instrument differs in an immaterial respect in form or mode of expression from the prescribed form, it is to be treated by the Public Guardian as sufficient in point of form and expression.

(2) The court may declare that an instrument which is not in the prescribed form is to be treated as if it were, if it is satisfied that the persons executing the instrument intended it to create a lasting power of attorney.

Part 2: Registration

Applications and procedure for registration

4 (1) An application to the Public Guardian for the registration of an instrument intended to create a lasting power of attorney–
   (a) must be made in the prescribed form, and
   (b) must include any prescribed information.

(2) The application may be made–
   (a) by the donor,
   (b) by the donee or donees, or
   (c) if the instrument appoints two or more donees to act jointly and severally in respect of any matter, by any of the donees.

(3) The application must be accompanied by–
   (a) the instrument, and
   (b) any fee provided for under section 58(4)(b).

(4) A person who, in an application for registration, makes a statement which he knows to be false in a material particular is guilty of an offence and is liable–
   (a) on summary conviction, to imprisonment for a term not exceeding 12 months or a fine not exceeding the statutory maximum or both;
   (b) on conviction on indictment, to imprisonment for a term not exceeding 2 years or a fine or both.

5   Subject to paragraphs 11 to 14, the Public Guardian must register the instrument as a lasting power of attorney at the end of the prescribed period.

Notification requirements

6 (1) A donor about to make an application under paragraph 4(2)(a) must notify any named persons that he is about to do so.

(2) The donee (or donees) about to make an application under paragraph 4(2)(b) or (c) must notify any named persons that he is (or they are) about to do so.

7   As soon as is practicable after receiving an application by the donor under paragraph 4(2)(a), the Public Guardian must notify the donee (or donees) that the application has been received.

8 (1) As soon as is practicable after receiving an application by a donee (or donees) under paragraph 4(2)(b), the Public Guardian must notify the donor that the application has been received.

(2) As soon as is practicable after receiving an application by a donee under paragraph 4(2)(c), the Public Guardian must notify–

(a) the donor, and

(b) the donee or donees who did not join in making the application,

that the application has been received.

9 (1) A notice under paragraph 6 must be made in the prescribed form.

(2) A notice under paragraph 6, 7 or 8 must include such information, if any, as may be prescribed.

Power to dispense with notification requirements

10   The court may–

(a) on the application of the donor, dispense with the requirement to notify under paragraph 6(1), or

(b) on the application of the donee or donees concerned, dispense with the requirement to notify under paragraph 6(2),

if satisfied that no useful purpose would be served by giving the notice.

Instrument not made properly or containing ineffective provision

11 (1) If it appears to the Public Guardian that an instrument accompanying an application under paragraph 4 is not made in accordance with this Schedule, he must not register the instrument unless the court directs him to do so.

(2) Sub-paragraph (3) applies if it appears to the Public Guardian that the instrument contains a provision which–

(a) would be ineffective as part of a lasting power of attorney, or

(b) would prevent the instrument from operating as a valid lasting power of attorney.

(3) The Public Guardian–

(a) must apply to the court for it to determine the matter under section 23(1), and

(b) pending the determination by the court, must not register the instrument.

(4) Sub-paragraph (5) applies if the court determines under section 23(1) (whether or not on an application by the Public Guardian) that the instrument contains a provision which–

(a) would be ineffective as part of a lasting power of attorney, or

(b) would prevent the instrument from operating as a valid lasting power of attorney.

(5) The court must–

(a) notify the Public Guardian that it has severed the provision, or

(b) direct him not to register the instrument.

(6) Where the court notifies the Public Guardian that it has severed a provision, he must register the instrument with a note to that effect attached to it.

Deputy already appointed

12 (1) Sub-paragraph (2) applies if it appears to the Public Guardian that–

(a) there is a deputy appointed by the court for the donor, and

(b) the powers conferred on the deputy would, if the instrument were registered, to any extent conflict with the powers conferred on the attorney.

(2) The Public Guardian must not register the instrument unless the court directs him to do so.

Objection by donee or named person

13 (1) Sub-paragraph (2) applies if a donee or a named person–
- (a) receives a notice under paragraph 6, 7 or 8 of an application for the registration of an instrument, and
- (b) before the end of the prescribed period, gives notice to the Public Guardian of an objection to the registration on the ground that an event mentioned in section 13(3) or (6)(a) to (d) has occurred which has revoked the instrument.

(2) If the Public Guardian is satisfied that the ground for making the objection is established, he must not register the instrument unless the court, on the application of the person applying for the registration–
- (a) is satisfied that the ground is not established, and
- (b) directs the Public Guardian to register the instrument.

(3) Sub-paragraph (4) applies if a donee or a named person–
- (a) receives a notice under paragraph 6, 7 or 8 of an application for the registration of an instrument, and
- (b) before the end of the prescribed period–
  - (i) makes an application to the court objecting to the registration on a prescribed ground, and
  - (ii) notifies the Public Guardian of the application.

(4) The Public Guardian must not register the instrument unless the court directs him to do so.

Objection by donor

14 (1) This paragraph applies if the donor–
- (a) receives a notice under paragraph 8 of an application for the registration of an instrument, and
- (b) before the end of the prescribed period, gives notice to the Public Guardian of an objection to the registration.

(2) The Public Guardian must not register the instrument unless the court, on the application of the donee or, if more than one, any of them–
- (a) is satisfied that the donor lacks capacity to object to the registration, and
- (b) directs the Public Guardian to register the instrument.

Notification of registration

15   Where an instrument is registered under this Schedule, the Public Guardian must give notice of the fact in the prescribed form to–
- (a) the donor, and
- (b) the donee or, if more than one, each of them.

Evidence of registration

16 (1) A document purporting to be an office copy of an instrument registered under this Schedule is, in any part of the United Kingdom, evidence of–
- (a) the contents of the instrument, and
- (b) the fact that it has been registered.

(2) Sub-paragraph (1) is without prejudice to–
- (a) section 3 of the Powers of Attorney Act 1971 (proof by certified copy), and
- (b) any other method of proof authorised by law.

Part 3: Cancellation of Registration and Notification of Severance

17 (1) The Public Guardian must cancel the registration of an instrument as a lasting power of attorney on being satisfied that the power has been revoked–

(a) as a result of the donor's bankruptcy or a debt relief order (under Part 7A of the Insolvency Act 1986) having been made in respect of the donor, or

(b) on the occurrence of an event mentioned in section 13(6)(a) to (d).

(2) If the Public Guardian cancels the registration of an instrument he must notify–

(a) the donor, and

(b) the donee or, if more than one, each of them.

18 The court must direct the Public Guardian to cancel the registration of an instrument as a lasting power of attorney if it–

(a) determines under section 22(2)(a) that a requirement for creating the power was not met,

(b) determines under section 22(2)(b) that the power has been revoked or has otherwise come to an end, or

(c) revokes the power under section 22(4)(b) (fraud etc).

19 (1) Sub-paragraph (2) applies if the court determines under section 23(1) that a lasting power of attorney contains a provision which–

(a) is ineffective as part of a lasting power of attorney, or

(b) prevents the instrument from operating as a valid lasting power of attorney.

(2) The court must–

(a) notify the Public Guardian that it has severed the provision, or

(b) direct him to cancel the registration of the instrument as a lasting power of attorney.

20 On the cancellation of the registration of an instrument, the instrument and any office copies of it must be delivered up to the Public Guardian to be cancelled.

Part 4: Records of Alterations in Registered Powers

Partial revocation or suspension of power as a result of bankruptcy

21 If in the case of a registered instrument it appears to the Public Guardian that under section 13 a lasting power of attorney is revoked, or suspended, in relation to the donor's property and affairs (but not in relation to other matters), the Public Guardian must attach to the instrument a note to that effect.

Termination of appointment of donee which does not revoke power

22 If in the case of a registered instrument it appears to the Public Guardian that an event has occurred–

(a) which has terminated the appointment of the donee, but

(b) which has not revoked the instrument,

the Public Guardian must attach to the instrument a note to that effect.

Replacement of donee

23 If in the case of a registered instrument it appears to the Public Guardian that the donee has been replaced under the terms of the instrument the Public Guardian must attach to the instrument a note to that effect.

Severance of ineffective provisions

24   If in the case of a registered instrument the court notifies the Public Guardian under paragraph 19(2)(a) that it has severed a provision of the instrument, the Public Guardian must attach to it a note to that effect.

Notification of alterations

25   If the Public Guardian attaches a note to an instrument under paragraph 21, 22, 23 or 24 he must give notice of the note to the donee or donees of the power (or, as the case may be, to the other donee or donees of the power).

SCHEDULE 1A: PERSONS INELIGIBLE TO BE DEPRIVED OF LIBERTY BY THIS ACT

Part 1: Ineligible Persons

Application

1   This Schedule applies for the purposes of–
(a) section 16A, and
(b) paragraph 17 of Schedule A1.

Determining ineligibility

2   A person ('P') is ineligible to be deprived of liberty by this Act ('ineligible') if–
(a) P falls within one of the cases set out in the second column of the following table, and
(b) the corresponding entry in the third column of the table–or the provision, or one of the provisions, referred to in that entry–provides that he is ineligible.

	Status of P	Determination of ineligibility
Case A	P is– (a) subject to the hospital treatment regime, and (b) detained in a hospital under that regime.	P is ineligible.
Case B	P is– (a) subject to the hospital treatment regime, but (b) not detained in a hospital under that regime.	See paragraphs 3 and 4.
Case C	P is subject to the community treatment regime.	See paragraphs 3 and 4.
Case D	P is subject to the guardianship regime.	See paragraphs 3 and 5.
Case E	P is– (a) within the scope of the Mental Health Act, but (b) not subject to any of the mental health regimes.	See paragraph 5.

Authorised course of action not in accordance with regime

3 (1) This paragraph applies in cases B, C and D in the table in paragraph 2.

(2) P is ineligible if the authorised course of action is not in accordance with a requirement which the relevant regime imposes.

(3) That includes any requirement as to where P is, or is not, to reside.

(4) The relevant regime is the mental health regime to which P is subject.

Treatment for mental disorder in a hospital

4 (1) This paragraph applies in cases B and C in the table in paragraph 2.

(2) P is ineligible if the relevant care or treatment consists in whole or in part of medical treatment for mental disorder in a hospital.

P objects to being a mental health patient etc

5 (1) This paragraph applies in cases D and E in the table in paragraph 2.

(2) P is ineligible if the following conditions are met.

(3) The first condition is that the relevant instrument authorises P to be a mental health patient.

(4) The second condition is that P objects–

  (a) to being a mental health patient, or

  (b) to being given some or all of the mental health treatment.

(5) The third condition is that a donee or deputy has not made a valid decision to consent to each matter to which P objects.

(6) In determining whether or not P objects to something, regard must be had to all the circumstances (so far as they are reasonably ascertainable), including the following–

  (a) P's behaviour;

  (b) P's wishes and feelings;

  (c) P's views, beliefs and values.

(7) But regard is to be had to circumstances from the past only so far as it is still appropriate to have regard to them.

Part 2: Interpretation

Application

6   This Part applies for the purposes of this Schedule.

Mental health regimes

7   The mental health regimes are–

  (a) the hospital treatment regime,

  (b) the community treatment regime, and

  (c) the guardianship regime.

Hospital treatment regime

8 (1) P is subject to the hospital treatment regime if he is subject to–

  (a) a hospital treatment obligation under the relevant enactment, or

  (b) an obligation under another England and Wales enactment which has the same effect as a hospital treatment obligation.

(2) But where P is subject to any such obligation, he is to be regarded as not subject to the hospital treatment regime during any period when he is subject to the community treatment regime.

(3) A hospital treatment obligation is an application, order or direction of a kind listed in the first column of the following table.

(4) In relation to a hospital treatment obligation, the relevant enactment is the enactment in the Mental Health Act which is referred to in the corresponding entry in the second column of the following table.

Hospital treatment obligation	Relevant enactment
Application for admission for assessment	Section 2
Application for admission for assessment	Section 4
Application for admission for treatment	Section 3
Order for remand to hospital	Section 35
Order for remand to hospital	Section 36
Hospital order	Section 37
Interim hospital order	Section 38
Order for detention in hospital	Section 44
Hospital direction	Section 45A
Transfer direction	Section 47
Transfer direction	Section 48
Hospital order	Section 51

Community treatment regime

9   P is subject to the community treatment regime if he is subject to–
(a) a community treatment order under section 17A of the Mental Health Act, or
(b) an obligation under another England and Wales enactment which has the same effect as a community treatment order.

Guardianship regime

10   P is subject to the guardianship regime if he is subject to–
(a) a guardianship application under section 7 of the Mental Health Act,
(b) a guardianship order under section 37 of the Mental Health Act, or
(c) an obligation under another England and Wales enactment which has the same effect as a guardianship application or guardianship order.

England and Wales enactments

11 (1) An England and Wales enactment is an enactment which extends to England and Wales (whether or not it also extends elsewhere).

(2) It does not matter if the enactment is in the Mental Health Act or not.

P within scope of Mental Health Act

12 (1) P is within the scope of the Mental Health Act if–
(a) an application in respect of P could be made under section 2 or 3 of the Mental Health Act, and
(b) P could be detained in a hospital in pursuance of such an application, were one made.

(2) The following provisions of this paragraph apply when determining whether an application in respect of P could be made under section 2 or 3 of the Mental Health Act.

(3) If the grounds in section 2(2) of the Mental Health Act are met in P's case, it

is to be assumed that the recommendations referred to in section 2(3) of that Act have been given.

(4) If the grounds in section 3(2) of the Mental Health Act are met in P's case, it is to be assumed that the recommendations referred to in section 3(3) of that Act have been given.

(5) In determining whether the ground in section 3(2)(c) of the Mental Health Act is met in P's case, it is to be assumed that the treatment referred to in section 3(2)(c) cannot be provided under this Act.

Authorised course of action, relevant care or treatment & relevant instrument

13 In a case where this Schedule applies for the purposes of section 16A–

'authorised course of action' means any course of action amounting to deprivation of liberty which the order under section 16(2)(a) authorises;

'relevant care or treatment' means any care or treatment which–

(a) comprises, or forms part of, the authorised course of action, or

(b) is to be given in connection with the authorised course of action;

'relevant instrument' means the order under section 16(2)(a).

14 In a case where this Schedule applies for the purposes of paragraph 17 of Schedule A1–

'authorised course of action' means the accommodation of the relevant person in the relevant hospital or care home for the purpose of being given the relevant care or treatment;

'relevant care or treatment' has the same meaning as in Schedule A1;

'relevant instrument' means the standard authorisation under Schedule A1.

15 (1) This paragraph applies where the question whether a person is ineligible to be deprived of liberty by this Act is relevant to either of these decisions–

(a) whether or not to include particular provision ('the proposed provision') in an order under section 16(2)(a);

(b) whether or not to give a standard authorisation under Schedule A1.

(2) A reference in this Schedule to the authorised course of action or the relevant care or treatment is to be read as a reference to that thing as it would be if–

(a) the proposed provision were included in the order, or

(b) the standard authorisation were given.

(3) A reference in this Schedule to the relevant instrument is to be read as follows–

(a) where the relevant instrument is an order under section 16(2)(a): as a reference to the order as it would be if the proposed provision were included in it;

(b) where the relevant instrument is a standard authorisation: as a reference to the standard authorisation as it would be if it were given.

Expressions used in paragraph 5

16 (1) These expressions have the meanings given–

'donee' means a donee of a lasting power of attorney granted by P;

'mental health patient' means a person accommodated in a hospital for the purpose of being given medical treatment for mental disorder;

'mental health treatment' means the medical treatment for mental disorder referred to in the definition of 'mental health patient'.

(2) A decision of a donee or deputy is valid if it is made–

(a) within the scope of his authority as donee or deputy, and

(b) in accordance with Part 1 of this Act.

Expressions with same meaning as in Mental Health Act

17 (1) 'Hospital' has the same meaning as in Part 2 of the Mental Health Act.

(2) 'Medical treatment' has the same meaning as in the Mental Health Act.

(3) 'Mental disorder' has the same meaning as in Schedule A1 (see paragraph 14).

SCHEDULE 2: PROPERTY AND AFFAIRS: SUPPLEMENTARY PROVISIONS

Section 18(4)

Wills: general

1 Paragraphs 2 to 4 apply in relation to the execution of a will, by virtue of section 18, on behalf of P.

Provision that may be made in will

2 The will may make any provision (whether by disposing of property or exercising a power or otherwise) which could be made by a will executed by P if he had capacity to make it.

Wills: requirements relating to execution

3 (1) Sub-paragraph (2) applies if under section 16 the court makes an order or gives directions requiring or authorising a person ('the authorised person') to execute a will on behalf of P.

(2) Any will executed in pursuance of the order or direction–

(a) must state that it is signed by P acting by the authorised person,

(b) must be signed by the authorised person with the name of P and his own name, in the presence of two or more witnesses present at the same time,

(c) must be attested and subscribed by those witnesses in the presence of the authorised person, and

(d) must be sealed with the official seal of the court.

Wills: effect of execution

4 (1) This paragraph applies where a will is executed in accordance with paragraph 3.

(2) The Wills Act 1837 has effect in relation to the will as if it were signed by P by his own hand, except that–

(a) section 9 of the 1837 Act (requirements as to signing and attestation) does not apply, and

(b) in the subsequent provisions of the 1837 Act any reference to execution in the manner required by the previous provisions is to be read as a reference to execution in accordance with paragraph 3.

(3) The will has the same effect for all purposes as if–

(a) P had had the capacity to make a valid will, and

(b) the will had been executed by him in the manner required by the 1837 Act.

(4) But sub-paragraph (3) does not have effect in relation to the will–

(a) in so far as it disposes of immovable property outside England and Wales, or

(b) in so far as it relates to any other property or matter if, when the will is executed–

(i) P is domiciled outside England and Wales, and

(ii) the condition in sub-paragraph (5) is met.

(5) The condition is that, under the law of P's domicile, any question of his testamentary capacity would fall to be determined in accordance with the law of a place outside England and Wales.

Vesting orders ancillary to settlement etc

5 (1) If provision is made by virtue of section 18 for–

(a) the settlement of any property of P, or

(b) the exercise of a power vested in him of appointing trustees or retiring from a trust,

the court may also make as respects the property settled or the trust property such consequential vesting or other orders as the case may require.

(2) The power under sub-paragraph (1) includes, in the case of the exercise of such a power, any order which could have been made in such a case under Part 4 of the Trustee Act 1925 (c 19).

Variation of settlements

6 (1) If a settlement has been made by virtue of section 18, the court may by order vary or revoke the settlement if–

(a) the settlement makes provision for its variation or revocation,

(b) the court is satisfied that a material fact was not disclosed when the settlement was made, or

(c) the court is satisfied that there has been a substantial change of circumstances.

(2) Any such order may give such consequential directions as the court thinks fit.

Vesting of stock in curator appointed outside England and Wales

7 (1) Sub-paragraph (2) applies if the court is satisfied–

(a) that under the law prevailing in a place outside England and Wales a person ('M') has been appointed to exercise powers in respect of the property or affairs of P on the ground (however formulated) that P lacks capacity to make decisions with respect to the management and administration of his property and affairs, and

(b) that, having regard to the nature of the appointment and to the circumstances of the case, it is expedient that the court should exercise its powers under this paragraph.

(2) The court may direct–

(a) any stocks standing in the name of P, or

(b) the right to receive dividends from the stocks,

to be transferred into M's name or otherwise dealt with as required by M, and may give such directions as the court thinks fit for dealing with accrued dividends from the stocks.

(3) 'Stocks' includes–

(a) shares, and

(b) any funds, annuity or security transferable in the books kept by any body corporate or unincorporated company or society or by an instrument of transfer either alone or accompanied by other formalities,

and 'dividends' is to be construed accordingly.

Preservation of interests in property disposed of on behalf of person lacking capacity

8 (1) Sub-paragraphs (2) and (3) apply if–

(a) P's property has been disposed of by virtue of section 18,

(b) under P's will or intestacy, or by a gift perfected or nomination taking effect on his death, any other person would have taken an interest in the property but for the disposal, and

(c) on P's death, any property belonging to P's estate represents the property disposed of.

(2) The person takes the same interest, if and so far as circumstances allow, in the property representing the property disposed of.

(3) If the property disposed of was real property, any property representing it is to be treated, so long as it remains part of P's estate, as if it were real property.

(4) The court may direct that, on a disposal of P's property–

(a) which is made by virtue of section 18, and

(b) which would apart from this paragraph result in the conversion of personal property into real property,

property representing the property disposed of is to be treated, so long as it remains P's property or forms part of P's estate, as if it were personal property.

(5) References in sub-paragraphs (1) to (4) to the disposal of property are to–

(a) the sale, exchange, charging of or other dealing (otherwise than by will) with property other than money;

(b) the removal of property from one place to another;

(c) the application of money in acquiring property;

(d) the transfer of money from one account to another;

and references to property representing property disposed of are to be construed accordingly and as including the result of successive disposals.

(6) The court may give such directions as appear to it necessary or expedient for the purpose of facilitating the operation of sub-paragraphs (1) to (3), including the carrying of money to a separate account and the transfer of property other than money.

9 (1) Sub-paragraph (2) applies if the court has ordered or directed the expenditure of money–

(a) for carrying out permanent improvements on any of P's property, or

(b) otherwise for the permanent benefit of any of P's property.

(2) The court may order that–

(a) the whole of the money expended or to be expended, or

(b) any part of it,

is to be a charge on the property either without interest or with interest at a specified rate.

(3) An order under sub-paragraph (2) may provide for excluding or restricting the operation of paragraph 8(1) to (3).

(4) A charge under sub-paragraph (2) may be made in favour of such person as may be just and, in particular, where the money charged is paid out of P's general estate, may be made in favour of a person as trustee for P.

(5) No charge under sub-paragraph (2) may confer any right of sale or foreclosure during P's lifetime.

Powers as patron of benefice

10 (1) Any functions which P has as patron of a benefice may be discharged only by a person ('R') appointed by the court.

(2) R must be an individual capable of appointment under section 8(1)(b) of the 1986 Measure (which provides for an individual able to make a declaration of communicant status, a clerk in Holy Orders, etc to be appointed to discharge a registered patron's functions).

(3) The 1986 Measure applies to R as it applies to an individual appointed by the registered patron of the benefice under section 8(1)(b) or (3) of that Measure to discharge his functions as patron.

(4) 'The 1986 Measure' means the Patronage (Benefices) Measure 1986 (No 3).

SCHEDULE 3: INTERNATIONAL PROTECTION OF ADULTS

Section 63

Part 1: Preliminary

Introduction

1   This Part applies for the purposes of this Schedule.

The Convention

2 (1) 'Convention' means the Convention referred to in section 63.

(2) 'Convention country' means a country in which the Convention is in force.

(3) A reference to an Article or Chapter is to an Article or Chapter of the Convention.

(4) An expression which appears in this Schedule and in the Convention is to be construed in accordance with the Convention.

Countries, territories and nationals

3 (1) 'Country' includes a territory which has its own system of law.

(2) Where a country has more than one territory with its own system of law, a reference to the country, in relation to one of its nationals, is to the territory with which the national has the closer, or the closest, connection.

Adults with incapacity

4 (1) 'Adult' means (subject to sub-paragraph (2) a person who–

(a) as a result of an impairment or insufficiency of his personal faculties, cannot protect his interests, and

(b) has reached 16.

(2) But 'adult' does not include a child to whom either of the following applies–

(a) the Convention on Jurisdiction, Applicable Law, Recognition, Enforcement and Co-Operation in respect of Parental Responsibility and Measures for the Protection of Children that was signed at The Hague on 19 October 1996;

(b) Council Regulation (EC) No 2201/2003 concerning jurisdiction and the recognition and enforcement of judgments in matrimonial matters and the matters of parental responsibility.

Protective measures

5 (1) 'Protective measure' means a measure directed to the protection of the person or property of an adult; and it may deal in particular with any of the following–

(a) the determination of incapacity and the institution of a protective regime,

(b) placing the adult under the protection of an appropriate authority,

(c) guardianship, curatorship or any corresponding system,

(d) the designation and functions of a person having charge of the adult's person or property, or representing or otherwise helping him,

(e) placing the adult in a place where protection can be provided,

(f) administering, conserving or disposing of the adult's property,

(g) authorising a specific intervention for the protection of the person or property of the adult.

(2) Where a measure of like effect to a protective measure has been taken in relation to a person before he reaches 16, this Schedule applies to the measure in so far as it has effect in relation to him once he has reached 16.

Central Authority

6 (1) Any function under the Convention of a Central Authority is exercisable in England and Wales by the Lord Chancellor.

(2) A communication may be sent to the Central Authority in relation to England and Wales by sending it to the Lord Chancellor.

Part 2: Jurisdiction of Competent Authority

Scope of jurisdiction

7 (1) The court may exercise its functions under this Act (in so far as it cannot otherwise do so) in relation to–

(a) an adult habitually resident in England and Wales,

(b) an adult's property in England and Wales,

(c) an adult present in England and Wales or who has property there, if the matter is urgent, or

(d) an adult present in England and Wales, if a protective measure which is temporary and limited in its effect to England and Wales is proposed in relation to him.

(2) An adult present in England and Wales is to be treated for the purposes of this paragraph as habitually resident there if–

(a) his habitual residence cannot be ascertained,

(b) he is a refugee, or

(c) he has been displaced as a result of disturbance in the country of his habitual residence.

8 (1) The court may also exercise its functions under this Act (in so far as it cannot otherwise do so) in relation to an adult if sub-paragraph (2) or (3) applies in relation to him.

(2) This sub-paragraph applies in relation to an adult if–

(a) he is a British citizen,

(b) he has a closer connection with England and Wales than with Scotland or Northern Ireland, and

(c) Article 7 has, in relation to the matter concerned, been complied with.

(3) This sub-paragraph applies in relation to an adult if the Lord Chancellor, having consulted such persons as he considers appropriate, agrees to a request under Article 8 in relation to the adult.

Exercise of jurisdiction

9 (1) This paragraph applies where jurisdiction is exercisable under this Schedule in connection with a matter which involves a Convention country other than England and Wales.

(2) Any Article on which the jurisdiction is based applies in relation to the matter in so far as it involves the other country (and the court must, accordingly, comply with any duty conferred on it as a result).

(3) Article 12 also applies, so far as its provisions allow, in relation to the matter in so far as it involves the other country.

10 A reference in this Schedule to the exercise of jurisdiction under this Schedule is to the exercise of functions under this Act as a result of this Part of this Schedule.

Part 3: Applicable Law

Applicable law

11 In exercising jurisdiction under this Schedule, the court may, if it thinks that the matter has a substantial connection with a country other than England and Wales, apply the law of that other country.

12 Where a protective measure is taken in one country but implemented in another, the conditions of implementation are governed by the law of the other country.

Lasting powers of attorney, etc

13 (1) If the donor of a lasting power is habitually resident in England and Wales at the time of granting the power, the law applicable to the existence, extent, modification or extinction of the power is–

(a) the law of England and Wales, or

(b) if he specifies in writing the law of a connected country for the purpose, that law.

(2) If he is habitually resident in another country at that time, but England and Wales is a connected country, the law applicable in that respect is–

(a) the law of the other country, or

(b) if he specifies in writing the law of England and Wales for the purpose, that law.

(3) A country is connected, in relation to the donor, if it is a country–

(a) of which he is a national,

(b) in which he was habitually resident, or

(c) in which he has property.

(4) Where this paragraph applies as a result of sub-paragraph (3)(c), it applies only in relation to the property which the donor has in the connected country.

(5) The law applicable to the manner of the exercise of a lasting power is the law of the country where it is exercised.

(6) In this Part of this Schedule, 'lasting power' means–

(a) a lasting power of attorney (see section 9),

(b) an enduring power of attorney within the meaning of Schedule 4, or

(c) any other power of like effect.

14 (1) Where a lasting power is not exercised in a manner sufficient to guarantee the protection of the person or property of the donor, the court, in exercising jurisdiction under this Schedule, may disapply or modify the power.

(2) Where, in accordance with this Part of this Schedule, the law applicable to the power is, in one or more respects, that of a country other than England and Wales, the court must, so far as possible, have regard to the law of the other country in that respect (or those respects).

15   Regulations may provide for Schedule 1 (lasting powers of attorney: formalities) to apply with modifications in relation to a lasting power which comes within paragraph 13(6)(c) above.

Protection of third parties

16 (1) This paragraph applies where a person (a 'representative') in purported exercise of an authority to act on behalf of an adult enters into a transaction with a third party.

(2) The validity of the transaction may not be questioned in proceedings, nor may the third party be held liable, merely because–

(a) where the representative and third party are in England and Wales when entering into the transaction, sub-paragraph (3) applies;

(b) where they are in another country at that time, sub-paragraph (4) applies.

(3) This sub-paragraph applies if–

(a) the law applicable to the authority in one or more respects is, as a result of this Schedule, the law of a country other than England and Wales, and

(b) the representative is not entitled to exercise the authority in that respect (or those respects) under the law of that other country.

(4) This sub-paragraph applies if–

(a) the law applicable to the authority in one or more respects is, as a result of this Part of this Schedule, the law of England and Wales, and

(b) the representative is not entitled to exercise the authority in that respect (or those respects) under that law.

(5) This paragraph does not apply if the third party knew or ought to have known that the applicable law was–

(a) in a case within sub-paragraph (3), the law of the other country;

(b) in a case within sub-paragraph (4), the law of England and Wales.

Mandatory rules

17   Where the court is entitled to exercise jurisdiction under this Schedule, the mandatory provisions of the law of England and Wales apply, regardless of any system of law which would otherwise apply in relation to the matter.

Public policy

18   Nothing in this Part of this Schedule requires or enables the application in England and Wales of a provision of the law of another country if its application would be manifestly contrary to public policy.

Part 4: Recognition and Enforcement

Recognition

19 (1) A protective measure taken in relation to an adult under the law of a country other than England and Wales is to be recognised in England and Wales if it was taken on the ground that the adult is habitually resident in the other country.

(2) A protective measure taken in relation to an adult under the law of a Convention country other than England and Wales is to be recognised in England and Wales if it was taken on a ground mentioned in Chapter 2 (jurisdiction).

(3) But the court may disapply this paragraph in relation to a measure if it thinks that—

(a) the case in which the measure was taken was not urgent,

(b) the adult was not given an opportunity to be heard, and

(c) that omission amounted to a breach of natural justice.

(4) It may also disapply this paragraph in relation to a measure if it thinks that—

(a) recognition of the measure would be manifestly contrary to public policy,

(b) the measure would be inconsistent with a mandatory provision of the law of England and Wales, or

(c) the measure is inconsistent with one subsequently taken, or recognised, in England and Wales in relation to the adult.

(5) And the court may disapply this paragraph in relation to a measure taken under the law of a Convention country in a matter to which Article 33 applies, if the court thinks that that Article has not been complied with in connection with that matter.

20 (1) An interested person may apply to the court for a declaration as to whether a protective measure taken under the law of a country other than England and Wales is to be recognised in England and Wales.

(2) No permission is required for an application to the court under this paragraph.

21 For the purposes of paragraphs 19 and 20, any finding of fact relied on when the measure was taken is conclusive.

Enforcement

22 (1) An interested person may apply to the court for a declaration as to whether a protective measure taken under the law of, and enforceable in, a country other than England and Wales is enforceable, or to be registered, in England and Wales in accordance with Court of Protection Rules.

(2) The court must make the declaration if—

(a) the measure comes within sub-paragraph (1) or (2) of paragraph 19, and

(b) the paragraph is not disapplied in relation to it as a result of sub-paragraph (3), (4) or (5).

(3) A measure to which a declaration under this paragraph relates is enforceable in England and Wales as if it were a measure of like effect taken by the court.

Measures taken in relation to those aged under 16

23 (1) This paragraph applies where—

(a) provision giving effect to, or otherwise deriving from, the Convention in a country other than England and Wales applies in relation to a person who has not reached 16, and

(b) a measure is taken in relation to that person in reliance on that provision.

(2) This Part of this Schedule applies in relation to that measure as it applies in relation to a protective measure taken in relation to an adult under the law of a Convention country other than England and Wales.

Supplementary

24 The court may not review the merits of a measure taken outside England and Wales except to establish whether the measure complies with this Schedule in so far as it is, as a result of this Schedule, required to do so.

25 Court of Protection Rules may make provision about an application under paragraph 20 or 22.

Part 5: Co-operation

Proposal for cross-border placement

26 (1) This paragraph applies where a public authority proposes to place an adult in an establishment in a Convention country other than England and Wales.

(2) The public authority must consult an appropriate authority in that other country about the proposed placement and, for that purpose, must send it–
(a) a report on the adult, and
(b) a statement of its reasons for the proposed placement.

(3) If the appropriate authority in the other country opposes the proposed placement within a reasonable time, the public authority may not proceed with it.

27 A proposal received by a public authority under Article 33 in relation to an adult is to proceed unless the authority opposes it within a reasonable time.

Adult in danger etc

28 (1) This paragraph applies if a public authority is told that an adult–
(a) who is in serious danger, and
(b) in relation to whom the public authority has taken, or is considering taking, protective measures,
is, or has become resident, in a Convention country other than England and Wales.

(2) The public authority must tell an appropriate authority in that other country about–
(a) the danger, and
(b) the measures taken or under consideration.

29 A public authority may not request from, or send to, an appropriate authority in a Convention country information in accordance with Chapter 5 (co-operation) in relation to an adult if it thinks that doing so–
(a) would be likely to endanger the adult or his property, or
(b) would amount to a serious threat to the liberty or life of a member of the adult's family.

Part 6: General

Certificates

30 A certificate given under Article 38 by an authority in a Convention country other than England and Wales is, unless the contrary is shown, proof of the matters contained in it.

Powers to make further provision as to private international law

31   Her Majesty may by Order in Council confer on the Lord Chancellor, the court or another public authority functions for enabling the Convention to be given effect in England and Wales.

32 (1) Regulations may make provision–
  (a) giving further effect to the Convention, or
  (b) otherwise about the private international law of England and Wales in relation to the protection of adults.

  (2) The regulations may–
  (a) confer functions on the court or another public authority;
  (b) amend this Schedule;
  (c) provide for this Schedule to apply with specified modifications;
  (d) make provision about countries other than Convention countries.

Exceptions

33   Nothing in this Schedule applies, and no provision made under paragraph 32 is to apply, to any matter to which the Convention, as a result of Article 4, does not apply.

Regulations and orders

34   A reference in this Schedule to regulations or an order (other than an Order in Council) is to regulations or an order made for the purposes of this Schedule by the Lord Chancellor.

Commencement

35   The following provisions of this Schedule have effect only if the Convention is in force in accordance with Article 57–
  (a) paragraph 8,
  (b) paragraph 9,
  (c) paragraph 19(2) and (5),
  (d) Part 5,
  (e) paragraph 30.

SCHEDULE 4: PROVISIONS APPLYING TO EXISTING ENDURING POWERS OF ATTORNEY

Section 66(3)

Part 1: Enduring Powers of Attorney

Enduring power of attorney to survive mental incapacity of donor

1 (1) Where an individual has created a power of attorney which is an enduring power within the meaning of this Schedule–
  (a) the power is not revoked by any subsequent mental incapacity of his,
  (b) upon such incapacity supervening, the donee of the power may not do anything under the authority of the power except as provided by sub-paragraph (2) unless or until the instrument creating the power is registered under paragraph 13, and
  (c) if and so long as paragraph (b) operates to suspend the donee's authority to act under the power, section 5 of the Powers of Attorney Act 1971

(protection of donee and third persons), so far as applicable, applies as if the power had been revoked by the donor's mental incapacity,

and, accordingly, section 1 of this Act does not apply.

(2) Despite sub-paragraph (1)(b), where the attorney has made an application for registration of the instrument then, until it is registered, the attorney may take action under the power–

(a) to maintain the donor or prevent loss to his estate, or

(b) to maintain himself or other persons in so far as paragraph 3(2) permits him to do so.

(3) Where the attorney purports to act as provided by sub-paragraph (2) then, in favour of a person who deals with him without knowledge that the attorney is acting otherwise than in accordance with sub-paragraph (2)(a) or (b), the transaction between them is as valid as if the attorney were acting in accordance with sub-paragraph (2)(a) or (b).

Characteristics of an enduring power of attorney

2 (1) Subject to sub-paragraphs (5) and (6) and paragraph 20, a power of attorney is an enduring power within the meaning of this Schedule if the instrument which creates the power–

(a) is in the prescribed form,

(b) was executed in the prescribed manner by the donor and the attorney, and

(c) incorporated at the time of execution by the donor the prescribed explanatory information.

(2) In this paragraph, 'prescribed' means prescribed by such of the following regulations as applied when the instrument was executed–

(a) the Enduring Powers of Attorney (Prescribed Form) Regulations 1986 (SI 1986/126),

(b) the Enduring Powers of Attorney (Prescribed Form) Regulations 1987 (SI 1987/1612),

(c) the Enduring Powers of Attorney (Prescribed Form) Regulations 1990 (SI 1990/1376),

(d) the Enduring Powers of Attorney (Welsh Language Prescribed Form) Regulations 2000 (SI 2000/289).

(3) An instrument in the prescribed form purporting to have been executed in the prescribed manner is to be taken, in the absence of evidence to the contrary, to be a document which incorporated at the time of execution by the donor the prescribed explanatory information.

(4) If an instrument differs in an immaterial respect in form or mode of expression from the prescribed form it is to be treated as sufficient in point of form and expression.

(5) A power of attorney cannot be an enduring power unless, when he executes the instrument creating it, the attorney is–

(a) an individual who has reached 18 and is not bankrupt or is not subject to a debt relief order (under Part 7A of the Insolvency Act 1986), or

(b) a trust corporation.

(6) A power of attorney which gives the attorney a right to appoint a substitute or successor cannot be an enduring power.

(7) An enduring power is revoked by the bankruptcy of the donor or attorney or

the making of a debt relief order (under Part 7A of the Insolvency Act 1986) in respect of the donor or attorney.

(8) But where the donor or attorney is bankrupt merely because an interim bankruptcy restrictions order has effect in respect of him or where the donor or attorney is subject to an interim debt relief restrictions order, the power is suspended for so long as the order has effect.

(9) An enduring power is revoked if the court–
(a) exercises a power under sections 16 to 20 in relation to the donor, and
(b) directs that the enduring power is to be revoked.

(10) No disclaimer of an enduring power, whether by deed or otherwise, is valid unless and until the attorney gives notice of it to the donor or, where paragraph 4(6) or 15(1) applies, to the Public Guardian.

Scope of authority etc of attorney under enduring power

3 (1) If the instrument which creates an enduring power of attorney is expressed to confer general authority on the attorney, the instrument operates to confer, subject to–
(a) the restriction imposed by sub-paragraph (3), and
(b) any conditions or restrictions contained in the instrument,
authority to do on behalf of the donor anything which the donor could lawfully do by an attorney at the time when the donor executed the instrument.

(2) Subject to any conditions or restrictions contained in the instrument, an attorney under an enduring power, whether general or limited, may (without obtaining any consent) act under the power so as to benefit himself or other persons than the donor to the following extent but no further–
(a) he may so act in relation to himself or in relation to any other person if the donor might be expected to provide for his or that person's needs respectively, and
(b) he may do whatever the donor might be expected to do to meet those needs.

(3) Without prejudice to sub-paragraph (2) but subject to any conditions or restrictions contained in the instrument, an attorney under an enduring power, whether general or limited, may (without obtaining any consent) dispose of the property of the donor by way of gift to the following extent but no further–
(a) he may make gifts of a seasonal nature or at a time, or on an anniversary, of a birth, a marriage or the formation of a civil partnership, to persons (including himself) who are related to or connected with the donor, and
(b) he may make gifts to any charity to whom the donor made or might be expected to make gifts,
provided that the value of each such gift is not unreasonable having regard to all the circumstances and in particular the size of the donor's estate.

Part 2: Action on Actual or Impending Incapacity of Donor

Duties of attorney in event of actual or impending incapacity of donor

4 (1) Sub-paragraphs (2) to (6) apply if the attorney under an enduring power has reason to believe that the donor is or is becoming mentally incapable.

(2) The attorney must, as soon as practicable, make an application to the Public Guardian for the registration of the instrument creating the power.

(3) Before making an application for registration the attorney must comply with the provisions as to notice set out in Part 3 of this Schedule.

(4) An application for registration–
   (a) must be made in the prescribed form, and
   (b) must contain such statements as may be prescribed.

(5) The attorney–
   (a) may, before making an application for the registration of the instrument, refer to the court for its determination any question as to the validity of the power, and
   (b) must comply with any direction given to him by the court on that determination.

(6) No disclaimer of the power is valid unless and until the attorney gives notice of it to the Public Guardian; and the Public Guardian must notify the donor if he receives a notice under this sub-paragraph.

(7) A person who, in an application for registration, makes a statement which he knows to be false in a material particular is guilty of an offence and is liable–
   (a) on summary conviction, to imprisonment for a term not exceeding 12 months or a fine not exceeding the statutory maximum or both;
   (b) on conviction on indictment, to imprisonment for a term not exceeding 2 years or a fine or both.

(8) In this paragraph, 'prescribed' means prescribed by regulations made for the purposes of this Schedule by the Lord Chancellor.

Part 3: Notification Prior to Registration

Duty to give notice to relatives

5   Subject to paragraph 7, before making an application for registration the attorney must give notice of his intention to do so to all those persons (if any) who are entitled to receive notice by virtue of paragraph 6.

6 (1) Subject to sub-paragraphs (2) to (4), persons of the following classes ('relatives') are entitled to receive notice under paragraph 5–
   (a) the donor's spouse or civil partner,
   (b) the donor's children,
   (c) the donor's parents,
   (d) the donor's brothers and sisters, whether of the whole or half blood,
   (e) the widow, widower or surviving civil partner of a child of the donor,
   (f) the donor's grandchildren,
   (g) the children of the donor's brothers and sisters of the whole blood,
   (h) the children of the donor's brothers and sisters of the half blood,
   (i) the donor's uncles and aunts of the whole blood,
   (j) the children of the donor's uncles and aunts of the whole blood.

(2) A person is not entitled to receive notice under paragraph 5 if–
   (a) his name or address is not known to the attorney and cannot be reasonably ascertained by him, or
   (b) the attorney has reason to believe that he has not reached 18 or is mentally incapable.

(3) Except where sub-paragraph (4) applies–

    (a) no more than 3 persons are entitled to receive notice under paragraph 5, and

    (b) in determining the persons who are so entitled, persons falling within the class in sub-paragraph (1)(a) are to be preferred to persons falling within the class in sub-paragraph (1)(b), those falling within the class in sub-paragraph (1)(b) are to be preferred to those falling within the class in sub-paragraph (1)(c), and so on.

  (4) Despite the limit of 3 specified in sub-paragraph (3), where–

    (a) there is more than one person falling within any of classes (a) to (j) of sub-paragraph (1), and

    (b) at least one of those persons would be entitled to receive notice under paragraph 5,

then, subject to sub-paragraph (2), all the persons falling within that class are entitled to receive notice under paragraph 5.

7 (1) An attorney is not required to give notice under paragraph 5–

    (a) to himself, or

    (b) to any other attorney under the power who is joining in making the application,

even though he or, as the case may be, the other attorney is entitled to receive notice by virtue of paragraph 6.

  (2) In the case of any person who is entitled to receive notice by virtue of paragraph 6, the attorney, before applying for registration, may make an application to the court to be dispensed from the requirement to give him notice; and the court must grant the application if it is satisfied–

    (a) that it would be undesirable or impracticable for the attorney to give him notice, or

    (b) that no useful purpose is likely to be served by giving him notice.

Duty to give notice to donor

8 (1) Subject to sub-paragraph (2), before making an application for registration the attorney must give notice of his intention to do so to the donor.

  (2) Paragraph 7(2) applies in relation to the donor as it applies in relation to a person who is entitled to receive notice under paragraph 5.

Contents of notices

9 A notice to relatives under this Part of this Schedule must–

    (a) be in the prescribed form,

    (b) state that the attorney proposes to make an application to the Public Guardian for the registration of the instrument creating the enduring power in question,

    (c) inform the person to whom it is given of his right to object to the registration under paragraph 13(4), and

    (d) specify, as the grounds on which an objection to registration may be made, the grounds set out in paragraph 13(9).

10 A notice to the donor under this Part of this Schedule–

    (a) must be in the prescribed form,

    (b) must contain the statement mentioned in paragraph 9(b), and

    (c) must inform the donor that, while the instrument remains registered, any revocation of the power by him will be ineffective unless and until the revocation is confirmed by the court.

Duty to give notice to other attorneys

11 (1) Subject to sub-paragraph (2), before making an application for registration an attorney under a joint and several power must give notice of his intention to do so to any other attorney under the power who is not joining in making the application; and paragraphs 7(2) and 9 apply in relation to attorneys entitled to receive notice by virtue of this paragraph as they apply in relation to persons entitled to receive notice by virtue of paragraph 6.

(2) An attorney is not entitled to receive notice by virtue of this paragraph if–

(a) his address is not known to the applying attorney and cannot reasonably be ascertained by him, or

(b) the applying attorney has reason to believe that he has not reached 18 or is mentally incapable.

Supplementary

12   Despite section 7 of the Interpretation Act 1978 (construction of references to service by post), for the purposes of this Part of this Schedule a notice given by post is to be regarded as given on the date on which it was posted.

Part 4: Registration

Registration of instrument creating power

13 (1) If an application is made in accordance with paragraph 4(3) and (4) the Public Guardian must, subject to the provisions of this paragraph, register the instrument to which the application relates.

(2) If it appears to the Public Guardian that–

(a) there is a deputy appointed for the donor of the power created by the instrument, and

(b) the powers conferred on the deputy would, if the instrument were registered, to any extent conflict with the powers conferred on the attorney,

the Public Guardian must not register the instrument except in accordance with the court's directions.

(3) The court may, on the application of the attorney, direct the Public Guardian to register an instrument even though notice has not been given as required by paragraph 4(3) and Part 3 of this Schedule to a person entitled to receive it, if the court is satisfied–

(a) that it was undesirable or impracticable for the attorney to give notice to that person, or

(b) that no useful purpose is likely to be served by giving him notice.

(4) Sub-paragraph (5) applies if, before the end of the period of 5 weeks beginning with the date (or the latest date) on which the attorney gave notice under paragraph 5 of an application for registration, the Public Guardian receives a valid notice of objection to the registration from a person entitled to notice of the application.

(5) The Public Guardian must not register the instrument except in accordance with the court's directions.

(6) Sub-paragraph (7) applies if, in the case of an application for registration–

(a) it appears from the application that there is no one to whom notice has been given under paragraph 5, or

(b) the Public Guardian has reason to believe that appropriate inquiries might bring to light evidence on which he could be satisfied that one of the grounds of objection set out in sub-paragraph (9) was established.

(7) The Public Guardian–
  (a) must not register the instrument, and
  (b) must undertake such inquiries as he thinks appropriate in all the circumstances.

(8) If, having complied with sub-paragraph (7)(b), the Public Guardian is satisfied that one of the grounds of objection set out in sub-paragraph (9) is established–
  (a) the attorney may apply to the court for directions, and
  (b) the Public Guardian must not register the instrument except in accordance with the court's directions.

(9) A notice of objection under this paragraph is valid if made on one or more of the following grounds–
  (a) that the power purported to have been created by the instrument was not valid as an enduring power of attorney,
  (b) that the power created by the instrument no longer subsists,
  (c) that the application is premature because the donor is not yet becoming mentally incapable,
  (d) that fraud or undue pressure was used to induce the donor to create the power,
  (e) that, having regard to all the circumstances and in particular the attorney's relationship to or connection with the donor, the attorney is unsuitable to be the donor's attorney.

(10) If any of those grounds is established to the satisfaction of the court it must direct the Public Guardian not to register the instrument, but if not so satisfied it must direct its registration.

(11) If the court directs the Public Guardian not to register an instrument because it is satisfied that the ground in sub-paragraph (9)(d) or (e) is established, it must by order revoke the power created by the instrument.

(12) If the court directs the Public Guardian not to register an instrument because it is satisfied that any ground in sub-paragraph (9) except that in paragraph (c) is established, the instrument must be delivered up to be cancelled unless the court otherwise directs.

Register of enduring powers

14 The Public Guardian has the function of establishing and maintaining a register of enduring powers for the purposes of this Schedule.

Part 5: Legal Position after Registration

Effect and proof of registration

15 (1) The effect of the registration of an instrument under paragraph 13 is that–
  (a) no revocation of the power by the donor is valid unless and until the court confirms the revocation under paragraph 16(3);
  (b) no disclaimer of the power is valid unless and until the attorney gives notice of it to the Public Guardian;
  (c) the donor may not extend or restrict the scope of the authority conferred by the instrument and no instruction or consent given by him after registration, in the case of a consent, confers any right and, in the case of an

instruction, imposes or confers any obligation or right on or creates any liability of the attorney or other persons having notice of the instruction or consent.

(2) Sub-paragraph (1) applies for so long as the instrument is registered under paragraph 13 whether or not the donor is for the time being mentally incapable.

(3) A document purporting to be an office copy of an instrument registered under this Schedule is, in any part of the United Kingdom, evidence of–
   (a) the contents of the instrument, and
   (b) the fact that it has been so registered.

(4) Sub-paragraph (3) is without prejudice to section 3 of the Powers of Attorney Act 1971 (c 27) (proof by certified copies) and to any other method of proof authorised by law.

Functions of court with regard to registered power

16 (1) Where an instrument has been registered under paragraph 13, the court has the following functions with respect to the power and the donor of and the attorney appointed to act under the power.

(2) The court may–
   (a) determine any question as to the meaning or effect of the instrument;
   (b) give directions with respect to–
      (i) the management or disposal by the attorney of the property and affairs of the donor;
      (ii) the rendering of accounts by the attorney and the production of the records kept by him for the purpose;
      (iii) the remuneration or expenses of the attorney whether or not in default of or in accordance with any provision made by the instrument, including directions for the repayment of excessive or the payment of additional remuneration;
   (c) require the attorney to supply information or produce documents or things in his possession as attorney;
   (d) give any consent or authorisation to act which the attorney would have to obtain from a mentally capable donor;
   (e) authorise the attorney to act so as to benefit himself or other persons than the donor otherwise than in accordance with paragraph 3(2) and (3) (but subject to any conditions or restrictions contained in the instrument);
   (f) relieve the attorney wholly or partly from any liability which he has or may have incurred on account of a breach of his duties as attorney.

(3) On application made for the purpose by or on behalf of the donor, the court must confirm the revocation of the power if satisfied that the donor–
   (a) has done whatever is necessary in law to effect an express revocation of the power, and
   (b) was mentally capable of revoking a power of attorney when he did so (whether or not he is so when the court considers the application).

(4) The court must direct the Public Guardian to cancel the registration of an instrument registered under paragraph 13 in any of the following circumstances–
   (a) on confirming the revocation of the power under sub-paragraph (3),
   (b) on directing under paragraph 2(9)(b) that the power is to be revoked,

(c) on being satisfied that the donor is and is likely to remain mentally capable,

(d) on being satisfied that the power has expired or has been revoked by the mental incapacity of the attorney,

(e) on being satisfied that the power was not a valid and subsisting enduring power when registration was effected,

(f) on being satisfied that fraud or undue pressure was used to induce the donor to create the power,

(g) on being satisfied that, having regard to all the circumstances and in particular the attorney's relationship to or connection with the donor, the attorney is unsuitable to be the donor's attorney.

(5) If the court directs the Public Guardian to cancel the registration of an instrument on being satisfied of the matters specified in sub-paragraph (4)(f) or (g) it must by order revoke the power created by the instrument.

(6) If the court directs the cancellation of the registration of an instrument under sub-paragraph (4) except paragraph (c) the instrument must be delivered up to the Public Guardian to be cancelled, unless the court otherwise directs.

Cancellation of registration by Public Guardian

17 The Public Guardian must cancel the registration of an instrument creating an enduring power of attorney–

(a) on receipt of a disclaimer signed by the attorney;

(b) if satisfied that the power has been revoked by the death or bankruptcy of the donor or attorney or the making of a debt relief order (under Part 7A of the Insolvency Act 1986) in respect of the donor or attorney or, if the attorney is a body corporate, by its winding up or dissolution;

(c) on receipt of notification from the court that the court has revoked the power;

(d) on confirmation from the court that the donor has revoked the power.

Part 6: Protection of Attorney and Third Parties

Protection of attorney and third persons where power is invalid or revoked

18 (1) Sub-paragraphs (2) and (3) apply where an instrument which did not create a valid power of attorney has been registered under paragraph 13 (whether or not the registration has been cancelled at the time of the act or transaction in question).

(2) An attorney who acts in pursuance of the power does not incur any liability (either to the donor or to any other person) because of the non-existence of the power unless at the time of acting he knows–

(a) that the instrument did not create a valid enduring power,

(b) that an event has occurred which, if the instrument had created a valid enduring power, would have had the effect of revoking the power, or

(c) that, if the instrument had created a valid enduring power, the power would have expired before that time.

(3) Any transaction between the attorney and another person is, in favour of that person, as valid as if the power had then been in existence, unless at the time of the transaction that person has knowledge of any of the matters mentioned in sub-paragraph (2).

(4) If the interest of a purchaser depends on whether a transaction between the attorney and another person was valid by virtue of sub-paragraph (3), it is conclusively presumed in favour of the purchaser that the transaction was valid if–

(a) the transaction between that person and the attorney was completed within 12 months of the date on which the instrument was registered, or

(b) that person makes a statutory declaration, before or within 3 months after the completion of the purchase, that he had no reason at the time of the transaction to doubt that the attorney had authority to dispose of the property which was the subject of the transaction.

(5) For the purposes of section 5 of the Powers of Attorney Act 1971 (protection where power is revoked) in its application to an enduring power the revocation of which by the donor is by virtue of paragraph 15 invalid unless and until confirmed by the court under paragraph 16–

(a) knowledge of the confirmation of the revocation is knowledge of the revocation of the power, but

(b) knowledge of the unconfirmed revocation is not.

Further protection of attorney and third persons

19 (1) If–

(a) an instrument framed in a form prescribed as mentioned in paragraph 2(2) creates a power which is not a valid enduring power, and

(b) the power is revoked by the mental incapacity of the donor,

sub-paragraphs (2) and (3) apply, whether or not the instrument has been registered.

(2) An attorney who acts in pursuance of the power does not, by reason of the revocation, incur any liability (either to the donor or to any other person) unless at the time of acting he knows–

(a) that the instrument did not create a valid enduring power, and

(b) that the donor has become mentally incapable.

(3) Any transaction between the attorney and another person is, in favour of that person, as valid as if the power had then been in existence, unless at the time of the transaction that person knows–

(a) that the instrument did not create a valid enduring power, and

(b) that the donor has become mentally incapable.

(4) Paragraph 18(4) applies for the purpose of determining whether a transaction was valid by virtue of sub-paragraph (3) as it applies for the purpose or determining whether a transaction was valid by virtue of paragraph 18(3).

Part 7: Joint and Joint and Several Attorneys

Application to joint and joint and several attorneys

20 (1) An instrument which appoints more than one person to be an attorney cannot create an enduring power unless the attorneys are appointed to act–

(a) jointly, or

(b) jointly and severally.

(2) This Schedule, in its application to joint attorneys, applies to them collectively as it applies to a single attorney but subject to the modifications specified in paragraph 21.

(3) This Schedule, in its application to joint and several attorneys, applies with the modifications specified in sub-paragraphs (4) to (7) and in paragraph 22.

(4) A failure, as respects any one attorney, to comply with the requirements for the creation of enduring powers–

(a) prevents the instrument from creating such a power in his case, but

(b) does not affect its efficacy for that purpose as respects the other or others or its efficacy in his case for the purpose of creating a power of attorney which is not an enduring power.

(5) If one or more but not both or all the attorneys makes or joins in making an application for registration of the instrument–

(a) an attorney who is not an applicant as well as one who is may act pending the registration of the instrument as provided in paragraph 1(2),

(b) notice of the application must also be given under Part 3 of this Schedule to the other attorney or attorneys, and

(c) objection may validly be taken to the registration on a ground relating to an attorney or to the power of an attorney who is not an applicant as well as to one or the power of one who is an applicant.

(6) The Public Guardian is not precluded by paragraph 13(5) or (8) from registering an instrument and the court must not direct him not to do so under paragraph 13(10) if an enduring power subsists as respects some attorney who is not affected by the ground or grounds of the objection in question; and where the Public Guardian registers an instrument in that case, he must make against the registration an entry in the prescribed form.

(7) Sub-paragraph (6) does not preclude the court from revoking a power in so far as it confers a power on any other attorney in respect of whom the ground in paragraph 13(9)(d) or (e) is established; and where any ground in paragraph 13(9) affecting any other attorney is established the court must direct the Public Guardian to make against the registration an entry in the prescribed form.

(8) In sub-paragraph (4), 'the requirements for the creation of enduring powers' means the provisions of–

(a) paragraph 2 other than sub-paragraphs (8) and (9), and

(b) the regulations mentioned in paragraph 2.

Joint attorneys

21 (1) In paragraph 2(5), the reference to the time when the attorney executes the instrument is to be read as a reference to the time when the second or last attorney executes the instrument.

(2) In paragraph 2(6) to (8), the reference to the attorney is to be read as a reference to any attorney under the power.

(3) Paragraph 13 has effect as if the ground of objection to the registration of the instrument specified in sub-paragraph (9)(e) applied to any attorney under the power.

(4) In paragraph 16(2), references to the attorney are to be read as including references to any attorney under the power.

(5) In paragraph 16(4), references to the attorney are to be read as including references to any attorney under the power.

(6) In paragraph 17, references to the attorney are to be read as including references to any attorney under the power.

Joint and several attorneys

22 (1) In paragraph 2(7), the reference to the bankruptcy of the attorney is to be read as a reference to the bankruptcy of the last remaining attorney under the power; and the bankruptcy of any other attorney under the power causes that person to cease to be an attorney under the power.

(1A) In paragraph 2(7), the reference to the making of a debt relief order (under Part 7A of the Insolvency Act 1986) in respect of the attorney is to be read as a reference to the making of a debt relief order in respect of the last remaining attorney under the power; and the making of a debt relief order in respect of any other attorney under the power causes that person to cease to be an attorney under the power.

(2) In paragraph 2(8), the reference to the suspension of the power is to be read as a reference to its suspension in so far as it relates to the attorney in respect of whom the interim bankruptcy restrictions order has effect.

(2A) In paragraph 2(8), the reference to the suspension of the power is to be read as a reference to its suspension in so far as it relates to the attorney in respect of whom the interim debt relief restrictions order has effect.

(3) The restriction upon disclaimer imposed by paragraph 4(6) applies only to those attorneys who have reason to believe that the donor is or is becoming mentally incapable.

Part 8: Interpretation

23 (1) In this Schedule–

'enduring power' is to be construed in accordance with paragraph 2,

'mentally incapable' or 'mental incapacity', except where it refers to revocation at common law, means in relation to any person, that he is incapable by reason of mental disorder . . . of managing and administering his property and affairs and 'mentally capable' and 'mental capacity' are to be construed accordingly,

'notice' means notice in writing, and

'prescribed', except for the purposes of paragraph 2, means prescribed by regulations made for the purposes of this Schedule by the Lord Chancellor.

(1A) In sub-paragraph (1), 'mental disorder' has the same meaning as in the Mental Health Act but disregarding the amendments made to that Act by the Mental Health Act 2007.

(2) Any question arising under or for the purposes of this Schedule as to what the donor of the power might at any time be expected to do is to be determined by assuming that he had full mental capacity at the time but otherwise by reference to the circumstances existing at that time.

[SCHEDULES 5–7 are not reproduced here.]

HUMAN RIGHTS ACT 1998 ss3, 6–8 and Sch 1

Legislation

Interpretation of legislation

3 (1) So far as it is possible to do so, primary legislation and subordinate legislation must be read and given effect in a way which is compatible with the Convention rights.

(2) This section–

(a) applies to primary legislation and subordinate legislation whenever enacted;

(b) does not affect the validity, continuing operation or enforcement of any incompatible primary legislation; and

(c) does not affect the validity, continuing operation or enforcement of any incompatible subordinate legislation if (disregarding any possibility of revocation) primary legislation prevents removal of the incompatibility.

Public authorities

Acts of public authorities

6 (1) It is unlawful for a public authority to act in a way which is incompatible with a Convention right.

(2) Subsection (1) does not apply to an act if–

(a) as the result of one or more provisions of primary legislation, the authority could not have acted differently; or

(b) in the case of one or more provisions of, or made under, primary legislation which cannot be read or given effect in a way which is compatible with the Convention rights, the authority was acting so as to give effect to or enforce those provisions.

(3) In this section 'public authority' includes–

(a) a court or tribunal, and

(b) any person certain of whose functions are functions of a public nature,

but does not include either House of Parliament or a person exercising functions in connection with proceedings in Parliament.

(4) [Repealed.]

(5) In relation to a particular act, a person is not a public authority by virtue only of subsection (3)(b) if the nature of the act is private.

(6) 'An act' includes a failure to act but does not include a failure to–

(a) introduce in, or lay before, Parliament a proposal for legislation; or

(b) make any primary legislation or remedial order.

Proceedings

7 (1) A person who claims that a public authority has acted (or proposes to act) in a way which is made unlawful by section 6(1) may–

(a) bring proceedings against the authority under this Act in the appropriate court or tribunal, or

(b) rely on the Convention right or rights concerned in any legal proceedings,

but only if he is (or would be) a victim of the unlawful act.

(2) In subsection (1)(a) 'appropriate court or tribunal' means such court or

tribunal as may be determined in accordance with rules; and proceedings against an authority include a counterclaim or similar proceeding.

(3) If the proceedings are brought on an application for judicial review, the applicant is to be taken to have a sufficient interest in relation to the unlawful act only if he is, or would be, a victim of that act.

(4) If the proceedings are made by way of a petition for judicial review in Scotland, the applicant shall be taken to have title and interest to sue in relation to the unlawful act only if he is, or would be, a victim of that act.

(5) Proceedings under subsection (1)(a) must be brought before the end of–
   (a) the period of one year beginning with the date on which the act complained of took place; or
   (b) such longer period as the court or tribunal considers equitable having regard to all the circumstances,
   but that is subject to any rule imposing a stricter time limit in relation to the procedure in question.

(6) In subsection (1)(b) 'legal proceedings' includes–
   (a) proceedings brought by or at the instigation of a public authority; and
   (b) an appeal against the decision of a court or tribunal.

(7) For the purposes of this section, a person is a victim of an unlawful act only if he would be a victim for the purposes of Article 34 of the Convention if proceedings were brought in the European Court of Human Rights in respect of that act.

(8) Nothing in this Act creates a criminal offence.

(9) In this section 'rules' means–
   (a) in relation to proceedings before a court or tribunal outside Scotland, rules made by the Lord Chancellor or the Secretary of State for the purposes of this section or rules of court,
   (b) in relation to proceedings before a court or tribunal in Scotland, rules made by the Secretary of State for those purposes,
   (c) in relation to proceedings before a tribunal in Northern Ireland–
      (i) which deals with transferred matters; and
      (ii) for which no rules made under paragraph (a) are in force,
      rules made by a Northern Ireland department for those purposes,
   and includes provision made by order under section 1 of the Courts and Legal Services Act 1990.

(10) In making rules, regard must be had to section 9.

(11) The Minister who has power to make rules in relation to a particular tribunal may, to the extent he considers it necessary to ensure that the tribunal can provide an appropriate remedy in relation to an act (or proposed act) of a public authority which is (or would be) unlawful as a result of section 6(1), by order add to–
   (a) the relief or remedies which the tribunal may grant; or
   (b) the grounds on which it may grant any of them.

(12) An order made under subsection (11) may contain such incidental, supplemental, consequential or transitional provision as the Minister making it considers appropriate.

(13) 'The Minister' includes the Northern Ireland department concerned.

Judicial remedies

8 (1) In relation to any act (or proposed act) of a public authority which the court finds is (or would be) unlawful, it may grant such relief or remedy, or make such order, within its powers as it considers just and appropriate.

(2) But damages may be awarded only by a court which has power to award damages, or to order the payment of compensation, in civil proceedings.

(3) No award of damages is to be made unless, taking account of all the circumstances of the case, including–

(a) any other relief or remedy granted, or order made, in relation to the act in question (by that or any other court), and

(b) the consequences of any decision (of that or any other court) in respect of that act,

the court is satisfied that the award is necessary to afford just satisfaction to the person in whose favour it is made.

(4) In determining–

(a) whether to award damages, or

(b) the amount of an award,

the court must take into account the principles applied by the European Court of Human Rights in relation to the award of compensation under Article 41 of the Convention.

(5) A public authority against which damages are awarded is to be treated–

(a) in Scotland, for the purposes of section 3 of the Law Reform (Miscellaneous Provisions) (Scotland) Act 1940 as if the award were made in an action of damages in which the authority has been found liable in respect of loss or damage to the person to whom the award is made;

(b) for the purposes of the Civil Liability (Contribution) Act 1978 as liable in respect of damage suffered by the person to whom the award is made.

(6) In this section–

'court' includes a tribunal;

'damages' means damages for an unlawful act of a public authority; and

'unlawful' means unlawful under section 6(1).

SCHEDULE 1: THE ARTICLES

Section 1(3)

Part I: The Convention

Rights and Freedoms

Article 2: Right to life

1 Everyone's right to life shall be protected by law. No one shall be deprived of his life intentionally save in the execution of a sentence of a court following his conviction of a crime for which this penalty is provided by law.

2 Deprivation of life shall not be regarded as inflicted in contravention of this Article when it results from the use of force which is no more than absolutely necessary:

(a) in defence of any person from unlawful violence;

(b) in order to effect a lawful arrest or to prevent the escape of a person lawfully detained;

(c) in action lawfully taken for the purpose of quelling a riot or insurrection.

Article 3: Prohibition of torture

No one shall be subjected to torture or to inhuman or degrading treatment or punishment.

Article 4: Prohibition of slavery and forced labour

1   No one shall be held in slavery or servitude.
2   No one shall be required to perform forced or compulsory labour.
3   For the purpose of this Article the term 'forced or compulsory labour' shall not include:
   (a) any work required to be done in the ordinary course of detention imposed according to the provisions of Article 5 of this Convention or during conditional release from such detention;
   (b) any service of a military character or, in case of conscientious objectors in countries where they are recognised, service exacted instead of compulsory military service;
   (c) any service exacted in case of an emergency or calamity threatening the life or well-being of the community;
   (d) any work or service which forms part of normal civic obligations.

Article 5: Right to liberty and security

1   Everyone has the right to liberty and security of person. No one shall be deprived of his liberty save in the following cases and in accordance with a procedure prescribed by law:
   (a) the lawful detention of a person after conviction by a competent court;
   (b) the lawful arrest or detention of a person for non-compliance with the lawful order of a court or in order to secure the fulfilment of any obligation prescribed by law;
   (c) the lawful arrest or detention of a person effected for the purpose of bringing him before the competent legal authority on reasonable suspicion of having committed an offence or when it is reasonably considered necessary to prevent his committing an offence or fleeing after having done so;
   (d) the detention of a minor by lawful order for the purpose of educational supervision or his lawful detention for the purpose of bringing him before the competent legal authority;
   (e) the lawful detention of persons for the prevention of the spreading of infectious diseases, of persons of unsound mind, alcoholics or drug addicts or vagrants;
   (f) the lawful arrest or detention of a person to prevent his effecting an unauthorised entry into the country or of a person against whom action is being taken with a view to deportation or extradition.
2   Everyone who is arrested shall be informed promptly, in a language which he understands, of the reasons for his arrest and of any charge against him.
3   Everyone arrested or detained in accordance with the provisions of paragraph 1(c) of this Article shall be brought promptly before a judge or other officer authorised by law to exercise judicial power and shall be entitled to trial within a reasonable time or to release pending trial. Release may be conditioned by guarantees to appear for trial.

4 Everyone who is deprived of his liberty by arrest or detention shall be entitled to take proceedings by which the lawfulness of his detention shall be decided speedily by a court and his release ordered if the detention is not lawful.

5 Everyone who has been the victim of arrest or detention in contravention of the provisions of this Article shall have an enforceable right to compensation.

Article 6: Right to a fair trial

1 In the determination of his civil rights and obligations or of any criminal charge against him, everyone is entitled to a fair and public hearing within a reasonable time by an independent and impartial tribunal established by law. Judgment shall be pronounced publicly but the press and public may be excluded from all or part of the trial in the interest of morals, public order or national security in a democratic society, where the interests of juveniles or the protection of the private life of the parties so require, or to the extent strictly necessary in the opinion of the court in special circumstances where publicity would prejudice the interests of justice.

2 Everyone charged with a criminal offence shall be presumed innocent until proved guilty according to law.

3 Everyone charged with a criminal offence has the following minimum rights:
   (a) to be informed promptly, in a language which he understands and in detail, of the nature and cause of the accusation against him;
   (b) to have adequate time and facilities for the preparation of his defence;
   (c) to defend himself in person or through legal assistance of his own choosing or, if he has not sufficient means to pay for legal assistance, to be given it free when the interests of justice so require;
   (d) to examine or have examined witnesses against him and to obtain the attendance and examination of witnesses on his behalf under the same conditions as witnesses against him;
   (e) to have the free assistance of an interpreter if he cannot understand or speak the language used in court.

Article 7: No punishment without law

1 No one shall be held guilty of any criminal offence on account of any act or omission which did not constitute a criminal offence under national or international law at the time when it was committed. Nor shall a heavier penalty be imposed than the one that was applicable at the time the criminal offence was committed.

2 This Article shall not prejudice the trial and punishment of any person for any act or omission which, at the time when it was committed, was criminal according to the general principles of law recognised by civilised nations.

Article 8: Right to respect for private and family life

1 Everyone has the right to respect for his private and family life, his home and his correspondence.

2 There shall be no interference by a public authority with the exercise of this right except such as is in accordance with the law and is necessary in a democratic society in the interests of national security, public safety or the economic well-being of the country, for the prevention of disorder or crime, for

the protection of health or morals, or for the protection of the rights and freedoms of others.

Article 9: Freedom of thought, conscience and religion

1   Everyone has the right to freedom of thought, conscience and religion; this right includes freedom to change his religion or belief and freedom, either alone or in community with others and in public or private, to manifest his religion or belief, in worship, teaching, practice and observance.

2   Freedom to manifest one's religion or beliefs shall be subject only to such limitations as are prescribed by law and are necessary in a democratic society in the interests of public safety, for the protection of public order, health or morals, or for the protection of the rights and freedoms of others.

Article 10: Freedom of expression

1   Everyone has the right to freedom of expression. This right shall include freedom to hold opinions and to receive and impart information and ideas without interference by public authority and regardless of frontiers. This Article shall not prevent States from requiring the licensing of broadcasting, television or cinema enterprises.

2   The exercise of these freedoms, since it carries with it duties and responsibilities, may be subject to such formalities, conditions, restrictions or penalties as are prescribed by law and are necessary in a democratic society, in the interests of national security, territorial integrity or public safety, for the prevention of disorder or crime, for the protection of health or morals, for the protection of the reputation or rights of others, for preventing the disclosure of information received in confidence, or for maintaining the authority and impartiality of the judiciary.

Article 11: Freedom of assembly and association

1   Everyone has the right to freedom of peaceful assembly and to freedom of association with others, including the right to form and to join trade unions for the protection of his interests.

2   No restrictions shall be placed on the exercise of these rights other than such as are prescribed by law and are necessary in a democratic society in the interests of national security or public safety, for the prevention of disorder or crime, for the protection of health or morals or for the protection of the rights and freedoms of others. This Article shall not prevent the imposition of lawful restrictions on the exercise of these rights by members of the armed forces, of the police or of the administration of the State.

Article 12: Right to marry

Men and women of marriageable age have the right to marry and to found a family, according to the national laws governing the exercise of this right.

Article 14: Prohibition of discrimination

The enjoyment of the rights and freedoms set forth in this Convention shall be secured without discrimination on any ground such as sex, race, colour, language, religion, political or other opinion, national or social origin, association with a national minority, property, birth or other status.

Article 16: Restrictions on political activity of aliens

Nothing in Articles 10, 11 and 14 shall be regarded as preventing the High

Contracting Parties from imposing restrictions on the political activity of aliens.

Article 17: Prohibition of abuse of rights

Nothing in this Convention may be interpreted as implying for any State, group or person any right to engage in any activity or perform any act aimed at the destruction of any of the rights and freedoms set forth herein or at their limitation to a greater extent than is provided for in the Convention.

Article 18: Limitation on use of restrictions on rights

The restrictions permitted under this Convention to the said rights and freedoms shall not be applied for any purpose other than those for which they have been prescribed.

Part II: The First Protocol

Article 1: Protection of property

Every natural or legal person is entitled to the peaceful enjoyment of his possessions. No one shall be deprived of his possessions except in the public interest and subject to the conditions provided for by law and by the general principles of international law.

The preceding provisions shall not, however, in any way impair the right of a State to enforce such laws as it deems necessary to control the use of property in accordance with the general interest or to secure the payment of taxes or other contributions or penalties.

Article 2: Right to education

No person shall be denied the right to education. In the exercise of any functions which it assumes in relation to education and to teaching, the State shall respect the right of parents to ensure such education and teaching in conformity with their own religious and philosophical convictions.

Article 3: Right to free elections

The High Contracting Parties undertake to hold free elections at reasonable intervals by secret ballot, under conditions which will ensure the free expression of the opinion of the people in the choice of the legislature.

Part III: Article 1 of the Thirteenth Protocol

Abolition of the Death Penalty

The death penalty shall be abolished. No one shall be condemned to such penalty or executed.

Secondary legislation[1]

COURT OF PROTECTION RULES 2007

Part 1: Preliminary

1 Title and commencement
These Rules may be cited as the Court of Protection Rules 2007 and come into force on 1 October 2007.

2 Revocations
The following rules are revoked–
(a) the Court of Protection Rules 2001; and
(b) the Court of Protection (Enduring Powers of Attorney) Rules 2001.

Part 2: The Overriding Objective

3 The overriding objective
(1) These Rules have the overriding objective of enabling the court to deal with a case justly, having regard to the principles contained in the Act.
(2) The court will seek to give effect to the overriding objective when it–
(a) exercises any power under these Rules; or
(b) interprets any rule or practice direction.
(3) Dealing with a case justly includes, so far as is practicable–
(a) ensuring that it is dealt with expeditiously and fairly;
(b) ensuring that P's interests and position are properly considered;
(c) dealing with the case in ways which are proportionate to the nature, importance and complexity of the issues;
(d) ensuring that the parties are on an equal footing;
(e) saving expense; and
(f) allotting to it an appropriate share of the court's resources, while taking account of the need to allot resources to other cases.

4 The duty of the parties
The parties are required to help the court to further the overriding objective.

5 Court's duty to manage cases
(1) The court will further the overriding objective by actively managing cases.
(2) Active case management includes–
(a) encouraging the parties to co-operate with each other in the conduct of the proceedings;
(b) identifying at an early stage–
(i) the issues; and
(ii) who should be a party to the proceedings;
(c) deciding promptly–
(i) which issues need a full investigation and hearing and which do not; and
(ii) the procedure to be followed in the case;
(d) deciding the order in which issues are to be resolved;
(e) encouraging the parties to use an alternative dispute resolution procedure if the court considers that appropriate;
(f) fixing timetables or otherwise controlling the progress of the case;
(g) considering whether the likely benefits of taking a particular step justify the cost of taking it;

(h) dealing with as many aspects of the case as the court can on the same occasion;
(i) dealing with the case without the parties needing to attend at court;
(j) making use of technology; and
(k) giving directions to ensure that the case proceeds quickly and efficiently.

Part 3: Interpretation and General Provisions

6 Interpretation

In these Rules–

'the Act' means the Mental Capacity Act 2005;

'applicant' means a person who makes, or who seeks permission to make, an application to the court;

'application form' means the document that is to be used to begin proceedings in accordance with Part 9 of these Rules or any other provision of these Rules or the practice directions which requires the use of an application form;

'application notice' means the document that is to be used to make an application in accordance with Part 10 of these Rules or any other provision of these Rules or the practice directions which requires the use of an application notice;

'attorney' means the person appointed as such by an enduring power of attorney created, or purporting to have been created, in accordance with the regulations mentioned in paragraph 2 of Schedule 4 to the Act;

'business day' means a day other than–

(a) a Saturday, Sunday, Christmas Day or Good Friday; or
(b) a bank holiday in England and Wales, under the Banking and Financial Dealings Act 1971;

'child' means a person under 18;

'court' means the Court of Protection;

'deputy' means a deputy appointed under the Act;

'donee' means the donee of a lasting power of attorney;

'donor' means the donor of a lasting power of attorney, except where this expression is used in rule 68 or 201(5) (where it means the donor of an enduring power of attorney);

'enduring power of attorney' means an instrument created in accordance with such of the regulations mentioned in paragraph 2 of Schedule 4 to the Act as applied when it was executed;

'filing' in relation to a document means delivering it, by post or otherwise, to the court office;

'judge' means a judge nominated to be a judge of the court under the Act;

'lasting power of attorney' has the meaning given in section 9 of the Act;

'legal representative' means a–

(a) barrister,
(b) solicitor,
(c) solicitor's employee,
(d) manager of a body recognised under section 9 of the Administration of Justice Act 1985, or
(e) person who, for the purposes of the Legal Services Act 2007, is an

authorised person in relation to an activity which constitutes the conduct of litigation (within the meaning of that Act),

who has been instructed to act for a party in relation to any application;

'legally aided person' means a person to whom civil legal services (within the meaning of the Legal Aid, Sentencing and Punishment of Offenders Act 2012) have been made available under arrangements made for the purposes of Part 1 of that Act);

'order' includes a declaration made by the court;

'P' means–

    (a) any person (other than a protected party) who lacks or, so far as consistent with the context, is alleged to lack capacity to make a decision or decisions in relation to any matter that is the subject of an application to the court; and

    (b) a relevant person as defined by paragraph 7 of Schedule A1 to the Act,

and references to a person who lacks capacity are to be construed in accordance with the Act;

'party' is to be construed in accordance with rule 73;

'permission form' means the form that is to be used to make an application for permission to begin proceedings in accordance with Part 8 of these Rules;

'personal welfare' is to be construed in accordance with section 17 of the Act;

'President' and 'Vice-President' refer to those judges appointed as such under section 46(3)(a) and (b) of the Act;

'property and affairs' is to be construed in accordance with section 18 of the Act;

'protected party' means a party or an intended party (other than P or a child) who lacks capacity to conduct the proceedings;

'respondent' means a person who is named as a respondent in the application form or notice, as the case may be;

'Senior Judge' means the judge who has been nominated to be Senior Judge under section 46(4) of the Act, and references in these Rules to a circuit judge include the Senior Judge;

'Visitor' means a person appointed as such by the Lord Chancellor under section 61 of the Act.

7 Court officers

(1) Where these Rules permit or require the court to perform an act of a purely formal or administrative character, that act may be performed by a court officer.

(2) A requirement that a court officer carry out any act at the request of any person is subject to the payment of any fee required by a fees order for the carrying out of that act.

7A(1) The Senior Judge or the President may authorise a court officer to exercise the jurisdiction of the court in such circumstances as set out in the relevant practice direction.

(2) A court officer who has been authorised under paragraph (1)–

    (a) must refer to a judge any application, proceedings or any question arising in any application or proceedings which ought, in the officer's opinion, to be considered by a judge;

(b) may not deal with any application or proceedings or any question arising in any application or proceedings by way of a hearing; and

(c) may not deal with an application for the reconsideration of an order made by that court officer or another court officer.

8 Computation of time

(1) This rule shows how to calculate any period of time which is specified–
   (a) by these Rules;
   (b) by a practice direction; or
   (c) in an order or direction of the court.

(2) A period of time expressed as a number of days must be computed as clear days.

(3) In this rule 'clear days' means that in computing the number of days–
   (a) the day on which the period begins; and
   (b) if the end of the period is defined by reference to an event, the day on which that event occurs,
   are not included.

(4) Where the specified period is 7 days or less, and would include a day which is not a business day, that day does not count.

(5) When the specified period for doing any act at the court office ends on a day on which the office is closed, that act will be done in time if done on the next day on which the court office is open.

9 Application of the Civil Procedure Rules

In any case not expressly provided for by these Rules or the practice directions made under them, the Civil Procedure Rules 1998 (including any practice directions made under them) may be applied with any necessary modifications, insofar as is necessary to further the overriding objective.

Part 4: Court Documents

10 Documents used in court proceedings

(1) The court will seal or otherwise authenticate with the stamp of the court the following documents on issue–
   (a) a permission form;
   (b) an application form;
   (c) an application notice;
   (d) an order; and
   (e) any other document which a rule or practice direction requires to be sealed or stamped.

(2) Where these Rules or any practice direction require a document to be signed, that requirement is satisfied if the signature is printed by computer or other mechanical means.

(3) A practice direction may make provision for documents to be filed or sent to the court by–
   (a) facsimile; or
   (b) other means.

11   Documents required to be verified by a statement of truth

(1) The following documents must be verified by a statement of truth–
  (a) a permission form, an application form or an application notice, where the applicant seeks to rely upon matters set out in the document as evidence;
  (b) a witness statement;
  (c) a certificate of–
    (i) service or non-service; or
    (ii) notification or non-notification;
  (d) a deputy's declaration; and
  (e) any other document required by a rule or practice direction to be so verified.

(2) Subject to paragraph (3), a statement of truth is a statement that–
  (a) the party putting forward the document;
  (b) in the case of a witness statement, the maker of the witness statement; or
  (c) in the case of a certificate referred to in paragraph (1)(c), the person who signs the certificate,
  believes that the facts stated in the document being verified are true.

(3) If a party is conducting proceedings with a litigation friend, the statement of truth in–
  (a) a permission form;
  (b) an application form; or
  (c) an application notice,
  is a statement that the litigation friend believes the facts stated in the document being verified are true.

(4) The statement of truth must be signed–
  (a) in the case of a permission form, an application form or an application notice–
    (i) by the party or litigation friend; or
    (ii) by the legal representative on behalf of the party or litigation friend; and
  (b) in the case of a witness statement, by the maker of the statement.

(5) A statement of truth which is not contained in the document which it verifies must clearly identify that document.

(6) A statement of truth in a permission form, an application form or an application notice may be made by–
  (a) a person who is not a party; or
  (b) two or more parties jointly,
  where this is permitted by a relevant practice direction.

12   Failure to verify a document

If a permission form, application form or application notice is not verified by a statement of truth, the applicant may not rely upon the document as evidence of any of the matters set out in it unless the court permits.

13   Failure to verify a witness statement

If a witness statement is not verified by a statement of truth, it shall not be admissible in evidence unless the court permits.

14 False statements

(1) Proceedings for contempt of court may be brought against a person if he makes, or causes to be made, a false statement in a document verified by a statement of truth without an honest belief in its truth.

(2) Proceedings under this rule may be brought only–
- (a) by the Attorney General; or
- (b) with the permission of the court.

15 Personal details

(1) Where a party does not wish to reveal–
- (a) his home address or telephone number;
- (b) P's home address or telephone number;
- (c) the name of the person with whom P is living (if that person is not the applicant); or
- (d) the address or telephone number of his place of business, or the place of business of any of the persons mentioned in sub-paragraphs (b) or (c),

he must provide those particulars to the court.

(2) Where paragraph (1) applies, the particulars given will not be revealed to any person unless the court so directs.

(3) Where a party changes his home address during the course of the proceedings, he must give notice of the change to the court.

(4) Where a party does not reveal his home address, he must nonetheless provide an address for service which must be within the jurisdiction of the court.

16 Supply of documents to a party from court records

Unless the court orders otherwise, a party to proceedings may inspect or obtain from the records of the court a copy of–
- (a) any document filed by a party to the proceedings; or
- (b) any communication in the proceedings between the court and–
  - (i) a party to the proceedings; or
  - (ii) another person.

17 Supply of documents to a non-party from court records

(1) Subject to rules 20 and 92(2), a person who is not a party to proceedings may inspect or obtain from the court records a copy of any judgment or order given or made in public.

(2) The court may, on an application made to it, authorise a person who is not a party to proceedings to–
- (a) inspect any other documents in the court records; or
- (b) obtain a copy of any such documents, or extracts from such documents.

(3) A person making an application for an authorisation under paragraph (2) must do so in accordance with Part 10.

(4) Before giving an authorisation under paragraph (2), the court will consider whether any document is to be provided on an edited basis.

18 Subsequent use of court documents

(1) Where a document has been filed or disclosed, a party to whom it was provided may use the document only for the purpose of the proceedings in which it was filed or disclosed, except where–
- (a) the document has been read to or by the court or referred to at a public hearing; or

(b) the court otherwise permits.

(2) Paragraph (1)(a) is subject to any order of the court made under rule 92(2).

19 Editing information in court documents

(1) A party may apply to the court for an order that a specified part of a document is to be edited prior to the document's service or disclosure.

(2) An order under paragraph (1) may be made at any time.

(3) Where the court makes an order under this rule any subsequent use of that document in the proceedings shall be of the document as edited, unless the court directs otherwise.

(4) An application under this rule must be made in accordance with Part 10.

20 Public Guardian to be supplied with court documents relevant to supervision of deputies

(1) This rule applies in any case where the court makes an order–
   (a) appointing a person to act as a deputy; or
   (b) varying an order under which a deputy has been appointed.

(2) Subject to paragraphs (3) and (6), the Public Guardian is entitled to be supplied with a copy of qualifying documents if he reasonably considers that it is necessary for him to have regard to them in connection with the discharge of his functions under section 58 of the Act in relation to the supervision of deputies.

(3) The court may direct that the right to be supplied with documents under paragraph (2) does not apply in relation to such one or more documents, or descriptions of documents, as the court may specify.

(4) A direction under paragraph (3) or (6) may be given–
   (a) either on the court's own initiative or on an application made to it; and
   (b) either–
      (i) at the same time as the court makes the order which appoints the deputy, or which varies it; or
      (ii) subsequently.

(5) 'Qualifying documents' means documents which–
   (a) are filed in court in connection with the proceedings in which the court makes the order referred to in paragraph (1); and
   (b) are relevant to–
      (i) the decision to appoint the deputy;
      (ii) any powers conferred on him;
      (iii) any duties imposed on him; or
      (iv) any other terms applying to those powers and duties which are contained in the order.

(6) The court may direct that any document is to be provided to the Public Guardian on an edited basis.

21 Provision of court order to Public Guardian

Any order of the court requiring the Public Guardian to do something, or not to do something, will be served by the court on the Public Guardian as soon as practicable and in any event not later than 7 days after the order was made.

22 Amendment of application

(1) The court may allow or direct an applicant, at any stage of the proceedings, to amend his application form or notice.

(2) The amendment may be effected by making in writing the necessary alterations to the application form or notice, but if the amendments are so numerous or of such a nature or length that written alteration would make it difficult or inconvenient to read, a fresh document amended as allowed or directed may be issued.

23 Clerical mistakes or slips

The court may at any time correct any clerical mistakes in an order or direction or any error arising in an order or direction from any accidental slip or omission.

24 Endorsement of amendment

Where an application form or notice, order or direction has been amended under this Part, a note shall be placed on it showing the date on which it was amended and the alteration shall be sealed.

Part 5: General Case Management Powers

25 The court's general powers of case management

(1) The list of powers in this rule is in addition to any powers given to the court by any other rule or practice direction or by any other enactment or any powers it may otherwise have.

(2) The court may–
  (a) extend or shorten the time for compliance with any rule, practice direction, or court order or direction (even if an application for extension is made after the time for compliance has expired);
  (b) adjourn or bring forward a hearing;
  (c) require P, a party, a party's legal representative or litigation friend, to attend court;
  (d) hold a hearing and receive evidence by telephone or any other method of direct oral communication;
  (e) stay the whole or part of any proceedings or judgment either generally or until a specified date or event;
  (f) consolidate proceedings;
  (g) hear two or more applications on the same occasion;
  (h) direct a separate hearing of any issue;
  (i) decide the order in which issues are to be heard;
  (j) exclude an issue from consideration;
  (k) dismiss or give judgment on an application after a decision is made on a preliminary basis;
  (l) direct any party to file and serve an estimate of costs; and
  (m) take any step or give any direction for the purpose of managing the case and furthering the overriding objective.

(3) A judge to whom a matter is allocated may, if he considers that the matter is one which ought properly to be dealt with by another judge, transfer the matter to such a judge.

(4) Where the court gives directions it may take into account whether or not a party has complied with any rule or practice direction.

(5) The court may make any order it considers appropriate even if a party has not sought that order.

(6) A power of the court under these Rules to make an order includes a power to vary or revoke the order;

(7) Rules 25.12 to 25.15 of the Civil Procedure Rules 1998 (which make provision about security for costs) apply in proceedings to which these Rules apply as if the references in those Rules to 'defendant' and 'claimant' were to 'respondent' and 'applicant' respectively.

26 Court's power to dispense with requirement of any rule

In addition to its general powers and the powers listed in rule 25, the court may dispense with the requirement of any rule.

27 Exercise of powers on the court's own initiative

(1) Except where these Rules or some other enactment make different provision, the court may exercise its powers on its own initiative.

(2) The court may make an order on its own initiative without hearing the parties or giving them the opportunity to make representations.

(3) Where the court proposes to make an order on its own initiative it may give the parties and any person it thinks fit an opportunity to make representations and, where it does so, it will specify the time by which, and the manner in which, the representations must be made.

(4) Where the court proposes–

(a) to make an order on its own initiative; and

(b) to hold a hearing to decide whether to make the order,

it will give the parties and may give any other person it thinks likely to be affected by the order at least 3 days' notice of the hearing.

28 General power of the court to rectify matters where there has been an error of procedure

Where there has been an error of procedure, such as a failure to comply with a rule or practice direction–

(a) the error does not invalidate any step taken in the proceedings unless the court so orders; and

(b) the court may waive the error or require it to be remedied or may make such other order as appears to the court to be just.

Part 6: Service of Documents

Service generally

29 Scope

(1) Subject to paragraph (2), the rules in this Part apply to–

(a) the service of documents; and

(b) to the requirement under rule 70 for a person to be notified of the issue of an application form,

and references to 'serve', 'service', 'notice' and 'notify', and kindred expressions shall be construed accordingly.

(2) The rules in this Part do not apply where–

(a) any other enactment, a rule in another Part or a practice direction makes different provision; or

(b) the court directs otherwise.

30 Who is to serve

(1) The general rule is that the following documents will be served by the court–

(a) an order or judgment of the court;

(b) an acknowledgment of service or notification; and

(c) except where the application is for an order for committal, a notice of hearing.

(2) Any other document is to be served by the party seeking to rely upon it, except where–

(a) a rule or practice direction provides otherwise; or

(b) the court directs otherwise.

(3) Where the court is to serve a document–

(a) it is for the court to decide which of the methods of service specified in rule 31 is to be used; and

(b) if the document is being served on behalf of a party, that party must provide sufficient copies.

31 Methods of service

(1) A document may be served by any of the methods specified in this rule.

(2) Where it is not known whether a solicitor is acting on behalf of a person, the document may be served by–

(a) delivering it to the person personally;

(b) delivering it at his home address or last known home address; or

(c) sending it to that address, or last known address, by first class post (or by an alternative method of service which provides for delivery on the next working day).

(3) Where a solicitor–

(a) is authorised to accept service on behalf of a person; and

(b) has informed the person serving the document in writing that he is so authorised,

the document must be served on the solicitor, unless personal service is required by an enactment, rule, practice direction or court order.

(4) Where it appears to the court that there is a good reason to authorise service by a method other than those specified in paragraphs (2) or (3), the court may direct that service is effected by that method.

(5) A direction that service is effected by an alternative method must specify–

(a) the method of service; and

(b) the date when the document will be deemed to be served.

(6) A practice direction may set out how documents are to be served by document exchange, electronic communication or other means.

32 Service of documents on children and protected parties

(1) The following table shows the person on whom a document must be served if it is a document which would otherwise be served on–

(a) a child; or

(b) a protected party.

Type of document	*Nature of party*	*Person to be served*
Application form	Child	–A person who has parental responsibility for the child within the meaning of the Children Act 1989; or
		–if there is no such person, a person with whom the child resides or in whose care the child is.
Application form	Protected party	–The person who is authorised to conduct the proceedings in the protected party's name or on his behalf; or
		–a person who is a duly appointed attorney, donee or deputy of the protected party; or
		–if there is no such person, a person with whom the protected party lives or in whose care the latter is.
Application for an order appointing a litigation friend, where a child or protected party has no litigation friend	Child or protected party	–See rule 145 (appointment of litigation friend by court order– supplementary).
Any other document	Child or protected party	–The litigation friend or other duly authorised person who is conducting the proceedings on behalf of the child or protected party.

(2) The court may make an order for service on a child or a protected party by permitting the document to be served on some person other than the person specified in the table set out in paragraph (1) above (which may include service on the child or the protected party).

(3) An application for an order under paragraph (2) may be made without notice.

(4) The court may order that, although a document has been served on someone other than the person specified in the table, the document is to be treated as if it had been properly served.

(5) This rule does not apply in relation to the service of documents upon a child in any case where the court has made an order under rule 141(4) permitting the child to conduct proceedings without a litigation friend.

33 Service of documents on P if he becomes a party

(1) If P becomes a party to the proceedings, all documents to be served on him must be served on his litigation friend or other person duly authorised to conduct proceedings on P's behalf.

(2) The court may make an order for service on P by permitting the document to be served on some person other than the person specified in paragraph (1) above (which may include service on P).

(3) An application for an order under paragraph (2) may be made without notice.

(4) The court may order that, although a document has been served on someone other than a person specified in paragraph (1), the document is to be treated as if it had been properly served.

(5) This rule does not apply in relation to the service of documents upon P in any case where the court has made an order under rule 147(2) (procedure where appointment of a litigation friend comes to an end–for P).

34 Substituted service

Where it appears to the court that it is impracticable for any reason to serve a document in accordance with any of the methods provided under rule 31, the court may make an order for substituted service of the document by taking such steps as the court may direct to bring it to the notice of the person to be served.

35 Deemed service

(1) A document which is served in accordance with these Rules or any relevant practice direction shall be deemed to be served on the day shown in the following table–

Method of service	Deemed day of service
First class post (or other service for next-day delivery)	The second day after it was posted.
Document exchange	The second day after it was left at the document exchange.
Delivering the document to a permitted address	The day after it was delivered to that address.
Fax	If it is transmitted on a business day before 4pm, on that day; or in any other case, on the business day after the day on which it is transmitted.
Other electronic means	The second day after the day on which it is transmitted.

(2) If a document is served personally–
(a) after 5pm, on a business day; or
(b) at any time on a Saturday, Sunday or a Bank Holiday,
it will be treated as being served on the next business day.

36 Certificate of service

(1) Where a rule, practice direction or court order requires a certificate of service for the document, the certificate must state the details set out in the following table–

Method of service	Details to be certified
First class post (or any other service for next-day delivery)	Date of posting
Personal service	Date of personal service
Document exchange	Date when the document was left at the document exchange.
Delivery of document to permitted address	Date when the document was delivered to that address.
Fax	Date of transmission.
Other electronic means	Date of transmission and the means used.
Alternative method permitted by the court	As required by the court.

(2) The certificate must be filed within 7 days after service of the document to which it relates.

37 Certificate of non-service

(1) Where an applicant or other person is unable to serve any document under these Rules or as directed by the court, he must file a certificate of non-service stating the reasons why service has not been effected.

(2) The certificate of non-service must be filed within 7 days of the latest date on which service should have been effected.

38 Power of court to dispense with service

(1) The court may dispense with any requirement to serve a document.

(2) An application for an order to dispense with service may be made without notice.

Service out of the jurisdiction

39 Application of Family Procedure (Adoption) Rules 2005

(1) The rules in Chapter 4 of Part 6 of the Family Procedure Rules 2010 ('the 2010 Rules') apply, with the modifications set out in this rule, to the service of documents out of the jurisdiction.

(2) References in the 2010 Rules to the Hague Convention shall be read in these Rules as references to the Convention on the International Protection of Adults signed at the Hague on 13th January 2000 (Cm 5881).

(3) References in the 2010 Rules to the Senior Master of the Queen's Bench Division shall be read in these Rules as references to the Senior Judge.

Part 7: Notifying P

General requirement to notify P

40 General

(1) Subject to paragraphs (2) and (3), the rules in this Part apply where P is to be given notice of any matter or document, or is to be provided with any document, either under the Rules or in accordance with an order or direction of the court.

(2) If P becomes a party, the rules in this Part do not apply and service is to be effected in accordance with Part 6 or as directed by the court.

(3) In any case the court may, either on its own initiative or on application, direct that P must not be notified of any matter or document, or provided with any document, whether in accordance with this Part or at all.

41 Who is to notify P

(1) Where P is to be notified under this Part, notification must be effected by–
   (a) the applicant;
   (b) the appellant (where the matter relates to an appeal);
   (c) an agent duly appointed by the applicant or the appellant; or
   (d) such other person as the court may direct.

(2) The person within paragraph (1) is referred to in this Part as 'the person effecting notification'.

Circumstances in which P must be notified

42 Application forms

(1) P must be notified–
   (a) that an application form has been issued by the court;
   (b) that an application form has been withdrawn; and
   (c) of the date on which a hearing is to be held in relation to the matter, where that hearing is for disposing of the application.

(2) Where P is to be notified that an application form has been issued, the person effecting notification must explain to P–
   (a) who the applicant is;
   (b) that the application raises the question of whether P lacks capacity in relation to a matter or matters, and what that means;
   (c) what will happen if the court makes the order or direction that has been applied for; and
   (d) where the application contains a proposal for the appointment of a person to make decisions on P's behalf in relation to the matter to which the application relates, details of who that person is.

(3) Where P is to be notified that an application form has been withdrawn, the person effecting notification must explain to P–
   (a) that the application form has been withdrawn; and
   (b) the consequences of that withdrawal.

(4) The person effecting notification must also inform P that he may seek advice and assistance in relation to any matter of which he is notified.

43 Appeals

(1) P must be notified–
   (a) that an appellant's notice has been issued by the court;
   (b) that an appellant's notice has been withdrawn; and
   (c) of the date on which a hearing is to be held in relation to the matter, where that hearing is for disposing of the appellant's notice.

(2) Where P is to be notified that an appellant's notice has been issued, the person effecting notification must explain to P–
   (a) who the appellant is;
   (b) the issues raised by the appeal; and

(c) what will happen if the court makes the order or direction that has been applied for.

(3) Where P is to be notified that an appellant's notice has been withdrawn, the person effecting notification must explain to P–

(a) that the appellant's notice has been withdrawn; and

(b) the consequences of that withdrawal.

(4) The person effecting notification must also inform P that he may seek advice and assistance in relation to any matter of which he is notified.

44 Final orders

(1) P must be notified of a final order of the court.

(2) Where P is notified in accordance with this rule, the person effecting notification must explain to P the effect of the order.

(3) The person effecting notification must also inform P that he may seek advice and assistance in relation to any matter of which he is notified.

45 Other matters

(1) This rule applies where the court directs that P is to be notified of any other matter.

(2) The person effecting notification must explain to P such matters as may be directed by the court.

(3) The person effecting notification must also inform P that he may seek advice and assistance in relation to any matter of which he is notified.

Manner of notification, and accompanying documents

46 Manner of notification

(1) Where P is to be notified under this Part, the person effecting notification must provide P with the information specified in rules 42 to 45 in a way that is appropriate to P's circumstances (for example, using simple language, visual aids or any other appropriate means).

(2) The information referred to in paragraph (1) must be provided to P personally.

(3) P must be provided with the information mentioned in paragraph (1) as soon as practicable and in any event within 21 days of the date on which–

(a) the application form or appellant's notice was issued or withdrawn;

(b) the order was made; or

(c) the person effecting notification received the notice of hearing from the court and in any event no later than 14 days before the date specified in the notice of the hearing,

as the case may be.

47 Acknowledgment of notification

When P is notified that an application form or an appellant's notice has been issued, he must also be provided with a form for acknowledging notification.

48 Certificate of notification

The person effecting notification must, within 7 days beginning with the date on which notification in accordance with this Part was given, file a certificate of notification which certifies–

(a) the date on which P was notified; and

(b) that he was notified in accordance with this Part.

49 Dispensing with requirement to notify, etc

(1) The applicant, the appellant or other person directed by the court to effect notification may apply to the court seeking an order–
- (a) dispensing with the requirement to comply with the provisions in this Part; or
- (b) requiring some other person to comply with the provisions in this Part.

(2) An application under this rule must be made in accordance with Part 10.

Part 8: Permission

50 General

Subject to these Rules and to section 50(1) of, and paragraph 20 of Schedule 3 to, the Act, the applicant must apply for permission to start proceedings under the Act.

(Section 50(1) of the Act specifies persons who do not need to apply for permission. Paragraph 20 of Schedule 3 to the Act specifies an application for which permission is not needed.)

51 Where the court's permission is not required

The permission of the court is not required–

(1) where an application is made by–
- (a) the Official Solicitor; or
- (b) the Public Guardian;

(2) where the application concerns–
- (a) P's property and affairs, unless the application is of a kind specified in rule 52;
- (b) a lasting power of attorney which is, or purports to be, created under the Act; or
- (c) an instrument which is, or purports to be, an enduring power of attorney;

(2A) where an application is made under section 21A of the Act by the relevant person's representative;

(3) where an application is made in accordance with Part 10; or

(4) where a person files an acknowledgment of service or notification in accordance with this Part or Part 9, for any order proposed that is different from that sought by the applicant.

52 Exceptions to rule 51(2)(a)

(1) For the purposes of rule 51(2)(a), the permission of the court is required to make any of the applications specified in this rule.

(2) An application for the exercise of the jurisdiction of the court under section 54(2) of the Trustee Act 1925, where the application is made by a person other than–
- (a) a person who has made an application for the appointment of a deputy;
- (b) a continuing trustee; or
- (c) any other person who, according to the practice of the Chancery Division, would have been entitled to make the application if it had been made in the High Court.

(3) An application under section 36(9) of the Trustee Act 1925 for leave to appoint

a new trustee in place of P, where the application is made by a person other than–

(a) a co-trustee; or

(b) another person with the power to appoint a new trustee.

(4) An application seeking the exercise of the court's jurisdiction under section 18(1)(b) (where the application relates to making a gift of P's property), (h) or (i) of the Act, where the application is made by a person other than–

(a) a person who has made an application for the appointment of a deputy;

(b) a person who, under any known will of P or under his intestacy, may become entitled to any property of P or any interest in it;

(c) a person who is an attorney appointed under an enduring power of attorney which has been registered in accordance with the Act or the regulations referred to in Schedule 4 to the Act;

(d) a person who is a donee of a lasting power of attorney which has been registered in accordance with the Act; or

(e) a person for whom P might be expected to provide if he had capacity to do so.

(5) An application under section 20 of the Trusts of Land and Appointment of Trustees Act 1996, where the application is made by a person other than a beneficiary under the trust or, if there is more than one, by both or all of them.

53 Permission–supplementary

(1) The provisions of rule 52(2) apply with such modifications as may be necessary to an application under section 18(1)(j) of the Act for an order for the exercise of any power vested in P of appointing trustees or retiring from a trust.

(2) Where part of the application concerns a matter which requires permission, and part of it does not, permission need only be sought for that part of it which requires permission.

54 Application for permission

The applicant must apply for permission by filing a permission form and must file with it–

(a) any information or documents specified in the relevant practice direction;

(b) a draft of the application form which he seeks permission to have issued; and

(c) an assessment of capacity form, where this is required by the relevant practice direction.

55 What the court will do when an application for permission to start proceedings is filed

Within 14 days of a permission form being filed, the court will issue it and–

(a) grant the application in whole or in part, or subject to conditions, without a hearing and may give directions in connection with the issue of the application form;

(b) refuse the application without a hearing; or

(c) fix a date for the hearing of the application.

56 Persons to be notified of the hearing of an application for permission

(1) Where the court fixes a date for a hearing under rule 55(c), it will notify the applicant and such other persons as it thinks fit, and provide them with–
  (a) subject to paragraph (2), the documents mentioned in rule 54; and
  (b) a form for acknowledging notification.
(2) The court may direct that any document is to be provided on an edited basis.

57 Acknowledgment of notification of permission application

(1) Any person who is notified of an application for permission and who wishes to take part in the permission hearing must file an acknowledgment of notification in accordance with the following provisions of this rule.
(2) The acknowledgment of notification must be filed not more than 21 days after notice of the application was given.
(3) The court will serve the acknowledgment of notification on the applicant and on any other person who has filed such an acknowledgment.
(4) The acknowledgment of notification must–
  (a) state whether the person acknowledging notification consents to the application for permission;
  (b) state whether he opposes the application for permission, and if so, set out the grounds for doing so;
  (c) state whether he proposes that permission should be granted to make an application for a different order, and if so, set out what that order is;
  (d) provide an address for service, which must be within the jurisdiction of the court; and
  (e) be signed by him or his legal representative.
(5) The acknowledgment of notification may include or be accompanied by an application for directions.
(6) Subject to rules 120 and 123 (restrictions on filing an expert's report and court's power to restrict expert evidence), where a person opposes the application for permission or proposes that permission is granted for a different order, the acknowledgment of notification must be accompanied by a witness statement containing any evidence upon which that person intends to rely.

58 Failure to file acknowledgment of notification

Where a person notified of the application for permission has not filed an acknowledgment of notification in accordance with rule 57, he may not take part in a hearing to decide whether permission should be given unless the court permits him to do so.

59 Service of an order giving or refusing permission

The court will serve–
  (a) the order granting or refusing permission;
  (b) if refusing permission without a hearing, the reasons for its decision in summary form; and
  (c) any directions,
on the applicant and on any other person notified of the application who filed an acknowledgment of notification.

60   Appeal against a permission decision following a hearing

Where the court grants or refuses permission following a hearing, any appeal against the permission decision shall be dealt with in accordance with Part 20 (appeals).

Part 9: How to Start Proceedings

Initial steps

61   General

(1) Applications to the court to start proceedings shall be made in accordance with this Part and, as applicable, Part 8 and the relevant practice directions.

(2) The appropriate forms must be used in the cases to which they apply, with such variations as the case requires, but not so as to omit any information or guidance which any form gives to the intended recipient.

(3) If permission to make an application is required, the court shall not issue the application form until permission is granted.

62   When proceedings are started

(1) The general rule is that proceedings are started when the court issues an application form at the request of the applicant.

(2) An application form is issued on the date entered on the application form by the court.

63   Contents of the application form

The application form must–

(a) state the matter which the applicant wants the court to decide;

(b) state the order which the applicant is seeking;

(c) name–

   (i)   the applicant;

   (ii) P;

   (iii) as a respondent, any person (other than P) whom the applicant reasonably believes to have an interest which means that he ought to be heard in relation to the application (as opposed to being notified of it in accordance with rule 70); and

   (iv) any person whom the applicant intends to notify in accordance with rule 70; and

(d) if the applicant is applying in a representative capacity, state what that capacity is.

64   Documents to be filed with the application form

When an applicant files his application form with the court, he must also file–

(a) in accordance with the relevant practice direction, any evidence upon which he intends to rely;

(b) if permission was required to make the application, a copy of the court's order granting permission;

(c) an assessment of capacity form, where this is required by the relevant practice direction;

(d) any other documents referred to in the application form; and

(e) such other information and material as may be set out in a practice direction.

65 What the court will do when an application form is filed

As soon as practicable after an application form is filed the court will issue the application form in any case where permission–

(a) is not required; or

(b) has been granted by the court; and

do anything else that may be set out in a practice direction.

Steps following issue of application form

66 Applicant to serve the application form on named respondents

(1) As soon as practicable and in any event within 21 days of the date on which the application form was issued, the applicant must serve a copy of the application form on any person who is named as a respondent in the application form, together with copies of any documents filed in accordance with rule 64 and a form for acknowledging service.

(2) The applicant must file a certificate of service within 7 days beginning with the date on which the documents were served.

67 Applications relating to lasting powers of attorney

(1) Where the application concerns the powers of the court under section 22 or 23 of the Act (powers of the court in relation to the validity and operation of lasting powers of attorney) the applicant must serve a copy of the application form, together with copies of any documents filed in accordance with rule 64 and a form for acknowledging service–

(a) unless the applicant is the donor or donee of the lasting power of attorney ('the power'), on the donor and every donee of the power;

(b) if he is the donor, on every donee of the power; and

(c) if he is a donee, on the donor and any other donee of the power,

but only if the above-mentioned persons have not been served or notified under any other rule.

(2) Where the application is solely in respect of an objection to the registration of a power, the requirements of rules 66 and 70 do not apply to an application made under this rule by–

(a) a donee of the power; or

(b) a person named in a statement made by the donor of the power in accordance with paragraph 2(1)(c)(i) of Schedule 1 to the Act.

(3) The applicant must comply with paragraph (1) as soon as practicable and in any event within 21 days of date on which the application form was issued.

(4) The applicant must file a certificate of service within 7 days beginning with the date on which the documents were served.

(5) Where the applicant knows or has reasonable grounds to believe that the donor of the power lacks capacity to make a decision in relation to any matter that is the subject of the application, he must notify the donor in accordance with Part 7.

68 Applications relating to enduring powers of attorney

(1) Where the application concerns the powers of the court under paragraphs 2(9), 4(5)(a) and (b), 7(2), 10(c), 13, or 16(2), (3), (4) and (6) of Schedule 4 to the Act, the applicant must serve a copy of the application form, together with copies of any documents filed in accordance with rule 64 and a form for acknowledging service–

(a) unless the applicant is the donor or attorney under the enduring power of attorney ('the power'), on the donor and every attorney of the power;

(b) if he is the donor, on every attorney under the power; or

(c) if he is an attorney, on the donor and any other attorney under the power,

but only if the above-mentioned persons have not been served or notified under any other rule.

(2) Where the application is solely in respect of an objection to the registration of a power, the requirements of rules 66 and 70 do not apply to an application made under this rule by–

(a) an attorney under the power; or

(b) a person listed in paragraph 6(1) of Schedule 4 to the Act.

(3) The applicant must comply with paragraph (1) as soon as practicable and in any event within 21 days of the date on which the application form was issued.

(4) The applicant must file a certificate of service within 7 days beginning with the date on which the documents were served.

(5) Where the applicant knows or has reasonable grounds to believe that the donor of the power lacks capacity to make a decision in relation to any matter that is the subject of the application, he must notify the donor in accordance with Part 7.

69 Applicant to notify P of an application

P must be notified in accordance with Part 7 that an application form has been issued, unless the requirement to do so has been dispensed with under rule 49.

70 Applicant to notify other persons of an application

(1) As soon as practicable and in any event within 21 days of the date on which the application form was issued, the applicant must notify the persons specified in the relevant practice direction–

(a) that an application form has been issued;

(b) whether it relates to the exercise of the court's jurisdiction in relation to P's property and affairs, or his personal welfare, or to both; and

(c) of the order or orders sought.

(2) Notification of the issue of the application form must be accompanied by a form for acknowledging notification.

(3) The applicant must file a certificate of notification within 7 days beginning with the date on which notification was given.

71 Requirements for certain applications

A practice direction may make additional or different provision in relation to specified applications.

Responding to an application

72 Responding to an application

(1) A person who is served with or notified of an application form and who wishes to take part in proceedings must file an acknowledgment of service or notification in accordance with this rule.

(2) The acknowledgment of service or notification must be filed not more than

21 days after the application form was served or notification of the application was given.

(3) The court will serve the acknowledgment of service or notification on the applicant and on any other person who has filed such an acknowledgment.

(4) The acknowledgment of service or notification must–
  (a) state whether the person acknowledging service or notification consents to the application;
  (b) state whether he opposes the application and, if so, set out the grounds for doing so;
  (c) state whether he seeks a different order from that set out in the application form and, if so, set out what that order is;
  (d) provide an address for service, which must be within the jurisdiction of the court; and
  (e) be signed by him or his legal representative.

(5) Subject to rules 120 and 123 (restriction on filing an expert's report and court's power to restrict expert evidence), where a person who has been served in accordance with rule 66, 67 or 68 opposes the application or seeks a different order, the acknowledgment of service must be accompanied by a witness statement containing any evidence upon which that person intends to rely.

(6) In addition to complying with the other requirements of this rule, an acknowledgment of notification filed by a person notified of the application in accordance with rule 67(5), 68(5), 69 or 70 must–
  (a) indicate whether the person wishes to be joined as a party to the proceedings; and
  (b) state the person's interest in the proceedings.

(7) Subject to rules 120 and 123 (restriction on filing an expert's report and court's power to restrict expert evidence), where a person has been notified in accordance with rule 67(5), 68(5), 69, 70, the acknowledgment of notification must be accompanied by a witness statement containing any evidence of his interest in the proceedings and, if he opposes the application or seeks a different order, any evidence upon which he intends to rely.

(8) The court will consider whether to join a person mentioned in paragraph (6) as a party to the proceedings and, if it decides to do so, will make an order to that effect.

(9) Where a person who is notified in accordance with rule 67(5), 68(5), 69 or 70 complies with the requirements of this rule, he need not comply with the requirements of rule 75 (application to be joined as a party).

(10) Where a person has filed an acknowledgment of notification in accordance with rule 57 (acknowledgment of notification of permission application) he must still acknowledge service or notification of an issued application form in accordance with this rule.

(11) A practice direction may make provision about responding to applications.

The parties to the proceedings

73 Parties to the proceedings

(1) Unless the court otherwise directs, the parties to any proceedings are–
  (a) the applicant; and
  (b) any person who is named as a respondent in the application form and

who files an acknowledgment of service in respect of the application form.

(2) The court may order a person to be joined as a party if it considers that it is desirable to do so for the purpose of dealing with the application.

(3) The court may at any time direct that any person who is a party to the proceedings is to be removed as a party.

(4) Unless the court orders otherwise, P shall not be named as a respondent to any proceedings.

(5) A party to the proceedings is bound by any order or direction of the court made in the course of those proceedings.

74 Persons to be bound as if parties

(1) The persons mentioned in paragraph (2) shall be bound by any order made or directions given by the court in the same way that a party to the proceedings is so bound.

(2) The persons referred to in paragraph (1) are–

(a) P; and

(b) any person who has been served with or notified of an application form in accordance with these Rules.

75 Application to be joined as a party

(1) Any person with sufficient interest may apply to the court to be joined as a party to the proceedings.

(2) An application to be joined as a party must be made by filing an application notice in accordance with Part 10 which must–

(a) state the full name and address of the person seeking to be joined as a party to the proceedings;

(b) state his interest in the proceedings;

(c) state whether he consents to the application;

(d) state whether he opposes the application and, if so, set out the grounds for doing so;

(e) state whether he proposes that an order different from that set out in the application form should be made and, if so, set out what that order is;

(f) provide an address for service, which must be within the jurisdiction of the court; and

(g) be signed by him or his legal representative.

(3) Subject to rules 120 and 123 (restriction on filing an expert's report and court's power to restrict expert evidence), an application to be joined must be accompanied by–

(a) a witness statement containing evidence of his interest in the proceedings and, if he proposes that an order different from that set out in the application form should be made, the evidence on which he intends to rely; and

(b) a sufficient number of copies of the application notice to enable service of the application on every other party to the proceedings.

(4) The court will serve the application notice and any accompanying documents on all parties to the proceedings.

(5) The court will consider whether to join a person applying under this rule as a party to the proceedings and, if it decides to do so, will make an order to that effect.

76 Applications for removal as a party to proceedings

A person who wishes to be removed as a party to the proceedings must apply to the court for an order to that effect in accordance with Part 10.

Part 10: Applications within Proceedings

77 Types of applications for which the Part 10 procedure may be used

(1) The Part 10 procedure is the procedure set out in this Part.

(2) The Part 10 procedure may be used if the application is made by any person–

(a) in the course of existing proceedings; or

(b) as provided for in a rule or practice direction.

(3) The court may grant an interim remedy before an application form has been issued only if–

(a) the matter is urgent; or

(b) it is otherwise necessary to do so in the interests of justice.

(4) An application made during the course of existing proceedings includes an application made during appeal proceedings.

78 Application notice to be filed

(1) Subject to paragraph (5), the applicant must file an application notice to make an application under this Part.

(2) The applicant must, when he files the application notice, file the evidence upon which he relies (unless such evidence has already been filed).

(3) The court will issue the application notice and, if there is to be a hearing, give notice of the date on which the matter is to be heard by the court.

(4) Notice under paragraph (3) must be given to–

(a) the applicant;

(b) anyone who is named as a respondent in the application notice (if not otherwise a party to the proceedings);

(c) every party to the proceedings; and

(d) any other person, as the court may direct.

(5) An applicant may make an application under this Part without filing an application notice if–

(a) this is permitted by any rule or practice direction; or

(b) the court dispenses with the requirement for an application notice.

(6) If the applicant makes an application without giving notice, the evidence in support of the application must state why notice has not been given.

79 What an application notice must include

An application notice must state–

(a) what order or direction the applicant is seeking;

(b) briefly, the grounds on which the applicant is seeking the order or direction; and

(c) such other information as may be required by any rule or a practice direction.

80 Service of an application notice

(1) Subject to paragraphs (4) and (5), the applicant must serve a copy of the application notice on–

(a) anyone who is named as a respondent in the application notice (if not otherwise a party to the proceedings);

(b) every party to the proceedings; and

(c) any other person, as the court may direct,

as soon as practicable and in any event within 21 days of the date on which it was issued.

(2) The application notice must be accompanied by a copy of the evidence filed in support.

(3) The applicant must file a certificate of service within 7 days beginning with the date on which the documents were served.

(4) This rule does not require a copy of evidence to be served on a person upon whom it has already been served, but the applicant must in such a case give to that person notice of the evidence upon which he intends to rely.

(5) An application may be made without serving a copy of the application notice if this is permitted by–

(a) a rule;

(b) a practice direction; or

(c) the court.

81 Applications without notice

(1) This rule applies where the court has dealt with an application which was made without notice having been given to any person.

(2) Where the court makes an order, whether granting or dismissing the application, the applicant must, as soon as practicable or within such period as the court may direct, serve the documents mentioned in paragraph (3) on–

(a) anyone named as a respondent in the application notice (if not otherwise a party to the proceedings);

(b) every party to the proceedings; and

(c) any other person, as the court may direct.

(3) The documents referred to in paragraph (2) are–

(a) a copy of the application notice;

(b) the court's order; and

(c) any evidence filed in support of the application.

(Rule 89 provides for reconsideration of orders made without a hearing or without notice to a person.)

Interim remedies

82 Orders for interim remedies

(1) The court may grant the following interim remedies–

(a) an interim injunction;

(b) an interim declaration; or

(c) any other interim order it considers appropriate.

(2) Unless the court orders otherwise, a person on whom an application form is served under Part 9, or who is given notice of such an application, may not apply for an interim remedy before he has filed an acknowledgment of service or notification in accordance with Part 9.

(3) This rule does not limit any other power of the court to grant interim relief.

Part 10A: Deprivation of Liberty

82A The practice direction to this Part sets out procedure governing–
  (a) applications to the court for orders relating to the deprivation, or proposed deprivation, of liberty of P; and
  (b) proceedings (for example, relating to costs or appeals) connected with or consequent upon such applications.

Part 11: Human Rights

83 General

(1) A party who seeks to rely upon any provision of or right arising under the Human Rights Act 1998 ('the 1998 Act') or who seeks a remedy available under that Act must inform the court in the manner set out in the relevant practice direction specifying–
  (a) the Convention right (within the meaning of the 1998 Act) which it is alleged has been infringed and details of the alleged infringement; and
  (b) the remedy sought and whether this includes a declaration of incompatibility under section 4 of the 1998 Act.
(2) The court may not make a declaration of incompatibility unless 21 days' notice, or such other period of notice as the court directs, has been given to the Crown.
(3) Where notice has been given to the Crown, a Minister or other person permitted by the 1998 Act will be joined as a party on filing an application in accordance with rule 75 (application to be joined as a party).

Part 12: Dealing with Applications

84 Dealing with the application

(1) As soon as practicable after any application has been issued the court shall consider how to deal with it.
(2) The court may deal with an application or any part of an application at a hearing or without a hearing.
(3) In considering whether it is necessary to hold a hearing, the court shall, as appropriate, have regard to–
  (a) the nature of the proceedings and the orders sought;
  (b) whether the application is opposed by a person who appears to the court to have an interest in matters relating to P's best interests;
  (c) whether the application involves a substantial dispute of fact;
  (d) the complexity of the facts and the law;
  (e) any wider public interest in the proceedings;
  (f) the circumstances of P and of any party, in particular as to whether their rights would be adequately protected if a hearing were not held;
  (g) whether the parties agree that the court should dispose of the application without a hearing; and
  (h) any other matter specified in the relevant practice direction.
(4) Where the court considers that a hearing is necessary, it will–
  (a) give notice of the hearing date to the parties and to any other person it directs; and
  (b) state whether the hearing is for disposing of the matter or for directions.
(5) Where the court decides that it can deal with the matter without a hearing it

will do so and serve a copy of its order on the parties and on any other person it directs.

85 Directions

(1) The court may–
  (a) give directions in writing; or
  (b) set a date for a directions hearing; and
  (c) do anything else that may be set out in a practice direction.
(2) When giving directions, the court may do any of the following–
  (a) require a report under section 49 of the Act and give directions as to any such report;
  (b) give directions as to any requirements contained in these Rules or a practice direction for the giving of notification to any person or for that person to do anything in response to a notification;
  (c) if the court considers that P should be a party to the proceedings, give directions joining him as a party;
  (d) if P is joined as a party to proceedings, give directions as to the appointment of a litigation friend;
  (e) if the court considers that any other person or persons should be a party to the proceedings, give directions joining them as a party;
  (f) if the court considers that any party to the proceedings should not be a party, give directions for that person's removal as a party;
  (g) give directions for the management of the case and set a timetable for the steps to be taken between the giving of directions and the hearing;
  (h) subject to rule 86, give directions as to the type of judge who is to hear the case;
  (i) give directions as to whether the proceedings or any part of them are to be heard in public, or as to whether any particular person should be permitted to attend the hearing, or as to whether any publication of the proceedings is to be permitted;
  (j) give directions as to the disclosure of documents, service of witness statements and any expert evidence;
  (k) give directions as to the attendance of witnesses and as to whether, and the extent to which, cross-examination will be permitted at any hearing; and
  (l) give such other directions as the court thinks fit.
(3) The court may give directions at any time–
  (a) on its own initiative; or
  (b) on the application of a party.
(4) Subject to paragraphs (5) and (6) and unless these Rules or a practice direction provide otherwise or the court directs otherwise, the time specified by a rule or by the court for a person to do any act may be varied by the written agreement of the parties.
(5) A party must apply to the court if he wishes to vary –
  (a) the date the court has fixed for the final hearing; or
  (b) the period within which the final hearing is to take place.
(6) The time specified by a rule or practice direction or by the court may not be varied by the parties if the variation would make it necessary to vary the date

the court has fixed for any hearing or the period within which the final hearing is to take place.

Allocation of proceedings

86 Court's jurisdiction in certain kinds of case to be exercised by certain judges

(1) The court will consider whether the application is of a type specified in the relevant practice direction as being one which must be dealt with by–
  (a) the President;
  (b) the Vice-President; or
  (c) one of the other judges nominated by virtue of section 46(2)(a) to (c) of the Act.
(2) The practice direction made under this rule shall specify the categories of case which must be dealt with by a judge mentioned in paragraph (1).
(3) Applications in any matter other than those specified in the relevant practice direction may be dealt with by any judge.

Disputing the jurisdiction of the court

87 Procedure for disputing the court's jurisdiction

(1) A person who wishes to–
  (a) dispute the court's jurisdiction to hear an application; or
  (b) argue that the court should not exercise its jurisdiction,
  may apply to the court at any time for an order declaring that it has no such jurisdiction or should not exercise any jurisdiction that it may have.
(2) An application under this rule must be–
  (a) made by using the form specified in the relevant practice direction; and
  (b) supported by evidence.
(3) An order containing a declaration that the court has no jurisdiction or will not exercise its jurisdiction may also make further provision, including–
  (a) setting aside the application;
  (b) discharging any order made; and
  (c) staying the proceedings.

Participation in hearings

88 Participation in hearings

(1) The court may hear P on the question of whether or not an order should be made, whether or not he is a party to the proceedings.
(2) The court may proceed with a hearing in the absence of P if it considers that it would be appropriate to do so.
(3) A person other than P who is served with or notified of the application may only take part in a hearing if–
  (a) he files an acknowledgment in accordance with the Rules and is made a party to the proceedings; or
  (b) the court permits.

Reconsideration of court orders

89 Orders made without a hearing or without notice to any person

(1) This rule applies where the court makes an order–
  (a) without a hearing; or

(b) without notice to any person who is affected by it.

(2) Where this rule applies–

(a) P;

(b) any party to the proceedings; or

(c) any other person affected by the order,

may apply to the court for reconsideration of the order made.

(3) An application under paragraph (2) must be made–

(a) within 21 days of the order being served or such other period as the court may direct; and

(b) in accordance with Part 10.

(4) The court will–

(a) reconsider the order without directing a hearing; or

(b) fix a date for the matter to be heard, and notify all parties to the proceedings and such other persons as the court may direct, of that date.

(5) Where an application is made in accordance with this rule, the court may affirm, set aside or vary any order made.

(6) Reconsideration may be by any judge of the court–

(a) including the judge who made the decision in respect of which the reconsideration is sought; but

(b) may not be by a judge who is not a prescribed higher judge within the meaning of section 53(3) of the Act in relation to the first-mentioned judge.

(7) No application may be made seeking a reconsideration of a decision that has been made under paragraph (5).

(8) An appeal against a decision made under paragraph (5) may be made in accordance with Part 20 (appeals).

(9) Any order made without a hearing or without notice to any person, other than one made under paragraph (5), must contain a statement of the right to apply for a reconsideration of the decision in accordance with this rule.

(10) An application made under this rule may include a request that the court reconsider the matter at a hearing.

Part 13: Hearings

Private hearings

90 General rule–hearing to be in private

(1) The general rule is that a hearing is to be held in private.

(2) A private hearing is a hearing which only the following persons are entitled to attend–

(a) the parties;

(b) P (whether or not a party);

(c) any person acting in the proceedings as a litigation friend;

(d) any legal representative of a person specified in any of sub-paragraphs (a) to (c); and

(e) any court officer.

(3) In relation to a private hearing, the court may make an order–

(a) authorising any person, or class of persons, to attend the hearing or a part of it; or

(b) excluding any person, or class of persons, from attending the hearing or a part of it.

91 Court's general power to authorise publication of information about proceedings

(1) For the purposes of the law relating to contempt of court, information relating to proceedings held in private may be published where the court makes an order under paragraph (2).

(2) The court may make an order authorising–
   (a) the publication of such information relating to the proceedings as it may specify; or
   (b) the publication of the text or a summary of the whole or part of a judgment or order made by the court.

(3) Where the court makes an order under paragraph (2) it may do so on such terms as it thinks fit, and in particular may–
   (a) impose restrictions on the publication of the identity of–
      (i) any party;
      (ii) P (whether or not a party);
      (iii) any witness; or
      (iv) any other person;
   (b) prohibit the publication of any information that may lead to any such person being identified;
   (c) prohibit the further publication of any information relating to the proceedings from such date as the court may specify; or
   (d) impose such other restrictions on the publication of information relating to the proceedings as the court may specify.

Power to order a public hearing

92 Court's power to order that a hearing be held in public

(1) The court may make an order–
   (a) for a hearing to be held in public;
   (b) for a part of a hearing to be held in public; or
   (c) excluding any person, or class of persons, from attending a public hearing or a part of it.

(2) Where the court makes an order under paragraph (1), it may in the same order or by a subsequent order–
   (a) impose restrictions on the publication of the identity of–
      (i) any party;
      (ii) P (whether or not a party);
      (iii) any witness; or
      (iv) any other person;
   (b) prohibit the publication of any information that may lead to any such person being identified;
   (c) prohibit the further publication of any information relating to the proceedings from such date as the court may specify; or
   (d) impose such other restrictions on the publication of information relating to the proceedings as the court may specify.

Supplementary

93 Supplementary provisions relating to public or private hearings
(1) An order under rule 90, 91 or 92 may be made–
- (a) only where it appears to the court that there is good reason for making the order;
- (b) at any time; and
- (c) either on the court's own initiative or on an application made by any person in accordance with Part 10.

(2) A practice direction may make further provision in connection with–
- (a) private hearings;
- (b) public hearings; or
- (c) the publication of information about any proceedings.

Part 14: Admissions, Evidence and Depositions

Admissions

94 Making an admission
(1) Without prejudice to the ability to make an admission in any other way, a party may admit the truth of the whole or part of another party's case by giving notice in writing.

(2) The court may allow a party to amend or withdraw an admission.

Evidence

95 Power of court to control evidence
The court may–
- (a) control the evidence by giving directions as to–
  - (i) the issues on which it requires evidence;
  - (ii) the nature of the evidence which it requires to decide those issues; and
  - (iii) the way in which the evidence is to be placed before the court;
- (b) use its power under this rule to exclude evidence that would otherwise be admissible;
- (c) allow or limit cross-examination; and
- (d) admit such evidence, whether written or oral, as it thinks fit.

96 Evidence of witnesses–general rule
(1) The general rule is that any fact which needs to be proved by evidence of a witness is to be proved–
- (a) where there is a final hearing, by their oral evidence; or
- (b) at any other hearing, or if there is no hearing, by their evidence in writing.

(2) Where a witness is called to give oral evidence under paragraph (1)(a), his witness statement shall stand as his evidence in chief unless the court directs otherwise.

(3) A witness giving oral evidence at the final hearing may, if the court permits–
- (a) amplify his witness statement; and
- (b) give evidence in relation to new matters which have arisen since the witness statement was made.

(4) The court may so permit only if it considers that there is good reason not to confine the evidence of the witness to the contents of his witness statement.

(5) This rule is subject to–
  (a) any provision to the contrary in these Rules or elsewhere; or
  (b) any order or direction of the court.

97 Written evidence–general rule

A party may not rely upon written evidence unless–
  (a) it has been filed in accordance with these Rules or a practice direction;
  (b) it is expressly permitted by these Rules or a practice direction; or
  (c) the court gives permission.

98 Evidence by video link or other means

The court may allow a witness to give evidence through a video link or by other communication technology.

99 Service of witness statements for use at final hearing

(1) A witness statement is a written statement which contains the evidence which that person would be allowed to give orally.

(2) The court will give directions about the service of any witness statement that a party intends to rely upon at the final hearing.

(3) The court may give directions as to the order in which witness statements are to be served.

(Rules 11 and 100 require witness statements to be verified by a statement of truth.)

100 Form of witness statement

A witness statement must contain a statement of truth and comply with the requirements set out in the relevant practice direction.

101 Witness summaries

(1) A party who wishes to file a witness statement for use at final hearing, but is unable to do so, may apply, without notice, to be permitted to file a witness summary instead.

(2) A witness summary is a summary of–
  (a) the evidence, if known, which would otherwise be included in a witness statement; or
  (b) if the evidence is not known, the matters about which the party filing the witness summary proposes to question the witness.

(3) Unless the court directs otherwise, a witness summary must include the name and address of the intended witness.

(4) Unless the court directs otherwise, a witness summary must be filed within the period in which a witness statement would have had to be filed.

(5) Where a party files a witness summary, so far as practicable, rules 96(3)(a) (amplifying witness statements) and 99 (service of witness statements for use at a final hearing) shall apply to the summary.

102 Affidavit evidence

Evidence must be given by affidavit instead of or in addition to a witness statement if this is required by the court, a provision contained in any rule, a practice direction or any other enactment.

103 Form of affidavit
An affidavit must comply with the requirements set out in the relevant practice direction.

104 Affidavit made outside the jurisdiction
A person may make an affidavit outside the jurisdiction in accordance with–
(a) this Part; or
(b) the law of the place where he makes the affidavit.

105 Notarial acts and instruments
A notarial act or instrument may, without further proof, be received in evidence as duly authenticated in accordance with the requirements of law unless the contrary is proved.

106 Summoning of witnesses
(1) The court may allow or direct any party to issue a witness summons requiring the person named in it to attend before the court and give oral evidence or produce any document to the court.
(2) An application by a party for the issue of a witness summons may be made by filing an application notice which includes–
    (a) the name and address of the applicant and of his solicitor, if any;
    (b) the name, address and occupation of the proposed witness;
    (c) particulars of any document which the proposed witness is to be required to produce; and
    (d) the grounds on which the application is made.
(3) The general rule is that a witness summons is binding if it is served at least 7 days before the date on which the witness is required to attend before the court, and the requirements of paragraph (6) have been complied with.
(4) The court may direct that a witness summons shall be binding although it will be served less than 7 days before the date on which the witness is required to attend before the court.
(5) Unless the court directs otherwise, a witness summons is to be served by the person making the application.
(6) At the time of service the witness must be offered or paid–
    (a) a sum reasonably sufficient to cover his expenses in travelling to and from the court; and
    (b) such sum by way of compensation for loss of time as may be specified in the relevant practice direction.
(7) The court may order that the witness is to be paid such general costs as it considers appropriate.

107 Power of court to direct a party to provide information
(1) Where a party has access to information which is not reasonably available to the other party, the court may direct that party to prepare and file a document recording the information.
(2) The court will give directions about serving a copy of that document on the other parties.

Depositions

108 Evidence by deposition

(1) A party may apply for an order for a person to be examined before the hearing takes place.

(2) A person from whom evidence is to be obtained following an order under this rule is referred to as a 'deponent' and the evidence is referred to as a 'deposition'.

(3) An order under this rule shall be for a deponent to be examined on oath before–

    (a) a circuit judge or a district judge, whether or not nominated as a judge of the court;

    (b) an examiner of the court; or

    (c) such other person as the court appoints.

(4) The order may require the production of any document which the court considers is necessary for the purposes of the examination.

(5) The order will state the date, time and place of the examination.

(6) At the time of service of the order, the deponent must be offered or paid–

    (a) a sum reasonably sufficient to cover his expenses in travelling to and from the place of examination; and

    (b) such sum by way of compensation for loss of time as may be specified in the relevant practice direction.

(7) Where the court makes an order for a deposition to be taken, it may also order the party who obtained the order to file a witness statement or witness summary in relation to the evidence to be given by the person to be examined.

109 Conduct of examination

(1) Subject to any directions contained in the order for examination, the examination must be conducted in the same way as if the witness were giving evidence at a final hearing.

(2) If all the parties are present, the examiner may conduct the examination of a person not named in the order for examination if all the parties and the person to be examined consent.

(3) The examiner must ensure that the evidence given by the witness is recorded in full.

(4) The examiner must send a copy of the deposition–

    (a) to the person who obtained the order for the examination of the witness; and

    (b) to the court.

(5) The court will give directions as to the service of a copy of the deposition on the other parties.

110 Fees and expenses of examiners of the court

(1) An examiner of the court may charge a fee for the examination and he need not send the deposition to the court until the fee is paid, unless the court directs otherwise.

(2) The examiner's fees and expenses must be paid by the party who obtained the order for examination.

(3) If the fees and expenses due to an examiner are not paid within a reasonable time, he may report that fact to the court.

(4) The court may order the party who obtained the order for examination to deposit in the court office a specified sum in respect of the examiner's fees and, where it does so, the examiner will not be asked to act until the sum has been deposited.

(5) An order under this rule does not affect any decision as to the person who is ultimately to bear the costs of the examination.

111 Examiners of the court

(1) The Lord Chancellor shall appoint persons to be examiners of the court.

(2) The persons appointed shall be barristers or solicitor-advocates who have been practising for a period of not less than 3 years.

(3) The Lord Chancellor may revoke an appointment at any time.

(4) In addition to appointing persons in accordance with this rule, examiners appointed under rule 34.15 of the Civil Procedure Rules 1998 may act as examiners in the court.

112 Enforcing attendance of a witness

(1) If a person served with an order to attend before an examiner–
   (a) fails to attend; or
   (b) refuses to be sworn for the purpose of the examination or to answer any lawful question or produce any document at the examination,
   a certificate of his failure or refusal, signed by the examiner, must be filed by the party requiring the deposition.

(2) On the certificate being filed, the party requiring the deposition may apply to the court for an order requiring that person to attend or to be sworn or to answer any question or produce any document, as the case may be.

(3) An application for an order under this rule may be made without notice.

(4) The court may order the person against whom an order is sought or made under this rule to pay any costs resulting from his failure or refusal.

113 Use of deposition at a hearing

(1) A deposition ordered under rule 108, 115 or 116 may be put in evidence at a hearing unless the court orders otherwise.

(2) A party intending to put a deposition in evidence at a hearing must file notice of his intention to do so on the court and serve the notice on every other party.

(3) Unless the court directs otherwise, he must file the notice at least 14 days before the day fixed for the hearing.

(4) The court may require a deponent to attend the hearing and give evidence orally.

Taking evidence outside the jurisdiction

114 Interpretation

In this Section–
   (a) 'Regulation State' has the same meaning as 'Member State' in the Taking of Evidence Regulation, that is all Member States except Denmark; and
   (b) 'the Taking of Evidence Regulation' means Council Regulation (EC) No 1206/2001 of 28 May 2001 on co-operation between the courts of Member States in the taking of evidence in civil and commercial matters.

115 Where a person to be examined is in another Regulation State

(1) This rule applies where a party wishes to take a deposition from a person who is–
    (a) outside the jurisdiction; and
    (b) in a Regulation State.

(2) The court may order the issue of the request to a designated court ('the requested court') in the Regulation State in which the proposed deponent is.

(3) If the court makes an order for the issue of a request, the party who sought the order must file–
    (a) a draft Form A as set out in the annex to the Taking of Evidence Regulation (request for the taking of evidence);
    (b) except where paragraph (4) applies, a translation of the form;
    (c) an undertaking to be responsible for the costs sought by the requested court in relation to–
        (i) fees paid to experts and interpreters; and
        (ii) where requested by that party, the use of special procedure or communications technology; and
    (d) an undertaking to be responsible for the court's expenses.

(4) There is no need to file a translation if–
    (a) English is one of the official languages of the Regulation State where the examination is to take place; or
    (b) the Regulation State has indicated, in accordance with the Taking of Evidence Regulation, that English is a language which it will accept.

(5) Where article 17 of the Taking of Evidence Regulation (direct taking of evidence by the requested court) allows evidence to be taken directly in another Regulation State, the court may make an order for the submission of a request in accordance with that article.

(6) If the court makes an order for the submission of a request under paragraph (5), the party who sought the order must file–
    (a) draft Form I as set out in the annex to the Taking of Evidence Regulation (request for direct taking of evidence);
    (b) except where paragraph (4) applies, a translation of the form; and
    (c) an undertaking to be responsible for the requested court's expenses.

116 Where a person to be examined is out of the jurisdiction–letter of request

(1) This rule applies where a party wishes to take a deposition from a person who is–
    (a) out of the jurisdiction; and
    (b) not in a Regulation State within the meaning of rule 114.

(2) The court may order the issue of a letter of request to the judicial authorities of the country in which the proposed deponent is.

(3) A letter of request is a request to a judicial authority to take the evidence of that person, or arrange for it to be taken.

(4) If the government of a country permits a person appointed by the court to examine a person in that country, the court may make an order appointing a special examiner for that purpose.

(5) A person may be examined under this rule on oath or affirmation in

accordance with any procedure permitted in the country in which the examination is to take place.

(6) If the court makes an order for the issue of a letter of request, the party who sought the order must file–

    (a) the following documents and, except where paragraph (7) applies, a translation of them–

        (i) a draft letter of request;

        (ii) a statement of the issues relevant to the proceedings; and

        (iii) a list of questions or the subject matter of questions to be put to the person to be examined; and

    (b) an undertaking to be responsible for the Secretary of State's expenses.

(7) There is no need to file a translation if–

    (a) English is one of the official languages of the country where the examination is to take place; or

    (b) a practice direction has specified that country is a country where no translation is necessary.

Section 49 reports

117 Reports under section 49 of the Act

(1) This rule applies where the court requires a report to be made to it under section 49 of the Act.

(2) It is the duty of the person who is required to make the report to help the court on the matters within his expertise.

(3) Unless the court directs otherwise, the person making the report must–

    (a) contact or seek to interview such persons as he thinks appropriate or as the court directs;

    (b) to the extent that it is practicable and appropriate to do so, ascertain what P's wishes and feelings are, and the beliefs and values that would be likely to influence P if he had the capacity to make a decision in relation to the matter to which the application relates;

    (c) describe P's circumstances; and

    (d) address such other matters as are required in a practice direction or as the court may direct.

(4) The court will send a copy of the report to the parties and to such persons as the court may direct.

(5) Subject to paragraphs (6) and (7), the person who is required to make the report may examine and take copies of any document in the court records.

(6) The court may direct that the right to inspect documents under this rule does not apply in relation to such documents, or descriptions of documents, as the court may specify.

(7) The court may direct that any information is to be provided to the maker of the report on an edited basis.

118 Written questions to person making a report under section 49

(1) Where a report is made under section 49 the court may, on the application of any party, permit written questions relevant to the issues before the court to be put to the person by whom the report was made.

(2) The questions sought to be put to the maker of the report shall be submitted to the court, and the court may put them to the maker of the report with such

amendments (if any) as it thinks fit and the maker of the report shall give his replies in writing to the questions so put.

(3) The court will send a copy of the replies given by the maker of the report under this rule to the parties and to such other persons as the court may direct.

Part 15: Experts

119 References to expert

A reference to an expert in this Part–

(a) is to an expert who has been instructed to give or prepare evidence for the purpose of court proceedings; but

(b) does not include any person instructed to make a report under section 49 of the Act.

120 Restriction on filing an expert's report

(1) No person may file expert evidence unless the court or a practice direction permits, or if it is filed with the permission form or application form and is evidence–

(a) that P is a person who lacks capacity to make a decision or decisions in relation to the matter or matters to which the application relates;

(b) as to P's best interests; or

(c) that is required by any rule or practice direction to be filed with the permission form or application form.

(2) An applicant may only rely upon any expert evidence so filed in support of the permission form or application form to the extent and for the purposes that the court allows.

(Rule 64(a) requires the applicant to file any evidence upon which he wishes to rely with the application form and rule 54 requires certain documents to be filed with the application for permission form.)

121 Duty to restrict expert evidence

Expert evidence shall be restricted to that which is reasonably required to resolve the proceedings.

122 Experts–overriding duty to the court

It is the duty of the expert to help the court on the matters within his expertise.

123 Court's power to restrict expert evidence

(1) Subject to rule 120, no party may file or adduce expert evidence unless the court or a practice direction permits.

(2) When a party applies for a direction under this rule he must–

(a) identify the field in respect of which he wishes to rely upon expert evidence;

(b) where practicable, identify the expert in that field upon whose evidence he wishes to rely;

(c) provide any other material information about the expert; and

(d) provide a draft letter of instruction to the expert.

(3) Where a direction is given under this rule, the court shall specify the field or fields in respect of which the expert evidence is to be provided.

(4) The court may specify the person who is to provide the evidence referred to in paragraph (3).

(5) Where a direction is given under this rule for a party to call an expert or put in evidence an expert's report, the court shall give directions for the service of the report on the parties and on such other persons as the court may direct.

(6) The court may limit the amount of the expert's fees and expenses that the party who wishes to rely upon the expert may recover from any other party.

124 General requirement for expert evidence to be given in a written report
Expert evidence is to be given in a written report unless the court directs otherwise.

125 Written questions to experts

(1) A party may put written questions to–
(a) an expert instructed by another party; or
(b) a single joint expert appointed under rule 130,
about a report prepared by such person.

(2) Written questions under paragraph (1)–
(a) may be put once only;
(b) must be put within 28 days beginning with the date on which the expert's report was served; and
(c) must be for the purpose only of clarification of the report.

(3) Paragraph (2) does not apply in any case where–
(a) the court permits it to be done on a further occasion;
(b) the other party or parties agree; or
(c) any practice direction provides otherwise.

(4) An expert's answers to questions put in accordance with paragraph (1) shall be treated as part of the expert's report.

(5) Paragraph (6) applies where–
(a) a party has put a written question to an expert instructed by another party in accordance with this rule; and
(b) the expert does not answer that question.

(6) The court may make one or both of the following orders in relation to the party who instructed the expert–
(a) that the party may not rely upon the evidence of that expert; or
(b) that the party may not recover the fees and expenses of that expert, or part of them, from any other party.

(7) Unless the court otherwise directs, and subject to any final costs order that may be made, the instructing party is responsible for the payment of the expert's fees and expenses, including the expert's costs of answering questions put by any other party.

126 Contents of expert's report

(1) The court may give directions as to the matters to be covered in an expert's report.

(2) An expert's report must comply with the requirements set out in the relevant practice direction.

(3) At the end of an expert's report there must be a statement that–
(a) the expert understands his duty to the court; and
(b) he has complied with that duty.

(4) The expert's report must state the substance of all material instructions, whether written or oral, on the basis of which the report was written.

(5) The instructions to the expert shall not be privileged against disclosure.

127 Use by one party of expert's report disclosed by another

Where a party has disclosed an expert's report, any party may use that expert's report as evidence at any hearing in the proceedings.

128 Discussions between experts

(1) The court may, at any stage, direct a discussion between experts for the purpose of requiring the experts to–
  (a) identify and discuss the expert issues in the proceedings; and
  (b) where possible, reach an agreed opinion on those issues.

(2) The court may specify the issues which the experts must discuss.

(3) The court may direct that following a discussion between the experts they must prepare a statement for the court showing–
  (a) those issues on which they agree; and
  (b) those issues on which they disagree and a summary of their reasons for disagreeing.

(4) Unless the court otherwise directs, the content of the discussions between experts may be referred to at any hearing or at any stage in the proceedings.

129 Expert's right to ask court for directions

(1) An expert may file a written request for directions to assist him in carrying out his function as an expert.

(2) An expert must, unless the court directs otherwise, provide a copy of any proposed request for directions under paragraph (1)–
  (a) to the party instructing him, at least 7 days before he files the request; and
  (b) to all other parties, at least 4 days before he files it.

(3) The court, when it gives directions, may also direct that a party be served with a copy of the directions.

130 Court's power to direct that evidence is to be given by a single joint expert

(1) Where two or more parties wish to submit expert evidence on a particular issue, the court may direct that the evidence on that issue is to be given by one expert only.

(2) The parties wishing to submit the expert evidence are called 'the instructing parties'.

(3) Where the instructing parties cannot agree who should be the expert, the court may–
  (a) select the expert from a list prepared or identified by the instructing parties; or
  (b) direct the manner by which the expert is to be selected.

131 Instructions to a single joint expert

(1) Where the court gives a direction under rule 130 for a single joint expert to be used, each party may give instructions to the expert.

(2) Unless the court otherwise directs, when an instructing party gives instructions

to the expert he must, at the same time, send a copy of the instructions to the other instructing parties.

(3) The court may give directions about–

(a) the payment of the expert's fees and expenses; and

(b) any inspection, examination or experiments which the expert wishes to carry out.

(4) The court may, before an expert is instructed, limit the amount that can be paid by way of fees and expenses to the expert.

(5) Unless the court otherwise directs, and subject to any final costs order that may be made, the instructing parties are jointly and severally liable for the payment of the expert's fees and expenses.

Part 16: Disclosure

132 Meaning of disclosure

A party discloses a document by stating that the document exists or has existed.

133 General or specific disclosure

(1) The court may either on its own initiative or on the application of a party make an order to give general or specific disclosure.

(2) General disclosure requires a party to disclose–

(a) the documents on which he relies; and

(b) the documents which–

(i)   adversely affect his own case;

(ii) adversely affect another party's case; or

(iii) support another party's case.

(3) An order for specific disclosure is an order that a party must do one or more of the following things–

(a) disclose documents or classes of documents specified in the order;

(b) carry out a search to the extent stated in the order; or

(c) disclose any document located as a result of that search.

(4) A party's duty to disclose documents is limited to documents which are or have been in his control.

(5) For the purpose of paragraph (4) a party has or has had a document in his control if–

(a) it is or was in his physical possession;

(b) he has or has had possession of it; or

(c) he has or has had a right to inspect or take copies of it.

134 Procedure for general or specific disclosure

(1) This rule applies where the court makes an order under rule 133 to give general or specific disclosure.

(2) Each party must make, and serve on every other party, a list of documents to be disclosed.

(3) A copy of each list must be filed within 7 days of the date on which it is served.

(4) The list must identify the documents in a convenient order and manner and as concisely as possible.

(5) The list must indicate–

(a) the documents in respect of which the party claims a right or duty to with-hold inspection (see rule 138); and

(b) the documents that are no longer in his control, stating what has happened to them.

135 Ongoing duty of disclosure

(1) Where the court makes an order to give general or specific disclosure under rule 133, any party to whom the order applies is under a continuing duty to provide such disclosure as is required by the order until the proceedings are concluded.

(2) If a document to which the duty of disclosure imposed by paragraph (1) extends comes to a party's notice at any time during the proceedings, he must immediately notify every other party.

136 Right to inspect documents

(1) A party to whom a document has been disclosed has a right to inspect any document disclosed to him except where–

(a) the document is no longer in the control of the party who disclosed it; or

(b) the party disclosing the document has a right or duty to withhold inspection of it.

(2) The right to inspect disclosed documents extends to any document mentioned in–

(a) a document filed or served in the course of the proceedings by any other party; or

(b) correspondence sent by any other party.

137 Inspection and copying of documents

(1) Where a party has a right to inspect a document, he–

(a) must give the party who disclosed the document written notice of his wish to inspect it; and

(b) may request a copy of the document.

(2) Not more than 14 days after the date on which the party who disclosed the document received the notice under paragraph (1)(a), he must permit inspection of the document at a convenient place and time.

(3) Where a party has requested a copy of the document, the party who disclosed the document must supply him with a copy not more than 14 days after the date on which he received the request.

(4) For the purposes of paragraph (2), the party who disclosed the document must give reasonable notice of the time and place for inspection.

(5) For the purposes of paragraph (3), the party requesting a copy of the document is responsible for the payment of reasonable copying costs, subject to any final costs order that may be made.

138 Claim to withhold inspection or disclosure of document

(1) A party who wishes to claim that he has a right or duty to withhold inspection of a document, or part of a document, must state in writing–

(a) that he has such a right or duty; and

(b) the grounds on which he claims that right or duty.

(2) The statement must be made in the list in which the document is disclosed (see rule 134(2)).

(3) A party may, by filing an application notice in accordance with Part 10, apply

to the court to decide whether the claim made under paragraph (1) should be upheld.

139 Consequence of failure to disclose documents or permit inspection

A party may not rely upon any document which he fails to disclose or in respect of which he fails to permit inspection unless the court permits.

Part 17: Litigation Friend

140 Who may act as a litigation friend

(1) A person may act as a litigation friend on behalf of a person mentioned in paragraph (2) if he–

    (a) can fairly and competently conduct proceedings on behalf of that person; and

    (b) has no interests adverse to those of that person.

(2) The persons for whom a litigation friend may act are–

    (a) P;

    (b) a child; or

    (c) a protected party.

141 Requirement for a litigation friend

(1) Subject to rule 147, P (if a party to proceedings) must have a litigation friend.

(2) A protected party (if a party to the proceedings) must have a litigation friend.

(3) A child (if a party to proceedings) must have a litigation friend to conduct those proceedings on his behalf unless the court makes an order under paragraph (4).

(4) The court may make an order permitting the child to conduct proceedings without a litigation friend.

(5) An application for an order under paragraph (4)–

    (a) may be made by the child;

    (b) if the child already has a litigation friend, must be made on notice to the litigation friend; and

    (c) if the child has no litigation friend, may be made without notice.

(6) Where–

    (a) the court has made an order under paragraph (4); and

    (b) it subsequently appears to the court that it is desirable for a litigation friend to conduct the proceedings on behalf of the child,

the court may appoint a person to be the child's litigation friend.

142 Litigation friend without a court order

(1) This rule does not apply–

    (a) in relation to P;

    (b) where the court has appointed a person under rule 143 or 144; or

    (c) where the Official Solicitor is to act as litigation friend.

(2) A deputy with the power to conduct legal proceedings in the name of the protected party or on the protected party's behalf is entitled to be a litigation friend of the protected party in any proceedings to which his power relates.

(3) If no one has been appointed by the court, or in the case of a protected party,

there is no deputy with the power to conduct proceedings, a person who wishes to act as a litigation friend must–

(a) file a certificate of suitability stating that he satisfies the conditions specified in rule 140(1); and

(b) serve the certificate of suitability on–

    (i) the person on whom an application form is to be served in accordance with rule 32 (service on children and protected parties); and

    (ii) every other person who is a party to the proceedings.

(4) If the person referred to in paragraph (2) wishes to act as a litigation friend for the protected party, he must file and serve a copy of the court order which appointed him on those persons mentioned in paragraph (3)(b).

143 Litigation friend by court order

(1) The court may make an order appointing–

(a) the Official Solicitor; or

(b) some other person,

to act as a litigation friend.

(2) The court may act under paragraph (1)–

(a) either on its own initiative or on the application of any person; but

(b) only with the consent of the person to be appointed.

(3) An application for an order under paragraph (1) must be supported by evidence.

(4) The court may not appoint a litigation friend under this rule unless it is satisfied that the person to be appointed satisfies the conditions specified in rule 140(1).

(5) The court may at any stage of the proceedings give directions as to the appointment of a litigation friend.

144 Court's power to prevent a person from acting as litigation friend or to order change

(1) The court may either on its own initiative or on the application of any person–

(a) direct that a person may not act as a litigation friend;

(b) terminate a litigation friend's appointment; or

(c) appoint a new litigation friend in place of an existing one.

(2) An application for an order under paragraph (1) must be supported by evidence.

(3) The court may not appoint a litigation friend under this rule unless it is satisfied that the person to be appointed satisfies the conditions specified in rule 140(1).

145 Appointment of litigation friend by court order–supplementary

The applicant must serve a copy of an application for an order under rule 143 or 144 on–

(a) the person on whom an application form is to be served in accordance with rule 32 (service on children and protected parties);

(b) every other person who is a party to the proceedings;

(c) any person who is the litigation friend, or who is purporting to act as the litigation friend, when the application is made; and

(d) unless he is the applicant, the person who it is proposed should be the litigation friend,

as soon as practicable and in any event within 21 days of the date on which it was issued.

146   Procedure where appointment of litigation friend comes to an end—for a child or protected party

(1) This rule applies–
  (a) when a child reaches 18, provided he is neither–
    (i) P; nor
    (ii) a protected party; and
  (b) where a protected party ceases to be a person who lacks capacity to conduct the proceedings himself.
(2) Where paragraph (1)(a) applies, the litigation friend's appointment ends.
(3) Where paragraph (1)(b) applies, the litigation friend's appointment continues until it is brought to an end by a court order
(4) An application for an order under paragraph (3) may be made by–
  (a) the former protected party;
  (b) his litigation friend; or
  (c) any other person who is a party to the proceedings.
(5) The applicant must serve a copy of the application notice seeking an order under this rule on all parties to the proceedings as soon as practicable and in any event within 21 days of the date on which it was issued.
(6) Where paragraph (2) applies the child must serve notice on every other party–
  (a) stating that he has reached full age;
  (b) stating that the appointment of the litigation friend has ended; and
  (c) providing his address for service.
(7) Where paragraph (3) applies, the former protected party must provide his address for service to all other parties to the proceedings.

147   Procedure where appointment of litigation friend comes to an end—for P

(1) This rule applies where P ceases to be a person who lacks capacity to conduct the proceedings himself but continues to lack capacity in relation to the matter or matters to which the application relates.
(2) The litigation friend's appointment continues until it is brought to an end by a court order.
(3) An application for an order under paragraph (2) may be made by–
  (a) P;
  (b) his litigation friend; or
  (c) any other person who is a party to the proceedings.
(4) The applicant must serve a copy of the application notice seeking an order under this rule on all other parties to the proceedings as soon as practicable and in any event within 21 days of the date on which it was issued.
(5) Where the court makes an order under this rule, P must provide his address for service to all other parties to the proceedings.

148   Procedure where P ceases to lack capacity

(1) This rule applies where P ceases to lack capacity both to conduct the proceed-

ings himself and in relation to the matter or matters to which the application relates.

(2) The litigation friend's appointment continues until it is brought to an end by a court order.

(3) An application may be made by–
(a) P;
(b) his litigation friend; or
(c) any other person who is a party to the proceedings,
for the proceedings to come to an end.

(4) The applicant must serve a copy of the application notice seeking an order under this rule on all parties to the proceedings as soon as practicable and in any event within 21 days of the date on which it was issued.

149 Practice direction in relation to litigation friends
A practice direction may make additional or different provision in relation to litigation friends.

Part 18: Change of Solicitor

150 Change of solicitor
(1) This rule applies where a party to proceedings–
(a) for whom a solicitor is acting wants to change his solicitor or act in person; or
(b) after having conducted the proceedings in person, appoints a solicitor to act on his behalf (except where the solicitor is appointed only to act as an advocate for a hearing).

(2) The party proposing the change must–
(a) file a notice of the change with the court; and
(b) serve the notice of the change on every other party to the proceedings and, if there is one, on the solicitor who will cease to act.

(3) The notice must state the party's address for service.

(4) The notice filed at court must state that it has been served as required by paragraph (2)(b).

(5) Where there is a solicitor who will cease to act, he will continue to be considered the party's solicitor unless and until–
(a) the notice is filed and served in accordance with paragraphs (2), (3) and (4); or
(b) the court makes an order under rule 152 and the order is served in accordance with that rule.

151 Legally aided persons
(1) Where the certificate of any person ('A') who is a legally aided person is revoked or withdrawn–
(a) the solicitor who acted for A will cease to be the solicitor acting in the case as soon as his retainer is determined under regulation 24 or 41 of the Civil Legal Aid (Procedure) Regulations 2012; and
(b) if A wishes to continue and appoints a solicitor to act on his behalf, rule 150(2), (3) and (4) will apply as if A had previously conducted the application in person.

(2) In this rule, 'certificate' means a certificate issued under the Civil Legal Aid (Procedure) Regulations 2012.

152 Order that a solicitor has ceased to act

(1) A solicitor may apply for an order declaring that he has ceased to be the solicitor acting for a party.

(2) Where an application is made under this rule–

    (a) the solicitor must serve the application notice on the party for whom the solicitor is acting, unless the court directs otherwise; and

    (b) the application must be supported by evidence.

(3) Where the court makes an order that a solicitor has ceased to act, the solicitor must–

    (a) serve a copy of the order on every other party to the proceedings; and

    (b) file a certificate of service.

153 Removal of solicitor who has ceased to act on application of another party

(1) Where–

    (a) a solicitor who has acted for a party–

        (i) has died;

        (ii) has become bankrupt;

        (iii) has ceased to practice; or

        (iv) cannot be found; and

    (b) the party has not served a notice of a change of solicitor or notice of intention to act in person as required by rule 150,

    any other party may apply for an order declaring that the solicitor has ceased to be the solicitor acting for the other party in the case.

(2) Where an application is made under this rule, the applicant must serve the application on the party to whose solicitor the application relates, unless the court directs otherwise.

(3) Where the court makes an order under this rule–

    (a) the court will give directions about serving a copy of the order on every other party to the proceedings; and

    (b) where the order is served by a party, that party must file a certificate of service.

154 Practice direction relating to change of solicitor

A practice direction may make additional or different provision in relation to change of solicitor.

Part 19: Costs

155 Interpretation

(1) In this Part–

    (a) 'additional liability' means the percentage increase, the insurance premium, or the additional amount in respect of provision made by a membership organisation, as the case may be;

    (b) 'authorised court officer' means any officer of the Supreme Court Costs Office, whom the Lord Chancellor has authorised to assess costs;

    (c) 'costs' include fees, charges, disbursements, expenses, reimbursement permitted to a litigant in person, any additional liability incurred under a funding arrangement and any fee or reward charged by a lay representative for acting on behalf of a party in proceedings;

(d) 'costs judge' means a taxing Master of the Supreme Court;

(e) 'costs officer' means a costs judge or an authorised court officer;

(f) 'detailed assessment' means the procedure by which the amount of costs or remuneration is decided by a costs officer in accordance with Part 47 of the Civil Procedure Rules 1998 (which are applied to proceedings under these Rules, with modifications, by rule 160);

(g) 'fixed costs' are to be construed in accordance with the relevant practice direction;

(h) 'fund' includes any estate or property held for the benefit of any person or class of persons and any fund to which a trustee or personal representative is entitled in his capacity as such;

(i) 'funding arrangement' means an arrangement where a person has–

    (i) entered into a conditional fee agreement or a collective conditional fee agreement which provides for a success fee within the meaning of section 58(2) of the Courts and Legal Services Act 1990;

    (ii) taken out an insurance policy to which section 29 of the Access to Justice Act 1999 (recovery of insurance premiums by way of costs) applies; or

    (iii) made an agreement with a membership organisation to meet his legal costs;

(j) 'insurance premium' means a sum of money paid or payable for insurance against the risk of incurring a costs liability in the proceedings, taken out after the event that is the subject matter of the claim;

(k) 'membership organisation' means a body prescribed for the purposes of section 30 of the Access to Justice Act 1999 (recovery where body undertakes to meet costs liabilities);

(l) 'paying party' means a party liable to pay costs;

(m) 'percentage increase' means the percentage by which the amount of a legal representative's fee can be increased in accordance with a conditional fee agreement which provides for a success fee;

(n) 'receiving party' means a party entitled to be paid costs;

(o) 'summary assessment' means the procedure by which the court, when making an order about costs, orders payment of a sum of money instead of fixed costs or 'detailed assessment'.

(2) The costs to which the rules in this Part apply include–

(a) where the costs may be assessed by the court, costs payable by a client to his solicitor; and

(b) costs which are payable by one party to another party under the terms of a contract, where the court makes an order for an assessment of those costs.

(3) Where advocacy or litigation services are provided to a client under a conditional fee agreement, costs are recoverable under this Part notwithstanding that the client is liable to pay his legal representative's fees and expenses only to the extent that sums are recovered in respect of the proceedings, whether by way of costs or otherwise.

(4) In paragraph (3), the reference to a conditional fee agreement is to an agreement which satisfies all the conditions applicable to it by virtue of section 58 of the Courts and Legal Services Act 1990.

156 Property and affairs–the general rule
Where the proceedings concern P's property and affairs the general rule is that the costs of the proceedings or of that part of the proceedings that concerns P's property and affairs, shall be paid by P or charged to his estate.

157 Personal welfare–the general rule
Where the proceedings concern P's personal welfare the general rule is that there will be no order as to the costs of the proceedings or of that part of the proceedings that concerns P's personal welfare.

158 Apportioning costs–the general rule
Where the proceedings concern both property and affairs and personal welfare the court, insofar as practicable, will apportion the costs as between the respective issues.

159 Departing from the general rule
(1) The court may depart from rules 156 to 158 if the circumstances so justify, and in deciding whether departure is justified the court will have regard to all the circumstances, including–
   (a) the conduct of the parties;
   (b) whether a party has succeeded on part of his case, even if he has not been wholly successful; and
   (c) the role of any public body involved in the proceedings.
(2) The conduct of the parties includes–
   (a) conduct before, as well as during, the proceedings;
   (b) whether it was reasonable for a party to raise, pursue or contest a particular issue;
   (c) the manner in which a party has made or responded to an application or a particular issue; and
   (d) whether a party who has succeeded in his application or response to an application, in whole or in part, exaggerated any matter contained in his application or response.
(3) Without prejudice to rules 156 to 158 and the foregoing provisions of this rule, the court may permit a party to recover their fixed costs in accordance with the relevant practice direction.

160 Rules about costs in the Civil Procedure Rules to apply
(1) Subject to the provisions of these Rules, Parts 44, 47 and 48 of the Civil Procedure Rules 1998 ('the 1998 Rules') shall apply with the modifications in this rule and such other modifications as may be appropriate, to costs incurred in relation to proceedings under these Rules as they apply to costs incurred in relation to proceedings in the High Court.
(2) The provisions of Part 47 of the 1998 Rules shall apply with the modifications in this rule and such other modifications as may be appropriate, to a detailed assessment of the remuneration of a deputy under these Rules as they apply to a detailed assessment of costs in proceedings to which the 1998 Rules apply.
(3) Where the definitions in Part 43 (referred to in Parts 44, 47 and 48) of the 1998 Rules are different from the definitions in rule 155 of these Rules, the latter shall prevail.

(4) Rules 44.1, 44.3(1) to (5), 44.6, 44.7, 44.9, 44.10, 44.11. 44.12 and 44.12A of the 1998 Rules do not apply.
(5) In rule 44.17 of the 1998 Rules, the references to Parts 45 and 46 do not apply.
(6) In rule 47.3(1)(c) of the 1998 Rules, the words 'unless the costs are being assessed under rule 48.5 (costs where money is payable to a child or a patient)' are removed.
(7) In rule 47.3(2) of the 1998 Rules, the words 'or a district judge' are removed.
(8) Rule 47.4(3) and (4) of the 1998 Rules do not apply.
(9) Rules 47.9(4), 47.10 and 47.11 of the 1998 Rules do not apply where the costs are to be paid by P or charged to his estate.
(10) Rules 48.2, 48.3, 48.6A, and 48.10 of the 1998 Rules do not apply.
(11) Rule 48.1(1) of the 1998 Rules is removed and is replaced by the following: 'This paragraph applies where a person applies for an order for specific disclosure before the commencement of proceedings'.

161 Detailed assessment of costs

(1) Where the court orders costs to be assessed by way of detailed assessment, the detailed assessment proceedings shall take place in the High Court.
(2) A fee is payable in respect of the detailed assessment of costs and on an appeal against a decision made in a detailed assessment of costs.
(3) Where a detailed assessment of costs has taken place, the amount payable by P is the amount which the court certifies as payable.

162 Employment of a solicitor by two or more persons

Where two or more persons having the same interest in relation to a matter act in relation to the proceedings by separate legal representatives, they shall not be permitted more than one set of costs of the representation unless and to the extent that the court certifies that the circumstances justify separate representation.

163 Costs of the Official Solicitor

Any costs incurred by the Official Solicitor in relation to proceedings under these Rules or in carrying out any directions given by the court and not provided for by remuneration under rule 167 shall be paid by such persons or out of such funds as the court may direct.

164 Procedure for assessing costs

Where the court orders a party, or P, to pay costs to another party it may either–
(a) make a summary assessment of the costs; or
(b) order a detailed assessment of the costs by a costs officer,
unless any rule, practice direction or other enactment provides otherwise.

165 Costs following P's death

An order or direction that costs incurred during P's lifetime be paid out of or charged on his estate may be made within 6 years after P's death.

166 Costs orders in favour of or against non-parties

(1) Where the court is considering whether to make a costs order in favour of or against a person who is not a party to proceedings–

(a) that person must be added as a party to the proceedings for the purposes of costs only; and

(b) he must be given a reasonable opportunity to attend a hearing at which the court will consider the matter further.

(2) This rule does not apply where the court is considering whether to make an order against the Legal Services Commission.

167 Remuneration of a deputy, donee or attorney

(1) Where the court orders that a deputy, donee or attorney is entitled to remuneration out of P's estate for discharging his functions as such, the court may make such order as it thinks fit, including an order that–

(a) he be paid a fixed amount;

(b) he be paid at a specified rate; or

(c) the amount of the remuneration shall be determined in accordance with the schedule of fees set out in the relevant practice direction.

(2) Any amount permitted by the court under paragraph (1) shall constitute a debt due from P's estate.

(3) The court may order a detailed assessment of the remuneration by a costs officer, in accordance with rule 164(b).

168 Practice direction as to costs

A practice direction may make further provision in respect of costs in proceedings.

Part 20: Appeals

169 Scope of this Part

This Part applies to an appeal against any decision of the court except where, in relation to those cases that are to be dealt with in accordance with Part 22 (transitory and transitional provisions), Part 22 makes different provision.

170 Interpretation

(1) In the following provisions of this Part–

(a) 'appeal judge' means a judge of the court to whom an appeal is made;

(b) 'first instance judge' means the judge of the court from whose decision an appeal is brought;

(c) 'appellant' means the person who brings or seeks to bring an appeal;

(d) 'respondent' means–

(i) a person other than the appellant who was a party to the proceedings before the first instance judge and who is affected by the appeal; or

(ii) a person who is permitted or directed by the first instance judge or the appeal judge to be a party to the appeal.

(2) In this Part, where the expression 'permission' is used it means 'permission to appeal' unless otherwise stated.

171 Dealing with appeals

(1) The court may deal with an appeal or any part of an appeal at a hearing or without a hearing.

(2) In considering whether it is necessary to hold a hearing, the court shall have regard to the matters set out in rule 84(3).

(Rule 89 provides for reconsideration of orders made without a hearing or without notice to a person.)

172 Permission to appeal

(1) Subject to paragraph (8), an appeal against a decision of the court may not be made without permission.

(2) Any person bound by an order of the court by virtue of rule 74 (persons to be bound as if parties) may seek permission to appeal under this Part.

(3) Permission is to be granted or refused in accordance with this Part.

(4) An application for permission to appeal may be made to the first instance judge or the appeal judge.

(5) Where an application for permission is refused by the first instance judge, a further application for permission may be made in accordance with paragraphs (6) and (7).

(6) Where the decision sought to be appealed is a decision of a district judge, permission may be granted or refused by–
   (a) the President;
   (b) the Vice-President;
   (c) one of the other judges nominated by virtue of section 46(2)(a) to (c) of the Act; or
   (d) a circuit judge.

(7) Where the decision sought to be appealed is a decision of a circuit judge, permission may only be granted or refused by one of the judges mentioned in paragraph (6)(a) to (c).

(8) Permission is not required to appeal against an order for committal to prison.

173 Matters to be taken into account when considering an application for permission

(1) Permission to appeal shall be granted only where–
   (a) the court considers that the appeal would have a real prospect of success; or
   (b) there is some other compelling reason why the appeal should be heard.

(2) An order giving permission may–
   (a) limit the issues to be heard; and
   (b) be made subject to conditions.

174 Parties to comply with the practice direction

All parties to an appeal must comply with any relevant practice direction.

175 Appellant's notice

(1) Where the appellant seeks permission from the appeal judge, it must be requested in the appellant's notice.

(2) The appellant must file an appellant's notice at the court within–
   (a) such period as may be directed or specified in the order of the first instance judge; or
   (b) where that judge makes no such direction or order, 21 days after the date of the decision being appealed.

(3) The court will issue the appellant's notice and unless it orders otherwise, the appellant must serve the appellant's notice on each respondent and on such

other persons as the court may direct, as soon as practicable and in any event within 21 days of the date on which it was issued.

(4) The appellant must file a certificate of service within 7 days beginning with the date on which he served the appellant's notice.

176 Respondent's notice

(1) A respondent who–
   (a) is seeking permission from the appeal judge to appeal; or
   (b) wishes to ask the appeal judge to uphold the order of the first instance judge for reasons different from or additional to those given by the first instance judge,
   must file a respondent's notice.

(2) Where the respondent seeks permission from the appeal judge, permission must be requested in the respondent's notice.

(3) A respondent's notice must be filed within–
   (a) such period as may be directed by the first instance judge; or
   (b) where the first instance judge makes no such direction, 21 days beginning with the date referred to in paragraph (4).

(4) The date is the soonest of–
   (a) the date on which the respondent is served with the appellant's notice where–
      (i) permission to appeal was given by the first instance judge; or
      (ii) permission to appeal is not required;
   (b) the date on which the respondent is served with notification that the appeal judge has given the appellant permission to appeal; or
   (c) the date on which the respondent is served with the notification that the application for permission to appeal and the appeal itself are to be heard together.

(5) The court will issue a respondent's notice and, unless it orders otherwise, the respondent must serve the respondent's notice on the appellant, any other respondent and on such other parties as the court may direct, as soon as practicable and in any event within 21 days of the date on which it was issued.

(6) The respondent must file a certificate of service within 7 days beginning with the date on which the copy of the respondent's notice was served.

177 Variation of time

(1) An application to vary the time limit for filing an appellant's or respondent's notice must be made to the appeal judge.

(2) The parties may not agree to extend any date or time limit for or in respect of an appeal set by–
   (a) these Rules;
   (b) the relevant practice direction; or
   (c) an order of the appeal judge or the first instance judge.

178 Power of appeal judge on appeal

(1) In relation to an appeal, an appeal judge has all the powers of the first instance judge whose decision is being appealed.

(2) In particular, the appeal judge has the power to–
   (a) affirm, set aside or vary any order made by the first instance judge;
   (b) refer any claim or issue to that judge for determination;

   (c) order a new hearing;

   (d) make a costs order.

(3) The appeal judge may exercise his powers in relation to the whole or part of an order made by the first instance judge.

179 Determination of appeals

(1) An appeal will be limited to a review of the decision of the first instance judge unless–

   (a) a practice direction makes different provision for a particular category of appeal; or

   (b) the appeal judge considers that in the circumstances of the appeal it would be in the interests of justice to hold a re-hearing.

(2) Unless he orders otherwise, the appeal judge will not receive–

   (a) oral evidence; or

   (b) evidence that was not before the first instance judge.

(3) The appeal judge will allow an appeal where the decision of the first instance judge was–

   (a) wrong; or

   (b) unjust, because of a serious procedural or other irregularity in the proceedings before the first instance judge.

(4) The appeal judge may draw any inference of fact that he considers justified on the evidence.

(5) At the hearing of the appeal a party may not rely upon a matter not contained in his appellant's or respondent's notice unless the appeal judge gives permission.

180 Allocation

Except in accordance with the relevant practice direction–

   (a) an appeal from a first instance decision of a circuit judge shall be heard by a judge of the court nominated by virtue of section 46(2)(a) to (c) of the Act; and

   (b) an appeal from a decision of a district judge shall be heard by a circuit judge.

Appeals to the Court of Appeal

181 Appeals against decision of a puisne judge of the High Court, etc

(1) Where the decision sought to be appealed is a decision of a judge nominated by virtue of section 46(2)(a) to (c) of the Act, an appeal will lie only to the Court of Appeal.

(2) The judge nominated by virtue of section 46(2)(a) to (c) of the Act may grant permission to appeal to the Court of Appeal in accordance with this Part, where the decision sought to be appealed was a decision made by a judge so nominated as a first instance judge.

182 Second appeals

(1) A decision of a judge of the court which was itself made on appeal from a judge of the court may only be appealed further to the Court of Appeal.

(2) Permission is required from the Court of Appeal for such an appeal.

(3) The Court of Appeal will not give permission unless it considers that–

   (a) the appeal would raise an important point of principle or practice; or

(b) there is some other compelling reason for the Court of Appeal to hear it.
(4) Nothing in this rule or in rule 181 applies to a second appeal from a decision of a nominated officer.

Part 21: Enforcement

183 Enforcement methods–general

(1) The rules in this Part make provision for the enforcement of judgments and orders.
(2) The relevant practice direction may set out methods of enforcing judgments or orders.
(3) An application for an order for enforcement may be made on application by any person in accordance with Part 10.

184 Application of the Civil Procedure Rules 1998 and RSC Orders

The following provisions apply, as far as they are relevant and with such modifications as may be necessary, to the enforcement of orders made in proceedings under these Rules–
(a) Parts 70 (General Rules about Enforcement of Judgments and Orders), 71 (Orders to Obtain Information from Judgment Debtors), 72 (Third Party Debt Orders) and 73 (Charging Orders, Stop Orders and Stop Notices) of the Civil Procedure Rules 1998; and
(b) Orders 45 (Enforcement of Judgments and Orders: General), 46 (Writs of Execution: General) and 47 (Writs of Fieri Facias) of the Rules of the Supreme Court.

Orders for committal

185 Contempt of court–generally

An application relating to the committal of a person for contempt of court shall be made to a judge and the power to punish for contempt may be exercised by an order of committal.

186 Application for order of committal

(1) An application for an order of committal must be made by filing an application notice, stating the grounds of the application, and must be supported by an affidavit made in accordance with the relevant practice direction.
(2) Subject to paragraph (3), the application notice, a copy of the affidavit in support thereof and notice of the date of the hearing of the application must be served personally on the person sought to be committed.
(3) Without prejudice to its powers under Part 6, the court may dispense with service under this rule if it thinks it just to do so.

187 Oral evidence

If on the hearing of the application the person sought to be committed expresses a wish to give oral evidence on his own behalf, he shall be entitled to do so.

188 Hearing for committal order

(1) Except where the court permits, no grounds shall be relied upon at the hearing except the grounds set out in the application notice.
(2) Notwithstanding rule 90(1) (general rule–hearing to be in private), when

determining an application for committal the court will hold the hearing in public unless it directs otherwise.

(3) If the court hearing an application in private decides that a person has committed a contempt of court, it shall state publicly–

(a) the name of that person;

(b) in general terms the nature of the contempt in respect of which the order of committal is being made; and

(c) any punishment imposed.

(4) If the person sought to be committed does not attend the hearing, the court may fix a date and time for the person to be brought before the court.

189 Power to suspend execution of committal order

(1) A judge who has made an order of committal may direct that the execution of the order of committal shall be suspended for such period or on such terms and conditions as may be specified.

(2) Where an order is suspended under paragraph (1), the applicant for the order of committal must, unless the court otherwise directs, serve on the person against whom it was made a notice informing him of the making and terms of the direction under that paragraph.

190 Warrant for arrest

A warrant for the arrest of a person against whom an order of committal has been made shall not, without further order of the court, be enforced more than 2 years after the date on which the warrant is issued.

191 Discharge of person committed

(1) The court may, on the application of any person committed to prison for contempt of court, discharge him.

(2) Where a person has been committed for failing to comply with a judgment or order requiring him to deliver any thing to some other person or to deposit it in court or elsewhere, and a writ of sequestration has also been issued to enforce that judgment or order, then, if the thing is in the custody or power of the person committed, the commissioners appointed by the writ of sequestration may take possession of it as if it were the property of that person and, without prejudice to the generality of paragraph (1), the court may discharge the person committed and may give such directions for dealing with the thing taken by the commissioners as it thinks fit.

192 Penal notices

(1) The court may direct that a penal notice is to be attached to any order warning the person on whom the copy of the order is served that disobeying the order would be a contempt of court punishable by imprisonment or a fine.

(2) Unless the court gives a direction under paragraph (1), a penal notice may not be attached to any order.

(3) A penal notice is to be in the following terms: 'You must obey this order. If you do not, you may be sent to prison for contempt of court.'.

193 Saving for other powers

The rules in this Part do not limit the power of the court to make an order requiring a person guilty of contempt to pay a fine or give security for his good behaviour and those rules, so far as applicable, shall apply in relation to an application for such an order as they apply in relation to an application for an order of committal.

194 Power of court to commit on its own initiative

The preceding provisions of these Rules shall not be taken as affecting the power of the court to make an order for committal on its own initiative against a person guilty of contempt of court.

Part 22: Transitory and Transitional Provisions

195 Transitory provision: applications by former receivers

(1) This rule and rule 196–
  (a) apply in any case where a person becomes a deputy by virtue of paragraph 1(2) of Schedule 5 to the Act; but
  (b) shall cease to have effect at the end of the period specified in the relevant practice direction.
(2) The deputy may make an application to the court in connection with–
  (a) any decision in connection with the day-to-day management of P's property and affairs; or
  (b) any supplementary decision which is necessary to give full effect to any order made, or directions given, before 1st October 2007 under Part 7 of the Mental Health Act 1983.
(3) Decisions within paragraph (2) include those that may be specified in the relevant practice direction.
(4) An application–
  (a) may relate only to a particular decision or decisions to be made on P's behalf;
  (b) must specify details of the decision or decisions to be made; and
  (c) must be made using the application form set out in the relevant practice direction.

196 Transitory provision: dealing with applications under rule 195

(1) The court may, in determining an application under rule 195, treat the application as if it were an application to vary the functions of the deputy which is made in accordance with the relevant practice direction made under rule 71, and dispose of it accordingly.
(2) In any other case, an application under rule 195 may be determined by an order made or directions given by–
  (a) the court; or
  (b) a person nominated under paragraph (3).
(3) The Senior Judge or the President may nominate an officer or officers of the court for the purpose of determining applications under rule 195.
(4) Where an officer has been nominated under paragraph (3) to determine an application, he may refer to a judge any proceedings or any question arising in any proceedings which ought, in the officer's opinion, to be considered by a judge.

197 Appeal against a decision of a nominated officer

(1) This rule applies in relation to decisions made under rules 195 and 196 by a nominated officer.

(2) An appeal from a decision to which this rule applies lies to a judge of the court nominated by virtue of section 46(2)(e) of the Act.

(3) No permission is required for an appeal under paragraph (2).

(4) A judge determining an appeal under paragraph (2) has all the powers that an appeal judge on appeal has by virtue of rule 178.

(5) An appeal from a decision made under paragraph (2) ('a second appeal') lies to a judge of the court nominated by virtue of section 46(2)(d) of the Act.

(6) A second appeal may be made from a decision of a nominated officer, and a judge to whom such an appeal is made may, if he considers the matter is one which ought to be heard by a judge of the court nominated by virtue of section 46(2)(a) to (c), transfer the matter to such a judge.

(7) An appeal from a decision made on a second appeal lies to the Court of Appeal.

198 Application of Rules to proceedings within paragraphs 3 and 12 of Schedule 5 to the Act

(1) In this rule, 'pending proceedings' means proceedings on an application within paragraph 3 or 12 of Schedule 5 to the Act.

(2) A practice direction shall make provision for the extent to which these Rules shall apply to pending proceedings.

199 Practice direction

A practice direction may make additional or different provision in relation to transitory and transitional matters.

Part 23: Miscellaneous

200 Order or directions requiring a person to give security for discharge of functions

(1) This rule applies where the court makes an order or gives a direction–

    (a) conferring functions on any person (whether as deputy or otherwise); and

    (b) requiring him to give security for the discharge of those functions.

(2) The person on whom functions are conferred must give the security before he undertakes to discharge his functions, unless the court permits it to be given subsequently.

(3) Paragraphs (4) to (6) apply where the security is required to be given before any action can be taken.

(4) Subject to paragraph (5), the security must be given in accordance with the requirements of regulation 33(2)(a) of the Public Guardian Regulations (which makes provision about the giving of security by means of a bond that is endorsed by an authorised insurance company or deposit-taker).

(5) The court may impose such other requirements in relation to the giving of the security as it considers appropriate (whether in addition to, or instead of, those specified in paragraph (4)).

(6) In specifying the date from which the order or directions referred to in paragraph (1) are to take effect, the court will have regard to the need to postpone that date for such reasonable period as would enable the Public Guardian to be satisfied that–

    (a) if paragraph (4) applies, the requirements of regulation 34 of the Public Guardian Regulations have been met in relation to the security; and

(b) any other requirements imposed by the court under paragraph (5) have been met.

(7) 'The Public Guardian Regulations' means the Lasting Powers of Attorney, Enduring Powers of Attorney and Public Guardian Regulations 2007.

201 Objections to registration of an enduring power of attorney: request for directions

(1) This rule applies in any case where–
   (a) the Public Guardian (having received a notice of objection to the registration of an instrument creating an enduring power of attorney) is prevented by paragraph 13(5) of Schedule 4 to the Act from registering the instrument except in accordance with the court's directions; and
   (b) on or before the relevant day, no application for the court to give such directions has been made under Part 9 (how to start proceedings).

(2) In paragraph (1)(b) the relevant day is the later of–
   (a) the final day of the period specified in paragraph 13(4) of Schedule 4 to the Act; or
   (b) the final day of the period of 14 days beginning with the date on which the Public Guardian receives the notice of objection.

(3) The Public Guardian may seek the court's directions about registering the instrument by filing a request in accordance with the relevant practice direction.

(4) As soon as practicable and in any event within 21 days of the date on which the request was made, the court will notify–
   (a) the person (or persons) who gave the notice of objection; and
   (b) the attorney or, if more than one, each of them.

(5) As soon as practicable and in any event within 21 days of the date on which the request is filed, the Public Guardian must notify the donor of the power that the request has been so filed.

(6) The notice under paragraph (4) must–
   (a) state that the Public Guardian has requested the court's directions about registration;
   (b) state that the court will give directions in response to the request unless an application under Part 9 is made to it before the end of the period of 21 days commencing with the date on which the notice is issued; and
   (c) set out the steps required to make such an application.

(7) 'Notice of objection' means a notice of objection which is made in accordance with paragraph 13(4) of Schedule 4 to the Act.

202 Disposal of property where P ceases to lack capacity

(1) This rule applies where P ceases to lack capacity.

(2) In this rule, 'relevant property' means any property belonging to P and forming part of his estate, and which–
   (a) remains under the control of anyone appointed by order of the court; or
   (b) is held under the direction of the court.

(3) The court may at any time make an order for any relevant property to be transferred to P, or at P's direction, provided that it is satisfied that P has the capacity to make decisions in relation to that property.

(4) An application for an order under this rule is to be made in accordance with Part 10.

MENTAL CAPACITY ACT 2005 (TRANSFER OF PROCEEDINGS) ORDER 2007
SI No 1899

Citation and commencement

1 (1) This Order may be cited as the Mental Capacity Act 2005 (Transfer of Proceedings) Order 2007.

(2) This Order shall come into force on 1st October 2007.

(3) In this Order 'the Children Act' means the Children Act 1989.

Transfers from the Court of Protection to a court having jurisdiction under the Children Act

2 (1) This article applies to any proceedings in the Court of Protection which relate to a person under 18.

(2) The Court of Protection may direct the transfer of the whole or part of the proceedings to a court having jurisdiction under the Children Act where it considers that in all the circumstances, it is just and convenient to transfer the proceedings.

(3) In making a determination, the Court of Protection must have regard to–

   (a) whether the proceedings should be heard together with other proceedings that are pending in a court having jurisdiction under the Children Act;

   (b) whether any order that may be made by a court having jurisdiction under that Act is likely to be a more appropriate way of dealing with the proceedings;

   (c) the need to meet any requirements that would apply if the proceedings had been started in a court having jurisdiction under the Children Act; and

   (d) any other matter that the court considers relevant.

(4) The Court of Protection–

   (a) may exercise the power to make an order under paragraph (2) on an application or on its own initiative; and

   (b) where it orders a transfer, must give reasons for its decision.

(5) Any proceedings transferred under this article–

   (a) are to be treated for all purposes as if they were proceedings under the Children Act which had been started in a court having jurisdiction under that Act; and

   (b) are to be dealt with after the transfer in accordance with directions given by a court having jurisdiction under that Act.

Transfers from a court having jurisdiction under the Children Act to the Court of Protection

3 (1) This article applies to any proceedings in a court having jurisdiction under the Children Act which relate to a person under 18.

(2) A court having jurisdiction under the Children Act may direct the transfer of the whole or part of the proceedings to the Court of Protection where it considers that in all circumstances, it is just and convenient to transfer the proceedings.

(3) In making a determination, the court having jurisdiction under the Children Act must have regard to–

(a) whether the proceedings should be heard together with other proceedings that are pending in the Court of Protection;

(b) whether any order that may be made by the Court of Protection is likely to be a more appropriate way of dealing with the proceedings;

(c) the extent to which any order made as respects a person who lacks capacity is likely to continue to have effect when that person reaches 18; and

(d) any other matter that the court considers relevant.

(4) A court having jurisdiction under the Children Act–

(a) may exercise the power to make an order under paragraph (2) on an application or on its own initiative; and

(b) where it orders a transfer, must give reasons for its decision.

(5) Any proceedings transferred under this article–

(a) are to be treated for all purposes as if they were proceedings under the Mental Capacity Act 2005 which had been started in the Court of Protection; and

(b) are to be dealt with after the transfer in accordance with directions given by the Court of Protection.

Avoidance of double liability for fees

4   Any fee paid for the purpose of starting any proceedings that are transferred under article 2 or 3 is to be treated as if it were the fee that would have been payable if the proceedings had started in the court to which the transfer is made.

COURT OF PROTECTION FEES ORDER 2007
SI No 145 (as amended)²

Citation and commencement

1 This Order may be cited as the Court of Protection Fees Order 2007 and comes into force on 1 October 2007.

Interpretation

2 In this Order–

'the Act' means the Mental Capacity Act 2005;

'appellant' means the person who brings or seeks to bring an appeal;

'court' means the Court of Protection;

'P' means any person (other than a protected party) who lacks or, so far as consistent with the context, is alleged to lack capacity to make a decision or decisions in relation to any matter that is the subject of an application to the court and references to a person who lacks capacity are to be construed in accordance with the Act;

'protected party' means a party or an intended party (other than P or a child) who lacks capacity to conduct the proceedings;

'the Regulations' means the Lasting Powers of Attorney, Enduring Powers of Attorney and Public Guardian Regulations 2007; and

'the Rules' means the Court of Protection Rules 2007.

Schedule of fees

3 The fees set out in Schedule 1 to this Order shall apply in accordance with the following provisions of this Order.

Application fee

4 (1) An application fee shall be payable by the applicant on making an application under Part 9 of the Rules (how to start proceedings) in accordance with the following provisions of this article.

(2) Where permission to start proceedings is required under Part 8 of the Rules (permission), the fee prescribed by paragraph (1) shall be payable on making an application for permission.

(3) The fee prescribed by paragraph (1) shall not be payable where the application is made under–

(a) rule 67 of the Rules (applications relating to lasting powers of attorney) by–

(i) the donee of a lasting power of attorney, or

(ii) a person named in a statement made by the donor of a lasting power of attorney in accordance with paragraph 2(1)(c)(i) of Part 1 of Schedule 1 to the Act,

and is solely in respect of an objection to the registration of a lasting power of attorney; or

(b) rule 68 of the Rules (applications relating to enduring powers of attorney) by–

(i) a donor of an enduring power of attorney,

(ii) an attorney under an enduring power of attorney, or

(iii) a person listed in paragraph 6(1) of Part 3 of Schedule 4 to the Act,

---

2 See also appendix G below.

and is solely in respect of an objection to the registration of an enduring power of attorney.

(4) The fee prescribed by paragraph (1) shall not be payable where the application is made by the Public Guardian.

(5) Where a fee has been paid under paragraph (1) it shall be refunded where P dies within five days of the application being filed.

Appeal fee

5 (1) An appeal fee shall be payable by the appellant on the filing of an appellant's notice under Part 20 of the Rules (appeals) in accordance with the following provisions of this article.

(2) The fee prescribed by paragraph (1) shall not be payable where the appeal is—

(a) brought by the Public Guardian; or

(b) an appeal against a decision of a nominated officer made under rule 197 of the Rules (appeal against a decision of a nominated officer).

(3) The fee prescribed by paragraph (1) shall be refunded where P dies within five days of the appellant's notice being filed.

Hearing fees

6 (1) A hearing fee shall be payable by the applicant where the court has—

(a) held a hearing in order to determine the case; and

(b) made a final order, declaration or decision.

(2) A hearing fee shall be payable by the appellant in relation to an appeal where the court has—

(a) held a hearing in order to determine the appeal; and

(b) made a final order, declaration or decision in relation to the appeal.

(3) The fees prescribed by paragraphs (1) and (2) shall not be payable where the hearing is in respect of an application or appeal brought by the Public Guardian.

(4) The fee prescribed by paragraph (2) shall not be payable where the hearing is in respect of an appeal against a decision of a nominated officer made under rule 197 of the Rules (appeal against a decision of a nominated officer).

(5) The fee prescribed by paragraph (1) shall not be payable where the applicant was not required to pay an application fee under Article 4(1) by virtue of Article 4(3).

(6) The fees prescribed by paragraphs (1) and (2) shall be payable by the applicant or appellant as the case may be within 30 days of the date of the invoice for the fee.

Fee for request for copy of court document

7 (1) A fee for a copy of a court document shall be payable by the person requesting the copy of the document.

(2) . . .

(3) The fee prescribed by paragraph (1) shall be payable at the time the request for the copy is made to the court.

Remissions and part remissions

8   Schedule 2 applies for the purpose of ascertaining whether a party is entitled to a remission or part remission of a fee prescribed by this Order.

9   . . .

Transitional provision

10 (1) In this article 'Court of Protection' means the office of the Supreme Court called the Court of Protection which ceases to exist under section 45(6) of the Act.

(2) Where a hearing that takes place on or after 1 October 2007 was listed by the Court of Protection before 1 October 2007, no hearing fee shall be payable under Article 6.

SCHEDULE 1

Article 3

Column 1	Column 2
Application fee (Article 4)	£400.00
Appeal fee (Article 5)	£400.00
Hearing fees (Article 6)	£500.00
Copy of a document fee (Article 7(1))	£5.00
. . .	. . .

SCHEDULE 2: REMISSIONS AND PART REMISSIONS

Interpretation

1 (1) In this Schedule–

'child' means a person–

(a) whose main residence is with a party and who is aged–

(i) under 16 years; or

(ii) 16 to 19 years; and is–

(aa) not married or in a civil partnership; and

(bb) enrolled or accepted in full-time education that is not advanced education, or approved training; or

(b) in respect of whom a party or their partner pays child support maintenance or periodic payments in accordance with a maintenance agreement,

and 'full-time education', 'advanced education' and 'approved training' have the meaning given by the Child Benefit (General) Regulations 2006;

'child support maintenance' has the meaning given in section 3(6) of the Child Support Act 1991;

'couple' has the meaning given in section 3(5A) of the Tax Credits Act 2002;

'disposable capital' has the meaning given in paragraph 5;

'excluded benefits' means any of the following–

(a) any of the following benefits payable under the Social Security Contributions and Benefits Act 1992 or the corresponding provisions of the Social Security Contributions and Benefits (Northern Ireland) Act 1992–

(i) attendance allowance under section 64;

(ii) severe disablement allowance;

(iii) carer's allowance;

(iv) disability living allowance;

(v) constant attendance allowance under section 104 as an increase to a disablement pension;

(vi) any payment made out of the social fund;

(vii)   housing benefit;

(viii) widowed parents allowance;

(b) any of the following benefit payable under the Tax Credits Act 2002–

(i)   any disabled child element or severely disabled child element of the child tax credit;

(ii) any childcare element of the working tax credit;

(c) any direct payment made under the Community Care, Services for Carers and Children's Services (Direct Payments) (England) Regulations 2009, the Community Care, Services for Carers and Children's Services (Direct Payments) (Wales) Regulations 2011, the Carers and Direct Payments Act (Northern Ireland) 2002, or section 12B(1) of the Social Work (Scotland) Act 1968;

(d) a back to work bonus payable under section 26 of the Jobseekers Act 1995, or article 28 of the Jobseekers (Northern Ireland) Order 1995;

(e) any exceptionally severe disablement allowance paid under the Personal Injuries (Civilians) Scheme 1983;

(f) any payments from the Industrial Injuries Disablement Benefit;

(g) any pension paid under the Naval, Military and Air Forces etc (Disablement and Death) Service Pension Order 2006;

(h) any payment made from the Independent Living Funds;

(i) any payment made from the Bereavement Allowance;

(j) any financial support paid under an agreement for the care of a foster child;

(k) any housing credit element of pension credit;

(l) any armed forces independence payment;

(m) any personal independence payment payable under the Welfare Reform Act 2012;

(n) any payment on account of benefit as defined in the Social Security (Payments on Account of Benefit) Regulations 2013;

(o) any of the following amounts, as defined by the Universal Credit Regulations 2013, that make up an award of universal credit–

(i)   an additional amount to the child element in respect of a disabled child;

(ii) a housing costs element;

(iii) a childcare costs element;

(iv) a carer element;

(v)   a limited capability for work or limited capacity for work and work -related activity element;

'family help (higher)' has the meaning given in paragraph 15(3) of the Civil Legal Aid (Merits Criteria) Regulations 2013;

'family help (lower)' has the meaning given in paragraph 15(2) of the Civil Legal Aid (Merits Criteria) Regulations 2013;

'gross monthly income' has the meaning given in paragraph 13;

'Independent Living Funds' means the funds listed at regulation 20(2)(b) of the Criminal Legal Aid (Financial Resources) Regulations 2013;

'legal representation' has the meaning given in paragraph 18(2) of the Civil Legal Aid (Merits Criteria) Regulations 2013;

'maintenance agreement' has the meaning given in subsection 9(1) of the Child Support Act 1991;

'partner' means a person with whom the party lives as a couple and includes a person with whom the party is not currently living but from whom the party is not living separate and apart;

'party' means the individual who would, but for this Schedule, be liable to pay a fee under this Order;

'restraint order' means–

(a) an order under section 42(1A) of the Senior Courts Act 1981;

(b) an order under section 33 of the Employment Tribunals Act 1996;

(c) a civil restraint order made under rule 3.11 of the Civil Procedure Rules 1998, or a practice direction made under that rule; or

(d) a civil restraint order under rule 4.8 of the Family Procedure Rules 2010, or the practice direction referred to in that rule.

(2) References to remission of a fee are to be read as including references to a part remission of a fee as appropriate and remit and remitted shall be construed accordingly.

Fee remission

2   If a party satisfies the disposable capital test, the amount of any fee remission is calculated by applying the gross monthly income test.

Disposable capital test

Disposable capital test

3 (1) Subject to paragraph 4, a party satisfies the disposable capital test if–

(a) the fee payable by the party and for which an application for remission is made, falls within a fee band set out in column 1 of Table 1; and

(b) the party's disposable capital is less than the amount in the corresponding row of column 2.

Table 1	
Column 1 (fee band)	*Column 2 (disposable capital)*
Up to and including £1,000	£3,000
£1,001 to £1,335	£4,000
£1,336 to £1,665	£5,000
£1,666 to £2,000	£6,000
£2,001 to £2,330	£7,000
£2,331 to £4,000	£8,000
£4,001 to £5,000	£10,000
£5,001 to £6,000	£12,000
£6,001 to £7,000	£14,000
£7,001 or more	£16,000

4   Subject to paragraph 14, if a party or their partner is aged 61 or over, that party satisfies the disposable capital test if that party's disposable capital is less than £16,000.

Disposable capital

5   Subject to paragraph 14, disposable capital is the value of every resource of

a capital nature belonging to the party on the date on which the application for remission is made, unless it is treated as income by this Order, or it is disregarded as excluded disposable capital.

Disposable capital–non-money resources

6   The value of a resource of a capital nature that does not consist of money is calculated as the amount which that resource would realise if sold, less–
(a) 10% of the sale value; and
(b) the amount of any borrowing secured against that resource that would be repayable on sale.

Disposable capital–resources held outside the United Kingdom

7 (1) Capital resources in a country outside the United Kingdom count towards disposable capital.
(2) If there is no prohibition in that country against the transfer of a resource into the United Kingdom, the value of that resource is the amount which that resource would realise if sold in that country, in accordance with paragraph 6.
(3) If there is a prohibition in that country against the transfer of a resource into the United Kingdom, the value of that resource is the amount that resource would realise if sold to a buyer in the United Kingdom.

Disposable capital–foreign currency resources

8   Where disposable capital is held in currency other than sterling, the cost of any banking charge or commission that would be payable if that amount were converted into sterling, is deducted from its value.

Disposable capital–jointly owned resources

9   Where any resource of a capital nature is owned jointly or in common, there is a presumption that the resource is owned in equal shares, unless evidence to the contrary is produced.

Excluded disposable capital

10   The following things are excluded disposable capital–
(a) a property which is the main or only dwelling occupied by the party;
(b) the household furniture and effects of the main or only dwelling occupied by the party;
(c) articles of personal clothing;
(d) any vehicle, the sale of which would leave the party, or their partner, without motor transport;
(e) tools and implements of trade, including vehicles used for business purposes;
(f) the capital value of the party's or their partner's business, where the party or their partner is self-employed;
(g) the capital value of any funds or other assets held in trust, where the party or their partner is a beneficiary without entitlement to advances of any trust capital;
(h) a jobseeker's back to work bonus;
(i) a payment made as a result of a determination of unfair dismissal by a court or tribunal, or by way of settlement of a claim for unfair dismissal;

(j) any compensation paid as a result of a determination of medical negligence or in respect of any personal injury by a court, or by way of settlement of a claim for medical negligence or personal injury;

(k) the capital held in any personal or occupational pension scheme;

(l) any cash value payable on surrender of a contract of insurance;

(m) any capital payment made out of the Independent Living Funds;

(n) any bereavement payment;

(o) any capital insurance or endowment lump sum payments that have been paid as a result of illness, disability or death;

(p) any student loan or student grant;

(q) any payments under the criminal injuries compensation scheme.

Gross monthly income test

Remission of fees–gross monthly income

11 (1) If a party satisfies the disposable capital test, no fee is payable under this Order if, at the time when the fee would otherwise be payable, the party or their partner has the number of children specified in column 1 of Table 2 and–

(a) if the party is single, their gross monthly income does not exceed the amount set out in the appropriate row of column 2; or

(b) if the party is one of a couple, the gross monthly income of that couple does not exceed the amount set out in the appropriate row of column 3.

Table 2		
Column 1	*Column 2*	*Column 3*
Number of children of party	*Single*	*Couple*
no children	£1,085	£1,245
1 child	£1,330	£1,490
2 children	£1,575	£1,735

(2) If a party or their partner has more than 2 children, the relevant amount of gross monthly income is the appropriate amount specified in Table 2 for 2 children, plus the sum of £245 for each additional child.

(3) For every £10 of gross monthly income received above the appropriate amount in Table 2, including any additional amount added under sub-paragraph (2), the party must pay £5 towards the fee payable, up to the maximum amount of the fee payable.

(4) This paragraph is subject to paragraph 12.

Gross monthly income cap

12 (1) No remission is available if a party or their partner has the number of children specified in column 1 of Table 3 and–

(a) if the party is single, their gross monthly income exceeds the amount set out in the appropriate row of column 2 of Table 3; or

(b) if the party is one of a couple, the gross monthly income of that couple exceeds the amount set out in the appropriate row of column 3 of Table 3.

Table 3		
Column 1	*Column 2*	*Column 3*
Number of children of party	*Single*	*Couple*
no children	£5,085	£5,245
1 child	£5,330	£5,490
2 children	£5,575	£5,735

(2) If a party or their partner has more than 2 children, the relevant amount of gross monthly income is the appropriate amount specified in Table 3 for 2 children, plus the sum of £245 for each additional child.

Gross monthly income

13 (1) Subject to paragraph 14, gross monthly income means the total monthly income, for the month preceding that in which the application for remission is made, from all sources, other than receipt of any of the excluded benefits.

(2) Income from a trade, business or gainful occupation other than an occupation at a wage or salary is calculated as–
(a) the profits which have accrued or will accrue to the party; and
(b) the drawings of the party;
in the month preceding that in which the application for remission is made.

(3) In calculating profits under sub-paragraph (2)(a), all sums necessarily expended to earn those profits are deducted.

General

Resources and income treated as the party's resources and income

14 (1) Subject to sub-paragraphs (2) to (5), the disposable capital and gross monthly income of a partner is to be treated as disposable capital and gross monthly income of the party.

(2) Where the partner of the party has a contrary interest to the party in the matter to which the fee relates, the disposable capital and gross monthly income of that partner is not treated as the disposable capital and gross monthly income of the party.

(3) Where proceedings are brought concerning the property and affairs of 'P', for the purpose of determining whether a party is entitled to a remission or part remission of a fee in accordance with this Schedule–
(a) the disposable capital and gross monthly income of the person bringing those proceedings is not treated as the disposable capital and gross monthly income of the party;
(b) the disposable capital and gross monthly income of 'P' is to be treated as the disposable capital of the party; and
(c) the disposable capital and gross monthly income of the partner of 'P', if any, is not treated as the disposable capital and gross monthly income of the party.

(4) Where proceedings are brought concerning the personal welfare of 'P', for the purpose of determining whether a party is entitled to a remission or part remission of a fee in accordance with this Schedule, the disposable capital and gross monthly income of a partner, if any, is not treated as the disposable

capital and gross monthly income of the party, where that partner is 'P' who is the subject of those proceedings in which the fee is payable.

(5) Where proceedings concern both the property and affairs of 'P' and their personal welfare, their disposable capital and gross monthly income shall be treated in accordance with sub-paragraph (3).

Application for remission of a fee

15 (1) An application for remission of a fee must be made at the time when the fee would otherwise be payable.

(2) Where an application for remission of a fee is made, the party must–
   (a) indicate the fee to which the application relates;
   (b) declare the amount of their disposable capital; and
   (c) provide documentary evidence of their gross monthly income and the number of children relevant for the purposes of paragraphs 11 and 12.

(3) Where an application for remission of a fee is made on or before the date on which a fee is payable, the date for payment of the fee is disapplied.

(4) Where an application for remission is refused, or if part remission of a fee is granted, the amount of the fee which remains unremitted must be paid within the period notified in writing to the party.

Remission in exceptional circumstances

16 A fee specified in this Order may be remitted where the Lord Chancellor is satisfied that there are exceptional circumstances which justify doing so.

Refunds

17 (1) Subject to sub-paragraph (3), where a party pays a fee at a time when that party would have been entitled to a remission if they had provided the documentary evidence required by paragraph 15, the fee, or the amount by which the fee would have been reduced as the case may be, must be refunded if documentary evidence relating to the time when the fee became payable is provided at a later date.

(2) Subject to sub-paragraph (3), where a fee has been paid at a time when the Lord Chancellor, if all the circumstances had been known, would have remitted the fee under paragraph 15, the fee or the amount by which the fee would have been reduced, as the case may be, must be refunded to the party.

(3) No refund shall be made under this paragraph unless the party who paid the fee applies within 3 months of the date of the order of the court which finally disposed of the proceedings.

(4) The Lord Chancellor may extend the period of 3 months mentioned in sub-paragraph (3) if the Lord Chancellor considers that there is a good reason for a refund being made after the end of the period of 3 months.

Legal aid

18 A party is not entitled to a fee remission if, under Part 1 of the Legal Aid, Sentencing and Punishment of Offenders Act 2012, they are in receipt of the following civil legal services–
   (a) Legal representation; or
   (b) Family help (higher); or
   (c) Family help (lower) in respect of applying for a consent order.

Vexatious litigants

19 (1) This paragraph applies where–

(a) a restraint order is in force against a party; and

(b) that party makes an application for permission to–

(i)   issue proceedings or take a step in proceedings as required by the restraint order;

(ii) apply for amendment or discharge of the order; or

(iii) appeal the order.

(2) The fee prescribed by this Order for the application is payable in full.

(3) If the party is granted permission, they are to be refunded the difference between–

(a) the fee paid; and

(b) the fee that would have been payable if this Schedule had been applied without reference to this paragraph.

Exceptions

20   No remissions or refunds are available in respect of the fee payable for–

(a) copy or duplicate documents;

(b) searches.

Precedents

1 Order for the appointment of a health and welfare deputy (single)

IN THE COURT OF PROTECTION   **Case No:**

IN THE MATTER OF THE MENTAL CAPACITY ACT 2005

In the matter of
[P's FULL NAME]

ORDER APPOINTING DEPUTY FOR HEALTH AND WELFARE

made by District Judge [   ]

at First Avenue House, 42–49 High Holborn, London, WC1V 6NP

on [   ]

UPON the court being satisfied that [P's full name] lacks capacity to make various decisions for himself in relation to a matter or matters concerning his personal welfare, and that the purpose for which this order is needed cannot be as effectively achieved in a way that is less restrictive of his rights and freedom of action.

IT IS ORDERED THAT:

1. **Appointment of deputies**
   (a) [Deputy's full name] of [Deputy's full address] is appointed as deputy ('the deputy') to make personal welfare decisions on behalf of [P's full name] that he is unable to make for himself, subject to any conditions or restrictions set out in this order.

   (b) The appointment will last until further order.

   (c) The deputy must apply the principles set out in section 1 of the Mental Capacity Act 2005 ('the Act') and have regard to the guidance in the Code of Practice to the Act.

2. **Authority of deputies**
   (a) The court authorises the deputy to make the following decisions on behalf of [P's full name] that he is unable to make for himself when the decision needs to be made :

   (i)   where he should live;
   (ii) with whom he should live;
   (iii) decisions on day-to-day care, including diet and dress;
   (iv) consenting to routine medical or dental examination and treatment on his behalf;
   (v)   making arrangements for the provision of care services;
   (vi) whether he should take part in particular leisure or social activities; and
   (vii) complaints about his care or treatment.

   (b) For the purpose of giving effect to any of these decisions the deputy may execute or sign any necessary deeds or documents.

(c) The deputy does not have authority to make a decision on behalf of [P's full name] in relation to a matter if the deputy knows or has reasonable grounds for believing that he has capacity in relation to the matter.

(d) The deputy does not have the authority to make the following decisions or do the following things in relation to [P's full name]:

    (i) to prohibit any person from having contact with him;

    (ii) to direct a person responsible for his health care to allow a different person to take over that responsibility; to make a decision that is inconsistent with a decision made, within the scope of his authority and in accordance with the Act, by the donee of a lasting power of attorney granted by him, or, if there is more than one donee, by any of them;

    (iii) to consent to specific treatment if he has made a valid and applicable advance decision to refuse that specific treatment;

    (iv) to refuse consent to the carrying out or continuation of life sustaining treatment in relation to him; and

    (v) to do an act that is intended to restrain him otherwise than in accordance with the conditions specified in the Act.

Reports

(a) The deputy is required to keep a record of any decisions made or acts done pursuant to this order and the reasons for making or doing them.

(b) The deputy must submit a report to the Public Guardian if and when required.

Service

(a) The requirement under Rule 48 of the Court of Protection Rules 2007 for the person effecting notification of the issue of this order to provide the court with a certificate of notification is dispensed with.

2 Order for the appointment of health and welfare deputies (joint, and joint and several)

IN THE COURT OF PROTECTION   **Case No:**

IN THE MATTER OF THE MENTAL CAPACITY ACT 2005

In the matter of
[P's FULL NAME]

ORDER APPOINTING JOINT [AND SEVERAL] DEPUTIES
FOR HEALTH AND WELFARE

made by District Judge [   ]

at First Avenue House, 42–49 High Holborn, London, WC1V 6NP

on [   ]

UPON the court being satisfied that [P's full name] lacks capacity to make various decisions for himself in relation to a matter or matters concerning his personal welfare, and that the purpose for which this order is needed cannot be as effectively achieved in a way that is less restrictive of his rights and freedom of action.

IT IS ORDERED THAT:

1. **Appointment of deputies**
   (a) [First Deputy's full name] of [First Deputy's full address] and [Second Deputy's full name] of [Second Deputy's full address] are appointed [jointly and severally] as deputies ('the deputies') to make personal welfare decisions on behalf of [P's full name] that he is unable to make for himself, subject to any conditions or restrictions set out in this order.

   (b) The appointment will last until further order.

   (c) The deputies must apply the principles set out in section 1 of the Mental Capacity Act 2005 ('the Act') and have regard to the guidance in the Code of Practice to the Act.

2. **Authority of deputies**
   (a) The court authorises the deputies to make the following decisions on behalf of [P's full name] that he is unable to make for himself when the decision needs to be made :
      (i) where he should live;
      (ii) with whom he should live;
      (iii) decisions on day-to-day care, including diet and dress;
      (iv) consenting to routine medical or dental examination and treatment on his behalf;
      (v) making arrangements for the provision of care services;
      (vi) whether he should take part in particular leisure or social activities; and
      (vii) complaints about his care or treatment.

(d) For the purpose of giving effect to any of these decisions the deputies may execute or sign any necessary deeds or documents.

(e) The deputies do not have authority to make a decision on behalf of [P's full name] in relation to a matter if the deputies know or have reasonable grounds for believing that he has capacity in relation to the matter.

(f) The deputies do not have the authority to make the following decisions or do the following things in relation to [P's full name]:

(i) to prohibit any person from having contact with him;

(ii) to direct a person responsible for his health care to allow a different person to take over that responsibility;to make a decision that is inconsistent with a decision made, within the scope of his authority and in accordance with the Act, by the donee of a lasting power of attorney granted by him, or, if there is more than one donee, by any of them;

(iii) to consent to specific treatment if he has made a valid and applicable advance decision to refuse that specific treatment;

(iv) to refuse consent to the carrying out or continuation of life sustaining treatment in relation to him; and

(v) to do an act that is intended to restrain him otherwise than in accordance with the conditions specified in the Act.

Reports

(a) The deputies are required to keep a record of any decisions made or acts done pursuant to this order and the reasons for making or doing them.

(b) The deputies must submit a report to the Public Guardian if and when required.

Service

(a) The requirement under Rule 48 of the Court of Protection Rules 2007 for the person effecting notification of the issue of this order to provide the court with a certificate of notification is dispensed with.

3 First directions order in welfare proceedings (made without a hearing)

IN THE COURT OF PROTECTION   Case No:

IN THE MATTER OF THE MENTAL CAPACITY ACT 2005

BETWEEN:

In the matter of
[P's FULL NAME]

ORDER AND DIRECTIONS

made by District Judge [   ]

at First Avenue House, 42–49 High Holborn, London, WC1V 6NP

on [   ]

WHEREAS

1) An application has been made by [   ] ('the Applicant') for orders under the Mental Capacity Act 2005 to determine the issues of [eg residence, care, contact].

2) It appears to the Court that the following issues arise as to [P]'s [capacity and best interests]:

   (a) [it can be very helpful to define the core issues in the case at the outset for the judge to consider when deciding what order to make by way of the first directions order]

IT IS DECLARED THAT:

3) Pursuant to section 48 of the Mental Capacity Act 2005, the Court has reason to believe that [P] lacks capacity to:

   (a) litigate

   (b) make decisions about [   ]

   (c) make decisions about [   ]

4) Pursuant to section 48 of the Mental Capacity Act 2005, and on the evidence before the Court, it is in [P]'s best interests to:

   (a) [eg reside at Y address]

   (b) [eg have contact with X, Y and Z]

IT IS ORDERED THAT:

1) Permission is granted pursuant to section 50(2) of the Mental Capacity Act 2005 to the Applicant to make this application.

2) The Official Solicitor is invited to act on behalf of [P] as litigation friend. If the Official Solicitor is currently unable to accept the invitation of the court to act as litigation friend the court will consider at the first hearing for directions who should be appointed to act as litigation friend for [P].

3) [X, Y and Z] are joined as parties.

4) The Applicant shall forthwith notify [A, B, C] of these proceedings, but they will be joined as a party only if he/she /they acknowledge[s] notification by filing form COP5 at the [regional] Court within 14 days of notification and indicates a wish to contest the proceedings.

5) [P] should be encouraged and assisted to participate in these proceedings by the parties insofar as he wishes and is able so to do.

6) These proceedings are to be in private. Nothing shall be published which identifies any party to these proceedings or may lead to the identification of any party or the residence of P.

7) The Applicant shall forthwith serve on each party and the Official Solicitor:

   (a) a copy of this order;

   (b) the application (form COP1, COP1B, COP2, COP3 and any witness statements filed)

   [The matter shall be transferred forthwith to the Regional Court sitting at [   ] County Court].[1]

8) The case shall be listed for a directions hearing and interim hearing on the first open date upon the direction of the nominated Judge with a time estimate of [   ].[2] The parties must attend at least 30 minutes before the hearing for final consultation.

9) The parties are encouraged to communicate with each other prior to the date of the first interim and directions hearing in order to identify and if possible narrow the issues to be decided by the court and to try to agree as far as possible the terms of the order that the parties will be asking the court to make.

10) Any statement which any party wishes to rely upon at the interim and directions hearing shall be filed at the regional court and served on all other parties no less than 3 working days before the first interim and directions hearing

11) The Applicant shall in compliance with Practice Direction 13B not less than 3 working days before the hearing file with the [Regional] Court and serve on the parties an indexed paginated case management bundle so far as the same has been obtained to date containing:

    (a) Applications and appendices;

    (b) Orders;

    (c) Witness evidence;

    (d) Medical evidence;

    (e) Other expert evidence;

    (f) Care plans

12) Not less than 2 working days before the directions hearing each party shall file with the court and serve on all other parties:

---

1 This can be at the request of the Applicant or on the court's own initiative.

2 It is usually sensible to suggest a time estimate of at least two hours for a first directions hearing.

(a) Position statements (which should succinctly on a single page identify the issues in the case and the party's stance on the issue);

(b) Drafts of any order or directions sought;

(c) Copies of any authorities relied on

13) No person shall disclose or publish any information in connection with these proceedings, including the text of the whole or any part of this order, save for the purpose of caring for [P] or for the purpose of communicating with a person exercising a relevant function authorised by statute or for the purpose of complying with an order of any court of competent jurisdiction.

14) Any person who is affected by this order may apply for reconsideration of the order within 21 days of the date on which this order was served by filing an application notice (form COP9) in accordance with Part 10 of the Court of Protection Rules 2007.

4 First directions order in welfare proceedings after attended hearing

IN THE COURT OF PROTECTION   Case No:

IN THE MATTER OF THE MENTAL CAPACITY ACT 2005

BETWEEN:

LA

Applicant

and

(1) PP
By his/her litigation friend, [the Official Solicitor]
(2) AA
(3) BB

Respondents

ORDER MADE AT HEARING ON [**]**[3]

made by District Judge [   ]

at First Avenue House, 42–49 High Holborn, London, WC1V 6NP

on [   ]

UPON hearing [counsel for the Applicant etc]

AND UPON the court having read [set out the documents that were brought to the judge's attention – included, in particular, any documents that are relevant to the question of funding of any expert reports for which permission is granted]

[**AND UPON** the [Party] conveying to the court its serious concern at the [X Local Authority's] conduct of these proceedings including its failure to comply with previous orders dated [   ] and reserving the right to make an application for costs and/or an application for the attendance of the [X Local Authority's] Head of Legal Services to attend future hearings in the event of further non-compliance.[4]]

AND UPON the court having made a separate order of even date concerning [disclosure from third parties]

AND UPON recording that the expert evidence provided for in this Order is reasonably required and necessary in order to resolve a significant issue in

---

3   This order is an compendious order setting out a substantial number of potential orders that may be made at the first directions hearing in a welfare case brought by a local authority – it would only be made at an attended hearing, and would not include all of the provisions. We are grateful to Michelle Pratley of Thirty Nine Essex Street for her assistance in the preparation of this draft order.

4   Where there has been non-compliance with previous orders.

these proceedings and to safeguard [P's full name]'s rights under Article[s 5 and[5]] 8 ECHR; and that the costs to be incurred in the preparation of such evidence are a wholly necessary, reasonable and proportionate disbursement on the funding certificate of [P]. Dr [Independent Psychiatrist]'s hourly rate of £[ ]and the estimated costs of his report are reasonable in the light of his qualifications, experience and expertise and in the light of the issues that arise in this case; Mrs [Independent Social Worker]'s hourly rate of £[ ] and the estimated costs of her report are reasonable in the light of his qualifications, experience and expertise and in the light of the issues that arise in this case;

IT IS DECLARED IN THE INTERIM PURSUANT TO SECTION 48 OF THE MENTAL CAPACITY ACT 2005, PENDING THE DETERMINATION OF THIS APPLICATION AND ON THE EVIDENCE BEFORE THE COURT THAT:

1. [P's full name] lacks the capacity to:

    (i)   litigate these proceedings;

    (ii)   decide where to live;

    (iii)   decide what care to receive;

    (iv)   decide what medication to take;

    (v)   decide what medical treatment to receive;

    (vi)   decide what contact to have with his/her family;

    (vii)   decide what contact to have with social and health care professionals;

    (viii) consent to or contract a marriage;

    (ix)   consent to sexual relations; and

    (x)   decide whether or not to use contraception.[6]

2. It is in the best interests of [P's full name] to reside at [   ] pursuant to arrangements made by the Applicant and set out in his/her care plan dated [   ].

3. It is in the best interests of [P's full name] to receive care at [   ] and have contact with social and health care professionals pursuant to arrangements made by the Applicant and set out in his/her care plan dated [   ].

4. It is in the best interests of [P's full name] to have contact with his/her family in accordance with Schedule 1.

IT IS ORDERED AND DIRECTED IN THE INTERIM PURSUANT TO SECTIONS 16 AND 48 OF THE MENTAL CAPACITY ACT 2005 AND AS A RELEVANT DECISION WITHIN THE MEANING OF SECTION 4A (3) AND (4) OF THE MENTAL CAPACITY ACT 2005 THAT:[7]

5. To the extent that the restrictions in place at [X care home] may be a deprivation

---

5   If the case involves a deprivation (or potential deprivation) of liberty.

6   Not all of these will apply in every case, but these are the most common declarations sought.

7   If questions of deprivation of liberty arise and the deprivation cannot be authorised by way of a standard authorisation under Schedule A1.

of [P's full name]'s liberty it shall be lawful and in [P's full name]'s best interests for no more than reasonable and proportionate force to be used for the least possible duration, and only if necessary, in order to ensure that [he/she] continues to reside there, and to return him/her in the event that [he/she] should leave of [his/her] own accord, or attend a planned activity in the community, and refuse to return.

6. The police may use reasonable and proportionate measures to return [P's full name] to [X care home].

7. The measures above shall be carried out in accordance with established protocols and the relevant care plans as dated [   ] periodically reviewed and updated by the Applicant, its employees or agents.

OR

IT IS ORDERED AND DIRECTED PURSUANT TO SECTIONS 4A(5), 21A(2)–(3) AND 48 OF THE MENTAL CAPACITY ACT 2005 THAT:

8. Pursuant to sections 4A(5), 21A(2)-(3) and 48 of the Mental Capacity Act 2005, the expiry date of the existing standard authorisation shall be varied from [   ] to [   ] and the applicant is excluded from any liability arising from the grant of that standard authorisation.[8]

OR

IT IS ORDERED AND DIRECTED PURSUANT TO SECTION 16 OF THE MENTAL CAPACITY ACT 2005 AND AS A RELEVANT DECISION WITHIN THE MEANING OF SECTION 4A (3) AND (4) OF THE MENTAL CAPACITY ACT 2005 THAT:[9]

9. To the extent that the arrangements [eg to transport P to X Care Home, including the possible use of oral sedation,] amount to a deprivation of liberty, it shall be lawful and in [P's full name]'s best interests for no more than reasonable and proportionate force to be used for the least possible duration, and only if necessary, in order to ensure that [eg. she is safely transported].

IT IS ORDERED THAT:

Permission

10. The Applicant is granted permission to bring these proceedings.

Parties

11. [P's full name] is joined as the First Respondent to these proceedings and the [Official Solicitor/   ], having consented, is appointed to act as his/her litigation friend.

12. [   ] is joined as the Second Respondent to these proceedings.

13. The parties to these proceedings are to be known as follows:

    (a) The Applicant: 'LA;'

---

8 This would apply where a standard authorisation was already in force, and the court exercised its power to extend the authorisation, following *Re UF* [2013] EWHC 4289 (COP).

9 This would apply where the authorisation is sought (and granted) for a single action that would amount to a deprivation of liberty.

(b) The First Respondent: 'PP;'

(c) The Second Respondent: 'AA.'

(d) The Third Respondent: 'BB.'

14. These proceedings shall be heard in private and no person shall publish or disclose any information to enable the identification of PP or any other party to these proceedings, save for the purpose of caring for PP or for the purpose of communicating with a person exercising a relevant function authorised by statute or for the purpose of complying with an order of any court of competent jurisdiction.

Section 49 reports

15. There shall be permission to the [party charged with responsibility] to obtain the following reports pursuant to section 49 of the Mental Capacity Act 2005. For the avoidance of doubt such reports are to be prepared in discharge of the relevant organisation's statutory functions and are not ordered as a private instruction for which experts' fees would be payable:

    (a) [A report from Dr ABC as to PP's psychiatric presentation and current and proposed treatment];

    (b) [A report from Dr DEF as to PP's neurological presentation and current and proposed treatment]; and

    (c) [A report from ABC CCG setting out the results of the review of PP's physical and mental health.]

16. The section 49 reports shall be sent to the [party] by 4:00pm on [   ]. The [party] shall file and serve a copy of the reports forthwith.

17. Any third party affected by paragraphs [15–16] shall have liberty to apply to the court to vary this paragraph of the order on three days' notice to the other parties.

Independent experts

18. The parties shall have permission jointly to instruct:

    (a) an independent expert consultant psychiatrist to report upon PP's capacity to decide upon [   ]; and

    (b) an independent expert social worker to report on upon PP's best interests with regard to [   ].

19. The Official Solicitor[10] shall send agreed letters of instruction to the experts by 4pm on [   ]. The Official Solicitor shall send drafts of the letters to the Applicant by midday on [   ] and shall consider any amendments to the letters of instruction suggested by the Applicant, if received by midday on [   ]. In the event of disagreement [the Applicant may send side letters to accompany the Official Solicitor's letters of instruction] [or] [the rival letters of instruction shall be sent, together with short written submissions, to the court for it to decide upon the content of the letter of instruction on the papers].

---

10 Or another litigation friend for P if the Official Solicitor has not been appointed. If the applicant in such a case is a public body, one would normally expect that the public body would take the lead in the instruction.

20. The experts' reports shall be provided to the Official Solicitor by 4pm on [   ] and the Official Solicitor shall forward them to the applicant forthwith.

21. The cost of the experts' reports shall be shared equally between the Applicant and PP. The proposed assessments, enquiries and reports (as set out in paragraph 5 of this order) are vital to the resolution of this case. The costs to be incurred in the preparation of such reports are wholly necessary, reasonable and proportionate disbursements on the funding certificates of PP. All invoices shall be settled within 28 days.[11]

22. The experts have permission to interview PP and be provided with and consider all documents disclosed in these proceedings including PP'ss records. The experts have permission to speak with any professionals and anyone else agreed between the parties regarding the matters upon which s/he is instructed to report. The independent expert social worker shall have permission to disclose information (the content and recipients of which shall be agreed in advance between the parties), about PP's circumstances in order to make necessary enquiries.

Evidence [residence, care and contact]

23. LA shall file and serve a statement by 4:00pm on [   ] addressing:

    (i)   the options available to the court in relation to PP's residence and care, including what placements and/or packages of care it is willing to fund;[12]

    (ii) whether or not it is willing to fund any alternative proposals for residence, care or contact proposed by any of the other parties;

    (iii) where it considers it is in PP's best interests to reside;

    (iv) the package of care it considers is in PP's best interests; and

    (v)   the frequency, duration and level of supervision for contact with PP's family it considers is in PP's best interests.

24. The other parties, with the exception of PP, file and serve a statement by 4:00pm on [   ] setting out:

    (i)   any alternatives for PP's residence, care and contact and how he/she proposes that any such alternatives should be funded;

    (ii) where he/she considers it is in PP's best interests to reside;

    (iii) the package of care that he/she considers is in PP's best interests; and

    (iv) the frequency, duration and level of supervision for contact with PP's family he/she considers is in PP's best interests.

25. PP's representatives shall, if so advised, file and serve a statement by 4:00pm on [   ].

---

11 This paragraph envisages that P is publicly funded. If not, then the provisions relating to the split of the costs and the settlement of the invoices would remain.

12 This is important so that the court is clear at quickly as possible what options are actually on the table: *A ACCG and another v MN and another* [2013] EWHC 3859 (COP) and *LBL v PB and P* [2011] EWHC 502 (COP), [2011] COPLR Con Vol 166.

Round-table meeting[13]

26. LA shall convene a round-table meeting between the parties to take place on the first available date in the week commencing [   ] at a venue to be agreed. The meeting shall consider [set out the areas for discussion].

27. The following directions shall apply to the round-table meeting:

(a) A draft agenda shall be circulated by LA at least five working days in advance of the meeting.

(b) The [independent social worker] shall attend the meeting, by telephone if not in person. The cost of and incidental to the attendance of the [independent social worker] at the round table meeting shall be shared [equally between LA, PP, and the other parties]. The reasonable costs to be incurred in the attendance of [the independent social worker] at the meeting are, in the opinion of the court, wholly necessary and proportionate disbursements on the funding certificates of the parties in receipt of public funding.

(c) LA shall use its best endeavours to arrange for relevant professionals involved in PP's social and health care to attend the meeting.

(d) LA shall arrange for a recording or a minute to be taken of the meeting and an agreed transcript or minute shall be filed no later than 10 days after the conclusion of the meeting.

(e) The costs of the attendance of legal representatives are in the opinion of the Court a wholly necessary and proportionate expense for the purpose of any party's public funding certificate.

Directions hearing

28. This matter shall be listed for a directions hearing before [   ] on [   ]/ on the first available date after [   ] with a time estimate of [   ] hours, at which time the declarations in respect of PP shall be reviewed and further case management directions will be made as necessary. The parties must attend at least 30 minutes before the hearing for final consultation. No hearing may be vacated save with the prior consent of a Judge of the Court of Protection.

29. The following directions shall apply to that directions hearing:

(i) LA shall send the other parties an updated index that is compliant with Practice Direction 13B together with paginated updates of any material to be added to the bundle by 4:00pm on [   ];

(ii) LA shall file an updated bundle that is compliant with Practice Direction 13B by 4:00pm on [   ];

(iii) LA shall file and serve a position statement by 4:00pm on [   ];

(iv) [the parties other than PP] shall file and serve their position statements by 4:00pm on [   ];

---

13 The court cannot order that such a meeting will take place, but as discussed in chapter 22, they can be a very useful tool.

(v) PP's representatives shall file serve a position statement by 4:00pm on [   ].

Fact finding hearing

30. This matter shall be listed for a fact-finding hearing before [   ] on [   ]/ on the first available date after [   ] with a time estimate of [   ] days. [   ] hours on [   ] shall be reserved for judicial reading time.

31. The following directions shall apply to that fact-finding hearing:

(i) LA shall file and serve a Scott Schedule setting out the specific findings of fact it seeks from the court, together with any further evidence in support of its case, by 4:00pm on [   ]. The Scott Schedule shall include a number for each finding that is sought, the page references for the evidence in support of each finding that is sought, a column for the [relevant party/parties] to respond, a column for any reply by LA, and a column to record the finding made by the court;

(ii) The [relevant party/parties] shall file and serve an updated version of the Scott Schedule, setting out its response to each finding that is sought, together with any further evidence in support of his/her case, by 4:00pm on [   ];

(iii) LA shall send the other parties an updated index that is compliant with Practice Direction 13B together with paginated updates of any material to be added to the bundle by 4:00pm on [   ];

(iv) LA shall send the other parties a draft witness list and witness template and a draft essential reading list by 4:00pm on [   ]. The other parties shall provide any comments by 4:00pm on [   ]. The LA shall file and serve a final version of the witness list, witness template and essential reading list by 4:00pm on [   ];

(v) LA shall file an updated bundle that is compliant with Practice Direction 13B by 4:00pm on [   ];

(vi) LA shall file and serve a position statement [and skeleton argument[14]] by 4:00pm on [   ];

(vii) [the parties other than PP] shall file and serve their position statements [and skeleton arguments[15]] by 4:00pm on [   ];

(viii) PP's representatives shall file serve a position statement [and skeleton argument[16]] by 4:00pm on [   ].

Final hearing

32. This matter shall be listed for a final hearing before [   ] on [   ]/on the first available date after [   ] with a time estimate of [   ] days. [   ] hours on [   ] shall be reserved for judicial reading time.

33. The following directions shall apply:

(i) LA shall send the other parties an updated index that is compliant with

14 This may be necessary if propositions of law are to be developed.
15 This may be necessary if propositions of law are to be developed.
16 This may be necessary if propositions of law are to be developed.

Practice Direction 13B together with paginated updates of any material to be added to the bundle by 4:00pm on [   ];

(ii) LA shall send the other parties a draft witness list and witness template and a draft essential reading list by 4:00pm on [   ]. The other parties shall provide any comments by 4:00pm on [   ]. The LA shall file and serve a final version of the witness list, witness template and essential reading list by 4:00pm on [   ];

(iii) LA shall file an updated bundle that is compliant with Practice Direction 13B by 4:00pm on [   ];

(iv) LA shall file and serve a position statement and skeleton argument[17] by 4:00pm on [   ];

(v) [the parties other than PP] shall file and serve their position statements and skeleton arguments by 4:00pm on [   ];

(vi) PP's representatives shall file serve a position statement and skeleton argument by 4:00pm on [   ].

Contact records[18]

34. LA shall arrange for a written record to be maintained of PP's contact with [AA and BB], recording the date the contact session took place, the time that the contact session began and ended, who attended and PP's presentation before, during and after the contact session. LA shall disclose a copy of the contact records to the parties on [eg the first Friday of each month].

Disclosure

35. LA shall disclose a copy of the [social services] records held in relation to PP from [   ] to date to PP's representatives by 4:00pm on [   ]. Thereafter LA shall disclose a copy of any updating [social services] records held in relation to PP on [e.g. the first Friday of each month].

36. PP's representatives shall provide the parties with a copy of any relevant documents obtained in these proceedings not already in their possession as soon as reasonably practicable and upon payment of their reasonable copying charges, save that PP's representatives may withhold relevant records from disclosure if they reasonably consider it is necessary to do so but shall provide the parties with a list of the relevant documents withheld on this basis.

37. LA has permission to disclose a copy of this order to [eg ABC Care Home].

Liberty to apply

38. Liberty to apply on [two days'] notice to the parties.

Costs

39. Costs reserved/No order as to costs save that there shall be detailed assessment of the costs of the parties in receipt of public funding from the Legal Aid Agency.

---

17 It would be usual for a skeleton argument to be prepared for a final hearing.
18 This would be needed if there are ongoing questions as to where P's best interests lie as regards contact.

SCHEDULE 1 – CONTACT ARRANGEMENTS FOR PP (EXAMPLE)

CONDITIONS OF CONTACT

1. The contact arrangements provided for in this schedule are conditional upon PP's wishes and feelings. In the event that PP communicates that [he/she] does not wish to attend a scheduled contact visit, or wishes to end a contact visit early, [his/her] wishes and feelings will be respected.

2. Contact shall take place in accordance with this schedule unless LA (or a member of the staff at ABC Care Home) determines that commencing or continuing a contact session is not in MN's best interests. Where LA (or a member of the staff at ABC Care Home) determines that commencing or continuing a contact session is not in MN's best interests, they shall inform AA and BB of the reason for this as soon reasonably practicable.

3. Where AA or BB are unable to attend a scheduled contact visit they shall endeavour to provide notice of this to ABC Care Home by telephone as soon as reasonably practicable.

4. AA and BB will be treated courteously and with respect by PP's carers at ABC Care Home and professionals involved in MN's care. AA and BB will also treat PP's carers and professionals involved in PP's care courteously and with respect.

CONTACT AT ABC CARE HOME

5. AA and BB may visit PP at ABC Care Home provided that:

   (i) AA and BB give at least 60 minutes' notice of an intended visit to ABC Care Home by telephoning and speaking to a member of staff;

   (ii) AA and BB and any other member of their family or any friend who attends the contact at ABC Care Home shall arrive no earlier than [XX.00am] and leave no later than [XX:00pm] to enable staff to prepare and complete the morning and night time routines of residents;

   (iii) The contact will take place at ABC Care Home unless it is agreed by a member of staff that it is in PP's best interests to go into the community with AA and BB. The duration, location and conditions of contact in the community are at the discretion of the staff at ABC Care Home;

   (iv) Staff at ABC Care Home will inform AA and BB of any change in PP's daily activities through either the Communication Book or in meetings; and

   (v) In the event that any requested contact with PP does not take place or is curtailed, AA and BB will be provided with an explanation of the reason why.

6. PP will be supported by a carer from ABC Care Home to ensure [his/her] care needs are met during contact with AA and BB but the visits will not be supervised.

CONTACT IN THE COMMUNITY

7. PP may have contact with AA and/or BB at such other venue as may be

agreed between LA and MM and FF if the LA considers this to be in PP's best interests. The frequency, duration, location and conditions of any contact in the community (including the attendance of staff from ABC Care Home and other residents from ABC Care Home) are at the discretion of the LA or the staff at ABC Care Home.

5 First directions order in a section 21A application

IN THE COURT OF PROTECTION   **Case No:**

IN THE MATTER OF THE MENTAL CAPACITY ACT 2005

BETWEEN:

[   ]

Applicant

and

[   ]

P and First Respondent

FIRST DIRECTIONS ORDER ON SECTION 21A APPLCIATION

made by District Judge [   ]

at First Avenue House, 42–49 High Holborn, London, WC1V 6NP

on [   ]

WHEREAS

1) [X Council] granted a standard authorisation for [   ] to be deprived of his liberty, until it expires on the [   ].

2) An application has been made by [   ] ('the Applicant') for an order under section 21A of the Mental Capacity Act 2005 to challenge the said standard authorisation.

IT IS ORDERED THAT:

3) Pursuant to sections 4A(5), 21A(2)-(3) and 48 Mental Capacity Act 2005, the expiry date of the existing standard authorisation shall be varied from [   ] to [   ] and the Applicant is excluded from any liability arising from the grant of that standard authorisation.[19]

4) [P's full name] is joined as a party and subject to his consent the Official Solicitor is appointed to act on [his/her] behalf as litigation friend. If the Official Solicitor is not in a position to be able immediately to accept the invitation of the court to act as litigation friend for [   ], the court will consider at the first hearing of the application the appointment of a suitable litigation friend to act on an interim basis.

5) The Applicant shall forthwith serve a copy of this order and of the application on (i) X Council; (ii) [relevant NHS bodies]; (iii) [any other relevant persons or bodies] who are joined as parties to these proceedings and who are to file form DLE Acknowledgment of Service within 7 days of service.

6) X Council is forthwith to file at court and serve on the parties (if they have not already done so) fully completed signed and dated copies of:

---

19 This follows the decision of Charles J in *Re UF* [2013] EWHC 4289 (COP).

i)   the standard authorisation

ii)   the age assessment

iii)   the no refusals assessment

iv)   the mental capacity assessment

v)   the mental health assessment

vi)   the eligibility assessment

vii)   the best interests assessment and

viii)   a copy of its current care plan or interim care plan in respect of the Applicant, together with copies of all previous urgent or standard authorisations made

7)   The case shall be listed for a directions and interim hearing on the first open date and within the next 14 days time estimate 2 hours at [First Avenue House]/[at the Regional Court of Protection sitting at [   ]. The parties must attend at least 30 minutes before the hearing for final consultation. No hearing may be vacated save with the prior consent of a Judge of the Court of Protection.

8)   Any statements of evidence that any party wishes to rely on at the initial hearing shall be filed at the regional court and served at least 3 days before the hearing. If oral evidence is to be given, the statements so served shall stand as evidence in chief.

9)   The Applicant shall not less than 2 working days before the directions hearing file with the regional court and serve on all other parties an indexed paginated case management bundle in accordance with Practice Direction 13B.

10)   Not less than 1 working day before the directions hearing each party shall file with the regional court and serve a position statement and draft of any order or directions sought.

11)   The parties are encouraged to communicate with each other prior to the date of the first interim and directions hearing in order to identify and if possible narrow the issues to be decided by the court and to try to agree as far as possible the terms of the order that the parties will be asking the court to make.

12)   No person shall disclose or publish any information in connection with these proceedings, including the text of the whole or any part of this order, save for the purpose of caring for [P's full name] or for the purpose of communicating with a person exercising a relevant function authorised by statute or for the purpose of complying with an order of any court of competent jurisdiction.

13)   Any person who is affected by this order may apply for reconsideration of the order within 21 days of the date on which this order was served by filing an application notice (form COP9) in accordance with Part 10 of the Court of Protection Rules 2007.

6 Order for the funding of a litigation friend for P

IN THE COURT OF PROTECTION   Case No:

IN THE MATTER OF THE MENTAL CAPACITY ACT 2005

BETWEEN:

[   ]

Applicant

and

[   ]

P and First Respondent

ORDER FOR FUNDING ARRANGEMENTS IN RESPECT OF OFFICIAL SOLICITOR[20]

made by District Judge [   ]

at First Avenue House, 42–49 High Holborn, London, WC1V 6NP

on [   ]

IT IS ORDERED THAT:

1) The Official Solicitor to the Senior Courts[21] [and local authority if appropriate are] [is] authorised to investigate the property and financial affairs of [P's full name and address] for the purposes of ensuring that the costs of [his/her] legal representation are provided to the Official Solicitor in these proceedings.

2) Any third party, including HM Revenue & Customs, is hereby directed and authorised to release to the Official Solicitor to the Senior Courts [and local authority if appropriate] such information and documents as he [they] may require on behalf of [P's full name] in the course of his [their] investigations within 7 days of any request.

3) In the event that [P's full name] is eligible for public funding (legal aid) the Official Solicitor is authorised in [his/her] name and on [his/her] behalf:

   a) to accept any offer of public funding made to [P's full name] by the Legal Services Commission;

   b) to sign the offer on [P's full name] behalf;

   c) to give any necessary notices of withdrawal (including establishing

---

20 These directions should form a separate single order to the main directions order as this order should be served on third parties who should not be informed of other aspects of the proceedings).

21 This order, suitably modified, can also be used where a litigation friend other than the Official Solicitor is appointed to act on P's behalf.

a standing order) to pay any public funding contributions from any amount standing to the credit of [P's full name] with any bank or building society;

4) In the event that [P's full name] is ineligible for public funding or to the extent that public funding does not cover the provision of legal services required by [P's full name], the costs of the Official Solicitor and of his solicitors of and incidental to the aforementioned proceedings are to be paid out of [P's full name]'s estate.

5) In the event [P's full name] has a Property and Affairs Deputy or Attorney then all invoices and fee notes/vouchers for disbursements on an interim basis shall be paid by [P's full name] s Deputy or Attorney within 28 days of receipt unless prior to such date the said Deputy/Attorney has applied to the court for directions in respect of the payment of the interim invoice/fee notes/vouchers for disbursement.

6) In the event [P's full name] does not have a Property and Affairs Deputy or Attorney then the Official Solicitor is authorised to give any necessary notices of withdrawal (including establishing a standing order) to pay solicitors' costs from any amount standing to the credit of [P's full name] with any bank of building society.

7) The Official Solicitor's costs to be assessed at the conclusion of the proceedings if not agreed.

7 Order for the provision of documents from a care home

IN THE COURT OF PROTECTION   Case No:

IN THE MATTER OF THE MENTAL CAPACITY ACT 2005

In the matter of
[P's FULL NAME]

ORDER FOR THE PROVISION OF DOCUMENTS

made by District Judge [   ]

at First Avenue House, 42–49 High Holborn, London, WC1V 6NP

on [   ]

[UPON HEARING   ][22]

IT IS ORDERED THAT:

1) By 4pm on 4 March 2014 the manager of [X Care Home, and address of the care home] shall provide to the Official Solicitor[23] its records relating to [P's full name].

2) Any person or organisation holding records concerning [P's full name] shall provide a copy of such records to the Official Solicitor, within 14 days of receiving any request from the Official Solicitor to do so.

3) The Official Solicitor shall serve a copy of this order forthwith upon the manager of X Care Home and shall have permission to serve a copy of this order on any person or organisation of whom a request under paragraph 2 is made.

4) The manager of X Care Home and any other person or organisation affected by this order shall have permission to apply, on notice to the Official Solicitor and the Applicant, to vary or discharge any relevant provision of this order.

5) No order as to costs.

---

22 If the order has been made following a hearing.
23 Or another litigation friend for P if the Official Solicitor has not been appointed.

8 Order for provision of documents by the police

IN THE COURT OF PROTECTION   **Case No:**

IN THE MATTER OF THE MENTAL CAPACITY ACT 2005

In the matter of
[P's FULL NAME]

ORDER FOR THE PROVISION OF DOCUMENTS FROM THE POLICE

made by District Judge [   ]

at First Avenue House, 42–49 High Holborn, London, WC1V 6NP

on [   ]

[UPON HEARING   ][24]

IT IS ORDERED THAT:

1) The [Chief Constable of [ABC Police]] is invited to in accordance with the local protocol[25]/shall provide the following information in respect of [P's full name and date of birth] to [P's full name]'s representatives within [ten] working days of receiving a copy of this order:

   (i)   The earliest date that it is anticipated that [XX] will be released and any subsequent revision of this date;[26]

   (ii)   The status of the charges in relation to the alleged assaults on P's full name;

   (iii) Any other investigations concerning [XX], including those that did not result in arrest or charge;

   (iv)   Confirmation of all convictions and non-convictions in relation to [XX];

   (v)   Details of arrests and charges – where, when and why – as well as recorded 'stop and search' incidents;

   (vi)   The age, gender, stature, defining features and extent of injury caused in respect of each victim of the offences for which [XX] has been convicted;

   (vii) Details of any sentences, including spent sentences and any applicable restrictions;

   (viii) Copies of any psychiatric/psychological reports prepared on [XX] prior to sentence or pre-sentencing reports where applicable/available.][27]

---

24 If the order has been made following a hearing.

25 Many police forces have in place a local protocol in relation to the disclosure of records in case involving children; this should be followed if possible. Such local protocols usually proceed on the basis that the police are invited to provide the documentation rather than being ordered.

26 This information would be sought so that the court can assess the risk posed by XX to P.

27 Not all of these will be applicable in every case.

2) The [Chief Constable of [ABC Police]] is also invited to in accordance with the local protocol/shall also provide within [ten] working days all documents held in relation to [P's full name], date of birth [   ], whose current address is:

[   ]

and whose previous addresses were

[   ]

and

[   ][28]

Liberty to apply

3) Any party affected by this order shall have liberty to apply to the court to vary this order on [e.g. three days'] notice to the other parties.

Costs

4) No order as to costs.

---

28 This provision would be used, for instance, where the records held by the police upon P are required.

9 Order for the instruction of experts

IN THE COURT OF PROTECTION   **Case No:**

IN THE MATTER OF THE MENTAL CAPACITY ACT 2005

BETWEEN:

[   ]

Applicant

and

[   ]

P and First Respondent

and

ORDER FOR THE JOINT INSTRUCTION OF EXPERTS[29]

made by District Judge [   ]

at First Avenue House, 42–49 High Holborn, London, WC1V 6NP

on [   ]

[UPON HEARING   ][30]

AND UPON recording that the expert evidence provided for in this Order is reasonably required and necessary in order to resolve a significant issue in these proceedings and to safeguard [P]'s rights under Article[s 5 and[31]] 8 ECHR; and that the costs to be incurred in the preparation of such evidence are a wholly necessary, reasonable and proportionate disbursement on the funding certificate of [P].

IT IS ORDERED THAT:

1) The parties shall have permission jointly to instruct:

   (a) an independent expert consultant psychiatrist to report upon [P]'s capacity to decide upon [   ]; and

   (b) an independent expert social worker to report on upon [P]'s best interests with regard to [   ].

---

29 Such an order would usually be included in a more wide-ranging directions order, most usually that made after the first attended directions hearing: see precedent 4 above.

30 If the order has been made following a hearing.

31 If the case involves a deprivation (or potential deprivation) of liberty.

2) The Official Solicitor[32] shall send agreed letters of instruction to the experts by 4pm on [   ]. The Official Solicitor shall send drafts of the letters to the Applicant by midday on [   ] and shall consider any amendments to the letters of instruction suggested by the Applicant, if received by midday on [   ]. In the event of disagreement [the Applicant may send side letters to accompany the Official Solicitor's letters of instruction] or [the rival letters of instruction shall be sent, together with short written submissions, to the court for it to decide upon the content of the letter of instruction on the papers].

3) The experts' reports shall be provided to the Official Solicitor by 4pm on [   ] and the Official Solicitor shall forward them to the applicant forthwith.

4) The cost of the experts' reports shall be shared equally between the Applicant and [P]. The proposed assessments, enquiries and reports (as set out in paragraph 5 of this order) are vital to the resolution of this case. The costs to be incurred in the preparation of such reports are wholly necessary, reasonable and proportionate disbursements on the funding certificates of [P]. All invoices shall be settled within 28 days.[33]

5) The experts have permission to interview [P] and be provided with and consider all documents disclosed in these proceedings including [P]'s records. The experts have permission to speak with any professionals and anyone else agreed between the parties regarding the matters upon which s/he is instructed to report. The independent expert social worker shall have permission to disclose information (the content and recipients of which shall be agreed in advance between the parties), about [P's] circumstances in order to make necessary enquiries.

6) No order as to costs.

32 Or another litigation friend for P if the Official Solicitor has not been appointed. If the applicant in such a case is a public body, one would normally expect that the public body would take the lead in the instruction.

33 This paragraph envisages that P is publicly funded. If not, then the provisions relating to the split of the costs and the settlement of the invoices would remain.

10 Injunction order

IN THE COURT OF PROTECTION   Case No:

IN THE MATTER OF THE MENTAL CAPACITY ACT 2005

BETWEEN:

LA

Applicant

and

(1) PP
By his/her litigation friend, [the Official Solicitor]
(2) AA
(3) BB

Respondents

ORDER MADE AT HEARING ON [   ]³⁴

IMPORTANT:

NOTICE TO THE [Relevant person to whom the injunction is addressed 'the Respondent']:
[Full name of the Respondent]

(1) This order prohibits you from doing acts set out in paragraph 1 of this order. You should read it carefully. You are advised to consult a solicitor as soon as possible. You have a right to ask the Court to vary or discharge this order.

(2) If you disobey this order you may be found guilty of contempt of court and may be sent to prison or fined or your assets may be seized.³⁵

made by District Judge [   ]

at First Avenue House, 42–49 High Holborn, London, WC1V 6NP

on [   ]

UPON the Applicant expressing its commitment to ensuring that the injunction orders below are enforced, and to this end the Applicant making it clear to all parties that, should [Full name of the Respondent] breach the injunction, then the Applicant will consider making an application for [Full name of the Respondent]'s committal to prison

---

34 An injunction order such as this would almost invariably only be made after an attended hearing.
35 It is essential that this Penal Notice is on the first page of the order.

IT IS ORDERED THAT:

1) Until [final judgment in these proceedings/further order of the court], [Full name of the Respondent] must not [set out precisely what the Respondent must not do].

2) [Full name of the Respondent] must not do the acts set out in paragraph 1 of this Order [himself/herself] and must not do those acts through others acting on [his/her] behalf or on [his/her] instructions or with [his/her] encouragement.

3) The Applicant shall arrange to personally serve [Full name of the Respondent] with a sealed copy of this order within five working days of receiving a sealed copy from the court.

4) [Full name of the Respondent] may apply to the Court at any time to vary or discharge this Order but if he/she wishes to do so, he/she must first inform the other parties' legal representatives in writing at least [72 hours] beforehand.

11 Order for the appointment of a property and affairs deputy (single)

IN THE COURT OF PROTECTION   **Case No:**

IN THE MATTER OF THE MENTAL CAPACITY ACT 2005

In the matter of
[P's FULL NAME]

ORDER APPOINTING A DEPUTY FOR PROPERTY AND AFFAIRS

made by District Judge [   ]

at First Avenue House, 42–49 High Holborn, London, WC1V 6NP

on [   ]

UPON the court being satisfied that [P's full name] lacks capacity to make various decisions for himself in relation to a matter or matters concerning his property and affairs, and that the purpose for which this order is needed cannot be as effectively achieved in a way that is less restrictive of his rights and freedom of action.

IT IS ORDERED THAT:

1) **Appointment of deputy**

(a) [Deputy's full name] of [Deputy's full address] is appointed as deputy ('the deputy') to make decisions on behalf of [P's full name] that he is unable to make for himself in relation to his property and affairs, subject to any conditions or restrictions set out in this order.

(b) The appointment will last until further order.

(c) The deputy must apply the principles set out in section 1 of the Mental Capacity Act 2005 ('the Act') and have regard to the guidance in the Code of Practice to the Act.

2) **Authority of deputy**

(a) The Court confers general authority on the deputy to take possession or control of the property and affairs of [P's full name] and to exercise the same powers of management and investment as he has as beneficial owner, subject to the terms and conditions set out in this order.

(b) The deputy may make provision for the needs of anyone who is related to or connected with [P's full name], if he provided for or might be expected to provide for that person's needs, by doing whatever she did or might reasonably be expected to do to meet those needs.

(c) The deputy may (without obtaining any further authority from the Court) dispose of money and property of [P's full name] by way of gift to any charity to which he made or might have been expected to make gifts and on customary occasions to persons who are related to or connected with him, provided that the value of each such gift is not unreasonable having regard to all the circumstances and, in particular, the size of his estate.

(d) The deputy cannot purchase any freehold or leasehold property on [P's full name]'s behalf without obtaining further authority from the court.[36]

(e) The deputy must not sell, charge or otherwise dispose of any freehold or leasehold property in which [P's full name] has a beneficial interest without obtaining further authority from the court.[37]

(f) The deputy may withdraw a sum not exceeding £25,000 a year from the funds of P without needing to obtain the prior approval of the Court of Protection. Leave for deputy to seek review of annual release upon filing detailed annual budget.[38]

(g) On [P's full name]'s behalf the deputy may take such steps as may be necessary to obtain (either alone or with a co-administrator) a grant of representation to the estate of [full name of deceased] and to use the share to which [P's full name] is entitled for his benefit.[39]

(h) For the purpose of giving effect to any decision the deputy may execute or sign any necessary deeds or documents.

3) Investments

(a) The deputy must exercise such care and skill as is reasonable in the circumstances when investing the assets of [P's full name].

(b) The deputy may make any kind of investment that the person absolutely entitled to those assets could make.

(c) This general power of investment includes investment in land and investment in assets outside England and Wales.

(d) In exercising the power of investment, the deputy must have regard to the standard investment criteria namely the suitability of the investments and the need for diversification in so far as is appropriate to the circumstances of [P's full name].

(e) The deputy must from time to time review the investments, and consider whether, having regard to the standard investment criteria, they should be varied.

(f) Unless the deputy reasonably concludes that in all the circumstances it is unnecessary or inappropriate to do so, before exercising any power of investment, the deputy must obtain and consider proper advice about the way in which, having regard to the standard investment criteria, the power should be exercised. 'Proper advice' is the advice of a person who the deputy reasonably believes to be qualified to give it by his ability in and practical experience of financial and other matters relating to the proposed investment.

---

36 This clause may apply in some cases.
37 This clause may apply in some cases.
38 This clause may be appropriate depending upon the size of P's estate.
39 This clause would only apply in specific cases.

4) Reports
(a) The deputy is required to keep statements, vouchers, receipts and other financial records.

(b) The deputy must submit a report to the Public Guardian as and when required.

5) Costs and expenses
(a) The deputy is entitled to be reimbursed for reasonable expenses incurred provided they are in proportion to the size of [P's full name]s estate and the functions performed by the deputy.[40]

(b) The deputy is authorised to pay the solicitors' fixed costs for this application, or, where the amount exceeds the fixed costs allowed, the deputy is authorised to agree the costs for making this application and to pay them from funds belonging [P's full name]. In default of agreement, or if the deputy or the solicitors would prefer the costs to be assessed, this order is to be treated as authority to the Senior Courts Costs Office to carry out a detailed assessment on the standard basis.[41]

(c) The deputy is entitled to receive fixed costs in relation to this application, and to receive fixed costs for the general management of [P's full name]'s affairs. If the deputy would prefer the costs to be assessed, this order is to be treated as authority to the Senior Courts Costs Office to carry out a detailed assessment on the standard basis.[42]

6) Security
(a) The deputy is required forthwith to obtain and maintain security in the sum of £[   ] in accordance with the standard requirements as to the giving of security.

(b) The deputy must ensure that the level of security ordered by the court is in place before discharging any of the functions conferred by this order.

7) Right to apply for reconsideration of order
Any person who is affected by this order may apply to the court for reconsideration of the order within 21 days of the order being served by filing an application notice (form COP9) in accordance with Part 10 of the Court of Protection Rules 2007.

8) Service
The requirement under Rule 48 of the Court of Protection Rules 2007 for the person effecting notification of the issue of this order to provide the court with a certificate of notification is dispensed with.

---

40 This clause would apply where a lay deputy is appointed.

41 This clause would apply where a lay deputy has instructed a professional to submit the application.

42 This clause would apply where a professional deputy is appointed.

12 Order for the appointment of property and affairs deputies (joint, and joint and several)

IN THE COURT OF PROTECTION   **Case No:**

IN THE MATTER OF THE MENTAL CAPACITY ACT 2005

In the matter of
[P's FULL NAME]

ORDER APPOINTING JOINT [AND SEVERAL] DEPUTIES FOR PROPERTY AND AFFAIRS

made by District Judge [   ]

at First Avenue House, 42–49 High Holborn, London, WC1V 6NP

on [   ]

UPON the court being satisfied that [P's full name] lacks capacity to make various decisions for himself in relation to a matter or matters concerning his property and affairs, and that the purpose for which this order is needed cannot be as effectively achieved in a way that is less restrictive of his rights and freedom of action.

IT IS ORDERED THAT:

1. **Appointment of deputies**
   (a) [First Deputy's full name] of [First Deputy's full address] and [Second Deputy's full name] of [Second Depuy's full address] are appointed [jointly and severally] as deputies ('the deputies') to make decisions on behalf of [P's full name] that he is unable to make for himself in relation to his property and affairs, subject to any conditions or restrictions set out in this order.

   (b) The appointment will last until further order.

   (c) The deputies must apply the principles set out in section 1 of the Mental Capacity Act 2005 ('the Act') and have regard to the guidance in the Code of Practice to the Act.

2. **Authority of deputies**
   (a) The Court confers general authority on the deputies to take possession or control of the property and affairs of [P's full name] and to exercise the same powers of management and investment as he has as beneficial owner, subject to the terms and conditions set out in this order.

   (b) The deputies may make provision for the needs of anyone who is related to or connected with [P's full name], if he provided for or might be expected to provide for that person's needs, by doing whatever she did or might reasonably be expected to do to meet those needs.

   (c) The deputies may (without obtaining any further authority from the Court) dispose of money and property of [P's full name] by way of gift to any charity to which he made or might have been expected to make gifts and on customary occasions to persons who are related to or connected with him, provided that the value of each such gift is not unreasonable having regard to all the circumstances and, in particular, the size of his estate.

(d) The deputies cannot purchase any freehold or leasehold property on [P's full name]'s behalf without obtaining further authority from the court.[43]

(e) The deputies must not sell, charge or otherwise dispose of any freehold or leasehold property in which [P's full name] has a beneficial interest without obtaining further authority from the court. [44]

(f) The deputies may withdraw a sum not exceeding £25,000 a year from the funds of P without needing to obtain the prior approval of the Court of Protection. Leave for deputies to seek review of annual release upon filing detailed annual budget.[45]

(g) On [P's full name]'s behalf the deputies may take such steps as may be necessary to obtain (either alone or with a co-administrator) a grant of representation to the estate of [full name of deceased] and to use the share to which [P's full name] is entitled for his benefit.[46]

(h) For the purpose of giving effect to any decision the deputies may execute or sign any necessary deeds or documents.

3. Investments

(a) The deputies must exercise such care and skill as is reasonable in the circumstances when investing the assets of [P's full name].

(b) The deputies may make any kind of investment that the person absolutely entitled to those assets could make.

(c) This general power of investment includes investment in land and investment in assets outside England and Wales.

(d) In exercising the power of investment, the deputies must have regard to the standard investment criteria namely the suitability of the investments and the need for diversification in so far as is appropriate to the circumstances of [P's full name].

(e) The deputies must from time to time review the investments, and consider whether, having regard to the standard investment criteria, they should be varied.

(f) Unless the deputies reasonably conclude that in all the circumstances it is unnecessary or inappropriate to do so, before exercising any power of investment, the deputies must obtain and consider proper advice about the way in which, having regard to the standard investment criteria, the power should be exercised. 'Proper advice' is the advice of a person who the deputies reasonably believe to be qualified to give it by his ability in and practical experience of financial and other matters relating to the proposed investment.

43 This clause may apply in some cases.
44 This clause may apply in some cases.
45 This clause may be appropriate depending upon the size of P's estate.
46 This clause would only apply in specific cases.

4. Reports

(a) The deputies are required to keep statements, vouchers, receipts and other financial records.

(b) The deputies must submit a report to the Public Guardian as and when required.

5. Costs and expenses

(a) The deputies are entitled to be reimbursed for reasonable expenses incurred provided they are in proportion to the size of [P's full name]'s estate and the functions performed by the deputies.[47]

(b) The deputies are authorised to pay the solicitors' fixed costs for this application, or, where the amount exceeds the fixed costs allowed, the deputies is authorised to agree the costs for making this application and to pay them from funds belonging [P's full name]. In default of agreement, or if the deputies or the solicitors would prefer the costs to be assessed, this order is to be treated as authority to the Senior Courts Costs Office to carry out a detailed assessment on the standard basis.[48]

(c) Any professional deputy is entitled to receive fixed costs in relation to this application, and to receive fixed costs for the general management of [P's full name]'s affairs. If the professional deputy would prefer the costs to be assessed, this order is to be treated as authority to the Senior Courts Costs Office to carry out a detailed assessment on the standard basis.[49]

6. Security

(a) The deputies is required forthwith to obtain and maintain security in the sum of £[ ] in accordance with the standard requirements as to the giving of security.

(b) The deputies must ensure that the level of security ordered by the court is in place before discharging any of the functions conferred by this order.

7. Right to apply for reconsideration of order

Any person who is affected by this order may apply to the court for reconsideration of the order within 21 days of the order being served by filing an application notice (form COP9) in accordance with Part 10 of the Court of Protection Rules 2007.

8. Service

The requirement under Rule 48 of the Court of Protection Rules 2007 for the person effecting notification of the issue of this order to provide the court with a certificate of notification is dispensed with.

---

47 This clause would apply where lay deputies are appointed.

48 This clause would apply where lay deputies have instructed a professional to submit the application.

49 This clause would apply where one of the deputies is a professional

13 Order for the investigation of P's finances

IN THE COURT OF PROTECTION   **Case No:**

IN THE MATTER OF THE MENTAL CAPACITY ACT 2005

In the matter of
[P's FULL NAME]

ORDER FOR THE INVESTIGATION OF P'S FINANCES

made by District Judge [   ]

at First Avenue House, 42–49 High Holborn, London, WC1V 6NP

on [   ]

WHEREAS

1. [X] ('the Applicant') has applied for an order under the Mental Capacity Act 2005.

2. The court has reason to believe that [   ] lacks capacity in relation to matters concerning her property and affairs and considers it in her best interests to make this order.

IT IS ORDERED THAT:

3. The applicant is directed to investigate as to the assets, property, income and liabilities of [   ] and report back to the Court of Protection by [   ].

4. Any person, including any bank or other financial institution, which possesses information concerning the property, finances or affairs of [   ] is hereby authorised and required to provide that information to the Applicant or their solicitors, Messrs [   ]

5. For the purpose of giving effect to this order the Applicant is authorised to execute or sign any necessary deeds or documents.

6. No order as to costs.

7. Any person who is affected by this order may apply for reconsideration of the order within 21 days of the date on which this order was served by filing an application notice (form COP9) in accordance with Part 10 of the Court of Protection Rules 2007.

14 Order approving a statutory will

IN THE COURT OF PROTECTION   **Case No:**

IN THE MATTER OF THE MENTAL CAPACITY ACT 2005

In the matter of
[P's FULL NAME]

**FIRST DIRECTIONS ORDER IN APPLICATION RELATING TO
SETTLEMENT OR DISPOSAL OF P'S PROPERTY**

made by District Judge [   ]

at First Avenue House, 42–49 High Holborn, London, WC1V 6NP

on [   ]

UPON the application of [   ] ('the applicant') for authority pursuant to section 18(1)(i) of the Mental Capacity Act 2005 to execute a statutory will on behalf of [P's full name].

AND UPON reading the draft of a statutory will proposed to be executed for [P's full name] (initialled by [the name of the judge] for the purpose of identification).

[**AND** without a hearing and without objection]

or

[**AND UPON** hearing (by telephone) [list those who have been heard]

IT IS ORDERED THAT:

1) The applicant is authorised in the name and on behalf of [P's full name] to execute a statutory will in the terms of the said draft.

2) The statutory will when executed is to be retained for safe custody by [solicitor's name] of [full address] and is to be held by them subject (during the lifetime of [P's full name]) to the directions of the court.

3) The costs of the applicant and of the Official Solicitor of and incidental to this application are to be assessed on the standard basis by the Senior Courts Costs Office and the certified amount of such costs is to be paid from [P's full name]'s estate.

4) Any person who is affected by this order may apply to the court for reconsideration of the order within 21 days of the order being served by filing an application notice (form COP9) in accordance with Part 10 of the Court of Protection Rules 2007.[50]

---

50 If the order was made without a hearing.

15 First directions order for applications concerning wills, settlements or approval of gifts

IN THE COURT OF PROTECTION   **Case No:**

IN THE MATTER OF THE MENTAL CAPACITY ACT 2005

In the matter of
[P's FULL NAME]

FIRST DIRECTIONS ORDER IN APPLICATION RELATING TO SETTLEMENT OR DISPOSAL OF P'S PROPERTY

made by District Judge [   ]

at First Avenue House, 42–49 High Holborn, London, WC1V 6NP

on [   ]

WHEREAS
An application has been made by [   ] ('the Applicant') for an order under the Mental Capacity Act 2005 to authorise [the execution of a trust/will/codicil/deed of variation] [and/or] [the making of a gift/gifts] on behalf of [P's full name]

IT IS ORDERED THAT:
1. [P's full name] is joined as a party to these proceedings and, subject to his consent, the Official Solicitor to the Senior Courts ('the Official Solicitor') is appointed to act on [his/her behalf] as litigation friend.

2. In accordance with paragraph 9 of Practice Direction 9F to the Court of Protection Rules 2007 the applicant shall, within 5 working days of the date of receipt of this order, serve on each party and the Official Solicitor copies of :

   (a) the application;

   (b) the statement of evidence (in form COP24) in support of the application; and

   (c) the exhibits and documents required pursuant to paragraph 6 of Practice Direction 9F to the Court of Protection Rules 2007.

3. Such statements of evidence that any party seeks to rely upon at final hearing shall be filed with the court and served on the other parties by the [6 weeks from the date of the order]. In the event that oral evidence is to be given, the statements so served shall stand as evidence in chief. Any statement of evidence on behalf of [P] shall be filed and served by the [8 weeks from the date of the order].

4. A disposal/directions hearing is listed on on the [first open date after 12 weeks] at [time] at the [Court of Protection, First Avenue House, 42–49 High Holborn, London, WC1V 6NP]/[the Regional Court sitting at [   ] County Court] with a time estimate of [   ]. The parties shall attend at least 30 minutes before the hearing for final consultation/[The hearing shall be by

telephone to be arranged by the Applicant]. No hearing may be vacated save with the prior consent of a judge of the Court of Protection.

5. No later than 3 working days before the hearing each party shall file at court and serve on all other parties a position statement and a draft of any order or directions sought.

6. Any person who is affected by this order may apply to the court for reconsideration of the order within 21 days of the order being served by filing an application notice (form COP9) in accordance with Part 10 of the Court of Protection Rules 2007.

If the Court is in a position to direct a final hearing at the initial directions stage, then the following directions will be made from paragraph 4 onwards

7. The application is to be listed for a final hearing on the [first open date after 12 weeks] at [time] at the [Court of Protection, First Avenue House, 42–49 High Holborn, London, WC1V 6NP]/[the Regional Court sitting at [   ] County Court] with a time estimate of [   ]. The parties shall attend at least 30 minutes before the hearing for final consultation. No hearing may be vacated save with the prior consent of a judge of the Court of Protection.

8. The parties shall agree not less than 5 working days before the final hearing the contents of the final hearing bundle. The bundle, together with any skeleton arguments and authorities, shall be filed with the Listing and Appeals Section of the Court of Protection by the applicant or their London agent not less than 3 working days before the final hearing

9. The parties shall agree not less than 5 working days before the final hearing the contents of the final hearing bundle. The bundle, together with any skeleton arguments and authorities, shall be filed with the regional court of the Court of Protection by the applicant not less than 3 working days before the final hearing.

10. Leave for any party to request further directions. The party requesting the directions shall file the application with the court and serve it on the other parties, and is to be responsible for the organisation of the telephone conference hearing.

11. Any person who is affected by this order may apply to the court for reconsideration of the order within 21 days of the order being served by filing an application notice (form COP9) in accordance with Part 10 of the Court of Protection Rules 2007.

Statements and letters

1 Position statement

IN THE COURT OF PROTECTION   Case No: 1289256

IN THE MATTER OF THE MENTAL CAPACITY ACT 2005

IN THE MATTER OF JOHN SMITH

BETWEEN:

ANY COUNTY COUNCIL

Applicant

and

JOHN SMITH
(P, by his litigation friend, the Official Solicitor)

first Respondent

and

JANE SMITH

second Respondent

**POSITION STATEMENT OF ANY COUNTY COUNCIL FOR
DIRECTIONS HEARING   2 APRIL 2014**

References in square brackets are to the page numbers in the bundle before the court

Essential re-reading:

(i)   Order of District Judge Bloggs 1 March 2014 [**B20–4**]
(ii) Report of Dr Williams of 1 February 2014 [**G1–9**]
(iii) Witness statement of Ms Cavanagh, Mr Smith's social worker, dated 15 February 2014 [**E1–15**]

A Introduction and dramatis personae

1. This position statement is filed on behalf of Any County Council ('the Council') ahead of the directions hearing listed before District Judge Jones on 2 April 2014. These proceedings concern Mr Smith, who is 33 years old. The medical report of Dr Williams of 1 February 2014 [**G1–9**] concludes that, as a result of an Acquired Brain Injury sustained on 1 December 2013, he does not have capacity to decide where he should live or as to his care arrangements. Dr Williams also considers that Mr Smith lacks the capacity to make decisions as to contact with his wife, Jane Smith (the Second Respondent), with whom Mr Smith is currently residing.

2. The Council has brought proceedings for (1) declarations as to Mr Smith's capacity to make decisions about his residence and care arrangements and as to contact with his wife; and (2) decisions/declarations as to where Mr Smith should live and receive care, and as future contact with his wife. The proceedings were initiated as a result of concerns as to quality of care being provided

to Mr Smith by his wife, detailed in the statement of Ms Cavanagh at [**E1–15**], which have led the Council to consider that Mr Smith's interests are best served by his moving into a specialist rehabilitation unit in Anytown.

3. Permission was granted to the Council to bring these proceedings by order of District Judge Bloggs on 1 March 2014, at which point John Smith, 'P', was joined as a party and – the Official Solicitor having consented – the Official Solicitor appointed to act as his litigation friend. As at 1 March 2014, Mrs Smith did not have legal representation but indicated that she was intending to seek such representation. District Judge Bloggs therefore made no substantive directions at the hearing on 1 March 2014, instead adjourning matters until the first open date after 1 April 2014 to allow Mrs Smith to obtain such representation.

B Issues for this hearing and the Council's position in respect of each

4. At this hearing, the Court will need to consider:

(1) What, if any, further evidence as to capacity is required in addition to the report of Dr Williams. The Council will say that there is no requirement for any further such evidence. The Council does not understand that either the Official Solicitor or Mrs Smith disagrees.

(2) What, if any, evidence is required as to Mr Williams' best interests. The Council understands that the Official Solicitor will invite the Court to agree to the instruction of an independent social worker to report upon Mr Williams' best interests as regards his future residence and care arrangements and contact with his wife. In principle, the Council would not object to such an instruction, but would wish it to be on a joint basis as between the Council, Mr and Mrs Smith.

(3) Further evidence. Mrs Smith has put in a detailed witness statement addressing matters raised by Ms Cavanagh; the Council would wish the chance to file a short supplemental statement responding to certain points in Mrs Smith's statement. The Council suggests that it would be sensible for this to be done prior to the report of any independent social work expert (if such is permitted) as this will allow the expert to have the complete picture before them.

(4) Further hearings. It is clear from the witness statement of Mrs Smith that she does not substantially dispute the factual matters outlined in the statement of Ms Cavanagh, but rather would invite the court to put a different interpretation upon those matters than those set out in Ms Cavanagh's statement. In the circumstances, the Council would submit that there is no requirement that a separate fact-finding hearing be listed, but rather that the court can proceed to list a final hearing to determine where Mr Smith's best interests lie. The Council would envisage that it will be necessary for such a hearing to be listed for 2 days in order to allow sufficient time for the giving of evidence, the making of submissions, and delivery of judgment.

C Directions order

5. A draft directions order is attached.[1]

---

1 A directions order, including some of the provisions of the order at precedent 4, appendix C above, would be attached.

2 Witness statement

Statement of the:

Statement no:

Signed:

Filed:

IN THE COURT OF PROTECTION	**Case No: 000**

IN THE MATTER OF THE MENTAL CAPACITY ACT 2005

AND IN THE MATTER OF JOHN SMITH ('P')

BETWEEN:

ANY COUNTY COUNCIL

Applicant

and

JOHN SMITH ('P')
(by [his/her] litigation friend, the Official Solicitor)

1st Respondent

and

JANE SMITH

2nd Respondent

STATEMENT OF JANE SMITH

I Jane Smith, of [   ] make this statement further to the order of District Judge Bloggs on 1 March 2014. I make this statement knowing and believing the contents to be true and in the knowledge it will be placed before the court.

1. I am the wife of John Smith who is the subject to proceedings by Any County Council. I will refer to him as 'John' in the rest of the statement.

2. I make this statement in order to provide information about my background, my relationship with John and my views as to his best interests.

3. The court will be aware that John is 33 years old and was born on [   ].

4. John and I met when we were both at university. We married when John was 23 and had therefore been together for 10 years. We have had a close and happy marriage until the injury sustained by John on 1 December 2013. Until then John worked as a computer programmer. I am a teacher but have been on compassionate leave since John's accident.

5. I would describe John as an energetic person, who threw himself in to his work and sporting activities, especially swimming which he has always loved.

Neither of us socialise very much and following our marriage we very much enjoyed spending time at home together.

6. Over the past five years we have been trying hard to have a baby. Sadly, up until now, I have not succeeded in becoming pregnant. However this period of time gave both of us an opportunity to reflect upon what we considered to be important. Both of us had concluded that being together and being part of a family was the most important thing for us both.

7. In recent years, we have spent much less time socialising with friends, and more time together, thinking about our future and spending time with our respective families, both of whom live near by. We looked forward to a future as a family, bringing up children together.

8. As the court will know, our lives were turned upside down when John was knocked over by a bus in December 2013. He sustained an acquired brain injury, which has led to a very severe impairment in his functioning. He has largely physically recovered from the physical injuries that he suffered. The problem is his complete change in the way in which he is able to manage and process information.

9. When I learnt of John's accident I was absolutely terrified. I went straight to the hospital where he was treated, and the records will show that I spent the next week by his side, at a time when his prognosis was unclear.

10. I agree that I was very keen for John to be discharged home as soon as possible. John is still able to communicate. I feel that he communicates particularly well with those who he knows well and who are prepared to spend time with him. He has made it very clear to me that he wants to return home and as far as possible resume living with me.

11. I have read the statement of Miss Kavanagh, who sets out a number of concerns about my care for John. I will not deny that looking after John since the accident has been an uphill struggle. Although my own mother has dementia and I have helped support her with personal care, I have never had to be a full time carer before. John needs assistance in many areas, not so much with his physical needs but simply being prompted to do things and to keep him safe. Because John is quite mobile, you have to keep an eye on him all the time.

12. I have tried very hard to manage but I confess that in recent weeks I have felt absolutely exhausted. I accept that I became very upset in a recent meeting with Miss Kavanagh, because I felt that the help I was being offered to look after John was completely inadequate. I was basically being offered 14 hours respite a week. This was just not enough to allow me to get basic household chores done, carry out the shopping and have a breather.

13. I am aware that Miss Kavanagh put forward the possibility of John going to a day centre. I have been to the day centre that she recommended. I found it extremely depressing. Most of the people there appeared to have much more severe disabilities than John and I feel he would just be miserable there and would feel that I am trying to get rid of him.

14. I do not believe that John needs to go in to a specialist rehabilitation unit. I believe that the intensive rehabilitation that Miss Kavanagh believes he needs could be provided to him at home.

15. I am aware that the local hospital has a day unit where there is rehabilitation and I would be very happy for John to attend this as a day patient.

16. In the meantime I would be very happy to accept more support in looking after John, if only it could be offered. I believe that I can manage, but not if I only have a few hours a week additional support. I need to be able to carry out basic household tasks, and occasionally to be able to have a bit of a break, in the knowledge that John is safe, and doing something that he enjoys.

17. For example John has always been a keen swimmer. I have asked for an assessment to see if he could go to the local swimming pool with someone to help him and this has never been carried out. I believe that he would find this very satisfying, and I do not believe that it is impossible to put this in to effect.

18. Rather than move John away from home, where he is happy, I would ask that Miss Kavanagh reconsiders the level of support she is prepared to offer to John. I understand that the council is thinking of having a fact finding hearing which I am advised is rather like a trial of the care that I have provided. Instead of going down this route, I would ask that the council considers giving John more support to remain at home. The court could then review the position and see how things have proceeded.

19. I believe this would be fairer both to me and particularly to John to see if I can manage.

20. I have tried to explain to John what is going on, and he was recently visited by the solicitor instructed by the Official Solicitor. She was very sympathetic and John was able to communicate with her to some extent. However after she left when he realised that he might have to move and go somewhere else, he had tears in his eyes. I do not believe it is necessary or reasonable for John to have leave home at this stage unless all alternatives have been tried.

21. Therefore I ask that the Council think again about how they are prepared to support John and me at home.

The contents of this statement are true to the best of my knowledge and belief

Signed: [   ]

Dated: [   ]

Anyfirm LLP
88–90 Wessex Street
London SE1 7EZ
DX DX 124 XDE
Tel: 020 7123 4567
Fax: 020 7123 4568
E-mail: office@anyfirm.com
Ref: 005808.001
Solicitors for Jane Smith

3 Letter of instruction to expert

[Mr/Ms   ]
Social Care Consultant
Anytown
AN1 5IL

Our ref: /005808.001
Your ref:
Date: 21 April 2014

PROTECT: PERSONAL DATA

Dear [Mr/Ms   ]

Re: Any County Council and (1) John Smith (by his litigation friend the Official Solicitor), (2) Jane Smith/Court of Protection number 000

Thank you for agreeing to prepare a report in this case. You are instructed by the parties below as an expert on an application by the Any County Council for declarations in respect of the best interests of Mr Smith. The Official Solicitor was appointed Mr Smith's litigation friend on 1 March 2014

By virtue of an order on 2 April 2014 the Court has given permission to the parties to instruct you to produce an independent report in these proceedings. You have permission to see all records and documents filed in these proceedings and to examine Mr Smith and read his social work medical and other records.

Your report must be filed and served by 30 May 2014. If you have any difficulties with that timescale please let me know straight away.

The final hearing has not yet been fixed. There will be a directions hearing at the Court of Protection on the first open date after 6 June 2014. I will keep you informed of any further hearings.

I am the lead solicitor in this case to whom you should look for instructions and information.

1. **The parties**

   (a) The applicant is Any County Council. The Council is represented by Mr James Burton, of Any County Council. Town Hall, Anytown. His direct dial is [   ] and his email address is [   ].

   (b) The 1st respondent is Mr Smith. He currently resides at the address above, which is the matrimonial home he shares with Mrs Smith. He is represented by me instructed by the Official Solicitor as litigation friend. My details appear at the top of this letter.

   (c) The 2nd respondent is Mrs Jane Smith. She resides with Mr Smith at the address above. She is represented by Mr Ian Brightspark, of Brightspark Solicitors LLP, High Street, Anytown. His direct dial is [   ] and his email address is [   ].

Mr Smith has an acquired brain injury, subsequent to a road traffic accident on 3 December 2013.

2. Documents

Please see my letter of today's date which lists the documents which you have been sent. I also attach copies of Mr Smith's records from Any County Council's Adult Social Care Team. Copies of his GP records and records from Anytown Hospital will follow.

3. Family structure

Mr John Albert Smith ('P') [DOB   ]
Parents: James and Elizabeth Smith, 25 The Lane, Anytown
Siblings: None
Wife: Jane Smith [DOB   ]
Parents-in-law: Janet and Bradley Marriott, 34 Fir Avenue, Anytown

4. Background history

You should note that the court has not made any findings of fact in this case. Mr Smith was born on [   ] and is thus 33 years of age. He achieved well at school and attended Any University where he achieved a degree in mathematics. Whilst at University he met Jane Marriott and they married in 2004. Mr and Mrs Smith have lived at their current address since April 2005. Mr Smith is known to have worked as a computer programmer and Mrs Smith is a teacher. Mrs Smith describes them as a couple who did not socialise much but enjoyed spending time together or with their respective families. Mr and Mrs Smith have no children but are believed to have been trying for a baby. Mr Smith was the victim of a road traffic accident on 3 December 2014, following which he sustained a brain injury which has resulted in a significant impairment. He is said to have made a good recovery from his physical injuries. He currently lives with Mrs Smith who is his main carer, with a care package provided by Any County Council; however following concerns about the quality of the care provided by Mrs Smith (set out in the statement of Ms Cavanagh at C1 in the trial bundle) the Council applied for permission to make an application to the Court of Protection.

5. Summary of the proceedings to date

These proceedings were commenced by the local authority who made an application (form COP1) on 10 March 2014. The application appears at page II 1 of the trial bundle. The local authority asked the court to decide the following questions:

- Does Mr Smith have capacity to make decisions about where he should live?
- Does Mr Smith have capacity to make decisions about whom he has contact with?
- Is it in Mr Smith's best interests to reside at the home he shares with Mrs Smith or at a specialist rehabilitation unit ?
- What should the contact arrangements with Mrs Smith be if Mr Smith moves to the rehabilitation unit?

The local authority set out the orders it sought:

- A declaration that Mr Smith lacks capacity to litigate these proceedings, and to make decisions about residence, care and contact with others.
- A declaration that it is in Mr Smith's best interests to move to a specialist rehabilitation unit for care and treatment.
- A declaration that it is in Mr Smith's best interests to have contact with Mrs Smith by agreement between Mrs Smith and the Unit.

District Judge Bloggs granted permission on 1 March 2014. At the same time he joined Mr Smith as a party and appointed the Official Solicitor to act as his litigation friend, the Official Solicitor having consented to act. Mrs Smith had indicated that she intended to instruct solicitors and you will see that she is now represented.

The first attended hearing took place on 2 April 2014. A copy of the order is with your papers at B30 of the trial bundle. You will see that DJ Jones made interim declarations that Mr Smith lacked capacity to litigate these proceedings and that he lacked capacity to make decisions about residence, care and contact with others. A number of case management orders were made, including provision for your instructions at paragraphs 12 and 13.

6. Diagnosis

The report of Dr Williams of 1st February 2014 contains Dr Williams' view that Mr Smith has an acquired brain injury which has led to an impairment in his cognitive function.

7. References to Mr Smith's capacity

Dr Williams' opinion is that Mr Smith lacks capacity to make decisions about his residence, care and contact, and to litigate these proceedings and that there is no prospect of his recovering such capacity.

At the hearing on 2nd April it became clear that all parties now agree that Mr Smith lacks capacity to make the decisions under consideration and it is likely that final declarations to this effect will be made at the next hearing.

8. Reference to Mr Smith's views

Mr Smith has said consistently that he would prefer to live with Mrs Smith. You are referred to the witness statement of Ms Cavanagh at E13, where she describes her interview with Mr Smith and to my attendance note of my visit to Mr Smith, when he became quiet emotional at the prospect of leaving home.

9. Assessment of capacity

Please note that you are not asked to assess Mr Smith's capacity and this section is for your information only.

The court is being asked to decide whether Mr Smith has capacity to make the following decision(s):

i) Where he/she should live (and consequential care arrangements).

ii) Who he/she should see.

iii) Litigation capacity in connection with the above areas.

The Mental Capacity Act 2005 s2(1) provides that a person lacks capacity if, at the time a decision needs to be made, he or she is unable to make or communicate the decision because of an 'impairment of, or a disturbance in the functioning of, the mind or brain'.

The Act contains a two-stage test of capacity:

1. Is there an impairment of or disturbance in the functioning of, the person's mind or brain?

2. If so, is the impairment or disturbance sufficient that the person lacks the capacity to make a decision in relation to the matter in question (i.e. the matters set out above)?

The assessment of capacity must be based on Mr Smith's ability to make a decision in relation to the relevant matter, and not their ability to make decision in general. It does not matter therefore if the lack of capacity is temporary, or the person retains the capacity to make other decisions, or if the person's capacity fluctuates.

Section 3(1) of the Act provides that a person is regarded as being unable to make a decision if he or she cannot:

• understand information about the decision to be made;
• retain that information;
• use or weigh the information as part of the decision-making process: or
• communicate the decision (by any means).

A lack of capacity cannot be established merely because of a person's age or appearance or his condition or an aspect of his behaviour. Similarly a person is not be treated as being unable to make a decision merely because he or she has made an unwise decision.

Practitioners are required to have regard to the statutory principles set out in section 1 of the Mental Capacity Act 2005 and the Code of Practice when assessing capacity and making decisions on behalf of a person who lacks capacity.

The statutory principles provide that:

s1 (2) A person must be assumed to have capacity unless it is established that he lacks capacity.

(3) A person is not be treated as unable to make a decision unless all practicable steps to help him to do so have been taken without success.

(4) A person is not to be treated as unable to make a decision merely because he makes an unwise decision'

(5) An act done, or decision made, under this Act for or on behalf of a person who lacks capacity must be done, or make , in his best interests

(6) Before the act is done, or the decision is made, regard must be had to whether the purpose for which it is needed can be as effectively achieved in a way that is less restrictive of the person's rights and freedom of action.

The Code of Practice is available on line at www.publicguardian.gov.uk. [Hard copies are available from The Stationery Office]. A booklet entitled *Making Decisions: a guide for people who work in health and social care* is also available online at www.justice.gov.uk/downloads/protecting-the-vulnerable/mca/opg-603-0409.pdf

Litigation capacity

Paragraph 4.33 of the Code states that the MCA's new definition of capacity is in line with, and does not replace the existing common law tests (including that for capacity to conduct proceedings, i.e. 'litigation capacity'). The common law authorities on capacity to litigate continue to provide a helpful guide when applying the test in sections 2 and 3 in the context of litigation capacity.

The common law approach to litigation capacity has been considered and developed in a number of cases. The leading case is *Masterman-Lister v Brutton & Co* [2003] 3 All ER 162 in which Lord Justice Chadwick stated the following:

> ... *the test to be applied ... is whether the party to legal proceedings is capable of understanding, with the assistance of such proper explanation from legal advisors and experts in other disciplines as the case may require, the issues on which his consent or decision is likely to be necessary in the course of those proceedings. If he has capacity to understand that which he needs to understand in order to pursue or defend a claim, I can see no reason why the law whether substantive or procedure should require the imposition of a next friend or guardian ad litem (or, as such person is now described in the Civil Procedure Rules, a litigation friend ... (para 75)*

> ... *a person should not be held unable to understand the information relevant to a decision if he can understand an explanation of that information in broad terms and simple language; and that he should not be regarded as unable to make a rational decision merely because the decision which he does in fact make is a decision which would not be made by a person of ordinary prudence.* (para 79)

In the same case Lord Justice Kennedy commented as follows (at para 26):

> ... *the mental abilities required include the ability to recognise a problem, obtain and receive, understand and retain relevant information, including advice; the ability to weigh the information (including that derived from advice) in the balance in reaching a decision, and the ability to communicate that decision ...*

He further observed at paragraph 27:

> ... *What, however does seem to me to be of some importance is the issue-specific nature of the test; that is to say the requirement to consider the question of capacity in relation to the particular transaction (its nature and complexity) in respect of which the decisions as to capacity fall to be made ... Of course as Boreham J said in White's case, capacity must be approached in a common sense way, not by reference to each step in the process of litigation, but bearing*

in mind the basic right of any person to manage his property and affairs for himself, a right with which no lawyer and no court should rush to interfere.

The Court of Appeal re-considered the *Masterman-Lister* test in *Bailey v Warren* [2006] EWCA Civ 51. At paragraph 126 of her judgment Lady Justice Arden set out the matters to be considered when assessing a person's capacity to conduct proceedings:

> *... The assessment of capacity to conduct proceedings depends to some extent on the nature of the proceedings in contemplation. I can only indicate some of the matters to be considered in accessing a client's capacity. The client would need to understand how the proceedings were to be funded. He would need to know about the chances of not succeeding and about the risk of an adverse order as to costs. He would need to have capacity to make the sort of decisions that arise in litigation. Capacity to conduct such proceedings would include the capacity to give proper instructions for and to approve the particulars of claim, and to approve a compromise. For a client to have capacity to approve a compromise, he would need insight into the compromise, an ability to instruct his solicitors to advise him on it, and an understanding of their advice and an ability to weigh their advice ...*

In the case of *The NHS Trust v Ms T* [2004] EWHC 2195 (Fam) Mrs Justice Bracewell when considering the issue of litigation capacity stated the following:

> *... There is no problem in this case in respect of Miss T's intellectual capacity. She is able to instruct solicitors, articulating well and with an approach which demonstrates that she knows there is a problem. But her difficulties arise in relation to processing information in order to give meaningful instructions to legal advisers. .... her wishes as expressed to her legal advisers are solely driven by a desire to kill herself which arises from mental disorder, that disorder involving a delusional belief that the blood within her body is evil ... Intellectually, she is able to acknowledge that that is a delusional belief, but she is driven by that belief by reason of her mental illness, which prevents her from processing information and giving reasoned instructions on the basis of that which she intellectually knows, but cannot understand by reason of her disability ... (at para 4)*

In considering therefore whether or not a person has capacity to conduct the proceedings it is accordingly important to focus on the particular proceedings in relation to which the issues arise, the complexity of that litigation and the issues to be determined.

Mr Justice Munby stated in *Sheffield CC v E & S* [2005] Fam 236, para 34:

> *The capacity to litigate is not something to be determined in the abstract. One has to focus on a particular piece of litigation in relation to which the issue arises. The question is always whether the litigant has capacity to litigate in relation to particular proceedings in which he is involved ... Someone may have the capacity to litigate in a case where the nature of the dispute and the issues are simple, whilst at the same time lacking the capacity to litigate in a case where either the nature of the dispute or the issues are more complex.*

We draw your attention to the further observations of Mrs Justice Bracewell in her judgment in *The NHS Trust v Ms T* referred to above about the relationship between litigation capacity and decision making capacity where she said at paragraph 2:

> ... *capacity to litigate ... is a separate issue from capacity to make decisions about medical treatment, although in many cases ... if there is no capacity to litigate, then by reason of the underlying matrix of factual evidence it would follow that there is no capacity to make decisions about treatment.*

At paragraph 5 of the same judgment she added:

> ... *although in some circumstances there may be a different answer to the question of capacity to litigate and capacity to make decisions about medical treatment, this is one of those cases in which the evidence is overwhelming that she lacks capacity to make medical treatment decisions, and it follows that a person who has a very unshakeable delusional belief about the very subject matter of the litigation cannot possess the ability to understand, retain, assimilate or act upon advice received as to the conduct of the litigation ...*

In the case of *Sheffield City Council v (1) E (2) S* [2004] EWHC 2808 (Fam) Mr Justice Munby, having considered the judgment of Mrs Justice Bracewell referred to above, went on to observe:

> *There is no principle either of law or of medical science, which necessarily makes it impossible for someone who has litigation capacity at the same time to lack subject-matter capacity. That said, however, it is much more difficult to imagine a case where someone has litigation capacity whilst lacking subject-matter capacity than it is to imagine a case where someone has subject-matter capacity whilst lacking litigation capacity ... I suspect that cases where someone has litigation capacity whilst lacking subject-matter capacity are likely to be very much more infrequent, indeed pretty rare. Indeed, I would go so far as to say that only in unusual circumstances will it be possible to conclude that someone who lacks subject-matter capacity can nonetheless have litigation capacity ...*

The following factors/questions therefore appear relevant when conducting an assessment of litigation capacity:

(i) The test is contained in sections 2 and 3 of the MCA 2005 but informed by the common law approach to litigation capacity set out in the above cases;

(ii) There is a presumption of capacity to litigate which can only be rebutted by clear evidence to the contrary;

(iii) Capacity to litigate is an issue-specific test so that a person may have capacity to conduct some litigation but not other litigation. Equally a person may have capacity to litigate but not have capacity to deal with (say) the administration of an award of damages;

(iv) The complexity of the particular litigation and the issues to be determined are significant;

(v) All practicable steps must have been taken to help Mr Smith conduct the proceedings without success; it follows that you need to consider the assistance and help that has been given to Mr Smith so far in the litigation and whether there are further practicable steps that could be taken;

(vi) Mr Smith must not be treated as unable to litigate merely because he makes unwise decisions;

(vii) A person can have a temporary lack of capacity and a person's capacity can fluctuate.

The diagnostic test

(1) The question is whether Mr Smith is suffering from an impairment of or disturbance in the functioning of the mind or brain which makes him unable to conduct the litigation.

The functional test

The questions are:

(2) Whether Mr Smith is unable to understand with the assistance of proper explanation and assistance, the issues on which his consent or decision is likely to be necessary during the course of the proceedings? Relevant matters to be understood include the nature of the decision/consent, the reason why the decision/consent is needed and the likely consequences of deciding one way or the other or failing to make a decision.

(3) Whether Mr Smith is unable to understand the issues in the proceedings? It is important to note that a person may have the intellectual capability to instruct solicitors or to act in person, but difficulties in relation to the processing of information may prevent the giving of meaningful or reasoned instructions (which was caused by a delusional belief in the *Ms T* case) or arriving at a meaningful or reasoned decision.

(4) Whether Mr Smith is unable to retain information and advice given to him during the course of these proceedings?

(5) Whether Mr Smith is unable to use or weigh the information in the balance as part of the process of making the decision? The Code notes that a person can understand information but an impairment or disturbance may stop them from using it (para 4.22);

(6) Whether Mr Smith is unable to communicate with any advisors, with the legal representatives or with the court? It is only if a person cannot communicate in any way at all that he or she should be treated as unable to make a decision through inability to communicate (see Code at para 4.23).

10. Assessment of best interests

The issue of capacity to make the relevant decision should be determined first. Only if the person is found not to have decision-making capacity will it be necessary to address the best interests issues.

The court is being asked to make a decision in Mr Smith's best interests. You are asked to advise the court and (the parties) on what is in Mr Smith's best interests given the circumstances outlined in this letter, in the documents accompanying this letter and from your own observations.

The term 'best interests' is not defined by the Act. MCA 2005 s4 however provides a statutory checklist of matters which should be taken into account and is set out below.

Best interests

4 *(1) In determining for the purposes of this Act what is in a person's best interests, the person making the determination must not make it merely on the basis of–*

  (a) the person's age or appearance, or

  (b) a condition of his, or an aspect of his behaviour, which might lead others to make unjustified assumptions about what might be in his best interests.

 (2) The person making the determination must consider all the relevant circumstances and, in particular, take the following steps.

 (3) He must consider—

  (a) whether it is likely that the person will at some time have capacity in relation to the matter in question, and

  (b) if it appears likely that he will, when that is likely to be.

 (4) He must, so far as reasonably practicable, permit and encourage the person to participate, or to improve his ability to participate, as fully as possible in any act done for him and any decision affecting him.

 (5) Where the determination relates to life-sustaining treatment he must not, in considering whether the treatment is in the best interests of the person concerned, be motivated by a desire to bring about his death.

 (6) He must consider, so far as is reasonably ascertainable–

  (a) the person's past and present wishes and feelings (and, in particular, any relevant written statement made by him when he had capacity),

  (b) the beliefs and values that would be likely to influence his decision if he had capacity, and

  (c) the other factors that he would be likely to consider if he were able to do so.

 (7) He must take into account, if it is practicable and appropriate to consult them, the views of–

  (a) anyone named by the person as someone to be consulted on the matter in question or on matters of that kind,

  (b) anyone engaged in caring for the person or interested in his welfare,

  (c) any donee of a lasting power of attorney granted by the person, and

  (d) any deputy appointed for the person by the court,

  as to what would be in the person's best interests and, in particular, as to the matters mentioned in subsection (6).

 (8) The duties imposed by subsections (1) to (7) also apply in relation to the exercise of any powers which—

  (a) are exercisable under a lasting power of attorney, or

  (b) are exercisable by a person under this Act where he reasonably believes that another person lacks capacity.

 (9) In the case of an act done, or a decision made, by a person other than the

court, there is sufficient compliance with this section if (having complied with the requirements of subsections (1) to (7)) he reasonably believes that what he does or decides is in the best interests of the person concerned.

(10) 'Life-sustaining treatment' means treatment which in the view of a person providing health care for the person concerned is necessary to sustain life.

(11) 'Relevant circumstances' are those–

(a) of which the person making the determination is aware, and

(b) which it would be reasonable to regard as relevant.

Again you are required to have regard to the Principles and provisions of the Act and the Code of Practice when considering and providing your opinion on Mr Smith's best interests (see in particular chapter 5 of the Code).

11. Your instructions

I hope the enclosures supply you with all the relevant documents. Please let me know if you need any further information or require clarification on any matters.

Please arrange to see Mr Smith. I am happy to arrange an appointment for you with Mrs Smith if this would assist. You will need to consider his social work and health records. You will need to speak to those responsible for his care. His care manager is Ms Cavanagh who can be contacted via the Council's solicitors.

You will need to meet Mrs Smith and Mr Smith's parents and father-in-law (his mother-in-law herself has dementia and it will not be appropriate for you to interview her). Having regard to section 4(7) in particular you should consider whether there is any other person engaged in caring for Mr Smith or interested in her welfare whom it would be practicable and appropriate for you to consult- for example other family members or social care professionals. If you need assistance in making arrangements to consult any other person please let me know. You should identify in your report all persons whom you have consulted during the course of your assessment.

Please provide a report covering the following areas:

Best interests

Please advise as to Mr Smith's best interests in the following areas.

1. *Care*

(a) Please set out Mr Smith's care needs. This should include the support needed in the following areas. If you are not able to comment on any of the areas below please say so:
Mental Health
Maximising independence
Daytime activities
Learning disability
Physical health
Cultural

(b) In what kind of setting can the needs you have identified under all the above headings best be met?

2. *Residence*

(a) What would the benefits be to Mr Smith's physical, mental, psychological, emotional and cultural wellbeing if he remains living with Mrs Smith?

(b) What are the disadvantages to Mr Smith's physical, mental, psychological, emotional and cultural wellbeing if he continues to reside with Mrs Smith.

(c) What would the benefits be to Mr Smith's physical, mental, psychological, emotional and cultural wellbeing if he moves to a specialist rehabilitation unit?

(d) What are the disadvantages to Mr Smith's physical, mental, psychological, emotional and cultural wellbeing if he moves to a specialist rehabilitation unit?

(e) Is it in Mr Smith's best interests to reside with Mrs Smith? If so please advise as to the package of care required to support this.

3. *Contact*

(a) If it is not in Mr Smith's best interests to live with Mrs Smith, is it in his best interests to have contact with Mrs Smith?

(b) What should the level and frequency of that contact be?

(c) Should there be any restrictions on such contact with Mrs Smith and if so what should these restrictions be?

12. Role of an expert

Additional to the documents referred to at (2) above I enclose for your ease of reference Part 15 (Experts) of the Court of Protection Rules 2007 and the supplemental practice direction together with a copy of guidance issued by Mrs Justice Pauffley in December 2010. I draw your attention in particular to rule 122 (paragraph 2 of the practice direction) with regard to the expert's duty to the court and to rule126 (paragraphs 8-11 of the practice direction) with regard to the content of an expert's report, and to paragraphs 8 and 9 of the December 2010 guidance.

13. Contact with others

It is essential to both your role as an independent expert and to the parties' perception of your independent status that there are no informal unrecorded discussions or correspondence with anyone involved in the case, particularly when you come to interview others such as the social care staff, etc. If you need further information, please contact me as I am the lead solicitor and I will provide information after consultation with the other solicitors involved. If documents are exchanged with one party, please copy them to all the others. Where possible, communication is best achieved by fax, letter or e-mail copied to all the parties.

Please maintain a careful record of all discussions with all persons with whom you discuss this case in the event that it is necessary to refer to them later.

It will be helpful if you would confirm in writing to me who you would like to have contact with, so that all parties are aware that meetings will be taking place in due course.

14. Proposed timescale and plan of work

If you require any help from me in arranging meetings or contacting the other solicitors, please let me know. Otherwise I shall assume that you will go ahead, organise visits and meetings, and will make your own arrangements. If at any time there is a delay in your plan and the timescale has to be altered, please inform me promptly so that I may inform the other parties and the court if appropriate

15. Factual issues and your report

You should express your opinion regarding your findings on the facts of the case, but you must not seek to resolve disputed facts, as this is of course the job of the court at the hearing. Where appropriate, it will be of assistance if you are able to express your opinion on the basis of alternative findings regarding the factual disputes. Your report may be subject to challenge by any of the parties. It is likely that one or more of the parties may put written questions to you following receipt of your report.

I am under a duty to disclose your report to the court and to the other parties and I will circulate your report on receipt. If you believe, as a rare exception to the general rule, that it should not be disclosed to any party, please let me know and I will seek the court's directions.

16. Trial date

The trial date has not yet been fixed. I will ask you closer to the next hearing to let me have details of your availability so that if a trial is fixed it will be on a date convenient to you.

17. Fees

The following terms and conditions apply:

The fees for your instruction will be shared, in equal shares between the instructing parties. . Some of the parties are in receipt of public funding and your fees will therefore be met through their public funding certificates.

Ultimately your fees will therefore be assessed by either the court or the Legal Aid Agency (LAA) at the conclusion of the case as to reasonableness in terms of both hourly rate and time spent. The parties' legal representatives cannot be responsible for any fees over and above those finally assessed and paid by the LAA.

On receipt of your invoice the legal representatives for the publicly funded parties are entitled to, and should promptly make a claim for payment on account of your fees to the LAA. Promptly upon receipt of such payment on account they should make this payment on account to you.

Such payments on account may, however, be recouped by the LAA at the end of the case following the final assessment of the bill. Such recoupment will only apply to any sum, paid on account, which exceeds the amount finally allowed on assessment by the Court or LAA. If your fees are reduced on assessment we will notify you within 7 days of receiving notification from the Legal Aid Agency or the court. If you wish us to make representations with regard to the reduction then you should notify us within 7 days, and provide us with the text or those representations, or the supporting documentation as the case may be.

In accepting this instruction you therefore agree that if your fees are subsequently reduced by the court or the LAA you will promptly reimburse the difference between the amount paid on account to you, and the amount finally allowed on assessment, to the parties' legal representatives.

Please bear in mind that although we, as the lead solicitors in instructing you, will do our best to assist you in obtaining prompt payment, we can only be responsible for the share of your fees attributable to our client. The other solicitors involved in this instruction to you are responsible likewise only for the share attributable to their client.

It is also important that during the course of your assessment you inform us immediately if you are likely to exceed your costs estimate. All public funding certificates have a cost limitation and we need to make an application to the LAA for any extension of this if it appears that the aggregate of the fees which are to be incurred in this case is likely to exceed the current costs limitation.. If you exceed your fee estimate without prior notification to us your fees may therefore not be met in full.

In addition, there are terms in the 2010 Unified Contract under which the publicly funded legal representatives must operate. In accordance with these if your fees are to exceed £250 you must keep accurate records of all the time spent on the work for which you have been instructed and of the work done. You must also permit the LAA to audit your records if necessary.

There is also certain work for which the LAA will not pay and limits on certain hourly rates.

The LAA will not pay:

(a) Any separate administration fee including, but not limited to, a fee in respect of offices and consultation rooms, administrative support including typing services, subsistence and couriers.

(b) Any cancellation fee where notice of cancellation is given more than 72 hours before the relevant hearing or appointment.

(c) Any travelling costs in relation to vehicle mileage in excess of 45p per mile.

(d) Any fee for travelling time in excess of £40 per hour.

(e) Any costs or expenses of or relating to the residential assessment of a child.

(f) Any costs or expenses of or relating to treatment, therapy, training or other interventions of an educative or rehabilitative nature.

(g) Any costs and expenses of independent social work provided outside England and Wales.

(h) Any costs and expenses in relation to contact activities including fees, charges and costs of contact centres and any reports or other assessments of contact between children and adults. However, please note that this exclusion does not apply to observation of contact which forms part of a psychological or parenting assessment.

You should therefore ensure that none of these costs are included in your invoice.

This letter of instruction has been agreed between the parties instructing you. I should be grateful if you would acknowledge receipt.

If there is anything at all which is not clear please do not hesitate to contact me.

Yours sincerely

Felicia Anysolicitor

ANYSOLICITORS LLP

4 Letter of instruction for testamentary capacity assessment from GP

Our ref:

Your ref:

Name

Address

Date:

Dear

Re: [Enter client name]

I am the property and affairs deputy for [X]. As deputy for [X] one of my duties is to ensure that appropriate testamentary provisions have been made on behalf of [X]. [X] is at present intestate/[X] has a will which has become outdated and I now wish to apply to the Court of Protection for the authorisation of a statutory will made on behalf of [X].

In order to make an application to the Court I need to obtain evidence that [X] lacks testamentary capacity. The relevant test to apply when assessing testamentary capacity is found in the case of *Banks v Goodfellow* which states that:

> 'It is essential ... that a testator shall understand the nature of the act [of making a will] and its effects; shall understand the extent of the property of which he is disposing; shall be able to comprehend and appreciate the claims to which he ought to give effect, and ... that no disorder of mind shall poison his affections, pervert his sense of right, or prevent the exercise of his natural faculties – that no insane delusion shall influence his will in disposing of his property and bring about a disposal of it which, if his mind had been sound, would not have been made.'

You need only decide on the balance of probabilities whether [X] has or does not have testamentary capacity, in other words, that it is more likely than not. I also request that you pay particular attention to the following points, and indicate whether [X] understands them.

- The nature of the act of making a will. This involves understanding that [s/he] will die and that when [s/he] does the will come into operation. Further, [s/he] can change or revoke the will before his/her death, but only for as long as [s/he] has the mental capacity to do so.

- The effect of making a will. This includes the appointment of executors, deciding who receives what, whether the gifts are outright or limited or conditional in some way, the consequences of a depleted estate, that a beneficiary may pre-decease [him/her], the effect on any previous will, and the reasonably foreseeable consequences of making or not making a will at this time.

- The extent of the estate. This includes the amount of property or money or investments [s/he] holds (although not necessarily the exact value) and the fact that some may be jointly owned, whether [s/he] has any debts, that some benefits may be payable only on [his/her] death irrespective of [his/her] will, and that the estate may change during [his/her] lifetime.

- The possible claims of others. This involves the ability to distinguish between individuals who may have some claim on the estate and to reach some kind of moral judgment in relation to them. Beneficiaries may be left out because they are otherwise well provided for, or because of personal reasons or preferences. [X] must be aware of these reasons and the possibility that these could be challenged.

I attach outline details of [X]'s estate for your reference.

I have requested you prepare this report because [X] informs me that you have been [his/her] doctor for a number of years. If, however, in the course of taking a psychiatric history and conducting a mental state examination you consider a specialist report is required (for example from a psychiatrist or psychologist), please let me know.

If you are of the opinion that [X] has the capacity to make a valid will, I would be grateful if you would confirm this in writing and indicate if you would agree to act as one of the witnesses when the time comes for [him/her] to sign it. If you conclude that [X] lacks testamentary capacity please complete the enclosed Form COP3 'Assessment of Capacity'.

I confirm that we have agreed the sum of £[   ] For the purposes of the examination and preparation of this report. or Please provide me with a note of your fees for providing this opinion. In the unlikely event that you are required to give evidence at court a further fee will be negotiated. Please mark your invoice with the reference stated at the top of this letter.

If you require any further information or clarification on any points please do not hesitate to contact me.

Yours sincerely,

Natasha Molloy

Checklists for best interests assessment, care planning and transition planning[1]

A Introduction

1) A common complaint from the court, other parties or the Official Solicitor is that there is insufficient written information about what is proposed for P, why the proposed option is considered to be in P's best interests, and the details of the care plan and transitional arrangements. Often, the relevant issues have in fact been considered by professionals working with P, but the written documentation such as care plans and witness statements does not reflect this adequately.

2) The checklists below list the sort of information and detail that is likely to be required to support an application to the court and within proceedings. They are of particular relevance for local authorities and health bodies considering making an application. They should not, however, simply be applied to every case since not every element will necessarily be relevant.

B Checklist for best interests evidence

1) *Clinical and social work information about P including diagnosis, prognosis, presentation, history*

   Although this information will be contained in the various records, it is helpful to have a summary of relevant details so that anyone unfamiliar with the case can have a picture painted of P and P's care needs.

2) *P's wishes (including IMCA reports if available)*

   P's wishes must be taken into account in making a best interests decision and it is therefore important to make sure that a clear record of P's wishes is kept, whether obtained directly from P, or through reports from third parties such as family members, paid carers, or advocates. This applies whether P expresses consistent or inconsistent wishes – in either case – the information about what P has said will need to be considered, although clearly in the former case it will likely be accorded more weight. Information should also be included about steps that have been taken to improve P's understanding of the issues in dispute, and to assist P in expressing his or her wishes.

---

1 This is taken from a paper originally drafted by Victoria Butler-Cole and Alex Ruck Keene, both of Thirty Nine Essex Street.

3) *Views of family members*

Careful recording of the views of family members is helpful, including family members who are not parties to proceedings. A record should also be kept of decisions taken as to why particular family members have not been consulted (if relevant).

4) *Details of every option considered for P*

The maxim 'show your working' is vital. If the team working with P have decided that a particular option is in P's best interests, it can be tempting only to explain in detail that preferred option. The other parties and the court need to know what all the possible options are, even if they include options that can immediately be discounted (for example, the option of doing nothing where P faces a serious risk to his or her wellbeing).

Make sure that options proposed by family members are included in the list of possibilities, even though they may not be recommended by the professionals working with P.

5) *Factors for and against each of the options under consideration*

For every option, details of the benefits and risks or disadvantages to P must be set out.[2] It is often easiest to do this in table form, or using bullet points, so that the reader can easily see the issues and can compare the various options under consideration. It is not important not to forget to include practical implications for P as well as less tangible factors such as relationships with family members and care home staff.

6) *The likelihood of the pros and cons of each option eventuating*

Give some indication of whether the risks and benefits identified are likely to occur or not, and this view is taken.

7) *The relative seriousness and/or importance of the pros and cons of each option*

It may not always be obvious which benefits and disadvantages the professionals place particular importance on and why. A common tension is

---

2   Following the well-established 'balance sheet' approach identified by Thorpe LJ in *Re A* [2000] 1 FLR 549 at 560: 'There can be no doubt in my mind that the evaluation of best interests is akin to a welfare appraisal ... Pending the enactment of a checklist or other statutory direction it seems to me that the first instance judge with the responsibility to make an evaluation of the best interests of a claimant lacking capacity should draw up a balance sheet. The first entry should be of any factor or factors of actual benefit. In the present case the instance would be the acquisition of foolproof contraception. Then on the other sheet the judge should write any counterbalancing dis-benefits to the applicant. An obvious instance in this case would be the apprehension, the risk and the discomfort inherent in the operation. Then the judge should enter on each sheet the potential gains and losses in each instance making some estimate of the extent of the possibility that the gain or loss might accrue. At the end of that exercise the judge should be better placed to strike a balance between the sum of the certain and possible gains against the sum of the certain and possible losses. Obviously, only if the account is in relatively significant credit will the judge conclude that the application is likely to advance the best interests of the claimant'. Whilst this pre-dates the coming into force of the Mental Capacity Act 2005, the Courts have continued to adopt the approach.

between avoiding risk and promoting independence: explain why more weight is given to one approach in the particular case.

8) *Reasons for identifying a particular option as being in P's best interests and for rejecting the other options*

Although it may seem clear in light of the analysis of benefits and disadvantages, it is helpful to set out separately a conclusion about which option is considered to be in P's best interests and why. This is particularly important where there is a dispute and where the proposed option entails significant disadvantages to P, such as a loss of independence, intrusion into a longstanding relationship, or inevitable distress caused by a change of environment.

9) *If proposed option entails risks or disadvantages to P, reasons why these are thought to be outweighed and steps to be taken to minimise them*

Having decided that certain risks are worth taking in P's best interests, or that certain disadvantages are outweighed by benefits, it is important to show that the professionals have considered what could be done to reduce these risks or disadvantages and set out detailed plans for dealing with them. This might include additional care or staff support for particular periods of time, or the provision of financial assistance to ensure that relationships can continue.

10) *Detailed contingency plans if the proposed option is implemented*

Where there is the prospect that a proposed option may fail in the short or medium term, there must be thought given to what will happen in those circumstances, to reassure the other parties and the court that hasty and off-the-cuff decisions will not suddenly be required, to the possible detriment of P.

C Checklist for Care Plans

1) Take into account the guidance given by Munby J (as then was) in *R(J) v Caerphilly County Borough Council* [2005] 2 FLR 860, (2005) 8 CCLR 255:

46 ... A care plan is more than a statement of strategic objectives – though all too often even these are expressed in the most vacuous terms. A care plan is – or ought to be – a detailed operational plan. Just how detailed will depend upon the circumstances of the particular case. Sometimes a very high level of detail will be essential. But whatever the level of detail which the individual case may call for, any care plan worth its name ought to set out the operational objectives with sufficient detail – including detail of the 'how, who, what and when' – to enable the care plan itself to be used as a means of checking whether or not those objectives are being met.

2) The assignation of specific responsibilities to individuals is particularly important in the Court of Protection context.

3) Take into account the factors set out in checklist A above wherever the care plan involves the making of decisions for or on behalf of P.

4) Ensure, where appropriate, that consideration is given to the person-centred planning approach.

5) Where the care plan involves any degree of restraint, identify the precise nature of the restraint, the rationale for it, plans to minimise the need for restraint (and contingency plans in case the need for restraint is escalated).

If, in the consideration of the need for restraint, it emerges that the requirement goes beyond restraint into a deprivation of the person's liberty then authorisation will be required for that deprivation (how this will be achieved will depend on the setting, and whether the DOLS procedures apply).

6) Be realistic. There is nothing that the Official Solicitor and Court of Protection likes less than to see a care plan founded upon optimism alone: if this means that it is necessary to set a series of apparently limited objectives on the way to a more distant goal, then so be it.

D Checklist for Transition Plans

1) Give details of P's current and proposed care, including full care plans for each setting.

2) Prepare a step-by-step account of how P will be moved from A to B including:

    (a) timing;

    (b) personnel involved;

    (c) who will take responsibility for the transition on the day and subsequently;

    (d) what will happen from P's perspective (eg moving possessions, arrangements for meals on the day etc);

    (e) whether police will be present and if so, details of their involvement (note that unless physical force and/or restraint and/or sedation are essential, it is best to plan on the basis that they will not need to be authorised by the court, and then to return to court in the event the transition does not work and further steps are required); and

    (f) monitoring in days/weeks immediately following move.

3) Where police will be involved in the removal, ensure that the transition plan includes information sufficient to satisfy the guidance given by Coleridge J in *Re MP; LBH v GP:*[3]

    In the event that it is expected that the assistance of the Police may be required to effect or assist with the removal of a vulnerable/ incapacitated adult ('P') which the Court is being asked to authorise, the following steps should generally be taken:

    (1) the Local Authority/NHS body/other organisation/person (the Applicant) applying to the Court for an authorisation to remove P should, in advance of the hearing of the Application, discuss and, where possible, agree with the Police the way in which it is intended that the removal will be effected, to include, where applicable, the extent to which it is expected that restraint and/or force may be used and the nature of any restraint (for example, handcuffs) that may be used;

    (2) the Applicant should ensure that information about the way in which it is intended that removal will be effected is provided to the Court and to the litigation friend (in cases where a person has been invited and/ or appointed to act as P's litigation friend) before the Court authorises removal. In particular, the Court and the litigation friend should be informed whether there is agreement between the Applicant and

3   [2009] FD08P01058. (2010) 13 CCLR 171.

the Police and, if there is not, about the nature and extent of any disagreement;

(3) where the Applicant and the Police do not agree about how removal should be effected, the Court should give consideration to inviting/directing the Police to attend the hearing of the Application so that the Court can, where appropriate, determine how it considers removal should be effected and/or ensure that any authorisation for removal is given on a fully informed basis.

Useful addresses and resources

Court of Protection	PO Box 70185 First Avenue House 42–49 High Holborn London WC1A 9JA DX 160013 Kingsway 7 Tel: 0300 456 4600 (Monday to Friday, 9am to 5pm) Email: courtofprotectionenquiries@hmcts.gsi.gov.uk
Court of Protection (emergency applications out of office hours)	Tel: 020 7947 6000 (Royal Courts of Justice enquiry number: ask for urgent business officer) or Tel: 020 7947 6260 (Royal Courts of Justice security)
Royal Courts of Justice	The Strand London WC2A 2LL DX 44450 Strand Tel: 020 7936 6000 The Clerk of the Rules (with responsibility for cases before judges of the Family Division sitting in the Court of Protection) 1st Mezzanine Queen's Building Royal Courts of Justice London WC2A 2LL DX 44450 Strand Tel: 020 7947 6543 The Chancery Judge's Listing Officer (with responsibility for cases before judges of the Chancery Division sitting in the Court of Protection) Room WG4 Royal Courts of Justice WC2A 2LL DX 44450 Strand Tel: 020 7947 7717

Official Solicitor and Public Trustee	Victory House 30–34 Kingsway London WC2B 6EX DX 141423 Bloomsbury

Tel: 020 3681 2751 (healthcare and welfare)/
020 3681 2758 (property and affairs)
E-mail: enquiries@offsol.gsi.gov.uk

Office of the Public Guardian	PO Box 16185 Birmingham B12 2WH DX 74424 Birmingham 79 Tel: 0300 456 0300 E-mail: customerservices@publicguardian.gsi.gov.uk

Court Funds Office	Court Funds Office Glasgow G58 1AB DX: 501757 Cowglen Tel: 0845 223 8500 E-mail: enquiries@cfo.gsi.gov.uk

Free legal resources

Website	Contents
www.gov.uk/apply-to-the-court-of-protection	Contains all the Court of Protection forms and current details as to fees
www.judiciary.gov.uk/publication-type/practice-directions/	Contains Practice Directions and Court of Protection Rules
www.bailii.org	British and Irish Legal Information Institute: transcripts of judgments including increasing numbers of decisions of the Court of Protection.
www.mentalhealthlawonline.co.uk	Extensive site containing legislation, case transcripts and other useful material relating to both the Mental Capacity Act 2005 and Mental Health Act 1983. It has transcripts for more Court of Protection cases than any other site (including subscription-only sites).
www.iclr.co.uk	Incorporated Council of Law Reporting website, includes a number of free case summaries and case reports.

Website	Contents
www.copcasesonline.com	Site maintained by Thirty Nine Essex Street Chambers with searchable database of cases relating to mental capacity law, as well as back issues of newsletter (available for free on a monthly basis. To be added to the mailing list email: marketing@39essex.com)
www.gardensocial.co.uk	Garden Court Chambers has a website and newsletter dedicated to social welfare, including community care, mental health and incapacity issues.
www.courtofprotectionhandbook. com	A free site accompanying *Court of Protection Handbook* with links to relevant statutory material and updates on practice and procedure cross-referenced to the book.
www.legalaidhandbook.com	A free site accompanying the Legal Action Group's *Legal Aid Handbook*, including updates to the handbook and resources relating to legal aid.
www.mhla.co.uk	Mental Health Lawyers Association website including list of members (and associate members) practising in the field of mental health and, increasingly, mental capacity law.
www.lawsociety.org.uk	Law Society website, which includes ability to search for solicitor by area of law.
www.barcouncil.org.uk	The Bar Council maintains a list of all barristers, and a further list of those offering public access, on its website There is also a dedicated telephone number and email address for questions about public access: Tel: 020 7611 1472 E-mail: PAenquiry@barcouncil.org.uk
www.chambersandpartners.com	Legal directory offering information about leading solicitors and barristers, including those specialising in Court of Protection work.

Website	Contents
www.legal500.com	Legal directory offering information about leading solicitors and barristers, including those specialising in Court of Protection work.
www.solicitorsfortheelderly.com	Solicitors for the Elderly (SFE) is an independent, national organisation of lawyers, such as solicitors, barristers and legal executives who provide specialist legal advice for older and vulnerable people, their families and carers. Their website includes a 'find a lawyer' function.

Other useful free resources related to mental capacity law

Website	Contents
www.scie.org.uk	The Social Care Institute for Excellence website includes good practice guidance in a number of areas relating to mental capacity and related law as well as a guide (SCIE Guide 42) to accessing the Court of Protection.
www.mentalcapacitylawandpolicy. org.uk	A website maintained by Alex Ruck Keene dedicated to improving understanding of and practice in the field of mental capacity law, including articles, papers and other resources on the MCA 2005 and discussion forums.
http://thesmallplaces.wordpress. com	Blog site maintained by Lucy Series, socio-legal researcher and expert commentator upon the Court of Protection.
www.communitycare.co.uk	Online magazine dedicated to community care matters, which frequently includes useful stories relating to the MCA 2005.
http://autonomy.essex.ac.uk	The Essex Autonomy Project is a research and knowledge-exchange initiative based at the University of Essex. It runs a number of projects (and a summer school) relating to the MCA 2005, from a philosophical angle.

Useful books

Practice and procedure

Gordon Ashton OBE (Ed), *Court of Protection Practice*, Jordan Publishing (annual publication)

The Hon Mr Justice Baker, editor-in-chief, *Court of Protection Law Reports*, Jordan Publishing

Christopher Johnston QC and Robert Francis QC (Eds), *Medical Treatment: decisions and the law – the Mental Capacity Act in action*, Bloomsbury Professional, 2nd edition, 2009

Denzil Lush and David Rees, consultant editors, *Heywood & Massey: Court of Protection Practice* (loose-leaf), Sweet & Maxwell

Mental capacity law generally

Caroline Bielanska and Martin Terrell (Eds), *Elderly Client Handbook*, Law Society, 4th edition, 2010

Lawrence Gostin, Jean McHale, Philip Fennell, Ronald D Mackay and Peter Bartlett (Eds), *Principles of Mental Health Law and Policy*, Oxford University Press, 2010

Richard Jones, *Mental Capacity Act Manual*, Sweet & Maxwell, fifth edition, 2012

Penny Letts (Ed), *Assessment of Mental Capacity: a practical guide for doctors and lawyers*, British Medical Association and Law Society, third edition, 2009

Denzil Lush, *Cretney & Lush on Lasting and Enduring Powers of Attorney*, Jordan Publishing, seventh edition, 2013

Michael Mandelstam, *Safeguarding Adults and the Law*, Jessica Kingsley Publishers, second edition, 2013

Court of Protection fees[1]

Note: at the time of writing, the Court of Protection Fees Order 2007 had yet to be amended to take account of the modifications to the fee structure outlined in the Government's response to its consultation on *Court Fees: Proposals for Reform*.[2] The table and supporting information below is taken from that response in which the Government indicated the levels of fees that are to be introduced.

Simple application fee	£220
Application fee (all other applications)	£410
Appeal fee	£410
Hearing fee	£515
Copy of a document (10 pages or less)	£10
For each subsequent page	50p
General application (on notice or by consent/ without notice)	£50

The division between 'simple' and other types of application is a new division.

Applications where the £410 fee will be applicable

- Applications relating to statutory wills codicils settlements and other dealings with P's property (practice direction 9D)
- Applications relating to the registration of lasting powers of attorney
- Applications relating to the registration of enduring powers of attorney
- Applications relating to the use or operation lasting powers of attorney
- Applications relating to the use or operation enduring powers of attorney
- Applications for permission
- Applications relating to P's personal welfare
- Applications made under section 21A of the Mental Capacity Act (Deprivation of Liberty Safeguards)
- All other originating applications
- Appeals against a decision of the court

---

1 See also the Court of Protection Fees Order 2007, reproduced in appendix B above.
2 See https://consult.justice.gov.uk/digital-communications/court-fees-proposals-for-reform/consult_view

Applications where the £220 fee would be applicable

The simple application fee would be charged in those applications relating to the appointment of a property and affairs deputy, applications where the deputy was applying for additional powers and New Trustee applications. These applications are usually non contentious, do not require judicial time and are dealt with by Authorised Officers of the Court, who are civil servants experienced in Court of Protection matters. Property and Affairs applications account for 94.5% of the court's work.

• Application relating to property and affairs including an application to appoint a deputy for property and affairs
• Application by currently appointed deputy relating to the deputy's powers and duties in connection with making decisions in relation to P's property and affairs
• Applications to appoint or discharge a trustee (practice direction 9G)

The fee for making an application within proceedings is also new. The Government has indicated that it will not be charged in the following circumstances:

• Applications relating to Hearings in accordance with Rules 90, 91 or 92 of the Court of Protection Rules
• Applications relating to the transfer of P's property under the control or ownership of another person when 'P' ceases to lack capacity
• Applications relating to the appointment of a litigation friend for 'P' or a protected party
• Applications relating to reconsideration of a court order made without a hearing or without notice to any person

Fee remission

With effect from 7 October 2013, the Courts and Tribunals Fee Remissions Order 2013 (SI No 2302) came into force. This Order introduced a new, standardised fee remissions system for courts and tribunals, including, materially, the Court of Protection (by virtue of paragraph 5 of the 2013 Order and amendments, including the introduction of a new Schedule 2 to, the Court of Protection Fees Order 2007). In summary:

1) Eligibility for remission or part remission of a fee will be based on two new tests - a disposable capital test and a gross monthly income test. Parties who satisfy the disposable capital test will receive a full fee remission, pay a contribution to the fee or have to pay the fee in full;

2) The gross monthly income test applies a series of thresholds to single people or couples, with an allowance for the number of dependent children they have. Parties with a gross monthly income below a certain threshold will receive a full fee remission. Parties will be required to pay a contribution of £5 towards their fee for every £10 of gross monthly income they earn over the relevant threshold. Parties with income in excess of £4,000 above the relevant threshold will not be eligible for any remission or part remission of a fee;

3) The disposable capital and gross monthly income of a partner is to be treated as disposable capital and gross monthly income of the party. However, where

the partner of the party has a contrary interest to the party in the matter to which the fee relates, the disposable capital and gross monthly income of that partner is not treated as the disposable capital and gross monthly income of the party;

4) Where proceedings are brought concerning the property and affairs of 'P', for the purpose of determining whether a party is entitled to a remission or part remission of a fee:

   (a) the disposable capital and gross monthly income of the person bringing those proceedings is not treated as the disposable capital and gross monthly income of the party;

   (b) the disposable capital and gross monthly income of 'P' is to be treated as the disposable capital of the party; and

   (c) the disposable capital and gross monthly income of the partner of 'P', if any, is not treated as the disposable capital and gross monthly income of the party.

5) Where proceedings are brought concerning the personal welfare of 'P', for the purpose of determining whether a party is entitled to a remission or part remission of a fee the disposable capital and gross monthly income of a partner, if any, is not treated as the disposable capital and gross monthly income of the party, where that partner is 'P' who is the subject of those proceedings in which the fee is payable;

6) Where proceedings concern both the property and affairs of 'P' and their personal welfare, their disposable capital and gross monthly income shall be treated in accordance with the rules governing property and affairs proceedings.

Costs proceedings

Special fees apply in relation to the determination in the Senior Court Costs Office of costs incurred in the Court of Protection (by virtue of the Civil Proceedings Fees Order 2008, as amended), as per the table below. The first two fees were increased following the consultation exercise set out above.

Paragraph of Civil Proceedings Fees Order	Type of case	Fee
6.1(a)	Where the amount of costs does not exceed £3,000	£115
6.1(b)	All other cases	£225
6.2	Appeal (detailed assessment proceedings)	£65
6.3	Request/application to set aside a default costs certificate	£65

Index